Inside the world of gambling's
most colorful (and controversial)
modern day casino boss

by Gary Green

Advice, lessons, history, and wisdom
for casino players, operators, vendors
analysts, and investors

SECOND EDITION and SECOND PRINTING
this edition © 2013 Penny Arcades Press

For several years, people have been saying "you should write a book about your casino experiences." As a former award-winning journalist, and never-quite-famous recording artist, the encouragement was not a stretch for my already sizable ego.

The problem was that I really had four casino books to write: one about my personal adventures, anecdotes, and experiences as a "gambling man"/ casino operator; a second that provided a behind-the-scenes look at casino operations and how casinos SHOULD be managed; a third that would provide a more accurate recent history than a lot of pop culture and cable television has proffered; and a fourth one that answers typical player questions about "beating the house," cheating, and winning streaks.

Instead, I decided to write one book based on years of marketing, operational, management, and finance experience. The challenge was to make it readable to all of those constituencies. In advance, I ask the reader's indulgence as I try to tie all of those aspects together; such is the nature of working in the "casino industry."

This is not, in any way, an autobiography. Nonetheless, I have elected to write much of this book as anecdotal narrative. At the same time, it is my hope that the breadth of the things I have learned about this business can in fact give insight, advice, lessons, history, and wisdom for casino players, operators, vendors, analysts, and investors.

Even before it went to press, parts of this book had been subpoenaed in civil and criminal court cases involving the definition of Class II slot machines and sweepstakes slot machines and a Superior Court judge appointed me to operate a court-seized casino in his state.

Portions of another chapter were published by Amazon's Kindle division under the almost pretentious sounding title "Marketing Donald Trump."

Between those two pre-publication uses, it would appear to me that there is at least some perceived value here from someone.

A close friend, himself a leading casino-industry figure who agreed to suffer through reading an early draft, commented "You have forgotten more about this business than most operators will ever know; you just wrote the greatest resume ever."

While I am not willing to go that far, I will assert to you that this book is filled with a lot of information, some pretty strange adventures, and life as a "Gambling Man."

—Gary Green
Boca Raton Florida

Table of Contents

♣ ♦ ♥ ♠ We don't have 13 anything in my business; No 13th floor of hotels, no 13 tables; no 13 machines in a bank; No 13s. So There is no chapter 13

Chapter One.

Just a roving gambler

"God help us, this is the life we have chosen."
— Lee Strasberg as Hyman Roth,
the Meyer Lansky character in *"The*
Godfather Part II" (via Mario Puzo
and Francis Ford Cappola)

It was one more late night in a smoke-filled coughing-corner of one of Atlantic City's first glitter-monster casinos; one of the 60,000 square feet of one-armed bandits, Big 6 wheels, and the table pits.

Back then, the late 70s or early 80s, THAT was a huge casino; and this was the biggest of all of them: *Resorts International* where people were standing in line three and four deep behind every slot machine waiting for an empty seat. By comparison, thirty years later, those 60,000 square feet cowered in the shadow of the 167,000 sq. ft. casino now next door at the *Taj Mahal* or the 344,000 sq. ft. casino four hours away at *Foxwoods* in Connecticut.

In 1980 I could have never predicted that in just a few months I would be working for or with a cast of somewhat dubious characters that the New Jersey Gaming Control Commission would recommend as *unsuitable* for a gaming licenses...or a few decades later I would be close friends with the chief investigator for that very Commission — who by then *owned* Resorts International... or that I would be part of a team working to buy one of those iconic Boardwalk casinos. Damn. *What a strange world.*

But at the time, I was a long-haired, oddly-dressed gambler sitting at a green-cheque ($25-chip) blackjack table's third base (last seat) trying to keep a true count as straight as my running count out of an eight-deck shoe. There were no famous M.I.T. count teams back then, no Dustin Hoffman *"Rain Man,"* and certainly no Kevin Spacey movies glorifying card counting; hell, *Sixty Minutes* had just done a cutting-edge piece "exposing" the mythological practice as being real.

As I was trying to focus, an old man sat down beside me, slid the ashtray aside, and began to give me the once over. I knew it was about time for me to leave. His eyes started with the cowboy Stetson on top of my head, and at first I thought he was trying to read the hatpins — *I used to stick dozens of them in my hat like travel decals on an old steamer trunk.* Rather than stop at my hat, his eyes followed the cut of my knee-length and waist-seamed frock coat, the bib of my custom-

1

made Victorian shirt, the strings of my tie and on downward to the toe covers of my pointy-toed cowboy boots. Then his eyes darted back up to my long brown hair with its Bill-Hickok-style ringlets falling on my shoulders. Maybe he just hated hippies dressed like 1880s cowboys.

"Who the hell would double-down on 16?" he growled at me in the tone of a disgruntled looser missing the third session of a boring convention a few doors down the boardwalk.

"Probably just a guy that knew there were no tens in a shoe that is rich in fives and low cards," I smirked with my southern accent, trying to sound more like a suave Rhett Butler than a trailer-park Jeff Foxworthy. *I had not lived in a trailer park in almost seven years, thank you very much.*

Already I had realized that he was just an obnoxious old punter and not a spy from the "eye-in-the-sky", but I also knew I actually *had* been made when the sweep of my hand brought a five from the dealer's shoe and he called "shuffle" after that hand.

"Son, there is no *Maverick Doc Holliday* gamblers no more. Don't you know you living outta your time," the old man told me. I rolled my eyes and pushed back from the table, thinking that apparently there were no more English teachers either. But he was right; I was theatrically costumed for the role I had chosen in life. Absurd as it was, it was a fun role and a profitable one, too.

I briefly made eye contact with the dealer, Vince, a short, tough Italian street kid from Philly, a few years younger than me. I was pretty certain that he knew what I was doing and rather than rat me out, he simply called for a shuffle of those eight decks.

I had tried to familiarize myself with all the dealers to memorize their eccentricities and weaknesses, hoping I could exploit their failures into maybe seeing a hole card or another slipup. This kid, Vince, was good and I had never been able to spot his hole card, even when he slid it to the little mirror to check it himself. I gave him a *"thanks-a-lot-motherfucker"* look for calling shuffle, not *even* able to imagine that someday he would be a top executive at one of America's best-known casino empires and I would be a Vice-President answering directly to him. I tossed him a red-cheque (five-dollar) tip and pushed back from the table to leave; I had no intention of starting over again on another eight-deck shoe. That was too mind-taxing.

"Where you going, cowboy?" a shill asked me as she put a cigarette in her lips and leaned toward me for a light. In Jersey, in those days, shills were actually required to wear a badge that read "shill."

I didn't even bother to color-up. I just pocketed the stack of porcelain greens along with the others I'd been hording, ignored her too-powdered face and casino-paid smile, and walked past Vince and the old man toward the cashier cages. I saw the arrogant smirk on Vince's face as if he had triumphed over some threat to "his" casino and I watched him look back toward the floor man — the "pit boss".

The "floor" was a way-too-slick looking guy in a black suit and an over-confident swagger that I instantly disliked when I had first spotted him months before. Unlike the dealers, he didn't wear a readily-visible name tag so I only knew him as "Brownie", the name Vince and the other dealers seemed to familiarly refer to him; and, fortunately, he did not seem to know me at all. None of us could have known that one day he would be CEO of the most high-profile casino in the country and later a Macau institution.

Just short of the cage, I shrugged and rather than cash-out, I walked toward a side door leading to the street (instead of the tourist-infested boardwalk). Outside, I took a long drink of crisp air and started to walk.

I was thinking that I'd been on the road so long — *since the day I was provoked to hit the road when a dissident student in a class I was teaching had said it couldn't be done in the second half of the 20th century* — that I probably could never come back in. Again, I could have had no clue that one day not only would I be back "in" but that I would be running (and owning) glitter-place casinos twice the size of this one. As I stepped along in the darkness, for one loses track of light and dark when one travels in the glitter jungle, it happened.

I'm not really sure where he came from. I know he was young, Hispanic, and New Jersey tough. My stooped, already small, five-foot and nine-inch frame with its then-only-150 pounds probably looked like an easy target for him, for in stature I am not the least bit imposing.

I begged him not to do it...at least I wanted to. But he left no time for that. It is much easier now to look back at what happened, to retrace the events and the thoughts, than to examine them in the midst of the action...of the violence...of the near tragedy of this man/boy's foolishness.

My natural paranoia made me certain that he had given it some thought; there *must* have been some plan. He couldn't have just chosen his target at random; he could not be that foolish. *Why can't people just THINK of the possible consequences before they do something stupid?*

He called to me and I ignored him. Perhaps I was in a daze from the glitter, perhaps that's what he wanted, or maybe I chose to ignore him. But he crossed my path in darkness, blocked my way and made his demand. He pointed something at me. He might have had a knife and he might have had a gun; and he had no idea that at this point in my life, it really did not matter. And when it was over he had no idea why he had been spared.

My mind halted its racing with eight-deck card-counting fixes and I felt my body recoil from the inertia of the braking. My reflexes snapped with the energy that had allowed me to survive all sorts of adversity. I certainly knew what was going to happen before it came to pass and if he had just looked at my eyes he would have seen the hungry gleam spark there; I knew it was there, *damnit*. I hated it when that happened; it was like the *Incredible Hulk* — I was going to lose control (without becoming huge, strong, nor green).

In my stomach I felt a burning acid roll around and start to climb my esophagus to my throat. I felt the muscles in my back flex and my spine stretch me to my full height from my normal half-stooped stand. And I felt my feet lock into the pavement and dig deeper for a firm hold. I knew the rage was coming; that damned temper of mine.

The first second had still not passed. Had any people stepped from the casino and had there been street lighting, they would have seen the blur of speed whip from my eyes and guide my body, but HE wouldn't have seen it. For by the time that first second had passed, he had been frozen by that gleam.

But by then the scrounge of human technology, the implement of no purpose but to take another human life; that which I had often donned during those years — my gun — was drawn from the seeming-nowhere behind my vest and was leveled directly at his head.

Still he couldn't see that the miles had indeed taken their toll and that neither his life nor my own meant anything to me; he had no idea how many murders I had been around, how many hacked, shot, stabbed, and mangled bodies were in my history. He looked at my eyes and broke only to look at the gun. Seconds passed that seemed like hours to me. Then he spoke.

"You're not the police," he demanded more in a scold for daring to stop his robbery than in question or from fear.

"Face your God, child," I warned in Victorian melodrama, breaking my own hard-learned survival law of never slowing to allow even motor actions, much less speech. *(Years earlier, when I had been riding in police cars at all hours of the night as a newspaper reporter covering all of those murders, Sergeant Andy Strain had warned me, "never pull a gun without pulling the trigger; never point it and never take the time to talk —just shoot and then announce that you were in fear for your life!")*

Yet, I could see that he was stunned enough that I could continue and possibly not take his life. Besides, I had slowed now and perhaps

4

30 seconds had elapsed; maybe we were now on even terms. He was still alive and I had not used my advantage.

"Your god forgives; I take revenge; CHOOSE," I offered. I tried to echo-chamber my voice as Lamont Cranston might have done before slouch-hatting himself to his *The Shadow* persona. It probably sounded more insane than threatening, but in either case, it served the purpose. *(At least I didn't mock-laugh "who knows what evil lurks in the heart of men".)*

He backed away, slowly, but backing. His own weapon dropped from sight, back into its hidden pouch or pocket or wherever.

"Who the hell are you?" he asked. He backed some more, turned, and then he was gone into the same shadows that had borne him.

He had asked..."Who the hell are you?"

Me?

Hell, I am just a roving gambler.

I am just a roving gambler,
I gamble all around
Whenever I meet with a deck of cards I lay my money down.

I've gambled down in Washington, I've gambled over in Spain
I'm goin' down to Georgia to gamble my last game.

—Traditional Folk Song

5

Chapter Two.
Casino Management *Philosophy*

> *"I have made more than $10 million in my life. Part of it I
> spent on gambling, part on booze, and part on women. The
> rest I spent foolishly."*
>
> **— Actor, George Raft**

Regardless of my personal flamboyance or standing in the middle of Las Vegas Boulevard holding a steel cutter while my pants are on fire; regardless of tic-tac-toe playing chickens, flying Elvis, and Donald Trump's apprentices; regardless of the dubious historical origins of the gambling *industry*; this is a VERY formulaic business.

What makes one casino more successful than another? What makes my joint successful and the one down the street suck?

Think about. At the end of the day we all have the same slot machines. Within the regulated parameters, the payout is the same; hell, in "Class II casinos" the payouts are identical. The table games are the same and the odds of winning are the same. We all have buffets, a gourmet room, cocktail waitresses, entertainment. We even have basically the same ugly-ass carpet on our floors. We all have players clubs. Christ, as incestuous as this industry is, even our employees are interchangeable.

So why is it that in Vegas, the Monte Carlo Casino's 2011 EBITDA was $57.4-million and the casino *literally next door*, New York-New York, earned $87.2-million while the City Center on the other side next door *lost* $56-million[1]?

Why is it that in Atlantic City in August 2012 the Borgata Casino's gaming revenue was $55.5-million and 2½-miles away the Trump Plaza's revenue was $10.7-million for the same month?

Why, in June of 2012, did the Isle of Capri in Pompano Florida make $10.3-million and Gulfstream Casino, 21 miles away, only made $4.5-million?

It cannot possibly be so simple that at one property they followed a set of rules and formulas and at the next property they did not. *Can it?* And if it IS that simple, why hasn't every operator, manager, investor, and analyst insisted that their casino(s) follow the rules? Why doesn't the University of Nevada teach this stuff?

From the get-go I will tell you again: *this is a formulaic business*. And unlike Coca-Cola, Bush's Baked Beans, Dr. Pepper, McDonald's Special Sauce, Famous Amos Cookies, or the Colonel's KFC recipe these formulas are *not* top secret. Yes, they do teach them at the University of Nevada, and at scores of seminars and workshops at every major casino industry trade show, and at dozens of industry conferences and trainings held every year.

6

Then what-the-hell…Why the discrepancies in revenue from one casino to the next?

I have heard every imaginable answer coming from general managers, marketers, operators, owners, and financial advisors. I have heard the blame leveled at the economy, too much competition, increased amenities at competing casinos, internal theft, inability to get quality incentives, changes in the restaurant menus, lack of adequate parking, too much debt to service, poor quality of the facility itself, marketing saturation, under capitalization and not enough cash in the cage, and (at one point) even sabotage. I have heard the blame pointed to *location-location-location* (hard to justify in the example of the Monte Carlo in Vegas).

All of these things are (or can be) problems; they can be contributing factors to these discrepancies, to under-performance, or even failure. When I was a mid-level casino employee, I have even suffered through some of these problems myself. But these are all symptoms.

I often use the analogy of someone getting hit in the head with a hammer. Every 30 minutes a guy walks up, smacks you in the head with a hammer, and then walks away. You keep taking aspirin, acetaminophen, ibuprofen, or the other headache cure of the day. That *IS* one way to deal with the pain, albeit temporary and pretty much avoiding the problem —a problem destined to come back worse and worse as long as that joker keeps showing up with the hammer. In *my* universe, we address the problem a little differently. We take the hammer away from that guy, make certain he is not going to ever come back with another hammer, and *then* treat the symptoms.

Get it? All of those "excuses" for the disparity are just that: excuses. They are all *symptoms* rather than causes. Okay, now it is time (this early in the book) to start pissing people off. The real issue is: *Bad Management*. And I am not talking about the departmental manager, the shift manager, the vice president of so-and-so, and in very many cases not even the general manager. I am talking about where "the buck stops"; I am talking about the operator, the owner, whoever the top policymaker(s) is (or are).

At that level, it is mandatory to stop masking the headaches with a few analgesics and shoot that hammer-wielding bastard through the heart. At that level, there really is no place of these lame excuses; yet it is at that level from which most of them emanate.

What about casinos in with the same ownership in the same proximity? The example of the Monte Carlo versus New York-New York is an example of next-door casinos owned by the same company with a $30-million difference. There must be some logical explanation of why the same operating company can have a successful property and a failing property within a block of each other. There is. It is: *Bad Management*.

In the same-ownership examples, the "bad" part is much more subtle because it does not involve *operational* management as much as *philosophical* management. In such cases, there is "bad management", even with the most

7

structured management practices in which executives in multiple casinos are interchangeable and as faceless as IBM blue-suiters, Ridley Scott's rows of marching minions in Apple's TV spot introducing the MAC, or in some sort of Orwellian mind-controlled dystopia.

In these cases, almost universally, there is a fundamental failure to understand the business that we have chosen. Application of business systems and methodologies from the "hospitality industry," from former Big-Eight-cum-Big-Six-cum-Big-Five-cum-Big-Four accounting / "professional services" firms, business school academics, and the lot, are a far cry from the *gambling joints* created by Benny Binion, Jackie Gaughan, Sam Boyd, or Tony Cornero, and Moe Dalitz.

The gambling racket *(or whatever euphemistic "gaming industry" pallet-washing term is chosen to hide our true business)* is about gambling. Moreover, it is about the public perception, fantasy, and experience of being a gambler; all of the mystery, naughtiness, and even latent evil of Las Vegas that popularized *"what happens in Vegas stays in Vegas"*, all of those movies and television shows, and the very term *Sin City*.

The perception of gambling (in Vegas, Atlantic City, Mississippi, or your local Indian casino) is some version of that Sin City fantasy of Elvis singing *"Well, there's black jack and poker and the roulette wheel; A fortune won and lost on every deal; All you needs a strong heart and a nerve of steel; Viva Las Vegas."* The perception of gambling is about a fortune waiting around the corner, flashy gangster-esque shows and showgirls, and mythical high rollers being treated like kings with everything "comped" by a nod to casino host.

Regardless of how little it resembles the accountant's tracking of revenue, players, and costs, it is the movie version of Las Vegas that people fantasize when they walk into the casino. Regardless of the reality behind the curtain, the *perception* of the gambling experience is what matters and my predecessors in the racket...er, business... understood that. One lesson that we all should have learned from national politics during the past 30 years is that perception is a lot more important than reality; that form *does* count more than content.

My old friend Bob Stupak knew this and exploited it better than anyone ever had. He took the fantasy of the "high roller" and extended it to almost everyone. Every single player could live that casino fantasy life, albeit through Stupak's very carefully created version of that fantasy.

Every year, from 1979 until early 1995, Stupak mailed millions of letters offering the Las Vegas high roller experience to regular people. In just one of those years he dropped more than 20-million pieces of direct mail, mostly to non-high rollers and many to people who had never been into a casino. In his letters he offered $1,200 in "cash and casino action" plus a free "fabulous" room at his *Vegas World* hotel on the Las Vegas Strip. The letters had some bullshit explanation of why that person was chosen, and they read like the recipient had already hit the jackpot just by being on "the list"—a very special "preferred" list. I got one of the letters; as did a uniformed patrol beat-cop named David

Cook, in Oklahoma City; as did a friend of mine who was then a salesman for Eastman Kodak in Rochester New York; as did another friend who as a steel-worker in Baltimore; as did millions of other people who were not even remotely casino high rollers or even particularly gamblers.

Stupak had calculated how much money he made from a typical casino visit from these low-roller, grind, or no-roller gamblers. He calculated how much of their own money they would drop into his slot machines if they were first seeded with some of his money. He calculated his costs for the mailing, the list purchases, the "free" food, and even the cost of that "free" hotel room. He then weighed those costs against the amount he would make per player and the **perceived** value of what he offered. It was from those calculations combined with that perception that he sent out the letters.

It was all customer perception and perceived value. The beauty of it was that his "offer" was not even free; it required hitting the customer's credit card for $398. Did it work? Hell yes! It was all about the perception of value and the perception of perks. Perception has amazing power as a motivator.

For several years I flew more than 150 flights annually on Delta Airlines, which qualified me as a "Platinum" frequent flyer. That meant: I always received a free upgrade to First Class; I always boarded before everyone else; if no seats were available on a flight that I needed, another (non-Platinum) passenger would be bumped to guarantee a seat for me; and if my flight was late for a connection, they would hold the next flight (within the legal gate-time limit) for my arrival and meet me at the arrival gate. Hell, if the connection was going to be really tight they would send a gate agent to ferry me to my next flight across the tarmac in a Porsche Cayenne. Additionally, everyone in first class everyone gets better meals, but I got SPECIAL amenities with my meals; and the gifts sent to me quarterly were amazing (one year they sent me a $500 Tiffany gift card). One day I had to fly a route that Delta did not serve; I had to switch airlines. On the other airline I was just another customer; just another number. Compared to the kid-glove Platinum treatment, it was like the *Greyhound bus* of airlines, No, actually, it was just a typical airline — but it really felt like a Greyhound Bus compared to Platinum. Changing airlines was a painful experience; a genuine pain-in-the-ass. Delta was MY airline and no other airline could do for me what Delta did.

Now, let's think about that rationally. I was paying an average of $300 per flight; times 150 flights a year. I was paying Delta airlines about $45,000 a year. If I had used discount carriers and ticket-bidding web sites, I probably could have flown for half that. So I was paying Delta a premium of probably $22,000 a year; and who knows what their actual cost would have been to fly that seat empty —certainly nothing near the $300 that I was paying.

Delta flies more than 160-million customers every year and there are 81-million members of their frequent flyers club. On a personal level, Delta Airlines has no idea who I am; but on a personal level, Delta is MY airline. They are the not only my preferred airline but they are the *only* airline that gives me all those perks. What a magnificent marketing coup! They created a personal relationship with me. *It is all perception.*

Bob Stupak's business model was all about *that* kind of perception. Even when he sprang the fact that the player owed him $398 (the $199 each for two people), he made it so palatable that the player felt like thanking him for taking the money; exactly the same way I felt like thanking Delta for customer service. I am not suggesting, *in any way,* that a modern casino be run *Stupak-style.* Still, there is no denying that he knew how to make a low-end player feel like VIPs; and he nickel-and-dimed his way into a fortune that way. He made potential players feel like special high-roller type Vegas guests; and they paid him for that feeling.

The technique was quite brilliant. First he promised $1,200 cash and "casino action"; only *then* did he talk about the fee of $199 (per person). The genius (and the bait) came in his breakdown of what he offered for the $398. First there would be $200 in actual cash; with that rebate, the "cost" was down to $198 for two people. Then he would give another $200 in one-dollar cheques (chips good for play at table games but not available for cashing). Then he threw in $400 in slot machine playable (non-cashable) credits, making the player $402 ahead just for accepting the offer.

To sweeten the package, he added four $100 entries to his slot tournaments (apparently non-invited guests actually paid that occasionally) and two free $5-entries to a million-dollar-jackpot contest. He added to that, five free Keno entries and topped it all off with a free hotel room for "three days and two nights." Then, because this was for a "favored guest", he would give four show tickets (good for two people to see two shows in the "fabulous Galaxy Showroom"). Finally, he threw in a promise of a guaranteed win of one of five "expensive gifts": a camcorder, a genuine $500 bill, a color television, a working slot machine with $300 cash, or a "bonus vacation" to Hawaii, Mexico, Arizona, or Florida. *(I will let you guess which "gift" most people "won"; based on his costs.)*

Just for icing on the cake, he tossed in a deck of cards and a pair of dice. Then as a "bonus", he offered a fourth day and third night plus another $50 in casino play if the offer was accepted midweek rather than on a weekend (the casino's slowest time). A copy of one of his letters is in the Endnotes to this book[2].

When customers arrived, they were given a level of customer service and personal attention that most of the recipients had never experienced and would never again see in their lives. For their two or three nights in Vegas these players were able to taste the other side; or at least their *perception* of how the other half lives. Bob Stupak understood that it was all about perception; he delivered the fantasy.

Again, I am not advocating the Stupak methodology but I am, very specifically, advocating that kind of focus on the players. In recent years casino operators have been all about the hard numbers with little regard for the player's perception. At many properties there has been a flagrant disregard for the individual player and her or his experience as a gambler. That is a dangerous, and foolish, way to do business. Yet it is pervasive throughout the "gaming industry."

In early 2011, I visited a supposedly-high-end Vegas strip hotel and stayed in a 1,600 sq. ft. suite with a rack-rate of close to $350 per night. Customer service was non-existent and the condition of the hotel itself abysmally showed a scandalous disregard for the customer experience. When I later had a candid conversation with the property's general manager I was told that his hands were embarrassingly tied by massive budget cuts to housekeeping and maintenance accompanied by an unofficial corporate philosophy that for every complaining customer there were two waiting in line for the room (apparently despite an average daily occupancy of only 74%).

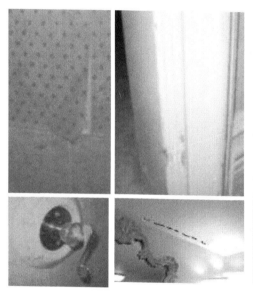

$285 a night: Typical lack of customer care in a "premier" Vegas hotel; symptomatic of a philosophy of an unending customer supply. **Far left top:** torn wallpaper in bathroom; **Left:** chipped doorframe between bedroom and sitting room; **Bottom far left:** Corroded-green shower knob; **Bottom center:** three-foot long string of green mildew on ceiling above the bed; **Below:** chipped paint along baseboard.

Casino management should revolve around the player experience. When I step into the operation of an existing casino to make the decision about which staff to keep or let go, the first thing I do is enter "under cover" to observe. I want to know if the general manager (and all of the managers) is on the casino floor during peak customer hours or if they are comfortably ensconced in their offices from nine to five on weekdays. British intelligence officer David John Moore Cornwell (writing under the pen-name John LeCaré) famously noted, "A desk is a dangerous place from which to view the world." If my managers are not on the floor at least some of that time, how on earth can they possibly know anything about the player experience?

In the "back of the house," away from players, is where the surgically-intense accounting and ulcer-giving analyses should be at work. A management philos-

11

ophy is indeed about customer service and marketing, but it is also about understanding uncountable nuances unique to the gambling racket. It is about our history, our behind-the-curtain secrets, how our machines operate, how regulation works, and in what business we actually operate.

What makes one casino more successful than another? Good management. The shocking discrepancies that I discussed are absolutely the byproduct of bad management; either bad operational management or bad policy-making management...either bad management in the trenches or in the corporate offices... or a combination of both.

Fortunately, players can learn to easily identify bad properties and either take advantage of them or ignore them. Likewise, operators, vendors analysts, and investors also can learn to easily identify bad properties and can take appropriate action.

However, I need to make it very clear that this is not a book about the *gaming business*; it is a book about the *gambling* business.

Chapter Three
Another typical day in the casino BUSINESS
(and what IS the casino business anyway?)

"There's a hold up in the Bronx,
Brooklyn's broken out in fights.
There's a traffic jam in Harlem
That's backed up to Jackson Heights.
There's a scout troop short a child,
Kruschev's due at Idlewild...
— **Nat Hiken,** theme from *"Car 54 Where Are You?"*
(and a typical *slow* day for a casino executive)

O n any given day there are a lot of things…a whole lot of stuff… that is constantly juggled through the brain of a casino executive. No day is a typical day; and every day is typical.

On this one, we had rented one of those big black stretch limos for Donald Trump's arrival (with his then soon-to-be wife Melania Knauss —*damn she is tall; 5'11" without those huge heels!*). Season One of NBC's *The Apprentice* had just ended and Donald Trump was a bigger "star" than he had been even in the 1980s with his *Art of the Deal* fame.

Even *I* was riding some of the show's fame because, for the final episode in April, KNBC in Los Angeles did a live-remote from the Trump Casino in Palm Springs with me as their featured color commentator and one of my staff as an in-house master of ceremonies — there I was in a celebrity-for-15-minutes adventure (ok, an hour) that had also landed me the gig as the guy who did the countdown for the west coast New Year's clock on December 31st. *(By the way, I had a childhood Times Square illusion shattered by that countdown: there is no "official clock"; the "celebrity" counter just starts counting whenever. There is not even a teleprompter or a big second-hand or a director. I just made up the numbers and if you set your clock by me, then your life may be a few seconds out of kilter.)*

Trump's gaming CEO, Mark Brown, had flown into Palm Springs with the celebrity couple to be met by his Operational Vice President (and my immediate boss) former Atlantic City dealer Vince Mascio, who had gone to the airport to brief Trump (and "Brownie") on the activities my staff had scheduled for the casino arrival.

Meanwhile, I was pacing back and forth (in my usual style) in front of the red carpet and the elephant-trunk velvet stanchions leading from the porte-cochere to the casino entrance. Out of the corner of my eye, I could see the roadie trucks for Charlie Daniels unloading for an unrelated concert that night in the casino showroom (which I called "my auditorium"). At the same time, I glanced back inside the casino toward my high-roller room to make certain that my man *Larry from Iowa* was still obliviously playing those $25-slots at $75 a spin.

Ostensibly (and for the press), "The Donald" was arriving to challenge Ginger, my tic-tac-toe playing chicken, to a $10,000 game for charity; but in reality, he was making a token appearance to appease the thirteen-member Indian tribe that actually owned the casino. Trump Hotels and Casinos had a management contract with the tribe. *(That management contract is really important in the big-picture of how Indian Casinos work and the direction I decided to go; and for that reason I have included it in the Endnotes to this book; it is public record* [3]. *But at the time, that contract was of very little interest to me.)*

When I arrived at the casino, a few months earlier, it was averaging "only" $45-million-a-month in slot machine play ("coin in"), but now that the property was pulling in $100-million in slot machine "coin-in" every month. The Tribe had tired of Donald Trump's expensive monthly fees for management, for use of the Trump name on the front of the building, for various consultants from the Trump organization, and who-knows what else; the Tribe depended on the Trump group to account for the fees being syphoned by the Trump group. But, as I said, I was not particularly concerned about all of that now; I had a casino event to operate and was much more focused on maintaining that $55-million change in fortune that I had brought the Tribe and Mister Trump.

Since the success of *The Apprentice*, the press (and especially the paparazzi) followed Trump everywhere — and I recognized the fame-wave as the ideal circumstance to stage a "media event." After all, I had a long history of staging bullshit media events. Twenty-one years earlier *Time*®, *Newsweek*®, the *Washington Post* and the *Baltimore Sun* had all lambasted me on the same day for setting up a photo-op *non-event* of Presidential Candidate Gary Hart's daughter making peanut butter and jelly sandwiches for campaign workers. *(Although it is most notable that no criticism was ever made of the media legion that showed up to film the sandwich making and eat the free food.)* At any rate, I was psyched for a media event to draw hordes of gamblers to our casino. *Publicity are us.* And whether he actually ever said it or not, "all press is good press" is often attributed to Donald Trump.

I rechecked all of the Trump arrival details: the showgirls were lined up along the entrance; the press was kept behind the ropes; Television celebrity Carson Daly's mother, Pattie Daly Caruso (a noted breast-cancer activist and Southern California television personality) was in front of the ropes for her promised "exclusive" with Don; my lead-showgirl/spokes-model, Kimmie, was waiting on the red carpet in her sequined gown to escort the VIPs; and my then-protégé, Will Wimmer (a former U.S. Border Patrol Agent), was ready to lead the security squadron through the packed crowd and to the chicken cage. I scanned the crowd looking for Tanya, my assistant, to be nearby in case anything went wrong and needed immediate action; she was in the private dining

14

room of the casino's gourmet restaurant putting finishing touches on the table where Trump was to sit with the Tribe to discuss their issues.

Yes, you have the scenario: Donald Trump, a tic-tac-toe playing chicken, a couple of thousand gamblers, and a few hundred members of the national and local press corps. Juggled against a Charlie Daniels concert, an angry 13-member Indian Tribe, and a high-roller slot player's $45,000 winning spree. You get the picture so far; *just another day in paradise.*

There was no way I could have peered into the future and seen that less than ten years later I would have be leading the casino due diligence to purchase one of the gems of the Trump empire and heading another group with hopes of financing a second casino for this Tribe (and step in as a replacement for Trump with my own management company for this very casino).

Yet that is exactly where this day's little adventures would lead me. In 2009, with the second or third collapse of his casino empire, Donald Trump resigned from *Trump Entertainment Resorts* (the successor company to my employer, *Trump Hotels & Casino Resorts),* leaving it in the hands of his creditors' holding company headed by *Avenue Capital Group,* one of the largest hedge funds focusing on distressed securities and private equity. A bankruptcy court ruled that Trump would receive 5% stock in the reorganized company and another 5% in exchange for the use of his name and likeness in perpetuity but Avenue would own the assets.

"I have nothing to do with it. I'm not in it; I'm not on the board. "It's a disaster and I see what's happened with so many others, and I don't want to be a part of it, " Trump told Blumberg's reporter.

What an understatement! But that is getting way ahead of the story. Meanwhile, true to their modus operandi, *Avenue* started selling off the three casino assets (The Marina, The Plaza, and The Taj Mahal). In February of 2011, after an interesting shuffle of assets and liabilities of the three properties, Avenue's Trump Entertainment Resorts unit sold the Trump Marina to Texas-based Landry's Restaurants which quickly rebranded that property as *The Atlantic City Golden Nugget.* By January of 2012, Avenue began the process of selling The Plaza and beefing up the Taj.

And that is where I re-entered the Trump world. The Trump Plaza was once operated by Donald Trump's wife, Ivana, and often the casino of ridicule amongst Trump staffers (primarily because of a perception of Ivana's lavish over-spending and the out-of-touch-with-reality management decisions that she made). Located in the center-position of the Boardwalk in Atlantic City, The property was a former Holiday Inn that became part of the Harrah's portfolio when the hotel giant morphed into a casino company. Harrah's had purportedly planned to partner with Bob Guccione and build the *Penthouse Hotel and Casino,* but when that deal fell apart, Trump stepped in. Donald Trump rebranded the property and purchased the adjacent *Playboy Hotel and Casino* (which he renamed the *Trump Regency* and later *The World's Fair at Trump Plaza Hotel and Casino).* Operating as *Trump Plaza,* The Donald had tapped Holiday Inn and

15

Harrah's marketing guru Gary Border to position the property as the ultimate luxury destination in Atlantic City.

After leaving Trump, Border had gone on to create the legend of Jack Binion and Horseshoe Gaming, and then created his own highly advanced marketing company.

The same day that I was doing a final edit of this chapter, I was doing a first-edit of the marketing plan for the to-be-rebranded Trump Plaza. Such deal-streams are typical in the casino world...as we will see. Armed with a proof-of-funds letter from Wells Fargo Bank and my due diligence agreement that assured me an operational contract for the casino, I found myself plowing through the bowels of The Trump Plaza less than a decade after the events of this "typical" day.

But back at my typical day and Trump and Brownie's arrival, Trump's limo arrived about twenty minutes late. I subsequently learned they had been driving in circles while Mark Brown and Vince Mascio outlined the Tribe's issues for Trump. After all, that was the *real* purpose of the visit anyway; my chicken promotion was pure subterfuge.

As the limo finally pulled up, someone cued the recorded music of the O'Jays singing their 1974 hit *"For The Love of Money"*, which was used as the theme for *The Apprentice* on NBC. The limousine stopped on its pre-arranged mark in front of the red carpet, my lead showgirl, Kimmie, opened the door and Donald Trump stepped out with Mark Brown immediately behind him. Vince and Melania followed, along with Trump's personal security team to work with the one provided by the casino. My aide, Will, stood with the security detail to hold the reporters behind the stanchions. I ran around the circumference to make sure everything was in place and ready for the media's pass to the next point.

The Press, Trump, Kimmie and Will at Gary's Trump29 Event

As soon as the two lead men stepped onto the red carpet with Kimmie leading the way, I could see the very tall Donald Trump lean over and whisper something to shorter Mark Brown as the two of them looked at the spectacle that I had created. *"Oh great,"* I thought, *"He has already found something wrong."*

As they stepped into the casino and the press began asking Trump questions about a recently-reported financial down-turn in his casino empire, I pulled Mark Brown aside to ask what had gone wrong. He looked at me puzzled and asked what I was talking about. I told him that I had seen Donald whisper to him as they walked along the red carpet. Brown laughed and said, *"Oh that. He looked at your model and told me, 'no panties'. I told him, 'no shit.'* I stared at him for a second, almost in disbelief before he re-assured me, *"You did good."*

That disaster averted, I ushered Mark to Tanya who took him to the private dining room while I rushed back to the crowd where Trump was taking questions. Eager to get my chicken promotion on the air, I slowly began guiding the Trump entourage through the crowd and toward the chicken booth. Amidst all the fluff questions about *The Apprentice* series, a reporter for the local CBS affiliate asked a tough question citing recently-released Wall Street numbers showing that the Trump casinos were losing money. The question pointedly asked if he was in California because the Tribe was concerned about losing money at this casino.

I had not expected the question but had years of "spin" experience, so I quickly fed an answer that include specific performance numbers to Will, who was still at Trump's side. He passed the numbers on to Trump who proudly announced that this casino was highly successful, the most successful in California and the most successful in the Trump empire. *Another disaster averted.*

Television fans and the press packed themselves against the stanchions as Trump approached the Chicken booth. Photographers climbed on top of slot machines to get a good shot of the game play. Our internal security team at the "eye-in-the-sky" surveillance was going crazy trying to watch the festivities as well as keep protective watch over the casino assets. Despite a prohibition and pre-event warnings, portable television lights and electronic flashes exploded in waves of strobes toward Trump and the group.

The crowd was pressing so tightly toward Trump that as soon as he got to the chicken booth we had to stretch more stanchions behind him and form a line of security guards just to give us enough room to breathe and turn around. I stepped into the little stanchion-made cage with him and triggered the tic-tac-toe game to begin. Joel inched around behind me to slide the loser tee-shirt into my hand.

Outside of a few bizarre misadventures, the tic-tac-toe chicken promotion ran pretty smoothly on a day-to-day basis. Nonetheless, I was always on alert for something to go wrong; I just did not need it to happen on the day that the national press and Donald Trump were huddled around my chicken booth.

17

Chapter Four
Meanwhile, Back At The Chicken Ranch...
...and slot machine random numbers

"Never work with animals or children; though anyone who hates animals and kids can't be all bad"
— **William Claude Dunkenfield,** better-known known as W.C. Fields

At the chicken booth, I had told Joel, the "chicken wrangler" to set the payouts at one in ten-million so that we could be assured that Trump would lose and fire the Apprentice chicken. Joel was even standing beside the booth, just out of camera range, to hand me a tee-shirt that said "I got beat by a chicken at Trump 29 casino." And I was ready to hand the shirt to Trump once he fired the chicken. Another Gary-made photo ploy guaranteed to garner headlines and airtime; but, alas, despite my own showmanship, I failed to heed the oft-quoted advice of W.C. Fields.

Enter my friend Bunky Boger and his chickens. From Lowell Arkansas, the man with the *I-couldn't-make-it-up-fiction* name made an entire life of working with and wrangling all sorts of animals. After a Warhol-esque 15 minutes of fame through a mid-1980s appearance on David Letterman's show with his life-long friend *Cody the Buffalo* (whom he allowed Dave to ride during the show), Bunky's twenty-first century wrangling was focused on a heard of chickens. No, really; I am serious.

Actually, it was a very cool gimmick designed for state fairs and the traveling carnival circuit. Despite initial trepidation from animal rights activists and assorted vegetarians (like myself), it made for a humane, clean, and fun promotion; and as Bunky likes to say *"these chickens retire with me in Arkansas which beats the heck out of their cousins that work for Tyson or Purdue and end up in the Colonel's bucket."*

Though Bunky had performed with Cody at hundreds of state fairs and arenas, his first career had been as a "bullfighter"—which I later learned was colloquial for *rodeo clown* (as opposed to a matador). Rodeo clowns, while dressed to entertain, are the heroes (or fools) who attract a charging bull's attention once it has bounced a rider in less than the eight-seconds to qualify for a rodeo ride. Bunky spent more than 30 years getting bones broken, skin gored, and saving the lives of dozens of bull riders.

Bunky Boger
Rodeo Clown

Sept. 30, 1985 Television Listing Showing
Bunky as guest on David Letterman Show

Incidentally, I had no idea how long that eight-second bull ride could actually feel until a few years later I was asked to ride a bull for a casino promotion. I was operating an Oklahoma Indian casino that had sponsored the finals for the PBR (that would be the *"Professional Bull Riders"*; and yes there IS such an organization). As part of the promotion to award the $10,000 check, I was decked out in a full tuxedo and escorted by two statuesque showgirls to a waiting bull. Although the poor Taurus-creature had been well-sedated and was long past his prime in life, it was still a harrowing experience to ride the bovine monster. Every time the damned thing took a step, I let out a little-girl-sounding yelp in anticipation of being bucked off his back and crushed under his past-his-prime weight. God bless those dudes that ride non-drugged bulls for their eight seconds!

Unlike my bull, Bunky Boger, though in his seventies, was not past HIS prime in life when he undertook chicken wrangling. First, he built a gilded box about 10-feet tall with a glass-front birdcage embedded in the left side of the box. Inside the cage, he built a feeding tray (where food would be sent once the chicken performed correctly) and a metal shield hiding a small light bulb from view outside the cage. Bunky painted, on the side of the shield that faced the glass front, the words "THINKING BOOTH" (with a tic-tac-toe board drawn beneath). Just to right of the cage, also embedded in the box, he placed a computer touch-screen with a tic-tac-toe board.

A player would walk up to the screen, touch a spot where their "X" or "O" would be placed and it would appear on the screen. Touching the screen would also turn on a light inside the chicken cage.

Bunky, his wife Connie, and their son Kelly trained the chicken(s) so that when the light came on the bird should look out the window at the computer screen then go behind the "thinking booth" and tap with its beak on a metal switch. When the switch was tapped, it would release a few pellets of food down a tube that led to the feeding tray. The bird would then get to eat.

19

More interestingly for the player, the bird's tap on the switch would trigger the computer to calculate the next move in the tic-tac-toe game. For the player, the illusion was that the chicken had looked at the screen, recognized the player's move and entered the thinking both to determine its own counter move. Once the computer...ah, the chicken...made the counter move, it would be the player's turn to make another move. This would continue until the chicken (computer) beat the player, or the game was tied, or the player beat the chicken.

Though the player saw one chicken at a time, there were actually 14 or 15 chickens with each bird working a three-hour shift before being replaced with a hungry bird. Still, the promotion was booked as "beat *the* chicken" as if it were one chicken named *Ginger*. Who amongst

ABOVE: Bunky Boger's Chicken Booth

us can tell one chicken from another, and who would know there were multiple "Gingers"?

As a variation of a less PETA-friendly sideshow from the 1940s, Bunky took this tic-tac-toe chicken on the road with him for the state fair circuit in the 1980s. Unfortunately, at a fair near Philadelphia (in the town of Bensalem) someone stole the entire coup of chickens. Apparently the city of brotherly love was also a city of chickenly love. *The Philadelphia Inquirer* had a field day with the story and turned it into a wire-service cutesy feed; and poor Bunky was out of business until he could train a new flock.

Meanwhile legendary casino regulator-turned operator Dennis Gomes spotted the story and wondered how the chickens would work as a casino promotion. Along with outside marketing gurus Frank Palmieri and Jan Talamo, he tested it and, for years, Bunky's chickens dominated the boardwalk at *The Trop* as the hottest promotion in Atlantic City.

"I thought it would be phenomenal. I told it to our people, our marketing people and (Trop President) Pam Popielarski and they all went crazy. There was a big laugh but they thought it would be big," Gomes said.

Linda Kassekert, the chair of the New Jersey Casino Control Commission, recalled Gomes' response when she asked him whether the chicken stunt would stir controversy among animal-rights advocates. "He told me, 'Listen, that chicken is living better than you and me.'"

In October of 2008 Gomes told Bunky that he considered his discovery of the chickens to be the high point of his career.

Despite my own trepidation over a side-show chicken playing Tic-Tac-Toe, I took a gamble, based on Gomes' endorsement and the tip, recommendation, *and insistence*, of Trump General Manager Mark Lefever. Mark is one of those unsung earth-movers of the gaming industry and insistence from him is generally a really good bet. I booked Bunky's birds as the *"$10,000 Chicken Challenge,"* promising the huge prize to anyone that could beat "Ginger" heads up at tic-tac-toe.

It would be free to play, but the caveats were that (1) you could only play once a day and (2) you were required to be a member of my players' club in order to challenge the chicken. The gamble paid off as Ginger became an instant hit with the chicken booth open 10 hours a day and a constant line (for the entire 10 hours) stretching through the casino and to the front door.

With one play taking approximately one minute, we had about 600 people a day challenging the chicken. I set up all the typical P.R. promotions with the local television news anchors playing against the chicken (and losing) as well as many of the celebrities that I would book into that 2,100 seat showroom.

More importantly, this particular promotion solved one of the biggest issues that face casino marketers in general. In order to target offers…to segment good customers from average customers from bad ones…the casino needs to monitor play. This is done by players inserting a club card into a slot machine while they play (or handing it to a dealer at a table game). The incentive to the player is that use of the card earns "points" that are traded for gifts, comps, cash, offers, and so on. The problem is that many players don't use the cards: they forget them; they are superstitious that the casino can somehow manipulate the payouts based on the cards; they don't want to bother standing in line to join the club; or the value proposition is not enough to motivate them.

When I first arrived at Trump29 Casino, less than 17% of the players in the casino were using tracking cards; only 17 out of every 100 people on the casino floor were using a player's card. That meant that at any given time, we had no idea who 83% of our players were. Not only did we not know their names, we didn't know how much each one was betting, how often they came in, how long they stayed, or what towns or neighborhoods they came from. How the hell can you run a business if you have no idea who 83% of your customers are; or worse yet, you have no idea how much money 83% of your customers are individually spending?

As a direct result of the tic-tac-toe chicken promotion, the number of players using their cards jumped from 17% to 44% the first month and rocketed to 74% by the end of the promotion; *a truly amazing phenomenon.* Equally impressive, our incremental slot revenue increased by 13%. This slot machine increase was directly traceable to so many people coming in at least once a week to challenge Ginger; once a week more frequently than they typically came by to play. The promotion was a phenomenal success for us; no wonder Dennis Gomes had dreamed it up! *I should have sent him a thank you card.*

As a consolation prize for the thousands of players who did not beat the chicken, I awarded them a tee-shirt with the words *"I got beat by the chicken at Trump29 Casino"* above a cartoon drawing of a muscular Ginger winning at tic-tac-toe. The tee shirts were being worn all over Southern California; I saw one in a fish house at Venice Beach one night and one at Magic Mountain all the way up in Valencia.

In the process, I became close friends with Bunky, his wife Connie, their children, and their chicken wrangler. I used the promotion over and over at casinos to such a degree that it became associated with me and one Tribal leader even argued that I owned the promotion. I do own Bunky's website (casinoChicken.com), but that is simply a favor to my good friends the Bogers.

At Trump29 it was a great promotion that was seen all over the state, thanks to the P.R. and a lot of paid television spots. The arrival of "Ginger" was promoted on television with the famous male strippers, *The Chippendales,* clad in shirtless tuxedos carrying the chicken into the casino inside a gilded emperor's carrying chair. (You can see these TV spots on YouTube as well as at www.GaryGreenGaming.com). It was my plan that Donald Trump's arrival on the heels of *The Apprentice* would catapult the promotion to national attention and draw even more players into the casino. And I had scripted everything perfectly…so I thought.

Neither *Ginger Number One* nor any of the 14 surrogate chickens actually played tic-tac-toe. As I explained earlier, the chickens were trained to tap a button that triggered the computer play. Customers were actually playing against computer software. Since it was computer controlled, I could also control how frequently (if at all) I paid out the prize — the $10,000, in this particular promotion.

I would simply tell the chicken wrangler how to set the payout, and he would adjust the computer. To avoid giving away $10,000 every day, I had him set the computer at 1 in 1,000,000. This did not mean that the game would have to be played 999,999 times before there was a payout, but it did mean that on the average one win would happen in every one million plays. That one winner could be player number one or it could happen anywhere between one and a million plays; it was random…within those set parameters.

That would seem simple enough, but the world of random numbers is a complicated maze for non-mathematicians; and I am certainly a non-mathematician. I had already learned the hard way about the randomness of such formulas, with the first $10,000 winner of the tic-tac-toe promotion.

The "chicken wrangler" that Bunky had chosen for the Trump casino was a thirty-something year old Oklahoma native named Joel Faulk. Joel had worked for Bunky for years in various capacities and was himself a seasoned rodeo performer and trick roper. In fact, Joel's rope tricks were so outstanding that after seeing one of his performances, Will Rogers Jr. presented Joel with one of the original ropes used by Will Rogers Senior. Joel had also gone on to work with the Royal Hannaford Circus as both a trick roper and as a ring master.

Shaved bald a lá Yul Brynner, Telly Savalas, Stone Cold Steve Austin, or Vin Diesel *(depending on your generation)* and with a deep radio-esque voice, Joel was ideal for several radio voiceovers and for announcing various promotions and player-participation stage events at the casino. I also hired him, some years later, to use his show-biz tent-filling expertise to craft a bus program for an Indian casino in Montana (similar to the one he had worked with in Southern California).

Joel Faulk and Ginger

Somewhere out on the web there is a great video of a younger Joel standing up on a galloping horse and jumping back and forth (with full knee-bend jumps) through a lasso loop. Apparently, at one time the young rodeo-champion Joel was all the rage. But, by this time in his life we was, at least temporarily, chicken wrangling for his old mentor, Bunky Boger.

Ginger had been on my casino floor for about 45 days and more than 25,000 games had been played. There was no sign of the promotion losing steam; but to keep interest high we decided to give away $10,000…to allow someone to *beat* the chicken.

The strategic problem was that we were 30 to 45 minutes away from the nearest television stations and I wanted to have evening news coverage of the win to get as much mileage as I could from spending $10,000. Why give away ten-large if I am not buying maximum player awareness?

So I developed a bogus news event and a press conference on some unrelated subject; a non-story to bring the television stations, radio news, and the newspapers to the casino. My plan was that just as the spurious event ended, someone would beat the chicken and the win ten thousand dollars. The attending press was sure to be disappointed from the non-news event and convinced they had spent all of this time and distance for a non-story with nothing in the film can. The "wild coincidence" that someone beat the chicken while they were packing up would just save the day for them.

As I said, we had been having about 600 people a day play against the chicken. I set the press conference for midday, so I instructed Joel to set the computer to pay out 1 in 300 rather than the one-in-a-million setting. My hope was that someone would win about midday. The press would be packing up and just about ready to walk by the chicken promotion when someone would win. *At least that was the plan.*

Five minutes before the end of the press conference, I rushed to the promotional booth to check with the chicken wrangler, Joel. Everything was set. I es-

23

timated that the press would begin walking by in about five minutes and would linger in the casino for no longer than 20 minutes.

At the rate of one player every 60 seconds, I told Joel to reset the payout to 1 in 20. I ran back to the press conference to watch it end on time, and then calmly walked back to the general vicinity of the tic-tac-toe chicken.

Joel signaled me that five people had played so I began counting the players as the press members walked my direction.

Fifteen — fourteen — thirteen — twelve — eleven — ten ... *getting close now...* nine — eight — seven — six — five — four — three — two ... *still no winner...* — one — zero... *what?* No winner? +1 — +2 — +3.

I rushed to the promotion booth, pulled Joel aside and frantically demanded that he reset the payout to 1 in 5. He did and I began the countdown as I watched the press mill through the casino and toward the door.

Five — four — three — two — one — zero — +1 — +2... still no winner!

Again I grabbed Joel, "reset it again. 1 in 3" I counted again:

one — two — three — four. *Still no winner.*

Random number generators are truly *random* and NOT predictable. *One-in-three* actually meant that on the average there would be one winner in every three players; which, of course, means that theoretically 200,000 people could play before there is a winner then there would be 100,000 winners in a row. And, there were an infinite number of mathematical possibilities of getting to that first winner.

Almost a half hour had passed and press members were packing to leave. I sent Tanya over to offer them free lunch in our buffet, knowing that most would not accept it but hoping to stall. I turned to Joel and pleaded "set it at 1 in every 2".

Again I counted — 1 — 2 — 3. *Damnit.*

I took a deep breath and told Joel, "See that woman, second in line? When she gets to the booth, she wins; make it pay 1 in 1; every player is a winner." Joel went behind the booth and inside the little closet where the computer was housed.

Not so amazingly, the woman won $10,000 by "beating" the chicken. As soon as she won the lights flashed, a siren sounded, and speakers began to blare Werner Thomas's classic German accordion melody *"The Chicken Dance"* song. An "explosion" on top of the booth launched a shower of brightly–colored confetti across the casino floor. Excited members of the press rushed toward the winner and I very dramatically feigned shock. *God, I love show biz!*

Unfortunately for my press purposes, the winner was not a "local"; she was a traveling nurse who was in the area for a six-month gig and had come to the casino on a dare to play against the chicken on her last day in California. There went the scores of her friends and neighbors rushing to my casino to play. More importantly, there went the follow-up stories, damnit.

Still, the winning was a huge success, the media coverage of the winner re-energized the whole promotion, and I learned a lot about the whole random-number process and how unpredictable it can be. No wonder slot machines seem to be such an enigma (more on that later).

ABOVE: Gary Green, the losing chicken and the first $10,000 winner; **BELOW:** Gary and the chicken are interviewed by a local television reporter shortly after the win.

Meanwhile, to take advantage of the media-generated excitement over a $10,000 winner and the success of Trump's hit television show, my staff and I created a new tic-tac-toe chicken promotion called *"The Apprentice Chicken."*

We filmed a very elaborate (and hilariously funny) television commercial in which a newscaster announced that Ginger the tic-tac-toe playing chicken had been beaten and had cost Donald Trump $10,000 at his casino. From outside a

25

door marked "Boardroom", you could hear Donald Trump's voice uttering his by-then famous tagline, *"You're fired."* A second later, I came out of the boardroom, my tie loosened and my hair mussed. Looking at the reporter I frantically gasped, *"He just fired Ginger. This is a total disaster."*

The next scene showed me in another boardroom saying, *"I know you are wondering why I called this meeting."* The camera pulled back to reveal the boardroom table was covered with live chickens, looking at me, clucking and doing whatever it is that chickens do. My dialogue continued, *"I know you are just Apprentice chickens, but you have to step up to the plate and fill the vacancy left by Ginger."*

Gary & Trump's Apprentice Chickens preparing for TV spot

A voiceover then explained that Ginger had been replaced by *Apprentices*. Players could challenge the apprentice chickens and each time one of the apprentices was defeated, that bird would be eliminated until there was only one winning chicken left.

Each time a chicken was defeated, the winning player would be awarded $250; a much smaller prize because these were *"just Apprentice chickens who were not tic-tac-toe masters like Ginger had been"*.

In conjunction with the new commercial (which you can see on *YouTube*), I provided free Buffalo wings at happy hour, reporting that players would be eating the late Ginger. I cut the hours back to eight hours a day (about 480 players a day) and had Joel set the payouts to 1 in 250 so that we would have an average of *at least* one winner every day.

To further mimic Trump's successful television show, I adopted the colors of the show and the background outline of New York City in all of my billboards and print ads.

One of Gary Green's Trump29 Apprentice Chicken billboards

My thought was to stretch the Apprentice program out for a month, until Trump arrived, have him beat an apprentice and utter live his now-famous tag line, *"You're fired"*, to the losing chicken. At that point, I would find a "winning" chicken and start the $10,000 chicken challenge all over again.

In addition to the billboards and television, we exploited *The Apprentice* television show, the $10,000 chicken prize, and Trump firing Ginger in every way I could possibly imagine. My March 2004 newsletter, mailed to all players' club members announced the hiring of the 15 apprentice chickens and I bombarded the Coachella Valley, Southern California and the national casino-player press with as many stories, pictures, and videos as I could create.

Casino Newsletter Reports Ginger Fired   Print Ad For Apprentice Chickens

Hence the stage was set to create a promotional front (and really good excuse) for Donald Trump's arrival in Palm Springs to meet with the members of the Twenty-Nine Palms Band of Mission Indians of Coachella California. Along

27

the way, it solved my problem of not enough players using their cards and it increased revenue even before the targeted mailings. The TV and print ads hit and we were on our way.

At my prompting, Trump made the first move, putting and "X" in the center square. The chicken/computer responded by putting an "O" in the upper right corner of the tic-tac-toe board. Trump, in turn, placed an "X" in the top center square, giving him two in a row.

As soon as I saw the computer respond to Trump's move by picking the top right square I could feel myself tense up. I had watched Joel set the damned thing to pay out only one in ten-million; but this move did not look like the typical patterns I had seen the computer play. Still, there was one blocking move for the computer to make, the bottom center square.

Instead, the computer picked the bottom right square. Unless Donald Trump was an absolute idiot it would be impossible for him to lose (except for the unlikelihood that he would throw the game). One in ten-million and that damned random number generator was going to get me again. In my mind I could already hear *"You're fired"* being aimed at ME.

I could also imagine people, not understanding the random number generators, scratching their heads in naïve dismay, and sincerely thinking *"That Donald Trump; no wonder he is so rich. He is just the luckiest man in America; he beat those chickens. He must be really smart too."*

ABOVE: Donald Trump ponders the Tic-Tac-Toe screen as Gary worriedly watches

Donald Trump is no idiot, and as soon as he realized what happened, he played off of it like a showbiz pro. He leaned slightly toward me and almost without moving his mouth, he muttered, *"what now?"*

I patted him on the back and said *"You fucking won; be happy. Smile."*

He turned toward the crowd, raised a power fist of victory, and gave a big smile. With only a slight hesitation, I began leading the crowd in cheering applause as we opened the stanchions and led Trump toward the private meeting with the Tribe.

To this day, most of the Tribal members as well as a majority of my staff are convinced that I had rigged the game for Trump to win. I think, at the end of the whole chicken ordeal, Trump took it in stride as just another promotional event; and he has had so many, I doubt if he even remembers this more than "just another day".

I, on the other hand, immediately put staff to work publicizing the *Donald Trump vs. the chicken* event. Think about it: I had taken an icon of New York serious business —*such an icon that he had the number one rated TV show about people wanting to work for him*— and reduced him to playing with

ABOVE: Donald Trump, Gary Green, and The Press react to Trump's unexpectedly beating the Tic-Tac-Toe playing chicken. Below: SNL script for Trump's chicken appearance.

chickens. What a story! The press was already there for his celebrity appearance, and so many pictures and videos were taken, we had created a massive national publicity event by "humiliating" the ever-so-serious business icon into a tic-tac-toe match with a chicken

Besides the local news, NBC's Nightly News picked up the story along with CNN, and even the business-stalwart CNBC. (Of course it helped that his *Apprentice* television show was on NBC). The wire services and hundreds of daily newspapers across the country picked up the story:

> Associated Press
>
> COACHELLA, Calif. — Without any specific strategy, dealmaker Donald Trump battled a live chicken and won.
>
> The real estate mogul showed up at his namesake Trump 29 Casino on Tuesday and played the Apprentice Chicken Challenge, a tic-tac-toe game with live poultry in a booth pecking its board selections while a gambler makes picks outside the box.
>
> The Donald beat the bird.
>
> Trump dropped in and spent a half-hour answering questions about his hit TV show, NBC's "The Apprentice," signed T-shirts and books and humored fans by spouting his catchphrase, "You're fired!"

Beyond the legitimate news media, *Entertainment Tonight, Extra,* along with that whole *National Enquirer* genre of television "entertainment news" shows) used the video footage provided by my staff.

Indeed, at the height of the "serious business" reality show, Donald Trump was challenging a chicken to a duel of tic-tac-toe! This was before *"Celebrity Apprentice"*, before Trump made a public spectacle out of jumping onto the silliness of *"where is Obama's birth certificate"*, and when *The Apprentice* was considered to be semi-serious reality television. In this light, the marvelously self-deprecating gimmick (and Trump was a pro about playing along) was beautifully crowned a week later when Trump hosted *Saturday Night Live,* dressed in a white suite, yellow shirt with a yellow tie, and surrounded by cast members dressed as chickens popping out of eggs. Though ostensibly the SNL appearance and skit had nothing to do with the tic-tac-toe adventure, in reality the national publicity gener ated by the chicken-challenge at Trump29 had for *that* particular 15-minutes identified the casino real estate mogul with... chickens.

SATURDAY NIGHT LIVE: Donald Trump's House of Wings

Donald Trump; David Crosby as Horatio Sanz; Dancing Chickens: Maya Rudolph, Amy Poehler, Kenan Thompson and Seth Meyers

[Cheap neon sign reads: TRUMP'S House of Wings. The synth-driven riff from the Pointer Sisters' hit 1984 pop song "Jump (For My Love)" is heard as we pull back and pan down to reveal real estate mogul Donald Trump in a spectacularly awful all-yellow suit and tie. He stands in front of a couple of diners and addresses the camera.]

Donald Trump: Cock-a-doodle-doo, folks. I'm Donald Trump.... And there's two things in the world I love -- a good deal and a good meal. So when I drove by a defunct Meineke Muffler Shop in Englewood, New Jersey ... I knew what I hadda do! I hadda buy it on the cheap and convert it into a restaurant specializing in buffalo chicken wings. ... So I did. And it's the most important thing I've ever done in my entire life. ... So, please, join me -- at Donald Trump's House of Wings!

[Trump gestures and four dancers, wearing goofy yellow and white chickens-popping-out-of-eggshells costumes, boogie into view and join him. They gesture energetically as they sing a parody of "Jump":]

Dancing Chickens: [sing]
Trump! You know our wings will make you happy!
Trump in! You know our wings will fill you up!
Trump! If you want a place with awesome chicken wings, yeah,
Donald Trump's House of Wings!

Following the publicity massive, I quickly eliminated the rest of the "apprentice chickens" through daily cash giveaways and a mark-off on an oversized score card that mimicked the one on the NBC Apprentice web site.

Utilizing the first chicken arrival Chippendale footage along with the news footage of Trump's win, and the follow-up commercial of my hiring the apprentice chickens, we created a third television spot to reintroduce a $10,000 giveaway and a replacement for "the

Donald Trump's chicken skit on *Saturday Night Live*

late" Ginger by a new winning chicken apprentice who we called "Ruby". You can view all three of the television spots on YouTube.

One might expect that after so much press exposure the excitement would die down and the glitter would wear off of the promotion. Instead, it became even bigger. Millions of people wanted to be like Donald Trump; almost no one could be. Millions more wanted to be on The Apprentice; very VERY few could be. But thousands and thousands could imitate Trump and play tic-tac-toe against the famous chicken in the very spot where they had seen Donald do it. Plus they could "connect" to The Apprentice by playing against Apprentice Chickens —all, seemingly, with Donald Trump's seal of approval.

Despite all of our successes with Bunky's promotion, we had been through some real harrowing times with the chickens; times that made the random number generator incidences seem minor.

From the onset, we had the issue of where the chickens would sleep. The Trump29 Casino was located in the middle of desert about 20 miles east of Palm Springs in the town of Coachella, east of Palm Desert, La Quinta, and Indio. Some days the temperature would be well over 110°. If we had kept their cages outside, we would have had roasted chickens available for the buffet. Besides, Bunky's contract *required* that we keep the chickens indoors in an air conditioned, clean, safe environment where the wrangler could have feeding, cleaning, and lighting access.

Have you ever smelled 15 caged chickens? *(I am from the rural South and I HAVE!)* There is clearly a reason that farmers keep their chicken coops far away from the house, over a hill, and down wind. To further complicate the smell issue, we were running a buffet/café, a gourmet restaurant, snack nooks, three bars, banquet rooms, a showroom, an employee dining room, and a five-restaurant food court that included a *McDonalds*. We could not put the chickens anywhere that their smell would reach customers or food services. After literally days of consternation we finally found a back-of-the-house room near the showroom and away from busy areas of the casino. The only problem was that the little room was one of the very few spots in the casino that was not covered by the eye-in-the-sky security system. Surveillance could not watch the chickens. Truly, finding a place to house 15 chickens inside an upscale casino almost caused us to cancel the whole damned contract. Chicken housing was a huge issue; and therein would be two additional problems.

The staff at this particular casino came, for the most part, from the nearby communities of Coachella and Indio. A large part of the staff was fluent in neither English nor Spanish, with "Spanglish"/"pochismo" being their actual language. Though a high school education was a requirement for a "key" license, many employees, especially in the housekeeping and maintenance departments, had not graduated from high school...or, sadly, even elementary school. Many who *had* graduated were not exactly at the top of their classes. That is not to imply they were not smart, that they were not great employees, or not great people; generally, they were all of those things. It simply means that that they formally were not well educated. Additionally, many of the employees were deeply steeped in border culture; a world unto itself.

Late one night a maintenance man stumbled across the secret room filled with chicken cages. He walked in, saw the chickens, and as an animal lover with chickens of his own, he determined that the birds were hungry. He rushed to the employee dining room and filled a tray with mashed potatoes, corn, and other veggies. He brought the tray back to the out-of-camera-sight chicken room and proceeded to feed all 15 of the birds. Unfortunately, he was not aware that the way the tic-tac-toe game worked was that the birds needed to be just hungry enough to want to tap the button to release pellets of food. Fattened well-fed birds were not apt to play the game; in fact, they were more likely to *sleep* in the booth. That is not to say Joel-the-wrangler starved the birds; they were well fed in their cages, but the timing of the meals as well as the amount of food was carefully calculated so that they would be hungry *enough* to participate in the game.

The day following the maintenance man's feeding of the birds, we had to close the promotion because none of the birds would perform. It took us more than 24 hours to figure out what had happened; and then we only understood after the same guy stopped by that night to check on the hungry birds. Fortunately, Joel was sitting with the birds all night, thinking they might be ill; he really was a nursemaid to Bunky's birds.

Once I explained how the promotion worked, the maintenance guy was completely cool with it and, of course, there were no consequences to him for his friend-of-animals gesture. He did offer us the "tip" that we should feed the birds more often and that he would be happy to care for them on Joel's days off (which he had none).

The most bizarre of the many chicken near-disasters came when another employee was found...ah...*with* ...one of the chickens. After the feeding incident we had asked the surveillance department to train a camera on the hallway that led to the chicken room; the last position where cameras could record at least anyone entering that hallway toward the room. That way they could see if anyone approached the room to feed the birds and surveillance could notify Joel if any unauthorized person did so. On one particular afternoon, the sharp-eyes of surveillance spotted an employee headed toward the chicken room. They called Joel, who was, unfortunately, off property at the time. When they finally located someone to check on the chickens, the employee was in the chicken room with his pants down around his ankles as he tightly held one of the chickens while he was apparently attempting to have sex with it. Poor Ginger!

At another casino where I employed Bunky and Ginger, Bunky called to tell me that Joel would not be available so he was sending another chicken wrangler who went by the name of "The Oklahoma Kid." No problem. As Bunky described the Kid's expertise he pitched, *"he was a bullfighter (rodeo clown) at Madison Square Garden for 30 years."*

32

I was silent as I considered how old "The Kid" must be to have worked anywhere for 30 years. Noticing my silence and thinking it was disappointment over not getting Joel, Bunky added, *"Since he left New York, he has spent the last 25 years handling animals at state fairs and rodeos."*

Finally I asked, *"Bunky, just how old is The Kid?"* Without missing beat, Bunky responded, "82 years young."

At my next casino, the 13 "Gingers" were wrangled by "The Kid."

Chapter Five

Behind the scenes of the stage...
(more of the "typical" day)

*"All the world's a stage,
And all the men and women merely players:
They have their exits and their entrances"*
— Shakespeare's As You Like It, spoken by
Jaques in Act II Scene VII.

On this day, Donald Trump had much more to be concerned about than Gary's little casino publicity tic-tac-toe chicken gimmick. The rest of that trip, for him, was all about the situation with the Tribe —which eventually resulted in the Tribe being released from their contract with Trump management. But MY day was still young; that "typical day" was far from over.

That night, unrelated and totally coincidental to the Trump visit, we had booked southern-rock/country legend Charlie Daniels to play in the 2,100-seat *Spotlight Showroom*. It was a different kind of show than our normal bookings; as a property so closely tied to the Trump image, we usually leaned toward the Rickles / Tony Bennett / Paul Anka set of Vegas acts or 1970s-80s rock bands (Peter Frampton, Doobie Brothers, Earth Wind and Fire) or (then) newer standup comics (George Lopez, Howie Mandel, Carrot Top).

As with all things casino and many things native, there had been some few minor awkward moments as the normal "Vegas" lineup of stars had made our showroom widely recognized as the premier concert venue in the Palm Springs area and added to the glitz and glamour of the Trump image. Though a well-known venue within Southern California, among many of the show business celebrities it was just another stop on the "Indian Casino" circuit to others. And, with Donald Trump's name gilded on the front of the building, few even knew that the reason the casino was called *Trump 29* because it was a partnership between the thirteen-member *29 Palms Band of Mission Indians* (who owned the casino) and *Trump Hotels and Casinos*, which had the management contract. Outside of the industry, few people understood that intricacy.

One notable exception was Howie Mandel, one of the smartest and most well-informed performers. Mandel opened his standup routine by saying *"I am happy to be here at Trump 29 Casino. It is not my favorite. Trump 28 is good. Trump 31 is better."* No one laughed. And some of the Tribal members were, apparently, offended that Trump 29 was NOT his favorite. No one got Mandel's joke; he was way too smart for the audience we had provided to him; and that was my fault for booking him to that audience.

On another night at a *"meet and greet"* backstage reception with Tribal members, Don Rickles, completely inadvertently, offended Tribal sensitivities

34

just by being the wonderful Don Rickles. Coming from his dressing room, already dressed in his tuxedo shirt and black tie, but without his pants on, Rickles had put on a smoking jacket/bathrobe before entering the "green room". Pretending to be dazed, he turned to his staff member and joked, *"What the hell are these people doing in my dressing room."* Rolling with the master's humor, the staffer said, *"These are the Tribal leaders."* After shaking hands with each of the attending members, Rickles was introduced to the Chairman (chief) of the Tribe; he quipped, *"All this is yours? That's great. Now get the hell out of my dressing room."* Instantly noting the surprise on the leader's face, Rickles quickly followed up, *"No, no, I mean no offense. You know how I am; now get the hell out of my dressing room. Really."* As part of the shtick, Rickles then turned to me, *"You. You are the guy that hired me right?"* I responded, *"Yes Sir."* He looked back at the Tribal leaders trying to make them understand the joke, and continued to address me *"Good. You have my check. You stay. The rest of you go."*

LEFT: Don Rickles with Gary Green backstage in the "green room" for a "meet and greet" at the Trump 29 Spotlight Showroom before one of Rickles appearances there.

It was classic Rickles and brilliantly delivered with perfect timing; but Tribal sensitivities being what they were at the time, this old white man blowing off the Natives to talk to another white man (supposedly with a check) was just symptomatic of a greater issue.

Don Rickles, of course, meant no offense, never would mean offense, and was not even aware that anyone would seriously take offense. In fact, so far into his well-known career, and having reached legend status, it is almost amazing that it would still be necessary to have this discussion to explain what he does for a living. After all, in advertising the coming of his concert, I had taken out a series of full page newspaper "teaser" ads that where totally blank except for a hockey puck in the bottom corner of the page and the caption *"Guess Who Is Coming To Trump29."* *"You hockey puck"* was one of Rickles' signature lines.

Yet two Tribal members seriously asked me if we were putting in an ice rink. Fortunately, the concert was a sellout, of course, and Rickles was brilliant and certainly never offensive.

Nonetheless, such minor little hiccups in smooth operation were typical crisis-du-jour and were (or should have been) little cause for further thought. The same was true for the Charlie Daniels issue to come...I thought.

There was a big country/rock following in the Coachella Valley and we had booked this concert several months before knowing of Trump's visit. We had missed the country music set altogether and I was hoping to bring in a different segment of after-show gamblers. At the time we booked the show, we had no idea that Trump and the New Jersey execs would be in town at the same time. So goes the typical day in the casino business.

It was a packed house and it even impressed the very east-coast-minded New Jersey Trump officials who had remained in town after Donald flew out that afternoon. Brown, Mascio, and the Jersey Trump group lined the back of the standing-room-only auditorium and cheered with the rest of the crowd as The Charlie Daniels Band went through their classic hits: *"The Devil Went Down To Georgia"*, *"Long Haired Country Boy"*, *"The South's Gonna Do It"*, and the others.

Then it happened. Midway through the rollicking show, Charlie Daniels dismissed his band. He pulled one solitary wooden bar stool mid-stage, picked up an acoustic guitar and took off his trademark Hoss-Cartwright-style hat, revealing his balding head.

"Ladies and Gentlemen, several years ago I gave my soul to the Lord Jesus Christ and I would like to share some of my favorite gospel songs with you," he announced from the stage.

The auditorium fell dead silent. Unsure if he was serious or not, the entire crowd did not even breath, waiting for him to either begin playing guitar or tell them it was a joke. It was so quiet you could hear the gurgle of the ice machine in the snack bar at the back of the auditorium. The longer the pause the more obvious it became that he was serious. At best, it was not an appropriate set list for a casino that positioned itself as a Vegas-like "sin city" / Trump-glitter gambling center.

Finally, the deathly silence was broken by one of the New Jersey Trump officials who boomed his voice through the entire auditorium in a heavy-Jersey accent, *"Get da fuck outta here. Dis is a casino not a fuckin' church."*

Shades of *Tony Soprano*! The auditorium erupted with laughter, including from Charlie on the stage. Unfortunately, Charlie was serious about his musical selection, and apparently about his religious conversion as well. Though he gave us one of the best renditions of *Precious Memories* that I have ever heard, the foul-mouthed Trump executive was correct and we were ordered never to book Daniels again...as much as I personally loved him.

Meanwhile my cell phone was vibrating with a text-message; there was a problem in the high-roller room. After this fucked-up day, if someone had pissed off Larry-the-high-roller I was not going to be a happy boy. I hoped that it was something simple like the buffet girl in the Platinum Lounge didn't come in for the late shift, again. Hopefully it was one of those *minor details*.

When I arrived at Platinum after getting the alarmed text at the Charlie Daniels concert, I was immediately corralled by one of my senior Casino Hosts who told me there had been a complaint from one of our quasi-high rollers, Eva. She was complaining that one of the Hostesses had been ignoring her and soliciting money from two other Platinum Members: Mr. Gimhae-Kim and my guy Larry. *Fuck; Not Larry.*

Eva was an interesting and typical, albeit sad, story. She and her husband had owned a small Midwestern chain of pharmacies and at retirement age had very fortunately sold out before the Walgreens and CVS's of the world drove the small owners out of business. With a very comfortable nest egg the couple retired to Palm Springs and settled into the life of the desert gentry. When her husband died, a few years later, Eva became quite the "woman-about-town" hobnobbing with the Palm Springs social registrants (Barbara Sinatra, President and Betty Ford, etc.). In her spare time, between social outings, she began gambling — high roller gambling — at Trump, Spa, Agua Caliente, and other upscale Southern California casinos; she was a premier member of my Platinum room for a long time. Then, like many gamblers' stories, she went bust; she lost most of her fortune. To pay her bills and living expenses, Eva took a job selling upscale real estate and living off of balloon commissions that would come with each multi-million-dollar sale. Soon her gambling habit ate up even that money, and she began to cut back. Her *coin-in* dropped from six-figures weekly to a few hundred dollars. She no longer qualified for Platinum membership, but we didn't have the heart to throw her out. The only down-side was that she was a constantly complaining busy-body and treated all casino employees as "the help" there to serve her. On this particular day, Eva was just being a busy-body and telling-on the Hostess for what she observed as "neglect".

Gimhae-Kim was a very wealthy Korean gambler who spoke very little English but gambled tens of thousands of dollars every week. He was actually assigned to and generally managed (because of the language issue) by my right-hand, Steve Sohng, a native Korean himself. Larry was a very-high roller gambler whose weekly play could easily alter the casino's winning numbers. Normally a whining complaint of neglect from Eva would have meant very little, but the very fact that this complaint involved some kind of problem with Gimhae-Kim and Larry was more than enough reason to call me.

I immediately called Steve to candidly talk with Mr. Gimhae-Kim. After a few moments of intense Korean discussion, Steve returned to brief me. Despite his less-than-fluent command of English, it seemed that the hostess had been talking with Gimhae-Kim about the fact that she lives alone. Regardless of the implication of that conversation, Gimhae-Kim had suggested that she buy a dog for companionship. When she complained that she did not make enough to afford a puppy, he offered to give her the cash to buy one. Apparently encouraged

37

by his offer, and oblivious to my policy of hosts and hostesses not being allowed to toke out (take tips), she whined to him that she could not afford to feed a growing puppy. Whether to dismiss her or to encourage her, Gimhae-Kim offered to give her cash for a year's worth of dog food. She thanked him, but turned down the offer and thus preserved her job (though ultimately she *did* buy a dog).

Larry had no complaint with the girl. In fact, he had no opinion one way or another; he was totally oblivious to her. All he wanted was to spin those slot machine reels. So there was no infraction there from Eva's complaint.

Then there was Larry. For weeks we had been trying to find something to comp to Larry. Those earned "players' club points" accrue on casino books and, since they can be traded in for food and gifts, they have a cash-equivalent value. Larry never took a comp so he had tens of thousands of dollars of cash equivalent on the books; that is a true nightmare for those CPA types…not to mention casino bosses. We had tried to give him showroom tickets, meals, trips, hotel rooms… he didn't want anything. We had been driving ourselves crazy pitching offers to Larry, though it was not like we were trying to buy his Platinum loyalty; we had that. We just wanted to keep him happy and get some of those damned points off the books.

This same hostess, well aware of management's problem, decided to take it on herself to find Larry's weakness. No one but she knows if the plan was for one of those weaknesses to be a roll in the hay with her; but the fact is she did spend more time with him than with busy-body non-revenue-generating Eva. Eva, in fact, *had* been neglected in that sense.

However the hostess was successful where none of us had been. It seems that Larry had at least one vice other than slot machines: a particular type of cigars. He had affection for something called *Cohiba Behike*, which we discovered sold for $440 a stogie (though I doubt it was actually a cheroot) or $17,600 a box. Apparently Larry did not subscribe to Mark Twain's observation, *"if it costs above 5 cents, I know it to be either foreign or half foreign and unsmokable."*

The hostess had in fact done what she was supposed to do, even in her neglect of Eva; she found a motivator for an important customer. Good job.

Fortunately, (for those of us with short anti-office attention spans) there are no "typical" days at casinos. If I had to be a Japanese *salaryman* or even a Midwestern CPA, I would be a total failure. I thrive in the constantly changing adventure, volatility, and intensity of the casino world. I love the universe of history, methodologies, and think-on-your-feet decisions that are part of every single day of casino life. Hell, I even enjoy the instability and volatility of the seemingly-lunatic characters that make up the casino universe of owners, board members, tribal officials, investors, and CEOs.

Once in the late 1990s IBM spent a lot of money flying me from Florida to San Francisco several times, courting me for a position in the Global Services

Practice. Many times I have been reminded what a miserable and short-lived career that would have been; *me in an IBM "uniform" and behavior pattern?*

I often tell new hires, at orientations, that everything they have seen in movies about casinos is not true AND is true at the same time. There are dozens of operational issues that "civilians" don't ever know or even think about:

- **Employees dying.** Happens all the time. Once at an Indian casino I had a short order cook die in my kitchen (from an overdose of cocaine). The Tribal Chief ordered the body moved out of the casino and off of Indian land before the cook could be pronounced dead. The Chief didn't want people to think the casino was haunted by evil spirits from having someone die there; he was afraid tribal members would not gamble in a place unlucky enough to have a death. I am serious; and this was in the 21st century.

- **Customers refusing to leave seat.** At one casino I had to keep an ever-changing supply of slot machine chairs because so many customers refused to leave their machines when they were on a "winning-streak". So when it was time for them to go to the bathroom, they would just urinate or defecate in their clothes and hence soil my chairs. My warehouse had a collection of seriously smelly chairs. And, there are those absurd Vegas stories of customers refusing to leave slot machines during the deadly MGM fire that killed 85 people in Las Vegas.

- **Casino running out of cash.** In January of 2004 one of Las Vegas' most recognized landmark casinos, *Binion's Horseshoe* was closed by regulators for not having enough cash. The Nevada Gaming Control Commission's *Regulation 6.150* very specifically sets formulas for how much cash a casino must have on hand. On a very busy day at a casino, unless the property is just obscenely cash flush, it is nearly impossible to keep up with the payout demand —especially if the machines are "loose" (i.e. there are lots of payouts). The only way to survive in this situation is to do multiple "drops" during the day; take cash out of the machines and recycle it for payouts at the cage. However that emergency-behavior does not meet the minimum legal guidelines for Nevada (and a number of well-regulated jurisdictions).

Some gaming jurisdictions, such as New Jersey, allow properties to dictate the actual cash on hand based on the property's experience. New Jersey regulations (N.J.A.C. 19:43-4.1) define the casino bankroll as daily average cash maintained in the casino, excluding any funds necessary for the normal operation of the casino, such as change banks, slot hopper fills, slot booths, cashier imprest funds and redemption area funds. Comparisons are made with the prior year's monthly daily average. If there are any significant reductions in cash, the property is required to provide an explanation. Negative trends in cash alert gaming authorities to watch for possible cash-flow problems.

When I opened a casino in rural Montana, the Tribal business committee had not budgeted for a full size casino's cash needs; they didn't have a clue and didn't ask anyone. The Tribal regulatory authority (the gaming commission) was kept in the dark by the business committee (not that they would have known any better anyway). And the bank syndicator that had funded the casino was deliberately lied to and misled. For 600 slot machines, eight table games, and Bingo, we opened with less than $5,000 in cash. If the grand opening was a total failure, then we could *possibly* get away with as little $30,000 to $45,000. If the grand opening was a success; we totally were screwed. Either way, having only five-thousand-dollars was a sick and painful joke.

Casinos (especially smaller poorly-regulated casinos, usually in Indian Country) run out of money all the time. The Nevada formula was designed to be a *minimum* operational figure to protect the public from a casino default. Even as a minimum, with those guidelines a small casino (500 machines and 8 table games) should figure their cage bankroll as follows:

GAME DESCRIPTION	NUMBER	MULTIPLIER	BANKROLL
Non-progressive slot machines	500	$50	$25,000
Total of all progressive jackpots	$10,000	1	$10,000
Table Games: number of games (8) times table limit ($300)	$2,400	100	$240,000
Bingo or Keno: number of games (12) times game top prize ($250)	12	$250	$3000
TOTAL *MINIMUM* BANKROLL REQUIRED:			$278,000

So, at least, my little Montana casino needed more than a quarter-of-a-million dollars in the cage. Even if we did not open the table games, and if we turned off the progressive jackpots, we would have needed a little more than $28,000 (that number is for 500 machines not 600). We had an insane $5,000.

I had already *walked on water* and raised $600,000 for the Tribal business committee to make up for their budget short falls which were keeping them from opening (more on that later). But the cage bankroll was another issue; they either hid the cash shortfall from me or they didn't understand it. Their plan was to use cash from their existing (and closing) mini-casino to bankroll the cage.

I was not privy to that cash number, but I had hoped it would be at very least mathematically sound; after all, the banking syndicator that had approved this deal was well-experienced in such matters. Mathematically, by comparison, my *Lil Vegas Arcade Casino* in Florida was approximately the same size as their small casino: 100 machines. In that case the math was:

GAME DESCRIPTION	NUMBER	MULTIPLIER	BANKROLL
Non-progressive slot machines	108	$50	$5,400

At unregulated *Lil Vegas*, I did it with $2,000 and a series of emergency (mini) drops.

In Montana, they actually were mathematically close in the old facility. Unfortunately, they had not taken into account cash for six-times that number of slots in the new casino ($32,400), for Bingo (another $3,000), their new slot progressives ($10,000), nor their table games ($240,000). In fairness, the bank syndicator had only approved 300 slot machines and was not aware of (and certainly had not approved) progressive slots nor table games; this was part of the deceptive stratagem the business committee was playing with the syndicator. Also, in fairness, the Tribe's business committee had planned on a locals-only casino but had hired me to go after an off-reservation tourism market (a strategy which failed miserably). Nonetheless, even by the syndicator's machine count, the cash-on-hand would mathematically have to be a minimum of $15,000 plus another $3,000 for the approved-Bingo.

Rather than opening with the $285,400 I needed (or even the non-table game and non-progressives a minimum of $45,400) I was given $5,000. So for that opening, there were two possibilities: I could have taken the regulatorily sane hardline and simply said *"no, it cannot be done without more cash, have a nice life"*; or I could find a way to open regardless of having no payout money. *That* way, I found, was to do a partial drop <u>every hour</u> for eight hours. Exactly like *Lil Vegas*, I did emergency drops; only instead of one a day, I did one an hour for eight hours.

David Cook, the well-known Oklahoma casino regulator who I had brought to Montana, was beside himself with outrage over the Tribal business committee's duplicity and/or ignorance. Retired from the Oklahoma City Police Department as the most decorated living officer in their history, Cook had become Executive Director of the gaming commission for that state's largest casino, moved on to a major casino accounting firm, and eventually settled into a consulting role to multiple Tribal casinos. His reluctance to come to Montana, where there were no state regulations and a totally unaware Tribal regulatory authority, was only reinforced by this multiple-drop strategy. While he recognized that my scheme was the only way to keep the doors open through a successful grand opening, he was outraged that these drops would be performed by brand new teams that had never been tested under fire. Moreover, he correctly forewarned that members of the Business Committee would not understand the issue and would be angry at long lines at the cashier cage windows; long lines that were destined to continue for months until cash flow could be stabilized.

To further complicate the issue, those bankroll figures are really not even minimum-on-hand cash under Nevada law. Though this was far from Nevada, regardless of the actual State, I have always tried to adhere to the Nevada minimums. Regulation 6.150 also requires a casino to have a bankroll for two weeks of accounts payable, two weeks of payroll, and one month of debt service.

In short, casinos really do often run out of money...even in Nevada, as the Bunion's' incident showed.

- **Customers dying.** This one, at least, is an industry hazard that hotel operators are familiar with; people die in hotel rooms all the time. On the casino floor, I am not talking about the rare newsworthy incidents like the horrific shootouts at Harrah's in Laughlin or Soboba in California or MGM Grand in Vegas or even nationally known slut-symbol Anna Nicole Smith dying in a casino hotel room at the Hard Rock Seminole in Florida. Rather I am talking about customers keeling over at a

41

slot machine or choking to death in the restaurant, or just dropping dead while walking across the floor. Happens all the time; get used to it.

- **Customer disguises.** For uncountable reasons, customers sometimes find it necessary (in their minds, anyway) to change identities during the course of a visit.

At Trump29, where we paid an average $35-per-visit bounty to bus riders, it was common for a bus rider to claim the thirty-five-bucks, step into the bathroom, put on a wig and change of clothes, and attempt to claim another $35. We caught one woman who had five changes-of-costume and wigs in her bag…along with five homeland security approved ID's in five different names.

That bizarre behavior combines with card counters, banned persons, and the sometimes notorious or famous, to make for an interesting array of disguised customers on a regular basis.

I used to have really famous one pop-star-diva *(and purported sex symbol, though I could never understand why)* who loved to play my penny slot machines at 4 a.m. several nights a week. Her disguises were so absurd that they looked like someone *pretending* to wear a disguise; the only thing she lacked was a plastic "Groucho" nose, glasses, and mustache.

Though I have yet to have an official black-book banned player show up at one of my properties *(though the late Frank "Lefty" Rosenthal used to claim that he did it all the time)*, I have many times caught persons I had banned or the property had banned, attempting to sneak back in under disguise.

Like I said, there are no "slow days" at the casino…even if revenue and traffic are slow. There are no *typical* days; there is no routine. And the mind of a casino boss is constantly filled with history, adventure, problems, solutions, numbers, formulas, cheats, hookers, tourists, winners…and losers.

The true irony of the entire "Trump29" adventure was that, again less than ten years later, through another series of contacts I was approached by a third-party broker to help the Tribe find financing for a new casino on Tribal land near the 29 Palms U.S. Marine Corps base. Part of the package I proposed along with the funding and development for the new property was that I be given a federally-submitted management contract for the new casino as well as for the older once-upon a time Trump casino.

Like most wanna-be development deals in the casino world, this one too was just another pipe-dream for adventurers who think there is nothing to making money at a casino other than opening the doors and turning on the slot machines. Other funding was located before the broker could follow-up on my offer.

TYPICAL DAYS:

LEFT: Gary Green (left) with Trump CEO Mark Brown (center) and Operations Vice President Vince Mascio (right) at a farewell ceremony for Mascio near Palm Springs.

ABOVE LEFT: Max (TV's Jethro Bodine) Baer Jr., a television reporter and Gary Green at the Tic-Tac-Toe Chicken booth at Trump29 Casino. *(The chicken beat Max handily.)* **ABOVE RIGHT:** Gary gets some last-minute staging instructions from the camera crew and director of one of a series of casino television spots. **BELOW:** Gary's assistant Tanya Beecroft with Gary Green and Vince Mascio at Trump29's celebration of Gary's 50th birthday.

Chapter Six.

A Little Casino History:

...NOT the movie version

"History repeats itself, first as tragedy, second as farce"
— **Karl Marx,** The Eighteenth Brumaire of Louis
Bonaparte (1852)

This racket (the casino gaming industry) is full of colorful personalities that have not shown up in movies (yet) and are far more colorful than some of those movie recreations of real life characters.

Keep in mind that this is a very young "industry" with a very sordid history. It was illegal for a corporation to own a casino until 1968 when Howard Hughes bought out Cleveland mob figure turned Vegas philanthropist, Moe Dalitz *(through a seemingly questionable deal with then-governor Paul Laxalt (later Ronald Reagan's "first friend") and often thought to be the model for Mario Puzo's fictional Senator Pat Geary portrayed by G. D. Spradlin in the films).*

Today's most-famous casino event, *Harrah's World Series of Poker* was founded by Texas mob boss (and twice-convicted killer) Lester "Benny" Binion. Until 1979 when Atlantic City's first casino opened, Nevada was the only state with legal casinos. In 1983 Major League Baseball threatened to kick Mickey Mantle out of the Baseball Hall of Fame if he did not sever ties with Atlantic City's Claridge Casino where he an advertising spokesman; they didn't want baseball's best known living legend associated with gambling. Native American (Indian) casinos were not "legal" until 1988.

The first Mississippi casino opened in 1992, the same year that the Mashantucket Pequot Tribe opened Foxwoods in Connecticut *(funded by Malaysian billionaire Lim Goh Tong after their Bingo hall had been funded by United Arab-American Bank; when they discovered no American financing was available to them).*

By July of 1999 the congressionally-created *National Gambling Impact Study Commission* determined there was no longer any significant presence of organized crime in legal gambling. And as of this writing, every American lives within a two-hour drive of at least one casino. Pennsylvania just legalized slot machines in 2004. Florida in 2006 (in Ft. Lauderdale only and 2007 in Miami). Maryland legalized in 2010, and many riverboat and state-by-state laws are still being debated into law in local jurisdictions.

It only stands to reason that there would be scores of colorful characters in such a young and fast-grown industry. I like to call them the true mad-men of gambling. I am not talking about the *tip-of-your-tongue* names like Steve Wynn, Donald Trump, Bugsy Siegel, Lefty Rosenthal, Benny Binion, or even the lesser-known but corporate important names like Kirk Kerkorian, Phil Satre or my old friend Bob Stupak. Instead, I am talking about characters like Dennis Gomes, Frank Haas, Steve Sohng, Mark Lefever, Tony Cornero, Billy Wilkerson, Billy Maizer Chief James Billie, Bill Bennett, and a roster of other insanely colorful madmen (and women) that shaped casino gambling in America. Wherever possible, I will introduce you to some of these madman geniuses who created the current casino world; some have been friends or colleagues others just industry-shapers.

As the Trump Vice President of Marketing, I initially vehemently opposed the tic-tac-toe chicken promotion as being campy and too "east coast" for Southern California. My favorite CPA-turned-casino-boss, Mark Lefever, was sitting in that General Manager chair at Trump29 and he had decided to bring the chicken promotion to California. Our friendly and often-joking debate over the chickens went on for months, delaying the signing of a contract with Bunky. Finally, near or shortly after the end of Mark's tenure with Trump, I relented and Bunky's troupe arrived at the Trump29 Casino. (Commenting on my endorsement of the promotion on Bunky's website, Mark emailed me *"stop lying; you hated it."*) He was right…at first.

Lefever is one of those great gaming characters that I am talking about. As notoriously low-key as I am flamboyant, the New Jersey native began his career as a CPA working for Arthur Anderson (long before the Enron scandal destroyed that firm).

At the time Mark Lefever began working for Arthur Anderson, gaming's aforementioned corporate infancy was just beginning to find its way into *Generally Accepted Accounting Principles*, traditional business patterns, organized marketing plans, and EBITDA-focused management models. The concept of an "investment grade" casino company was a total non sequitur. Though there is a strong argument that the Teamsters Central States Pension Fund and other "golden age" Vegas investment interests were extremely business minded; there was, without a doubt, comparatively little (if any) true regulatory monitoring of these enterprises.

Law enforcement in these newly regulated jurisdictions had no clue what to look for in controlling LEGAL gambling and legitimate business people knew only the tenets of their respective businesses. *Drop, hold, cage,* and the universe of casino policies and procedures were foreign language terms to them. The newly-flexing industry was hungry for business expertise and several large accounting firms developed Casino/Hospitality practices to answer the call. Most were as adept at it as a typical hotel companies would be, though some few lucked out with good talent on staff.

One of the youngest, brightest, and most ambitious of the number crunchers for a (then) *Big 8* accounting firm, Mark Lefever was assigned to audit casino operations all over the country, including presiding over the ITT-Sheraton property in Tunica Mississippi.

Sheraton Hotels, like the Holiday Inn, Ramada, and Hilton, oh-so-had tried to jump into the casino racket and found themselves out of their neat little corporate league. In a typical overkill backlash to years of casino companies neglecting even basic business-practices (and Sheraton's not having a clue about gaming), ITT for all practical purposes turned the operation of their casino acquisitions —*and the casino floor*— over to the accounting firm of Arthur Anderson. As absurd as that sounds to us in the post-Enron universe, at the time it seemed like a prudent (if not cutting-edge) business decision.

In 1913, Arthur Andersen and Clarence Delaney, both juniors at Price Waterhouse, bought *The Audit Company of Illinois* to form Andersen, Delaney & Company which five years later became Arthur Andersen & Co. For the next 71 years, the Anderson motto *"Think Straight; Talk Straight"* helped make the company a leader in accounting standards. Despite the corporate arrogance that bred the Enron and other scandals, as of this writing Arthur Andersen has neither dissolved nor filed bankruptcy. From a onetime army of 85,000 employees, Anderson today has about 200 Chicago-based employees focused on the scores of lawsuits against the company (and what will most likely be the dissolution). The company currently is a general partnership shaped by four LLC's called "Omega Management One" through "Omega Management Four." Omega, of course, is the last letter of the Greek alphabet and in Christian iconography means the end at Armageddon; someone at least had a sense of the derisively mockery for the fiasco...a sense of humor that is even more appropriate in the context Anderson's involvement in gaming.

The parent of Sheraton, ITT (*International Telephone and Telegraph*) was one of the "legitimate corporations" that entered the casino business following the Dennis Gomes-era legal putsch. Founded in 1920 by a US Army Lieutenant Colonel named Sosthenes Behn to operate telephone service in Puerto Rico, the company began buying Bell-neglected phone companies throughout Latin America and Europe.

As a *legitimate* business, ITT's record made the mafia look like little leaguers...or at best Irish pikeys. While future Vegas Strip founders Meyer Lansky, Benny Siegel, Frank Costello, Tony Cornero and other "organized criminals" were serving their apprenticeships running rinky-dink grey-market casinos in Covington Kentucky, Louisiana, Saratoga Springs, and off-shore, *legitimate* ITT was making large cash payments to Heinrich Himmler and becoming the first American business received by Hitler after he took power. While Vegas financier Charles "Lucky" Luciano was using his influence from prison to stop Nazi sabotage on the New York docks, *legitimate* ITT (through its Focke-Wulf subsidiary) was building the Nazi Luftwaffe's most successful fighter planes used to shoot down American and British airmen. ITT also owned Huth, a company that supplied radar and radio parts to the Nazi military. I am sorry; perhaps *I just have a warped sense of legitimacy, but I find that much more distasteful than operating an unlicensed gambling hall.*

By the 1970s, a few years before Dennis Gomes began chasing Lefty Rosenthal's skims at the Stardust, legitimate ITT (according to declassified CIA documents) financially backed opponents of Salvador Allende's legally elected

Chilean government prepare a military coup and the assassination of Allende. And, in 1972 newspaper columnist Jack Anderson printed a memo from ITT's Washington lobbyist, which revealed a relationship between ITT's providing funds for the Republican National Convention and a republican Justice Department settlement of an antitrust suit favorable to ITT.

You know, Meyer Lansky looked at Cuba and suggested that what his business needed was the co-operation of a government. And Honoré de Balzac's *Father Goriot* proclaimed of his daughter's fiancée, Rastignac, *"Le secret des grandes fortunes sans cause apparente est un crime oubli, parce qu' il a t proprement fait"* paraphrased in *The Godfather* as "behind every great fortune is a great crime." Apparently *legitimate* ITT was, from the onset, way more libertine than Lansky *or* the French playwright-turned-novelist.

In 1968, ITT purchased the Sheraton Hotel chain, which it owned for thirty years until it sold off all of its non-hotel businesses (including all the communications and manufacturing companies) and merged with Starwood Resorts. Starwood, a well-respected hotel operator was originally a Westchester County REIT *(more recently in the news after their CEO Steven J. Heyer was ousted by the hotel company's board amid allegations that he had sent inappropriate and suggestive e-mails and text messages to a female employee)*.

Against this backdrop, and probably oblivious to it, Mark Lefever of Arthur Anderson was anointed acting general manager of the Tunica Sheraton Hotel and Casino, as ITT quiet appropriately allowed the auditors to run the whole show. Mark was making all the decisions, from finance to gaming to marketing to food & beverage. Apparently, he showed a remarkable aptitude for running a casino; Mark, at least since I have known him, seems to be a natural "casino guy."

From his Tunica successes, Lefever was sent by Anderson to Vegas to handle the audit for Sheraton's hopeful unloading/sale of the famed *Desert Inn*. Representing ITT-Sheraton/Starwood as an Arthur Anderson operative, Mark was appointed Chief Operating Officer of the legendary hotel and tasked with both profitably operating it *and* negotiating a successful sale. During the next couple of years, he went through what must have been ulcer-giving negotiations and a near-sale to South African hotel operator, *Sun International* for $275-million. Ten months after that announced sale, Sun pulled out; however, the Sun agreement provided that if they withdrew their offer and ITT subsequently sold the property for less than $275-million, Sun would pay the difference up to $15-million. *(Nice work, Mark!)*

By April of 2000, Lefever was escorting the already near-legendary Steve Wynn through the Desert Inn and dodging reporters' questions about the meetings. Rumored to be a birthday present for his wife, Elaine, Wynn paid ITT $280-million for the DI; a mere 6½% of the $4.4-billion in proceeds from selling his Mirage resorts to MGM...and $5-million more than Sun had agreed to pay. The reportedly fragile ego of Steve Wynn had already been bruised by reports that Kirk Kerkorian had bested him in the purchase of the Mirage; young

Mark Lefever had the good sense to keep his mouth shut that he too had out-negotiated the Vegas giant.

Frankly, I am not certain that either Kerkorian or Lefever out foxed Wynn; Steve Wynn is the incarnation of *"he who laughs last laughs best."* And, like Liberace, Wynn is laughing all the way to the bank. The man, who built his empire with Michael Milken's junk bonds but avoided the tainted shadow when Milken went to prison, has the touch to outfox most. Still, there is no denying that Lefever's negotiation was stroke of pure genius.

Always one to recognize talent and ambition, Wynn offered Lefever the continuation as Chief Operating Officer of his newly-purchased Desert Inn; a position Lefever kept until he and Wynn closed the venerable old property. *(Wynn's two towering properties, Encore and The Wynn, sit on the old DI site today.)*

Hence, by his 35th birthday, Mark Lefever joined the ranks of the Las Vegas legends by taking the helm of the former residence of Howard Hughes and former domain of longtime Meyer Lansky friend Moe Dalitz. Now, for god sake, an *accountant* was running one of the Strip's legendary casino hotels. And, he has some great stories about the transition from the "old" Desert Inn to one being run by a straight-as-an-arrow accountant.

There is a great picture that Mark used to have on the wall just to the right of his desk at Trump29, featuring a 1950 Life Magazine® centerfold spread showing the opening-day staff of the Desert Inn framed by a craps table on the casino floor. In the same picture frame was a photo from the year 2000 of Mark's closing-day staff posed fifty years later in the same positions. For his 40th birthday, I launched a massive archive search to find that original issue of Life® and presented it to Mark.

The DI (as it was called, at least by the locals and Vegas regulars), was the fifth casino to open on the strip and was known for its 170-acre 18 hole golf course on the strip —a professional course which not only did Mark often play, but kept open until the very end...even after the casino closed. Mark is a hell of a golfer; in Southern California, he lived inside PGA West at La Quinta.

The DI story began in 1927 when a 19–year-old kid from Illinois named Wilbur Clark dropped out of high school and hitchhiked to San Diego to find his estranged father. He found his father and stayed in Southern California where he got a job as a bellhop and four years later drifted up to Reno where he learned to be a craps dealer at the Nevada Bank Club (in 1931 that was the largest casino in the United States).

By 1939, Clark had returned to Southern California and was an investor in Tony Cornero's notorious SS Rex *cruise-to-nowhere* gambling ship. For 25¢, a gambler could leave from Los Angeles' Santa Monica Pier on a water taxi ride to the Rex, anchored three miles outside US territorial waters off the Santa Monica Pier. The Rex, unlike many of the modern cruises-to-nowhere off the coasts of Florida, South Carolina, and Texas, was not a run-down garbage scow with indoor/outdoor carpet glued to its desks and poop decks. The S.S. Rex was a luxury casino with thick carpet, rich mahogany rooms, and an opulence that far surpassed any casino in America at the time; even Reno's famed Nevada Bank Club. It truly was the finest casino in America.

I am not sure how Clark got the opportunity to invest with Cornero; and I have not found anyone who could *authoritatively* tell me how that connection came to be. Some people say it was from connections Clark made while dealing in Reno. Clearly, by this time Clark had become pretty well known in gambling circles in California and Nevada and like today, perhaps even more so in those days, the "insider" casino world was a pretty incestuous clan. Even today, most of us know someone who knows someone who has worked with almost every top-name casino professional or hanger-on. *In fact, talk to almost any casino executive in the early 21st century and we have all worked for Harrah's, Trump, or Wynn at one time or another.*

Tony Cornero, himself a colorful character, was portrayed in a caricature by Cary Grant (as "Joe Adams") in the 1943 film *Mr. Lucky*. He was the original builder of the *Stardust* on the Vegas Strip (the casino which launched my friend Dennis Gomes' career direction). After an assassination attempt in 1948, his alleged assailant, a former casino host on the S.S. Rex, was identified by the *Las Angeles Mirror* as the lead suspect in the infamous *Black Dahlia* case. Tony survived the shooting.

The LA Times Report Of Cornero's Shooting

Though the LA Times simply called him a "big time gambler," when he is *Googled* in the 21st century Cornero comes up as a Las Vegas and Southern California *organized crime figure*. True or false, we do know that he was not a pal of law enforcement and politicians. California Governor Earl Warren (later Chief Justice of the US Supreme Court) promised *"to call the Navy and Coast Guard if necessary"* to shut down the gambling ships outside of California waters. A former State Prosecutor, Warren specifically cited the use of wood for the luxury interior of SS Rex owned by Tony Cornero proclaiming, *"It's an outrage that lumber should be used to build such a gambling ship, when veterans can't get lumber with which to build their homes."*

Cornero died in 1955 under, at best, "suspicious" circumstances while playing craps at the Desert Inn. Presumably, he had a heart attack, but he was pronounced dead *by a pit boss* (rather than a coroner or medical professional). His body was taken off the casino floor before the coroner or Sheriff's Department was called and the glass from which he had been drinking was immediately taken away and scrubbed. There was never an autopsy.

As the *Las Vegas Review-Journal* has pointed out, most of the Strip's founding fathers had been involved in manufacturing or distributing illegal liquor in the 1920s. It is more than a coincidence that the early names in organized crime files are the same names that founded (at least portions of) the Las Vegas Strip: Meyer Lansky, Ben Siegel, Gus Greenbaum, Jake Friedman, Jack Entratter, Moe Dalitz, Milton Prell, Davie Berman, Milton Jaffe... *and Tony Cornero.*

A full-page ad for the SS Rex

The great epiphany scene in Warren Beatty's film Bugsy, *(where Beatty looks out into the desert and dreams of magnificent resorts rising from the sand)* was, in reality, more like a moment in Cornero's life. Unlike movie mythologies, the fact is that Siegel simply found himself playing a role as part of a mob investment group's involvement in the already-under-construction Flamingo; he did not create it.

Cornero, on the other hand, actually had the vision, conceived, and began building what he called *"The Meadows"* resort Cornero's gambling ships were already bigger and more luxurious than any casino in the country, and his vision was to create equal carpeted-luxury in the desert town full of sawdust-floor joints. Why the hell isn't there a big budget Hollywood film about Tony? Wait; maybe I should write the treatment...or at least copyright the concept. *(I think I just did.)*

50

"Bugsy" Siegel, by contrast, was merely a front man who had been sent to the West Coast by Meyer Lansky and Lucky Luciano to work with Gus Greenbaum and Moe Sedway in setting up a racing wire for the legal casinos in Nevada. In short order the trio (with Lansky calling the shots) legally bought (and held the license for) the El Cortez Casino in downtown Vegas. The El Cortez was what we would today call the "proof of concept" for their racing wire; and it provided a venue for glory-hog Siegel to play big shot casino boss as the more-polished front man of the group.

I recently watched a cable television "mob exposé" of Las Vegas in which an "expert" asserted that after Siegel's death, when Greenbaum showed up to run the Flamingo, no one knew who he was. *What bullshit!* Everyone knew who he was; he was an equal partner.

Lansky, despite the clear mob role, was known even among the gangsters as a guy who ran very "business-like" casinos, fair games, and managed extremely professionally. The best portrait of Lansky management that I have ever read is in the very well footnoted book, *Havana Nocturne: How the Mob Owned Cuba and Then Lost It to the Revolution* by T. J. English[4]. It really shows a true picture of what it meant for Lansky to run a casino; and it was his precision management and bookkeeping that would help obscure history and create Vegas legend for Cornero-like desert dreams.

Tony Cornero was not the only dreamer to have an epiphany in the Nevada desert. Billy Wilkerson, publisher of the famed *Hollywood Reporter* and owner of the *Ciro's* nightclub hot spot in Los Angeles, began building his dream of a luxury casino in Vegas. (Ciro's, by the way, at 8433 Sunset Boulevard, is as of this writing the location of the famed *Comedy Store*.) Wilkerson envisioned an even more upscale version of his famous celebrity-attracting nightclub; this one with a European-style casino attached. His planning expanded to include a showroom, a bar-lounge, restaurant, cafe, luxury hotel, indoor shops, and a health club. Remember, at this time, a Vegas casino was what today we would call a motel with a really large lobby for games; 1,000 square feet for the "casino" would be large. Wilkerson was thinking about 50,000 square feet of casino space; 50 times the size of the average casino.

All of these dreams of grandeur from the golden days are so much like the modern-day dreams that I hear from dozens of wanna-be casino impresarios every year that it is… scary. I probably get a dozen or more "business plans" every year from people looking for money to finance casino projects; some know what they are doing, most do not. They all sound like these early dreamers…and THAT is exactly why I keep talking to them.

The driving force behind many less-grandiose nightclub projects of that era, Wilkerson hired world-class architects to outline his dream. A prolific traveler, whenever Wilkerson would begin one of his numerous new projects he would give the design a project code name, usually taken from exotic birds he had seen during his vast travels. Sometimes the name would stick and remain the name of the business and sometimes it was there just for project identification; much in the same way that today Microsoft code-names its new versions of Windows before release *(Windows Vista was called Longhorn, Windows 7 was called Vienna, XP was called Whistler, and so on.)*

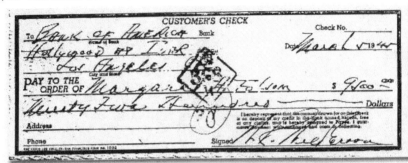

Billy Wilkerson's 1945 check for downpayment for the land for the flamingo project

For this project, he chose the bird and the name **Flamingo** and liked it so much that he commissioned Hollywood graphic artist Bert Worth to design a logo. *No, the Flamingo was definitely not named for the allegedly long legs of Bugsy Siegel's nasal-whining ("I got money from lots of them fellers") Alabama mistress/girlfriend, Virginia Hill.*

Though he got the construction started, Wilkerson soon ran out of money with his insistence on such luxuries as: an air-conditioned building (there were none in Nevada); custom-made gaming tables (with rounded corners like modern tables, instead of old-style sharp corners); cushioned stools at all tables (instead of standing up to play the games); and other "revolutionary" amenities that are today essentials of any casino.

Meanwhile, Moe Sedway, at the El Cortez, heard some of the gamblers talking about the financial shortfall. Without even having met Wilkerson, Sedway took the project to Meyer Lansky who set about finding a manner to approach Wilkerson in some way that the developer would not feel "threatened by organized crime". He sent an intermediary, Harry Rothberg, to propose an investment contract under which Wilkerson would retain one-third ownership of the project but would have 100% creative and managerial control.

Though my telling of this radically differs from the pop culture version and the very slick Warren Beatty movie, the fact is that soon after Wilkerson signed with the New York investment group, Rothberg's local associates Gus Greenbaum and Moe Sedway introduced Wilkerson to their "project liaison," the well-dressed Ben Siegel. Siegel begin showing up on the construction site daily; and while Wilkerson was back in Los Angeles Siegel was making decisions without discussing them with Wilkerson. When the inevitable conflicts and arguments developed, Siegel suggested that Wilkerson sell out his 33% to a corporation owned by Siegel (not the rest of the mob group — just Siegel and his girlfriend).

It doesn't take a genius to see why Luciano and company felt screwed by Siegel. *THAT is the REAL story.*

Ben Siegel's assassination was so sensational and created so much publicity that it did, ultimately, make him partially responsible for the success of Las Vegas; just not in the way the movies played it. The sensationalist attention that his death brought to Vegas, the mythology surrounding him as a character, his palling around with movie stars, all served to let the world know that there were casinos in Las Vegas and there was something luxuriously Hollywood-naughty about them. America does love Hollywood naughty and gangsters.

Hence, modern Las Vegas was not *even* the dream of "Bugsy" Siegel; it *might have been* the dream of Billy Wilkerson but it was <u>definitely</u> the dream of Tony Cornero.

The string of connections in Cornero's life is at least industry-incestuously interesting. Cornero died inside the casino that belonged to his former investor Wilbur Clark (and Moe Dalitz). At the time of his death, Cornero was about 75% finished building what he called the largest and most plush casino

At left are advertisements from two different eras of the Stardust Hotel and Casino in Las Vegas

in Nevada, the Stardust. Moe Dalitz took over that project, finished it and opened it.

The Stardust Hotel and Casino was the real-life model of the fictional *Tangiers Casino* in the Martin Scorsese film *Casino*…and was ultimately the real-life target of Dennis Gomes' original investigation. *(Though the movie ac-*

53

tually was shot at the Riviera, across the street from the now-demolished Stardust.)

In November of 2006, I walked the empty halls of the ghostly Stardust, a few days before the fixtures were auctioned off and about four months before it was imploded.

ABOVE: The Stardust Boardroom in 2006: *note the open door at the head of the table; it is a disappearing 'secret' exit door that folds seamlessly into a wall.*

The Stardust's old hard count room... where the infamous coin weight skim took place.

Beyond the hotel hallways, I wandered through the casino cage, into the count room (where Rosenthal's legendary skims took place). I rambled through the surveillance room, backstage at the Wayne Newton showroom (where I had toked out many doormen over the years for great tables), into Lefty's old office, the boardrooms, the hidden stairways, the marketing offices, and in every off-limits nook and cranny that I could find.

The Stardust "drop" room/vault and safe; small in size compared to most of the rooms I have had built in casinos I developed.

All that remained Frank "Lefty" Rosenthal's old office at the Stardust; stained carpet and bleak walls. *I thought of the scene from Casino where DeNiro gets up from behind his desk with his pants off and walks over to a wooden valet to put them on before taking a meeting.*

Admittedly, I was looking for the ghosts of the past 48 years just as I had at the DI on its closing day a few years earlier; but this time I had unprecedented access to every square foot of the historic property. Thirty years earlier, I would have had to be juiced in through Lefty to have this kind of access; 25 years earlier, I would have had to be Dennis Gomes to have this kind of access. On this day, I was just the GM of an obscure Indian casino taking a handful of his staff members through a few pages of history that few of them could appreciate with the intensity that I carried for it.

The abandoned floor of the main casino walkway at the Stardust in 2006

The equally-abandoned blackjack pit at the Stardust in 2006

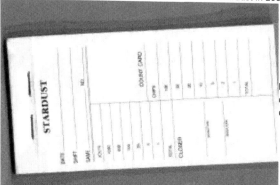

LEFT: A casino shift-manager's cash-count book from the final days of The Stardust.

Fortunately, on this exploration and tour of the spirit-filled hallways, I had the forethought to take my camera with me...so a few weeks before implosions, I was able to take a few digital pictures of a fading part of Vegas legend from vantage points that few had been able to chronicle ... or even visit.

There is no point in my taking the time to go through the sordid history of the Stardust, the infamy of Rosenthal, the legitimate management by Boyd Gaming in its latter years; several books have done that quite well. I probably *could* lecture on Boyd's series of 21st century management misfires that culminated with the implosion of the Stardust, the planning (and delay) of the Echelon project, botched Dania Jai Alai project, under-utilization of the Borgata in Atlantic City and more. And I love to talk about the absurd arrogance of Boyd executive staff, as they scratch their heads and asses wondering what went wrong.

During their ponderings over the legality of gaming in Broward County Florida in the early 21st century, the executives of Boyd somehow accidentally *(I am now guessing it was accidental, though at the time I thought it was intentional)* put me on their internal email list. They accidentally made me privy to their internal discussions of the legislative process, their thoughts on taxation, and operational issues of their Dania Florida project. Without revealing proprietary content, I am comfortable saying that the group in those "analyses" did not know their asses from a hole in the ground...as their eventual total failure revealed. I *really* wanted to buy the property from them.

Nonetheless and despite all of these sidebars rolling around inside a casino exec's head, they are all a far cry from the flurry of activity on the Strip a half-century earlier when the DI was conceived.

Eleven years before the Stardust construction began and ten years before Tony Cornero's death, when the SS Rex was sold, Wilbur Clark took his profits, moved to Vegas and became the second person to own a hotel called the *El Rancho*. Buying out founder Thomas Hull, Clark became the sole proprietor of the first resort casino on Highway 91 outside of Las Vegas —the highway that eventually became known as *"The Strip." (As of this writing, there is a Hilton timeshare sitting on that location, about a stone's throw from my old penthouse condo at The Turnberry.)*

Wilbur Clark also bought the lease to operate the *Monte Carlo Club* on Fremont Street and thus created another Vegas practice by installing the first flashing-lights sign in Vegas history. In 1946 he sold both properties for $1½-million and bought the *Players Club Jungle Casino*, further down U.S. Highway 91.

Seeing the frantic work that Billy Wilkerson was doing to build the *Flamingo* even further down Highway 91 and having talked with Cornero about the vision in the desert, Clark immediately began remodeling the Jungle to create the equally-chic *Wilbur Clark's Desert Inn*. His original vision was to mimic the famed (and posh) Desert Inn of Palm Springs, long time a haunt of the powerful and famous (both presidents Hoover and Roosevelt vacationed there, as well as scores of Hollywood stars). Clark began construction immediately but found himself competing for scarce building materials with Ben Siegel, as well as the under-construction Thunderbird; but the real materials shortage was caused by the post-war boom of home-building for returning GIs.

The allegation and rumor has always been that the primary Las Vegas contractor in those days, *The Del Webb Company*, profiteered from the shortage by scamming the non-construction-savvy managers, like Siegel. Allegedly and according to the Vegas rumor-mill, Webb's company would make a big production of delivering materials to the Flamingo (and other sites), assuring the owners that by paying a premium price they were bypassing the post-war shortages. The story goes that after a major production of unloading the truck, once the owner was significantly impressed with the "black market" materials, workers would reload the materials to another truck and drive out the back gate. Supposedly, the same material would be redelivered the next day or delivered to the next project down the street. There is, of course, no real evidence that this sort of thing happened, but if it did, that would certainly explain some of the mountainous cost over-runs Siegel suffered at the Flamingo and that might have ultimately contributed to his murder.

That is certainly not to argue that Del Webb (in any way) would have been involved in such swindles or even unwitting complicity in Siegel's death. After all, Del Webb owned the New York Yankees (from 1945 until 1964); and who doesn't have a friend or relative that lives in a Del Webb "Sun City" retirement community somewhere in America? We have already seen that *legitimate* companies, like Webb (or ITT for example) would *never* be involved in questionable activities like common mobsters that ran Vegas gambling joints. *(For those who miss the sarcasm, please forgive my poor writing for not making the point.)*

Shortage or scam, by 1948 Wilbur Clark had only $25,000 left in the bank and needed $90,000 to finish the rooms, another $750,000 to finish the casino/resort, $250,000 for FF&E (furniture, fixtures and equipment)... and all of that did not even include cage and operational cash that he would need. For help, he began floating proposals to raise $3½-million to finish his dream; one report had him applying to the Roosevelt New Deal *Reconstruction Finance Corporation* for a loan; another said that he offered a mortgage on the property to a Virginia insurance company. Apparently, neither came through.

I can relate; I have been in the same boat, exactly, both on behalf of various Indian Tribes and for myself trying to finish projects. Running out of money in the midst of a project is gut-wrenching at the least.

In 1949, he finally met Morris ("Moe") Dalitz (allegedly of Cleveland's Mayfield Road Gang), who in turn put together a group of investors from Cleveland (including Sam Tucker, Thomas McGinty, and Morris Kleinman) to guarantee a loan from the Teamsters Union's Central States Pension Fund. In exchange, the Dalitz group bought 75% interest in the casino and agreed to keep Clark on as a figurehead and promoter for his share.

It is a model I used myself a half-century later, sans the Teamsters and gangsters, for my own *Gary Green's Lil Vegas Redemption Casino* when it fell short of my original investors' purses. I ended up owning 12½% of a property that had my name on the sign. On the other hand, that is not a lot different from Trump, Wynn, and the big names that take their companies public and end up with 5% of their own stock. For a second casino, Gary Green's Lil Vegas Two, I was ready to give up 40% to one investor, 30% to another, 10% each to two others, and 5% to management...ending up owning 5% of a second casino with my name on the sign.

In 2008, I met a few times with Dalitz's bookkeeper, who in his 80s was a frequent player in one of *my* properties. Despite the pop-culture and movie depiction of those days in Vegas being free-reign frolicking of wise guys skimming at every turn, this guy was a straight-as-an-arrow accounting machine, even in his ninth decade of life. He could calculate a fairly accurate picture of earnings by watching a casino floor, estimating hold, counting the number of players, and estimating operating costs; Definitely a casino guy that knew the BUSINESS of casinos (as opposed to a hotel accountant who thought it was all the same). There may not have been Arthur-Anderson-Big-Eight standards in place in the Dalitz days, but I can assure you that there were world class accounting procedures for every penny.

The *DI* finally opened in 1950 with Edger Bergen (and, of course, Charlie McCarthy [Candace was only 4 years old]) as the first performers in the Painted Desert Room (soon-to-be rebranded as the Crystal Showroom). The two-day gala was the first production for legendary showman Donn Arden. The media-blitz (public relations) was handled by Hank Greenspun (who would resign a few months later to found the *Las Vegas Sun*); he pitched the opening to the national press as *the biggest party in history*.

The Crystal Showroom eventually became one of the grandest showrooms in Vegas. Over the years, it hosted Don Rickles, Sinatra, Dean Martin, Liberace, Tony Bennett, Wayne Newton, Tina Turner, The Smothers Brothers, Paul Anka, Neil Sedaka, Dionne Warwick, Cher, Buddy Hackett, Bobby Darin, Bob Newhart, Barry Manilow, Roseanne Barr, Garry Shandling, and dozens of others.

Like tens of thousands of gamblers and Las Vegas visitors, the first Vegas show I ever saw was in the Crystal Showroom; my first *"proper dress required/two-drink minimum"* show was Rich Little (with Petula *("Downtown")* Clark as his opening act). In the 1980s when most of the showrooms bucked the musician's union and switched to taped music, the grand old Crystal Showroom stayed true to the image and kept a live orchestra in a pit in front of the stage. And in the ultimate twist of Vegas fortunes, Rich Little ended up four-walling my old venue of the *Euro-Circus Casino* in Myrtle Beach South Carolina for a year in the 1990s.

In 1956, Wilbur Clark, suffering a stroke and unable to move freely, sold his remaining 25% interest to Moe Dalitz.

Dalitz, by anyone's history of Vegas, was one of the most colorful characters of the city in the desert. Personally, I have always liked his famous exchange with Estes Kefauver during the Senate's hearings on organized crime and gambling:

> **KEFAUVER:** *"As a matter of fact, you had been making a great deal of money in recent years, so I suppose from your profits from one investment you would then go ahead and make another investment. Now, to get your investments started off you did get yourself a pretty good little nest-egg out of rum running, didn't you? "*
>
> **DALITZ:** *"Well, I didn't inherit any money, Senator ... If you people wouldn't have drunk it, I wouldn't have bootlegged it."*

Kefauver, incidentally, a creation of my adopted home state of Tennessee, initially was not *so* interested in tackling organized crime. He was leading a crusade against the "social and moral decay" caused by comic books (no, I am not kidding). Even the publisher of the *New York Times* privately warned him that Kefauver-endorsed local government-sponsored book burning (even comic books) was probably not something a United States Senator should be supporting...given that pesky first amendment thing. Nevertheless, Kefauver was ambitious and wanted to lead *something*. Finally, the publisher told the Senator that the newspaper would support him for Vice President in the upcoming election if he would go after a more palatable target: some like organized crime, for example. Hence the Senator put aside his Davy Crockett coonskin cap (yes, he was actually known for wearing a coon skin cap at the United States Senate), turned his back on the post-war book burnings (albeit "only")

Kefauver on the March 24, 1952 cover of Time Magazine

comic books), and set his sights on Moe Dalitz rather than on Superman, Batman, and the Flash[5].

My friend Howie Gold, the somewhat (but not nearly enough) celebrated Vegas lounge-lizard piano man, tells me that Dalitz used to drop him $100-bills as tips...in the early 70s. This would seem to be consistent with almost all of the Vegas histories that describe the generosity of the Moe Dalitz personality. The historically prolific *Las Vegas Review-Journal* reporter Jon L. Smith wrote, *"The life of Moe Dalitz is perhaps the best example of a gambling man existing in sunshine and in shadow."* I love it; perhaps I should have titled this book *"in sunshine and in shadow."*

By his own accounts, Dalitz began his career as a depression-era bootlegger running illegal casinos in Kentucky and Ohio. Smith quotes him as joking, *"How was I to know those gambling joints were illegal? There were so many judges and politicians in them; I figured they had to be all right."*

In Vegas, he was widely regarded as a respected patron of café society and near the end of his life, was named *Humanitarian of the Year* by the American Cancer Research Center and Hospital. In 1982, he received the Torch of Liberty Award from the Anti-Defamation League of B'nai B'rith. In 1979, he set up the *Moe Dalitz Charitable Remainder Unitrust*, a fund that allowed 14 nonprofit organizations to split $1.3 million when he died.

Long reputed to be the Cleveland mob's "man in Vegas," he openly acknowledged that he was close to Jimmy Hoffa, Meyer Lansky, the Mayfield Road Gang, Jimmy *"Blue Eyes"* Alo, the Cellini brothers, and an encyclopedia of infamously alleged mobsters. Yet, announcing his death, the Las Vegas Sun called him *"Las Vegas' most distinguished citizen for four decades."* Indeed, in the sunshine and the shadows.

Beside the DI and the Stardust, Dalitz was also the driving force behind the Las Vegas Convention Center, the Las Vegas Country Club, Sunrise Hospital, the Boulevard Mall, Commercial Center, Winterwood Golf Course, several UNLV buildings, Fitzgerald's Hotel casino in downtown Vegas, the Nathan Adelson Hospice and entire residential neighborhoods of low-come housing. He also founded the Las Vegas Convention and Visitors Authority.

One of the supposed "mob experts" on an A&E television "exposé" of Vegas recently claimed, without substantiation or documentation, that Dalitz used Teamsters' money to build a Vegas hospital for the sole purpose of smuggling cash out of Las Vegas in ambulances and (apparently) have the ambulance drive the cash to Cleveland to distribute it amongst mafia bosses. What*EVER* !

Many who wrote about Dalitz have said that he was the quintessential example of Las Vegas' reputation as a place where people can reinvent themselves. From Benny Binion to Steve Wynn and from Frank Sinatra to Moe Dalitz himself, it would seem that Vegas has been indeed just that. *And that is probably the most important thing about Vegas for me as well.*

Clearly one who did *not* need a reinvention, Howard Hughes arrived in Vegas by private train on Thanksgiving Day 1966 and checked into the top two floors of Dalitz's Desert Inn. Encamped there for more than a month, Hughes' business manager and public face, Bob Maheu, recalled that they had been asked to vacate the hotel before New Year's Eve to make room for high rollers. None of the Hughes party gambled and, in those days, hotel rooms and restaurants were not the huge revenue centers that they are today; back then casinos made their money from gamblers *(what an outrageous concept!)*. If Dalitz had adopted modern-Vegas' philosophy of property management, there would have been plenty of revenue from the hotel rooms, food, phone calls, and so on. (Of course there might have never been a Las Vegas in the first place if those early operators thought they were not in the gambling business.)

The Hughes group refused to leave, according to Maheu, and by March, three months later, Dalitz's attorneys were angrily threatening to evict the group. Perhaps surprisingly to the gullible reader of Vegas pseudo-history or A&E "exposés" (and to those wags that think millions are rolled out in ambulances), there were no gangsters or guys with silk suits showing up to threaten to bury Maheu in the desert. In a video interview recorded shortly before his death in 2008, Bob Maheu said that Dalitz's <u>attorneys</u> *were* literally screaming at him and threatening both loss-of-income litigation and sheriff's department eviction. I don't know, to me, that seems to be a far cry from a mobster threatening to bury someone in the desert.

Rather than face legal eviction, Hughes told Maheu to buy the hotel. Dalitz at first said the DI was not for sale; then he off-the-cuff demanded a (then-outrageous) price of $13-million, knowing that no one in their right mind would pay such an absurd price. Hughes ordered Maheu to pay the price. However,

60

Hughes refused to be photographed, fingerprinted or even fill out financial disclosure papers required to own a Nevada casino.

Nonetheless, the State of Nevada was eager to oust the mob and bring in "legitimate business," so the State quickly passed the *Corporate Gaming Act*, to permit corporations to become casino license holders.

Actually, there never had been a formal prohibition of corporate casino ownership; but until the Hughes issue arose, every shareholder of a company that owned a casino had to be licensed (and hence photographed, fingerprinted, and fill out financial disclosures). State legislation to remove that condition was considered as early as 1963, but never passed. However, the fear that gangsters would use a public company as a "front" disappeared with Howard Hughes' involvement. *(I won't go into the litany of allegations about Hughes' activities in the Second World War nor the battle with Juan Trippe and Pan Am, or the Nixon-connection through Don Nixon; there are endless volumes on those subjects.)* And, of course, this Corporate Gaming Act allowed for and led to the current corporate control of the gaming industry.

When Hughes died in 1976 his Summa Corporation imploded in a fight between the Maheu forces and the so-called "Mormon Mafia" caretakers of Hughes in his last days. The estate was finally settled in 1983 and the DI was sold off with other Summa assets in 1986.

The new owner was Kirk Kerkorian, who a mile away had developed the largest hotel in the world (at the time) both in terms of number of room and its height, The International Hotel. *(In fact, it was the tallest building in Vegas from 1969 until 1979 when Dalitz's Fitzgerald's Casino surpassed it.)*

In 1969 Kerkorian opened The International, a block off the Strip, (originally with 1,512 rooms and expanding to 3,174 rooms) with a four-week party featuring Elvis' famous $100,000-a-week return to Vegas (the beginning of the white-jumpsuit fat-Elvis era). The 2,000-seat showroom *(slightly smaller than my Trump29 showroom in Palm Springs)* was considered a behemoth at that time; who BUT Elvis could sell-out that many seats in Vegas!

Decades later, after the turn of the century, dressed in one of

Gary Green in Elvis costume at Las Vegas Hilton

Elvis's original white-polyester jumpsuits and white platform shoes that had belonged to Roy Horn *(of Siegfried and Roy)*, I filmed an award-winning television commercial on that very stage. *(Damn, Roy has tiny feet and the shoes about killed me to walk in.)* Using Elvis's actual dressing room, my feeling of an eerie trip of nostalgia, was heightened by the fact that celebrated Elvis impersonator Trent Carlini was headlining in the room at the time. There was just some Elvis-ghost overkill going on as I pranced around on the stage.

By then the property had changed hands twice, and had suffered a murderous fire. In 1970 Kerkorian sold *The International* to Baron Hilton, who changed its name to *The Las Vegas Hilton* (where, incidentally, I lived for several months right after the turn of the century). Hilton operated it until 2004 then sold it for almost $300-million to Resorts International (which was then headed by Nick Ribis, Trump's former attorney and marketing VP), an affiliate of Colony Capital —the largest privately held gaming company until Harrah's went private.

As I began this writing, the Las Vegas Hilton *name* was franchised to Resorts and run for Ribis by Rudy Prieto, another top Trump alumna and a first class operator. By the time we were editing this book, Prieto was gone from the property; we are in an ever-changing industry. Though at the time I didn't personally know Ribis, I knew his son who was a casino marketer working for my friend Frank Palmieri; and though I do not know Prieto, I have observed his work for years. As I keep saying, we are in a very incestuously small business world.

Since I began this book, the Las Vegas Hilton again changed names, losing the *Hilton* flag and rebranding as the LVH ("Las Vegas Hotel"). By 2012 the LVH had been remodeled multiple times and featured 2,956 rooms and suites along the 12 restaurants and 6 bars. It was the only hotel physically attached to the Las Vegas Convention Center; and the hotel itself had more than 200,000 sq. ft. in its own convention center. It also owned a nine-hole putting green as well as tennis courts.

Above all else, this is THE hotel attached to the Las Vegas Convention Center—one of the largest and busiest convention centers in the world. And, unlike MY performance there, the property also will always be remembered as Elvis' home in Vegas; the venue where he performed. A bronze statue of "the King" stands near the entrance to the hotel lobby. However, beyond the legacy of Elvis, the property has one of the last of the old Vegas grand showrooms and a rich history tied to it. Barbra Streisand was the opening-night performer, along with Peggy Lee performing afterwards in the hotel's lounge. In 1969, right after Streisand's engagement, Elvis performed for 58 consecutive sold out shows, breaking all Vegas attendance records, (130,157 paying (and ostensibly gambling) customers in the period of one month), with stellar reviews coming from both critics and the public. He broke his own attendance record in February 1970, and again in August 1970, and August 1972. When playing Las Vegas, he lived in the penthouse suite (room 3000), located on the 30th floor, until his last performance there in December of 1976.

Elvis was due to perform there again in 1978, to celebrate the opening of the North tower, but the singer died in August 1977. His manager, Colonel Tom Parker, lived in the hotel on the 4th floor from the 1970s to mid-1980s. Liberace headlined in the showroom during the 1970s drawing sold-out crowds twice per night. When he signed his contract at the Hilton in 1972 he earned $300,000 per week, a record amount for individual entertainers in Las Vegas.

It was the site in 1978 where Leon Spinks defeated Muhammad Ali for the World Heavyweight Championship. It was also the site in which Mike Tyson defeated Tony Tucker to become the Heavyweight Champion in 1986. Also, Donald Curry defeated Milton McCrory at the Las Vegas Hilton to become the Welterweight Champion in December 1985.

Its physical attachment to the Convention Center has consistently kept occupancy above 80% year round. For the past few years, net room revenue consistently has hovered around $80-million with F&B revenue providing another $56-million. Colony Capital management operated the rooms at a 60.5% margin. The casino contributed another $60-million to the bottom line. On top of the almost $300-million purchase price, Colony spent more than $200-million on renovations and upgrades.

In 2011, the casino alone earned approximately $56-million from its 74,000 square foot gaming space with 1,200 slot machines, 50 table games, and one of the last super-sized sports books in Las Vegas. Nonetheless, the property posted losses of $8.864 million in the second quarter of 2011 vs. a loss of $9.851 million in 2010's second quarter. In their SEC filings, Colony attributed the losses to tough competition and an oversupply of hotel rooms in Las Vegas, driving their net revenue of $45.5 million was down from $47.5 million for the period. At the same time, casino revenue of $14.2 million declined 9.1 percent. The casino's table games hurt for the quarter, with their win declining by $800,000, while slot play declined $1.2 million. Hotel room revenue was steady at about $19.3 million, while food and beverage revenue fell 8.6 percent to $14.4 million.

In the face of these losses, colony defaulted on a $252 million loan in 2010 and used operational expenses to make payments during three months of 2011 while it tried to restructure debt. However, the combination of the debt service and apparent managerial incompetence/malfeasance were impossible to overcome under the existing Colony structure.

The Wall Street Journal, which first reported the foreclosure filing against the property, noted investment banking giant Goldman Sachs was both a lender to and investor in the property. Goldman Sachs foreclosed in December of 2011 and took control of the facility except for the casino itself (because the gaming license belonged to Colony).

Colony Resorts reported that it chose not to make monthly interest payments totaling $3.5 million for June, July and August of 2011 on its $252 million term loan "in order to conserve liquidity for operating and other needs." The loan made up the bulk of the company's $296 million in debt and liabilities. Public record confirms that the term loan lender was Goldman Sachs Commercial Mortgage Capital L.P. Another Goldman Sachs affiliate was an investor in Colony Resorts LVH and this was not the first time the term loan has been in default, with the last default resolved in July 2010. That affiliate *Whitehall Street Real Estate Funds*, was through Goldman's purchase of American Casino & Entertainment (ACE) from Carl Icahn, which included the Stratosphere along with three other properties. Hence, Goldman had the ability and structure to operate the property should they choose to go that route.

Clark County District Court Judge Elizabeth Gonzalez on December 14, 2011 approved the appointment of longtime gaming executive and ACE employee Ronald Johnson as receiver, but only for the nongaming operations of the LVH; that was after Tom Barack, the billionaire chief of Los Angeles-based Colony Capital, testified it would be untenable for him to have Johnson operate under his gaming license while he had no authority over Johnson's actions. However, the Nevada Gaming Commission on December 22 2011 approved plans for Johnson to operate the casino under the existing gaming license.

The Gaming Commission decision sent the issue back to Gonzalez's courtroom, where Goldman Sachs and Colony announced they had agreed they would stop fighting the receivership effort. After enduring years of losses at the Hilton during the recession, Barrack testified that his company had lost all its equity in the property. The receivership order signed by Judge Gonzalez included protections for workers, requiring the receiver to seek court approval before initiating any mass layoffs.

In July 2012, operating under trusteeship, the LVH lost $2.485 million on an EBITDA basis as net revenue was reported at $10.275 million. In September of 2012 the chief creditor and a partner announced plans to buy it out of foreclosure in November 2012 and continue operations.

Privately, Goldman had indicated that they wanted to sell the asset, which at the time Colony purchased it, was valued at $800-million. Private word from Goldman was that they would sell the property (including the casino) for around $185-million. At the time it was my opinion that it would have taken another $10-million to $25-million to fund and license the casino. While no hotel renovation was immediately needed, there were branding and marketing costs associated with the property. I believed the "all in" cost for the property to be a little less than $250-million; however the $185-million figure was neither official nor firm and there was some indication from insiders that the number may be even less.

It was at the Hilton on a Tuesday night in mid-February of 1981 when my friend and one-time coworker Ed Buchwald had his dinner interrupted by a fire alarm about 8pm. Flames burst from the 8th floor of the east wing of the three-wing hotel giant and quickly engulfed the building to the upper floors. Officials interrupted the showroom where Juliet Prowse was performing, telling the audience only *"there is an emergency — please leave immediately."* Money was locked in boxes at the casino tables and gamblers were evacuated.

Three bodies were found on the 8th floor face down in an open elevator; a man and woman were found smoke-inhalation suffocated in a bathroom on the 10th floor; other bodies were found in front of closed elevator doors. Enormous smoke clouds billowed from the hotel as onlookers rushed from the Strip over to Paradise Road to mill around the disaster. Ultimately, eight people died and 200 were injured.

For starting the fire, and thus causing the deaths, a room service bus boy, apparently motivated by a desire to be a hero rescuing people, was eventually sentenced to eight life terms without the possibility of parole. Apparently, he set curtains on fire with a really large marijuana doobie.

My friend Ed and his party escaped unharmed but were separated for a few hours in the outdoor panic.

Besides building the *International*, Kirk Kerkorian is best known amongst Vegas watchers as the owner of three hotels that have been called MGM Grand (the first now carries the Bally's brand and the second is still called MGM Grand). Today he owns the MGM/Mirage conglomerate of casino/hotels. He is the guy credited with besting Steve Wynn in the purchase of Wynn's Mirage empire (but as previously noted, I am not certain how accurate that assessment actually is). Kerkorian renamed the DI as "MGM Desert Inn" and held onto it for seven years before selling it for $160-million to ITT Sheraton.

For three years beginning in 1978, all of America peeked into the lobby, casino, pool, and grounds of the DI every Wednesday night, thanks to the ABC television series *Vega$*. The show starred Robert Urich as fictional private detective Dan Tanna, who worked for the DI, drove a red 1957 T-bird around Vegas, and lived in a DI-owned warehouse next door to Circus-Circus. *Mission Impossible* star Greg Morris played a Metro Police Lieutenant, and 1950s & 60s movie icon (and my friend) Tony Curtis played the silk-suited owner of the DI.

I was in Vegas on August 28, 2000, spending the DI's last open day in a blackjack pit with two employees who had been at the DI for decades. There were literally tears streaming down their faces as they talked about the "good ole days" under Dalitz and what bastards Steve Wynn and Mark Lefever were... as if Mark had somehow personally decided to close the DI. (Though in reality he DID close it almost a month before the previously announced closing date).

As I have said, Mark is one of the greatest case studies of the transition of old Vegas to new Vegas; of mob Vegas to Wall Street Vegas; of "the boys" running things to accountant-bean-counters managing things.

One of the best and most colorful Las Vegas transition stories I have ever heard is Mark Lefever's description of the turmoil he caused when he first became GM at the DI. In one split-second, on his first day, he instantly changed Vegas employee culture forever by refusing (and ending) the traditional "envelope" (of kickback cash from everyone's tokes) being brought to the General Manager. Mark tells the story as a humorous anecdote, seemingly without any thought of what a major positive impact he put into motion for the day-to-day lives of thousands of casino industry employees. And that makes the story all-the-better.

Until that fateful day Mark took the helm of the DI, every toked out casino employee (employees whose income was dependent on tips), had to pay a portion of their daily tips to their immediate supervisor, to the department head, to the casino manager, and all the way up the ranks to the General Manager himself. So, basically, whatever a rank-and-file employee earned in tips, they had to discount it by about 50% (half of their pay) because of all the kickbacks they had to pay in order to keep their job. This was a lot of untaxed kickback money.

My recollection of the story goes that Mark was sitting at his desk when one of the CM's (casino mangers — i.e. shift manager) walked in and tossed an envelope onto his desk and turned to walk out.

Mark looked up and asked *"what is that?"*

"Your envelope for the day," the CM answered.

"What the fuck does that mean?" Mark pressed; I am sure in his best New Jersey tone.

The CM explained to Mark that every employee paid a portion of their tips as "under the table" (i.e. unreported) cash to the General Manager.

Straight-as-an-arrow Mark wanted no part of it. To further complicate matters, he ordered the CM to redistribute the funds to the employees and put out word to all managers and supervisors that anyone accepting an envelope would be fired.

The poor casino manager ...and all the supervisors... had to be thinking that the most inexperienced, naive, and YOUNG general manager in history had just arrived. They had no idea that Mark had just set a standard that would change the casino industry forever. But that is exactly what he did; and he tells the story as if it was just another day of adapting his style and integrity to casino culture...rather than bending casino culture to his style and integrity. Knowing Mark, I suspect he would argue with me that it was not that big of a deal; but it was.

One of the very few public pictures of Mark LeFever

Think about it... the entire way of life for thousands of casino employees (and for an entire industry) was changed forever on that day. And Mark Lefever is never thought of or mentioned in even the most esoteric and obscure histories of Vegas.

Mark hired me at Trump, I think against his own instincts and better judgment. It was certainly against the recommendations from part of his senior marketing staff, but perhaps caving to the insistence of his H.R. department (and my array of friends and references *(not the least of which was my real estate tie back to Trump himself in New York)* and my long history with Native American activism).

Though I remained both friendly and loyal to Mark and visited his golf-course home several times at PGA West in La Quinta California, I never felt that Mark ever really *liked* me. I think he was uncomfortable with how unconventional, unstructured, un-accountant-like, I am (not to mention the fact that I don't drink wine or play golf). He never said anything to indicate that, but it is not like we send Christmas cards either. I don't think Mark, as the very best of 1990s-style accountants, was ever 100% comfortable with what *Casino Journal* called my "(PT) Barnum-like vigor" or what *Indian Gaming Business* called my "Las Vegas flamboyance."

Though, it *is* notable that Mark seemed to have no issues with the flamboyance surrounding his 40th birthday party. The Trump corporate VP of slots (a wild man named Lou, for whom on several occasions I had provided cab fare home for his various barroom pick-ups girls that he had eventually terrified with threatened supposedly debaucherous sex acts) arranged a party at a local hotel for Mark's 40th birthday. I arrived late and the veranda around the pool more resembled an already-drunken bachelor party than a birthday party. The attendees were a handful of Trump's Atlantic City Vice Presidents from various divisions, Mark Brown, and ... Lou's "special" invited guests. I have no idea where Lou had gotten all the girls. I *do* know that he had called some agency in either Palm Springs or LA and that the girls were all professional models and actresses some had actually appeared in Playboy. They had all brought along their portfolios and books of head shots, credits, and publicity material. Several of the girls brought screen shots of their websites which were, apparently, pay-to-view soft porn sites. Flamboyance? Hmmm. I think it is safe to say that the stereotypical Las Vegas style or Hollywood style "party" was certainly orchestrated by Lou that night. For the record, the wild portions of the party seemed to amuse Mark but true to his straight-as-an-arrow form, he did not participate in anything unacceptable or in the least bit questionable; he let the other guys do their thing, but he was a perfect gentleman. *Gotta love this guy.*

Mark Lefever is a great guy and would make a superlative chief executive of any gaming resort operation. With Arthur Anderson, the DI, the Riviera, and even the restructuring of debt for the Trump-managed Palm Springs tribe, he has repeatedly proven his genius. But, having said that, I think Mark would be much more comfortable with a less risk-taking marketer whose pendulum swings closer to the conservative side of definitive projections than toward the more risky fine-line between *"wow"* and *bullshit*. I could be wrong, but at the end of the day, I don't think he likes gamblers... at least ones that gamble away from the casino floor.

Mark was one of the first of a long succession of accounting gurus to move into casino operations. Very few of have succeeded; Mark is a rare example. Of course it sounds a lot more compatible to the Vegas mythology if I call them "numbers guys" instead of accountants. Use that euphemism, I can cite Meyer Lansky and any number of bottom-line "guys" contrasted to the flamboyant "guys" like Siegel, Stupak, Bennett, Binion, and others.

67

If the concept of a bookkeeper running a glitzy casino seems out of sync, then the notion of a hero-accountant running a glitter palace may be off the charts. You may remember that Dennis Gomes had told Bunk that the tic-tac-toe chicken was his personal high-point. If that is accurate, then it must rank pretty high in the big scheme of things. I note, too, that both of the big promoters of the chicken in my life were accounting guys running casinos: Mark and Dennis.

Dennis Gomes, in his first career as a regulator, was the leader of the case that brought down Lefty Rosenthal and became the book and movie *Casino*. He also developed the casino internal control guidelines and investigative procedures that are still required both in New Jersey and Nevada ...and have been the model for regulation and consumer protection in almost every state that has legal casinos.

Gomes' far-reaching impact on gaming began in 1971 when the 27-year-old CPA was hired as the chief of the audit division of the Nevada Gaming Control Board. Like most somewhat boring auditors, he easily could have been doomed to a stereotypical career of a green-visor nerd checking on tax payments *(which is pretty much what the job description called for before he arrived –sans green visor and sleeve garters)*. But something in Denny apparently raised what I used to tell him was his *"spider sense"* to wonder what exactly was going on with the Argent Corporation's hiring of some unsavory (to say the least) characters. *(Argent was the parent of the Stardust, Fremont, and Hacienda casinos in Vegas.)*

Dennis Gomes

Legend has it that on his own initiative, genius, or madness, he transformed his job and the mission of the division to an investigative / law enforcement role and in the process became one of principal architects of Nevada's continuing drive to eliminate organized crime from casinos. He became known for an undisputed reputation for integrity; and as recently as August of 2007 he testified in the largest organized crime case in the history of the United States.

I have to admit that I have never read his entire 700-page report that began an entire chapter of Nevada's seemingly never-ending war against organized crime. *(Though I have doubts about the entire nature of what they seem to call "organized crime. In my naïve youth, I once asked a very high ranking Trump official about "organized crime" in the New York City building trades where Trump was best known. He replied to me, deadpan "What, you asking if we worry about the Mafia? We ARE the fucking Mafia." Little did I know how thin that line was, though I doubted then (and now) that he was doing little more than sounding tough).*

But there is no doubt that Denny Gomes made that 700-page report happen and changed the face of casino gaming forever. And THIS is the guy that turned

Bunky's tic-tac-toe playing chickens into a casino marketing promotion; go figure.

I also have to admit that I am remiss in not having sought out Gomes to meet him and pick his brain until the end of 2010 and only two years before his death; though a number of my co-workers and employees had worked with or for him over the years and our paths continually crossed. When we finally did meet, he readily told me that he had heard my name for years and wondered why we never met; and I, of course, had heard of him since my early days in Atlantic City right after Resorts opened their doors.

Dennis Gomes was one of the most unsung movers and shakers in the history of casino gaming. We should be seeing movies about Dennis Gomes rather than about Bugsy Siegel. Shortly before his death in 2012, he told me that his daughter, Danielle, was working on a book to correct that oversight.

Riding the success of Gomes' Nevada triumph and fame, he was lured to New Jersey to create gaming control (and some of the toughest licensing requirements in the industry) for the then-recently legalized casinos there. Officially he was hired as chief of special investigations for the New Jersey Division of Gaming Enforcement. Once again, he probably would have remained in *that* job forever had it not been for his unyielding integrity. Apparently tired of the political nonsense that then surrounded the licensing of the Mary Carter Paint Company as Resorts International *(that is whole other story)*, by 1977 he had been quoted saying that enforcement in New Jersey was a sham (at least that is what *Baron's Financial* quoted him as saying). This time, he headed back to Nevada…to try his hand as a casino operator rather than a regulator. It is one of the greatest ironic twists of our industry Dennis Gomes eventually <u>owned</u> Resorts International…far more ironic than my contract to operate the Trump Plaza property.

Probably the first of the high-profile transition leaders from mob-management to CPA management, Gomes went on to operate at least 13 casinos in Nevada and New Jersey. The *New York Times* once called him the casino world's *"Mister Fixit."* He ran Hilton's casino properties, answering directly to Baron Hilton; he was president of the famed Golden Nugget; worked for Trump (running the Taj Mahal); and became the president of the Atlantic City Tropicana…where he discovered my friend Bunky and the chickens.

Industry rumor was always that Aztar, then the parent company of the Tropicana, had been grooming Gomes to become Chairman whenever top-boss Paul Rubeli retired… and that somehow Gomes had been screwed out of that position during board jockeying for spoils of a hostile takeover by the Columbia Sussex Corporation. Though Rubeli and I shared a stage as panel members several times, I have no clue what the real deal was; but I do know that historically speaking, Gomes was never stymied by others' incompetence or misrepresentations. He moved forward and eventually created *Gomes Gaming,* ran a riverboat somewhere in the Midwest…and (as noted) owned Resorts International in Atlantic City.

Several executives who have worked for Gomes, including the CFO I worked with at Trump29, talk about a requirement that they attended his karate, yoga and meditation classes every morning before reporting to work. Giant-of-a-man George Toth, who apparently worked alongside Gomes in the creation of Gomes Gaming *(and himself the former GM of the Sands and a veteran of eccentric Carl Icon's organization)* never mentioned to me such a "requirement" — though I have never asked him specifically about it. Personally, I think it is a pretty good idea; but I *would* think so; *Kwai Chang Caine* was a role model for me and I thought Han Bong-Soo *(Bong Soo Han)* was much cooler than Billy Jack.

ABOVE: Dennis Gomes with one of Bunky's Chickens

The Atlantic City Sands, by the way, is where two very large goons threatened to break my legs in multiple places if I continued my earlier card-counting career at their casino. (More on that later.)

What I DO know is that Dennis testified before the New Jersey Casino Control Commission *"There's something in the martial arts called chi, the life energy that guides you. I think I give energy. I think love is the most powerful force in the universe. If you do everything from love, you can tap into that energy; those Wall Street guys hate that."* And, he told the *Wall Street Journal* that he studied martial arts and had a tattoo of a fist on his arm, *"to symbolize the idea of using power only "to maintain peace and harmony."*

Denny's reign at Aztar itself makes for an interesting story. As an absolute byproduct of the Gomes legacy of trying to chase organized crime out of gaming, several large hotel companies decided to jump into casino gaming with both feet. There was a *sort-of* logic to the thought: hotel casinos are like hotels in *some* way; doesn't it follow that the best hotel operators would be the best legitimate casino operators? *(By the way, the answer to that is NO it does NOT follow.)*

I began seriously talking with Dennis in February and March of 2011, about six months after he bought Resorts (more on that later). We were exploring a mutual vision for marketing resorts based on its history and the history of Atlantic City.

Either then or now, the bizarre history of *Resorts International* is just an incredible hanamusubi of confusion. That story alone, regardless of the parts of it that have been litigated over and over, is soap-opera typical of exactly the kind of intrigue that keeps people so excited about casinos. If I had to write an elevator-pitch "treatment" for a *fictionalized* Hollywood movie of the Resorts story, I would pitch a crusading young Eliot-Ness-type casino regulator who single-handedly drove the mafia out of Las Vegas, launching a fight against the CIA, a corrupt US President, the last Mafia boss, and crooked government bureaucrats all controlled by an evil crime lord. Here is the outline that I would pitch:

Company founder sets up a front (from a hardware paint company) with ties to CIA covert operations, a leading mafia boss, and illegal finance of a Presidential campaign;

Founder steals a private Caribbean resort from the heir to the largest grocery store chain on the planet, bribes third-world government officials, and sells a private toll-bridge to access their island;

Founder manipulates law to legalize gambling near New York City so that only his casino qualifies as legal;

Our hero begins fight against licensing of founder and accuses company of corruption;

Our hero is defeated and driven out of the state into exile;

Founder of company dies at 58 and company becomes part of a hostile takeover by country's most famous real estate mogul;

Dissident stockholders headed by legendary television producer fight mogul and win settlement;

New company quickly sells to South African group that plans $500-million renovation but the fall of racist apartheid creates a financial crisis for buyer and forces him to sell to mogul's former lawyer;

Former mogul's lawyer bankrupts company and sells it to...

... our crusading young casino regulator.

The non-fiction version is a close parallel of the movie treatment. As I said, Dennis Gomes had been lured from his quasi-clerical role where he had brought down Lefty Rosenthal in Nevada to head New Jersey Gaming Control's "special investigations."

In May of 1978, Resorts became the first legal casino outside of Nevada. Back then Resorts, their initial licensing, and their ownership (as well as control) were at very least *"less than clear,"* as Dennis later described it to me.

Resorts International, under CEO James Crosby, had changed its name from the *Mary Carter Paint Company* after acquiring the Paradise Island Casino from A&P Grocery heir Huntington Hartford. Beyond that, as Dennis said it is unclear what is true and what is not. In 1977 *Rolling Stone Magazine* had run an "exposé" of Resorts, which they later had to retract; and Hartford himself filed and dropped a number of allegation-filled lawsuits against the casino company. True or false, over the years the company had been linked to: Thomas Dewey (as in *"Dewey Wins"* over Truman) the mob persecutor who supposedly put $2-million into the company; his nemesis Meyer Lansky, who supposedly controlled a Miami Bank that financed the company and used the paint company as a front; employees who were part of the Bay of Pigs Invasion; Watergate hard-

71

ass G. Gordon Liddy; a partnership with Nixon friend and financier Charles Gregory "Bebe" Rebozo owning the only bridge to Paradise Island; Howard Hughes; and the CIA...and those are just the ones I have read about; there are probably more (not to mention the ones that have been whispered).

We *do* know that resorts owned a private intelligence company called *Intertel* that was set up by former Justice Department lawyer Robert Peloquin. We know that Intertel did detective, security and surveillance work for Howard Hughes' right hand man Bob Maheu as well as for ITT, Anastasio Somoza, and the Shah of Iran's SAVAK organization. Beyond that, there have been, at worst, libelous allegations about mob ties and, at best, "Blackwater" like tales of mercenary black-bag jobs for the CIA. Almost fifty years after the fact who the hell knows or cares anymore.

We do know that when I first stepped into Resorts in 1979, just a few days before the near-mugging outside the casino, there were people lined up behind every slot machine, waiting for a seat. Despite the unprecedented cash flow from that success (about $730,000 casino win per day), Resorts did nothing to upgrade their property and by the early 1980s (when I was working in Atlantic City casinos) there were nine casinos along the boardwalk. Resorts was a run-down 1920s building (formerly known as Haddon Hall Hotel and Rooming House) competing with Steve Wynn's over-the-top glitter at his *Golden Nugget Casino* at the other end of the boardwalk and the new Aztar Vegas-style *Tropicana*.

When I met Resorts CEO James Crosby over dinner in Resort's gourmet room in 1981, he was deeply concerned about those other properties encroaching on what he considered his personal domain. Between chain-smoking coughs during the meal, Crosby lectured me (I was his 27-year-old non-smoking casino bus marketer) on how he had single-handedly brought casinos to New Jersey when Myer Lansky, Baron Hilton, Holiday Inns, and "every politician in the state" had failed. He told me, "don't you worry about it; I have a plan that will make those Las Vegas boys pack up and go home."

In 1986 Crosby decided to respond to the competition by buying land near resorts and launching plans to create the *Taj Mahal Casino*: his vision of the largest, most glittery, over-the-top casino outside of Vegas; a project to rival Wynn's Vegas *Mirage*. But in August of 1986 Crosby, died at 58 years old during an operation combatting his emphysema.

It was only after his death that the financial labyrinth of Resorts began to unravel and it became clear that the Taj Mahal would never be completed; at least not by *that* company. By early 1987 the company was targeted for a hostile takeover by Donald Trump who purchased controlling interest during a Crosby heirs' feud and made an offer to buy all outstanding shares. Before he could follow through with that offer, Trump became embroiled in a legal challenge from other stockholders headed by television legend Merv Griffin (the creator of *Jeopardy* and *Wheel of Fortune,* who already owned the Beverly Hilton and a chain of other hotels). The battle ended with a settlement agreement in which

72

Griffin won Resorts and Trump would take control of the Taj Mahal development property...and eventually hire Dennis Gomes as his CEO.

Disillusioned with the gaming industry and the Trump-esque name-calling bravado, Griffin sold the Paradise Island property to Sol Kerzner's South African *Sun International*. After $90-million in renovations, eight years of marginal operating, and politically the overthrow of South Africa's apartheid, Griffin sold Resorts to Kerzner as well (reportedly for around $350-million). Though Kerzner had announced a $500-million renovation plan, in reality he only invested less than 10% of that in Atlantic City, opting instead to transform the Paradise Island property from "Resorts International" to "The Atlantis" (which itself was bankrupt in 2011).

Without the now decades-over-due full renovations, Resorts continued to lose money and in 2001 Kerzner sold the property for less than half what he paid for it. In another incestuous twist of the gaming industry (many of which we will see in the following pages), the buyer was Colony Capital — headed by Nick Ribis.

Colony headed a division of Colony that focused on buying failing casinos at fire-sale prices and operating them without investing much. Besides Resorts, they bought the Las Vegas Hilton, as well as casinos in East Chicago, Tunica Mississippi, and another Atlantic City property. Still not investing in a full renovation of Resorts, Colony too failed as an operator. As noted, in December of 2009, Wells Fargo foreclosed on Colony and announced that on December 31 2010, they would at long last close the property unless a buyer came forward. Since that foreclosure, Colony's other properties also took dives. As noted earlier, in September 2011, Colony skipped three mortgage payments of $3.5-million each due on the Las Vegas Hilton, promoting Goldman Sachs to foreclose on its $252-million term loan to Colony. A year later, in September 2012, Goldman Sachs formed a JV with New York REIT Gramercy Capital to buy the LVH out of foreclosure (Hilton pulled their name from the property in early 2012 forcing a rebranding to LVH).

Almost a year before the failure of the Las Vegas Hilton, Wells Fargo agreed to sell Resorts in Atlantic City to Dennis Gomes and his partner Morris Bailey for only $35-million; 10% of what Sun had paid and about 25% of what Colony had paid.

Dennis gained control of Resorts in 2010 and early in 2011 he had asked me to come to Atlantic City to meet with him (as well as his writer-daughter Danielle). Unfortunately I did not meet Danielle before Dennis' death, but I was able to be sort of an un-official receptacle of Dennis' last year of marking and promotional vision for Resorts in Atlantic City.

From the "roaring twenties" style exploitation of Terence Winter's successful HBO series *"Boardwalk Empire"*; to *"Cirque Risque —The Naked Circus"* at Dennis's Superstar Theater; to the casino's rebranding of a million-dollar stakes races at Monmouth Park racetrack to the *Resorts Haskell Invitational*; to my urging that he re-contract with my old friend Frank Palmieri's Media and

Marketing Group as his advertising and marketing agency... Gomes and I talked at least a couple of times a month about marketing, brand positioning, and the future of Resorts.

I was told that in January of 2012, back in Vegas and around the time of the death of his oldest son Doug, Dennis fell while moving a marble table top. He knew he felt some pain afterwards and as he later described a conversation with his doctor: *"He asked me, 'Did you ever break your back? He told me, 'Dennis, you're the toughest SOB I've ever seen in my life. You're the only person I know who's walked around for one solid month with a broken back.'"* He had four broken vertebrae. Either in conjunction with or after the fall (and the subsequent painful back brace that he was issued), Dennis told me that he was undergoing temporary kidney dialysis.

On Friday February 24, 2012, Dennis, only ten years my senior, died in a Philly hospital from complications of that dialysis.

As noted, Dennis Gomes had run all of Baron Hilton's Nevada properties (including the legendary Flamingo and the Las Vegas Hilton; He had run the

Golden Nugget in downtown Vegas; As CEO of Trump's Taj Mahal between 1991 and 1995 he increased operating profits from about $85-million to more than $145-million; at Aztar he spearheaded growth that took the stock price from $4 a share to $40; all of this from the Nevada Gaming Control Board chief of the audit division who brought down Las Vegas organized crime.

Shortly after his death, Resorts announced that Gomes' turn-around strategies had brought the company out of the red and turned a profit for the first time in years. By July of 2012, Resorts was still posting more than $13-million a month in slot revenue, compared to only $10.9-million at the competing Trump Plaza.

I had thought of contacting his son Aaron (who I have never met) and Mo Bailey shortly after Dennis' death and offer to continue the vision; but I opted against it as too ghoulish. Nonetheless, in August of 2012 the Mohegan Tribe of Connecticut, operators of the Mohegan Sun Casino (itself reportedly $1.6-billion in debt amid their auditor's "going concern warning") agreed to take over management of Resorts. The tribe also agreed to buy a piece of Resorts and finance a $35-million expansion to bring a Margaritaville restaurant. New Jersey law requires that a management company be invested in a casino they operate.

Back in the 1980s, the hotel-industry lust for casinos, clearly spawned by Gomes' bringing a new flavor of legitimacy to the industry, had begun in a big way. Holiday Inns, the Memphis Tennessee motel giant billed as *"The Nation's Innkeeper"* bought Harrah's. *(That by the way is why the massive and award-winning Harrah's player database is still maintained in Memphis at the former Holiday Inn reservation center...on the same damned NEC computers from the 1970s!)* Around the same time, Baron Hilton jumped into the business forging alliances first with Trump and later with Bally. And in the same decade Holiday Inn wanna-be-clone, Ramada Inns, bought the Tropicana casinos in Vegas and in Atlantic City while Sheraton bought the Desert Inn and others.

While Harrah's and Hilton became incredible successes, Ramada was not so well-run or fortunate (depending on your perspective). There was no Phil Satre (Harrah's now-retired visionary chairman who currently sits on the board of the world's largest slot machine manufacture) at the helm of Ramada to guide the hotelier's entry into gaming. Right away there was a hotel-type remodeling of the Atlantic City Tropicana and creation of a two-story casino with a "Tivoli Pier" theme and rebranding of the strong Vegas/Havana brand to some hotel marketer's vision: *"Trop World"*.

The bleeding of Ramada cash was instantly clear as company profits fell from $17.2-million in 1985, to $10.3-million in 1986, and only $4.9-million in 1987. On the way to posting a $5.1 million loss with $260-million in debt, in 1988, the Ramada *hotel* brand was split from the casino brand and sold for $540-million to Hong Kong based New World Development Company. *(How one sells a company for a multiple of 106 times earnings is beyond my limited financial abilities; never mind the fact that they were losing money.)* At the same time, Ramada sold its *Marie Callender* restaurant chain for another $54½-million.

(Incidentally, since we were talking about Dennis Gomes and the adventures that became the movie "Casino" — it was in the parking lot of the Marie Callender restaurant at 600 West Sahara Avenue in Vegas where Lefty Rosenthal's car bomb exploded — rather than in the hotel parking lot as shown in the movie.)

Ramada's remaining casino division was spun into a publicly traded company called *Aztar Corporation* which hired Dennis Gomes as guru (and, as noted, he increased share price by 10-times). Nonetheless, from that fiasco loss of its core business, an outside observer might hope that the corporate world (or at least investment bankers) would have learned that running a casino is NOT "the same as running any other business" and certainly not the same as running a hotel. Nonetheless, the most vehement and fervent soap box orators for *"it is just like any other business"* seem to be people who have entered the casino business, have ridden high on its cash flow, and then found a scapegoat for why they failed in the end.

True to form, Aztar decided to operate their new casino empire from the *hotel company* headquarters in Phoenix…and run it like a really big hotel project; despite Dennis' objections. Once Gomes became President of the "resort" (read "casino") division, the company seemed to be on a road to recovery. Just before the William Yung (Columbia Sussex) takeover, Gomes-driven Aztar had turned around their losses to a $212-million EBITDA against $915-million in revenues. Aztar was trying to pay down and refinance debt as well as repurchase their own stock.

Alas, hoteliers have still not learned the lessons Dennis was teaching; even as of this writing, just take a look at the taking-private of Harrah's with hedge fund money and their two false starts at new IPOs. (As a friend of mine noted in November of 2010, *"those guys aren't in the casino business; they are in the hedge fund and capital management business."* Amen.)

In fairness, I should point out that Aztar *did* try to expand by "testing the waters" (pun intended) in the *riverboat* casino business. One of my former business partners, Frank Haas *(at this writing GM of an Oklahoma casino that he and I developed),* opened a Caruthersville Missouri riverboat casino in 1995 for Aztar as its creator and first acting General Manager. He ran a profitable, albeit small, operation and he ran it well; but it was not enough to save Aztar and it did not become a business model for them.

A decade later, I hired Haas as well as his Aztar riverboat captain/pilot, his Aztar IT manager, Aztar's slot manager, Aztar's marketing manager, Aztar's table games manager, and Aztar's games trainer to help me rebuild business at another Oklahoma casino. It was from that experience that Haas and I formed a short-lived development company to build our second foray into *Oklahoma* Indian gaming; the Ottawa Tribe of Oklahoma's High Winds Casino.

Frank Haas is another of those colorful casino characters that began as "a numbers guy". Not an accountant, but a numbers analyst that came to gaming through the hotel side of Ramada Inns with business experience in a family business far from gaming or hotels. Frank was the last of several generations of a Pennsylvania Dutch coffin making dynasty; and he has some really interesting stories about that business *(is the pillow stuffed with cotton, poly-fiber, or shredded newspapers? And does it matter?)*. Rather than continue in the family craft, Frank took his cost-focus and accounting analytical skills to the hotel/casino world which in turn took him from Pennsylvania to Arizona where he landed at Aztar's Phoenix headquarters (almost by accident after his wife had applied for a different job there and discovered they needed a numbers guy).

At Trump (a few years after he left Aztar), Frank had been career-stagnated as a comptroller, politically bypassed for promotion to CFO (in favor of another former Gomes employee), and hence excluded from the top management circles. Seeing a lot of talent in Frank (as well as his just being a great guy that deserved a seat at that table), I began inviting him to join the meetings of our Trump management triumvirate (myself, the CFO, and the Jersey-based liaison) at the almost-nightly off-site dinners and strategy sessions. I had already seen Frank in action on the job and knew he was one of those unsung heroes that kept the business going. His addition to the management group could only enrich our group with his genius and focus on details.

A few months later, when I left Trump to become GM of the then-largest casino in Oklahoma *(more on that in a later chapter)*, I brought Frank along as CFO. In fact, that was a pretty goofy-situation itself. At the Trump29 casino, as I prepared to leave, Frank told me that for several years he had been planning to visit Oklahoma to look at ranch and farm property for eventual retirement. As an off-the-cuff comment of mere politeness I said, *"Well, hell, if you ever get out that way, give me a call and I am certain I can find a job for you."*

My second week in Oklahoma, Frank called me — from the Will Rogers Airport in Oklahoma City; he was ready to take me up on the "job offer". Caught completely off guard but surrounded by crooks, thieves, sharks, and liars (more on that, too, in a later chapter), I needed *somebody* to watch my back, so I hired him on-the-spot for a few thousand dollars more than he had been making at Trump. I trusted him unreservedly and needed a guy like that! I needed a Frank Haas focus. He went back for a two-week notice, but in our industry that is merely a formality and executives at that level are immediately escorted from the property (regardless of the circumstances of the departure).

Coming to Oklahoma from Trump, in addition to Frank, I also hired three lower-level hourly-wage employees who wanted to move. I hired the parking valet supervisor (a 23-year-old Black Muslim from East LA) and one of the switchboard operators (a near-minimum-wage Mexican-American from Indio California who was a close friend of the prostitute in Indio who briefly had brought down televangelist Jimmy Swaggart). I also brought along the night supervisor of the players club, Will, who I had been grooming as my protégé

77

since before he led the security team for the aforementioned Trump visit. I later heard that after Frank's departure, there were accusations that the Trump staff had been "raided" for Oklahoma. (Though no one ever seriously believed that, the Tribal Chairman *did* complain to the Governor of the Oklahoma Tribe).

A few years later, when Frank and I jointly built that northeastern Oklahoma casino, I personally wrote the *General Manager* job description to match Frank's resume (and *only* Frank's resume). That was actually not necessary, because Frank's background was so rich and so laser-focused on the day-to-day functions of top management that even if a top-notch candidate had come along, that person would have had a tough time matching the superior merits of Frank Haas and his skillset.

I also single-handedly wrote the Tribal Gaming Commission's policies and procedures to favor not only a general manager's needs, but specifically toward Frank's own personal eccentricities. I sat in on all candidate interviews and trashed the mediocre ones (there were no *good* ones)...all to make certain Frank was hired; again not a stretch given his quality — even as a standalone he could compete head-to-head with any G.M. in the country and come out on top. Yes, Frank was "juiced" into the job (in the parlance of the casino world) and it was perfect for him; though, again, he needed no juice for the gig.

Six years later, when I visited him in Oklahoma, Frank had pictures of his cattle *(yes his cattle!)* as the wallpaper on his computer; his daughter, AJ, told me about chasing stray cows while she was wearing high heels; and Frank could not attend the *National Indian Gaming Association* convention in 2010 because his cows or bulls or something were doing something cattle-like at the old ranch. *Gotta love it.*

LEFT: Frank Haas (left), Gary Green (center), and Will Wimmer (right) examine plans for development of a new Oklahoma casino. *Circa 2004.*

During the building of that casino, Frank and I had agreed that it did not matter which of us was *"Number One"* and which was *"Number Two."* In fact, I had argued strongly to the Tribal leadership, over several objections, that I should take the Number *Two* slot rather than the top title. I reasoned that this would give the Tribe the least amount of controversy once they opened a new casino (after all, I DO seem to cut a wide strip of controversy wherever I land...as you will soon see). Hence, I was able to write that job description and the regulations to match Frank exactly. Once Frank was in the GM position, he discovered that he did not have the budget to afford both of us and funneled the *Number Two* role to a former employee for a third of my cost. But, known only to Frank and none of his naysayers, I never had any intention of actually living in rural Oklahoma (I had stayed in a Marriott 20 miles away in Missouri for the 11 months of construction) and I had plans to develop other casinos across the country in other short-term assignments like that one. By contrast, as noted, it was Frank's long-time dream to own a ranch in Oklahoma and ride his horses. And, as noted, as of this writing, he has accomplished those things.

I see him for a week once a year either at the annual *Global Gaming Expo* in Las Vegas or the *National Indian Gaming Association* in New Mexico, Arizona, or California, and we talk periodically by email. Unannounced, I occasionally drop in on him in Miami Oklahoma (pronounced Miam-ah) at his casino there and pitch him slot machines, tracking systems, and free marketing advice; reminding AJ of the Lionel Trilling quote (usually attributed to Picasso) *"Immature artists imitate. Mature artists steal."* I, of course, bastardize it for her (and for Frank) to *"good marketers borrow ideas from other casinos; great marketers steal them."*

In 2009 I attended his daughter's, AJ's, chapel-wedding at the *Paris Casino* in Las Vegas and even paid two-thirds of the preacher's fee because absent-minded-professor Frank forgot to bring cash.

Over the years, as I have become more finance-savvy, Frank has focused more and more on marketing his casino and moving from exclusive number-crunching to adding some creative flair. At the same time, he has shown the good taste not to be flamboyant, colorful, nor controversial and as that sharp contrast to me he remains steady. His daughter AJ adds the real creative flair and together they have effectively branded the property

ABOVE: Frank Haas moves to the marketing side, posing with showgirls to send a video greeting to Gary Green from High Winds Casino in Oklahoma.

and have taken it to the proverbial "next level" with the help of the aforementioned marketing gurus Frank Palmieri and Jan Talamo.

♣ ♦ ♥ ♠

79

Chapter Seven
I Run *fucking* Casinos: Gambling Halls;
...NOT "Hospitality Industry" Hotels

"...hospitality industry, a euphemism for organized prostitution..."
— **Annette Fuentes and Barbara Ehrenreich,**
Women in the Global Factory

Listen to me... VERY CAREFULLY: running a casino is _**not**_ the same as running a hotel. "Gambling" is *not* a dirty word. And it *is* ok to call one of these "entertainment experience properties" a gambling joint. Oh, and we don't have "same store sales" like the retail business.

Look, people do not fly to Aspen for the hotels or the entertainment "experience"; they go to Aspen to ski. They do not go to Orlando for the hotels and the shopping experience; they go to Orlando for Disney. All the other millions of dollars of amenity revenue is *icing on the cake*. Take away the cake and the icing is useless. Take away the snow or Disney or whatever the primary draw is... and you have disjointed nothing. Eat just the icing and you are eating hollow junk that will ultimately just make you sick (even if it does seem to taste good at the time).

Get it? The practice of basing a business model in Orlando *assuming* customers may or may not go to Disney or in Aspen *assuming* customers may or may not be there for the snow...is...at best flawed and at worst moronic. Yes, there are companies that will make LOTS of money with that model —for a short while and until the day they are shocked to learn that people did not come to Orlando because they have a nice hotel there.

Sands Las Vegas (Venetian Hotel) founder Sheldon Adelson (once listed as the third wealthiest man in the world) made his fortune on the periphery of the gaming industry promoting conventions and hotel rooms in Las Vegas —where people wanted to come to gamble. In 2010, he emphatically insisted that he was not in the gambling business. But like Louie is *Casablanca*, shocked to learn that there is gambling going on, the depression of the late 00's caused at least many Wall Street analysts to rethink Adelson's apparent disdain for the rackets that bring people to his hotels and conventions. More on that shortly.

People come to Las Vegas to gamble. People don't come to a casino for the euphemistic "entertainment and hospitality experience" —especially non-destination local casinos that do not have hotels. People come to a casino to gamble. Period. *Now, how do I explain that to an investment analyst?* Wait; maybe I just did.

In the transition of taking casinos from mob ownership to legitimate business operations, there was only one way that Wall Street and the investment

80

community could justify getting involved: through established business models that bankers could understand. Those complex casino-world distinctions between *coin-in*, *drop*, and *hold* were not part of expected valuation formulas. Instead, Wall Street looked for a perceived "similar" industry to understand these enormous cash-flow generators. Hence, "casino" and "gambling" euphemistically became "hospitality property" and "gaming." Under the new leadership of a Harvard Business School professor, even Harrah's eventually began referring to their casino floors with such Wall Street friendly terms as "same store sales," "up sell" and "cross sell." And, across the industry, rather than merely amenities for gamblers, all of the rooms, food, alcohol, entertainment, and in some places even valet parking, each became revenue centers with their own P&L responsibilities.

The focus moved from running a *gambling hall* to being "in the hospitality industry." There was already a SIC code for hospitality, and even today if you search for a code for "casino" at the government's SIC website (http://www.osha.gov/pls/imis/sicsearch.html) you find:

> **7011 Hotels and Motels:** Commercial establishments, known to the public as hotels, motor hotels, motels, or tourist courts, primarily engaged in providing lodging, or lodging and meals, for the general public. Hotels which are operated by membership organizations and open to the general public are included in this industry.
>
> — U.S. Department of Labor, Occupational Safety & Health Administration, Standard Industrial Classification (SIC) System *latest revision: 1987*

If that is where the United State Government classifies casinos, then it also is something bankers can understand, pitch to investors, and not worry about having to be creative. In that line of thinking, it seemed like a natural expansion for "hospitality" companies (hotels) to move into "gaming" as another same-store revenue stream. Some hotels have spas, some have gourmet restaurants, some have amusement parks, some have swimming pools *...and some would have these casinos*. (What a fucking bone-headed idea!)

Think about it. Let's reduce casinos to just another variation of a hotel, ok? Now let's add this little twist to it: at my Trump29 Casino, when I left, we had an average "coin-in" of a little more than $100-million a month. Let's use that as a model rather than actual numbers from there:

> *Ok, now picture yourself as an investor in "hotels" (we didn't have one there); your $25-million investment <u>grosses</u> $100-million a month! Holy shit! Of course you can sell that to the investment community. Hell, since this is the HOTEL/HOSPITALITY industry, you don't have to explain those pesky little things like hold (that reduces your actual gross revenue to $8.5-million)...if anyone ever actually questioned it, you can call it "cost of goods sold." Never mind casino operational costs at that time totaled about 40% (reducing that earnings number down to $5.1-million); oh and since you have already used "cost of goods sold", I am not sure how you explain away the manufacture's*

rev share that reduces your number to $2.9-million. Oh and let's not forget the taxation (including tribal taxes) that reduces your number to $1.5-million. Ah, and the management fees that reduce the number to $1.04-million. Oh, let's not forget promotional costs, separate from that operational number which could reduce your actual monthly earnings to $640,000. So, let's not think about those casino-industry specific little things that would yield an annual earnings of about $8-million. Instead, let's focus on a HOTEL that has $100-million cash flow monthly ($1,200,000,000: One-point-two-BILLION annually). It is a hell of a lot easier to get investors to line up behind a HOSPITALITY business that has $1.2-billion in annual cash flow than it is to get them on board with a casino that has a monthly EBITDA of $640-thousand. Thank God this is the legitimate business world now involved in "gaming" rather than those "casino guys."

As far back as 1999 or 2000 at the World Gaming Congress & Expo (the forerunner of the current industry trade show *Global Gaming Expo* —G2E), I debated average daily rate (ADR) of hotel rooms on the Strip as part of one of the casino-industry panel forums. I sat on the dais along with then Mandalay Resort Group President/CFO Glenn Schaeffer, and Aztar Chairman Paul Rubeli. How I got on the podium with those industry heavies was more about force of personality than pedigree; I certainly didn't have anywhere near the credentials those guys had. However, I did have a dissertation-like booklet on revolutionizing casino marketing methodologies and that booklet not only contained "inside information" given to me by executives at Harrah's, Mandalay, and Hilton but it had been widely circulated in the industry amongst the analysts. I suppose, then, that I was a minor buzz figure amongst the giants.

In those days, Schaeffer was a darling of the Wall Street boys (and in every right still is a brilliant operator/financier today). Even before that panel, I had always been impressed with his no-nonsense, albeit arrogantly brash, direct approach to complex issues. The fact that he is a patron of literature and holds an MFA in fiction writing, just impressed me even more; while Steve Wynn was playing at the arts by over-spending for masterpieces (and punching holes in canvasses), Glenn Schaeffer was a genuine renaissance executive who personally bankrolled writers and libraries.

At the time, Schaeffer's Mandalay Bay Hotel and Casino was one of (if not THE) most upscale properties on the Strip and he was a torchbearer for the multiple-revenue stream argument. (Hell, the top floors of the Mandalay were operated by *The Four Seasons*; it was a first class "joint" all the way.)

Schaeffer, on that panel, suggested that eventually Mandalay would like to see a $600+ per night rate for rooms on the Las Vegas Strip. I argued that the best ADR ("average daily rate") would be zero; I wanted hotel rooms to be a place to put gamblers to bed at night. Rubeli, agreeing with neither of us, but leaning toward Schaeffer, sang the woes of "giving away revenue" but agreed that the focus should be on gaming. (He had come a long way for a Ramada Inns hotel guy.)

Don't get me wrong: I am a big fan of revenue...anywhere we can get it. But my argument was that an average visitor to Vegas had a finite amount of money to spend and that we could capture the entire amount at gambling (and comp everything else) while creating a <u>loyal return guest</u> for the specific property; I wanted return customers. The idea was that we would build a long-term customer, with brand loyalty, who would come back to us again and again rather than a room-deal-hunting whore who would hop from property to property.

Schaeffer's argument was that capturing a portion of that finite budget was certain with room rate and less certain with the casino; and the huge (and seemingly never-ending) customer base made the brand loyalty issue more a function of the "complete package" than of the gaming experience.

I could only counter that the certainty for *casino win* is a function of marketing, because once a player begins, there is a mathematical certainty of the casino's long term win. Schaeffer, apparently, preferred the more definite, albeit perhaps short-term, capture of those dollars without regard to my loyalty issue. In fairness to him, at the time the industry truly believed there was an unlimited number of new customers –one of many reasons customer service suffered at so many casino hotels. *Who cared? There was always another customer waiting in line.*

In fact, today, even in the 21st century, I still see that impersonal lack of customer service... sadly it prevails even amongst the industry giants who claim they are leaders in customer service; as I showed in the second chapter of this book with the series of photos of the rundown "resort" in Vegas.

And, of course, in the non-resort "locals" casinos, there is absolutely no argument to support the "destination resort" school of thought.

As far as revenue stream from sources other than gambling, I go back to Sheldon Adelson's "vision". In July of 2010 *The Economist* magazine reported that Adelson claimed that he is not in the gambling racket and that 70% of his revenue came from non-gaming revenue centers. The magazine reported:

> *"Mr. Adelson, the head of Las Vegas Sands and for some years the world's third-richest person, insists that he is not in the gambling business, nor even in the gaming business (a distinction he and Michael Leven, Las Vegas Sands' president, consider important; the difference between gaming and gambling, according to Mr. Leven, "is the difference between having a cocktail and going out drinking").*"[6]

The same issue of the magazine reported that only 17% of the visitors to Vegas do NOT gamble. Please don't make the logical fallacy of misunderstanding the statistical data and think that the magazine reported that Adelson makes 70% of his money from 17% of the people (a variation of the Pareto principle and traditional sales "wisdom" that 80% of the sales come from 20% of the customers). Hell, if it was that simplistic, just give me the other 83%! Of course, it does not break down that simply since everyone has to eat and sleep…but there is still something unsettling if not out-and-out fucked-up about that report — even more than a decade after my panel with Schaeffer.

After that panel debate, we all shook hands and I have neither seen nor talked to Schaeffer since; and I am sure he has forgotten all about the little encounter and all about me (if he even remembered me at all for a minute). Rubeli and I talked a few times, mostly about Dennis Gomes.

In the short run, Adelson and back then, Schaeffer, absolutely were correct. After orchestrating the almost $8-billion sale of Mandalay Resort Group, Schaeffer moved on to head the Fontainebleau project with my old friend Mark Lefever as his CFO…and of this writing I have no idea what either are doing since the bankruptcy of that project.

Meanwhile and unrelated to Glen Schaeffer, many Vegas hotel/casinos separated their amenities into independent revenue centers, with each being responsible for its own bottom line, and even its own continuation in business; each (financially) independent of the other revenue centers. The long-held practice of liberally giving gamblers free rooms, food, and drink, ("comps") morphed into a complex accounting labyrinth that would have impressed even the mob's greatest subterfuges of shell companies.

In fact, the delivery of *any* player comps at all has become so complex that most "properties" either contract out the calculation or employ a highly skilled team of mathematicians and database analysts to prepare the computations. When I first arrived at Trump29, we actually paid a company about eight-grand a month to analyze our player tracking data and recommend what comps would go to which players. THAT is how complex this bullshit had become over the years.

Technology guru Tom Trimble and I even created software that would automate the process. Called *LogicComps*, it took the tedious (and expensive) process of weighing the economic variables and automated/mechanized the progression of decisions so that even a clerical employee would be able to "issue comps" while still having decisions based on the overly-complicated business rules developed by the wags. In short, LogicComps allowed casinos an inexpensive way to utilize those over-priced player-tracking systems, without having to hire a staff of non-gaming technicians to calculate room costs vs. player value. Even that calculation is a head-scratcher.

On paper, if for example, the "rack rate" (what you and I would pay if we just walked up asked for a room) for a hotel room was $600, then that room might have a "wholesale" value of $300 *(we will get to THAT a little later)*. If the casino had a player who generated, for example, $1,000 in profit for the casino, then a portion of that profit would be used as promotion to build player loyalty and to keep the player at this "property" rather than sleeping at a competing "property" and possibly gambling there. Studies show people tend to gamble where they lay their heads at night. So consider that promotional money an "advertising" expense.

That promotion might be in the form of a "discounted" hotel room, allowing the gambler to rent the room at, say, $100 a night — a perceived huge discount (from $600) to "reward" the gambler for their loyal play. The hotel then would collect $100 from the gambler and send the casino a bill for $200 — the difference between what was paid for the room and where the wholesale rate had *seemingly*-arbitrarily been set.

Hence, collecting a total of $300 a night for the room, the hotel could show a profit and stay in business. Try to forget the fact that the $200 came from a different department of the *same company* and ultimately *out of the same pocket*. How phony-baloney is that corporate creative accounting? No wonder the world has forensic accountants; oh wait, this is *legitimate* business...I almost forgot... "Mob" duplicity is not part of the casino world anymore. This is that new model of 70% of revenue coming from non-gaming sources!

Add to this seeming absurdity, 15 or 20 other variable factors (from zip code of the guest which allows a comparison of the historic spending behavior to other guests from that zip code; to frequency of visits; spending in other revenue centers of the property; propensity to accept free drinks; interest in shows; and on and on). The calculation quickly becomes unruly and in some cases scientistic rather than scientific. *(In a later section of this book, I make some sense out of these schemes...as well as show some examples of the non-sense in some versions of them.)*

Even more complex, that "wholesale" rate for the room is not totally arbitrary; it too is actually formulaic.

In the traditional hotel management world, not everyone pays the same price for identical rooms... just like with airplane seats. You have heard the stories of two people sitting side-by-side on a plane; one person paid $500 for their seat and the person in the next seat paid $200. The same types of pricing discrepancies exist rampantly in the hotel industry.

There are special discounts for travel agents, reservation services, advertising promotions, corporate rates, government per diem rate, senior citizen rates, organization rates (AAA, AARP, CAA, etc.), convention & group rates, seasonal rates, weather-related rates, and scores of other variables...and those are just the "published" rates. Moreover (and most insidious to consumers) there are daily variations in non-published room rates determined by occupancy and other factors (more on this below).

And, in the Casino world, we have very large discounts given to known casino players ("casino rate"). That, within itself, created a problem for those "multiple revenue centers" sycophants. Typically, a hotel does not give away free rooms to big spenders in other operational units (someone that orders a big meal in a restaurant; someone that buys a lot in the gift shop; even someone who spends hours riding a ski lift); you do not get a room discount just because you ordered a big dinner. Right out of the box, the hotel model needed some adjusting...despite insistence that gaming is less than a third of the revenue stream and that to be near the gaming just MIGHT be the reason someone rented the hotel room.

Remember how Howard Hughes came to be in the casino business in the first place —and opened the industry to corporate America: he and his crew were paying for hotel rooms that Moe Dalitz wanted to GIVE to high-roller players (rather than collect revenue for renting rooms).

A rented ("sold") hotel room has a fixed cost that can be associated with it. There is the cost of the housekeeping service: *if a housekeeper is making $10 an hour (and 30% in benefits) and can clean a room in 15 minutes, then there is a $3.25 cost associated with the room.* Add the cost of linens for the room, utilities, peripheral staff *(a percentage of front desk, security, and so on)*, even debt service and depreciation for the room's square footage... and so on. The bottom-line number is the actual cost per room per day and (generally speaking) that number *plus* a fixed markup percentage (for R.O.I.) is considered by the hotel industry to be the *minimum* that can be charged for a room.

As of this writing, in Las Vegas that *cost per room per day*, less the fixed mark-up percentage, is somewhere between $15 and $75 ...depending on location, occupancy percentage, condition of property, etc. This number, notably, does **not** include the pro-rated per room per day per square foot amount of money to cover financing the property, cost of the money, and other finance-related expenses that have become so exorbitant with some of the newer properties caught in the money lending frenzy of the first decade of the 21st century. So a room that cost $15 to maintain, may have a minimum needed daily rate of $150 because of exorbitant financing.

Nick Ribis was famously quoted after his purchase of the Las Vegas Hilton as saying, "I paid $90,000 per room, and Wynn's rooms cost $1 million! If I charge $130 a night I make tons of money! He has to get over $300!"[7]

Just as operating costs dictate the *minimum* charge for a room, an entirely different set of factors that determine the *maximum* a hotel can effectively charge. These include:

- Hotel demand, directly tied to the microeconomics of the travel industry (and this is another area where the hotel model does not *exactly* match the economic engine that drives travel to Las Vegas or Atlantic City and especially to those locals casinos);

- Competition *(supply & demand; degree of saturation; extent of rate-cutting and room-comping; differences in physical facilities (including condition); even customer service level);*

- Internal Elasticity *(the airline industry calls this **Yield Management**) based on near-desperation of hotel management to assure a high occupancy percentage by using reservation center computers to adjust the price minute-by-minute based on projected occupancy for that date. To see this in action, visit* Marriott *or* Hilton *websites twice (a few days* *apart) and price the same room in the same hotel on the same date at each website visit. You will find different prices for the same room.)* For example, I recently booked a room online for seven nights at Marriott.com. The AAA discount rate came to $1,876. I returned to the website six hours later and booked the same room for the same dates for $1,526 (and cancelled the previous reservation). The next day I went back to website and got a price of $1,284 for the same room and same days. Again, I made the change. Two days later, I was able to book the same room for the same dates for $1,120.52. The next day the hotel was sold out for some of my days so my taking advantage of the system came to an end. These price changes were a result of "yield management" pricing systems.

Just from the standpoint of accurate revenue projections, how fucked up is that? So, instead of accurate projections, the industry takes occupancy percentage (hence the fanatical focus on keeping that number high) and multiplies that by the Average Daily Rate (ADR) of these all-over-the-place prices.

In other words, even though I would be paying $160 a night for the room, some analyst somewhere would be reporting "projected revenue" for that room at $268 per night (at least). And, THIS is "legitimate" business…wait till you see the reason behind this madness!

These are the factors used in the traditional hotel management and combined with one of several rate calculation formulas to create the actual cost of a room to the hotel. *A typical hotel-industry formula process is contained in the endnotes of this book.*[8]

One of the many devices brought from the hotel industry to casinos *(ah, I mean to the new "hospitality industry")* is to announce the price of rooms even greater than the "rack" (published) rate. We did this at the Trump organization. For example, if a room costs the hotel $50 a night and the rack rate is $95 a night, then management publishes a rate (and posts it in the room) of $125 a night. Even though almost no one will *ever* be charged that $125 rate, every guest (even rack-rate customers) will think they were treated special and got a "deal." (Even though in some circles that might be considered fraud; this is legitimate business in the "hospitality" industry.)

Even more importantly, all this also makes a tasty little tax loss because we "had to" rent our room at a $30 loss. *(But THAT thievery from the IRS is certainly not conspiracy or "organized" crime… right?).* Such is the world of traditional hotel management and pricing…and such was the world of the new mangers coming into the casino industry.

I used to periodically stay in a very large suite at the *Paris* in Vegas; when, on the rare occasion, I actually paid for the room, the rate was somewhere between $75 and $95 a night. The rate posted on the back of the door was $3,500 per night. *Right; like ANYONE has ever paid that!*

So the rate charged by the hotel to the casino, absurd as it may sound, is based on some complex analysis of room costs. Never mind that all of this transaction between the hotel and the casino is merely on paper, and certainly never mind that $100 for a room is a hundred-dollars less with which to gamble. Never mind the debate over consumer perception and marketing value of a discount room versus a VIP free room.

Never mind the fact that a customer now perceives that there is a "cost" to gamble (hotel and food) when in the mind of a typical gambler there is no cost to the activity itself. Despite the bankers' insistence on sugar-coating gambling as mere entertainment (the *gaming* word versus "gambling"), gamblers play the games to win money...not to game like a video game on a computer. People gamble thinking they CAN win. They don't *hate* losing if there are other benefits; but charging high rates for rooms and food takes away at least some of those benefits. *I even argue that setting players' club tier-levels too high for average gamblers is a mistake; but that is another discussion.*

One of my partners recently considered making an offer to purchase the high-end ($4-billion project) Cosmopolitan hotel/casino in Vegas. Owning casinos was never part of Deutsche Bank's strategy and the bank told the *Financial Times* the Cosmopolitan was "neither a strategic nor a long-term investment"; yet they were stuck with it. The property lost $54.3 million during the second quarter of 2011, slightly less than the $56.8 million it lost during the first quarter. The casino opened on Dec. 15, 2010, so no previous second quarter numbers exist for comparison. During the first six months of operation, The Cosmopolitan, lost $111.1 million on net revenues of $231.08 million.

Primarily recognized for its trendy nightclub and restaurant offerings, quarterly gaming revenue fell to $28.2 million from $31 million in the first quarter. But more to my point, Hotel revenue rose in the second quarter as the property continued to ready new hotel rooms for use. Food and beverage revenue climbed significantly and continued to be the Cosmopolitan's largest source of revenue. In fact two of the bars at the Cosmo are among the top 10 grossing bars in the U.S. and one is THE highest grossing bar in America (*The Marquis Bar*).

Yet the casino is losing money and therefore the entire project is losing money...so much so that privately (and yes I AM revealing privileged information at the time of this writing), Deutsche Bank indicated they would unload their $4-billion nightmare for $1-billion.

The ultimate argument is about the attraction itself: do people come to gamble or do they come for the hospitality experience...or in the specific example for the Marquis Bar; do they come to *Sin City* or do they come for an entertainment venue? Again, do they go to Aspen for singers in the auditoriums or for the snow? Do they go to Orlando for Disney or for the hotels? Do they go to Myrtle Beach for the beach or for the nice hotel (what? there are no nice hotels in their hometown?) And, by God, they come to Vegas to gamble; shows and food are *amenities*.

Again, in the short-run, Schaeffer's outlook was right on target and made some pretty significant fortunes for a good group of people...and made me look like a dinosaur...though chronologically I am decades younger.

Sheldon Adelson's model (of not being in the gambling business at all) has made the man a third or fourth fortune and by 2007 had him listed by *Forbes* as the third richest man in the world. In 2012 he was the single largest contributor to the presidential campaign of Mitt Romney; by July of that year he had put $10-million into a Romney "super pac" and Forbes Magazine predicted that by the actual number was ten times that and closer to $100-million[9].

At least one of Adelson's fortunes came from his creation of the huge COMDEX technology trade show of the 1980s that brought tens of thousands of computer goomers to Vegas to fill hotel rooms, eat, drink, go to topless bars, and attend his trade show. Booked, accurately at the time, as the largest trade show in the world, Adelson and his partners invented the show specifically to bring non-gamblers to Vegas where they had bought the Sands hotel (once upon a time the "home" of the Sinatra Rat Pack).

Vegas old timers and cab drivers used to laugh at the COMDEX computer nerds, popularly saying *"they come to town with five dollars and one pair of underwear and never change either one."*

In fact, Adelson's 2010 proclamation that he was not in the gambling business was just the most recent of curious interpretations of the man with almost as much money as Bill Gates or as the "Oracle of Omaha."

Adelson's life history was that of a wheeler-dealer; not necessarily in a bad way. *The Las Vegas Review Journal* reported that he made his "first million" as a middleman teaching small companies how to go public and became a self-described "venture capitalist" and owner of more than 70 companies. The 1960s stock market crash destroyed that fortune and Sheldon moved into the mortgage brokering business focusing on condominium conversions. He attended a condominium-market trade show that had been advertised in an industry magazine. There he discovered that the magazine actually owned the trade show, and sold booth space as expensively as advertising space in the magazine. Apparently, he liked the business model.

With a crash of the real estate market, he purchased a small publishing company in Boston and launched a trade show based on one of the magazines: a highly-specialized field called "Data Communications"... the computer industry. A Dallas Texas show in 1978-79 was the first personal computer trade show. Mildly successful as it was, the show was not enough to stave off a dispute between Adelson and his partners and they parted ways with Sheldon keeping the trade show and the partners taking the publishing company.

Adelson launched a trade-show production company with a new group of partners, Richard Katzeff, Ted Cutler, Jordan Shapiro and Irwin Chafetz. In 1979 they rebranded their computer trade show as the Computer Dealers Expo

(COMDEX) and booked into Bally's (at that time known as the MGM Grand, before the current MGM was built) in Vegas. Though it was just one of several dozen trade shows the company produced, the timing was right for COMDEX: the PC explosion was beginning. Within a couple of years that one show had outgrown both Bally's and the Las Vegas Convention Center.

Adelson was making a another very large fortune: the Las Vegas Review Journal reported that he was renting convention space at 10¢ a square foot and selling it at COMDEX for $50 a square foot. Adelson even financed the building of the expansion to the Vegas convention center and sold it to the Las Vegas Convention and Visitors Bureau.

Realizing the pull of that convention and not seeing and end to it in the near future, he set out to buy his own hotel in Vegas where he could build his own convention center. After unsuccessful runs on the Landmark, the Dunes, the Frontier, and the Aladdin, he finally was able to buy the Sands.

The Sands had been the old mobbed-up hangout of the super-cool Rat Pack during the filming of *Oceans 11* and at one time was THE symbol of Vegas. In the mid-60s Howard Hughes bought the hotel; in 1988 Kirk Kerkorian bought if from the Hughes estate and seven months later flipped it to Adelson's *Interface Group* trade show company.

From his standpoint, Sheldon Adelson now had a hotel (and, alas, apparently to his chagrin, a casino) to be amenities to his primary business: *owning and producing trade shows*. He now had a place to put trade-show attendees to bed at night. And it even had restaurants and one of those casinos. Clearly the computer nerds did very little gambling so Sheldon apparently was right.

The model worked and brought a new kind of visitor to Vegas, ultimately changing the entire paradigm of Las Vegas visitors. Adelson really was the poster-boy for non-gambling revenue and in 1995 he sold the convention (COMDEX) to a Japanese company for $862-million. That was for the name only; he retained the Sands convention center and hotel, built the Venetian, and in 2004 took the company public while retaining 90% of the ownership.

Of course, the downside of moving away from the business of running *a gambling joint* is the very model itself. By separating the casino from its amenities, the businesses depended on the typical competitive and economic forces of those businesses...the Marquis Bar competes with other bars. And Las Vegas, for example, has somewhere upwards of 150,000 hotel rooms to rent ever night. That is a lot of competition — especially if one begins with the premise that these are "just hotel rooms" rather than places to put gamblers to bed. There are, also, more than 2,500 licensed restaurants in Las Vegas.

Sheldon Adelson's empire based on non-gaming has certainly suffered those ups and downs. Apparently, his investors, at least the ones who buy the stock, foolishly think he is in the casino business. *(I guess people DO go to Macau for the weather and NOT to gamble.)*

His stock has roller-coastered and from October 2007 to October 2008 his stock price fell from $148 a share to $4.70 while his market capitalization plummeted from $49-billion to $3-billion, forcing Adelson to personally invest an additional $525-million into his company. His investment followed a Bloomberg headline that warned *"Las Vegas Sands Plunges on Default, Bankruptcy Risk"* and a letter from PricewaterhouseCoopers, warning of a potential default on loans that would cause "substantial doubt about the company's ability to continue as a going concern." Nonetheless, by April of 2009 the stock was trading at $2.25 a share.

Of course, such are the ups and downs of the non-gaming sectors that Adelson (and others) had chosen along with the financial market freewheeling to finance expansion (that I might call, at best, dubious) in the early 2000s. As of this writing his stock is trading somewhere back up around $43 a share, down from $60 in 2011.

Despite the economic downturn of the last years of the Bush presidency and first years of Obama's, those Vegas room numbers were still increasing (though some mildly stalled). There has long been an argument that Vegas has "too many" hotel rooms —it was even argued that the Flamingo was "too big" to support itself when it opened in 1946; and Steve Wynn's original Mirage was thought by wags to be a monstrous waste in 1989. That has NEVER been my argument.

I simply argue that people come to casinos to gamble and we are in the gambling business. The entertainment, restaurants…and yes, hotel rooms…are merely amenities to make sure the gamblers stay in my joint instead of the one next door. Further (and MOST alarming about the business model adopted by some casino operators), I argue that the Schaeffer-Adelson Las Vegas model of not being in the gambling racket can NOT be exported to casinos outside of Las Vegas. Please trust me here…no one is going to Shawnee Oklahoma, Coachella California, Black River Falls Wisconsin (or scores of other casino locations) for the nice hotel, the great show lineup, the gourmet restaurant, or the magical fingers of the masseuse: they go there for the fucking casino. They go there to gamble! Yet some of these casino managers have exported what they learned in the corporate hotel world to their new jobs in Indian Country or at remote casinos.

In the longer run, we will have to rely on the fallout and aftermath of the extremes adopted by these operators; the total separation of casinos from the amenities.

Nonetheless, we CAN thumbnail-look at the recent history of the melding of the hotel/hospitality with casino gaming halls and while noting some significant successes, many have been to the determent of the original hotel brands (and those amazing valuation multiples):

HOTEL OPERATOR	CASINO COMPANY	RESULTS
Holiday Inns	Caesars Entertainment (formerly known as	**CASINOS HUGE SUCCESS; HOTELS FAILED.** Went from icon with 1,400+ hotels, Trailways buses, and other companies to the hotel brand being sold off to a British beer company, and after several splits became the InterContinental Hotels Group.

91

HOTEL OPERATOR	CASINO COMPANY	RESULTS
	Harrah's)	Primarily because of the leadership of former hotel executive Phil Satre and the business-school expertise of his replacement, Gary Lovemann, Harrah's, of course, became one of the most successful casino operators, and as of this writing the largest casino company in the world, purchasing Caesars Entertainment in 2005. Holiday Inns, on the other hand, became an "also ran". This, of course, is notwithstanding the Harrah's 2006 management-led buy-back of the company with financial instruments tied to mortgage securities at the end of the first decade of this century and a Apollo Global Management switch of equity and debt.
Hilton	Bally's	**CASINOS SPLIT OFF.** Hilton Hotels spun off its casinos, including the Las Vegas Hilton and Bally's, into publicly traded *Park Place Entertainment* to get the casinos more value from Wall Street. Park Place bought Caesars Palace, renamed themselves *Caesars Entertainment* (and was bought by Harrah's in 2005 for $9 billion). Thriving Hilton Hotels gave the world Paris Hilton and by the end of the first decade of the 21st century a P/E Ratio of - 0.010, not tied to any gaming operations.
Sheraton	Desert Inn & others	**HOTELS SPLIT OFF/MERGE.** Sold casinos; split parent company; merged hotel into large hotel operator.
Ramada Inns	Tropicana	**HOTELS FAILED.** Sold hotel brand to Asian company; sold restaurants; started casino spin-off (Aztar) which was sold off as board chairman retired.
Columbia Sussex	(Aztar) / Tropicana	**CASINO FAILED.** Highly successful manger of hotels for Marriott, Holiday Inn, Sheraton, Radisson, Hilton and 8 other brands. Purchased Aztar in 2006; casinos filed for bankruptcy in 2008.

In Autumn of 2008, the divergence between hotels and casinos became even more dramatic when MGM/Mirage's then-Chief Executive Officer, Terry Lanni, told a conference call of investors that the company might consider splitting its nongaming hotel subsidiary into a separate publicly traded company. *Reuters Financial, Dow Jones,* and *Bloomberg* all reported that (then) Deutsche Bank gaming analyst Bill Lerner observed, "What MGM Mirage is looking at is almost a reverse of the Hilton move."

During that conference call, my friend Lerner noted that the *Four Seasons* upscale hotel chain had a valuation of 28 times cash flow before it was taken private. So the issue seems to be two-fold:

- Firstly, my assertion that operating a hotel is not only NOT a prerequisite to operating a casino, but it is in fact detrimental to operating a casino in several cases; and
- Secondly, pure hotel groups (hotel pure-plays, to use "Street" slang) have consistently shown more favorable earnings multiples than casino-hotel companies.

In fact, the second issue seems to support my first assertion.

Of course this was (a month or so) before the late Terry Lanni resigned (at the time of a *Wall Street Journal*-reported controversy around USC's denial that Lanni had an MBA from their school). Thank goodness these new corporate executives are pillars of integrity and veracity, unlike those organized crime guys that started this industry. To me, Lanni always behaved as a gentleman and an evangelist for his outlook (though we radically disagreed in management philosophy). He died in July of 2011 (at the same age Gomes was at his death: 68).

The philosophical split in the industry is between "casino guys" and "non-gaming guys". I entered the industry on the casino side and learned the business side. Hence, I run casinos rather than hospitality experiences; and I am a *Gambling Man* rather than...

Chapter Eight
Pay no attention to that man behind the curtain

OZ'S VOICE: Oh - I - Pay no....
LS -- Shooting past the Four at left to the Curtain in b.g. – Dorothy goes over to it and starts to pull it aside --
OZ'S VOICE: ...attention to that man behind the curtain. Go - before I lose my temper! The Great and Powerful ---....
MCS -- Dorothy pulls back the curtain to reveal the Wizard at the controls -- he reacts as he sees Dorothy -- Dorothy questions him -- the Wizard starts to speak into the microphone -- then turns weakly back to Dorothy -- CAMERA PULLS back slightly as the Lion, Scarecrow and Tin Man enter and stand behind Dorothy --
OZ'S VOICE: ... -- Oz -- has spoken!
— The Wizard Of Oz Movie Script

During my very first week working for *The Donald*, I was sitting in Mark Lefever's office lamenting over a string of losing nights for the property. I knew there was a problem at the blackjack tables; Mark had told me that. And, I knew enough to realize that if table games had been losing for months then there was either a legitimate card-counting team or an inside-job crime of some sort. That was an issue within itself and Mark had asked me to watch the tables and see what I could find. But on this particular afternoon we were discussing the seemingly impossible: a recent string of losing days from the slot machines...in the high-limit area.

Based on my own fairly substantial understanding of slot machine math, I knew that machines could *not* lose over the long haul, though a losing day here and there is totally typical; my business revolves around that premise. I also knew that, from an accounting standpoint, if the slots take in a couple of million dollars for a day and some lucky stiff hits a $5-million jackpot, then *there* is a losing day. Hell, the tic-tac-toe chicken adventures with random number generators showed *that* kind of volatility. But, for several consecutive consistently losing days at the Trump property to happen and without any huge jackpots being won...then something must have been up. What was happening to my "long term" confidence level?

Here we were on a day in the middle of a week (the slowest time at the casino) with barely $2-million in "coin-in" for the day and we were suffering from an actual multiple-day *loss* on the slot floor. Was someone stealing from us...again?

Just a few weeks earlier, the "eye-in-the-sky" surveillance staff had nailed a two-person team of a slot attendant and a change girl that had managed to scam over a hundred-grand in a slight-of-hand during hopper fills and customer hand-pays. So we were all alert to possible crime. To be honest, I sort of hoped *that* was the problem; at least it would be easy to explain.

In the casino world, we have a movement that we call "washing hands" that was designed to show the eye-in-the-sky that we are being honest anytime we touch money. The best way to observe the move is to go to the cashier's cage and watch what the clerk does after he or she counts out your winnings. They will lay the money on the counter and then spread their palms face down in front of their body, flip their hands to the palms-up position, clap/scrape their palms together (as if they were washing their hands) and then again show their flattened palms. The various cameras in the ceiling (and other places — often hidden to even them) watch the hand-washing, and can clearly see (and record) that no money is being misplaced (or deliberately hidden). By the way, if you go to a casino where they do NOT do that at the cashier's cage, I recommend leaving and never returning—something is not right (more on THAT later too).

These two morons were stealing dollar-tokens from our dollar slot machines when they would do a hopper-fill (adding coins to an empty machine). When they would "wash their hands", they would each hold one coin against their palm with their thumb and slight-of-hand hide it from the cameras. One dollar at a time, one machine at a time, they took more than $100,000 by averaging 250-hopper fills a-day over the course of a little more than a year and a half.

When we finally nailed these two assholes, we made an executive decision to make a statement. We arrested them on the casino floor, in front of customers and their coworkers. We handcuffed them and very forcibly led them to the back of the house, loudly announcing for all to hear "no one steals from the players in a Trump casino". In the back of the house we separated the duo and took each to a dark room with one bright spotlight in it.

Alas, yes many casinos DO still have those "backrooms" you see in the movies. In one casino I had a guy on my staff whose entire job was to look scary in backroom interrogations. He was a great happy-go-lucky guy and as friendly as you'd ever want to know; but when he was playing the role he was a hulking giant of man who could make a priest confess to the Kennedy assassination. He was one scary motherfucker and he was on my payroll for that reason.

At Trump29 we made each of these thieves believe that we were going to resort to all the myths they had heard about from old Vegas: cut off their fingers, torture them, and maybe even bury them in the desert. In no time, after wetting their pants (literally), they confessed.

Was it legal? Was it admissible in court? Was it kidnapping and illegal arrest? Well... not exactly. We were in a sovereign Indian nation and exempt from many State and Federal laws.

When one runs a casino, amid the hundreds of thoughts constantly barraging the brain, various ways people will steal is always on the front burner. During this particular week, with almost $2-million churning through the machines on this "losing" day, the casino should have grossed a neat $170,000 for the day. Instead, we lost $35,000 and that fact was what was giving both Mark and me heartburn.

I came from the world of cards; blackjack card counting and poker (not the newly-fadded Texas Hold'em world, but hardcore draw poker). If the problem had been with table games, I would have (as I had in the past and did many times in coming years) gone to the pits and found the problem. Though most surveillance teams are well-trained, there is nothing like a player's perspective to spot traditional cheats like past posting, signaling, gadgets, mucks, chops, switches, shiners, stacking, cuts, pitches, crisscrosses, riffles, passers, teams, shuffle tracking, a dozens of other old-style cheats.

To spot worst-case scams, or to train staff, I would call my old friend George Joseph. The Detroit native has run surveillance for Bally's, Paris, Aladdin, Dunes and other Vegas properties. He is the author of at least three books and constantly on television as an authority on casino scams (I have seen him on *48 Hours; America's Most Wanted; CNBC; Criss Angel Mind Freak; Dateline NBC; The Discovery Channel*; several *A&E* shows; *The Learning Channel*; and just about any show that talks about "inside" Las Vegas). He is by far one the most brilliant card mechanics and card magicians that I have ever watched. I have attended a half-dozen of his seminars and I have used his services several times to train my staff. In fact, in Oklahoma City I brought him in to train surveillance and Gaming Commissions from a dozen casinos.

George is the guy who caught the notorious gang of computer scammers that had been stealing hundreds of thousands from Indian casino blackjack games all over California and New Mexico. Though I had read the details many times and had heard him describe it in seminars, there is nothing like hearing his personal reminiscences of how he made the capture.

Over pizza one night in Biloxi, George, dressed in all black, gave me a detailed recap of the whole adventure —even down to a malfunctioning computer mother board taped to the back of a player, setting the player's shirt on fire. In the midst of the general conversation, George casually rolled off, *"I was telling Mohammad Ali about this, one night at dinner and..."* I interrupted. *"Whoa, you know Mohammad Ali?"* It was then that I learned that George is married to Joe Lewis's daughter and Ali was a close family friend.

At any rate, if there were a card scam or slight-of-hand that I had not seen in casinos over the years or learned from my father and his carny days, then I would call on George to spot it and to train my staff to spot it. I've never seen one slip by him. But...

Master gaming protection advisor George Joseph

this was a slot machine problem, not a table games scam so I was reluctant to call George (though he is an expert there too).

From my standpoint, as The Donald's new marketing Vice President, this was MY problem and specifically meant I was down $205-thousand for the day;

not just the loss of $35-large, but on top of that the $170,000 that I should have been ahead. Thank goodness, this was before Trump popularized *"you're fired"* and that flick of his wrist imitated by millions of TV viewers; otherwise I would have been seriously worried about my near-term employment options. And this was not a one-day volatility issue; it had been going on for one week and two days. *How the fuck does a slot floor lose money over the long term?*

As the top casino executives scratched our collective heads (and proverbial asses) over the issue, our database manager wandered into the office and casually asked a question that solved the mystery: *"Was Larry here playing last night?"* You remember Larry...my high-roller from the "typical day"; this was my first encounter with him.

Our database manager, Steve Sohng, was at that time one of the finest and most under-utilized marketers in the industry. Born in Korea (where his parents still lived), Steve spoke with a heavy Korean accent which made him difficult to understand for many people; I always suspected *that* is why his talents had never been fully utilized; not exactly an underlying racism, but certainly a language issue. Frankly, rather than hire me to market that particular Trump property, someone should have promoted Steve to the position (though he might not have been *ready* at that point). I eventually helped with that little oversight by officially making him my Number One and bumping his salary as high as was allowable under company guidelines. There was definitely a noticeable growth in his confidence level (as well as the way he dressed for work) after I began to rely on him so heavily. In fact, many of the staff decisions that I made (or were attributed to me) were actually made by Steve and implemented by me.

I have often used the management technique of allowing subordinates to make unpopular decisions within their realm of responsibility and then personally taking the heat for the unpopularity in order to shield them. I did that with Frank Haas at our first casino in Oklahoma, I did it for Steve Sohng at Trump29, and I would repeat it many times to foster growth, development and especially self-confidence when ambitious detractors might otherwise stymie it. Sometimes a good manager has to protect his subordinates from their coworkers as well as from boards of directors (or Tribal councils).

Steve was another real life casino industry *character*; he was a caricature of what every non-casino employee imagines casino life must be like. He drank a lot, he gambled a lot, and he had the *reputation* of a "ladies' man." His adventures, while typical of many casino employees, were the extreme version of the conglomerate of all employee stories. If I wanted to create a fictional character to amalgamate the extreme casino stories of a dozen lives, I would create Steve. He did it all...for real. He is one of those figures that most people would not want to actual-

The should-be legendary Steve Sohng

ly know but love to hear about; he was like the Rolling Stones' Keith Richards —the extreme of all things in his genre. If USA Network television as part of their *"characters welcome"* promotion asked me for the BEST casino character, I would give them Steve Sohng; he is a great guy!

During the grand opening party for the Agua Caliente Tribe's *Spa Casino* in downtown Palm Springs, Steve drank enough that my secretary, Tanya, and I decided that he should not be driving. Even before we arrived at the six-hour party, I literally pick-pocketed his car keys and rolled him into the backseat of my car (leaving his car at my condo). At a get-together at the home of two of my player development staffers, before the party, Steve drank enough that we were able to convince him that one of my hosts was going to handcuff him, blindfold him, and hoist him in the air on a BDSM *(a combination of 3 acronyms, BD for Bondage Discipline, DS for Domination and Submission and SM for Sado Masochistic)* pulley system and have her way with him. By the end of the night we had to pull over twice for Steve to open the car door and vomit. By the time we got back to my building he had passed out and we carried him up a flight of stairs to my condo. He did not regain consciousness as I tucked him in on my couch, and I confidently left his car keys on my kitchen counter, before retiring to my own bedroom. The next morning I arose to find the apartment empty. There were stale stains of recently-cleaned wine-filled vomit all over my couch and carpet, the car keys were missing, and Steve's car was gone. I had parked inside the gated community, but his car was just outside the gate. The fence was 12-feet high, topped with coils of razor-wire, and could be exited only through a keyed gate; and the key was with me. Hours later Steve called me to tell me that his clothes were in shreds, his arms were bloody, and he could not remember how he got home from the party.

On another occasion, Halloween, I took Steve and Tanya out to dinner to the gourmet room at a rival casino. Steve drove. Being the consummate gentleman, when he returned to the car he held Tanya's door in the back seat and then my door in the front sheet. Unaccustomed to having men (or anyone, for that matter) hold a door for me, I slammed the car door shut once I was in my seat. Unfortunately, Steve's hand was still in the door-jam when I slammed it. Five hours later, we finally navigated the Emergency Room's absurd bureaucracy to get him to a gurney in front of a doctor. To calm Steve and take his mind off the pain, the physician began to make small talk about the Trump casino and our showroom. As if he was not in severe pain with a bloody nail-less thumb, Steve reached into his pocket and produced two complementary tickets to the next night's concert in the showroom and presented them to the doctor. *"If you will come in and play for a couple of hours, then I would be honored for you to be my guest to see Tony Bennett tomorrow night,"* Steve told him. Steve Sohng never stopped prospecting for customers.

Like me, Steve began his casino career because he was first a player. He once told me that when he first came to the United States to attend college at the University of Nevada at Las Vegas, his father had given him money to pay the first year's tuition, books, and room & board. Steve, being a true gambler, lost all of the money…every dime…at baccarat… before school started. *Gotta love that kind of gambler!*

By the time I knew him, Steve's game of choice was video poker and he had the fastest reaction time I have ever seen playing those machines. Many times I have thought of writing to Bob Dancer, or one of the other video poker gurus just to introduce the amazing Steve. Once I timed him playing at the Augustine Casino in Southern California — he hit those frigging buttons on the average of a full game (holds included) every second: 60 games a minute; 3,600 games an hour. He was playing full coin-in on a 25¢ machine, which translates to $1.25 per game or gambling $4,500 per hour. Over the course of four hours that night, Steve went through $18,000 in coin-in. The machines were set to "hold" 4% (without *perfect* play) so his theoretical win was about $17,280; hence he was losing an average of $720 over the course of the evening. But besides being fast, Steve was good; VERY good and very accurate. He only played very select 9/6 or better machines (*more on what that means in a later chapter*), and his play was near theoretically perfect. So in fact, he was actually winning about 103% of his play; meaning that he had a new profit for the evening of about $540. That equates to being paid about $135 an hour for sitting at a video poker machine. And the fucker did it consistently. That is not to say he never lost; but damn, he was definitely a *player*.

Dressed in a dark suit and on the casino floor on a busy Friday or Saturday night, Steve was one of the best casino hosts I have ever seen. Because his "day job" was our database manager (before I made him my assistant and then *Director of Marketing*) he would run an analysis of players' who were active on the floor and then set about one-on-one contacts loaded with offers and inducements targeted to each player specifically. Far more targeted in offers than even I could develop for direct mail, his personal contact consistently increased the average play of any customer he targeted by about 35%; a phenomenal increase. Armed with show tickets, restaurant comps, and credit approval, make no mistake about it, when Steve Sohng was on the casino floor he was almost always personally responsible for double-digit percentages increases of that day's bottom line profit. So much for a language barrier, Steve was a fucking money machine for the casino and anyone that does not use him for that is an idiot.

On the database side, Steve and I clashed from the onset over his traditional (and proven successful) use of "theoretical" win for the casino to segment customers. I had developed a somewhat controversial player-targeting methodology that was based on *actual win* rather than *theoretical win* and combined it with frequency of visits to the casino as well as how recently a player had visited. Instead targeting customers from a two-dimensional linier graph with traditional "X" and "Y" axes, I was using a 3D model similar to the "RFM" model that the paper catalog industry used to segment customers. My method flew in the face of standard casino wisdom, but was supported early on by Mark Lefever (who as a number-cruncher probably saw the abstract mathematical soundness in it).

Steve and I continued to debate the method until we finally tested it against a third-party database analysis. Once it was proven, Steve and I became fast friends on the professional level. In fact, that behind-the-scenes database modeling was the key to not only Steve's friendship but the entire success of that Trump property.

Steve Sohng was hard-playing, but he was also brilliant on the business side. To this day, I argue that Steve is one of the most under-appreciated geniuses in the industry. He is well worth deep into a six figure salary and more.

During that first week of my work with Trump, I could see the light come on in Mark Lefever's eyes as he heard Steve's question. Mark wheeled his chair around toward his computer and typed in a query for a list of players on the floor the night before. Indeed, "Larry" had been playing. Who the hell was Larry? (And, by the way, does it worry you that he got a list of customers that fast? Don't let it; that is what we do.)

"Well that explains it; and he has been here all week," Mark sighed with relief. A few calculations later, between the computer screen and the electronic adding machine on his desk (remember he is a CPA and THOSE guys love 10-key adding machines), we discovered that on this one day — *excluding Larry's play* — the slots had actually held almost 12% (a gross profit for the casino of $240,000 instead of the revenue projection of $170,000 for the day). Without "Larry's play" I was not at all $205-thousand in the hole; I was $240,000 ahead and even $70,000 ahead of *projections* for the day. But damn. That meant *"Larry"* had won enough to put us in the hole; he had to have won some large part of that $240,000 *plus* the $35,000. A phone call to the cashier cage and a review of Federal W2-G tax forms indicated that the speculation was correct as the computer screen showed. And I felt like a complete novice who had no idea of how a casino operates.

Also, now I was feeling like Butch or Sundance staring in the distance at a white hat and asking *"Who the hell IS that guy?"* What was the secret of one guy whose slot play could change the fortunes of a casino for the day or the week? What is it that he could do that would send the executive staff (or at least me) running for bottles of Maalox? He did not cheat. He was not a mathematician that understood formulas and Pascal's probability tables. He didn't have a "system". He was not an industry insider that knew of a weakness in a computer chip.

He was just a guy; a guy who won tens of thousands of dollars of the casino's money on a regular basis. True, he did play $25-machines (slot machines where the minimum bet was $25) and he played full coin-in (meaning he played the maximum number of bets per spin of on some machines was $625). Larry would often play four or five hours a night, rarely stopping except for a bathroom break or to drink from a bottle of water brought to him at the slot machine; but on other days he would play for less than an hour and leave.

A really *busy* slot machine (not being played by a mad genius like Steve Sohng) can spin between 600 and 700 times an hour and that meant Larry was betting *at least* something greater than $45,000 an hour and as much as ten times that per hour. During the course of his five-hour of nights, he was gambling a minimum of a quarter of a million dollars. If he had been playing my penny video slot machines I could have expected to keep about $27,000 a night of his money. If he had been playing my regular quarter or dollar slot machines, I would have expected to keep a little more than $19,000 of his money per night. If he had been playing Steve-perfect strategy on my video poker machines, I would have had a problem; but fortunately there are few people that can concentrate on a skill game for that many hours and stay focused enough to beat the house...to beat me. Larry was playing a mindless slot machine; and on top of that an older reel-style machine.

I have used a lot of jargon so far and I probably should take a minute to talk about some important terms that surface over and over (and are important in understand the "Larry problem"): *win, drop, hold,* and *coin-in.* All three refer to money played, but all three are distinctly different measurements.

Like Steve Sohng and hundreds of other casino executives, I started in casinos as a player... and truth be known, I am still a gambler. To the world of us casino *players*, the word WIN means how much money we make when we play. If we come into the casino with $100 and leave with $125 then our WIN is $25. Of course some gamblers would claim they won $125 and lost $100. It is all relative, I suppose, but for a player the WIN is how much more I have in my pocket when I leave the casino than when I arrived. Anything *less than what I arrived with,* is a LOSS rather than a WIN.

But in the terminology of a casino boss, WIN is how much money the *casino* made, not the player. The term is totally upside down for the casino compared to what it means for the player. At the end of the day, a week, or a month, or any gaming period, casino WIN is how much players LOST. For a casino operator WIN is gross profit.

Just remember this: when a player has a WIN then the casino has a LOSS; and when the casino has a WIN then the player loses. It is just a matter of switching hats...or in this case switching "sides of the table." *(Often, when people ask me what I do for a living, I tell them "I am a gambler who plays both sides of the table.")*

You have seen signs over some slot machines that announce things like *"92% payout".* For a player, that sign is supposed to make them think that they win 92% of the time they play... or at least that 92% of every dollar played is paid back as a win. But for the casino that sign means that the long-term WIN is only 8% of all the money played in the machine. That 92% player payout (often mistakenly called "par") is the opposite of *hold.*

The *hold* is the percentage of money that the casino makes in the long term from a game. If the hold is (for the above example) 8%, this means that the slot machines pay out 92% to the customer. On the average, then, over the life of the machine, for every $100 played, the casino keeps (or wins) $8 and the remaining $92 are paid back to players.

What makes slot machines interesting to play is that the 92% (in this example) is not predictably consistent. A machine could take in $10,000 without a single payout and then suddenly pay one winner $9,200. If that person had just walked up to the machine and this was their first spin, he or she would proclaim how "loose" the machine is. On the other hand, if several other people played a cumulative $10,000 without winning anything, they would be cursing how "tight" the machine is.

In reality slot machines are set for neither extreme. Rather, they payout based on a complex table of probable minimum payouts. This table takes into account such things as the layout of the physical and virtual reels; odds for each of the winning combinations; the payout amounts for each of the combinations; combinations of some large and some small payouts; and other mathematical formulas.

The spreadsheet for this complex payout schedule is called a *Payout And Retention* (PAR) *Sheet* (often incorrectly called *Pay Table and Reel* or *Probability Accounting Reports* or *Percentages And Returns* —all indicating just how "mysterious" this industry is). Every machine manufacturer provides casino operators with a PAR sheet for each slot game they offer. (Well at least every manufacture SHOULD and is compelled by law to do so in many jurisdictions; but some rinky-dink companies don't do it or don't have them to give). In many jurisdictions there is a licensing requirement that PAR Sheets must submitted to the regulatory body overseeing casinos. For example, in my home state of Florida, state law very specifically (and typically) addresses PAR sheets:

"No slot machine game shall be certified for play by a licensed independent test laboratory if the manufacturer's Payout and Retention (PAR) sheet does not indicate a probable minimum payout percentage of at least eighty-five percent (85%) of all credits played over the mathematical cycle of the game at a ninety-five percent (95%) level of confidence. The licensed independent test laboratory shall test the slot machine to certify that the slot machine game meets the probable minimum payout indicated on its PAR sheet at a ninety-nine percent (99%) level of confidence. The manufacturer or distributor shall also provide a PAR sheet with each slot machine game delivered to a slot machine licensee."

—Rule 61D-14.038, Florida Department of Business & Professional Regulation, Division of Pari-Mutual Wagering, Pari-Mutual Facility Slot Machine Operations

Needless to say, these PAR sheets are guarded fanatically by the manufactures. As a casino operator, I have been offered tens of thousands of dollars by manufacturers to provide them with the PAR sheets from their competitors. For every one legitimate operator like me, there are probably a half dozen that gladly provide PAR sheets. When we get around to talking about how slot machines work, you will see why the math of these PAR tables is so valuable.

One of my favorite games, in terms of bonus rounds, is the IGT *Price Is Right Game.* Unfortunately the damned thing has to pay a percentage to the owner of the theme of the game and hence the hold is usually an absurd 14.955%; a great number for the casino but a horrible number for the player. You can compare that par sheet to the publically-available par sheet in the endnotes [10].

That hold we talked about (8% in the example) is called *theoretical* hold because it is the *mathematical formula* for which the machine is set. But like that damned tic-tac-toe playing chicken, just because the machine is *set* to pay-out 92% of the time, does NOT mean that 92 out of every 100 spins are winners for the players. While it is true that over the long-run that formula itself will be 95% to 99% accurate, in a short period of time it can be way off.

Several times I have opened new casinos and on opening day, after less than $100 of play, a machine would hit a jackpot $10,000 or more. If that machine never allowed a player to win another penny, it would still take three months to recover that payout (at $100 play per day). Add into the equation that there would be hundreds of minor payouts, and that machine would be "upside down" with a negative *actual hold* for a long time. The theoretical hold would eventually cause a long term correction but in the meantime the cumulative hold of the machine would be a negative number.

If we measure hold for one hypothetical day and on that day only have 100 people in the casino with each one playing exactly $10 then our theoretical hold for the day should be $80 (100 people x $10 each = $1000 and 8% of that is $80). But, if in that same day with those same bets, someone hit that $10,000 jackpot then the actual hold for the day would be a *negative* 1000% hold. Of course that $10,000 jackpot would be part of the theoretical payouts defined by the PAR sheet and would be the accumulation of many plays to mathematically work out in the long run to 92% of the money put into the machine. But in the short run and for the day... ouch.

If you are not a math person, don't let your eyes glaze over; I am about to show you which slot machines pay out better.

Okay... As I said, there is a difference between *theoretical hold* and *actual hold*. Hence there is a difference between actual win and theoretical win (thus, the debate that Steve Sohng and I had about targeting customers based on their "theo" (theoretical) vs. their actual losses).

Now that you understand the terms *hold* and *payout*, you can see the usefulness of this information to a player who wants to decide which casino or which machines to play. The chart below shows a recent Nevada state report of the average Las Vegas slot machine payouts and holds.

Location	Denomination	Payout	Hold
Strip	$25	96.51%	3.49%
Downtown	$1	94.55%	5.45%
Downtown	$5	94.16%	5.84%
Downtown	Quarters	93.8%	6.2%
Strip	$5	93.46%	6.54%
Downtown	$25	93.28%	6.72%

Location	Denomination	Payout	Hold
Strip	$1	92.48%	7.52%
Downtown	Nickels	90.41%	9.59%
Strip	Quarters	89.96%	10.04%
Downtown	1¢	88.81%	11.19%
Strip	Nickels	88.27%	11.73%
Strip	1¢	87.48%	12.52%
Strip	IGT Mega-	86.09%	13.91%
Downtown	IGT Mega-	85.95%	14.05%

From this chart you can see that for a player, the best chances of winning are the $25 machines on the strip, the $1 machines downtown, $5 machines downtown, and the 25¢ machines downtown. The best machines for the casino *(and worst for players)* are the IGT Megabucks $1 machines anywhere, penny machines anywhere, and nickel machines on the strip.

Actually, for the player, the very best slot machine bets in the Las Vegas area are the $5 machines in North Las Vegas and:

Location	Denomination	Payout	Hold
North Vegas	$5	98.55%	1.45%
Strip	$25	96.51%	3.49%
North Vegas	Quarters	95.8%	4.2%
Clark County	$5	95.56%	4.44%

As of this writing, the North Las Vegas casinos include: Bighorn Casino; Cannery Casino and Hotel; Five Star Tavern 53; Fort Cheyenne Casino; Jerry's Nugget; Opera House Casino; Poker Palace Casino; PT's Gold; Silver Nugget Casino; Speedway Casino; Texas Station Gambling Hall and Hotel; and The Beverly Hillbillies Gambler Casino. Should a Vegas-novice reader decide to venture that direction, I recommend that you dress very casually and blend; the area has not historically been without street crime. Guys in Armani suits and driving Jaguars probably shouldn't go there; trust me, that is the voice of experience speaking.

It is also *very* important to emphasize that this description of *hold* is strictly for slot machines. *Hold* for table games is a far more complex calculation that almost no one observing the industry, and few inside the industry, ever get right. With slot machines we are measuring hold percentage against every single bet by the player *(the coin-in that we will talk about in a minute)*; at table games, we only measure against the *drop*.

To understand this, let's go back to slots, the primary revenue source: Remember that $1000 cash that was fed into the machines by the players for us to understand hold percentages? At the end of the gaming day when that money is taken out of the machines... it is called the *"drop"*. Simply stated, *"drop"* is the amount of *cash* put into the machines, by the players (regardless of payouts). Apart from of how much money is paid out of the machine in player win (casino loss), the *drop* is the amount of money put into the machine and stored there.

The whole issue of *drop* has gotten really complicated in recent years with technological advances. In the golden olden days (which I have spent so much time talking about to let you into my mind) drop was relatively simple: there were paper money and coins.

Coins were counted in what we call "hard count" because it was "hard" money (as opposed to soft paper). There were complex machines, scales, and verification devices that were all part of the count room process to assure that no one was stealing money. Hard count requires lots of labor to deal with the massive weight and space taken up by relatively small amounts of cash (compared to paper money). Additionally, because of the weight of coins there are more frequent employee injuries and workers comp claims.

This is separate and apart from normal change coinage. There is a vast different in the number of coins needed to make change for point-of-sale or even change for slot winnings versus the number of coins needed for all payouts to be in coins dropped from a machine hopper. The former merely requires standard cashier coin procedures; the latter requires an entire room of equipment and storage as well as heavy-duty carts and bins to hold all the heavy coins. A quarter weighs about two ounces (5.67 grams), so a thousand dollars in quarters weighs about 12 pounds; thus the $375,000 required to operate a floor with 1,500 slot machines would weigh two-and-a-quarter tons (4,500 pounds). Try carrying that around on a casino floor...without dropping any bags of coins on a foot and breaking it.

In one of my early naïve days I made the mistake of trying to get a cashier at the Las Vegas Hilton to tell me how much a bag of silver dollars weighed. This general curiosity question caused her to call security to question me as to why I wanted to know. One of the Gomes-discovered *Stardust* skims involved an employee of a the company that provided coin-weighing scales adjusting the scales to give an incorrect weight in the hard count room so that crooked employees could then steal the overage without it being tracked.

Paper money is counted in rooms called "soft count"... meaning that paper is softer than coinage. The soft count room is filled with machines that count the bills and sort them by denomination. The process of counting paper money from slot machines involves a casino function called "drop and count".

Though there are variations from casino to casino and regulatory jurisdiction to jurisdiction, basically the drop & count process is uniform and designed for efficiency, security, and integrity of the cash. After all, this is where all the cash is.

The following section outlines a *typical* drop and count process, if not procedure:

Gary's Drop & Count Process

DROP: Members of the casino drop team dress in brightly colored jumpsuits (a lot like you see prisoners wearing when they are brought into court); this way they are readily identifiable by security and surveillance. The drop team members are not allowed to have pockets, purses, or anything that would provide a place to stash the money they are taking out of the slot machines.

1. The drop team uses stanchions to cordon off a group of slot machines on the floor.
2. Uniformed security officers stand guard at the stanchions to keep the public from crossing into the drop area.

3. Once several banks of machines are cordoned off, the drop team rolls a large metal drop-cart *(at right)* *into* the roped-off area. These heavy-duty carts can hold 3,500 to 6,500 pounds of money. The carts are loaded with empty "drop boxes".

4. Each slot machine has several sets of specialty keys that unlock various parts of the machine. The keys are color-coded for their different functions. *At the left is a typical key used in the process.*

5. Typically the "belly glass" holder is dropped down to a 90° angle in front of the machine, revealing the "drop door" inside the machine. The picture above shows two of the locks; the picture at the right shows a Bally slot machine cabinet with the belly glass holder dropped open.

6. Once the door is revealed, another key is used to unlock the door, revealing a *drop box*. There are a minimum of two drop boxes assigned to every machine; one is actually in the machine and a second is loaded onto the drop cart before the cart is rolled onto the casino floor. The drop box on the cart is empty. *The picture at the left shows the drop-box inside the slot machine.*

7. This drop box is removed from the machine and placed in the chair in front of the machine. The drop box has money in it, from the "drop" that players have put into the machine.

   Depending on the machine manufacturer and on jurisdictional regulations, an audit report is printed out at the machine when the box is removed. *(This report can also be printed via a server from an audit office, in some jurisdictions.)*

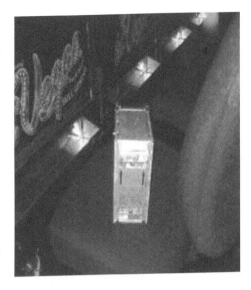

8. Each slot machine has a number affixed to it (called an "asset number"). Each drop box has an asset number that matches the asset number of the slot machine. For example, if the machine is number 1234, then one drop box will be numbered 1234-A and the next will be numbered 1234-B.

   The drop team picks the full drop box up from the chair and replaces it with the corresponding empty drop box. In other words, if cash-full box 5432-B is taken from the machine, then empty box 5432-A is placed in the chair. The cash-filled box is then placed in the drop cart and the empty box is put back into the machine. The door is locked and the belly glass door closed.

   This process is repeated for each machine until the section is finished. The drop cart is then locked and rolled back into the soft count room.

COUNT: Count rooms/vaults are generally protected by a man-trap set of doors (see drawing at right). A man trap is a small waiting room with a locked door at each end. The first door must be closed and locked before the second door can be unlocked. This keeps unauthorized people from walking through a single door to get to the count room and vault. Generally a man trap uses both surveillance camera identification and an

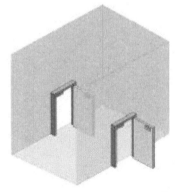

electronic key for each door, often with different locks or key codes for each door. With electronic locks, the second door cannot physically open until the first has closed.

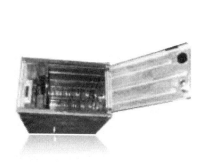

9. Once inside the count room, each drop box is removed from the cart, unlocked with a special key, and the cash from that box is counted (at least twice) and compared to the machine-audit number. Counts are done either by bank-style cash counting machines or manually. This process continues until the cash matches the audit number for each machine; if there is no match then an exception report is filed for the overage or underage (and in MY casinos someone is going to be fired). When completed, the emptied drop boxes are loaded back onto the cart for the next drop. *The picture at the left is an open (and empty) drop box. Note the springs ... which are pushed down by the weight of the cash.*

What I have just described is the process for "soft count" ... without coins. But the soft count process has become a little more complex in the past few years, from an accounting standpoint. Casinos have almost universally moved away from slot machines that accept coins; so *hard count* has all but disappeared.

In its place, most slot machines accept both paper money and *printed payout tickets* called a TITO (ticket in / ticket out). These tickets are bar coded slips of paper, which can be redeemed for cash, or inserted into the bill acceptor for play at other machines. Since these tickets have a cash value (both in other machines and at the cage), and since they are inserted through bill acceptors into the drop box, they necessarily become part of the drop and count.

From the audit side, there needs to be an entry for cash drop as well as an entry for ticket drop. Suddenly the drop is perverted from real cash to cash *plus* paper tickets.

Hence to fully understand the daily play through a slot machine we need another measure; one that combines the cash and the tickets as well as non-cashed-out credits played through the machine. This is the measure of *"coin in."*

(Even though there are likely no coins involved, the term is a throwback to the early slot days).

Indeed, for many, the most complicated measure of casino money is *"coin in."* The concept is so complicated and misunderstood that I have noticed several top-notch casino text books and lecturers get it wrong. In fact, one of the very best casino text books, often used at the University of Nevada, gets it totally wrong.

This is *exactly* why casino operators are different from hotel operators, operators of other businesses, and even academics. It is a highly complex and specialized business.

In a nutshell, *coin-in* is the amount of money wagered or played through a machine. In that sense, it is gross revenue of a machine—before payouts. Simple as that seems, it is not so simple to wrap your head around because it gets confused with drop.

Let's slowly go through the concept so that it is clear. To do this, I will run through several scenarios.

1. You sit down at a slot machine, insert a $10 bill, make 10 consecutive $1-plays and lose each one. You get up and leave. **In this case, the *coin-in* was $10; and the *drop* was $10.**

2. In a second example, you sit down at a slot machine, insert a $10 bill, and decide not to play at all. You instantly cash out and get your $10 back. **In this case, the coin-in is Zero; but the drop was $10** (because when the cash can is emptied there will be a $10 bill in it — even though $10 was paid out in either a ticket or some other device).

3. For a third example, you sit down at a slot machine, insert a $10 bill, make one $1 bet, lose it and decide to leave with your remaining $9. **Coin-in, in this example, is $1; but the drop was $10.**

So far it is easy to follow: coin-in is the amount of money that is actually bet. It does not relate to win nor even drop. It is simply the amount played. But let's look at a fourth, more complex and more realistic example:

4. You sit down at slot machine, insert a $10 bill:

ACTIVITY:	COIN IN	DROP	CASH HOLD	HOLD %
You make a $1 bet and lose it. Your cash available is now $9; **your coin-in is $1;** and the drop is $10.	$1	$10	$1	100%
From that remaining $9, you make another $1 bet and win 75¢. Your cash available is now $8.75, You have bet a total of $2; your coin-in is $2.	$2	No additional	$1.25	63%
From the remaining $8.75 you make another $1 bet, reducing your bankroll to only $7.75. You win $10, upping your bankroll	$3	No additional	-$9.75	-258%

ACTIVITY:	COIN IN	DROP	CASH HOLD	HOLD %
to $17.75. You now have a net win of $7.75 (over the original $10) However, your coin in is only $3.				
From your $17.75 bankroll you make 17 more $1 bets losing each one. Your bankroll is down to 75¢. Your net loss is $9.25; the casinos net win is $7.25. But your coin-in is $20; (the 17 one-dollar bets in this example, plus the $3 coin-in from the above three bets).	$20	No additional	$9.25	46%

In this example, your actual cash bankroll was only $10. The actual *drop* into the machine was only $10. The casino *win* was only $9.25. But… *the coin-in was $20* (double the drop in this case).

An actual break-down of the progress of this example looks like this:

DROP	bet #	Bet amount	total of all bets made	player win (this hand)	player cumulative win	player bankroll (credits available for cash out)	Total coin in	Casino Win	Casino Cum Win	Hold %
$10.00	1	$1.00	$1.00	$0.00	($1.00)	$9.00	$1.00	$1.00	$1.00	100%
	2	$1.00	$2.00	$0.75	($1.25)	$8.75	$2.00	$0.25	$1.25	63%
	3	$1.00	$3.00	$10.00	$7.75	$17.75	$3.00	($9.00)	($7.75)	-258%
	4	$1.00	$4.00	$0.00	$6.75	$16.75	$4.00	$1.00	($6.75)	-169%
	5	$1.00	$5.00	$0.00	$5.75	$15.75	$5.00	$1.00	($5.75)	-115%
	6	$1.00	$6.00	$0.00	$4.75	$14.75	$6.00	$1.00	($4.75)	-79%
	7	$1.00	$7.00	$0.00	$3.75	$13.75	$7.00	$1.00	($3.75)	-54%
	8	$1.00	$8.00	$0.00	$2.75	$12.75	$8.00	$1.00	($2.75)	-34%
	9	$1.00	$9.00	$0.00	$1.75	$11.75	$9.00	$1.00	($1.75)	-19%
	10	$1.00	$10.00	$0.00	$0.75	$10.75	$10.00	$1.00	($0.75)	-8%
	11	$1.00	$11.00	$0.00	($0.25)	$9.75	$11.00	$1.00	$0.25	2%
	12	$1.00	$12.00	$0.00	($1.25)	$8.75	$12.00	$1.00	$1.25	10%
	13	$1.00	$13.00	$0.00	($2.25)	$7.75	$13.00	$1.00	$2.25	17%
	14	$1.00	$14.00	$0.00	($3.25)	$6.75	$14.00	$1.00	$3.25	23%
	15	$1.00	$15.00	$0.00	($4.25)	$5.75	$15.00	$1.00	$4.25	28%
	16	$1.00	$16.00	$0.00	($5.25)	$4.75	$16.00	$1.00	$5.25	33%
	17	$1.00	$17.00	$0.00	($6.25)	$3.75	$17.00	$1.00	$6.25	37%
	18	$1.00	$18.00	$0.00	($7.25)	$2.75	$18.00	$1.00	$7.25	40%
	19	$1.00	$19.00	$0.00	($8.25)	$1.75	$19.00	$1.00	$8.25	43%
	20	$1.00	$20.00	$0.00	($9.25)	$0.75	$20.00	$1.00	$9.25	46%

We measure *coin-in* because it truly is a reflection of amount of money bet during the session. At any point during the play you could have cashed out and left. Instead, you chose to play $20 worth of bets…even though you only paid $10 in actual cash from *your* pocket for those bets. The additional $10 in bets came from money you won from the casino and could have cashed out.

In this fourth example, the numbers for measuring one player's monetary performance are complex and look like this:

Theoretical Hold	Actual Hold	Drop	Coin-In	Casino Win	Casino Loss
12%	7½%	$10	$20	$9.25	0
Machine Win	Machine Loss		Performance	Player Win	Player Loss
$18.25	75¢		+4½%	0	$9.25

We will deal with that "theoretical hold" number later.

Assuming this player was using a players club card, I have this information as well as such things as the length of this playing session, the theme of the machine, how many spins per hour the player made, and a lengthy recitation of other benchmarks.

Knowing your *coin-in* number tells me what kind of gambler you are and consequently tells me what sort of offers I can present to you in order to entice you to reach into your own pocket and further contribute to my drop. My drop, on the other hand, gives me a basis for a simple mathematical function for my win for the day. Keep in mind that hold and win/loss for the casino, are the same calculation.

Through subsequent chapters and anecdotes, coin-in will be a key term. And in the industry itself, it is a lifeline. That coin-in number gives me an indication of any particular player's propensity to gamble; but more importantly, it gives me a snapshot of how much play a particular slot machine is getting. At Trump, for example, all executives were texted the previous day's coin-in number as soon as the drop and count teams finished; that would give us a snapshot of how we did the previous day. On the other hand, I have worked for some Indian casinos and some charitable casinos that had no regard whatsoever for coin-in and don't even track it.

In the case of my high-roller rooms, that coin-in number determines who gets the comps and who gets an invitation to join my "Platinum Club." Designed to be like the airlines' frequent flyer program, tiered players clubs have a proven history of increasing play. I have always made it a point to make the various tiers of my player's clubs to mimic my experiences with Delta Airlines (that I discussed earlier). Whenever players visit another casino, I want them to feel separation anxiety from me.

A casino's "high roller room" (or Platinum Room, as I always brand them), is designed to do help that happen. It is a tool to make good players (measured by high coin-in) feel PAIN if they go to another property. My platinum players are coddled in *any* way that it takes to *own* their loyalty. ANY way that it takes; understand the full implication of that necessity as you "read between the lines" here.

During the period of time that I was working for Trump, I was at an off-site gourmet restaurant for one of our many *Platinum Members Only* parties hosted by members of the Tribe and my staff of Casino Hosts and Hostesses. One of my Hostesses was a 21-year-old extremely flirty girl who had been "surgically enhanced" (breast implants, butt-reshaping, nose job, and whatever else she had done). After observing the girl's enhancements and her flirty mannerisms, one key tribal member (a female) pulled me aside and seemingly-scolding asked *"Is that the new Hostess that you hired?"* I respond, *"Yes M'am it is."* She (the tribal leader), whistled and said, *"Gary, that little cunt is going to make us a fucking fortune. I want you to pimp her ass out to every dirty old man on our*

112

Platinum list. She needs to give that stuff away to everybody. She will make this tribe a fucking fortune. Good work"

Unlike Nevada, prostitution is not legal in Southern California; and we had gone to great extremes to repeatedly chase hookers out of our casino. Don't think for a minute that I have some moral objection to the profession, much more simply I believed that if gamblers are spending money on whores then that is money they could be spending at my tables or machines. If they have to have a hooker, I would much prefer that it be a marketing expense offset against their play than have them put that precious gaming cash into the prostitute's coffers. (Steve Sohng and I chased a working girl out one night, only to have her offer her "services" to all of casino management in exchange for allowing her to stay and "work." *How do you spell "ewwww"?*)

Chapter Nine

How do you fit "gambler" into the ole resume?
(and what do slot machines have to do with it?)

"MORGAN: Going into business for ourselves. Wyatt just got us a Faro game.
DOC: Since when is faro a business?
WYATT: Didn't you always say gambling's an honest trade?
DOC: I said poker's an honest trade. Only suckers buck the tiger. The odds are all with the house.
WYATT: Depends how you look at it. I mean it's not like anybody's holding a gun to their heads
— **fourth draft of Kevin Jarre's 1993 screenplay "Tombstone"**

Kirk Douglas was wearing a suit...much nicer clothes than the other men at the card table. He also appeared to have had a bath and a shave; another thing lacking from his "gaming" companions.

My grandfather used to sell 30-minutes in the bathtub and shower for 25¢ at his barber shop in rural North Carolina; so I knew the significance of a recently-bathed dandy in the midst of men who purchased a bath *maybe* once a week on a Saturday night.

A flashily-powdered girl with a too-low-cut brocade dress was at Kirk's left side and a glittering diamond-studded stiletto was in his right boot. He was Doc Holliday in the 1957 film *Gunfight At The OK Corral* and he was one cool cat...clearly the coolest dude in the whole film (probably the *only* cool guy in the whole film).

A few moments later Burt Lancaster's Wyatt Earp was told that Holliday was "*a professional gambler.*" From that moment on I wondered just exactly how one gets to be a "professional gambler" and how that works into the resume. At that point I had no clue that one day I would know exactly the answer to that and would be considered one of the biggest (or at least most controversial) "casino bosses" in America.

As the years passed from my childhood into adolescence, more specifically and less flippantly I wondered how one could actually make a living as a "*gambler*". These professional gamblers seemed to have a hell of a good time. Even "*Bond, James Bond*" was often seen at a baccarat table. How cool was *that*? (And never mind the fact that in the 2006 remake of *Casino Royal*, they changed the game from baccarat to Texas Hold 'em.)

114

Early in my adult life, I had been a theatre manager, a journalist, a recording artist and touring musician, a union official, a public relations political operative... *why the hell couldn't I be Doc Holliday?*

The biographers of Mafia gambling mastermind Meyer Lansky repeatedly tell of *his* pondering the very issue of *professional gambling* and coming to the conclusion (at the age of 12) that the only way to "win" in gambling is (as he put it) *"to own the joint."* This revelation came, apparently, after he had lost the family's hard-saved weekly nickel for Sabbath "cholent/ hamin" by being taken at a street-corner craps game around 1915. *Come on seven!*

I won $800 from a Director of Operations for one of my casinos —*a gaming professional* — rolling dice until he finally noticed that one die only had fives on it and the other only had sixes and twos. Even the best are gullible at times; what can I say? *(Yes, I gave him the money back.)*

Though I had several close encounters with the man I was told to call "Mister Meyer" (Lansky) and his business interests about 65 years later, it took me a while to understand the error of his early adolescent pronouncement. *(And for the record —especially for gaming control commissions— my "close encounters" in no way reflect an association in any manner.)*

Nonetheless, as a southern boy I was much more attuned to the colorful Georgian, Doc Holliday, than the New York Jewish gangster, even if my business sense was with the bookkeeper's philosophy. Even today there is a three-foot poster of Doc Holliday's face on one wall of my office. Long before Val Kilmer's brilliant portrayal of Holliday in the film *"Tombstone,"* I was totally dazzled by the very concept of a "professional gambler," but everything I knew about business made me think that there must be SOME reason that Wall Street invests in gaming.

Today at least three casino companies are still in the Fortune 500 list of America's largest corporations; and I know from my IPO's during the dot-com era that the investment banking community doesn't get involved unless they can examine viable metrics and realistic financial projections. If a Wall Street financial analyst is going to recommend an institutional buy of a stock, you can bet your sweet bippie that the numbers are as solid as any other SEC-approved public corporation; hence my willingness to lean toward the Lansky school alongside the Holliday school.

On the other hand, I am totally amazed, stunned, and bewildered that so many gaming companies based their early 21st century expansion on mortgage-backed instruments pooled in trusts for bond holders to call when the real estate industry crashed. More on this later, but this is what happens when MBAs and accountants run casinos instead of gambling men (and women).

But, alas, I was indeed a child of the 1950s, raised on a healthy dose of both historical and fictional western passion plays seven nights a week on television. So I was used to hearing of colorful 19th century characters that had no visible means of support other than gambling. And these guys always had the fanciest clothes, the hottest chicks, the fastest guns, hearts of gold, and by God they were just *cool*. I mean, who could argue that anyone in the entire old west was cooler than James Garner's Brett Maverick, Jack Kelley's Bart Maverick, or their British cousin Roger Moore's Beau Maverick? What about Rhett Butler? Other than that unfortunate little gun-running incident, Clark Gable's character was nothing more than a professional gambler...and a damned cool one.

God! America loves a scoundrel. But beyond these fictional characters, John Henry "Doc" Holliday was a real life breathing human being...*and a professional gambler.* Get this: The sickly-sweet character of *Melanie* in Margaret Mitchell's *Gone With The Wind* was based on the author's great aunt who had a love affair with her first cousin. The great aunt, in shame, retreated to a convent and as a nun became the model for Ashley Wilkes' wife. Her real-life cousin paramour: John Henry "Doc" Holliday, who fled Georgia in disgrace to begin his life as a gambler. And that dashing gambler was the model for Rhett. *In the world of gamblers and scoundrels, truth is often stranger than fiction.*

American historical frontier lore (fact and fiction) is well-spiced with those characters whose only income seemed to be from "games of chance and skill." Like I said, Doc Holliday was just cool.

My running some of the most successful gambling halls in the country has given me amazing insight into both that thin line between folk lore / reality and Lansky's conclusion that the only way to make money is to own the casino. And my expert opinion, as a gambler who has taken that seat on both sides of the table, is that many times the lore is correct and Lansky was wrong.

Oh don't get me wrong...casinos do always win *in the long run*. That is what the whole exercise about "hold" was all about; and that, of course is how we build all these fancy glitter palaces. But on any given day...any given hour...or God-forbid, any given minute; I make no guarantees to you about which side wins.

Remember every time Larry from Iowa came in, my coin in would go up but my bottom line was always in jeopardy. Nine times out of ten, the son-of-a-bitch would beat the house for more money than the rest of the players would lose all added together.

The scary thing is that almost any successful casino operator will still explain losing days by tell you *"that is why they call it gambling."* Even the tightest run house has losing nights. Even the most Wall Street-savvy gaming executive will use words like "luck" and "chance". Even the most hardened Chief Financial Officers will talk about "winning" days and "bad luck."

Oh yes, Lansky WAS wrong. And I love to point to the most ironic example of his being wrong. In 1948 Lansky financed the fourth casino to open on Highway 91 (the Las Vegas Strip): *The Thunderbird*. On the north end of the Strip across from what is now Circus-Circus, the Thunderbird Casino opened in September of 1948 with Meyer's brother Jake running the joint. Opening night was a Las Vegas style disaster even more impressive than the day-after-Christmas 1946 disastrous opening of Benny Siegel's Flamingo that made *that* hotel close two weeks later. It was a disaster's disaster that proved Mister Meyer wrong. By the end of *that* opening night, the casino had lost so badly and paid out so much money that two players ended up owning the casino ... *literally.* The owners lost the fucking casino in a craps game![11]

The point is that the house does NOT always win. Larry showed it, the damned tic-tac-toe playing chickens showed it, Thunderbird showed it, and I see it all the time at casinos all over the country. It *is* true that in the long run, mathematically, the house always wins. But as we have seen, the "short term" can last a really long time.

Remember, when I first met Mark Lefever, his blackjack tables had been on an 11-month long losing streak. Now think about that: if the house loses for that long a period of time, then players are beating the house for that long. So, at least in that "short" term, it very clearly **IS** possible to make money by beating the house.

In fact, if the house has winning AND losing days...then the house too is "gambling for a living;" just as much as the players are gambling for a living. So, in fact, professional gamblers *do* sit on both sides of the table. The trick is learning how to identify the winning and losing streaks and maximize them...even make them happen. THAT "trick" is what makes one a *professional* gambler. And it is the trick of figuring out which side of the table to be on at any given time.

Let me define "gambling" just a little further. Gambling is not about being stupid. It is about taking risks...and good gamblers take *calculated* risks.

Laying $50,000 on a hard way 4 at a craps table is not gambling; it is stupidity. Playing a Steve-Sohng-special 9:6 video poker machine with a 1% hold with perfect strategy, shooting for a Royal Flush is much more like gambling. Going "all in" at a $25/$50 Texas Hold'em table with a non-suited K-6 before the flop is not gambling; it is entertainment (or a totally whacked-out tournament strategy for someone watching way too much television). Above all, let's not confuse amusement and entertainment with true gambling.

On the other side of the table (or machine), properties that rely totally on promotions are not gambling; they are just pissing money at the wind and hoping some of it blows back to them. I know, I have done that too.

There is a fairly well-known lunatic in casino marketing circles who is recognized not for his successes but for his incredible failures at promotions. One among my favorite absurdities was his giveaway of a huge pots-and-pans set to anyone who would bring in a post card (targeted based on a player's *theoretical* loss). Hundreds of players received the mailing and lined up at the players' club to claim the cookware. Each was given an oversized 22-pound box which was impossible to carry around the casino from machine to machine. So, the players promptly took their boxes to their cars and drove home. He *had* successfully brought hundreds of players into the casino. It got them into the casino but it was as if he had devised a scheme to force them to leave without playing. Basically the casino spent a ton of money on the design of the post card, the cost of mailing, the cost of the cookware, the staffing for the promotion...and received zero return on that investment. THAT is not gambling; it is flushing money down the toilet.

Frank Haas, my once CFO and once partner in a casino management company, tells me about a promotion one GM created where a radio spot advertised a "secret word". Anyone coming to the casino and mentioning that word would get $20...in <u>cash</u> (and **not** in *playable credits*). To make matters worse, the redemption center was in a different building from the casino. AND, this obviously-for-locals promotion was targeted to lower income and unemployed people. As a sensible person might deduce, the low income folks went to the out building, said the secret word, took their $20 and went home. Even worse, the word was distributed at a local homeless shelter. Almost no one went into the casino. That was not gambling; it was simply madness.

Look, I have been responsible on a day-to-day basis for several thousand slot machines. By some accountings, I have overseen a conglomerate of more slot machines than anyone else in the world. In *any* accounting I have had a LOT of slot machines. In recent times I have even worked for a slot machine developer and have co-owned a slot manufacturer. Believe me, I know slot machines. Some days I <u>DO</u> lose. And THAT is what makes it gambling. But I am not stupid. In the long-haul, I win because on the average, nationwide, I *hold* about 8½ % of whatever is put into my machines...and in some jurisdictions a lot more than that.

That does not mean that there are not days when you may show up, put a twenty-dollar bill into a machine and walk away with two-million-dollars. It happens. But it is a *gamble* that I am willing to take with you because in the long run, I win more money than I pay out. Even when I pay out thirty or forty thousand or even a million all to one person... in the long-haul I still win. One key to my winning in the long run is my having a large enough bankroll to weather the storm of paying out guys like Larry or guys and gals like you.

When I was on the other side of the table (as a player), I counted cards, collected Bingo hot cards, found 9:6 (and even 10:7) video poker machines with a 1% or less hold, got inside information about slot holds (and PAR sheet frequencies) and used any number of other tricks to even out the odds or sometimes to shift the long-term odds to my favor and for my bankroll. I was still gambling, but I made calculated gambles not idiotic bets. Gambling and betting are two different things, as that Kevin Jarre script echoed.

So how did gambling get to be MY honest trade? You remember that the Jersey tough boy had asked *"Who the hell are you?"* A second later he had backed away, turned, and then was gone into the same shadows that had borne him. Not many weeks had passed since the day I took the side door out of *Resorts* to Pennsylvania Avenue and almost shot the would-be mugger. At that time, the *Taj* and *Showboat* had not been built and that side street was not so tourist-friendly as it became in later years. On my subsequent twice-a-week trips to Atlantic City I had carefully avoided the side streets except Iowa Avenue beside the Trop (when I took the cheap buses rather than luxury coach).

Baltimore based, at the time, I had been bouncing around the east coast playing guitar and promoting my third album on New York's small but prestigious *Folkways Records*. I used to tell people that there was good news and bad news about that: the good news was that I made about $750-an-hour on stage; the bad news was that I played about an hour a month.

I had just come off of a very cold New York City tour when I read that a stock exchange hot shot had won $145,000 in just ten days playing blackjack at the one casino that had opened in Atlantic City New Jersey. This guy, named Ken Uston, supposedly had an IQ of 169 and had written a book about playing *Pac Man*.

Hell, I supposedly had an IQ of 180 and loved *Pac Man* (actually I preferred *Ms. Pac Man* and really preferred *Space Invaders*), and had been playing blackjack since before I was in elementary school. As a child, I learned addition from adding the face value of cards. Why the hell didn't I make $145,000 in two weeks?

I was living in Baltimore at the time running a folk music coffeehouse bar and commuting to NY for guitar gigs. Atlantic City, a little more than two hours away from Baltimore, had just legalized casino gambling. After this last series of coffee house gigs in New York, I was unemployed, past due on the rent, and not real sure from where the week's groceries might come. The unemployment rate was high enough that my job searches had not yielded anything and there was little market for a guitar-playing recording artist and newspaper reporter...with a ponytail.

This guy Ken Uston got me thinking again about the whole concept of a "professional" gambler. From my enthrallment with the black-and-white television westerns and big-screen gamblers, early on it seemed to me that either (1) most of these gamblers cheated to win; or (2) gambling games have changed and gotten harder over the years; or (3) one CAN in fact beat the house and win. Now, Ken Uston was reinforcing the latter.

There is in fact, a plethora of historical evidence that the first two were somewhat true. The first and second propositions are clearly substantiated by the disappearance of *Faro* as a casino game and by any gambling museum's collection of card cheating devices.

Nonetheless, there was even greater evidence (as well as scientific data) that showed my latter supposition is absolutely true. Doctor Edward O. Thorp's famous book *Beat The Dealer* began to prove that to be true.

Driven more from desperation than recreation, I began reading about this alleged "science" of *card counting* for blackjack. Convinced, by the *60-Minutes* Uston story that the research made sense, I shuffled eight decks of cards together and began following various systems and modifications for counting cards. To my total amazement, in practice, I came out ahead of the house almost every time.

Even better than Uston's pop-culture book and Dr. Thorp's computer-geek book, I found most useful Lawrence Revere's *Playing Black As A Business*[12].

119

Revere is the pseudonym of the late Griffith Owens, a pit boss who played both sides of the game as both the house and a player. He worked closely with computer guru Julian Braun who helped Dr. Thorp develop *his* models. Revere's book was written in common English without the need of my understanding mathematical models. His book told me what to do without the need to understand why it worked (at that point).

After absorbing Revere and the other authors, I began some reconnaissance trips to Atlantic City. To feed my desperation I responded to an ad in the *Baltimore Sun* selling trips to Atlantic City. The excursion was basically *free*; a $19.95 bus ticket was refunded with $20 in quarters upon arrival at the casino. I borrowed the $19.95 and headed into my foray as a *professional gambler*. I even dressed for the role, donning a Victorian shirt and an Edwardian frock coat for my adventure...and for my test.

Two decades before actor Val Kilmer's Doc Holliday would warn *"I'll be your huckleberry,"* I was decked out to be the huckleberry of all huckleberries. I sat silently on the bus ride up Interstate 95 and then east along rural southern Jersey roads. Letting my imagination roam to the finest Gene Rodenberry *Paladin* (Have Gun Will Travel) script, I tried to ignore the hunger in my stomach and the potential eviction if I failed. From a stake of $20 in quarters I needed to raise $350 for rent and another $100 for groceries and other expenses. At the time, this wild west adventure to the Jersey shore was a life or death mission. But first I needed to understand the "lay of the land."

Ten hours later I was back on the bus hearing, *"Turned that roll of quarters into $7,000 in thirty minutes; I bet 'em the hard way; five at a time."* The speaker was a 64-year-old retired schoolteacher from south Baltimore, recently widowed and feeling really good about a "huge" win on a 25-cent slot machine.

"I've been coming to this casino every week for two years and this is the third time I've hit the big one: $250 on a roll of nickels! Of course, I've probably put twice that much into these machines on the weeks I didn't hit." This laughing speaker was a security guard who visited Atlantic City every weekend from his home in Washington, DC.

Sitting quietly near the back of the bus, sipping Jack and Coke from a wax deli cup, was the owner of a chain of small fruit stands. He was friendly and full of smiles, but had very little to say about winning or losing. Privately he flashed a pocket full of returned "markers" totaling almost ten thousand dollars in checks that he had written to the casino and won back. And unlike most markers issued to players, these were not for table games but for slot machines. He had been playing the $25 slot machines in the "high rollers" slot area and had more casino credit than most typical slot players made at their daily jobs in six months. On the other hand, his possession of the cancelled markers simply meant that he had won back (or paid off) some portion of the checks he had written.

Beginning in 1979, every day of the week between 35 and 70 buses, all operated by private tour companies, rolled out of Baltimore to Atlantic City. Even

120

larger fleets pulled out of Philadelphia, Washington, New York, and Newark...all Atlantic City bound. The average casino-bound bus filled about 60 percent of 47 seats, though several companies often booked 160% of capacity and on many days added a second bus during the most popular travel times.

"*The casinos do not pay for these buses,*" explained the owner of one of the mid-sized bus companies. "*One of the biggest misconceptions about this business is that these are hotel buses. People expect bus drivers to be able to answer hotel questions for them,*" He added, explaining that his company sent between 35 and 40 buses a week to Atlantic City. Pointing out that most of his runs are chartered for churches, clubs, civic groups and other organizations, he concluded, "*It is a day of entertainment; it is glitter, glamour and in some ways a sort of escape for people who otherwise would never be able to have this kind of luxury.*"

A young nurse on a 6 p.m. to 6 a.m. roundtrip explained her junkets, "*I don't expect to win anything. I made $200 twice. But that's not what I'm really going for. I mean, I only take about $15 with me and I get the twenty or so they give. That's all. I just enjoy the excitement of playing the slot machines. I love that sound when the coins hit the tray*"

A typical bus trip offered cash and voucher payment to bus riders: $15 in quarters for day trips; $17 in quarters at night; with up to a $22 voucher for a free return trip. Some also offered free buffet meals. A trip generally cost the rider $17.95 (I don't know why they didn't just charge $18) and with those rebates from the casino a rider actually came out up to $4.05 ahead. During busy times at the casinos, a return voucher might be as little as a $2-discount off of the next trip.

In my case, after shopping around I had found a $19.95 bus ticket and was rewarded a $20 roll of quarters, a $5 buffet credit, a $5 return-trip cash voucher (which meant I could get $25 on my next trip), and a $2 discount for my next trip.

ABOVE: A May 1979 $2 return voucher from Baltimore to Atlantic City for a line run bus casino trip in 1979. Notice the voucher is called a "deferred discount."

121

"People do choose which bus company to take by how much they get back," one operator told me, adding, *"They don't all go by the incentives, but a (large) number of them do."*

"Hell, if I could afford to go twice a week, I wouldn't have to gamble; I'd have money," one woman told a friend who was talking about a second trip in one week.

Among the riders on my first month of bus trips to Atlantic City were a large percentage unemployed people, those with no income, people with very low income and older people with fixed income. Thinking that if my gambling expedition failed I would at least be able to write an article about it, I took copious notes on the trip:

- More than three-quarters of the people on each of eight midweek bus trips that I surveyed were low income African American women, most widowed, divorced or simply single;
- One 24-year old had hocked a stereo at a pawn shop to take the trip in hopes of winning enough money to pay the month's rent and get the stereo back;
- Two older men, sharing a case of beer, discussed cashing unemployment checks to go gamble;
- A sad-eyed 44-year-old cashier hoped to make enough money to buy a car so she could stop riding buses to work every day;
- And a very eager (and incredibly overweight) bag-lady-looking woman belted out Baptist hymns in freedom-bus style (reminiscent of the civil rights era bus trips), punctuating her loud songs with almost-comical prayers to win at the slot machines.

At the end of each trip, sad eyes were even sadder. In my own focus-group-like poll taken on my first three Atlantic City bus trips I found only two winners; one with a $25 win on quarter machines and one with a $10 win on a nickel machine (penny machines were very rare in those days). Everyone else I talked with had lost. Even the ones who had loudly boasted of turning rolls of coins into hundreds (or thousands) of dollars had fed those winning right back into the hungry slots until they had lost it all and then lost the change in their pockets.

All-in-all, this was not the romantic image that I had hoped to find; it was not the *Doc Holliday legend*. At the time I was not even sure if it was gambling. This is not what I wanted to find and it certainly was not looking terribly encouraging for my card-counting adventure.

As one casino bus marketing manager explained of the passengers, *"They will give us the $20 back as well as $20 or $30 of their own money."* He added, *"Las Vegas is in the middle of a desert; there is nothing around it. But within three or four hundred miles of Atlantic City there are literally millions of people. With the bus programs we can bring those people into the casino for six hours to play the slots and have them back home the same day. No pain-in-the-ass hotel rooms to fuck with."*

He added, "*The marketing strategy here is easy to see. It is volume and we have just scratched the surface. There are hundreds of cities and towns outside of the metropolitan areas. Once we reach into those little towns we open up a whole new field of customers.*"

When I began my adventure, more than 5,000 buses rolled into Atlantic City every week to deposit a quarter-million riders from the Northeast for non-overnight day trips; as far south as Washington and as far west, incredibly, as Detroit (11 hours by bus). The Atlantic City casinos, during prime bus hours (noon to 7:30 p.m.), were packed with slot machine players.

"*I've been on this one for three hours and the best it has done is a $5 payoff. It's due for the big one anytime now: Good luck,*" a woman cheered on a waiting player as she finally ran out of quarters and gave up her machine.

"*Don't you touch my damned machine; I'll knock your lights out honey,*" warned an overweight, chain-smoking woman as she stood idle in front of a nickel machine, waiting for change. (The seeming correlation between chain smoking and grind joint slot-machine pullers is at best interesting and at worst choking.)

"*I don't want that machine; it just paid big. It'll eat up my money and not hit good again for a week,*" a mother of four said after waiting an hour in line to get to an open machine.

"*This one ain't no good. It must have paid off yesterday; it's not doing a thing for me*" pouted another player as she gave up her machine.

Meanwhile change attendants continued to bring fresh rolls of nickels and quarters to the machine worshippers. In those days there was no TITO (ticket in ticket out) and very few bill acceptors; so most everything was coin-driven. The cocktail waitresses continued to stop by every half hour with free mixed drinks to further numb the brains watching the spinning symbols. The players continued to wait for a machine to "hit". And the buses keep rolling to the casino bus lounge door and then pulling way. I was definitely getting an education.

In that early world of slot players, I fortunately discovered a different set of "VIP" buses providing sharp contrast to these every-nickel-counts trips. These buses were not the 47-seat modified Greyhounds but were 15-seat luxury coaches. Rather than "paying" the riders, the riders did the paying…$50 for the privilege of taking such a bus and no roll of quarters waiting at the other end. These sleek super-coach trips included two onboard meals, all the free drinks anyone could hold, and an ever smiling hostess (who on at least on one bus was a 20-year-old alleged former Playboy Playmate).

Experienced junket masters with a history of high roller junkets to Las Vegas and the Bahamas ran most of the VIP bus trips. Upon the player's arrival at an "embarkation point" *(rather than a "bus station", like the line-runs)* a secretary assigned seats while the Playmate/on-board hostess took orders for breakfast. There were no tickets, waiting rooms, or boarding numbers on these upscale buses. Unlike on the 5,000 slot-buses, each passenger was personally welcomed with chitchat and small talk. And, of course, each player was expected to drop $1,000 or more at the casino...as opposed to the $30 to $60 per player average on the "herd" buses.

By the time the junket master made his greeting rounds from seat to seat, spent a few minutes getting to know his "guests" and returned to his own enlarged four seat section in the back of the bus, breakfast was long over and the hostess was coming out of the on-board kitchen and passing along the aisle to serve pre-lunch drinks. And by the time lunch was finished and the hostess had talked and joked with the gamblers (as she offered beverages from soda and beer to wines and liquors), the bus had arrived at the casino.

Since players' clubs and player tracking had not been adopted yet, passengers on these VIP trips were required to attach tiny cloth logo pins to their jacket lapels (gentlemen were *required* to wear jackets) which identified them to casino employees as being with a specific junket master and able to sign the check for all the complimentary food and drink they wanted while at the casino. This, of course, was before the creation highly-structured points-for-comps policies now in place.

The real perk of these luxury bus trips was the complimentary dinner (by reservation only) in the members-only gourmet restaurant high above the casino and a world away from the bus lounges, sneeze-guard buffets, and the rolls of quarters. (In fact these buses didn't even drive to the bus-lounge area; they stopped at the front door of the hotel.) While several of the low end line-run (as they were called) bus trips offered a very nice buffet dinner with the traditional roll of quarters, none came near the elegance and service offered to these players. The VIPS could order anything on the menu, including the high-end wine list...all free of charge. There were no lines in which to wait and there was constant service; though I did note that several of the restaurants had two sets of menus and wine lists; one for giving the free-meal customers and a different one with the $500+ wines.

For the line-run bus rider, a role of quarters could last hours at the 25¢ slot machines; almost all day at the nickel slots. But that role of coins would not cover even one bet for the VIP passengers.

Finally, this bus group was a lot closer to what I had in mind for the gambler's life; though I was still having a rough time equating even the luxury VIP buses to taking the stage coach into a movie set Tombstone Arizona.

So with my own observed lay-of-the-land, a few "test trip" bus rides up to Atlantic City, my rent due, and my electricity past due, I borrowed that $19.95 from a friend and hopped on a mid-week line-run bus from Baltimore to the Boardwalk.

Just outside of Atlantic City the bus pulled into the staging area and took its place waiting in line behind a dozen other buses scheduled to arrive at the same time. Once it was our turn, the bus inched forward to park beside a singlewide mobile-home trailer with a vinyl *"Tropicana"* sign attached to the door. A twenty-something-year-old woman stepped into the bus and gave us a rah-rah speech about how wonderful the *Trop* was. After she finished her canned sales pitch, she gave us some basic instructions about the time and location to re-board the bus; it was the same speech I heard every time I had taken a scouting trip to check out the gambling. As she reminded us of the bus number and the loading time, she walked along the aisle and handed each of us three vouchers: one for the roll of quarters; one for an additional $5 on our next trip; and one for the reduced-price buffet.

Line-run bus riders were discouraged from playing table games, after all these were slot runs. Nonetheless, I traded the coin voucher for a role of quarters, opened the roll and dumped it into a plastic coin cup beside a slot machine. I carried the coin cup to the cashier and watched as a cashier poured the cup of quarters into giant coin-counting machines. It stopped at $19.75 and the cashier slapped the side of the machine with her fist. Apparently this jarred loose the final lodged quarter and the LED screen registered $20. She handed me a twenty-dollar bill and I walked toward the $2-tables.

Three hours later, to my dismay and amazement, I had won my rent money, my utilities, and enough groceries for a month; $501. That was the goal I had set as my greatest expectation and had vowed if I reach that number I would walk away. The truth is…rather than walk way I more like skipped and danced away! I was thrilled (and stunned that it worked).

At the cage I fished into my pockets for four black ($100) chips, three green ($25), four red ($5) and three white (normally one-dollar chips but in Atlantic City they represented $2) and collected the five one-hundred-dollar bills and the one *George Washington.*

Almost trembling, I made a beeline for the exit door feeling as if I had just robbed a bank and wanted to get out before I was nabbed. I still had three hours before the bus was due to take me back to Baltimore…but I was literally afraid to go back into the casino, fearful that someone might discover what I had done and make me give back my rent and groceries.

By the time the bus had crossed the Maryland state line, I had calmed enough to realize that I had broken no laws and had not even done anything immoral or unethical. Still, it had seemed *too* easy.

Just like the pusher who says, *"The first one is free, after that you pay me,"* the rush (and the money) had sucked me in. I spent the next couple of years learning everything I could about gambling, casino operations, and all the other tenets of my new profession. Before I walked away from the tables, I was running high-roller junkets to Atlantic City, the Bahamas, and Vegas. I graduated far from the $2 tables and was comfortable at hundred-dollar-minimum tables varying bets to as much as $3,000 bet on the turn of one card. The most I had played at the time was $60,000 on one roll of dice.

One afternoon I was sitting at a $25 table at the *Sands* in Atlantic City. I had been making minimum table bets and the count began to turn to my favor. For some reason (or in hindsight: some *insanity*) I didn't increase my bets as the deck got better; for one thing, I suspected that I had attracted the attention of the pit boss by doing that earlier. I was feeling very paranoid and was almost sure that the "suit" had discovered that I was a card counter.

As the deck got better and better I still made the minimum table bet of $25 per hand. Still the pit boss was hovering and I felt eyes on me. Imaginary or not, my stomach was churning and I felt like I was about to have a very serious fight. There were absolutely no tangible signs of any danger at all... but it just did not "feel" right. And like everyone, I had heard the stories of card counters being dragged into "the backroom" and having their knuckles broken...or worse.

Finally the actual count became absurdly high in my favor; one of the best shoes I had ever seen favoring the players. *"Fuck-em if they can't take a joke,"* I thought as I begin fishing hidden chips from my pockets; lots of greens ($25) and blacks ($100). The Sands (and much of Atlantic City) was so poorly managed in those days that there were no top-end limits on many of the table games; a player could bet the table minimum as low as $2 sometimes (but $25 in this case) and could bet an unlimited maximum. And THAT is just what I did; after digging through all my hidden pockets I increased my previous hand's $25 bet by 720 times. I bet $18,000. I was dealt 15 and did not hit it.

A second after I moved my hand across the cards to indicate "stay", I was tapped on the shoulder. I turned to see two VERY large men dressed in the cheapest J.C. Penney off-the-rack suits I had seen in a long time. *"Mr. Green, we would like to talk with you,"* one of them said in a comically stereotypical New Jersey "mob" accent. I was thinking this could be bad since no one here knew my name.

"Let me grab my money here, first," I said.

"OUR money", the speaker said, attempting to "correct" me.

"Naw, trust me on this one; it is MINE, hoss," I said to him in my very best combative Southern drawl.

The second man firmly grabbed my left shoulder and began backing me from the table. I stepped toward him, a little quicker than he was expecting and it caused his grip to loosen just enough for me to twist my body under his massive arm and back toward the table. I was now facing him and thinking of how I was going to take out his equally large friend after I would give this one roundhouse kick to the celiac plexus. Two uniformed security guards appeared from behind a bank of slot machines before I had the opportunity to deal with either issue.

"Well hell," I sighed as I prepared to get my ass kicked severely, *"why waltz when you can rock and roll?"*

I stepped into a "T" stance and pulled my hands up prepared to strike at the jugular veins of the first suited man and poke out the eyes of the second... knowing full well that I was going to seriously lose this confrontation. I also knew that once they discovered that I was armed, this was going to get very ugly. My mind began racing to all of the scenarios of a shootout in the casino, the arrests, the deaths (including mine), and a dozen other possibilities. Fuck. This was a no-win.

ABOVE: The late Sands Hotel/Casino in Atlantic City (right) and the Claridge (left) next door. *circa 1980s.* The Sands was imploded in 2007 and the Claridge was sold to Hilton, nee Bally, nee Park Place, nee Harrahs, nee Claridge at Ballys.

LEFT: Three $25 green cheques (chips) from the Atlantic City Sands blackjack tables.

Before I had to worry about the outcome, the first man spoke again, *"Mr. Green, there is no problem here. Let's all just be calm. Your play is just a little too rich for the Sands. We would like for you to leave."*

"My money..." I began.

"We will escort you to the cage to cash out the cheques and then you will have to leave," he said in a calm and controlled voice. Out of the corner of my eye, I spotted a New Jersey Gaming Control Board agent overseeing the entire event. Well, at least it would be safe and my gun would remain hidden.

I was escorted around the people waiting in line at the cage and taken directly to a waiting cashier. He carefully counted my chips, handed me the cash, and washed his hands in the air in front of the cameras. My entourage of escorts then walked me to the side door, and closed it behind me with the one speaker saying, *"You will no longer be welcome at The Sands. Please never attempt to return."*

"*Eh screw 'em,*" I thought as the door closed, "*There are eight more casinos on the boardwalk.*"

Since I was already off the boardwalk, I walked next door, just across the alley-street into the Claridge Casino and Hotel. As I stepped through the revolving door a uniformed security officer blocked my path and waved his index finger from left to right while shaking his head no. Damn. Less than two minutes and I was already barred from the property next door.

Except for how fast it happened, I was not terribly surprised at being barred from the casino directly next door. They were mere steps apart and shared a common alleyway.

I walked back up Park Place and to the Boardwalk to enter Bally's from the Boardwalk entrance. Through the tinted-glass doors I walked into the maze of slot machines. Except for a benign security guard watching the door, there was no sign of "heat" and in my full Victorian gambler's attire (carefully designed to *attract* attention) I made my way through the casino. Instead of walking directly to the blackjack pits, I milled around a few slot machines dropping three quarters here and a dollar there. Slowly and methodically, I played machines in several banks as I worked my way toward the blackjack pit.

I decided to start small, and I walked up to a $5 table, sat down, and handed the dealer a twenty-dollar bill. "*Cheque change twenty,*" the dealer chimed out to the pit boss. The pit floor-manager suit answered an automatic "*okay changing a twenty*" but then did a double-take as he glanced toward me.

"*Mister Green, you are welcome to play our slots or at any of our other table games, but I am afraid you are just a little too lucky to play blackjack at Bally's,*" the floor (manager) very politely said.

It was the same story at every casino on the boardwalk. From the *Golden Nugget* to *Tropicana* down to the *Playboy* on down to *Caesars*, (I already knew about *Bally'*, *Claridge,* and the *Sands*), back down to *Resorts International*. All eight casinos had blacklisted me.

On my walk back down to Resorts to wait for the bus back to Baltimore, Bob Goulet brushed by me and stopped just long enough to say, "*evening Gary; you ok? You look like they finally caught you counting.*" He kept walking and before I could respond he was gone. I had run into Broadway legend Robert Goulet about a half dozen times in Atlantic City, but only small talk; it is not like we were close friends. Christ, did everyone in AC know that I was counting cards?

In a depressed fog, I walked into the lobby of *Resorts* to wait for the bus departure time. I had taken one of the luxury coaches, with the hostess and gourmet dinner; but I was not feeling much like a gourmet dinner (or any food for that matter). I sat down on a plush sofa in the hotel lobby and decided to just wait.

I had only been sitting there for a minute or so when an elderly Jewish man sat down beside and began nodding his head at me as if acknowledging the answer to some question he had asked. I recognized him immediately as Willie

128

Maizer, the owner and host of the luxury bus junket company. In fact, his name was painted on the side of the bus.

"They finally caught you didn't they?" he asked.

"What are you talking about? Caught me doing what?" I shrugged.

"Look kid, don't bullshit a bull shitter," he smiled, *"you were good. Maybe one of the best I have ever seen; but it was just a matter of time until they caught your ass. I knew it was coming."*

"Well why the hell didn't you warn me?" I asked, trying to decide if I wanted to take offence to being called "kid". I was barely over 25 and he was almost 50 years older than me, so I concluded that it was probably ok.

"You had to learn it for yourself. You wouldn't have listened to me," he smiled grandfatherly. *Tell me, do you know other gamblers in Baltimore that would come to Atlantic City?"*

I shrugged again, *"I guess so; some."*

"I don't mean nickel slot players. I am talking about table players. Craps players. Not whales, but people who will gamble $300 to $500 in a day. Do you know people like that?" he asked.

"It can't be that hard to find them," I said, knowing full well that he was talking about my entire rent for a month being gambled on a roll of the dice. Despite my success with big numbers at blackjack, I did not consider *that* gambling. The idea of anyone betting even $100 dollars on *a roll of the dice* was just bizarre to me, even though I had seen Mister Maizer gamble thousands at a time and had done it myself on a "don't" bet.

In fact, all of that hoopla and yelling around dice tables gave me the creeps. I mean, my father had taught me to play craps before I was in the first grade, and I certainly knew all the cool code words for the dice combination.

ROLL	SLANG
TWO	Snake Eyes
THREE	Acey-Ducey
FOUR	little Joe from Kokomo
FIVE	Fever
SIX	sixie from Dixie
SEVEN	Come on seven
EIGHT	eighter from Decatur
NINE	Nina from Carolina
TEN	Pair of roses
ELEVEN	six five, no jive; craps out
TWELVE	boxcars

I had played craps in street games, office games, and neighborhood games. Figuring the odds doesn't take a genius; there are 36 different ways the dice can come up and a seven can come up six of those 36 times. There are five ways to roll a six or an eight; four ways to roll a five or nine; three ways to roll a four or a 10; two ways to roll three or 11; and only one way to hit two or 12. Beyond that, it is just a matter of figuring odds and the chance of rolling any given number; not something I wanted to depend on for my rent. And those proposition bets that so many dice players go for…were just insane.

129

Nonetheless, I was honest when I told Mr. Maizer that it should not be hard to find gamblers willing to play at the levels he was asking about. As he continued to talk to me, he led me up two flights of escalators to the gourmet Italian restaurant near the showroom.

We spent all of dinner, a couple of hours after dinner and the long ride back to Baltimore talking about the junket business. By the time the bus dropped me off at the Shell station where I had parked my car on Reisterstown Road in Pikesville near Baltimore, Maizer had offered to hire me on a commission-basis to fill buses with gamblers.

Before I agreed to accept the offer he warned me that the bus junket business in Baltimore was dominated by a man named *"Captain John"* (I later learned that he meant the legendary gambler/business man Captain John Kassap who in 2004 helped two internet nerds *(ok, one of them was a seasoned Vegas guy)* buy the Golden Nugget in Vegas). Mister Maizer told me that he had worked either with or for The Captain but had some sort of falling out before going out on his own. He went on to tell me to avoid The Captain because he was "connected to the wrong people" (incidentally, there has never been any evidence whatsoever of that being true).

Most curiously, and forebodingly, Mister Maizer told me that his operation was "protected" by his silent partner in Miami Beach Florida, a *"Mister Meyer."* He said that "Mister Meyer" had arranged that *Willie Maizer Casino Tours* would have the exclusive bus rights for high-roller bus trips to *Resorts International* because Mister Meyer was also a silent partner in the ownership of Resorts, as well as Maizer's junket racket. Maizer went on to tell me that while the "other" bus operators deal with marketing departments and bus mangers, he bypasses all of those people and deals directly with the CM (casino manager) or even Resorts' President Jack Davis and CEO Jim Crosby (who became my friend).

It was clear that Willie Maizer did enjoy very special treatment for his high roller buses from Baltimore and later Washington DC; treatment that no other bus operator received. I know that long before player tracking existed, each of Mister Maizer's players were rated. It was not until just before Meyer Lansky's death in 1983 that Willie Maizer told me that his "Mister Meyer" was in fact Meyer Lansky who allegedly owned a piece of all junket business going to Resorts in both Atlantic City and on Paradise Island in the Bahamas.

In relatively short order, following a haircut, a shave, and a strategic change of wardrobe, I began hanging out with Willie Maizer, his high-roller clientele, and Crosby. It was a never-ending fast-ride flume of adventures and education through the junket racket with Maizer and the (at best) shady slough of *Resorts International* and its complexities. While guys that I would later know (and answer to in some cases) were making their bones as break-out dealers and floors, I was hob-knobbing with the headline makers who were totally removed from the day-to-day floor operations and more concerned about dodging Denny

Gomes. While those guys were learning to be steady and solid earners, I was honing the flamboyance and showmanship and calculating gambles to take.

In fact, my "aerial" view of Resorts gave me a perspective of the full operation and not the limitation of the pits, or the slots, or accounting or what-have-you. My education was "global" and casino-wide not "local" or about how-to-stack-cheques-for-a-pit-boss-quick-count.

On the other hand, it probably was *not* the best industry route for someone seeking a "career" in the business. I was not in the "trenches"; I was in the executive offices.

Because of the things my father had taught me, Maizer's "revelations" to me that *games of chance* are not necessarily so much "chance"... was never a news flash to me. Most interesting in that education was the fact that the casinos could mitigate losses through a series of advanced but very subtle manipulations of games, of player data, and even offers to players. And even that data was...suspect at best. It is no wonder Gomes was less-than-amused.

Let's say, hypothetically and for example, the owner or executive of a large casino (or group of casinos) wanted to take his girlfriend on a shopping spree about which his wife should not find out. Well...somewhere in the player database there is, dormant, a player whose action earned him a huge amount of cash-value comps. Those comps are carried on the casino's books as a liability, because at any time the player could show up and claim them (and the casino would have to pay out). Now, let's suppose the player died or got pissed off at the casino, or for whatever reason was *never* going to return. In theory, that liability stays on the books either forever or until some random date management picks to "expire" the liability.

Above: Gary Green, with hair pulled back in pony tail, days before the shave & haircut to start work in the industry. **Below:** Casino operative, Gary after the haircut and shave. *Same 1980s glasses.*

So let's suppose a bad-haired casino owner wanted to waltz his southern-beauty-queen girlfriend through the high-end shopping mall in the casino concourse for a quick Harry Winston necklace or two. In theory it would be possible for him to charge the purchase to the casino and for a casino executive to pay for the purchase from an open liability account of a player who had died or otherwise disappeared. Liability off the books; girlfriend happy; no money out of pocket. How is that for living large?

131

What an education I got! Being Maizer and Lansky's token *Shabbat goy* was not a bad gig. In fact it was graduate school casino training in so many areas that I would later put to use in finding bad operators, corruptions, and out-and-out thievery that most casino bosses just didn't have the training or experience to spot. UNLV can teach the theory and George Joseph's workshops can train amazingly. But nothing beats hands-on global understanding from *both* sides of the table.

Lansky died in early 1983, the business started slowing down, and Maizer (who had long been in ill health) also died; leaving me Vice President of nothing. Mister Maizer drove one of those ridiculous Cadillac's that GM made as an eight-cylinder that changed to six-cylinder that changed to four-cylinders operating, depending on the acceleration; I always wondered who got stuck with that in his will.

Based on Maizer's training and Lanksy's blueprint, I expanded my casino sphere into associations. Using a combination of their influence and my own folk-music reputation, I took a paid gig as a business agent for a large labor union. In less than a year I was representing more than 40 unions as both a business agent and a "public relations manager", in which role I was able to arrange junkets to *Paradise Island* (the Bahamas) and to Atlantic City for my *Resorts* friends; all without the necessity of a gaming license.

Reaching beyond labor unions and trade associations, I took my music days experience of running a folk club/ coffee house and opened the *Sht Creek Casino* with the uncle of a family friend. Maryland, at that time, had one of those typical laws which allowed charities to have "casino night" to raise money. Of course none of the charities had casino equipment or expertise; so, a guy like myself could create an all table-games casino, bring a following of players, and provide tables, dealers, and a percentage of profits for a different charity every night of the week. A temporary alcohol license allowed me to serve beer and wine for any three-day event and I got two of those every week... so in effect ran a full scale casino with the exception of slots.

When there was no charity available, we stored the equipment in Baltimore's historic *Fells Point* district in an apartment that my partner rented there. Rumor had it that he was running the games from his apartment with topless blackjack dealers and cocktail waitresses turning tricks in his back bedroom. To get into the apartment there was an elaborate B-movie-style entrance up a long dark hallway and two flights of stairs; hence giving rise to saying that one was *"up Sht Creek"* when they visited. Beyond the hallway there were three sets of doors, a man-trap, and to get inside a set of code words that changed daily. Whether the rumor was true or not, was lost forever when my partner and a one-night-stand girlfriend fell asleep in the apartment with cigarettes burning. They set the entire half-block on fire, destroying all the contents of the apartment. He flew to California the next day and I only saw him once again, about 10 years later. A few years after that I heard he had been murdered in Tampa Florida.

I spent the next few years bouncing around various marketing functions in the commercial casino world and eventually ended up running a casino-circus (along the lines of Vegas' Circus-Circus). When the Soviet Union came to a crashing end, the new Russian government began selling-off state assets. Amongst the many things they sold was the 100-year-old state-owned Moscow Circus. Elements of that circus ended up at an entertainment complex in Myrtle Beach South Carolina. I had written a semi-best-selling travel guide about Myrtle Beach[13] and I was co-publishing a magazine touting the Myrtle Beach area as a tourist attraction. The circus, rebranded *"Euro-Circus"* had purchased several full-page advertisements in my magazine. When they defaulted on the advertising payment, I (by virtue of a *printers' lien*) became a partner in the venture.

Above Left: Back cover of *Insider's Guide To Myrtle Beach*. **Above Center Top:** The magazine owned by Gary Green and his father, which resulted in a printer's lien on the circus and Gary's ownership. **Above Center Bottom:** Television and stage personality Mickey Finn's promotional material. **Right:** Myrtle Beach newspaper business page article about Gary Green's ownership of the Russian circus.

At some point during that venture piano-playing legend Fred "Mickey" Finn showed up in Myrtle Beach looking for a venue after his shows closed in Vegas and Atlantic City. After giving him a tour of the entertainment venues of this 12-million-tourist-a-year Mecca, he asked me why I didn't have slot machines in my circus. *Duh.*

South Carolina, like most bible-belt states, outlawed gambling, of course; however the State did allow limited video poker machines *"for amusement only"* under certain limited conditions *(more on that —MUCH more— in a later chapter)*. Mickey Finn's idea of running a casino circus may have been very Vegas-esque to the non-gaming world; but it was a natural grey-area-of-the-law fit for Myrtle Beach South Carolina — long recognized as the *"Redneck Rivera of Sin"*.

Shortly after taking one-third interest in the circus, my other two partners disappeared from the scene. One, a septuagenarian, suffered a massive stroke at an airline ticket counter on his way back to Myrtle Beach from his winter home in Vermont. The second partner was a Russian national and well-connected entrepreneur who started from nearly nothing and got rich through connections to the corrupt, but elected, government of Russia during the state's transition to a market-based economy. That partner, like many of the Russian oligarchs, abruptly disappeared during a visit to Moscow during Vladimir Vladimirovich Putin's rise at the end of the Boris Yeltsin administration.

The international intrigue of THAT adventure would, within itself, make for a good adventure novel, but the "bottom line" was that it left me as the sole owner of the circus/casino. With the two partners, I had been merely the marketer of the venture. The older guy had been the showman and the Russian had been the liaison to the Russian performers. Full operation was a little more than I bargained for. Shortly after the Russian's death I was visited by a guy that I can only describe as Russian mobster, offering to buy me out for one-dollar *"and other considerations."* The other considerations, he explained, were that I would not disappear the way my partner in Moscow had done.

Before I could respond to his generous offer (he had given me 24 hours), I was visited by an emissary for Saudi Arabian billionaire arms dealer Adnan Khashoggi who told me that the gun runner had a romantic interest in one of the aerialist in my trapeze act, and Khashoggi wanted to buy the show and move it to Vegas.

The U.S. Department of Justice recommended that I accept the Russian's offer and with a South Carolina a political climate that was likely to outlaw the games soon, I thought it best to accept the Russian "offer" (that I couldn't refuse) rather than choose suicide.

The non-Russian partner had been a showman and producer for more than a half century. Among his many triumphs was the production of several Super Bowl halftime shows and World's Fair main pavilion shows. Before his death, he introduced me to a friend who had partnered with former Louisiana Governor "Fast" Eddie Edwards to produce the 1984 scandal-plagued New Orleans World's Fair. At the time of the demise of my circus this friend was knee-deep in a new extravaganza project in the Philippines.

Philippines Vice President Doy (Salvador Roman Hidalgo) Laurel had a plan for casinos in his country; six years before the anticipated centennial celebration there and 10 years before western investment in Macau casinos. Laurel was planning to leave office and be appointed by incoming President Fidel Ramos as the chairman of the Philippine National Centennial Commission. Fast

Eddie's partner was the developer, ATT and FedEx had signed on has sponsors and plans were underway to create a centennial entertainment complex.

The United States had just closed the naval base at Subic Bay in Olongapo Zambales in the Philippines and the land was under treaty to be returned to the government of the Philippines. Laurel was eyeing a spot for a casino-complex at the huge concrete circle that had been the Navy's southeast Asia radar array. After several trips to Washington to visit the Philippines Embassy and the U.S. State Department I accepted Laurel's invitation to spend a week with him in Manila.

The casino was to be owned and operated by the Philippine Amusement and Gaming Corporation (PAGCOR), a government monopoly that had been created by President/dictator Ferdinand Marcos. Ostensibly Laurel was looking for American casino expertise to develop the project for the seemingly haplessly managed PAGCOR. However after a few days of meetings in Laurel's office, at the hotel, and at the Subic location, it became clear that the Vice President was actually looking for an underwriter to fund the project. At that time I did not have access to that level of funding —and not a lot of interest in gaming in the Philippines. I returned to the United States after thanking Doy Laurel for his offer, but passing.

As a diversion I had been exploring the new communications medium, the Internet. Before the circus adventure, as a personal friend of then-United States Senator, Al Gore, I had read his 1991 *High Performance Computing and Communication Act* and thought there might be some future marketing potential there. By 1993 I was an early user of Marc Andreessen's Mosaic web browser and created one of the first few web pages. By 1996, I had created early advertisements and ticket sales for my circus using America on Line (AOL) and the early internet.

Pursuing a plan to sell merchandise on-line through a software development company, I called some old friends in the IT department of Mirage Resorts in Vegas. I asked for an audience with them to pitch an "online store" to sell casino chotskies around the world. In the midst of presentation, which for the time was pretty technical, Steve Wynn walked into the room with two large dogs at his sides. My host told me to continue and everyone in the room, though visibly tense, continued to take notes as if their CEO had not walked into the room. In the midst of my babbling some technical jargon, Wynn spoke, *"Well that's all good but what-the-hell can you do about my player tracking problem?"*

Wynn explained his problem like this: He had high-roller customers staying at and playing at the Mirage Resort. These players were "rated players" and entitled to thousands of dollars in comps from the casino. They would occasionally wander next door to his other property, Treasure Island. They were, of course, sophisticated enough to know that Wynn owned both properties. They had a players club card that was good at the Mirage but at the Treasure Island the card did not work. The pit bosses could not see player history and the card did not work in the slot machines...even identical machines. The player tracking com-

135

puter systems at the two properties were two different systems and could not communicate with each other; even if they had been the same brand on the same kind of servers, none of the systems had a method to communicate with each other.

Today that is a "no brainer" issue but in the mid-1990s it was a major issue; though not so much for an Internet company that relied on client-server computing. *"Nonsense,"* I blurted. *"I can solve this in 15 seconds."* I pulled the paper napkin I had been using as a coaster out from under a water bottle and quickly sketched a solution using ASCII message files and constantly updating the two systems every minute or so via internet protocol. I tossed the napkin toward Wynn, who did not move nor reach for it. Instead, the IT manager looked at it, looked at me, and then turned to Wynn. *"This guy just saved us a hundred thousand,"* he told Wynn. (I suspect it was closer to millions.)

Shit. I should have sold it to them. I quickly learned my lesson. I arranged meetings with Harrah's and with Mandalay Resort Group. The other two large multi-property operators on the Strip refused to meet with me: MGM and Park Place Entertainment. I quickly learned that the buzzword in casino marketing and management circles was "a one-card" system; a players club card that players could use at all the properties of a particular operator. Wynn only had two properties; the other operators had lots of properties and the problem was magnified exponentially.

I detailed my napkin-sketched solution in a patent application and added an element to automatically sort the player tracking data the same way that catalog companies had sorted customer data for years. In addition to filling out the patent application, I self-published that little 100-page dissertation booklet outlining the solution; the booklet that had gotten me on the speaking stage with Schaeffer and the big boys at the trade shows like the *American Gaming Summit* in Las Vegas (the forerunner of G2E) and a serious of industry-media interviews.

Above Left: Yahoo Finance announcement of the pending patent of Gary Green's casino management system. **Above Right**: the cover of Gary's booklet outlining the methodology.

136

Wynn immediately implemented my "one-card" strategy and began serving their customers better. Harrah's decided that their communication issue could be resolved using their old Holiday Inns reservation system with dedicated phone lines from each of the property transmitting data overnight (not real time) to and from their data servers in Memphis Tennessee (the former headquarters of Holiday Inns). Park Place continually refused to talk with me even though the gaming analyst at their investment bank insisted that their CFO read my booklet. MGM never returned my calls and at a trade show their CEO, Terry Lanni, told me that MGM had no interest in a system that would share player point liabilities between properties. Mandalay Resort Group continued to bring me back again and again as they struggled to created their one-card solution.

But the real interest came from Las Vegas pioneer Bill Bennett. Bennett was the leader of the 1980s and 1990s push to make Las Vegas a "family attraction." His *Circus-Circus* expanded to create the Egyptian-themed *Luxor*, the Camelot-themed *Excalibur*, and then the luxury *Mandalay Bay*. He expanded to other cities, rebranded his company as *Mandalay Resort Group*, and took the company public launching a post-Wynn love-affair between Wall Street and the casino industry. He acquired Gold Strike Resorts and brought that company's executives into the leadership of the Mandalay; that group included Glenn Schaeffer (who I had debated over hotel ADR) and Michael Ensign (father of now-disgraced United States Senator John Ensign. The history of Circus-Circus and its madman founder Jay Sarno is a book-length adventure story, but Bill Bennett's chapters ended when Ensign, Schaeffer, and their younger generation of operators forced him to resign.

He sold his stock and purchased the legendary Sahara Hotel Casino at the north end of the Strip. The Sahara, in 1952, had been the fifth casino to open on the Strip. Among many distinctions, it was the home of the Jerry Lewis Labor Day telethon for decades.

Shortly after he bought the Sahara, Bennett wrote to me about the advances Harrah's had made in database management and how those advances might differ from my methodology. He wanted in:

"I don't know if you have a copy of Harrah's last annual report...I understand they are not doing very well. I am interested in having something similar to Harrah's (database). If it is as good as you have stated, I can contact three or four more friends of mine who have casinos. I merely tell you this so that you will know the potential of doing business with us."

Until his death in December of 2002, Bill Bennett mentored, guided, trained, and directed my development as a casino marketer and operator. More than anyone else or any other company, he influenced my marketing systems.

We often fought loudly and bitterly over the issue of bringing families to Las Vegas; I hated the idea. He eventually admitted that he had gone that direction *only* because the one casino that he could get his hands on was Circus-Circus and mere ownership of that property doomed him to that demographic. Despite that acknowledged concession, his arguments could be vicious, loud, and at times ash-try-throwing violent. But his arguments were also informative, revealing, and provided hours and hours of personalized Las Vegas history and casino operating and marketing tips.

When he entered the casino industry he was a furniture salesman who worked as a casino host. By the time I knew him, *Forbes Magazine* estimated his net worth at $600 million, naming him one of the 400 richest Americans at the time.

After hours, days, and months of direction, guidance, and conversations, on April 16 of 2002, he wrote to me:

> "Unfortunately, I fell down a small mountain and lost my left leg half way between the knee and foot and lost one half of my right foot. I have been trying to learn how to walk again, and I am sure I'll get it done some day."

On June 2, Mister Bennett wrote me again to tell me that he had given up trying to recover:

> "I am going to UCLA tomorrow, as they specialize in the type of ailment that I have. I am sorry to have to tell you this, but, under the circumstances, I don't see that I can do anything more, unless UCLA comes up with a way to cure my problems."

Those "problems", actually tied to alcoholism and related illnesses, resulted in his death in another few months at 78. He died almost exactly a month after the death of his friend Ralph Engelstad, owner of the Imperial Palace Casino.

Following Bill Bennett's death, I continued to hone my marketing system and teamed with technologist Tom Trimble to fully automate it to a module that could augment any player tracking system and continued to offer the methodology to Indian casinos from Washington State to California to Oklahoma. It was one of those pitches that ultimately brought me to Trump29 casino.

Meanwhile, lest anyone think I retired from being a casino *player* after my encounter with the two goons at *The Sands* in Atlantic City, I continued to play at casinos (where I was not licensed) and continued to play in the World Series of Poker *(until it started getting thousands of amateurs playing in it and then I moved to the side games).* Look beside you at your next blackjack table; I may be there...you never know.

Above: One of Gary Green's World Series of Poker registration tickets.

"Jed, only one man in a hundred plays poker by the odds. Luck's only important when you sit down with men who play as tight as you do. When I find that out, I quit. It's gambling." — **James Garner as Bret Maverick, 1957**

138

Chapter Ten

Can You Beat These Damned Machines?

"I ain't sayin' I beat the devil, but I drank his beer for
nothing. Then I stole his song."

— **Kris Kristofferson**

As much as I would like it otherwise, the truth is that the house does NOT always win; you (the player) actually can beat the house. Really. Larry showed it...remember? The damned random number generator on the tic-tac-toe playing chickens showed it with the visiting nurse and with Trump himself; random number generators ARE random. I see it all the time at casinos all over the country.

It *is* true that in the long run, mathematically, the house always wins. But as we have seen, the "short term" can last a really long time. Remember, when I first met Mark Lefever, his blackjack tables had been on an 11-month long losing streak?

When I talked about the definition of gambling I noted that if the house loses for a long a period of time, then players are beating the house for that long. So, at least in that "short" term, it very clearly *IS* possible to make money by beating the house.

What about those huge-payout wide-area-progressive (WAP) slot machines; gambling or entertainment? Before you rush out and start pumping money into those progressive slot machines, let me tell you that the chances of winning these things are...well... let's say not real favorable to the player. Your chances of winning the IGT MegaBucks® jackpot is around 50-million to one; your chances of winning an average Nevada "linked progressive" is about 16,777,000 to one. By comparison, according to the National Oceanic and Atmospheric Administration, your chances of getting hit by lightning are one in 280,000 in any given year or one in 3000 over your lifetime. You are a lot more likely to get hit by lightning than you are to win that huge progressive. According to the National Transportation Safety Board you have a 1 in 7.6-million chance of dying in car accident; better than twice your chances of winning an average WAP. So, don't bet your mortgage payment on hitting the wide area progressive. And even if you DID win, the payout is usually over a 20 year period; not all at once.

Still, the casino operator in me has to tell you: you can't win unless you play the game and it is a small bet for a huge payoff. *That is why they call it gambling.*

The other issue we have to address before we can talk about winning against the casino is the entire collection of myths concerning the layout of a typical casino floor (though no slot floor is typical). These casino myths are more about great psychological manipulations using floor layout by some devious evil-genus of behavioral science and architecture. *Who the hell ever heard of someone being both an architect and a psychologist and how do I advertise in the paper to hire someone for that job?*

Actually, in most new casinos (outside of the Vegas strip or the Atlantic City boardwalk) here is how floor configuration works: The casino manager gets a copy of the architect's "as built" floor plan of the room where the slot machines are to be placed. He sends that floor plan, with the specific measurements of walls and electric supply, to a slot machine manufacture; usually IGT or Bally. Someone at those companies has a Computer Aided Design (CAD) program. They are given the instructions that "this casino wants to fit 800 machines in this room; find the best way to do it." Thus is born the general layout of the typical casino floor.

In some small casinos, it is often even more absurd; machines are just fit in anywhere they can be stuck; that is why they look like giant warehouses of rows of slot machines. I even know of several cases where vendors gave casino bosses substantial kickbacks to put their machines in high-traffic areas (usually when slot machine companies are sharing machine daily revenue with the casinos). The kickback ... er ... I mean "placement fee"...to the casino or slot managers is offered in much the same way soft drink companies pay fees for shelf space at the grocery store. The slot machine vendor then makes up for the kickback by charging the casino more (a higher percentage revenue share) for the machines.

"Revenue share" or "participation" is a euphemism for ways that slot machine companies lease games rather than sell them to the casinos. An understanding of rev-share vs. purchase is important to players because it can be a clue to a machine's hold...leased games are sometimes worse for the player (though not always).

Casinos obtain slot machines one of two ways: they can purchase them or lease them. The purchase price of a new slot machine (as of this writing) ranges from about $7,500 to about $18,000, depending on the manufacture, the features, popularity and the theme of the machine. With a purchase, there is a separate annual contract for upgrades and maintenance. And, if a specific game does not perform well on the casino floor, there is an additional fee to change the game to another title or theme. By contrast, the cost of leasing a slot machine is generally based on a percentage of the revenue that a machine generates (or a flat daily fee, loosely based on revenue).

Revenue, for this calculation, is certainly not *coin-in* or *drop* but, rather, is based on win (cash drop minus payouts). Typically a revenue share is structured so that the casino keeps 80% of the revenue and the slot vendor keeps 20%. These revenue share deals can be couched as revenue share or as leases or as lease-to-purchase or any number of other catchy phrases for sharing the income.

Depending on the clout of the casino and the popularity of the slot machine (and the vendor), that percentage split can be as low as 85% & 15% or as high 62½ % & 37½%. Most contracts fall in between those extremes with the 80% and 20% being typical.

Think about the math. If the average win per machine per day is $100, then the slot machine company gets $20. Multiply that time 365 days and the slot machine vendor gets $7,300; multiply that by a typical three year contract, and the vendor collects $21,900 for the game that cost them $7,500 to $18,000. More interestingly, if the game is on a "rev-share" at a high-grossing casino (like Hard Rock in South Florida, or Cherokee in North Carolina, or dozens of other highly successful casinos around the country), then the games are winning around $350 per machine per day or an annual take of $25,550 for the slot machine company or $76,650 over three years for their machine.

Now double those top-end numbers. The Indian Gaming Regulatory act prohibits Tribes from entering into rev shares of seven years or longer; so many vendors lease to Tribal casinos for six years and eleven months! (At $350 win per machine per day, that is a take of $176,721 per machine over the term of the lease; or $17.6-million for every 100 slot machines—as just the vendor's share!)

Not bad. In fact, I often pitch investors by asking *"What is better than owning a casino? Owning the slot machines inside the casino!"*

In those lease arrangements, it is in the interest of the manufacturer to provide games that have a higher hold for the casino (a lower payout) so their 20% is a higher actual dollar amount (giving a higher win per unit per day). Especially in smaller casinos that hold is totally controlled by the manufacturer rather than by the casino. Hence in those cases, the smaller casinos, it really is beneficial for the player to know if the casino owns the games or if they are on a revenue share basis. *(More on that when we talk about "Class II" games.)*

Some slot titles are not for sale at all and can only be obtained through revenue share agreements. These titles, generally, are ones that are either extremely popular or have third-party proprietary themes. The immensely popular *Wheel of Fortune* machine, for example, is not for sale; IGT has to pay a royalty —a percentage of each win— to Merv Griffin Enterprises, which owns the rights to *Wheel of Fortune.*

There are also a number of third-party companies that do not manufacture slot machines but only purchase them and lease them to casinos under a revenue share plan. Many of these third party companies will also loan casinos (especially Indian casinos) money to build or expand. The loans then are repaid by increasing the revenue share (say, up from 20% to 37½%). With those deals the additional percentage does not go down once the loan is paid off; they are in perpetuity (for the term of the lease).

Regardless of kickback or loan schemes and the higher hold of leased machines, there is still an entire collection of myths concerning the layout of a typical slot floor (though, as I said, no slot floor is typical). Generally these myths are specific to how we place loose or tight machines on the slot floor. I have heard from players or read (as supposedly factual information from "experts" and web sites). Let's look at some of these myths. In advance, I want to thank several web sites and "tip books" from Amazon.com for providing me these myths as supposed "tips" of "how to win" against slot machines. *What bullshit!*

SLOT MACHINE MYTHOLOGY 101:

1. Machines with a car sitting on top of them or a high progressive jackpot are placed in high traffic areas. Nope. Some people do it; some do not. It is not a hard and fast rule and you should make no decisions about play based on any supposition about it. My Ford Mustang giveaway at the Trump property was stashed away in a corner of the casino that had almost no traffic except during showroom nights once a month. *(By the way, as an aside, it took three years for anyone to win that car; then it was won three times in one week. Damned random number generators and Bunky's chickens.)*

2. New machines with higher holds are always placed in high traffic areas. Not even true. Sometimes we place new machines in low traffic areas to drive traffic back to them; sometimes we put them in high traffic areas because we want to replace machines that are already in those areas. There is no rule; and new machines don't necessarily have higher holds.

3. Dollar and Five-Dollar machines are always near the table games. Nope. In fact many casinos put those games in special areas for "high limit" slot players. They are usually nowhere near the game pits. One casino in Southern California even puts their $5 games in a special room that only club members who have reached a certain level of play may enter. The general public could not play them even if they wanted to.

4. The best payout machines are put in areas obnoxious to players (like at bathroom entrances, near concert halls, near smelly food courts, or where people are standing in line to attend some other attraction). This is supposed to discourage play on the good machines. I have to ask, why would I want to discourage play on any machine I put on my floor? If wanted to discourage play, I would just take the machine out. There is fierce competition amongst vendors for my floor space and I put games on my floor based on how much they will win per day[based on lots of play.

5. The most popular machines are set near the entrance to the casino so passersby can see people playing and be encouraged that there must be "loose" machines there. A little contradictory to the previous myth, but most myths are a series of contradictions. With the exception of clusters along the boardwalk in Atlantic City or Fremont Street in Vegas or State Street in Reno, I can't think of any areas where the casino floor is visible to a lot of foot traffic. In fact, once I have someone in my casino, getting them to play the machines is not really the issue; I am more interested in how

long they play and how many coins they play...and bringing them back.

6. TV themed machines pay off better near entertainment halls, video poker machines pay off better near a poker room, keno machines pay off better near the keno parlor. No.

7. Better paying machines are put near the table games pit so as to create an atmosphere of excitement around the table games; and

8. Worse paying machines are put near the table games pit because the people who play near table games are hanger-ons who come to the casino to wait on the person at the table. These games will keep them busy while the "real" gambler plays at the tables.

No to both #7 and #8. Besides being mutually exclusive, both are silly. As for the latter, in the 1950s and 1960s slot machines were considered amenities sometimes thought to be only for "girlfriends and wives" of "real gamblers" that played at the tables. The boyfriends and husbands could keep an eye on the girls without being bothered during their supposedly serious gambling. As I said, some casino managers subscribed to that strategy; but that was before slot machines were responsible for most of the revenue of the hall. As for the former assertion, I feel like there is excitement enough around table game pits with craps players yelling like Irish Banshees every time they get a pass.

9. The loosest machines are in busy parts of the casino to give an illusion of lots of casino activity. This is another one of those myths that I scratch my head about and say "Duh." If an area of the casino is busy, it is probably because the loosest machines are there, not the other way around. The area was not automatically crowded with players at tight machines and a casino boss one day said "Gee, lots of people are already playing there on our best machines, so let's put our worst machines there so everybody will be excited." *Yeah right.*

10. Loose machines are at the beginning and end of traffic patterns but not in the middle. Just not true. There is no universal strategy or rule about where to put tight or loose machines. Everyone does it differently.

11. Loose machines are placed on elevated carousels so they can be seen; and

12. Loose machines are placed near the diner or restaurant so people will hurry and finish eating and get back to playing; and

13. Loose machines are near the cashier cage so people waiting in line can see more winners and be encouraged to play more.

In answer to numbers 10, 11, 12, and 13 above: a resounding Bah Humbug.

What one slot manager may choose to do does not make it a universal rule. There are no universal rules for placing slot machines. Most slot managers lack the knowledge or lack the willingness to get that complicated. The good slot managers have more important things to think about. Ultimately the casino always wins; it is a function of arithmetic. The slot manager needs to get people to play all of his machines, so the issue of where the "good" ones are is far less important to him than it is to players.

14. Casino managers spend hours and hours with human behavior studies to plot where to place machines. Nope. Outside of mega-casinos, placement of machines at most smaller casinos is at best haphazard; as noted, at some casinos it is based on floor plans manufacturers provide.

15. Casinos pump 100% pure oxygen into the slot floor to keep you awake all night, playing the machines.

I love the work of author Mario Puzo; like many of my generation I can quote long passages from *The Godfather* verbatim. Hell, I have quoted him repeatedly in this book. His book *Fools Die* is one of the best Vegas novels I have ever read. However, despite my respect and affection for him, his creation (or at least perpetuation) of this myth is just silly. Firstly and foremost, do you have any idea how flammable the casino would be if pure oxygen was pumped onto all those cigarette smokers? Remember rockets launch burning pure oxygen. Jeeze. Now what IS true is that many casinos do pump scented air freshener through the air condition systems. While there is an aromatherapy science of what scents make people more alert, think more clearly, or put them to sleep, the actual reasons for these air fresheners are much less dubious: Casinos are places where people smoke constantly, stay for long periods of times without baths, and drink and eat god-knows-what. Without a little air freshener, they would seriously stink. And I should note that there are a couple of companies pitching pheromone technology to casino to modify behavior; but as of this writing I know of no evidence it works or any company actually doing it.

The single most important thing that I can tell you about slot machine floor layout myths is to forget everything you have ever heard and forget every "feeling" you have about machines. To this day I will tell people facts about machines, based on my years of experience with them, and they will still respond, *"Yes I know that, but my neighbor always plays the third machine from the end in every casino she goes to and she wins all the time."*

The problem with these, and most, gambling myths is that a few coincidences seem to give credence to them. It is a lot like the millions of people who follow the daily newspaper for astrology tips on how to live their lives. In fact, the very behavior that gives rise to these myths is the behavior that the slot machine business depends on to exist.

The psychologists who follow the works of the late B.F. Skinner (and others of the "behaviorist" school) have learned that "intermittent reinforcement" is a more powerful behavior modifier than constant reinforcement. In English, that means that if you push the button on a slot machine 100 times and one of those times you get a big payout, you will be psychologically encouraged to push the button 100 more times; as opposed to pushing it every time and getting a small payout every push, which would become boring very fast. That theory of gaming, watched by manufacturers of games, is about as complex as we get.

Except for marketing gimmicks (like "up to 95% payback" signs), slot managers tend to set all the machines of a like denomination and of like platform with the same hold. If you come on a bank of eight or 16 machines that are all the same theme and same denomination, most likely every machine in the bank will have the same payout. It is very rare that a slot manager bothers to deviate from that; it is too complicated to keep up with; especially in smaller casinos. This, of course, is ever-changing as technology advances.

However, there are some facts (in contrast to myths) about floor placement that you do need to know; these facts are based on a number of independent tests and tracked play:

- Bright signage over banks of machines tends to get customers to play the machines more, regardless of the machine's payout.
- Machines that can easily been seen across the floor are played more often, regardless of their payout.
- The higher the ceiling from the top of the machine, the more the machine is played, again regardless of payout.
- The taller the machine, the more the machine is played.
- Floors that are designed as "warehouses" of long rows of slot machines tend to get less play than floor layouts of individual little "cubbies" of slot machines that encourage exploration or direct traffic patterns. However, the cubbies have to be open enough so that players can see other machines.
- Slot machines that are near the table games pit do get more play, regardless of their hold.
- The attractiveness of cocktail servers has been shown in repeated academic studies to increase the level of play of both sexes (regardless of the seeming sexism of the assertion).
- Brighter lighting, better air circulation (pulling smoke away, even from smokers), and cooler air temperature all cause more play on the machines.

This information, and a ton of other data and scientific studies, are available to most slot directors, casino managers, and operators. But the sad truth is that few have the time or patience to use this kind of information. Remember, in most casinos, a manufacturer designs the floor layout and the slot manager orders all the machines to pay out the exact same as all the other machines of a particular style, theme, and denomination.

So is it real or is it Memorex®; is it gambling or is it entertainment? Is it myth or is it reality? Can you beat the casinos?

Several years ago, I hired a very young guy to be a shift manager at my players' club. He was totally inexperienced in casinos, had some minor sales experience, had played some college-buddy poker games, but had a great attitude and incredible customer service skills. Somehow I just sensed he was "one of us"; and he wanted to put *professional gambler* on *his* resume. He did indeed excel at the job and was soon promoted through the ranks.

One night, when he was on duty, he overheard that Steve Sohng, Mark Lefever, and I were going to play at a nearby competing casino. He began asking me about the games at that casino; he was looking for tips for winning. Though the hold on the games at that casino was (at the time) pretty good (from the player standpoint) I was not certain that I wanted to encourage him to drop his paycheck into slot machines.

In the industry, those PAR sheets, the actual payout percentage of my machines, your odds at hitting one of the huge progressive jackpots, floor layout strategies, and the location of my best-paying machines are all considered *proprietary* information. I know many casino operators that have fired staff for even *hinting* to players at these "secrets". For the record, I think that all the secrecy is absurd and *wrong-wrong-wrong*; and I also think that those columnists and writers (like the great John Robison and others) who teach about these machines are *right-right-right* in doing so. Hell if it was up to me, I would print everyone's par sheets right here; many are on the internet anyway.

As I have pointed out repeatedly, mathematically and in the long run, *slot machines always win*; THAT is how we build multi-million (and now billion) dollar casinos. Casinos are not built on winners; they are built from the profits from losers. Not to sound like a *Star Trek* character or like *Sheldon Cooper* discussing *Heisenberg's uncertainty principle of quantum fluctuation*, but ... in the short term, just like with those damned Bunky Boger chickens, that random number generator is totally unpredictable. And, that of course, is why people keep playing the machines.

See, here is the thing: if I have a slot that has an 8½% hold (paying out 91½%) a really uninformed player can change my hold to three or more times that; paying out closer to 70% instead of the 91½%. That is because with many slot manufactures, that *hold percentage* is based on playing "full coin-in" (meaning, maximum number of lines with the maximum bet per line). In other words, on a penny machine that typical 8½% hold is based on playing 25 lines at up to 18-cents per line. Thus a "penny" slot machine is actually a $4.50 slot machine. In order to get that 8½% hold, each bet would have to be $4.50. However if you bet only one line (instead of 25) and just one cent (instead of 450-cents)

146

then the hold is entirely different. I have one group of machines where that hold climbs to 27½% if you play just one penny at a time. *I love uninformed players.*

For one manufacturer of an especially fun line of slot machines, I personally designed their math pay tables (the frequency and volatility). Since I designed the math, my first thought is to include those par sheets here; but they *are* the proprietary intellectual property of that company and not really mine anymore. Nonetheless, take my word for it; planning pay schemes IS a science.

In slot machine pop literature, the really good writers generally offer very legitimate insight and tips that serve to answer a lot of the mythology about slot machines. More importantly, for players, while the machines cannot be "beaten", following the legitimate tips from legitimate experts (as opposed to con men peddling "systems") can at least give a player chance of losing less.

I decided to have a little fun with that hungry-for-action new-hire and share with him some basic industry information that would seem to the less-informed to be valuable "inside information" that I was offering. So, I gave the young plebe a check list of a thirteen "insider secrets" to slot play:

Gary Green's Bakers' Dozen Slot Tips for the New Hire

1. The most popular slot machine in the country is the IGT-manufactured **Wheel of Fortune**[*] machine. It comes in a variety of styles, denominations, and even generations of the machine. Walk into to your favorite casino and find an old-style *Wheel of Fortune* slot machine; not one of the newer ones, but one of the older reel-type in an aging, fat, dirty, black cabinet. *(A reel machine has physical reels instead of a video screen. The older reel machines can be spotted by their dirtier, slightly-beat-up reels instead of the translucent new reels that light up from behind.)* Wait until you see one on which someone has just hit a *"Spin The Wheel"* bonus jackpot and walked away. People often walk away right after they hit a bonus round because they, mistakenly, believe that another bonus is not "due". Generally and usually, this is totally untrue; but due to some really bad programming, there is occasionally an exception. Sit down at that machine and play *minimum* coin-in (usually a quarter) for 40 spins. At the most it will cost you $10 (if you lose on every spin), but it will probably not even cost you that because you will win a few mini-payouts along the way. Beginning with the 40th spin of the reels, play the maximum number of coins (three coins are required on those old machines in order to trigger a bonus round). Here is the "big secret": on those older machines, the *"Spin The Wheel"* bonus was set to pay off between every 40 and 50 spins ... consistently; no random number generators, no few-million spins. The bonus round was triggered between 40 and 50 spins. Period. With the required maximum bet in place, you will spin the wheel and win more money than you started with. Cash out. Walk away. The end; you just beat the house. You may not win the top payout, but you will trigger the bonus round and win a minimum of 25 coins ($6.25 on those old quarter machines) and you will be ahead of where you started.

If you don't walk away, you have another 40 spins to wait and there is always the chance that in those 40 spins you will lose the whole $10 it takes to spin 40 times...thus putting you in the hole. Walk away after the bonus round. You won.

Short of this flaw, the *Wheel of Fortune* machine generally holds 15.486%; a miserable payout for the player. Moreover, your chance of winning the "top" jackpot is one in 15,728,640 and despite the player's "hope" of hitting on any of the multiple lines, it is available only on the 400th coin and the 1st line. For the player, despite its popularity, the game sucks.

2. **Choose where you play wisely.** On the average, slot machines in Las Vegas pay off twice as well as slot machines in Mississippi (Tunica, Biloxi, and Gulfport). Vegas machines pay off up to three times better than the machines at Foxwoods and some of the other Indian casinos and 20% better than Colorado. Vegas machines pay off about 60% better than most riverboat casinos. And we won't even talk about how poorly the captive-audience cruise ships pay! Additionally, in Vegas, *(as we have seen in earlier chart)* the suburbs in North Las Vegas payout better than Fremont Street (downtown) which in turn pays out better than the Strip[14]. This is all based on public record; not mythology.

3. Look for a *"Jacks or Better"* **video poker** machine and examine the posted payoff table for the machine; this is usually printed on the glass at the top of the machine above the video screen or on the screen itself. Look in the column for "one coin" and the lines for *Full House* and for *Flush*. Ignore the rest of the payout table. Most machines will indicate that Full House pays 8 coins (or credits) and Flush pays 5 credits. In the business we call that an 8/5 machine. Avoid those machines. Look for a 10/7 machine: Full House pays 10 coins and Flush pays 7 coins. When you find a 10/7 machine, there is a negative house advantage; the pay table is set in favor of the player and not in favor of the house. *The closer that ratio is to 10/7, the better your odds.* It does not matter (at this point "why"...just believe me. Most likely the best you will find will be a 9/6 machine. Play it.

However, understand that even playing that kind of machine, to get a positive return consistently you need to play nearly perfect strategy...which at times definitely flies in the face of what would seem to be common sense. Nonetheless it is not SO difficult to learn. The very best training aid I have ever seen is a software program created by Video Poker genius Bob Dancer: *Video Poker For Winners*. I have no affiliation whatsoever with it or with him; but I will tell you that it absolutely is THE tool to learn to make money at video poker. His books are great too, but his software is phenomenal.

4. If you find yourself in an **Indian Casino**, ask any employee if the slot ma-

148

chines are "Bingo Machines" (also known as "Class II" machines). If they are "Class II" then the payout is most always set by the manufacturer of the machine who shares in the revenue with the Indian Tribe. These machines, generally speaking, are much less favorable to the player than standard slot machines (or "Class III" machines). Avoid playing the Bingo Machines altogether if you can. *Play only the Class III machines in an Indian casino.* There are a couple of exceptions to this...but they are rare.

5. If your only casino choice is an Indian casino that only has **Bingo Machines** (some in Florida, some in Oklahoma, Texas, Alabama, Washington State, New York, and a handful of others as of this writing), then look closely at each machine and see the copyright © notice printed on the glass plate at the front of the machine. The copyright notice will tell you the name of the company that manufactured the machine (and thus the company that set the payout). In Bingo Machines, as of this writing two companies set their payouts more favorable to players than the other companies: VGT and AGS. Look for their branded machines (*Red Hot Ruby, Mr. Money Bags, Gems & Jewels, Star Spangled Sevens*, and a handful of others for VGT; *Royal Reels, Liberty Sevens, and The Mouse Game*, for AGS). The VGT *Mr. Money Bags* machines at the $5 denomination with maximum coin-in ($15 per spin) have an amazingly high payout level; probably the best I have seen at Class II casinos. If you can handle a couple of hundred dollars loss, the payouts are really good on this machine. In fact, their Money Bags and Red Hot Ruby mechanical reels, M-1 series holds only 2.33% with three credits ($15) paid and only 2.85% with one credit played; their M-2 series games at $5 pay out 98.1% (holding only 1.90%). Any way you slice it, that is an amazing player-favored payout scheme.

6. Look for IGT's *Megabucks Jackpot* slot machines. When you find them, **run the other direction**. They are historically the worst payout of any slot machine in America. They get away with it because they also have the *highest* payoff for the smallest bets. For a $3 bet you *could* win millions of dollars...*potentially*. But in the short term, you will lose more on those machines than on any other machines. The IGT Megabucks machines account for about 20% of the revenue of Las Vegas casinos, yet they account for a relative tiny percentage of number of games on the floor.

7. **Look for multi-denomination** slot machines. These are machines where you choose to play either 1-cent, 5-cents, a quarter, a dollar, or even $5. Two rules about these machines: (a) they historically payout better than any other machines and (b) the higher denomination you play on these machines, the better the payback[15].

8. **Look for branded games**; slot machines themes with a TV show, a movie, a celebrity, or some other pop culture icon. These themes are licensed by the manufacturers and the casino has to pay a license fee (and often shared revenue) to the person or company that owns the theme. That

makes these machines more expensive for the casino to operate than non-themed machines. While the themed machines are by far the best entertainment, the extra cost for the machines is passed along to the player as the lowest payout. That fact disappoints even me; as a player my favorites over the years have included the *Elvis, Regis Philbin, Price Is Right, Sinatra,* and *Beverly Hillbillies* machines. I loved them for entertainment value and at times even felt it was worth the few extra percentage points in payout just to go through the entertainment bonus rounds on those machines. But the fact is somebody has to pay the royalties on those machines; that someone is always the player who gets a worse payout.

9. **Look for signs** above groups of machines that advertise high payback; but this is a little tricky. If a sign says something like "up to 95% payback" then you definitely do not want to play the machines; the trick is in the phrase *"up to."* In casino operators' minds, that language actually means that (at least) one of the machines in the group pays back that much; the rest of the machines under the sign could payback some terrible amount. Despite my earlier explanation of how difficult it is to switch up a bank of machines, it is relatively easy to have one or two high-paying machines mixed in with a bank of "regular" machines. The correct language is just a reference to the payback percentage without *"up to"* or *"some machines"* or similar wording. Actually, in Nevada and in New Jersey there are legal restrictions on the use of such wording on signs. If the signs say "95% payback" (without the additional words) then every machine in that group must have that payback level. *(Though remember our earlier discussion, though, about volatility.)* Look for signs that payback 96% to 99%. You have a better chance of winning those machines. *(This supposed strategy of having just one machine in a bank that pays out at that level is very "old school" thinking and most casinos are getting away from it.)* However, be aware that even with such a high payout, the frequency/volatility issue is still there: if a game pays out 99% it could pay out nothing for the first $100,000 played through it and then suddenly pay out $99,000 to one person OR there are thousands of math schemes that allow that payout percentage without giving you the frequency. Be careful.

10. **Look for busy banks** (rows) of machines and watch the players at them. Usually banks of machines are busy because the regular (frequent) players know the machines payout well. *This is not always the case, and there are times that I have used all sorts of deceptions to give players the illusion that machines payout better than they actually do.* However, in general, local regular players know which machines payout the best. Walk through the casino and see which banks of machines seem very busy. Before you start playing in one of those banks of machine, stand behind a few machines and watch the players. If the machines seem to be paying out pretty frequently, then chances are the locals have spotted the best

machines in the casino (and have not been duped by some marketing guru like me).

11. **Players' Club Cards.** The first thing I do when I go to a new casino is join the players' club. At this writing, a number of Las Vegas give you $10 in free play just for joining the club. At very least, in almost any club, you earn points that are good for cash back and all sorts of freebies. While using a club card has absolutely no impact whatsoever on your play, the freebies have a cash value that clearly offsets some of the losses you may have. Consider the $10 just for joining. Let's say you are playing a 25-cent machine with the maximum number of coins you can play at a time being three (75-cents). You put in a $10 bill and spin six times, losing each time; this has your bankroll down to $4.50. On the 7th spin you win $2.50, getting your bankroll back up to $7. That means you have lost 30% of your starting money. But if you include the $10 in free play that the casino gave you, then rather than minus 30%, you are up positive 70%. Even if you are playing dollar machines instead of quarter machines, the benefits of players clubs actually increase the value of your play. When I joined the club at the *Aladdin* (now called *Planet Hollywood*) in Las Vegas, there was no cash bonus but my 45 minutes of play on $1 video poker machines brought me a buffet for two (valued at almost $40), a free jacket ($20), a hat (2.50), and a few other trinkets. All in all, they rewarded my 45-minutes of play with about $65 in value. Join the players' clubs; there is no negative impact on the machines and there are plenty of positives that help make you a winner.

In the larger sense, if you find a game that pays 98% and a players club that gives you a 3% rebate cash back (or comps) then from the get-go you are already at 101% of what you gamble. Lots of casino glitter-houses were built on margins as small as 1%. And, on top of that, you contribute to that magical database that I have talked about.

Additionally, in late 2012 based on slot play I was comped 4 nights at four different hotels in Las Vegas. Based on average rack rate for those rooms, the equivalent cash value of those 16 nights was a total of $1,842. Since that money would have come from my gambling budget, we can count that as a "win". That means that if I played the slots and lost $500, I would still be "up" more than $1,300 because I didn't have to pay for the rooms. JOIN THE PLAYERS CLUBS!

12. **Tom's Rule.** When my friend Tom Trimble (the brilliant technologist who at one time designed slot machines for one of the largest manufacturers and designed systems for a mid-level manufacture) was leading design teams to create new slot machine games he had a rule for his guys: *if a player puts a $20-bill into a machine and the play on that twenty dollars does not initiate at least one bonus round, then the game sucks and should not be produced.* Actually, as Tom explains it, his $20 rule was used by his development team to determine any possible play problems

with a game, *"Multiple failures normally meant there was a math problem and the bonus frequency had to be lowered. In some cases discussion led to the test being over ruled. I don't think there was ever a real popular game (during my work there) that failed that test, even though several were released."* When visiting a new property *(remember new-age casino executives call casinos "properties")*. Tom and I both always use Tom's Rule as we scope out the machines looking for the good bonus rounds. While it is almost impossible to determine how good (or bad) a machine is based on only a few spins, the *Tom's bonus rule* is still a really good measure. Look for some of the games Tom worked on in varying roles (some were near completion when he arrived): Aristocrat's *One Big Cheese, Pick Pocket, Big Shot, and Looney Sevens*. Also, I insisted on Tom's Rule being applied to the development of games for Synergy Gaming, so on those games look for *Caribbean Island, Desert Nights, Winter Carnival, Miami Heat, M-O-N-E-Y, Platinum Blonde,* and others.

13. **Baker's Dozen Bonus Tip #13.** Look for $1 denomination *Blazing Sevens* branded mechanical reel one-line machines manufactured by Bally and play $3 per spin on them. In setting these machines up, one of the options that slot managers have is a slightly better (for the player) payout than many other slot machine models. Since so many players know about *Blazing Sevens* machines, several manufactures (including Bally themselves) produce knock-offs with similar names. *Accept no substitutes.* Though slot directors don't always exercise this option, in many properties these machines have outstanding payout. Watch other players on the machines *(tip number 10 above)* and see if those machines are crowded.

Extra Tip #14 In Case You Didn't Like Any One Of The Above. The math is a little flawed on certain bonus features on some machines at certain denominations. The flaws are not bad enough that they warrant either taking the machines off the slot floor or even reprogramming them; but they are significant enough that you can exploit them to make a little money...if you walk away immediately after you hit them. For example, IGT's original *Lucky Larry's Lobstermania* in the nickel game video version (only the five-reel 15 line version): when you hit the bonus round there is a disproportionate bonus payout to the number of credits played if you play *one level below maximum coin in*. Maximum coin-in is 75 nickels but if you play at 45 nickels instead (three coins per line instead of five) the bonus feature pays out a little too much and gets you ahead of where you started. When that happens: take your money and walk away. IGT discovered this flaw and on newer *Lucky Larry's* they have corrected it; however the new ones are easy to spot because they have gone to 90-nickels rather than 75. Also from IGT, their five-reel, twenty-line original *Cleopatra* video slot played at the penny denomination with maximum coin-in has a killer bonus round if you can last long enough to trigger it. The nine-line version does not seem to have this issue; and Cleopatra II simply sucks. Almost always the 20-line bonus gets you ahead of where you started, regardless of how long it took you to trigger it. The best we can tell, this only seems to be a problem on the penny machines when you play full coin in ($2 per spin). Even in normal play the 20-line 300-coin game pays out 97.993%; a 2.007% hold compared to that 15% hold of Wheel of Fortune. This is generally speaking a GREAT game for players.

I should point out that computer (and hence slot machine) technology changes constantly and many of these "tips" refer to older games —which, make no mistake about it, are still widely available and dozens of casinos across the country. However, in most modern games many of the mistakes or oversights that caused these seeming flaws in the games have been correct. For example, except for buy-a-pay or multiplies most modern slot machines maintain the same payout (and hold) percentage regardless of the number of credits played.

All of these seeming tips are simple operational facts that we know from the experience of operating these games on various casino floors. Actually, the best tip I could give the young newbie was to walk away as soon as you are ahead of where you started; even if you are only ahead by a few dollars.

Let me tell you something, the guys – *like me* – that run casinos for a living were not usually your high school valedictorians; hell, without spell-check we can't even *spell* valedictorian. We don't have brilliantly-conceived slot machine plots to trick you out of your money and very few of us would know *when* to change the payout on a slot machine even if we knew *how*...and believe me, we don't know how. (Okay, actually I do...but most operators do not...and most have not also been in the slot manufacturing business). So beating us should not be rocket science if you were going one-on-one against most casinos bosses *(which, unlike bad movies or the late Benny Binion, never happens)*.

Of course we rely on the computer and the math to take care of winning, but one more reason that our casinos consistently beat you is that we count on players being absorbed with ignorance, myths, "systems", and (as Nero Wolfe liked to say) *"flummery"*. As long as you cling to the flummery, my casinos (and lots of others) are going to keep making money off of you; but if you know as much (or more) than my staff then you are going to lose less and even beat us more frequently than other players.

I cannot repeat nor emphasize enough to the novice that over a period of time it is mathematically impossible for a casino to lose money on the slot machine floor. But in the short run, a savvy player can spot the most favorable machines and walk away better than average players. And as a casino operator, I don't mind...much.

Slot machines are, without debate, the most simple casino games to play. They also happen to be the most complex to understand. They offer the highest potential payoff for players with the lowest wager of any casino game; where else can you *(possibly)* win tens of millions of dollars for a 75-cent bet? Most importantly for me, slot machines are responsible for more than 80% of my revenue on any given day ... unless a particularly savvy and flummery-liberated player comes into my property. *Remember that bastard, Larry.*

Everyone knows that there are always *some* big winners. Jackpots are so common that we have three-part jackpot "hand pay" forms that slot attendants carry around with them in stacks of 25. Besides, who would come back to a casino if everyone lost?

Remember that payouts are a lot more frequent than the general public thinks. Author and columnist John Robison fielded a letter from a player who complained that he knew "factually" a local Indian casino was only paying out 19% (that would be an 81% hold —*I WISH!*). He ranted on that payouts changed at different times of day, from one tribe to the next, and that such a payout scheme was an outrage and no one should ever play at that casino. Despite a well-thought-out and well-written response by John, I too had to respond to the players' outrage. John was kind enough to print my response in his column:

John:

Saw your column of letters on slot payouts (casino hold). Specifically the person claiming that the casino was holding 81% (or rather "pays 19%" as the person said). The specific casino they cited was the Hard Rock in South Florida...owned by the Seminole Tribe of Florida.

A good part of that floor is filled with IGT Class II (Bingo server) machines. Those machines, unlike standard commercial or Indian Class III machines, do not have a flexible way of controlling the hold. In fact, they have three settings and that is it. The most hold that can be set on those machines is 14% and I don't think ANYONE is doing that.

As you know, of course, a 14% hold means an 86% payout.

As an operator I would LOVE to have machines that hold those absurdly high numbers like 80-something percent HOLD, but we all know that if machines only paid out so poorly, no one would ever play them. The delightful thing for operators is that we don't NEED those huge holds that people imagine. The low-ball industry standard 8.5% is a delightful number that pleases me well.

Finally, as you know, some Class II machines (like those manufactured by VGT and AGS) have manufacturer-set holds and they are as low as 3.5% with the casino (or Tribe) having no control whatsoever. Hence, of course, the perception that times-of-day or even one tribe to the next having "better" payout is pure mythology. But then again, THAT is why I love this business. As long as there are "believers", my machines will keep making money!

Gary Green

And John kindly added, in his column:

As I have said, typically I only keep eight dollars out of every $100 that you gamble in my joint. It takes a lot of hundred-dollars-gambled to build billion dollar hotel casinos. Almost all of the money that you put into a slot machine gets paid back out of the machine to you or to other players. Of course that payout may come after you put in five $20-bills and lose every bit of it, the person behind you does the same, and a third person puts in only $5 and wins a jackpot of $188. In that example, overall, the machine paid out about $92 for every $100 played ... but it did so over several players and not to every single person that put in $100.

In fact, a more realistic (albeit simplistic) pay schedule is probably even more complicated:

- You may put in your five $20 bills and lose all of it.
- The next player puts in $100 and wins $10.
- There is still $174 (92% the $200) that has to be paid out in some undefined combination and to some undetermined number of players. It could come as a $174 win to the next player or it could come as $1 wins to the next 174 players or any combination in between.

If only it were so simple! But the truth is, the mathematical possibilities get to a headache level; especially for me. Let's take for example that *Blazing 7s Double Bonus* machine from Bally. With its basic settings *(out-of-the-box without a casino altering settings)* the game pays out 91.96% with one credit played and 92.7% with maximum (three) credits played. Let's take just two possible outcomes for example: out of a total of 1,038,054 possible plays of the game there are 38,976 opportunities for the reels to line up blank-blank-blank (nothing) but only 3,248 possibilities for blank-blank-double jackpot symbols to appear. That is one very basic and very simple example of math tables for slot payouts. Keep in mind that all of these payout possibilities are themselves merely the volatility *within the limitation of the hold.*

In other words, taking into account that 92.7% AND recognizing that some players will only play one credit or two (which lowers the payout and changes the volatility table), just those two outcomes fluctuate. Specifically, in only 1,000 spins of the reels there is a *"margin of error"* of +/-104.69% that those outcomes may or may not be accurate. However in ten-million spins of the reels that possibility changes to a *"margin of error"* of only +/- 1.05%:

Number of Spins	Margin Of Error
1,000	104.69%
10,000	33.11
100,000	10.47%
1,000,000	3.31%
10,000,000	1.05%

There is an episode of *Star Trek Deep Space Nine* in which *Chief Miles O'Brien* (played by the Irish actor Colm Meany) is confronted by an abnormality in the space time continuum and frantically complains, *"thinking about this gives me a headache."* I can relate, when it comes to slot machine math. After a harrowing bout with algebra in the 7th grade, I successfully avoided math classes until I was 30 years old. It was only then that I began to understand patterns, and became addicted.

Fortunately, you don't need to be a mathematician to own, operate, or even beat slot machines; the game designers handle that stuff. All you need to understand is the theory of how they work and how casinos use that theory. Successful players understand these things a whole lot better than average players and better than most casino executives. If you really are interested in the math behind games (not just slots but casino games in general), my friend (and at times my attorney) *Tony Cabot* has written THE book on the subject: *Practical Casino Math* by Anthony N. Cabot and Robert C. Hannum, published by the *Institute for the Study of Gambling and Commercial Gaming* at the University of Nevada in Reno.

For my young novice friend wanting to tag along with the "big boys", before I could introduce him to that "bakers' dozen" so-called "tips" and the supposed minutia of slot strategy, I first had to get rid of some more of the bad information and out-and-out nonsense about machines:

- Slot machines are never, ever, ever, *"ready to hit."* In modern times, there is no such thing as a machine being "due." Just because a slot machine has been played for a long time and not given a payout does *not* mean a payout is due. If this was *ever* true, it is not true with computer-controlled slot machines.
- The temperature of a machine has nothing to do with the payout. A "hot" machine is not physically hot. Seriously, there is one internet "beat the slots" system that sells for $49 that tells you to feel the temperature of the machine. *Don't even believe it.*
- Casino bosses do not loosen or tighten the payout of a machine on a whim or at will. As I said before, most of us don't even know how and in many jurisdictions it takes State approval and supervision to make such a change. Have you ever been around *any* state bureaucracy? It is never a quick process to do anything with government supervision; I can assure you that even if I wanted to change payouts based on the time of day, I could never get through

156

the government bureaucracy in time to get it done. That aside, it is just not part of our strategy. The notable exception to this is the recent introduction of new game platforms like IGT's sbX® and downloadable server-based platforms from WMS, Bally, and other manufactures which allow "on the fly" changing of titles *and holds* (in some cases) from server downloads.

- Putting a player card in a slot machine does not in any way affect the payout. I wish-to-hell it did so I could control the "Larrys" of the world; but it does not. At one of my casinos I had a really good high-roller slot player. (*"Really good"* for me means that she lost a lot of money every time she played.) She absolutely refused to use her players' club card. Yet she insisted that my casino hosts give her all kinds of freebies including gourmet meals, prizes, cash back, and the whole range of goodies we "comp" to good players. Empirically we could observe that she was a good player; but with the absence of hard computer data, we had no accounting process against which we could charge off the costs of these freebies. She refused to use the card because she was certain that insertion of the card changed the payout of the machine. Not only is it technologically impossible to do so (with current machines), but it is also illegal to do so. I never could beat this into her head; some myths refuse to die.

- Articles that tell you how to hit huge jackpots and find *ready-to-hit* machines are generally a waste of time and money; ones that tell you how the machines work are perhaps more worth reading.

- A newly opened casino does not have "looser" slots that tighten up after the opening...for all the complicated reasons I just stated. However, by contrast, occasionally when I open a new property, I do monkey with the locally-controlled options. For a casino that I opened in the spring of 2006, I decided to set the payouts on the machines about 4% higher than the payouts at the six competing casinos in the area. Subsequently someone probably DID change that hold at some point later, but if they did, it was not a quick nor easy process (that casino was Class II and did not the sbX® or similar platform).

I should add to this list the fact that betting-management systems don't work at table games and are absolutely silly when applied to slot machines (the Martingale, the Double-Pyramid, and so on). Just forget about them; they are *really* stupid.

I have a good friend (if not one-time mentor) who has been managing table games for almost three decades. He knows more about card players and table games than almost anybody I know, with the sole exception of gaming guru Vic Taucer (the author and former Caesars Palace table games manager turned college professor). This friend of mine loves to play blackjack. Now you might think that he either counts cards or does some other "advantage" play; after all, he has run the card pits at one of the largest casinos on the planet in Macau. Nope. He uses the Martingale betting system. *Un-fucking-believable.*

The Martingale system is an asinine (and antiquated) betting system usually associated with roulette but periodically popping up at other games (even, amazingly enough, at slot machines). The way it works is: he bets a minimum table bet, say $25. If he loses he then bets $50. If he loses that, he then bets $100; and you guessed it if he loses that, he bets $200. If he wins, he takes his winnings and starts over at the minimum. When he finally wins, after a series of double-ups, his net win is one unit of the table minimum. In other words after that series I just described, with $400 on the table (the $200 bet plus $200 won) his NET WIN is only $25. But...he *is* ahead. The problems, of course, are monumental. Even if he was only on a $5 table, if he had 20 consecutive losses, his bet would need to be $2,621,440; *it is just like the old story of doubling pennies every day for a month and on the 30th day the days' number is $5,368,709.12 with the total save being $10,737,418.23.* On a $25 table that figure becomes more than $13-million just to win a net $25.

Even during one of the worst weeks of the economic crisis, I received an email announcing that six-month T-bills had fired off at 1.2% that would have meant a profit of a pitiful $156,000 on a $13-million investment. But even THAT abomination would be 6,240 times better than the return on his thirteen-million at a $25 blackjack table using the Martingale system. Hell; just buy a casino. I will make you considerably more than $25 for every $13-million you invest.

Besides, no table games boss in his right mind is going to allow unlimited bet maximums. That is what cost Jake Lansky the Thunderbird and it is what cost me a career as a card counter.

My friend would argue that the chances of him losing 20 games in a row are pretty slim; but assuming a blackjack pit has a $300 maximum bet on a $5 table, only six losses in a row would put him out of business. Additionally he would argue that that the likelihood of blackjacks, doubling-down, and other specialty pays would make up for the minor $25 wins. If he is making a $200 bet and wins, he would win a net $25 (lose 25 + lose 50 + lose 100 = total loss of $175 then win $200 for a net gain of $25); however if a blackjack pays 3 to 2 (150% of the original bet) then he wins $300 for the hand and a net win of $125 instead of just $25. Don't hold your breath for that. Besides remember he is out of Martingale double options after four hands at many $25 tables.

Most system players would blame even that many consecutive losses on a "losing streak"...which even I have referenced in this book. But I need to be clear: There is absolutely no such thing as a *winning streak* or a *losing streak*. The whole concept is totally flummery.

The myth is based on a belief that winning or losing is not random and not independent. There is actually a belief that bets are somehow (mystically? technologically? religiously?) connected to each other and therefore all wins should be balanced out by losses. So, according to the myth, if there has been a long string of losses on a machine, then a long streak of wins is due.

Legend has it that my gambling hero, Doc Holliday, would never shoot a man if Doc was on a winning streak; but God help you if he was on a losing streak.

The fact is, the issue was solved in 1654 by the mathematician Blaise Pascal when he worked out the first Craps theory for a gambler named *Mom's Knight* (Chevalier de Mere). (*Who says only modern day poker players have cutesy names?*) Though it has been a mere 350 or so years, this is one of those gambler myths that refuses to die...and what we know about changing odds at blackjack (blackjack ONLY) serves to confuse the muddled-thinkers even further. I am not going to give you a math lesson here (*remember I hated math in school*), but if you really want to cling to the idea of a streak, please go buy a probability text book from a college bookstore. *There really are no streaks in gambling.* (Oh, and by the way, the world is round not flat either).

Finally, on the subject of *slot machine mythology*, I want to refer you to actor Everett Sloane playing *"Franklin Gibbs"* in *"The Fever"* episode (1.17) of *The Twilight Zone*, from January 29, 1960:

> *"Franklin Gibbs: (after maniacally playing a slot machine for nearly 24 hours, it "deliberately" breaks down on him)... Give me back my dollar, you miserable dirty... That's my last dollar! (He attacks the machine and pushes it over; it crashes to the floor) GIVE ME BACK MY DOLLAR! (he is dragged out of the casino by security guard)."*

A casino measures revenue within 24-hour *gaming days*. Most casinos are open 24 hours a day, seven days a week; however the actual *gaming day* is rarely from midnight to midnight. In fact, the start and end point of the 24-hour period is a carefully-guarded secret by most casinos and differs from property to property. This has nothing at all to do with your ability to win or lose, but is directly tied to Federal money-laundering laws (*specifically Title 31 of the US Code and more recently (Public Law 107-56) The Patriot Act*).

The Internal Revenue Service requires you to pay taxes and the casino to file a tax report on any player who wins more than $1,199 in one gaming day. If you had several payouts that totaled $1,200 or more and you knew precisely when my gaming day ended, then you could cash-out up to $1,199 one minute before the gaming day ended and then cash-out another $1,199 one minute after the gaming day began; thus evading Federal taxes and the tracking of that money.

Massive amounts of cash move in and out of casinos so fast that for the purpose of transaction reporting, we are treated as *financial institutions* in much the same way as banks and are subject to money laundering regulations. So any transaction of more than $10,000 has to be reported in a "suspicious activity report" (SAR) just like a bank transaction. So if you "laundered" $9,000 before the end of the gaming day and another $9,000 a minute later, technically you would be legal but certainly a red-flag.

159

Hence to make certain that a player is not siphoning cash to Al Qaida, $2,000 at a time, casinos keep our gaming day secret. One casino might end the gaming day at 4am and another might end it at 10pm. The time is of no importance whatsoever. What *is* important is that we measure slot win in terms of the gaming day. This is important because you need to understand the mindset of a casino boss when it comes to machine payout; even if it *IS* archaic to think a money laundering scheme would involve only $2,398 ($1,199 times two gaming-days)[16].

Many of the terms of the slot machine world (like *"coin-in"*) are indeed similarly archaic throw-backs to the origins of the devices, so I will give you a another two-minute history lesson here. Initially, slot machines were not the big-time revenue generators that they have become in the 21st century.

Slot machines began as chewing gum and candy vending machines; some even dispensed cigarettes...one at a time. A "player" would put a penny (or nickel) in a machine and pull a handle. Driven by clanking gears, three mechanical reels would spin around, viewable through a glass window. Each reel had a series of symbols representing *flavors of the gum or candy*. If each reel stopped spinning so that three cherry-symbols were visible in the center of the glass window, then the "player" won cherry-flavored gum or candy; if the reels stopped on three lemons, then the prize would be lemon-flavored gum or candy. If the reels stopped without having all three reels lined up on matching symbols, then the player got nothing. Since the cost of one piece of gum or candy was negligible, owners of these machines counted their profits by counting the number of coins put into the machine. Hence *coin-in*. And, inevitably, many times the "player" would not take the gum at all, instead opting to take the cash-price for the gum; thus making them very grey-area gambling machines.

Eventually those machines evolved into true gambling devices that paid out cash rather than just gum. A nickel machine from the 1930s would typically payout: two nickels for one cherry appearing in the window; four nickels for two-cherries; ten nickels for three oranges; 14 nickels for three blueberries; eighteen nickels for three bells; and a "jackpot" of $7.50 (150 nickels) for three bars; all for a five-cent bet. *(There were no multiple-coin plays originally.)*

The guy who invented slot machines in 1895, Charles Fey, patriotically put a cracked liberty bell as a symbol on each of his reels and soon slot machines became known as "Liberty Bells." That is why many slot machines today still have bells as one of their symbols... along with the fruit flavors of the gum and candy. The modern machines still look like the old ones in many ways; cherries and liberty bells are as popular as ever; but many other symbols have been replaced by various marketing themes of the machines (characters from movies or television shows, cartoon or other pop-culture icons, and so on). Instead of taking one penny or one nickel, machines now take multiple coins and bills (as well as printed tickets).

In those early days, slot machines had three mechanical reels that rotated and stopped...all controlled by a series of gears. After starting the gear motion by pulling the handle on the side of the machine *(giving birth to the term "one armed bandit")*, you could listen for all three gears to lock and the coin to drop into place.

There were five very distinct "click" sounds from the machine and old-time casino hands will tell you that slot players used to listen very carefully to those clicks like a safecracker listens to lock tumblers. When I play the antique slots in my own collection I often close my eyes and wait for each distinctive "click."

Even if those "safecracker" players could somehow predict the outcome of the game by the sound of the gears, those days are long gone...and so are the gears.

The slot machines you will find in casinos today are computers. They are not *run by* computers or *controlled by* computers; they *ARE* computers. At the same time I am writing this description for you, I have just ordered 400 new slot machines for casino I am building in the Midwest. The internal workings of those slot machines are Intel Core i7® computers, with the exact same chip as the one I am using to write this chapter.

ABOVE: The internal mechanical works of a vintage Buckley nickel slot machine from the Gary Green Collection. Note all of the mechanical parts.

LEFT: The front view of that same Buckley machine nickel slot machine (maximum payout $7.50) from Gary Green's collection. Note the handle on the right side; the only way to make the reels spin. Also note at the top the coin slot for one (and only one) nickel.

The same computer that "Little Johnny" uses to sign on to the internet and research his homework (or play video games and look at online porn) is the exact same machine that is inside every single slot machine at your local Indian casino or on the Strip in Vegas. Even in the slot machines that still have spinning reels inside, rather than video screens, there are computers.

As I said earlier, some early casino managers considered slot machines to be a nuisance on their floor only as something to keep "wives and girlfriends busy while then men gambled" (presumably at the tables). Regardless of such dated thinking, initially slot machines were put into casinos as only minor revenue sources, not unlike vending machines.

Somewhere between those first *Liberty Bells, Buckley* and other original slot machines and the computers that they have become today, there were several intermediate stages that eventually led to computer chips controlling mechanical reels. Those intermediate steps produced a host of strange part-reel and part electronic machines as well as many quasi-video hybrid machines, pre-touch screen video poker machines, and quite a few pure electronic test machines. A lot of those are still around (as of this writing) in older casinos.

The way a modern slot machine works is a little unsettling when one thinks about how much money is fed into each one of things; at least it is unsettling once you realize that most of what you see (spinning reels or videos) is just a show and has nothing to do with determining the outcome of the bet. That's right, the outcome has been determined *long* before the reels (or video) stops spinning. The spinning is just a show to make you feel like something is happening.

On a modern slot machine, a computer program begins running the instant the machine is turned on and "booted up." The program continues to run until the machine is turned off. The entire time, thousands...tens of thousands...of games are being played; but are not being displayed.

A computer program called a Random Number Generator (RNG), usually embedded on a special government-regulated chip in the computer, constantly calculates a series of number combinations (for example, two-billion is not an

162

unreasonable series — some programs generate far fewer combinations, but the method is the same). The number of combinations is determined by a mathematical formula that corresponds to the number of different symbols and blank spots in the video or on the reel.

Each one of these numbers is equal to one (and only one) combination of positions on the reels. For example the reel-alignment of a cherry on the first reel, blank spot on the second reel, and bar on the third reel might be represented by the number 27. In the same series, the number 10,928 might represent a cherry on the first reel, a different blank spot (from another position on the reel), and a different bar on the third reel. These numbers are randomly picked at the rate of thousands of combinations per minute (if not per second).

ABOVE: The insides of an "intermediate" era slot machine; note the mechanical reels *(this one was "themed" by Coca-Cola® —notice their logo on the first reel)*. Notice also the two areas of computer components in this "hybrid" era slot machine.

ABOVE: The insides of a modern (as of THIS writing) video slot machine; no reels. Notice the back of the flat-screen computer monitor to the left and the fan at the right to cool the Intel chip. Both of these slot machines are from Gary Green's personal collection.

Okay, so now you walk up to a slot machine, feed your $10-bill into it and push the button to start playing. When you push that button you may *think* you are starting the wheels to spin until they randomly (or *magically* or what-EVER) stop on symbols. In reality, you are "freezing" the program for the tiny fraction of the second it took you to push the button. Whatever number combination was on the program at that particular fraction of a second when you pushed the button becomes the outcome of your bet.

It is all over before the reels (or video) even begin spinning. The *only* reason the reels spin is to create a show for you. It does not matter how long it takes for them to spin, the outcome of the bet has already been determined by the computer. *The reels will stop at the combination that you "froze" when you pushed the button.*

You look at the screen and think, *"Wow, I almost won the top jackpot because that one reel is just a half-inch off."* Nonsense; you are just looking at a show. The outcome was determined an eternity (in computer time) before the reels even started spinning; between the time you pushed the button and the time the show stopped running, the program probably ran 100,000 other number combinations.

While all of that applies to either video or spinning reel machines, a video-only slot machine can get even more complex. On a video slot machine, hitting the button not only freezes the number, but it also starts the video movie running. Those movies look like spinning reels and there may be all sorts of options for various angles of play (diagonals, horizontal, reverse, multiple lines, and so on), but the fact remains that the outcome (whether you win or lose has been determined) long before the movie ended...and in fact before the movie even started.

Oh, by the way: some modern slot machines still have the old "one-armed bandit" handle on the side of them, and you can pull the handle to get the reels spinning. Inside the slot machine there is a tight spring on the handle and even a sound device that simulates pulling a handle to start the gears turning and wheels spinning. The truth, of course, is that pulling the handle simply triggers the button that freezes the program the same way pushing the button does. The outcome is already determined and it makes no difference if you push a button or pull a handle.

Even more headache-giving complexly, the introduction of multiple coins playable in a machine opened up all sorts of mathematical *and psychological* possibilities. Getting a payout from a machine does not necessarily mean that you win more than you gamble; a payout is not necessarily a *winning* payout.

Let me tell you about my favorite payout gimmick; I call it the *"IGT trick"*, because it is most often masterfully presented by the largest slot machine company in the world, *International Gaming Technologies* (IGT). *(IGT has their own name for it.)* Let's say you bet the maximum number of coins on a particular machine, maybe 45 nickels per spin. Every few spins you "win"...maybe 20 nickels. Psychologically, YOU ARE A WINNER and all sorts of videos, bells, and whistles sound on the machine. Factually, you bet $2.25 and you lost $1.25 of it; or *you "won" $1* back. Either way, the technique is designed keep you playing. The game pays out frequently and you win frequently; just not an amount more than you had bet. *(And just imagine what this does to your "coin-in" number if you replay those "winnings" in hopes of getting a bigger win.)* Technology changes fast; five years ago this was only true on video slot machines but today reel machines can have the same gimmick. Four years ago it was primarily IGT's gimmick; today WMS Games has taken this methodology to entirely new levels.

There were just a few more basics that my novice slot player needed to understand: the different kinds of games that were available on modern slot machines.

- **Buy-the-payout.** Remember those *Bally Blazing Seven* machines I talked about? They are three-coin machines. They are generally $1 machines with a maximum bet of $3. The symbols on the reels are bars and fiery ("blazing") sevens. If you land on various bar combinations you win a few coins, but if you land on three sevens you win $100, $200, $300, or a bigger jackpot. However, if you land on three sevens and have only played $1 or $2, then you win nothing at all. In order to "qualify" for the prizes associated with the 7's you have to play three dollars. This is called maximum coin in. On these *buy-the-payout* machines, the payout options are directly tied to the number of credits you play on the machine.

- **Multipliers.** These machines also encourage you to play maximum credits, but all symbols pay — regardless of whether you play one credit or the maximum. These machines multiply and increase the amount of the payoff based on how many coins you put in the machine. For example, with one credit played, the winning symbol of one cherry might pay two credits. But if you played maximum coins (three in this case), the same one cherry symbol would pay off maybe 6 credits. For example, the *same multiplier* (x2) for any given symbols would be:

CREDITS PLAYED	PAYOUT	MULTIPLIER
One	Two	X2
Two	Four	X2
Five	Ten	X2

However, some machines have different multipliers that increase with the coins played and might payout like this:

CREDITS PLAYED	PAYOUT	MULTIPLIER
One	Two	X2
Two	Six	X3
Five	25	X5

- **Lines.** If you don't have a headache already from the complications of these games, get ready for a guaranteed headache. Line games allow you to activate different payout lines depending on how much money you put in the machine. For example, one credit might activate *the center line only* so that you only win if three symbols line up across the middle of the glass and along the center line. A second coin might activate another line just above the center line. A third coin might activate a line just below the center. A fourth coin might activate a diagonal line from bottom left to top right. A fifth coin might activate a diagonal line from top left to bottom right. Any winning combination of symbols that show up along one of the lines pays out *only* if you have activated that line. As of this writing, most machines on a typical slot floor are 25-line machines. To get to those 25-lines, however, there are some seemingly-wacky payout patterns.

165

There are also combinations of these three basic game types. For example, line games are usually also multipliers. Many nine-line games can be played from one to 45 credits; one credit activates only the center line with a multiplier of one while 45 credits activates nine lines with a multiplier of 5. Often bonus rounds (see below) are only triggered when all lines are played with full coin in per line (maximum bet). In fact, there are also a number of pretty common gimmicks that are added to these basic game types by most manufacturers:

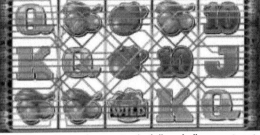

The above lines show a typical "wacky" payout patterns on a multi-line slot machine; note that the patterns are not all straight lines.

- **Bonus rounds.** If you remember the first quick-and-easy tip I gave the newbie employee, the old-style IGT *Wheel of Fortune* machines go into a bonus round every 40 or 50 plays. *The Tom Rule* (also from those quick tips) was also about bonus rounds. Bonus rounds are little mini jackpot games within the slot game itself. On the original *Wheel of Fortune* machine a player spins a large wheel at the top of the machine to win from 25 to 1000 credits. Various spinning wheels are popular bonus features (*Wheel of Fortune, Monte Carlo,* etc.). Video cartoons are also popular, as are actual film clips from TV shows (*Beverly Hillbillies, Munsters, Alfred Hitchcock,* Twilight Zone, *Elvis's 1968 Comeback Special, Green Acres, Hee-Haw, M*A*S*H,* etc.). There are a host of other bonus rounds; one of my favorites is Bally's original $1 *Millionaire Sevens*, which features a rising-bar of jackpot numbers. Most of these bonus features are interactive features between player and machine that take time away from the standard game. Bonuses payoff higher (or *appear* to be greater) than the standard spins..

- **Nudge machines.** These are cute and fun. The reels stop spinning, and you notice you *"almost"* won, but the reels are completely stopped. Then suddenly the reel that is only one position away from your win, nudges forward to line up perfectly with the other two symbols on the pay line. *You win.*

- **Bonus Multipliers.** IGT's *Double Diamonds* machine is the archetypical model for this gimmick, though there are scores of imitations both from IGT and from other manufacturers. Let's say that on the pay line you get a bar on the first reel, a second bar on the second reel, but on the third reel you get the special *"Double Diamond"* symbol. You still win, but rather than the standard payout for three bars, you get double that payout. These special bonus multipliers come in double-payout,

166

three-times payout, five times, seven times, ten times, 20 times, 50 times, and even 100 times the payout.

- **Scatter.** The scatter feature is a combination one two or more of a particular symbol *anywhere* on the screen —not just on the pay lines. A scatter either triggers a specific larger payout than typical matching symbols or triggers one of the bonus features.

Usually the payouts from all of these "bonuses" figure into the overall hold of the machine; hence there may be very few or very small payouts in the "regular game" if there are frequent and larger bonus payouts. On the other hand, some bonus features are totally independent of the game's hold and draw from a special prize pool. It is important to read the game's rules (usually available on one of the video screens of the game) to know if the bonus money comes from the hold or is independent.

Also, understand that all of these special features, gimmicks as I call them, are designed to encourage you to play more...with you hoping to reach a bonus level, a multiplier, or a special nudge. And studies have shown that they all work in increasing your time-in-play at machines. The outcome of the game is still determined the same way; but the gimmick gets you to play more.

Again, it is important to know, however, if the special increased payouts of these gimmicks are all figured into my hold percentage and are mathematical functions of that relationship between frequency and volatility of the machine. As a marketing inducement to get you to play more, they may look like opportunities to win proportionately large payouts; but factually they payout no more or no less than the machine hold is set for the game.

Among the most notable independent bonuses are those *Wide Area Progressive* (WAP) that I discussed earlier. A progressive payout takes a very small percentage of every credit played in a machine and puts that into a prize pool. For a 25-cent machine, the progressive share is usually 1¼ cents per 25¢ bet; for dollar machines it is about two-cents per dollar or six-cents for three-coin-in dollar bets. *(This may be top secret information that casino bosses don't like to give out, but I don't see the big deal in telling you.)* One of my partners has created a WAP for games in the country of Chile. The games grab 1½% of the bet with ½ of a percentage point going to the payout on the progressive jackpot, ½ of a percentage going to fund future WAP jackpots, and ½ of a percentage as a "management fee" to my partner and his group. Now remember that the WAP contribution is based on the play —*the coin-in*— rather than the win.

Think about *that* WAP scheme. If each machine is winning $100 per machine and the hold is 8% that means the coin-in on the machine is $1,250 per day. The WAP contribution then is $18.75; which is 18¾% of the win or hold. Now, if there are 1,000 machines on the WAP then the WAP contribution is $18,750 per day; times 365 days is almost seven-million dollars a year ($6,843,750). The "management fees" for that comes to $2.28-million a year. And that number is based on only $1,250 coin-in with only 1,000 machines on the network; the formulas increase as the coin-in increases and the number of machines increases. Consider 10,000 connected machines across multiple casinos with an average coin in of $3,750 (around $300 win per unit per day); then suddenly that contribution would jump to $13-Billion a year.

As noted, *What is better than owning a casino? Owning the slot machines inside the casino!*

The WAP machines are almost always *buy-the-payout* games in which you have to play maximum coin-in to qualify for a chance to win the Progressive Jackpot...even though the contribution to the jackpot comes from coin-in at all levels. The slot machine is linked, by computer networking (just like a network at an office), to other slot machines casinos all over the particular state in which you are playing. With the jackpot coming from a few cents per bet per machine at every casino on the network, in almost no time these progressive jackpots are hundreds of thousands of dollars and even millions in some cases.

Along the same lines of gimmicks to encourage play, in addition to the wide-area progressives, some casinos often have their own internal progressives (LAP: *Local Area Progressive*) that operate in the same way. Like WAPs, the local progressives use a separate computer program to payout the progressive jackpots. To begin a local progressive, we usually seed the pot with $10,000 to $150,000 to encourage play. We let the progressive play build up to that seed amount, adding the percentage of each bet and then building to it. Your chances of winning a local progressive are usually better than winning the huge Wide Area Progressives.

In many cases, while the standard payouts on these machines are functions of the hold; the payout of the Progressive Jackpot is a separate computer program (or *algorithm*) that is not really related to the standard payout schedule. That means your chances of winning the WAP or a LAP are unrelated to the machine's payout schedule. Whether the WAP/LAP payout is connected to the machine's volatility, frequency, hold and other payout measures is strictly a matter of manufacture's preference and the rules of the governing regulatory authority. *(It is important, too, to recognize that progressives found in "grey area" games are rarely (if ever) regulated and hence there is no consumer protection or guarantees whatsoever. More on that in a later chapter on "grey area gaming".)*

You usually can spot WAP machines by the big, brightly-flashing LED signs over the bank of progressive machines; a sign with a constantly changing number showing some huge payout potential. Because the machines are typically linked to play at several casinos, the number changes several times per second.

At the very second I am writing this to you, there is a Progressive Jackpot of almost $3-million available on my friend Max Baer Jr.'s[17] IGT *Beverly Hillbillies* slot machine but that number is subject to change as quickly as I type the next paragraph. The *Elvis* quarter machine is offering about a million dollars; and the huge *MegaBucks* jackpot is set to pay out more than $10-million to one person. And the list goes on with different, constantly changing progressives.

In each of the cases, which I just checked by looking at the slot screens, the actual number is calculated down to the penny and quite literally changes several times per second based on play across the state (or across the country in some cases). For example, the largest MegaBucks jackpot ever paid from one of these machines was $39,710,826.36 paid in March of 2003 at the *Excalibur Casino* in Las Vegas. (A 25-year-old Los Angeles software developer was visiting Vegas to bet on college basketball's March Madness. He pumped about $100 into the machine before it hit[18].)

Clearly the value of these machines, to my casinos, is that I can advertise the huge potential jackpots to attract players to come try their chance on the machine. Again, in most cases the normal hold is different from the Progressive Jackpot. I keep more of your money on these machines than on any others; *remember the chart I showed on machine hold in Las Vegas.*

I have also, by design, not taken the time here to go into the details of how to play (and allegedly take advantage of) table games. There are scores of books on the subject...and some of them are actually good. Frankly, I suggest you learn to count cards.

So, can the machines be beaten by players? In the short term yes. But, you really need to remember to walk away when you win —even if it is only a small win.

Chapter Eleven

What the hell is an "Indian Casino"

(or how did I get a casino in my neighborhood?)

"I am a red man. If the Great Spirit had desired me to be a white man he would have made me so in the first place."
— **Sitting Bull**, Lakota Medicine Man & Chief

Make no mistake about it: there are actually 562 little independent countries INSIDE the geographic borders of the USA. When you walk into an Indian casino you are leaving the United States of America and entering another nation. Not figuratively, not because of the glitter of casinos lights; not because of some cultural romanticism about Native Americans; not because of the tragic history of the "vanishing American"; but quite literally you are on foreign soil. Tribes existed as sovereign nations long before white Europeans arrived.

In most cases there are no border crossings and no customs agents, yet when you step into that casino it is just the same as if you crossed through the revolving steel gates in San Diego to enter Tijuana or across the bridge from Detroit to Windsor.

By sheer numbers, most of the casinos in the United States are "Indian Casinos". Of the purported 1,500 *"gaming establishments"* in the country, all but about 800 are (to put it nicely) less than what we would generally describe as a "real" casino; those are more akin to the South Dakota-style store-fronts *(where there are 51 "casinos" with a statutory maximum of 30 slot machines each)*. My count of less-than "real" casinos includes "charitable gaming", pari-mutuel off-track betting, lottery rooms, cruise-to-nowhere ships, and California-style card-rooms. Of the 800 or so "real" casinos (that look like a Vegas tourist attraction), about 122 are in Las Vegas (with another 266 in the rest of Nevada), 16 are in Atlantic City, 33 are in Mississippi, and a smattering in other states (Detroit's three casinos; Philly's; Pittsburgh's; Baltimore's; Fort Lauderdale's; etc.), and a few riverboats across the country (like Missouri's 13 stationary "riverboat" casinos). But there are more than 300 *Indian* casinos spread across the country.

The 562 "federally recognized" tribes (and the hundred or so that have been "decertified" by the U.S. Government) make up only about one-percent of the U.S. population. Only a little more than a third of those Tribes have casinos; and population-wise the members of *those* tribes barely make up one-third of the Native American Indian population, or about 1/3 of 1% of the national population. And those 201 casinos are hardly equally distributed amongst the participating Tribes; the Chickasaw Nation (of Oklahoma) alone has 13 casinos; the Cherokee (of Oklahoma) have eight; the Seminole (of Florida) have four; and several other tribes own multiple casinos. In fact, only 22 Indian casinos produce 56% of the revenue of Indian gaming.

The reality is that a vast majority of Native Americans do NOT benefit from gaming revenue. Despite the incredible wealth of *some* of the tribes that have casinos, the majority of Native Americans are still struggling in a centuries-old cycle of poverty. According to the U.S. census, more than 30% of all Indians earn less than $6,300 a year. The myth of rich Indians making millions from casinos is just that: a myth. Most Native Americans are still fighting to pull themselves out of a centuries-old cycle of poverty. Centuries of US Government programs have repeatedly failed (for uncountable reasons); but casinos —*the first economic development program to actually be controlled by the Tribes themselves*— have been the first real hope of reducing the poverty cycle. Though not a magic pill, there has been genuine progress from casino revenues, especially for education, elders, and health care programs.

Having recognized that dire situation, unarguably inflicted by the U.S. Government over the centuries, it is at very least interesting to frame that poverty within the context of the tribes that DO have casinos; of all the programs to fight Native poverty, gaming truly is the only economic development that has worked for the Indian Nations. However, before I share some of those incredible numbers with you, let me further set aside the notion of "rich Indians" that is often used to claim that *"assimilation is complete"* (as if such digestion was even a desirable thing).

The poverty-level numbers are themselves alarmingly compelling; and they stand in stark contrast to reports of the Tribal Council of the Florida Seminole paying $965-million cash to purchase the Hard Rock Cafe, hotel and casino business while a local newspaper claimed that Tribal Council members have spent more than $280-million on luxury vehicles, televisions and stereo systems, as well as for cosmetic surgery for tribal members.

The abject, miserable (if not hopeless) poverty on some of the New Mexico reservations where the only home stove is outdoors (as is the toilet) and the houses are still mud/straw adobe walls and floors, stands in incredible disparity to the $80-plus-million paid by six tribes to disgraced lobbyist Jack Abramoff to "protect" Indian gaming interests.

The near-squalor of living conditions in Native North Dakota, western Montana, and even coastal North Carolina are hard to generalize in the same breath as the popular Jeff Benedict book that viciously claims that tribes assimilate out of existence and are replaced with "fake" Indians who scam their way into owning casinos.

In that kind of pop-culture bastardization of reality, there are, even today, those who seriously argue that there should be no more "recognized" Indians. Similar to saying "there is no racism in America because a black man was elected president and there are African American multi-millionaires", the argument is that rich Tribal nations (like the Florida Seminole) are not suffering enough to have sovereignty or even be recognized as a Tribe.

There are strong (though not necessarily valid) arguments that the obscene-ly foul 1887 Congressional General Allotment Act, was finally successful (in the 21st century) to "civilize," "de-Indianize," and assimilate native peoples into "mainstream" (read "white") society. The only step left, according to that thought, is to continue the Roosevelt through Kennedy policies to terminate the government's trusteeship of Indian lands and integrate the Indian population into white America.

Within that backdrop, according to the National Indian Gaming Associa-tion, in 2011 Indian gaming produced $26.2-billion in gross revenue and another $3.2-billion from related hospitality and entertainment services (resorts, hotels, restaurants, golf, entertainment complexes, travel centers, etc.). Indian casinos generated 628,000 jobs and paid $9.4-billion in Federal taxes and $2.4-billion in state taxes, revenue sharing, and regulatory payments. THAT is a hell of a lot of money; but it is not an "answer" to the reality of Native America.

The single most important thing to understand about Indian casinos is *sov-ereignty*. Indian casinos exist because of it. Native American gaming is the story of one of the most illogical, sometimes tragic, and always absurd chapters of American history. The rise, proliferation, and operation of Indian casinos is a paragon of the preposterous becoming reality.

I have organized, developed, built, and operated Indian casinos all across America. And for the record, I am a white baby-boomer male, raised in the rural South on a healthy dose of 1950s black-and-white *cowboy and Indian* television shows, and educated in Tennessee where Andrew Jackson is considered a hero rather than a devil-incarnate that he is to many Native Americans. Following my Tennessee introduction to Johnny Cash's *Bitter Tears* album of Peter Lafarge songs, in college I distributed the Mohawk Warrior Society's radical newspaper *Akwesasne Notes* (and after college indexed it for the Alternative Press Index), and was a major organizer (and alleged gun-runner —if you believe FBI inform-ants) for the *American Indian Movement's* siege of Wounded Knee in the early 1970s.

As an activist for Native American rights, I helped write the first iteration of the Shumway Bill (that eventually became the *Indian Gaming Regulatory Act*). I had *some* role (though often minor) in every *nationally-publicized* Native Amer-ican Indian civil rights struggle of the second half of the 20th Century. My friend Russell Means spent days educating me my 1974 American Indian Movement Support Group as we distributed the Oglala *Declaration of Continuing Inde-pendence* asserting, *"The United States of America has continually violated the inde-pendent Native Peoples of this continent by Executive action, Legislative fiat and Judicial decision. By its actions, the U.S. has denied all Native people their International Treaty rights, Treaty lands and basic human rights of freedom and sovereignty. This same U.S. Government, which fought to throw off the yoke of oppression and gain its own inde-pendence, has now reversed its role and become the oppressor of sovereign Native peo-ple."* So it should be clear to the reader where my politics are at least on the ques-tion of Native American issues.

As an adult, I have been key in some of the most publicized Indian casinos in the country: I was a vice-president for Donald Trumps' one foray into running Indian casinos; I was the television and billboard spokesman for one of the Midwest's most successful Indian casinos; and I have been a frequent speaker on effective Indian casino operation & management at casino industry trade shows including the *National Indian Gaming Association* as well as a front-cover poster boy for the official publication of that organization. Two of my companies, as of this writing, are associate members of that organization.

One cornerstone of my business has been the fact that you —*the casino players*— *were* coming into a different nation when you came into one of the casinos that I operated for tribes.

So exactly how is it that the 5,726 people in Wetumpka Alabama woke up one morning to find a 16,000 square foot casino with one slot machine for every ten

Gary Green on the Cover *of "Indian Gaming Business"* — the official publication of the *National Indian Gaming Association* (also the picture used on the cover of this book).

residents in their little rural town? Their answer is the same answer for scores of small towns that have suddenly and unexpectedly become gambling centers; and *that* answer is the story I will tell you here. It *really is* a story of cowboys and Indians.

The story is not about good guys and bad guys. It is certainly not about "rich" Indians taking advantage of *anything* and it is not even about genocide or perceived *new* imperialism by white government. While there are inevitably elements of all of that in any history of American expansion and Native American Indians, this story is about a string of improbabilities, oversights, and blunders that brought America's favorite vice to within a two-hour drive of every citizen.

We all know and understand that if we travel to Canada, to Mexico, to Europe or Asia, we are in a different country. US laws do not apply there; we have no "constitutional rights" there; and in many countries there is no concept of *"innocent until proven guilty"*. These nations have their own laws and what may be legal here in the United States may be a major crime in some of those countries. Likewise what is a major crime here in the USA may be totally legal in some of those countries. *(How many college kids visit Amsterdam where the sale of small quantities of marijuana is allowed by 'licensed' coffee shops?)* It is all because each country is its own sovereign nation. Each is an autonomous state exercising supreme power and controlling influence over the body politic with freedom from external control.

In the United States, under current law, those 562 Native American Indian tribes[19] in the country are recognized as sovereign nations just as surely as Japan, Canada, or France are sovereign nations. Despite many state and local governments fighting them at every turn, these Indian tribes are entitled to their own governments, police departments, court system, housing authorities, health care systems, roads departments and...casinos. Historically these governments have been "wards" of the United States' Bureau of Indian Affairs; but in recent decades that chancery-esque legal guardianship or custody has been redefined to allow more (if not yet complete) autonomy to the 562 nations. This is not unlike the U.S. occupation of Germany, Japan, and Italy after the Second World War; but unlike those countries, the U.S. never released Native America.

For entertainment this weekend you may go to the local movie theatre, next week you might go to the civic center for a concert, and the following weekend you might visit a local Indian casino to play the slot machines. All may be within a few minutes' drive of your home and the same greenback dollars are good at all three. Few Americans realize that when they go to that casino they have become international travelers.

All-in-all more than 5.2-million people identified themselves as American Indians in the 2010 Census and more the 2¼-million people identified themselves as part Indian or Native American. The 562 "recognized" sovereign Indian Nations are dotted across almost every state, with Oklahoma and California having the most recognized nations within their borders.

Some of these "nations" are huge and have many citizens. The Navajo Nation, for example, is made up of more than 16-million acres, about the size of Maryland, Massachusetts and New Jersey combined. And there are at least 80,000 Navajo who live in that nation. Others are somewhat smaller, wiped out by white expansion, disease, poverty, or even warring with other tribes. The Augustine Band of Cahuilla Mission Indians has one member and her "nation" is about 500 acres that no one lives on[20] (though the casino there is open 24-hours-a-day and seven days a week). California's *29 Palms Band of Mission Indians* (where I worked under the Donald Trump contract), as noted, has 13 members with none living in the Nation.

If an Indian Nation is located within the boundaries of a State in which casino gambling is illegal, the Tribal Nation can still operate its own casinos. THAT shocking fact is just the beginning of the implications of the sovereign power of these Indian Nations within the borders of the United States. In every state in the Union, murder is a serious felony; on at least one Indian Nation in the State of Oklahoma, it is a misdemeanor punishable by no more than one year in jail[21]. When I was running an Indian casino in California, we would periodically have customers threaten to sue us for various negligence issues or violations of California law. As a matter of routine, managers would tell the customers, *"Get a life, you are in a Sovereign Nation you have no rights here and California law doesn't apply. Get the hell out of here."* A tribe in New Mexico has its own speed limits (44, 34, 24, and 14) as you drive up the roadway toward the casino. Tribal police write tickets, payable to Tribal Court, if you drive 35 instead of 34. If you need emergency services at an Indian casino, don't expect to dial 911 on your cell phone; local police are forbidden (by Federal law) from entering the Sovereign nation to provide police, fire, or ambulance service without Tribal invitation or pre-signed agreement to allow them there. When celebrity-tramp Anna Nicole Smith died at the Hard Rock Hotel on the Seminole Nation near Ft. Lauderdale Florida, it was the Seminole Tribal Police and Seminole Tribal Rescue that answered the call; not the Florida or Broward County officials.

The examples go on and on. But the point is clear: Indian casinos are located within independent Indian *Nations* – sovereign countries within the borders of the United States. You don't need a visa; you don't need an official government travel warning (because there really is nothing to be concerned about); it is just a political structure that evolved to allow you to gamble close to home.

Historically speaking, there should be no question in anyone's mind about the brutality and out-and-out genocide that white colonist waged against Native American Indians as this country was being settled. There is even strong documented evidence that the western-movie staple of "scalping" settlers was actually a practice that white Texans began against Indian settlers rather than the other way around.

Whatever the case, most people accept that white treatment of Indians has been historically shameful. Even long after the establishment of the United States Government, white people continued a history of "Indian wars", exploitation, and the seemingly deliberate and systematic destruction of racial, political, and cultural groups of Indians. War of 1812 hero Andrew Jackson, father of the modern Democratic Party, and leadership guru of my adopted home state of Tennessee, still today is viewed by many Native Americans with the same despise as Adolph Hitler for the genocidal *Trail of Tears* removal of Natives from their Eastern homelands. *(For my entire life annual Democratic fundraiser dinners in every state were called the Jefferson-Jackson Dinners; in 2009 Jackson's name was dropped from many —over that political sensitivity.)*

In residual effect, those tribes that were not reduced to a handful of members by sheer brutality did suffer from being at the lowest economic rung of society. The poorest health care, widespread malnutrition, alcoholism, and a scourge of externally inflicted social and physical maladies all explain the true reasons for the *"vanishing American"*. There is strong evidence that the genetic

175

propensity toward alcoholism was further exploited as a genocidal tool by white imperialists. The life expectancy in the 21st century for Native Americans is the late 40s (compared to the late 70s for white Americans).

In half-hearted efforts to appease, atone, apologize, or perhaps deceive, the United States Government adopted the official policy that the former tribes were *like* independent nations conquered in war. Under this policy the tribes were treated as independent and sovereign nations just as a foreign land "under our protection" would be treated following a war; not unlike the occupation of Germany by the US, England, and the USSR following the Second World War or Iraq immediately following our invasion and removal of Saddam Hussein. Tribal members were considered "wards of the nation," incapable of making their own decisions.

Just like with military foreign occupation, the administration of tribal matters was assigned to the War Department (in a special *Bureau of Indian Affairs,* until that bureau was moved to the Department of Interior in 1949 when the War Department was abolished). Without a doubt, the Bureau's role in dealing with Indians has changed as American political sentiment has changed; sometimes hurting Indians and sometimes helping them. Currently the bureau's mission has moved from subjugation and assimilation to social services and partnership...at least as far as their official mission is described.

In an effort to help (or force) tribes establish BIA-acceptable governments, the 1934 *Indian Reorganization Act* created US-like constitutions for the Tribal Nations. Under that law some tribes kept a traditional "chief" as their head of state while others adopted more white-society titles like California tribes' "Chairman" or Midwestern tribes' "President" or Oklahoma tribes' "Governor" and Tribal Councils called everything from Council to Congress to Parliament to Legislature.

The complexities of Tribal rule, Indian sovereignty and US motivations are probably good fodder for someone's dissertation, but for us the issue revolves around how this special status allowed casinos to pop up in places that they were seemingly outlawed...like that little Alabama town or Eagle Pass Texas where the Kickapoo Indian Nation operates one-thousand slot machines and twenty table games for 22,000 people.

Indian sovereignty was not invented for casinos; and Indian *gambling* was certainly not invented because of sovereignty (though Indian *casinos* were). In fact, each of those statements is so emotionally-charged in the Indian world, that they have obscured the financial foundations that eventually allowed those casinos to exist.

Time Magazine, in an emotion-inducing (and at times factually inaccurate) cover story lambasted by most Indian rights activists, reported in December of 2002:

> "Imagine, if you will, Congress passing a bill to make Indian tribes more self-sufficient that gives billions of dollars to the white backers of Indian businesses— and nothing to hundreds of thousands of Native Americans living in poverty. Or a

bill that gives hundreds of millions of dollars to one Indian tribe with a few dozen members—and not a penny to a tribe with hundreds of thousands of members. Or a bill that allows select Indian tribes to create businesses that reap millions of dollars in profits and pay no federal income tax—at the same time that the tribes collect millions in aid from American taxpayers[22]."

In an equally emotionally-charged response to the *Time* article, the president of the *National Indian Gaming Association* lambasted *Time* for defamed Indian gaming and Tribes with the article. President Ernie Stevens, who I have called friend and have supported often, blasted back:

"Your story is based on the false and offensive premise that "Washington" created Indian gaming as a "cheap way to wean tribes from government handouts." Indian gaming is not a federal program. Instead, it is one tool that Tribes use to generate revenue for their communities. The Federal programs that you refer to as handouts represent an attempt by the federal government to live up to thousands of treaty obligations incurred when establishing the land base for this Nation. American Indians have been victimized by federal policies supporting genocide and assimilation, which took millions of lives and millions of acres of Indian land, and caused economic and cultural destruction. Our grandfathers, Pontiac, Tecumseh, Crazy Horse, Chief Joseph, Geronimo, and so many others, fought for our rights – especially our right to self-government on our own land. The U.S. Constitution, the President, Congress, and the United States Supreme Court all recognize Indian Tribes as governments. Indian gaming is self-reliance.[23]"

As I said, the emotions run high on both sides and consequently the facts sometimes get blurred in the furor. The history of Indian gaming and the structure of Indian sovereignty are both in the midst of that blur. For the local gambler, or the struggling casino operator, it only adds to the amazing plot of the story; but in this case Ernie was absolutely accurate.

It is a fact that Indian gambling has been around for centuries. California's Chumash Tribe, for example, gambled for centuries in special areas called *malamtepupi* – roughly a casino for several ancient games of skill and of chance[24]. This and dozens of other ancient tribal games have been used as a strong emotional argument that "gaming" is therefore a part of Native American Indian culture and any attempt to limit Tribal gaming by tribes is a racist and imperialist assault on their culture. Be that as it may, nobody in their right mind believes that roulette, craps, blackjack, and slot machines (or even Bingo) are old Indian traditions.

More complexly on the emotional level, is the fact that the concept of Indian sovereignty was apparently endorsed by the US Constitution; at least that is the way courts have upheld it over the years. Specifically the Constitution excludes, in two places, Indians from taxation[25] and gives Congress the power to regulate commerce with Indians Tribes just as it does with any foreign government[26]. These constitutional references have been interpreted to endorse tribal sovereignty as part of the "conquered foreign lands" philosophy.

Based on this repeated interpretation, most of the laws, War Department regulations, and US Supreme Court cases have dealt with the administration of the conquered land. Ultimately the administration of that land is the key issue of sovereignty and of building casinos. Even today the BIA's mission statement begins with:

"The Bureau of Indian Affairs (BIA) responsibility is the administration and management of 55.7 million acres of land held in trust by the United States for American Indians, Indian tribes, and Alaska Natives. There are 562 federal recognized tribal governments in the United States. Developing forestlands, leasing assets on these lands, directing agricultural programs, protecting water and land rights, developing and maintaining infrastructure and economic development are all part of the agency's responsibility.[27]"

There is no doubt that most of these policies historically have been wrought with paternalism, anti-Indian racism and out-and-out land grabbing for white farms, transportation, and later oil. The financial rape *(and despicable as the term is, that accurately describes the violation and emptiness left)* of the Osage people in Oklahoma by oil companies and the court-ordered payment to tribal members a quarterly royalty check (sometimes of mere pennies), is a prime example. But regardless of the perhaps less-than-honorable motivations, the US Government for more than 200 years has been officially a proponent of at least some form of the Sovereign status of the Indian Nations within our borders.

The emotional question has been the issue of how far the cover of *"dependent* sovereignty" goes. Both the Tribes and the US Government have pushed that question in every imaginable direction through thousands of court cases, public laws, and agency directives.

For a casino operator, or for a gambler, there is almost nothing that I can think of that is more boring than legal history. I have always loved quoting Dick the butcher, from Henry VI, *"The first thing we do, let's kill all the lawyers[28]"*. But in understanding how casinos started showing up in your neighborhood, it really *is* interesting to see how court rulings impacted day-to-day life. The lawyers' debacle actually coincides with the romanticized but often brutal Wild West era that we know so well from television and film.

In the 1830 the US Supreme Court set the stage for the battle with a definition of Tribal Nations as "domestic dependent nations.[29]" That decision severely limited the idea of total sovereignty and gave state, local, and Federal authorities all sorts of jurisdiction on tribal land. In fact, that 175-year-old ruling is what allowed the Bible-belt white families in south-central Alabama to find a casino in their backyards and what allowed New York City to find the largest casino in the world only 139 miles from midtown Manhattan.

The most provocative land issue raised by that ruling was the *ownership* of Tribal land. Based in part on this ruling, Indian lands are *owned by* the United States Government but held in *trust* for the Tribes. The Indian Nations cannot sell the land but can use it for their own nation as their tribal government sees fit. A Tribal Nation or an individual Indian can buy land just like anyone else buys land, but it does *not* automatically become part of the BIA-administered trust land. The only land in "trust" is the Indian "homeland" assigned by the

178

BIA to be the reservation and home for the tribe. That assigned trust land is not necessarily the *ancestral* homeland of the tribe (as is clearly evident from the Cherokee Nation's trust land in the State of Oklahoma where they were driven from their actual homelands in North Carolina, Georgia, and Tennessee).

Occasionally a tribe will purchase land and ask the BIA to place that land into trust. In those situations, the argument is that the land purchased was originally part of the tribal homeland ("aboriginal home") but was stolen from the tribe, in one way or another, and by historical justice needs to be returned to the Nation. Land purchased that is *not* put in trust is called "fee land." Land assigned by the BIA (whether purchased or granted and whether to a Tribal Nation or to an individual Indian) is the trust land. This definition of "trust land" became the single cornerstone to placement of casinos a century and a half later.

There are uncountable variations of Trust Land that have been played with over the years; some have stuck and others have disappeared, with new ones popping up all the time. One example is that in addition to Tribal Trust lands, there are issues involving individual allotments of land held in trust by the Department of Interior not for an entire Tribe but for specific members or families within a Tribe.

Though tribal lawyers spent the next 150 years fighting the results of that 1830 Supreme Court decision, it wasn't until the last half of the 20th century that any headway was actually made and the door was opened enough for casinos to sneak through.

The modern history of the tug-o-war began, perhaps appropriately, in a trailer park and with a 1976 United States Supreme Court case called *Bryan v. Itasca County*[30]. Itasca County Minnesota had sent Mr. Bryan (who was a Chippewa Indian) a personal property tax bill for the mobile home in which he lived. The trailer was located on land held in trust by the United States for members of the Chippewa Tribe on Leech Lake Indian Reservation. Bryan's attorneys argued (and won) that his personal property was exempt from taxation because it was on trust land; it was in the sovereign Nation of the Chippewa Tribe and the United States cannot tax foreign countries. This seemingly was a very literal interpretation of the US Constitution by the High Court; but the dude got to keep his trailer when the tax collectors tried to seize it for unpaid taxes.

In 1979 the Seminole Tribe in Florida decided to push the sovereignty issue to the limit. You may remember from high school or college history that the Seminole are a tribe that never signed a treaty with the United States. It seems the blue coats weren't all that interested in chasing natives through alligator-infested swamps of South Florida. The aforementioned Andrew Jackson was the Florida governor who, despite his reputation as an "Indian Fighter" was not so keen on chasing the Seminole into the swamps. At this writing, I am living in South Florida so I can relate to that other Tennessean's reluctance to wrestle gators.

In the 1970s, the State of Florida allowed charities to run Bingo games as fundraisers provided that the games had certain limits on the size of the prize and the times the game could be played. The Florida law provided for criminal penalties against anyone operating a Bingo game outside of those regulations.

The leadership of the Seminole Tribe started their own Bingo games, without regard to the State's rules and regulation for charitable Bingo games...especially the limit on size of payouts. The Tribe's high stake Bingo games were immensely popular with the Ft. Lauderdale/Miami retiree community and the publicity was massive. The Broward County Sheriff raided the Bingo hall and charged Tribal leaders with violation of State criminal laws.

The case went to Federal Court with the Tribe suing the State of Florida over the issue of *sovereign immunity*. The Court ruled that the State's rules about Bingo were <u>regulatory</u> and hence just because there was a criminal penalty attached did not make the Bingo *game* illegal. Rather, the court said, Bingo is legal *but regulated*. And, the court concluded, since the issue was regulation, then the Bryan trailer tax decision applied: Florida did not have the jurisdiction to regulate on tribal land[31]. The US Supreme Court agreed and refused to hear the case.

The fallout from the case was landmark. Suddenly, by approval of Federal Court and the tacit approval of the United States Supreme Court, Indian Nations could operate high stakes Bingo games free from State regulation. In fact, suddenly any regulation from any State was in question when applied to Indian lands.

Eight years later, in 1987, the high Court further opened the floodgates and caused a tidal wave by deciding in favor of Tribal sovereign immunity for a high stakes Bingo hall in California[32]. In that case the Supreme Court expanded on the Seminole case and added that once a state had legalized any form of gambling then Indian Nations within the boundaries of that state could offer the same game but without any State governmental restrictions. That meant that if the state allowed legal "casino night" operations (like I ran in for charities in Maryland), then Indians (whose "trust land" was within their state) could have the same games without the regulations and limitations imposed by the State.

The prospect of *unregulated* gaming of any kind is a dark and scary storm cloud; just wait till you get to my chapter on "grey area" gaming! Remember that gambling is a cash business with millions of dollars changing hands. At that Donald Trump operated casino in California we handled about $100-million in cash a month in "coin-in." That much cash floating around with no regulation...especially given the dark history of casino gambling...is an open invitation to God-only-knows what sort elements. Clearly the United States Congress had to act fast to protect both the Tribes and the rest of the US population from people like... well, frankly, like my first employers in the gaming industry.

The resulting Pandora's Box was twenty-one pages of complex legalese woven into a Federal Law that Congress clearly thought would be an insignificant piece of legislation to appease the States as well as the Tribal Bingo halls. It was one of those pieces of Federal legislation where no one stopped to think about the implications before Congress approved it and Ronald Regan signed it.

As I said earlier, as 1985 I was working with tribes to support a bill introduced by Congressman Mo Udall of Arizona and by California Congressman Norm Shumway to affirm Indian Nations' right to have *any* form of gambling regardless of whether or not a state had any form of gaming regulation. Regardless of the motivation of the Congressmen, our motivation was two-fold.

As a longtime advocate of Indian Sovereignty, I wanted US law clearly and specifically to state that Indian Nations were sovereign enough to be independent of the rules, laws, and regulations of State governments. My involvement in this issue predated my casino career and went back to my college days when I headed a 10,000-member coalition put together to support the Oglala Lakota Nation "siege" of Wounded Knee in the early 1970s. For me, it was simply an issue of self-determination for people we had abused; and perhaps one day an expatriated location for me.

Secondly, by then I was an Atlantic City junketeer with the legendary Willie Maizer (and by extension Meyer Lansky), and I viewed the possibility of Indian casinos as a new market for me to deliver eager gamblers.

Though our bill was defeated, a couple of years later Congress *did* pass a compromise put together by Senator Daniel Inouye of Hawaii and Daniel Evans of Washington. The new law greatly reduced the scope and freedom offered by our bill and was probably expected to appease all sides enough for Indian Bingo to disappear as a troublesome political issue.

The *Indian Gaming Regulatory Act* (IGRA) tried to answer all of the emotional as well as legal questions that had been raised since the Bryan decision and more importantly since the Seminole decision. And, on the surface, the new law seemed to serve both goals well.

Addressing the emotional issue that games of chance and skill were a centuries-old part of Indian culture, IGRA defined games into three "classes[33]":

1. **Class I** gaming was defined as "social games played solely for prizes or minimal value.[34]" The law explained these as the traditional forms of Indian gaming played in connection with tribal ceremonies or part of tribal culture. The Act affirmed that the Indian Nations could conduct these games at their will and without interference or interest from any outside government. Wagering on these games was the private matter of the Tribe and the Individuals and would not be subject to any state or federal gambling laws.

Addressing the Seminole and California (Cabazon) issues of unrestricted Bingo prizes, IGRA set up a very specific category for Bingo and even allowed for the emerging 1980s technology that was beginning to allow electronic Bingo games.

2. **Class II** gaming was defined as "Bingo or lotto whether or not electronic or computer or other technologic aids are used.[35]" The law allowed the Indian Nations to run these games free of interference or regulation from any government. In fact, this section proved to be the most radical allowance of the law, affirming the sovereignty of the tribal nations by

181

noting that this Bingo right exists *whether or not states have legalized Bingo in any form and regardless of a state's approval or disapproval* of Bingo within its borders. Class II games were in fact the cornerstone of sovereignty and put to rest any issues still surrounding the Seminole and the Cabazon lawsuits as well as their fallout.

Finally, the law went on to totally quash any fears of unregulated Las Vegas style gaming-gone-wild by banning certain games except in very special circumstances:

3. **Class III** gaming was defined as "all forms of gaming that are not class I gaming or Class II gaming.[36]" These are the traditional Las Vegas style games like blackjack, pai gow, baccarat, *slot machines*, sports betting, roulette, craps, keno, lotteries, and so on. Once they were defined, the law went on to say that an Indian Nation could have these "Class III" games *only* if the State in which they are located allowed these sorts of games already *and* if the State entered into a specific contract with the tribe to allow the tribe to have these "Class III" games. The law called these "international" contracts a "compact".

In effect, the lawmakers apparently thought, the issue of unregulated games was dead since only Nevada and New Jersey had legalized "Class III" games. New Jersey had zoned casinos to only Atlantic City and Nevada was, well, *Nevada is Nevada*. But in 1988 the likelihood of any other state legalizing casinos did not seem very probable.

Just for good measure, IGRA went on to establish an independent federal regulatory agency; the National Indian Gaming Commission (the NIGC) was charged with a seemingly noble mission:

"The Commission's primary mission is to regulate gaming activities on Indian lands for the purpose of shielding Indian tribes from organized crime and other corrupting influences; to ensure that Indian tribes are the primary beneficiaries of gaming revenue; and to assure that gaming is conducted fairly and honestly by both operators and players.

To achieve these goals, the Commission is authorized to conduct investigations; undertake enforcement actions, including the issuance of notices of violation assessment of civil fines, and/or issuance of closure orders; conduct background investigations; conduct audits; and review and approve Tribal gaming ordinances.[37]"

Made up of a chairman (appointed by the President and confirmed by the Senate) and two commissioners appointed by the Secretary of Interior, at least two of the three had to be members of a federally recognized Indian Nation. Then, seemingly to give teeth to the law, the NIGC created 141 pages of fine-print rules and regulations published in Chapter 25 of the Code of Federal Regulations that already dealt with "Indians."

Advocates of IGRA and the NIGC insist that "Indian gaming is more heavily regulated and more secure than commercial gaming.[38] When the law was passed, almost three-decades ago, most everyone agreed that with Class III games virtually untouchable, the actual regulation of Bingo halls was a no-brainer job.

Then *it* happened. In March of 1989, less than a year after the passage of IGRA but four years before the first NIGC was appointed, the Governor of Connecticut received a certified letter demanding that his state comply with the new *Indian Gaming Regulatory Act* and enter into negotiations for a state compact with the Mashantucket Pequot Nation to establish Class III games.

Both the Governor and the Attorney General were at a loss. Their reading of IGRA defined Class III games as Vegas-style casino games. Casinos were illegal in Connecticut and the law required a state to negotiate a compact *only* if the State allowed these sorts of games already.

The attorney for the Pequot Nation reminded the Governor that Connecticut law did allow "Las Vegas Nights" to be held as fundraisers for charities; *the same kind of casino nights that allowed for MY grey-area SHT CREEK Casino in Baltimore at about the same time.* The Seminole and Cabazon questions of whether or not the Indian Nation could therefore have the same games but without the State's limits and regulation had been clearly addressed by IGRA. Moreover, IGRA had put teeth into the legislation by requiring that if a State government refused to negotiate a compact with a Tribe, then the Federal Government would negotiate on behalf of the State and enforce the State's compliance.

Five months later, in August of 1989, the Pequot Tribe filed suit in Federal Court against the State of Connecticut to force the Governor to negotiate a compact with the Tribe for a Class III casino. In mid-May of the following year, a Federal judge ordered Connecticut to negotiate a compact with the Tribe. In September, the US Court of Appeals upheld the ruling and in May of 1991, the US Supreme Court concurred.

In the same month, despite a flurry of anti-casino lobbying and scare tactics that included stories of an AIDS epidemic in casinos, mafia infiltration of Connecticut, and people losing their homes to gambling debts, the Bureau of Indian Affairs and the State of Connecticut agreed to a compact with the Tribe. Nine months later the largest casino in the world, *Foxwoods*, opened its doors in Connecticut —minutes from New York City. (Never mind the allegation that since no one lived on Tribal land at the time and the "Tribe" only had one member, Skip Hayward, who had spent his lifetime claiming to be white.)

The creation of Foxwoods, of course, set the precedent for Indian Nations within the border of any state that allowed charity "Vegas Nights," legal card rooms, off track pari-mutuel betting, state lotteries, or any other form of gambling…including Bingo halls. Overnight states found themselves compelled to enter into compact negotiations to allow casino gambling within in their states.

Suddenly, unintended and without warning, full-blown casinos were springing up in states that *thought* they had outlawed them.

Currently there are 249 Class III Indian casino compacts with states. Yet only twenty-eight of the 50 states have tribally-owned casinos...either Class III or Class II. These casinos have created more than 400,000 jobs, 75% of which are held by non-Indians, though in states of high unemployment (like the Dakotas) 80% of the tribal casino employees *are* Indians. Seventy-five-percent of Tribal casinos devote all of their revenue to Tribal governmental services, economic development, and charity. Only 73 of the tribes involved in gaming distribute the profits to their membership. Before IGRA there had been no successful Federal economic development programs on reservations.

Still, detractors of Indian casinos claim: that the casinos are legal shields for white con men to operate otherwise illegal casinos; that tribal gaming is an unregulated magnet for organized crime; that Indian people do not pay income taxes; that the casinos drain resources from surrounding non-Indian communities; and that a host of moral issues challenge areas that have voted opposition to gambling.

Despite hard evidence to counter each of these fears, and overwhelming non-Indian-support of casinos, many communities are still troubled by a taste of Las Vegas suddenly appearing down the street from their schools or churches. Even more troublesome to some, the states that did not have charitable "Vegas Nights," no state lotteries, and no racetrack betting found casinos popping up within their borders. States like North Carolina, Texas, Florida and Alabama, deep in the Bible belt found that Bingo halls were being transformed into what appeared to be full-fledged casinos. And in that "Class II" world, states were powerless to do anything at all about these casinos. After all, they were just playing Bingo...so it seemed.

Chapter Twelve

Bingo? It LOOKS like a slot machine to me
(invisible Bingo cards and virtual ping-pong balls)

"It depends on what your definition of "IS" is."
— President Bill Clinton

Shortly after the dot-com bubble began in the mid-1990s, I was standing at a booth at a casino trade show looking at an "electronic Bingo game" that made my eyes want to jump out of my head. For all the world, this game looked like a slot machine. I couldn't believe it was Bingo.

I walked up to the machine, put my coins in, pulled a handle (like an old one-armed-bandit handle), and watched video-game-looking slot machine reels spin. Bar-Bar-Cherry. No winner. I put another three coins in to spin again. Bar-Bar-Bar. I won! *It was a fucking slot machine!*

But it was not EVEN a slot machine. My putting the coins in the machine triggered a series of computer processes that were totally invisible to me but were happening in a fraction of a second on the computer.

Putting the coins in the machine "bought" me an *invisible* ("virtual" in computer lingo) Bingo card; a card that was only on the computer and running as a program in the background that I could not even see. I am serious: an INVISIBLE Bingo card!

Pulling the handle on the slot machine triggered two functions in the invisible computer program. First, it drew invisible (again "virtual") ping-pong Bingo balls from an invisible ("virtual") ball hopper. Seriously, follow me here: *we are talking invisible ping-pong balls too.* Then it *automatically* virtually (or invisibly) "daubed" my invisible Bingo card for any matching

virtual (invisible) numbers. Again, all unseen by me.

Pulling the handle also started a video cartoon movie running; which is all I was aware of (and, frankly, didn't know it was just a movie or a cartoon). The "movie" was of three slot machine reels spinning...looking like a real slot machine in Las Vegas, Atlantic City, Tunica, Biloxi, Reno or any other "real" casino. I thought I was playing a slot machine, not running a movie of a slot machine. When my invisible Bingo card "won", on my second play, the video movie stopped with three bars on the "pay line" so that it looked just like a slot machine.

The salesman explained to me that three bars on the video screen were an "electronic facsimile" of an *invisible* (virtual) diagonal Bingo on the virtual (invisible) Bingo card. Three cherries would have been an electronic facsimile of a vertical Bingo. Three lemons would have been an electronic facsimile of a horizontal Bingo. The top jackpot on the machine, several thousand dollars, would have been won by an electronic facsimile of a full-card cover Bingo... on that invisible Bingo card, of course.

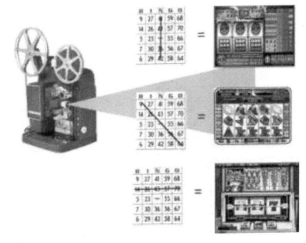

Welcome to Indian gaming Class II slot machines! Hell, welcome to the entire State of Alabama a few years later in 2007. Little did I expect that one day I would have more than 1,500 of these machines operating in an Indian casino in Oklahoma, convincing players they were gambling on "Las Vegas style slot machines;" or that I would be ordering ten thousand of these machines to place in "charitable Bingo halls" in Alabama in 2009. If I had not experienced this myself, I am not sure even I would believe it. In fact, to make things even more bizarre, when IGT, the largest slot machine company in the world, decided to get into the "Class II" market, I became their first and *single largest* customer with the first 600 of their first-generation "Class II" machines on my casino floor.

The existence of these invisible ping-pong balls revolves around a loophole in the law, how Bingo is played, and the U.S. Department of Justice's interpretation and enforcement of a federal slot machine law for Indian tribes. It also involves the necessity to clear up a lot of technical jargon; bear with me as we do so. While it may initially seem like gobbledygook, in reality creating this invisible Bingo is probably one of the most significant develops in gambling history.

IGRA firmly established the rules: if the state does not already allow gambling games and if the state is not interested in entering into a "compact" with a tribe, then the law limits Tribal Nations to only Class I and Class II games. That means a tribe is stuck with a Bingo hall if the citizens of a particular state do not want casinos in their backyard and if the state does not already have charitable "Vegas Nights" or a state lottery. *Or so it might seem!*

Here comes that amazing "Bingo" slot machine that I played at that trade show. Remember that little section of the Class II description that says *"whether or not electronic or computer or other technologic aids are used"?* Therein is the issue ... and the root of the seeming deception. And that is how such conservative states as Alabama, Oklahoma and Florida ended up with huge casinos.

Back when the Indian Gaming Regulatory Act was written, there was no Internet, there was no technology boom, there were relatively few personal computers, and there was no client/server computing that could exchange data. Bingo halls, especially in Nevada (and other states that allowed large-scale commercial Bingo) used primitive electronic aids to make Bingo games go faster. An electronic aid was as much a part of Bingo at that time as paper cards were a generation earlier; but by today's technological standards those late-1980s electronics look like watching reruns of the 1960s version of *Star Trek*.

In Bingo, since someone wins every game, the way the house (the casino) makes money is to play a lot of games or, rather, sell lots of cards per game. "Technologic aids" and "electromechanical facsimiles" of Bingo were invented to allow players to buy and play hundreds of cards at a time (and allowing the Bingo halls to sell "packs" of cards instead of individual Bingo cards).

In the early 1960s when I first started playing Bingo in commercial halls, cards were ten-cents each per game. Typically, a good player could accurately play four or six cards when a number was called. *(And since the cards were permanent and belonged to the house, I would wander from seat to seat collecting "hot" cards so I could win more frequently; a practice that pissed off the operators to no end.)*

In those days we covered the house-owned plastic cards with a popcorn kernel but by the early 70's that had evolved to disposable paper cards marked with an ink blotter called a "dauber" (to "daub" the number on the card). The house would make about 60-cents a game off of me or about six-bucks an hour before they took out the costs of payouts. After payouts, the house would make about $4.50 an hour off of my play. Multiply that by 100 players and the house is making $450 an hour operating the game; not bad in 1960s dollars if the joint is open eight hours a day seven days a week for a little more than three-grand a week. Add to that the additional revenue of selling me the ink-filled daubers as well as food & beverage, and it made for a nice little business.

By the late 1980s when IGRA was written, "electronic daubers" had been invented which would allow players to keep track of hundreds of cards at once. Suddenly the cost of playing one game of Bingo went up from a dime to 60-cents up to as much as $25 or $30 for a "session" of maybe 12 different games. But proportionally the chance of winning went up as well...and the length of time between winners went down.

In the 1980s a player could rent an dauber electronic unit and pay for a fixed number of Bingo cards for the unit; from one to several hundred. The most common electronic units (manufactured by really good companies like GameTech and others) looked like an over-sized calculator, but rather than calculator keys they would have numbers from 0 to 9. When a Bingo number was called, the player would press the keys for that number *(there was no need to have the letters B-I-N-G-O since they were virtually assigned to the proper numbers)*. The electronic unit then would search all the cards loaded into the unit (hundreds possibly) and if any of the cards contained the entered number, the card would be marked or "daubed" automatically. The player did not have to ever look at the cards; the machine did it all.

Circa 1989 GameTech's TED *(The Electronic Dauber)* that represented electomechanical facsimile of Bingo cards.

Once a unit "won" a Bingo, a floor runner would come to the player and visually confirm the winning electronic card to pay the prize or money to the player. All machines then would be automatically reset for the next game.

This was the most advanced "technologic aid" that existed when IGRA was written and what was *probably* expected to exist in Indian casinos under the "Class II" definition originally created by lawmakers. The addition of a video display of the slot-machine-like movie was established in a landmark 2001 court case created by a brilliant Chickasaw Indian lawyer named Jesse Green. Green had spent a career fighting to expand gaming on behalf of his tribe and other Oklahoma tribes and ultimately argued and won the landmark cases that defined electronic Bingo. Even up until his untimely death (from cancer) in 2012, my friend Jesse (no relation) continued fighting for innovate ways to defend sovereignty and Indian gaming.

The history of Bingo itself still plays a vital role in understanding what goes on in tribal casinos. Bingo itself was neither the invention of church fundraisers nor of carnivals, though both had a hand in it. The game apparently began in the 16th century with an Italian state-run lottery that featured a ball-draw and some letters printed in columns on a card with numbers under the letters. At least by the early 1900's a version of the game had found its way to the carnival circuit in the USA and was being played in horseshoe shaped booths covered with numbered cards and small piles of beans. When my father first joined traveling carnivals to working the gambling sides in the early 1940s, he began running these BINGO games.

The caller would draw a small wooden square from a cigar box, call out a number that was printed on the square, and wait for players to check their cards to see if the number called matched a number on their card. If it matched they would place a dried bean on the card over that number. Once a player filled a line of numbers on their card, either horizontally, vertically or diagonally, they would call out *"Bean-o!"* (because of the beans they were using to cover the numbers). Winning players would get a doll or some other carnival prize.

The folklore of Bingo tells us that in 1929 a traveling salesman named Ed Lowe bought some dried beans, a rubber numbering stamp and some cardboard to start his personal home version of the game. During one party at his house, one of his players was getting more and more excited as she got close to winning. When she finally won, she jumped from her seat, became tongue tied, and instead of shouting "Beano," she wildly stuttered "B-B-B-BEAN-GO!" There was such excitement and laughter about it all that Lowe decided to market the game and call it "BINGO".

While there probably is *some* truth to that version of the story, let's cynically also consider that "beano" was probably a public domain game and word associated with the game and the new "Bingo" word was something that could be copyrighted, patented, and sold. We *are* talking about a *business*, after all.

Regardless of the origin of the name, several months after Bingo hit the market as a home party game, Lowe was approached by a priest from Wilkes-Barre, Pennsylvania with an interesting Bingo problem. The priest had bought several sets of Lowe's two-dollar Bingo games to use as a fundraiser for his church, but each game produced half a dozen or more winners because of the duplication of winning combinations in each box and then even more duplication because he bought several game sets. Salesman Lowe could immediately see the tremendous market in fundraising with Bingo if he just could work out that little kink.

At an absurdly high fee (a charge per card of up to $100 near the end) he hired a Columbia University mathematician to devise 6,000 different card combinations for him. Suddenly BINGO was a real business and Lowe was marketing to churches, schools, and civic groups. From there it was a short step to commercial Bingo halls and the tremendous popularity of the game.

In the 1950s and early 60s when I was growing up, American Bingo was played with 75 ping-pong balls, each of which was imprinted with a number from one to 75. In addition to the number on each ball, there was also a letter on the ball (either B, I, N, G, or O). Of note, "Brazilian" Bingo (popular in all of Latin America) is a 90-ball game with no "free space"; this game has crept into the U.S. in a few electronic devices.

Basic Bingo has not really changed since those days. A Bingo player's card has 25 squares which are arranged in five rows and five columns. Each column is headed with a letter (either B, I, N, G or O) and each square has a number in it. The "B" column has five numbers randomly from the range of 1 to 15; the letter "I" has five numbers from 16 to 30; "N" has only four numbers from 31 to 45 (with the center space on the card in the "N" column as a "free" space); "G" has five numbers in the range of 46 to 60; and "O" also has five numbers taken from the range of 61 to 75.

The 75 ping-pong balls are put in a wire drum or a plastic air-blower and are drawn out one by one until someone wins. A caller reads the letter and number on each ball. Players look for a matching number on each of their cards and when they get a match of adjacent numbers in a row spelling B-I-N-G-O or get numbers in a row under any letter, they win.

Bingo differs from many gambling games in that someone always wins at Bingo; *the game continues until there is a winner.* With slot machines and other gambling devices (roulette for example) it is possible that all players lose and only the house wins. With Bingo, it is a contest against other players; the game continues until one player gets a "Bingo". This is a very important concept.

Since there has to be a winner of every game, the mathematical odds for how much money you can win at Bingo vary from hall to hall and are based on the difference between what the hall takes in and what is paid to the players. In other words, if the house pays prizes of $75 for every $100 taken in, the game operates at a 25% house advantage. That means the players can expect to lose 25-cents of each dollar they spend on "card packs". An average $25 purchase of "card packs" lasts for a one-hour session of Bingo. Hence, the house can count on winning $6.25 per hour per player. Average 250 players in a Bingo session and the house average win is $1,625 per hour. Four sessions per day and the house gross win is $6,500 a day.

This method of payoff is very similar to horse tracks or dog tracks that allow pari-mutuel betting. The players vie for cash generated by other players and *not from a house bank.* This, too, is a very important concept in Indian Gaming.

In other words, the players are playing against *each other* and not against the owners of the Bingo hall. The profit for the Bingo hall comes from the difference between what is paid out in winnings and the commission kept (the $25 in the above example).

Now we get a little technical, but follow me here and you will see why the invisible Bingo scam came into being. In casino terms, all of that payout math means that Bingo has a 25% "hold" (in this example)…higher than almost any table game, slot machine, or other game of chance in a casino.

However, in terms of revenue *per hour*, the number is vastly different. A traditional Bingo hall, to seat 300 or so players needs about 16,000 square feet. So the casino's daily win-per-square-foot-per-gaming day for Bingo is only about $4.06 (in this example) compared to a win-per-square-foot-per-gaming-day of anywhere between $12.50 and $50 for slot machines taking up the same amount of space.

In short, slot machines make from three to 12 times more than Bingo makes per square foot, despite the higher percentage win-per-game. Moreover, slot machines require fewer personnel to operate. Clearly, anyone with half a brain would want to have slot machines instead of a Bingo room. However, of course, the way IGRA was written, a slot machine would be classified as a "Class III" game rather than a Bingo game.

190

All this is well and good and makes for interesting lore on how Bingo works and where it came from, but it doesn't explain the virtual Bingo cards. What the laws did not anticipate was the incredible technology boom of the 1990s spurred by the dot-com bubble and the amazing graphic video games that can be played on almost any personal computer. It was *that* technology windfall that gave birth to the "virtual Bingo" or "invisible Bingo" slot machines that I first encountered at that trade show.

It seemed, at the time, that the only thing keeping Indian casinos from installing thousands of these "Bingo" slot machines (euphemistically called *"Class II machines"*) was a little-used federal law called "The Johnson Act[39]."

In the best of legalese, the Johnson Act attempts to outlaw slot machines by giving jurisdiction to the Federal Trade Commission and the FBI over manufacture, transportation, and usage of slot machines. The Act goes on to say, *"It shall be unlawful to manufacture, recondition, repair, sell, transport, possess, or use any gambling device in the District of Columbia, in any possession of the United States, within Indian country ... or within the special maritime and territorial jurisdiction of the United States...including on a vessel or documented under the laws of a foreign country.[40]"*

It then list pages of exceptions to that "general rule of law", most of which are for shipboard gaming but also contains the exception for any state that has legalized slot machines. Hence, states like Nevada, New Jersey, Mississippi, Missouri, Colorado, and so on are exempt.

The authority of the Johnson Act gets even murkier in its definition of a slot machine. Like the Indian Gaming Regulatory Act, this law was written at a time long before the technology explosion. The definition of a slot machine covered by this federal law gives an accurate description of antique slot machines like those in my collection, but doesn't come anywhere near describing a modern day slot machine in Las Vegas. The law defines a slot machine specifically:

"**(1)** any so-called "slot machine" or any other machine or mechanical device an essential part of which is a drum or reel with insignia thereon, and (A) which when operated may deliver, as the result of the application of an element of chance, any money or property, or (B) by the operation of which a person may become entitled to receive, as the result of the application of an element of chance, any money or property; or

(2) any other machine or mechanical device (including, but not limited to, roulette wheels and similar devices) designed and manufactured primarily for use in connection with gambling, and (A) which when operated may deliver, as the result of the application of an element of chance, any money or property, or (B) by the operation of which a person may become entitled to receive, as the result of the application of an element of chance, any money or property; or

(3) any subassembly or essential part intended to be used in connection with any such machine or mechanical device, but which is not attached to any such machine or mechanical device as a constituent part."[41]

Arguably, today's slot machines are far from the old mechanical reel devices. In fact, it is really hard to find a mechanical reel slot machine in most juris-

191

dictions; and even when you CAN find reels in a slot machine they are not mechanical, but are controlled by a computer chip and a random number generator. Again Chickasaw attorney Jesse Green came to rescue. Through judicial review, Greene forced the Federal government to exempt Tribes from the Johnson Act.

There you have the loopholes in the law. Moreover, if the laws are taken literally *...not on "intent" of the authors or predictions of future technology...* then The Johnson Act only deals with antique mechanical slot machines and their successors.

In the same literal style of interpretation, the IGRA regulations for "technologic aid" refer to any technological version of classical Bingo – *which would include even those invisible "virtual" Bingo cards and invisible ping-pong balls.*

Initially, when the technology of invisible Bingo was first devised it was widely seen as such a slimy interpretation of loopholes that the major slot machine manufactures would not have anything to do with it at all. The large, respectable, publicly-traded corporations like IGT, Bally, Aristocrat, and the others totally ignored that market.

"That market" was potentially huge. All of those sovereign Indian nations located in states with no form of gambling could now have slot machines. Prime among such states was Oklahoma which had dozens of Tribes that had been relocated to BIA trust lands. Even in states where Tribes had the ability to enter into compacts, placement of Class II Bingo machines would mean that the revenue from the games would not be taxable under state laws. As I said, the market was potentially huge.

Still, the large manufacturers avoided at best a grey legal (and at worst an out-and-out scam) area of these invisible Bingo cards. Thus the fabrication of these machines at first fell to a handful of garage manufacturers based in Georgia, South Carolina, and other traditionally non-gaming states. Moreover the sales schemes and marketing of these machines to Tribal casinos were initially in the hands of a group of companies that *Harpers Magazine* characterized as "rinky-dink, homegrown, "and "sinister.[42]"

The history of those companies was as bizarre as the "Class II" market they came to serve. Many of them began by manufacturing Windows® based video poker terminals in basements, garages, and mini-warehouses in South Carolina. That state, like most others, has had a decades long battle with "unregulated" (read: illegal) slot machines in backrooms at bars, gas stations and fraternal clubs like VFW, Elks, Moose, Eagles, and so on. South Carolina became so saturated with such games that in the early 1990s the state actually passed a law to regulate the games[43].

The bizarre law stopped short of legalizing casinos but allowed any business to have up to five (but not more) video poker or blackjack machines (not slot machines) but no advertising, promotions, nor comps for the games. The law went on to limit payouts to any one person to $125 per day, and to impose a tax on the machines and a tax on the winnings of the machines. No other regulation was attached to the law and almost immediately mini-casinos began popping up around South Carolina.

Each mini-casino was a building filled with small rooms with five machines in each room. Each room was its on Limited Liability Company and had its own electric meter. It was very common to see a 3,000 square foot triple-wide trailer with sixty electric meters behind it to support 300 video poker machines inside, with five machines per meter/room.

Beyond the whole spirit-of-the-law "grey area" issue (beyond the number of machines), these mini-casinos and the machines were not regulated. Non-regulated meant that the public was not protected from absurdly high holds, being cheated, validation that the games even played accurately, and a host of other machine-related issues. Non-regulated casinos meant that there was no protection from skimming, minors could gamble, there were no requirements for any internal control standards, no taxes on winning, no requirements that players even actually had to be paid if they won a big jackpot.

Least you brush off this South Carolina scheme as rinky-dink nickel-and-dime racket, the State of South Carolina reported that revenue from those video poker mini-casinos was $2.8-billion per year. That is BILLION with a "B"…and that is *reported* income in a jurisdiction that doesn't require reporting. Those unregulated machines were holding about 35% so the actual coin-in for a year was something near $7-Billion; Seven Billion dollars CASH was passing through South Carolina video poker machines every year. You can imagine the unscrupulous elements that flock to large unregulated amounts of cash and thus what South Carolina was like. I was there, and know exactly what it was like (and in a later chapter in this book I will discuss the unregulated gaming world).

Despite those huge numbers, wisely IGT, Bally, Aristocrat, WMS, and the legitimate slot machine companies that were licensed to provide games in regulated jurisdictions wanted no part of such at atmosphere. Even the *possibility* of questioning the legal operation of their games anywhere could result in the company losing its license to do business in a legitimate, protected, regulated jurisdiction. The *Dennis Gomes'* of the world had fought long and hard to clean up the gaming industry. Legitimate operators and legitimate vendors could not afford —nor *did they want*— to be involved in unregulated gaming. The casino world has come a long way from the Meyer Lansky days.

With so much cash flow there were all of the controversies one might expect and the overt sleaziness of having banks of electric meters behind converted mobile homes was a little much for almost *anyone* to swallow. Finally, in July of 2000, after almost ten years of operation, the Supreme Court of South Carolina ruled to outlaw video poker. This decision in a relatively unnoticed southern state seems, at first glance, neither particularly interesting nor germane to anything having to do with Indian Gaming. But a closer look at the video poker industry in South Carolina reveals some amazing precursors and shows how a handful of vendors ended up leading the charge into Indian country; vendors

193

characterized by an analyst at the University of Nevada at Reno as *"the lowest rung" of the casino industry[44]*.

Up until that ban, South Carolina – *which most people probably didn't know even had legalized casinos* – had more places to gamble than any other state...INCLUDING NEVADA. With more than 7,000 places to gamble, South Carolina had 36,000 slot machines (more than any state other than Nevada, New Jersey, and Mississippi)[45].

South Carolina's gambling empires were born of small businesses finding those absurd loopholes in the law like the electric-meter scam; of taking advantage of the fact that technology changed faster than laws changed; of the darkest, most consumer-exploitive gaming in the country. This is a familiar theme that we will see repeated as it was perpetuated against Indian tribes...and especially in other unregulated markets.

Since those huge publicly traded slot machine companies were nowhere to be seen in South Carolina, the dominant companies in South Carolina had names that ended with "Music Company," "Amusements" or "Coin Machines"; names that would at least be changed (though the owners and managers would remain the same) once they reached the Indian Tribes.

The names themselves give clue to the company origins and hence the origins of the transformation of Indian gaming a decade later. By the end of the 1960s the dozens of jukebox route vendors in the South were losing business. There were fewer and fewer jukeboxes as American music became more portable with cassette tapes (and eventually even CD's and ultimately iPods and MP3s). In search of another route business, many of these vendors initially entered the pinball machine route business. The business model was the same as jukeboxes had been: the vendor would own the machines, place them into various businesses (like gas stations, convenience stores, and bars) and split the profits with the owners of those businesses.

Additionally, pinball machines could become gambling devices of sort, with cash payouts given for "free games" won by players. Of course this practice was eventually outlawed by most states because of that gambling (or "skill game") aspect of it; nonetheless, the practice persisted. I recall as early as 1964 in East Tennessee watching guys play a pinball machine in the garage at a gas station my father owned; if they reached some magical number of points they would win a dime or multiple dimes for other point values. The dimes were paid out of my father's cash register. I quickly became a n*erd pinball wizard.*

By the late 1970s the early days of video games, like *"Pong"* and *"Space Invaders,"* had appeared. This also allowed traditional mechanical pinball machines, with their steel ball bearings and spring flapper-arms to be replaced or upgraded to video arcade games and video pinball games. By the early 1980s video arcades were all the rage for the former jukebox route jobbers and there familiar business model.

Under some state laws, "pinball" machines could become anything that could be represented on a video screen as long *as it was a skill game*. It might be

194

a representation of actual pinball with video balls and flappers, or it might be a Space-Invaders-kind of game where your "skill" allows you to kill more aliens than some players, or it might be...say...a video representation of five playing cards where your "skill" at playing video poker could earn you a higher score than other players. Get it?

South Carolina law outlawed games of chance, like most states. However, pinball was considered a game of "skill" because you "win" by playing the game better than other players. The law allowed that if a pinball player obtained certain scores they could "win" a free game on the machine. That definition of a "skill game" became very important by the 21st century on Indian reservations.

Now, follow this amazing leap of logic:

- If it cost a quarter to play pinball, then winning a free game must have a cash value of 25-cents. (That *cash value* will be very important.)

- If one possible outcome of a game is that you qualify for *one* free game, then another possible outcome could be that you qualify for 400 free games (or any number picked by the owner of the machine).

- If one free game has a cash value of 25-cents, then 400 games would have a cash value of $100.

- So if you played a 25-cent video arcade game you could possibly (though your amazing skill) win $100 from that one play. And THAT sounds a lot like slot machines to some people.

Though the law specifically banned distributing money to a player for winning, there was nothing in the law that banned distributing a free game to the player. Moreover, of course, since each free game had a cash value of 25-cents, there was nothing to keep the player from selling his "free games" back to the company for their face value.

So, instead of dropping coins into a winning tray (like an old-style slot machine) or dispensing a ticket-in/ticket-out coupon (like the newer slot machines), these machines simply paid off with a printed receipt indicating the number of "free games" or "credits" won; actually the words "free games" were usually replaced with the word "credits". A player that hit a jackpot of $1,000 would actually receive a printed receipt for "4000 credits". The winner would then take the printed credit voucher to the cashier cage and "sell" it to the cashier for a thousand bucks. Just to make certain the player (and the State) understood these were playable credits and not a cash payout; the machine stored those playable credits and allowed the player to actually use them as free games. The voucher was only printed if and when the player decided to "print a receipt"...a multi-step function initiated by the player through touching a series of spots on the video screen.

For enterprising trailer owners that wanted to be in the casino racket, the vendors were happy to enter into a standard jukebox style revenue share agreement and even teach the operator how to skirt the law. *"Think of it like a flea market renting out little stalls to different people,"* one South Carolina machine vendor explained to me at the time. *"It is totally legal; you payout to the customer by buying their game credits from them at the cash value of a free game,"* one vendor explained to me as he tried to convince me to install 300 games. The revenue share was normally 50/50 but in some cases the vendor took as much as 80% of that almost $3-billion dollars.

Once the games were outlawed, those vendors were losing a whole lot of money. They needed a "new South Carolina" to ply their trade. Most set their sights on Indian Tribes. The plan was to use the same strategy of finding legal loopholes and jump head first into the fastest growing gaming market in America: tribal casinos. Let's consider the South Carolina elements they could bring to Indian tribes:

SOUTH CAROLINA ELEMENT	INDIAN COUNTRY VERSION
In South Carolina, these vendors found a loophole in the definition of pinball machines and through video technologies created video poker.	For Indian reservations these very same guys found a loophole in the definition of *"electronic aids to Bingo"* and created slot machines with invisible or virtual Bingo.
In South Carolina, the vendors owned the machines and placed them in the businesses at no charge, splitting revenues with the business proprietor on a 60%-40% basis or in best cases a 50%-50% basis.	This same method was used for Tribes which were not able to buy machines – they were not for sale. That sleazy aspect of the scheme often turned into an illegal and usury way of financing entire casinos for poverty-stricken Tribes.
In South Carolina the vendors helped business proprietors set up dozens of independent enterprises to each house five machines separate and apart from the other machines. Besides skirting the law limiting the number of machines, this system forced each small group of machines to have its own accounting records; maintained by the vendor and not by the business. In such a system, it was impossible for the proprietor to know exactly how the machines were doing.	Vendors used the same technique of keeping games from any central accounting by keeping game machines separate from any other vendor's games. This way, the Indian casinos could not have any sort of central accounting system to analyze all games from all vendors (or *any* games from some vendors). In fact, some vendor's machines would only allow performance and revenue reports to be run by the vendor's employees who had the right passwords.
In South Carolina the pay tables for the machines and the frequency a customer could win was set by the vendors and not by casinos. Unlike Vegas, where casinos compete with each other by adjusting the payouts of machines, in South Carolina every machine from any one vendor paid out the exact same percentages at any casino in the State.	The exact same system remained in place when these vendors moved to Indian gaming.

This is one of several absurdities of the first forays into Indian Gaming, exploiting Tribe's desperate need for games since the "legitimate" vendors avoided Class II; and it was a model that made me, at very least, unpopular with a number of machine vendors. I required a centralized accounting system and MY access to it. As recently as 2007 I was having that argument with Class II vendors and calling the president of one of the companies *an asshole* for not allowing it; I got taken off his Christmas card list (though his wife and his vice president of sales both continued to sleep with one of my key operational executives (all three at the same time) to hold *his* interest in their company).

Not particularly surprising, among the first vendors of the Class II "revenue share" machines to rush to the Indian casinos were permutations of South Carolina and Georgia gaming companies: *VGT* (Video Gaming Technologies) then of Roebuck South Carolina; *Nova Games* of Piedmont South Carolina; *Cadillac Jack Gaming* of Duluth Georgia; *World Touch Gaming* of Cumming Georgia; *SED* (Select Electronic Devices) of Greenville South Carolina (and later Duluth Georgia) and a handful of others. Amongst those first movers, VGT almost alone stood out as company that from its beginnings worked to differentiate itself from the sleaziest elements of the industry by focusing on quality, hands-on client service, and regulated-quality integrity of their games.

The biggest of these companies was *Leisure Time Technology* of Norcross Georgia with their popular "Pot-O-Gold" game. In 2012, looking back on those days, the founder of that company confessed to me that he personally made close to a billion dollars over several years in that era. In 2001 that company filed a bankruptcy following the end of South Carolina gaming as well as accusations by Arizona authorities that in their State the company (1) was selling gaming devices to tribes that lacked state gaming compacts, (2) illegally moved slot machines across state lines, and (3) provided false information to regulators and misrepresenting its financial condition in documents filed with the SEC[46]. Nonetheless, the reorganized company (as Vision Gaming and Technology) sold and re-licensed their games to pop up at Indian casinos all over the country. In 2008, Vision was purchased by the aforementioned SED Gaming which itself was deep into Indian Country as well as other grey markets like Alabama.

By far the shadiest of any of the companies were a group of middle-men who neither owned technology nor machines. They were merely salesmen at best (con men at worst) who used sweetheart contracts, cash-payments, prostitutes, and old-fashioned kickbacks to develop and exploit relationships with Tribal officials and management. In the big historical picture, these *Route Operators* (as most called themselves from the old jukebox term) did not differ substantially from the *Comancheros* who cheated, exploited, and stole from the Pueblo, the Comanche, the Apache, the Kiowa, and the Navajo a century earlier.

These companies would negotiate an "exclusive territory" to be the distributing agents for a particular manufacturer or several manufacturers. The "exclusive territory" was a business model that former jukebox rack-jobbers fully understood and encouraged. Among other benefits, it meant that the manufactures did not have to hire expensive sales and support staff; those would be furnished by the jobber...er..."exclusive territory company".

The middlemen, or jobbers, would agree to distribute a minimum number of machines in exchange for their exclusive territory. The manufacturer would agree, as part of such a deal, to reduce the revenue share to a more standard 20% going to the manufacturer: still a pretty substantial figure as we will see shortly.

Think of it like this: A company agrees to put one machine in your gas station (for example). The machine wins $100 a day. The owner of the machine takes $20 of that and leaves you a daily profit of $80. Now, the owner of the machine has so many machines that he will not deal with anyone who wants less than 100 of his machines. Your gas station can't handle that many machines so a middleman steps in. The middleman takes 100 machines from the owner and agrees to assign one to you. The middleman needs to be paid too, so he takes another 20% of that $100 for himself. That leaves you with only $60 out of every $100 taken in.

With only 20% of gross revenue needed to pay the manufacturer/owners, the jobbers were free to negotiate whatever deal they could arrange by whatever method they found necessary. Consequently it was not uncommon to see revenue shares with numbers like 37½%, 32.6%, 40%, or in some cases totally upside down deals with the middleman taking as much as 60% and leaving only 40% for the tribe. The lopsided jobber commissions were used, among other things, to fund the "marketing expenses" of the jobbers.

What kind of marketing expenses? At the 2005 convention and trade show of the *National Indian Gaming Association*, at least one of the jobber middleman companies flew three prostitutes from Nevada to the convention site in San Diego to "entertain" select Tribal officials and casino managers. The services of the girls were offered to members of my own staff in exchange for placement of machines on the casino floor; unfortunately for the jobber, my slot manager was a gay man and had no interest in that particular gratuity.

In this bizarre discussion of invisible Bingo, I have not even touched on the *other* type of Class II machine, the virtual "pull-tab" machine; but these machines are so scarce and generate such little revenue that they hardly merit more than a paragraph or so. These machines dispense paper pull tabs (legal under Class II definitions) like any vending machine.

Pull tabs are small cards that either have printed "no winner" or indicate a prize amount won. A pull tab session contains a fixed number of cards, say for example 1,000 cards. Each card is sold to the player for a fixed price, say one dollar. The lot of 1,000 cards will contain, for example, $750 in cash winning tickets ranging from $1 prizes up to a $500 prize. The total of all winning tickets adds up to only $750 (in this example) even though $1,000 worth of tickets would be sold in a cycle. The casino keeps the remaining $250; a 25% hold.

Traditionally pull tabs were sold manually to players. However there are pull-tab dispensing machines that will also sell the cards to the player. These machines often have video screens that look like slot machine play or look like video poker play (without the player's ability to "hold" cards for the outcome). Clearly dispensing machines (they actually drop the little card-ticket into a tray with each purchase), pull tab machines do not carry the "invisible game" stigma carried by virtual Bingo machines.

As I said, pull tab machines are such a small part of the landscape that they are insignificant other than to understand that many Indian casinos do have these machines; but they are the basis for the 21st century grey-market of "sweepstakes" machines across America (more on this later). For the "Class II" world consider pull tabs a niche market that comes nowhere near competing with slot machines but are often confused with slot machines because of their video screens. Many vendors take advantage of this confusion to argue that their machines are not slot machines (as defined by the Johnson act) but merely vending machines like pull tabs; the electronic Bingo argument.

For the Leisure Time bankruptcy, the "middleman" companies, and for the remaining southern-based companies, South Carolina's multi-billion dollar industry was a mere drop-in-the-bucket compared to Indian country's growing $14, $15 or $16-*Billion* industry. So it was not long at all before a second tier of manufacturer/vendors jumped into the Class II market.

Two companies quickly rose to the top of the pack amongst the myriad of new (non-South Carolina) vendors to rush into Class II: (SDG)*Sierra Design Group* (later purchased by Bally) and *Multimedia Games* of Austin Texas. In radically different ways, these two companies totally changed the landscape of Class II casinos and ultimately opened the doorway for the larger manufactures to step into the market.

The stage was set for big business to enter Indian gaming by three disparate events.

First and foremost was the size of the cash market itself. I don't think the average American has any grasp of how much actual cash flow we are talking about in just one casino. The numbers are staggering even to me as an insider. If a casino has 2,000 slot machines on its floor winning an average of $150 per machine per day, that is a daily gross profit of $300,000 or an annual gross of $109,500,000 (that is almost $110-million) profit for just one casino...all in cash and all in small bills. If we extrapolate that win to coin-in then there is more than $1.2-*Billion* dollars of cash flow per year for just one casino...CASH MONEY. And someone had to count that $3.28-million that came through the machines every single day; that would be more than 164,000 twenty-dollar bills.

We discussed the cost of buying a slot machine. But in the Indian Country model imported from South Carolina, the games were not for sale. In a revenue-share deal the vendor took 20% and the tribe kept 80%. In that arrangement, slot machine vendors would take home $21.8-million per year per casino of the size I used in the example above. Hence rather than a one-time $26-million for the sale of slot machines, the vendor company would take the $21.8-million a year for six years and 11 months; or a total of almost $150.7-million for their trouble of providing financing. *(Moreover, the wholesale actual cost for those second-*

tier machines was much less than that $13,000 average retail figure; it was closer to $5,000). That is certainly enough return to get big business' attention, after all..

Secondly, IGT, Bally, and the other large publicly-traded corporations that manufacture slot machines were already heavily involved in Indian gaming before these invisible Bingo schemes came along. Remember the entire world of Class III games, which includes real Las Vegas style slot machines. The Indian Gaming Regulatory Act allows tribes to have that type of game provided the tribe enters into a compact with the State. Tribes located in "compacted" states, like California, had access to real slot machines from real vendors.

For years, through its South Dakota subsidiary, SODAK Gaming (SO-South; DAK-Dakota) IGT offered tribes a lease-purchase agreement so that the tribes did not have to come up with millions of dollars upfront to get started in the casino business. A typical revenue share pioneered by SODAK and copied by the other big boys in the industry was that 80/20 split with SODAK taking 20% of the win-per-unit and the tribe taking 80% over the term of five years to finance the machines. With a $150 average win-per-unit-per-day, IGT would finance a $13,000 machine for a mere $54,750. Calculating that as simple interest, it is 300% charged to the tribe. And THAT is the model used by LEGITIMATE, large publically traded corporations.

That, keep in mind, is the standard deal *without* the whole scheme of Class II invisible Bingo balls and taking 30% to 40% of revenue rather than 20%.

Meanwhile even in the Class III market with regular Vegas-style slot machines, individual state compacts varied on how many slot machines could be installed. In California for example, the pre-Schwarzenegger (under Governor Gray Davis)compacts with tribes limited each tribe to no more than 2,000 machines (regardless of the number of casinos a tribe might own). The only way around that 2,000 machine limit was to add Class II machines to the mix; the state compacts had no jurisdiction over Class II machines (and hence no tax could be collected for them).

If Class II machines could be made to look like and act like regular slot machines, then who would know the difference? And THAT was clearly a market demand for invisible Bingo balls. The fact that IGT's SODAK was already among the biggest vendors in Indian gaming at very least made IGT closely watch the Class II market.

The third factor that set the stage for the big boys to enter the market was a series of decisions from the IGRA-created *National Indian Gaming Commission*. By the early 2000's the NIGC was carefully looking at invisible Bingo and apparently scratching their collective heads wondering what happened to good old-fashioned Bingo. At first they questioned the whole concept of invisible Bingo by disallowing certain games, fining casinos and their operators, and closing down some casinos.

But the grey-area vendors were old hands at skirting government regulations and they were quick to respond to the NIGC. When the NIGC insisted that "invisible Bingo" was absurd, the manufacturers responded by making video-movies of miniature Bingo cards *visible* on the screens of the slot machines. Hence it was still *virtual* but no longer *invisible*. When the NIGC raised the same issue about invisible ping-pong balls, the manufacturers responded in the same way. They made an animated cartoon ball draw appear on the screen.

The Indian Gaming Regulatory Act very specifically further defines electronic aids to Bingo as something that "broadens participation by allowing *multiple players to play with or against each other* rather than with or against a machine." No problem. The vendors simply expanded the client-server technology so that all the players were playing from the identical ball draw by networking the slot machines like personal computers in an office.

Simple as THAT sounds, it is one of the most perverse complications that led to the big boys coming into the market. A normal slot machine, in Vegas, is a stand-alone unit. That means that if every other slot machine in a casino is unplugged and only one remains plugged in, that one can still operate. That is NOT the technology that the South Carolina boys used in Indian Country.

For a "stand alone" slot machine, the computer in the machine must have the entire game program, accounting of the money, and all the elements on that one machine. If you have 1,000 machines in a casino then those programs must be replicated 1,000 times. Even more complex, each of those 1,000 machines must have its own random number generator chips (that randomize the outcome of each game). That is a damned expensive and technologically complicated process; no wonder they get $13-large for selling the machines!

For years the large manufacturers advocated a more simple technology that would allow one copy of the programs and one control chip to sit on one computer server. Each slot machine would be just a terminal, receiving everything from the server. It would work just like the Internet. In fact "server based gaming" is the big trend that slot vendors are pushing right now in their sales departments and at this writing is the current "state of the art" offering from IGT, WMS, and others.

In their wisdom, the *Nevada Gaming Control Board*, as well as other regulatory agencies around the country, has been very slow to approve this technology because...well, at best, its integrity and security seems a little questionable. In short, if someone can hack into a web site, it is not unreasonable to think that they *possibly* could hack into a slot machine that uses the same technology as the internet. Nonetheless, a version of server-based games is all the rage currently amongst the slot manufacturers.

But our boys, late of South Carolina and Georgia, had been using "client server" technology all along. Who wanted to be bothered with those cumbersome individual chips for each slot machine or having to replicate the program hundreds of times? After all, it is not as if these games were subject to pesky regulations that verified game integrity. From the onset, many of their models *required* a server with the slot machines being just dumb terminals. Those that did not use the server model used stand-alone machines that did not meet even the basic minimum requirements for Nevada or other tightly regulated jurisdictions; some were actually written in MSDOS-based programming code and some were hard-coded boards from Taiwan with built-in reset cheats and 35% holds. (See my upcoming chapter on grey-area gaming).

The companies who at that time were using server technology had it easy: when the server program picked the virtual ping-pong balls *(now visibly represented on the screen by a video cartoon of balls with numbers on them)*, it was a simple step to have the same pick of balls for every single machine. After all, it was just one program doing it. *So another NIGC objection was answered by technology.*

From afar, the major manufacturers continued to watch Tribal gaming. However, it would take two more developments to get them to jump into the fray. Those two developments would set the final stage for corporate America to enter Indian gaming in a big way.

If we accept, as somehow legitimate, the leap of logic that allows the invisible Bingo cards and virtual ping-pong balls to be replaced by video cartoons of Bingo then the next steps in development of the Class II market makes perfect sense. If we reject the legitimacy of invisible Bingo, then we might have a hard time believing the bizarre spiral of events and inventions that came next. It is important to remember that this entire business is based on the loophole of the *electronic facsimile* of Bingo.

The final stage begins with a relatively amazing way to convert regular slot machines to the virtual Bingo format. Sierra Design Group (SDG) was a brilliant little technology company founded by a casino industry veteran who created a methodology that would allow familiarly branded slot machines to operate in a Class II environment.

The Bingo-only Indian casinos could use the SDG platform so that players now could play slot machine titles they recognized from Vegas, Atlantic City, Tunica, or any of the Class III Indian casinos. Suddenly players in states where slot machines were outlawed could play IGT's stalwart brands like *"Double Diamonds"* and *"Lucky Larry"*, Bally favorites like *"Blazing 7's"*, Aristocrat market leaders like *"Jumping Joeys"*, and scores of other proven titles.

Up to this point Class II games had brand-names that no one particularly knew or had any loyalty toward…outside of the small grey-market areas where they were played. The only consistent brand had been the *"Pot-O-Gold"* machines, which were branded as much by the animation in its bonus rounds as any other feature and they were not EVEN class II. But the new SDG innovation allowed Bingo hall casinos to lose that South Carolina-like atmosphere that Harper's Magazine had called *dark, depressing, and as un-Vegas-like as possible*[47]. Instead, these Bingo hall casinos could be alive with recognizable and exciting branded games. A television advertisement for Florida's Seminole Tribe's Class II casino (before they added Class III) summed it up perfectly, *"Real Games; Real Fun."*

Using SDG's servers and Bingo platform (or video lottery platform in some states), two major break-throughs were accomplished. First, the branded titles were brought to the players in areas where those very titles had been outlawed. Much more importantly for the development of the industry was the licensing of game programs that IGT, Bally, Aristocrat, and others leased to SDG. This allowed the big companies to see how well their games would do in the Class II market...without having to risk the investment of developing server-based games with *phony-baloney* Bingo back ends. (And without endangering their licenses in regulated states.) If the SDG experiment was a success, then it would be a positive metric for the big boys to consider entering the market.

Equally as important to the landscape being tilled for the big boys was the contribution of publicly-traded Multimedia Games (MGAM). Primarily a technology company focused on gaming (rather than a gaming company looking for technology), MGAM brought a number of technological improvements to the landscape. This Austin Texas based company led some major fights with NIGC regulators to define the nature of Bingo facsimile. They won some and they lost some.

Publicly traded on NASDAQ since 1996, MGAM's CEO Gordon Graves moved Bingo-based games light years ahead of the old South Carolina model that had sprung from lesser companies' survival desperation. Like SDG, Graves and MGAM licensed branded games from Nevada-popular slot machine companies and adapted them to the Class II requirements with MGAM's own proprietary protocols.

He replaced the old South Carolina printed receipt of game credits with a slick high-tech EFT (electronic funds transfer) card that appeared to store the "credits" like an ATM card but (like a real ATM card) merely stored a customer ID number and recorded the cash transaction (and player data) on a server. This allowed players to take the EFT card out of one machine and move to another and play credits stored on their server account and identified on the card...either from credits won on the previous machine or cash deposits onto the card.

Graves also successfully mimicked IGT's thriving pay table formula of giving frequent payouts of small values.

MGAM also created an "instant Bingo" platform called "MegaNanza", which still played "invisible Bingo" but was much more slot-machine like in its internal workings. It also pitted the players against the casino rather than against each other. Though rejected by NIGC's Class II scrutiny, it did set the standard for how an instant Bingo machine should and *could* work for players. In 2002 the NIGC informed tribes that the most-popular game in play in many Indian casinos, MGAM's "MegaNanza" machines, were Class III and any tribe using them without a compact would be fined. In some cases these machines were winning in excess of $400 a day for the Tribes. This setback, of course, wounded MGAM and the Tribes but it also fueled the company to find a new way to generate revenue.

However, by far, all technology aside, Gordon Graves and MGAM's most important contribution to the landscape of Indian gaming was the company's own business model. More than anything else they or any other company did, MGAM's business model opened the door for the major companies to take the market seriously.

In the world of slot machine sales (or leases for that matter), there is fierce competition between manufacturers. Offering *branded* machines gives a competitive advantage, but equally important for obtaining market share is customer perception of the machines; the belief by customers that the machines payout well. Machine manufacturers pay for promotions in casinos, give away tee-shirts and trinkets to players, and advertise their brand-specific games locally for casinos. On the wholesale side, the manufacturers offer special discounts, incentives, and a whole host of inducements to get market share...to get floor space...to get more games on a casino's floor.

MGAM created a relatively unique way to guarantee floor space for their machines: they financed the casino, built it, directed construction, managed it, and marketed it for the tribes...all in exchange for a guarantee of floor space for their machines. Of course the company denied that they managed and marketed and argued about building, but the facts were pretty clear.

In the tiny town of Thackerville Oklahoma, one mile from the Texas border on Interstate 35, MGAM "financed," hired designers, and assigned a construction project manager to build a 1,300-machine casino for the Chickasaw Tribe. It became the closest casino to the 1.2-million people an hour away in Dallas Texas. In exchange, the Tribe gave approximately 80 percent of the floor space to MGAM's machines, plus shared 30 percent (rather than 20%) of gross revenues from those machines with the company[48].

The casino was so successful that MGAM repeated the process all across the country both for the Chickasaw Tribe and for other tribes. MGAM created finance deals for the Osage Nation, the Peoria Tribe, and the Kickapoo Tribe. In fact, in November of 2004, MGAM (through its subsidiary company, "Mega-Bingo") even went so far as to buy land for a tribe; a tract of 216 acres and another of 118 acres[49]. Additionally, Multimedia Games owned the fixtures (lights, seats, etc.) in the building until the end of the contract[50]. And, on top of the 30% revenue share, MGAM wanted another 2% to put into a special "marketing fund" to promote their games at the casino.

Let's do some quick math. There were (at that time —*a LOT more now*) approximately 1,300 games at Thackerville and Multimedia had 80% of those...or 1,040 machines. Thackerville drew patrons from Dallas and had a win per unit per day of around $600, but let's be very conservative and assume a daily win-per-unit of only that same $150 figure we have been using. That is a daily win per unit for MGAM (at 30%) of $45. Multiplied by 1,040 machines, that is a daily take for the company of $46,800 or an annual take of $ 17,082,000. Over the course of the five-year agreement, that is a total of $ 85.41-million for

204

MGAM. *(Of course you can actually multiply that time four for a more accurate number: $342-million. That is a hell of a return on the investment.)*

In addition to that huge revenue, the "development deals" (as MGAM liked to call them) also required tribes to pay an additional daily fee back to Multimedia based on the number of other gaming manufacturers' machines[51]. This sort of penalty fee at just the Thackerville facility covered about 260 slot machines and forced the tribe to compute that penalty fee into the cost of operating any machines other than MGAM's; in short, any other vendor was penalized from the onset.

In 2004 when I talked to Summit Structures, the company that built the fiberglass tent-like structure that became the Thackerville casino, I was quoted a price of about $13-million to build a similar facility. Again, in terms of simple interest, MGAM makes a cool 85% interest for loaning the tribe money to build a casino…and that does not include the penalty fees charged by MGAM against those vendors' games.

There of course is no applicable Federal usury ceiling for this kind of transaction and the State of Oklahoma has a maximum rate for business loans of 45%[52]. But, as we have discussed, Indian tribes are sovereign nations and in most cases immune from State or Federal law. So such a "loan" was certainly legal.

Tribes, generally speaking, are unable to get more traditional business loans for a number of reasons. Firstly, many financial institutions don't want to fund casinos or other "sin businesses." Secondly, and more importantly, under the Federal "sovereign nation" status that allows the casinos to exist, the land and building cannot be used as collateral for a loan because they cannot be sold. This is a complex issue, but for now it is sufficient to recognize it as a significant roadblock to traditional financing. Finally, tribes cannot be sued for default on a loan or a contract unless a specific waiver allowing them to be sued is signed; remember the bank would be trying to sue a "foreign country" in that nation's court system —in "Tribal Court".

With nothing for the banks or traditional financial institutions to latch onto for collateralizing their loans or setting recourse, there were no sources of funds other than "development deals" like the MGAM deal…or handfuls of other far less scrupulous deals (if you can imagine *that*). I will discuss these deals in more detail in my chapter on managing, financing, and marketing casinos.

The Chickasaw had few or no other options (at that time) than to play with MGAM. And the income from that one Thackerville casino accounted for about 15% of MGAM's revenue for 2003. It is no wonder that seven other similar deals were started by the company[53]. In Goldsby Oklahoma the machine revenue share for MGAM "financing" was reported to be a 40% share for MGAM. Stock in the slot machine company jumped from a 2002 low of $17.82 a share following the NIGC's "MegaNanza" decision to a high of $49.05 by January of 2004 with the Thackerville deal as the new business model.

By their own business model, MGAM had become a casino developer, a casino manager, a land management company, a finance company, a slot machine company, a fixture supplier, a marketing company, and who knows what else. *In short, MGAM became a casino company with the Chickasaw Tribe fronting for them.*

In late April of 2004, NIGC Acting General Counsel Penny Coleman sent MGAM and the Chickasaw Nation a "letter of determination" informing them that the NIGC had determined that the Thackerville "development" agreement was actually a management contract under the definition of IGRA and 25 C.F.R.

On the surface and to an industry outsider or a casino player this might seem like some industry technical mumbo-jumbo. However, an understanding of this distinction shows how it changed Indian gaming forever. For one thing, at the shallow-most level, it helped MGAM's stock to plummet below $7 a share. While I note that as the shallowest of the impacts of the decision, most of my analyst friends would tell you that a loss of 86% market cap is devastating to most companies. *(Market cap is a measure of the total dollar value of all outstanding shares of a company, computed as shares times the current market price. This is a pretty standard measure of corporate size and strength.)*

Up until the decision letter, other vendor companies had begun to follow the successful MGAM model. Georgia-based Cadillac Jack Games bought prefabricated buildings for casinos in exchange for floor space[54] and other companies investigated the same model.

Cadillac Jack (CJ) moved away from that business model after they were purchased by Russian oligarch and casino mogul Oleg Boyko. But CJ's troubles in Indian Country were far from over; Oklahoma's Indian Gaming casino regulator, David Cook, repeatedly had said he would not license Cadillac Jack for Tribes he represented because of Boyko's alleged Russian organized crime ties. The company *was* able to get licensed through its CEO, Russian Gene Chayefsky, a Boyko associate without his boss' publicity baggage. Cook had been troubled by published reports by a group of Russian journalists that claimed Boyko and the Russian First Deputy Finance minister Andrey Vavilov had created a "National Reserve Bank" to run a large financial fraud. According to the journalists, in February 1995 Vavilov signed an agreement with Boyko to transfer $92-million U.S. dollars to "National Credit" for financing Boyko's foreign investments. Vavilov allegedly sent $45-million Boyko in return for a home in Los Angeles and a penthouse in New York.

Meanwhile, Chayefsky and Cadillac Jack became embroiled in a control issue with founder (and 30% stakeholder) Mike Macke as the company began pitching Class II games in Mexico. Finally in 2012 the cloud over CJ completely disappeared when the Canadian *Amaya Gaming Group* purchased the company. A highly-respected publically-traded company (on Canada's TSX Venture Exchange), Amaya is a straight-as-an-arrow company focused on multiple verticals within the *regulated* gaming world. Once Cadillac Jack was part of Amaya, the old (and perhaps questionable) business practices disappeared and CJ focused on regulated gaming.

Back in Oklahoma, MGAM's management issues were coming to a head. A "management contract" under the *Indian Gaming Regulatory Act* is far more than a simple agreement to manage a casino. Just the *definition* of the contract takes up nine pages of the tiny-print Code of Federal Regulations. The 4,833 words that define a management contract are backed up by an extremely complex approval procedure. At this writing, the approval process for a management contract is taking 18 months to two years. *(See the Trump management contract in the Endnotes of this book).*

An NIGC-approved management contract also must adhere to very specific regulations, which include among other things, limiting the amount of money the management company can make and restricting the scope of activities in which the management company can participate. The regulations also prohibit a management company from owning or transferring ownership of any land or other real property. Even more complexly, a management contract requires submission of three years of detailed financial statements, detailed background and personal information of the officers of the company (even down to misdemeanor and traffic convictions), and specific limitations on the activities of the officers of the company. Moreover, IGRA requires that tribes maintain "sole proprietary interest" in their gaming enterprises.

In short, the NIGC destroyed the MGAM[55] business model. MGAM responded with a bevy of chest-pounding statements claiming that the NIGC acted beyond their scope and that NIGC's decision was not presented in a timely manner[56].

Additionally, MGAM had its client tribes raise as much political pressure as possible to defend the business model by characterizing it as some sort of charitable effort by MGAM to help poor tribes that could otherwise not afford to enter into the lucrative world of casino gaming. Lobbying was so powerful that the leadership of the Senate Indian Affairs Committee, Senator Ben Nighthorse Campbell and Senator Daniel Inouye fired off a two-page letter "warning" the NIGC that the commission was having a *"chilling effect"* on *"those who would come forward to assist tribes."* The letter continued, *"As you well know, for many tribes entering the gaming arena, their only means of providing compensation to those who are involved in the start-up and development of gaming enterprises is to commit a percentage of future net revenues to pay for these non-management agreements."*

This "charitable enterprise" argument, as humanitarian as it might have sounded at the time, was a hard pill to swallow when it came to a close look at the Thackerville issue. The Chickasaw Tribe and MGAM owned more casinos than any other Tribe in the country and at the time was expanding with several multi-million dollar projects.

The destruction of the development contracts further opened the doors for other manufactures to step into Indian gaming. With the *"other vendor penalty"* removed for properties, the new opportunity to lend money to tribes, and most importantly the destruction of the single-vendor monopoly, the stage was finally set for the major vendors to step into Class II gaming. *And it happened quickly.*

Bally Gaming, the Reno Nevada based giant (and *among* the inventors of video poker), bought Sierra Design Group (SDG) and instantly was in the market; and in fact dominating the State of Washington by taking control of SDG's large customer base. The former owner of third-largest commercial slot machine manufacturer Aristocrat, joined with Bally's former CEO to found an exclusively Class II company called *C2 Gaming* (and those founders, Steve Wiess and Lowell Hansen (respectively) are two of the industry's stalwarts of integrity, unlike many of the companies' that were already in Class II gaming on the roadway from Georgia and South Carolina).

Frank Haas and I traveled repeatedly to Reno and to South Dakota to try to convince the 900-pound-gorilla, IGT, to enter into the Class II universe. When at long last they agreed, I took the very first 600 machines off the Reno assembly line. Shortly afterwards IGT abolished their SODAK Indian gaming division (which they had not founded in the first place), folding it into the primary company and began large scale manufacturing of their own Class II platform with placements almost immediately in Florida, Alabama and Oklahoma.

All the doorways were open and all the roadblocks were cleared for corporate America to enter Indian gaming. But it was not instantly smooth sailing for the corporate giants. At dinner one night in Oklahoma City's *Mickey Mantel's Steakhouse*, an IGT executive confessed to me that part of the reason IGT did not have more Class II games on casino floors was that *"the other guys"* ... he moved his fingers in the motion of counting money... *"and we are not willing to pay people off to get our machines in there."* Large publicly-traded companies really can't afford to participate in that sort of duplicity...the South Carolina model.

Still, even with the SEC-watched corporations in the market, one should not forget the foundation of this entire business: cartoon representations of invisible Bingo cards and invisible ping-pong balls. There is actually a fucking multibillion dollar business of taking YOUR money that is based on that concept. *Get it?*

Aware of many of the seeming-absurdities and loopholes in the regulations, beginning on March 31, 2004 and by mid-2005 the NIGC had finished a fifth rewrite of the Class II regulations that would, among other things, do away with the loophole of invisible Bingo. In their proposed revision of 25 CFR, the NIGC wrote *"These standards for classification are intended to ensure that Class II gaming using "electronic, computer, or other technologic aids" can be distinguished from forms of Class III gaming that employ "electronic or electromechanical facsimiles"* of a game of chance or slot machines." They went on to say *"Electronic or electromechanical facsimile means a game played in an electronic or electromechanical format that replicates a game of chance by incorporating all of the characteristics of the game."*

After reviewing the lengthy proposed changes, attorneys for well-respected Indian gaming law firm Hobbs & Strauss reported that the new regulations would disallow every existing Class II slot machine and turn Class II gaming back into paper Bingo and dauber facsimiles of it. Still, the United States Department of Justice sharply criticized the proposed new regulations as not going nearly far enough to curtail the *Johnson Act violations* that they perceived to exist in Indian gaming...especially in non-compacted states (moving gambling devices across state lines).

Even the first proposed rewrite of the regulations, in 2004, set the stage for devastation of the industry and of casinos for tribes in states without compacts. Hobbs & Strauss as well as other tribally-hired law firms spearheaded a major push for compacted games in every state. In November of 2004, partly due to the law firms' push, voters in Florida and Oklahoma (two huge Class II states) approved ballot measures for the state to enter into gaming compacts for Class III games and totally bypass the whole Class II debacle.

Yet the Class II games remained in casinos all over the country; and again on November 10, 2008 the NIGC published (in the Federal Register) their "final" new technical standards for Class II games. Specifically, the "final" standards added new parts to the Class II regulations: requiring independent laboratory certification of games; and amending the definition of "facsimile." Very specifically, the published rules made it clear that *"the rule does not attempt to distinguish Class II gaming from Class III gaming. Rather, the rule assumes that games played on Class II gaming systems are, in fact, Class II."*

The NIGC added, *"The rule also seeks to permit flexibility in the implementation of technology and to embrace the development of future technologies unforeseen and undeveloped."*

I would not say that I played a "significant" role in these clarifications, but I was certainly a part of a number of the hearings, comment sessions, and reviews beginning in 2004 and for several years. And, I ghost-wrote tribal commentary to proposed changes for two different Oklahoma Tribes, having Tribal Governors or Chiefs sign their name to my commentary arguing that Class II should not be tampered with by the NIGC on the grounds of Sovereignty rather than on the grounds of technology advancements. I note that some of my comments made it into the Federal Register published October 10, 2008.

It appeared that those proposed changes would die before actually becoming regulations with the coming of the Obama administration beginning in January of 2009. However, the same standards came back to the forefront in 2012, though they still did not become law nor regulation.

The "bottom line" (as the accountants say) was that that there were no substantial changes in Class II for a five-year "grandfather" period that ended in 2012. And, ultimately, as two Oklahoma IGT employees told me at a Global Gaming Expo convention, the large companies like IGT were getting out of the Class II business and focusing exclusively on compacted states and the Class III model. At the same event, the son of one of C2's founder confirmed to me that their company, founded exclusively for Class II (as their name indicates), was developing Class III games. And the giant of all Class II companies, VGT, originally of South Carolina but lately of Nashville Tennessee, introduced their own Class III games at the Global Gaming Expo trade show in 2012.

Meanwhile, concerning electronic Bingo and facsimiles of Bingo, it really is as President Clinton said on another subject: *it depends on what your definition of "IS" is.*

Chapter Fourteen

How I killed Elvis in Indian Country

"Hell, we don't have to worry about genocide from your people anymore. We Indians are going to kill ourselves off before you have a chance to do anything else to us. Since we have casinos and a little money, white people can just sit back and watch us destroy each other over this bullshit."

— **Russell B. Ellis, former Treasure of Absentee Shawnee Tribe**

In Indian Country I killed Elvis. I pissed off almost all of those Class II slot machine companies from South Carolina. I "conspired" with the FBI to destroy a casino-finance plan. I raised one Tribe's revenue by $55-million dollars for the sole purpose of seeing my name in print. Oh, and I apparently screwed an oxycodone addict out of a $2-million-a-year job at a casino. At least those are among the most common rumors, stories, legends, and complaints about me.

Undeniably, I have spent a lot of years in Indian Country; first as a displaced 1960s radical following the post-Wounded Knee struggles for sovereignty and later as a developer and operator of casinos on behalf of various Tribes across the country. I have been either fortunate or cursed, depending on one's perspective, to have avocation and skills in both arenas.

Remember, I am a white Southerner with an obvious fixation on 1950s westerns as the passions plays of my culture; and I grew up thinking the unrelated Jackson boys (Andrew and Stonewall) were the good guys. So I suspect my *original* journeys to Native America were probably less about historical reparation and more about the romanticism of reliving Sam Houston's being adopted into the Cherokee Nation, Davy Crockett's fight with Andrew Jackson against the notorious *Indian Removal Act*, or some other fanciful (if not paternally racist) imagination of my gambler hero Doc Holliday's time living with the Ute.

While distributing *Akwesasne Notes*, playing guitar and singing *"Custer Died For Your Sins"* on stage with my friend Kanghi Duta (Floyd Westerman), or raising money, support, and "supplies" for *Wounded Knee*, the romanticism melded with the zeitgeist of early 1970s political radicalism. Organizing and demonstrating with AIM leadership, TAIMSG, and AIMSG[57]; secret meetings with Tuscarora leaders; and a whirlwind of rallies, gatherings, and protests; all facilitated that transition a decade and a half before IGRA.

It is just one of those oddities of historical circumstances that this backdrop eventually melded so well with my career *as a professional gambler* to bring me to Indian Country to develop and operate casinos.

Still, I really do not know how even to begin describing the transition I observed in Native American life in the 20th and 21st centuries. Consider the middle-America white ethos of *"work hard and get out of poverty,"* against some-

211

thing more akin to being jerked from the lowest depths of degradation to seemingly overnight controlling and self-regulating hundreds of millions of dollars in cash flow.

Regardless of one's politics, almost everyone can agree that there is a culture of poverty that is outside the mainstream of America. Regardless of racial demographics, poverty itself is a culture-delineator and breeds, encourages, and almost-requires certain behaviors from health and hygiene to alcohol and drug abuse to failings of education to a host of criminal activities. Add to that the ethos of more than 500 years of undeniable holocaustic attempted genocide (and "decertification") of an entire race. That skin-and-bone noir bleakness is not a glass house that easily is shattered by sudden communal ownership of a casino that barely pays for health care.

The revelation of more than 500 little sovereign nations is disconcerting to some. The concept of invisible Bingo cards and virtual ping pong balls seems inexplicable to most. The abject poverty and attempted annihilation of hundreds of nations and an entire race is unconscionable to most.

Given *that* backdrop, just imagine, then, what life is like operating casinos in that environment. While the collection of anecdotes in this chapter is an accurate picture of some of those tribulations, these stories are very specific to the Tribes involved and very special circumstances that gave rise to each one — *even my killing Elvis*. At the same time, some of the issues that I will explore in these accounts are symptomatic of complications that would inevitably plague those complex circumstances that have given us modern Indian Gaming.

Since it is anecdotal, I will present this chapter as a narrative continuation of the day Trump showed up to play against Ginger, the tic-tac-toe chicken. Picture that Indian Tribe with only 13 members left alive —and their very own casino of 2,000 slot machines and 20 table games. From casino revenue, each member of the Tribe collects a per capita payment close to $48,000 a month plus a nearly-one-million-dollar annual Christmas bonus. Yet it was not unusual for some Tribal members' bank to call casino management complaining that the members' checking accounts were overdrawn or that they surpassed their credit card limit and did not pay the bill. Draw your own conclusions as to why this was.

Travel four miles down the street and there was another Tribe…with *only one* full-blooded surviving member and five partial-blooded members. They also owned a casino; but with *only* 500 slot machines. Let's see: 500 machines winning an average of $100 per-unit-per-day is $50,000 a day or $1.5-million a month or $18.25-million a year. At even a 40% operational cost, that would be a net profit of almost $11-million a year for the "Tribe's" six members. Their *Augustine Tribe* was a band of the Cahuilla that have inhabited California for more than 2,000 years. White imperialism, purchase of land by unscrupulous developers, and marriages (and assimilation) into Mexican culture apparently destroyed the band, except for the lone surviving full-blood and her five relatives.

212

The *larger*, 13-member, *29 Palms Band of Mission Indians* is also part of the Cahuilla. According to one of the 13 members, their band was known as the shaman and medicine-man sect of the Tribe. So in addition to suffering the same extinction forces as *the Augustine*, they also were attacked, rejected, ostracized, and often killed by other Cahuilla bands. Their extinction, like the *Pequot* who own Connecticut's *Foxwoods* was less at the hands of General-Custer-like "Indian fighters" and more at the hands of their own and other Tribes.

This does not imply, even for one thought, that these two examples are typical of Indian gaming. In fact the *Augustine Band* is the smallest of the federally recognized Tribes and both are an exception rather than the rule: especially when it comes to wealth.

My gig with Donald Trump was in conjunction with Trump Hotels and Casinos having the management contract for the casino belonging to that 29 Palms Band of Mission Indians. Dubbed *Trump29* Casino, for that reason, it was my second foray into Indian Gaming since helping ramrod the original federal law, the Indian Gaming Regulatory Act. It was also "The Donald's" first foray into Native American casinos.

The oldest of the thirteen members had, in their youth, suffered the poverty, racism, and outcast status that I had observed in the 1970s. One member had spent decades as a housekeeper and was worn down from years of scrubbing other peoples' toilets and mopping their floors. She would periodically conduct spot inspections of the casino bathrooms to see if our housekeeping employees were doing the job that she knew so well. Nearly toothless from years of inability to afford dental and health care, she spent many days drinking and complaining about how white mangers were robbing her.

The youngest of that thirteen were spoiled in cash, drugs, sex cults, and the dregs of Southern California Mexican-American street culture. One member actually boasted of having the largest pornographic video collection in California. One member bought a new Hummer the day they became available to the public but parked it in her front yard never to be driven after the first 40 miles when she discovered that she had to *climb up* into the cab in her high-heels. Another member was away; allegedly serving what we were told was "drug time" in prison. Several of the 13 were prone to fits of rage, seemingly unprovoked, at staff members of all levels…from housekeeping through management. I was once told to fire a marketing manager because a Tribal member thought the young blonde woman was too pretty *(Sovereign Nation: no U.S. employment law protections)*. Others were mild-mannered and seemingly beaten back in defeat…except for their half-million dollar annual paychecks.

Still, the educational level (actually lack thereof), the generations of victimization, the propensity toward alcoholism, the behavior that many of today's teens would call "ghetto"…were all unshakable simply by pumping massive amounts of money into members' pockets.

This Tribe especially, but almost all of the smaller Tribes that got into gambling early, had been (at one time or another) victims of those grey-area vendors, of the various "development" schemes we have discussed, and almost every con-man scam I have ever seen or read about. Just as white speculators, thieves, conmen, and "expansionists" had invaded Indian Country in the 19th century to steal land, butcher buffalo, and assault Tribal wealth and resources in every way imaginable, so too hordes of 21st century white men invaded Indian country's new-found casino riches. From Abramoff-style conmen to less silver-tongued out-and-out thieves, to job-hunters, white America once again descended on Indian country's treasures after isolating them for a century.

Consequently, the Tribe (as a personality itself) was at best leery and at worst highly suspicious of anything not Native. That especially included the slick New York Donald Trump and his band of professional operators and gamblers.

In the eyes of some of the Tribal members, Trump had promised to transform their small Bingo Hall and Class II casino into a world-class property bearing the Trump name and bring in high roller gamblers from around the world. Their own (white) General Manager had brokered the Trump deal and in addition to the hefty salary they were already paying him, negotiated himself a lifetime annuity based on the revenue of the casino. Rather than pumping millions of New York dollars into Coachella California, Trump's company guaranteed the first several million of a loan package for the Tribe through a large Midwestern syndicator; but the Tribe itself was on the line to pay off the loan. In short, the Trump "deal" wasn't *that* much of a "deal" for the Tribe.

RIGHT: Trump29 Casino in Coachella California, near Palm Springs, circa 2004.

The syndicator, in turn, having a long track record of financing Indian Casinos required specific limited waivers of sovereign immunity that included control of the bank accounts where daily drop funds were deposited. The loan document was so restrictive that biweekly payroll, food & beverage purchases, and *anything* spent had to have prior approval of the syndicator. All other debt was subordinated to the syndication and even slot machine updates had to be approved.

At first I thought these loan-covenants to be absurd, repressive, and racist-paternalistic; and apparently federal banking regulators eventually agreed with me, since a few years later they had taken control of that particular syndicator and forced it out of business. *(For banking issues and not NIGC related issues.)*

Bankers often argued that the perils of sovereignty and the less-than-stellar track-record that many Tribes had in paying back loans made such covenants the absolute *minimum* necessary to assure loan repayment; covenants borne of years of defaults, bad experiences, and in some cases deliberate (and perhaps retaliatory) fraud, against white bankers.

To add to the uneasiness between the Tribe and *The Donald*, Trump's contract required a 30% share of all revenue. From that fee only the General Manager's salary was paid; the rest of the executive and subordinate staff was paid from the Tribe's 70% share of the revenue (even though ALL employees *answered to* the Trump organization). That within itself is a formula for resentment. Moreover, Trump was paid an additional fee for the licensing of his name and image for the property. The entire Trump management contract (at least the portions that are public record) is contained in the endnotes of this book.

By the time Donald Trump arrived to play *tic-tac-toe* with my chicken, the Tribe was openly hostile toward him and his contract. Several of the 13 wore tee-shirts with his catch phrase *"you're fired"* and his name scrawled beneath. As I said earlier, the true purpose of his visit was for the Tribe to express that they wanted out of the contract. They sincerely believed that the Trump organization was providing them nothing for their fees. (Never mind the fact that I had increased their revenue by more than double; the Tribe considered me "theirs" and not Donald's).

This hostility and belief that they were wasting their payments was partially fueled by a California Tribal attorney (himself white) who had a long history of involvement in Tribal ventures beyond just casinos. He had, in fact, found ways to create huge legal fees from an entire cafeteria-list of "investments" for many nouveau millionaires amongst California Native Americans. *(I was especially amused about his getting the Tribe involved in an EPA-controversial tire-recycling project, supposedly "protected" from environmental regulation by sovereignty.)* One of his key assertions was that the Tribe could handle professional managers equal to or better than Trump's choices for a fraction of the costs. Unfortunately he was not proven wrong until long after I, Trump, and the management contract were long gone; revenue plummeted to pre-Trump levels and vastly below pre-Gary Green levels.

While Trump had indeed brought the loan syndicator to the table, guaranteed a portion of the loan, and provided top-notch staff and advisors; it was not unreasonable to conclude that those functions might have had a somewhat steep price tag that, at least in part, paid for the Trump mystique. It was in *that* context

215

that I began to ponder just how much value the Trump mystique brought to the table versus what portion of it was simply good staffing.

In the midst of these conflicts, Donald's Vice President of Casino Operations (and my good friend), Vince Mascio decided to experiment with the Trump29 branding and appeal. For the first two years of the Trump management contract the appeal and focus had been Donald Trump himself. Using that strategy, the casino was doing about $45-million-a-month in "coin-in".

With the employment of the tic-tac-toe chicken and our brand shifting from Trump to *Ginger the Chicken*, the coin-in had grown to an average of more than $70-million. This led us to discussions about the cartoonish image of a branding character in general. We were enjoying the benefit of Trump and *The Apprentice* brand combined with the *Ginger* branding. Vince wondered aloud what would happen if we threw a couple of other faces into the branding mix.

First we hired a "spokes model", the aforementioned Kimmie, to appear on all of our billboards, newsletters, TV, and print ads. Located in a Twilight-Zone existence between the poverty of Coachella and Indio California and nearby affluent Palm Springs, Palm Desert, and La Quinta, we had picked a Mexican-American model that also carried an exotic Anglo look. Her success was difficult to gauge initially but clearly she was tied to the brand.

We then began to wonder about the actual power of Donald as the total brand. To test our suspicions, our next direct mail piece was divided into two versions; identical letters with identical offers. One was signed by Donald Trump; the other by me —*Gary Green, Vice-President Trump Hotel and Casino Resorts*. We wanted to see if one signature drove more revenue than the other. I, of course, expected to be trounced by "The Donald." To my total amazement, the letters bearing my signature brought in 21-times the revenue of the letters signed by Trump. Stunned, we repeated the test with the following week's mailing, reversing the two groups and remarkably achieved similar results.

ABOVE: Gary Green as the larger-than-life casino boss, taking a sledge hammer to a poorly-paying slot machine on a billboard for Donald Trump and The 29 Palms Band of Mission Indians casino near Palm Springs California.

It was time to pull together a focus group of respondents and find out what-the-hell was going on. Almost universally we were told *"I knew Donald Trump was not sending me a personal letter, so I considered it "junk mail" from the casino; but this guy, Gary Green, is obviously a real person and a personal letter from him is probably really a personal letter."*

From that day forward, the official marketing strategy of Trump Hotels and Casinos for Southern California was to brand the casino with Gary Green's signature and face. I signed all the direct-mail letters. I was on billboards. I was the official face in the television commercials. I became a larger-than-life cartoon character of a "casino-boss".

We had no idea what a monster we were creating but we DID know that the $45-million-a-month coin-in that had climbed to $70-million, now *rocketed* to $100-million-a-month. While Trump's casino properties in Atlantic City were taking a financial dive, his California managed-property was posting metrics that were beyond reason. There was no change in the economy; there was no physical change; there was no shift in competitive strategies. The only measurable change was the rebranding.

The more that the revenue climbed the more the Trump organization insisted, frankly over my objections, that I become the branding face of the casino. My advertising face expanded to public appearances, a cameo walk-on in an Indy film about a couple that meets in a casino, to the aforementioned New Year's Eve countdown for a Los Angeles television station. A celebration of my 50th birthday was transformed by the Trump organization to a high-roller party inviting 300 of our best players along with celebrity look-a-likes (Sinatra, Elvis, Dean Martin, Sammy Davis Jr., and the same "Marilyn Monroe" actress (Susan Griffiths) who had appeared in *Pulp Fiction*), as well as pages of B-list Hollywood per-

The Trump29 high-roller invitation to Gary Green's 50th birthday celebration.

sonalities who lived in or near Palm Springs. My good friend *Eddie Garrett*, who had played the photographer for the Los Angeles coroner's office on NBC's *Quincy,* sat at my table.

It was during the preparation of this party that I learned the Hollywood racket of celebrities being paid to attend parties. Once word got out that there was a big party being planned for Gary Green, the casino was approached by a number of celebrities (or their agents) wanting to attend *for a fee*. The two standouts in my mind were David Spade who offered to show up and sit at my table for $15,000 and former *Batman* Adam West, who offered to spend the evening at the party for a mere $7,500. We rejected all pay-to-attend offers; though I would have loved for Adam West to have visited (back in 1966 he had been my hero).

Using me as a branding tool would have seemingly reinforced the Tribe's anti-Trump argument that Donald's name and image was not nearly as valuable as its price tag. But instead of seizing on the value of that momentum, several of the 13 members complained that

Above: Actress Susan Griffiths reprises her most famous role as she sings *"Happy Birthday Mister (Vice) President"* to Gary Green. **Left:** Veteran character actor Eddie Garrett (late of *Quincy* and of *Ironsides*) at Gary's birthday party table.

rather than use Gary Green as branding, the image on the billboards should be a tribute to the Tribe's history and culture. Trump's Vince Mascio strongly argued that I was a caricature, a cartoonish branding image. His words would have fallen on deaf ears had he not also been armed with hard metrics that showed the effectiveness of the campaign. He then argued that the White, Asian, and Mexican gamblers, who collectively were responsible for that $100-million a month, would not be enticed to gamble by a lecture on Native American history but would continue to be enticed by fun gambling images.

Even though I was spending more cash on marketing than a typical casino should spend, my results were undeniably effective. With my seemingly exorbitant marketing expenses, the casino still was operating at a very healthy 42% (rather than my then-optimal 39%). More importantly I was $700,000 ahead of revenue projections for the fiscal year and a million dollars ahead of the previous year. *Those are the kind of results to write home about!*

Casino financials are generally confidential information but because of the Trump bankruptcy and because of the management contract, certain financials are actually part of the public record (if one can find them). The following shows my January 2004 financials. This snapshot gives you a good insight into the revenue and expenses of running a mid-sized Indian casino. *(By the way the "M" at the end of EBITDA takes into account the Trump management fee.)*

Trump 29 Casino
MTD Highlights

Description	MTD 1/31/04 (Estimate)	MTD 1/31/04 (Budget)	Var (Unfav)	MTD 1/31/03 (Actual)	Var (Unfav)
Slot Revenue	6,258,044	5,874,047	$383,997	5,421,195	$836,849
Table Revenue	510,905	575,050	(64,145)	493,759	17,146
Gaming Revenues	6,768,949	6,449,097	319,852	5,914,954	853,995
F & B Revenue	486,148	461,160	24,988	377,422	108,726
Rattlesnake Revenue	110,218	177,521	(67,303)	163,688	(53,470)
Entertainment	224,035	199,406	24,629	433,524	(209,489)
Retail	30,718	31,603	(885)	24,369	6,349
Other	6,975	16,791	(9,816)	13,750	(6,775)
Non-Gaming Revenues	858,094	886,481	(28,387)	1,012,753	(154,659)
Gross Revenues	7,627,043	7,335,578	291,465	6,927,707	699,336
Promotional Allowances	205,291	184,326	(20,965)	286,016	80,725
Net Revenues	7,421,752	7,151,252	270,500	6,641,691	780,061
Total Operating Expenses	3,834,564	4,249,231	414,667	4,102,889	268,325
EBITDAM	$3,587,188	$2,902,021	$685,167	$2,538,802	$1,048,386
Slot Handle	80,987,137	76,428,431	4,558,706	75,731,428	5,255,709
Table Drop	3,519,451	4,248,418	(728,967)	3,692,689	(173,238)
Slot Hold %	7.7%	7.7%	0.0%	7.2%	0.6%
Table Hold %	14.5%	13.5%	1.0%	13.4%	1.1%
Operating Expenses:					
Salaries & Wages	1,861,000	1,494,065	233,065	1,613,289	152,289
Benefits	438,300	506,019	67,719	460,042	21,742
Supplies	129,054	129,074	20	114,121	(14,933)
Professional Services	80,076	80,076	0	39,973	(40,103)
Entertainer Fees	126,550	169,800	43,250	293,803	167,253
Advertising	173,050	175,050	0	245,271	72,221
Bus Program Cash Back	250,610	325,000	74,390	250,900	290
Marketing	185,350	168,350	(17,000)	142,043	(43,307)
Utilities	167,639	167,619	0	196,470	28,851
Other	121,553	121,583	30	70,844	(50,709)
	3,133,162	3,534,636	401,474	3,426,756	293,594

	Jan 2004 (Estimate)	Jan 2004 (Budget)	Var (Unfav)	Jan 2003 (Actual)	Var (Unfav)
EBITDAM	3,587,188	2,902,021	685,167	2,538,802	1,048,386

Meanwhile, I was now more convinced that the value-added by having Donald Trump's name on a casino was probably initially worth the price tag but certainly *not* long term except to firmly hold the brand. This was not an opinion I openly shared and certainly did not mention it to anyone. Nonetheless, it was becoming clear to me that a highly-branded and segment-targeted marketing campaign tied in with Trump could be more powerful than a licensing fee to Donald J. Trump alone. Clearly branding from The Apprentice did add value.

Between that realization and the handwriting on the wall for the future of the relationship between the Tribe and Trump, I began quietly looking at the job market without actually floating resumes. Since my 15-minutes-of-fame, I had received about a dozen job offers and had turned them all down out of loyalty to Trump; and while that loyalty was not wavering, I saw an inevitable parting between the 29 Palms Band of Mission Indians and Trump Hotels and Casinos. Given the failing state of the Trump properties everywhere else (and the uncertainty of Mark Brown's job) I suspected there would be no place left for me.

There had been an unwritten "promise" that I would be given the General Manager position at Donald's new casino at *Trump Island Villas* on Canouan Island. *(Tiny four-square-mile Canouan is one of the Grenadines Islands belonging to St Vincent; it was 3,000 miles closer to my home than Southern California.)*

During my consideration of Trump's offer, I was contacted by a headhunter for an Indian casino near Oklahoma City. Never a fan of the fly-over states and certainly not interested in the heart of the Midwest, I at first tossed the offer with the others that had dropped at my doorstep. After I ignored the email, the headhunter made a follow-up phone call dropping a salary figure that was 75% more than what Trump was paying me *and* contained a quarterly bonus offer that was a many-times multiple of the salary. *That,* at least, got my attention and I agreed to accept their plane ticket to Oklahoma for an initial interview.

The headhunter met me at the airport dressed in jeans and a Harley-Davidson leather jacket. I was whisked away in her black Mustang at about 85-miles-per-hour to meet with an accountant for the Tribe who explained to me that the hiring authority, the Tribal Treasurer, had fallen into a *diabetic coma* while I was on the plane and he was not expected to live. This accountant, I was told, would nonetheless interview me and report her findings to the Tribal Council. Ooooook. Given the high incidences of diabetes amongst Native Americans, this troubling news was not shocking; just disturbing.

She explained that the position was not *actually* to be General Manager of their existing to casino but to become the General Manager and *developer* of a proposed new casino...which had not yet even been financed. On that charming revelation I was dropped off at the *Marriott Courtyard* in downtown Oklahoma City and told that we would resume the "interview" the next day. I accepted that it had been a wasted trip to middle America and was content to see the tourist sites including the scene of the infamous Timothy Mcveigh bombing as well as the National Cowboy Hall of Fame.

The next morning she took me to a walk-in health clinic for a "drug test" that was supposedly pre-arranged. None of the clinic personnel had heard of me, the Tribe, or the headhunter; I ended up paying out-of-pocket for the urinalysis drug test. Next she drove me to a downtown hospital which I recognized from the television news broadcast of the bombings. At the hospital I was told to put green scrubs on over my Armani suit and don a facemask as I was led into the intensive care unit of the hospital to meet the treasurer. Even with intravenous tubes running in and out of his arms and with his face gaunt from the disease, Russell B. Ellis looked like a force to be reckoned with.

First, he was every white boy's ideal vision of a Native American. He looked as if he had been chiseled on the face of a buffalo nickel or had been the stand-in for Iron Eyes Cody; from his long grey pony tail to his classic facial bones, he looked *so* "Indian" that I almost gasped at the sight. He was a man that obviously stood well over six-feet, when he could stand. Despite the pronouncement to me that I was meeting him on his death bed, I could see that this was a man that would be around for a long time.

"Well how the hell are you?" he asked me as I stepped beside the hospital bed.

"A damned sight better than you are," I answered this complete stranger.

"Look, I am going to be out of here in a couple of days and I want you here in Oklahoma helping me. I have a fucking mess that needs to be cleaned up and I need somebody that can market the hell out of this thing as well as manage it. I want you to come," he said in stern seriousness.

"Just like that? No formal interview?" I asked.

"Hell I know more about you than your damned mother does and that is why I flew you here. I want you to start in two weeks," he answered.

The truth is that he *did* know a hell of a lot about me. The Tribe had recently hired David Cook, just four months retired from the Oklahoma City Police Department as the most decorated living officer in the history of the city. Cook had been asked to secretly *"find out everything you can about this guy,"* and being a former undercover agent accustomed to building RICO and other major cases, he took the orders very literally. Cook immediately ran all of the routine investigations (one of his favorite sayings is *"In God we trust; everyone else we run through NCIC"* –National Crime Information Center).

Above: Russell B. Ellis, *who went to great extremes to avoid being photographed,* is almost caught in this picture at an NIGC hearing with Gary Green.

David told me recently that those investigations were just the beginning. Using his network of police contacts he had an undercover agent in Palm Desert California verify that my condo actually existed and that my car with a Florida license plate was actually parked there or at the casino. *"I was used to people giving phony addresses, and I was not going to take any chances with you,"* he told me.

"By the time I was finished with you, you could have gotten a top secret clearance with the Federal Government," David told me as I was preparing to write this book.

He checked every state where I ever had lived, talked to even casual acquaintances, and knew even where I regularly took my meals. At point he called me about my Folkways /Smithsonian record albums and in perfect Midwest police style questioned, *"Now about these records you allegedly have recorded; what exactly is on them."*

He prepared a detailed dossier on me and delivered it to Treasurer Ellis before the decision was made to fly me to Oklahoma.

David went on to serve a number of Tribes and commercial casinos in investigative, enforcement and compliance matters, as well as a few casino operational positions. In 2008 he was a finalist for the *Chief of the Enforcement Division* of the National Indian Gaming Commission and is widely recognized as one of the casino world's top compliance investigators and trainers.

Above: Renowned Tribal casino regulator David Cook.

I told Ellis that I would consider the offer and contact him after I returned to California. He told me that he had already decided that I was taking the position and he needed an answer within the week because (as he put it) *"I have so much crime, rip-offs, and fucked up people that I need you here now."*

The truth is, I had serious misgivings about being in Oklahoma, wasn't excited about leaving the metro-Los Angeles area, and wanted to give Trump the opportunity to sweeten *his* offer to me. I remained loyal to Vince, Mark Brown, and (of course) Donald. I liked my coworkers and my subordinates at Trump29. And, I was sort of non-paternalistically bemusedly fond of the disfunctionality of thirteen members of the 29 Palms Band of Mission Indians.

The headhunter was prepared to take me back to Oklahoma City's Will Rogers Airport, which I noticed was at Wiley Post Field and on Amelia Earhart Drive; it was a tad disconcerting that the airport was named for three victims of plane crashes. Before leaving for the airport, I asked the headhunter to drive me to the Tribes' existing casino so that I could get a general "lay of the land." She drove south of Oklahoma City in the town of Norman, on State Road 9, passed the University of Oklahoma (which for some inexplicable dyslexic reason is called OU rather than UO).

Along the way we passed the United States Postal Service's national training center; the location that had made an indelible mark in the national culture when a crazed worker lost control and shot several of his coworkers... causing the coining of the term *"going postal."*

Ah yes, Oklahoma!

Another seven to ten miles and we arrived at the Absentee Shawnee Tribe's *Thunderbird Wild Wild West Casino.*

Rural and removed from the population center as it was, the visual stunned me. It was a genuine themed casino with an old-West-town façade attached to the steel building. All it needed was a stage coach out front (which I later added) and it would have looked ready for the Las Vegas strip or at least for a Disney World attraction. I quietly wished that the GM position available were for *this* casino and not a new one not-yet-under-construction.

As we pulled into the parking lot, the head hunter asked me, *"Did Russell tell you that the General Manager here would be reporting to you?"*

"Ah, no," I answered.

"Well that is the plan. I don't want to say too much. You make your own decisions," she said as she decided to sit in the car while I visited the casino.

Given *that* information, I decided it best to be totally "undercover" as I perused the casino. I took off my jacket and tie, unbuttoned my shirt, took out my cuff links and rolled up my sleeves and stepped inside the casino. In the

ABOVE: Exterior theme of the *Thunderbird Wild Wild West Casino* near Norman Oklahoma (circa 2004); note the horse sculptures "hitched" in front of the casino. **BELOW:** The "Shawnee Overland Stage Coach" filled with showgirls, added by Gary Green.

next few minutes I observed more graft, scams, rip-offs, skim operations, *Federal Minimum Internal Control Standards* violations, safety hazards, and questionable procedures than I had ever seen, cumulatively in my entire life or even in books and movies. I wandered around the casino stunned and in amazement.

In Southern California, someone would have gone to prison over any number of these violations. At Trump29 I was once called before a Gaming Commission inquiry to explain why a spot check of a marketing-give-away of stereo systems apparently had one more stereo than was on the list of schedule recipients. *(It was, by the way, for a wild-card drawing.)* The point is, I was from a world where strict policies and procedures had to be written and followed for every action. The most outstanding thing to be said about the 29 Palms Band of Mission Indians is that they operated a gaming commission that should be held as a model for every Tribal regulatory body in the country; they were meticulous.

In Norman I was walking through a world that looked as if James Cagney's grapefruit-in-the-face gangster and his sidekick George Raft were running the joint. It scared the hell out of me.

Appalled, I caught myself "washing my hands" in front of the surveillance cameras as if I believed any legitimate surveillance had been in place. I was totally at a loss for words to describe the number of independent criminal activities, operational violations, and just stupid procedures that I observed. I returned to the waiting car and said nothing other than *"well that was interesting."*

The headhunter pressed me and I honestly responded, *"That is probably the most fucked up casino I have ever been inside."*

She smiled and said that Russell was really going to like working with me and I should definitely let him know what I had seen.

Back on the plane, I decided to not accept the offer but to write Ellis a scathing letter detailing what I had seen and my reasons for turning down his offer. In my office at Trump29, I put together a four page letter of blunt bullet points outlining the horrors I had observed. In that letter, datelined from Palm Desert, I began:

"First, I want to again thank you for taking the time and the energy to meet with me from the Intensive Care Unit of the hospital. THAT act alone said a lot to me and showed me a man whose vision and spirit are stronger than any of the limitations that usually make people say "impossible." That speaks volumes about the potential success of this project.

I continued:

Russell, you will find that I speak very frankly and very directly. I am going to do that now. I toured the Thunderbird property. From what I have seen I strongly believe that either (1) it has some very very serious management failures or (2) someone is stealing from you."

The letter then continued into my bullet points of issues.

I dropped the letter in the mail and decided to accept the Trump offer as soon as Vince returned to town at the end of the week. The day before Vince's scheduled arrival Russell Ellis telephoned me. He said that he had read my letter.

"You cut right to it, didn't you?" he asked with a grinning-sounding tone.

"Well, yes Sir, I figured there was no reason to beat around the bush about it," I answered.

"That casino started out making us a fortune 13 years ago and it has been going downhill ever since. Last month I had to loan the casino $18,000 from the Tribal treasury just to make payroll. It is more fucked up than you can imagine. I want you to come in here, take it over and clean the fucking house. You will have absolute authority backed by me and I want every one of the thieving bastards out of there," he said in a spewing of excited tones.

What he did not tell me was that former police officer Cook now officially had been appointed Executive Director of the Tribal Gaming Commission and was already deep into his investigation. Cook's initial reports identified exactly the same issues that my bullet-point letter had raised. This validated both me and Cook; it also totally convinced the Treasurer that it was time to make a change.

He also did *not* tell me that he had hired investigators from *The Fidelis Group* (former FBI and IRS forensic auditors and investigators) to find out what was going on at the casino... and their initial findings were identical to my walk-through.

Ellis' excitement suddenly put the project in a whole new light for me and just to drive home the point he sweetened the offer by increasing the bonus structure.

"Our Tribe charges the casino a six-percent tax on the daily drop," he began.

"On the drop?" I interrupted; *"don't you mean on the "win", on the "hold"?*

"Hell no. We want our cash off the top; if we waited for the win, that bunch of fucking crooks in there would tell us we weren't winning anything. We depend on that damned money to operate the Tribe so we take it off the top," he continued.

I interrupted again, *"but if you take six-percent off the drop that is an effective tax rate of 70% of the revenue; leaving the casino to operate on 30% of the revenue. A typical casino operates on 39% to 40% of revenue."*

"Hell, we own the building. There is no loan. If they can't operate that place on 30% then somebody is stealing something," he added.

"Well you are definitely right on that point," I told him.

"Right now we aren't getting a damned thing out of that casino. I am highly confident that you can turn that around and make us some money. Since our money is tied to the drop then I want your bonus to be tied to us making money. I am offering you one-half-of-one-percent of the taxable drop as a bonus. If we don't make money; you don't make money. And if we get rich then you do too," he concluded his offer.

I did some quick math and realized that if the drop is even $30-million a month then my bonus would be $150,000 a month. There was no TITO (ticket-in / ticket-out) so coin-in would be drop plus replays. Forgetting coin-in, even going absurdly low, if each machine averaged only $50 a day in drop cash, then

225

my bonus would still be $54,000 a year on top of my base salary. I had just seen the win results for the Claridge in Atlantic City; they had about the same number of games as Thunderbird and they *won* for the year $109,574,000 (before expenses). Okay, even ½ of 1% of *win* at that rate would be a half-million dollar bonus. And if the casino did what Trump29 was doing, that would translate to an annual bonus of $6-million. I was getting a headache. I told the treasurer I would get back to him but I needed to give Trump at least a 30 day notice.

The next day I sat down with Vince Mascio and told him about the offer. Vince's advice was *"jump at it"*. He told me that even if the job only lasted a year, it would be well worth it and he did not think Trump would survive a full year either in Atlantic City or in his contract with the Indians. There was a clause in the contract that allowed for termination if either party became insolvent and THCR was on the brink.

Trump also responded. After initially offering to match whatever Oklahoma tendered, upon hearing of the bonus structure the word came from Trump, *"I hope you enjoy your new position."* I laughed.

I formally tendered a 30-day notice, knowing that in the casino industry it is traditional to immediately escort a resigning employee off property, to protect assets. It turned out, though, that I was so entrenched in the property, so key in its operation, and so tied to the brand, that my month-notice was accepted.

Working with Mark Lefever, Vince Mascio, Steve Sohng, and a dozen other really good people was an experience which I was not eager to leave behind. Leaving the prestige of being a Vice President for Donald J. Trump was a major step as well. Though I took with me the valet guy, one of the phone operators, Will (from the players club), and Frank Haas…it was not like I was raiding the staff. And since there was no shared customer base between Coachella California and Norman Oklahoma, there was not much chance of leaking any proprietary information between the two. *(I did, however, as a matter of security remove the SIMS card from my company cell phone and replace it with a blank one.)*

I began using my remaining month to rebrand the property from "me" to the new General Manager; but he lacked the force of personality or the larger-than-life attitude to be an actor on *that* stage. The effort quickly fizzled and I then began instructing the management staff on how to stick to the direct mail formulas I had created; and I obtaining their promises that they would not deviate from those formulas. I wanted to make certain the transition was smooth and that revenue did not dip back to that lower level just because Gary Green left. My focus was to keep the property at its current level, position it to grow, and maintain a close relationship with the Tribe, with Trump, and with the staff.

But a week later David Cook called me. David's investigation further had confirmed many of the bullet points I had sent to Treasurer Ellis and the Tribe had appointed David "interim General Manager" of the Thunderbird Casino with the charge of securing tribal assets. In doing so, Cook had fired the General

Manager and 110 other employees. He was recommending criminal prosecution and had met with the FBI twice.

Meanwhile, Ellis had announced his contract with the forensic accounting firm. Cook was calling me to ask, *"Mr. Green, can you come to Oklahoma earlier? I am a little over my head here. I am a police officer and an investigator and I don't know a thing about running a casino. I have started cleaning it up for you here, but I need somebody in here that knows how to operate a casino. Can you please get out here sooner?"*

At a Trump "going away" party for me, the newly appointed General Manager asked if there was anything he could do to convince me to stay. The Tribe's Chairman, Dean Mike, asked the same question. There was nothing either could do by then.

My arrival at the Absentee Shawnee Tribe's *Thunderbird Wild Wild West Casino* SHOULD have coincided with my departure from the *Thunderbird Wild Wild West Casino* as well. Any operator in his (or her) right mind would have run the other direction after the first day. I, on the other hand, either out of a sense of challenge, adventure, or temporary insanity, decided to stick with it. I am far beyond the racist concept of *"the great white hope,"* but damn these people *seriously* needed help.

Shortly after my arrival, and before actually reporting to the casino, Treasurer Ellis revealed to me the details of that $18,000 loan from the Tribal treasury to the casino; funds needed to make up a shortfall in making payroll; and he was expecting that trend to continue until revenue increased or expenses went down. As if that were not enough, then he hit me with the classic *"oh-by-way."*

In this case, the *oh-by-the-way* was that the Tribe owed the National Indian Gaming Commission more than $4-million in fines for operating illegal blackjack games and illegal Class III re-spin slot machines and refusing a *cease-and-desist* order following a *Notice of Violation*. Apparently, the (now-former) General Manager had refused the order and was actually arrested *and* ordered to wear ankle bracelet while he was under house arrest.

Unlike their neighbors at the nearby Seminole Tribe, where the NIGC took over management and operation of the casino, the Absentee Shawnee had attorneys that were able to keep the casino under "Tribal" control. However, because of the shortfall in cash flow, the Tribe was now behind in their payments to the NIGC and in danger of closure by regulators.

I found this out before I knew that Frank Haas was on his way to Oklahoma, and I reached back into my memory of what little I had observed of how Frank had implemented Mark Lefever's payoff negotiations with that evil loan syndicator for Trump29. I called Lefever to get his suggestions of how to get out of this mess. His first comment to me, before offering advice, summed up the situation absolutely accurately, *"you're fucked."* Oh swell; but that is what I like about Mark —to the point and no bullshit.

I finally met the Governor of the Tribe, Kenneth Blanchard, who shared with me three years of independent audit reports showing that the casino had been "flat" for all three years. Blanchard, correctly, asked the question, *"How can they make the exact same amount of money, to the penny, every year?"*

Governor Blanchard was hard to get to know. It took several months to understand what he was all about; but when I did, I came to respect him more than any other member of that Tribe. Blanchard had an amazingly down-to-earth focus on economic development; he was constantly pursuing ways to improve life for his Tribal members.

Traveling with my parents through the hills of our Appalachian homeland during the 1950s and 60s, I had seen, firsthand, some of America's most dire rural poverty: wood frame houses with the cracks between the wallboards "insulated" with wadded newspapers shoved into the holes; cardboard boxes cut in the shape of window panes to keep the blowing snow out; no running water and toilets a few yards behind the house, with a hold dug into the ground and an "outhouse" overtop of it; one bucket of coal to fire the only heat in the house for the entire winter. If it had not been for President Johnson's "war on poverty in Appalachia," many kids would have never tasted pasteurized milk. In one east Tennessee elementary school we attended, my brother Ron came home one day to report a little boy in his first grade class has urinated in his pants rather than pee into "that pretty white bowl" where he was taken to the bathroom; he had never seen indoor plumbing.

On his desk in Shawnee Oklahoma, Ken Blanchard kept a notebook filled with photographs of the homes and living conditions of his people before the recent casino-funded economic development programs. The stark images of poverty from the travels of my childhood were practically images of luxury compared to the bleakly severe deficiencies and abject poverty suffered by the Absentee Shawnee Indians of Oklahoma. Page after page of Blanchard's scrapbook served to remind him and show me the necessity of economic development programs, health care, housing, and jobs provided by casino gaming on his Tribal land.

Not only was my mission clear, from talks with Ken Blanchard, but his vision was clear; more clear than that of any leader of any Tribe I had talked with before or since. Ken Blanchard had a mission in life and this casino was part of that mission. Talks with him were among those few-in-a-lifetime defining moments and my decision to stick with the *Thunderbird Wild Wild West Casino* rather than run back to Trump or back to commercial gaming was driven by Blanchard's sincerity, his vision, and the mission he had given me.

A little more than a year later, after a long and expensive battle, when the voters of Oklahoma finally empowered *their* governor to sign a gaming compact with Tribes, Governor Blanchard was with Oklahoma Governor Brad Henry at one minute after midnight on January First when the law went into effect. The two Governors signed the history-making document and Blanchard became the first Tribal leader to sign with the State, allowing his casino to offer Class III games and legal blackjack (or at least an Oklahoma version of it).

It was this kind of visionary leadership that should have made Kenneth Blanchard a legend among his people and for generations have his name spoken with the same reverence as the first great Shawnee leader, Tecumseh. But, alas, such was not to be the fate of Blanchard's self-less dedication to his Tribe and to his people. Such was not to be the legacy of either the Compact with Oklahoma nor the Thunderbird Casino...but before that legacy could be explored, there were more serious issues facing the casino than merely flat revenue and the casual observations I had made to Treasure Ellis.

Absentee Shawnee Governor Kenneth Blanchard (right) with Oklahoma Governor Brad Henry (left) at one minute after midnight signing the first Tribal Gaming Compact for any Tribe in the history of Oklahoma.

First, *but not even foremost*, there were the issues of a huge American Express bill and of charge accounts at clothing stores all over Oklahoma City. Ellis told me that the previous General Manager had opened an American Express account in the casinos' name without the Tribal Council's knowledge or consent and had issued cards to several employees. *(I later learned that the former Governor of the Tribe had in fact authorized the account if not how the cards were ultimately used. His administrative assistant told me, however, that he was bedridden and not aware of what he was signing at the time the GM visited him in a hospital with the form to sign, shortly before his death.)* Additionally, several marketing department employees had confessed to Cook (the ex-cop was a master of getting confessions) that they had purchased personal clothing and household furnishings from department stores and charged the items to casino accounts, authorized by the Director of Marketing (who was married to that General Manager).

The NIGC fine, these bills, questionable management, and a pretty fat staff (the marketing department had almost 20 employees) all combined to paint a clear picture of the financial status of the business. I added to my inquiries of Ellis only the daily cash flow, drop, and hold.

I also wanted to review, in detail, those "flat" casino audits for the past three years. The NIGC requires that Indian casinos submit to an independent outside audit and this Tribe had contracted with one of the most respected firms in the industry. However the audits were a woeful disappointment; the last pages detailed the casino management's refusal to release financial data and refusal to give access to auditors. Ellis was baffled and the audits were worthless; they had no data. *Something was definitely up.*

After the status report from Ellis, I finally met David Cook in person. Cook had been given the task of leading me around the casino, introducing me to staff, and briefing me on what he had discovered in his investigations...as well as who he had already fired and why. The first fired had been the General Manager; the GM had already fired his own wife when he was *"shocked to discover that she misused the American Express account."* (Shades of Rick Blane paying Louie's gambling winnings just as Louie was ordering *Café Americain* closed).

My first stop was the GM's office, which still had a cloud of stale cigarette smoke hovering in the air. The desk was coated with a thick, yellow, sticky film of nicotine and when I rested the side of my hand on it, my palm became coated with a yellow stain. I had already observed that the separate administration building was a two-story wood-frame structure with no sprinkler system nor smoke detectors; and most of the employees in that building smoked at their desks. Several of the offices had burning cigarettes in ashtrays but no one in the office. Walking through the casino to the GM's office with David Cook, I noticed there was no fire suppression or sprinkler system over most of the area. And so my inspection began.

Just outside the rear entrance to the casino, a long refrigeration trailer (from an 18-wheel tractor-trailer rig) was parked. Electric wires ran from the casino to power the refrigeration unit on the truck. There was a small padlock on the doors to the trailer. David Cook told me that *he* had put the padlock on the trailer after learning that it had at one time been totally filled with frozen restaurant-quality steaks. When he opened the doors, there was only one pallet of the meat left; in less than two months the small casino and its tiny coffee shop had gone through an entire truck load of steaks. OR...with the door not having a lock and no surveillance camera in the back of the casino, someone possibly had been stealing the meat. That was one of the oldest rackets in stealing from a restaurant. I think Nicholas Pileggi detailed that scam in *Wise Guys* as did Demaris Ovid in *The Last Mafioso; Jimmy the Weasel Fratianno.* This was the first time I had actually seen it in action.

As I walked along the outside of the casino, I noticed electrical wires and CAT-5 network cable looped along the side of the building without conduit or even ties to hold it from the wind or weather. Subsequent examination revealed that these were the cables that carried the game outcomes (from the Virtual Bingo draw) from the server rooms to the slot machines. I asked Cook, *"What is to keep someone from slicing one of those lines and changing the outcome of the game?"*

"You mean like that?" he responded as he pointed to a ball of black plastic electrical tape wrapped around an obvious splice point. *"Oh you haven't seen anything yet,"* Cook told me as he read the pained expression on my face.

I scanned the parking lot and the back acreage of the property, looking for backup generators (in the event of loss of power). Running 600 server-based slot machines could be a big problem if customers had money in play during a power outage; unless there was a generator in place to pick up where a local UPS would fail. Most Minimum Internal Control Standards required backup generators. Here there was no such requirement and no generators.

As we walked toward the door to go back inside, I got a hefty whiff of what smelled like a freshly-fertilized pasture. I looked at Cook who laughed and led me to an open cesspool. *"Please don't tell me that is the raw sewerage from the casino,"* I almost pleaded. *"Totally legal here; you are on a sovereign nation,"* he reminded me, adding *"it is only bad when the wind changes direction."*

"Shit," I said. *"Exactly,"* David laughed.

As soon as we stepped back inside the casino, David pointed me toward two closets near the back door. Each had a series of barn-hinge hasps with padlocks through them. Cook, who had a ring of keys that looked like something the high school janitor used to carry around, did not have a key to these "secure" closets.

The NIGC, trying to effectively protect tribal assets, requires that the virtual ping-pong-ball Bingo servers are locked away from the general public and requires:

"physical security measures restricting access to agents, including vendors, must exist over the servers, including computer terminals, storage media, software and data files to prevent unauthorized access and loss of integrity of data and processing."
These two closets were the "secure sever rooms" for the casino.

"Do I EVEN want to see this," I asked Cook, rhetorically. He called for the "IT Department" to allow us access. I can't think of the words to describe what I saw in these closets. For my older readers, you will remember the sound of the contents of Lum and Abner's closet falling out when the door opened. For younger readers, imagine a closet packed with: wires; old computers (working and not working); oily rags; scraps of paper; half-empty soft drink cans; molded coffee floating in months-old cups; broken furniture parts; and even a mousetrap with peanut butter bait. Imagine all of that balanced so that if the door opened too quickly, everything would lose balance and fall out the door. Add to that lovely visual, a spider-web of network cables, unlabeled or otherwise identified, each coming from a network hub underneath one of the banks of slot machines. Approximately 75 cables were strung to one (or both) of the closets, all without conduit or labels. The cables were draped, pulled, looped, and strung seemingly haphazardly and intertwined through each other without organization. I cringed and continued my tour.

As I walked across the gaming floor toward a section of the building called the "Nickel" something or another, I tripped on a weak section of the floor (and wondered about slip-and-fall accidents).

"Oh that is where the forklift fell through the floor when it was lifting the sculpture to the top of those slot machines," a housekeeping employee told me, adding *"people fall there all the time. We just never got it fixed"*

Ellis had already told me that the casino had spent $75,000 to buy a solid bronze sculpture from a Seminole leader (who was also a State Senator) as a sort of political tribute.

The" Nickel Corral", I discovered, was not actually part of the casino structure; rather, it was made of four doublewide mobile-home trailers stitched together and attached to a side doorway from the main casino. The lights had been taken out and replaced with one "black light" tube in every other fixture. The room was so dark that I could see the people at slot machines only because of the glow of the slot machine video screens and not from room lighting.

I scanned the room for security cameras. There were smoked-bubbles for them, but I seriously doubted that anyone could see an image from the cameras (if there even were any). The room was dangerously dark and the construction of the trailers did not seem solid enough to support the weight of the slot machines; the floor buckled as I walked across it (and I only weighed 160 pounds at the time).

I looked at the front of the slot machines and noticed that many of the machines did not have cam locks on the drop door of the belly glass. This meant that an unscrupulous customer or dishonest employee could open the front of the slot machine, and get to the cash drop box without a key...you remember my pictures of how a drop team removes money from slot machines. As I opened the glass, I discovered there was no lock on the cash box either. This meant that not only could anyone reach the cash box, but they could get to the cash as well. I glanced up to the camera covers and again realized that even during a drop, there would be no way to observe cash taken from the machines. I wondered how much had been out-and-out stolen.

Since I was already inside the machine, without a key, I checked the meters...or rather I tried to check the meters. There were none. Hence there was no physical record (hard meters) of how much cash went into the machine or was paid out; it was as if these machines had been designed to be stolen from.

I closed the slot machine, shook my head again, and turned to David to continue my tour. As I slammed the machine shut, I commented, *"These are some seriously fucked-up slot machines."* A nearby slot technician ran up to me and warned, *"You can't call these slot machines; you have to call them video machines."*

"Horseshit. They are Class II slot machines," I said. The tech replied, *"we were told to never call them that, it is a secret. We have to call them video machines. Nobody knows they are slot machines."*

"A secret? You were told that by an asshole. What you call the machines does not change what they are or what they are not. They ARE slot machines; just Class II type slot machines." I explained as I walked to the front of the room.

At the front side of the trailers, there was a construction area that looked like it had at one time been the bathrooms for the mobile homes. Workers had installed a bullet-resistant Plexiglas window and were busying themselves measuring for sheet rock walls. Inside the construction area I could see the Cage and Cashier Manager directing the work crew. As I opened the hollow door to step into the room with Cook, the manager asked me what I thought of the new location of their "satellite" cage. Hiding my shock, all I could immediately respond was, *"ah...No."*

The Federal Register has published (in 25 C.F.R. chapter 500) a detailed set of *Minimum Internal Control Standards* (MICS) for protecting tribal assets at a casino; these are *minimum* standards and they are very detailed. It was those standards that had made me cringe at the "server room" closets and the dangling wiring outside the building.

This violation, however, was totally absurd. A casino cashiers' cage is the "bank" inside the casino; however in an average day a cage handles a lot more money than a typical branch bank. There are very specific guidelines (as well as common sense) about how such an area is to be secured. Drop ceiling panels, hollow doors, paper-thin trailer walls, and pressed-wood floors above cinder blocks do not really make for the most secure of banks. Frankly, I thought they were joking when they told me that this area was going to be a bank/cage. *"How exactly are you going to protect the Tribe's cash in this configuration?"* I rhetorically asked no one.

Years later, when I developed a casino for the Ottawa Tribe of Oklahoma (the diametrical opposite of THIS Tribe in terms of functionality, integrity, and harmony), I personally wrote a set of Tribal Internal Controls (TICS) that was adopted by their gaming commission, approved by the NIGC, is still in use today, and has been copied by me many times over the years for less-regulated casinos. Internal Controls are so essential for legitimate operation of a casino that I have included that entire Ottawa set in the endnotes of this book.[58]

I continued my tour through the casino, stopping long enough to admire an indoor rock waterfall with ivy growing through it. *"I wouldn't get too close to that,"* a maintenance man warned me, *"just a couple of months ago we found a momma rattler had hatched six baby rattlesnakes there."* I turned to Cook, who just shrugged his shoulders as he continued my tour.

Our next stop was through a doorway that led to a bar and a racing book; a classic OTB (off track betting) parlor with wide screen televisions, a remote access *Amtote* machine, and lots of trophy cups, jockey colors, and track decoration (as well as a full service bar). It was, truly, a beautifully designed room. I immediately spotted a guy handicapping races for a number of players and then collecting a percentage of their winnings as a toke. *Who is the tic-tac artist,"* I asked Cook. *"The what?"* he responded. *"The dude working our room for a cut of the winnings,"* I said pointing to the guy. *"Oh, that is the manager of our OTB,"* David explained. *"Get-the-fuck-outta-here,"* I heard myself say in Trump-esque slang. Great, the manager of the OTB is illegally handicapping for players. Never mind the ethical violations of that; never mind the MICS violations of licensed employees participating in the outcome of a bet; it is just a sleazy-looking practice. I shook my head and made another mental note.

I watched two of the bar maids return "spillage" (that had not spilled at all) and pocket the price of the drink themselves without hitting the cash register. Christ, even the bar was ripe with criminal pilferage. Behind the bar and in a side room I examined the rack and gun system and observed the inventory set-up. I would bet *dollars-to-donut-holes* that the inventory was being short-reported. *(I later learned that not only was that true, but the alcohol distributor was giving cash kickbacks to at least two of my bar shift managers for their orders.)* And why in the hell had surveillance not caught that?

As we continued the tour, we walked through the main casino through another set of glass doors into the Bingo hall. Behind me was a balcony overlooking the room. As I climbed the stairway toward the balcony I could feel each step give a little and I listened to the creak each time I put weight on a step. The balcony itself bowed and bent as I walked across the floor; so much so that I *really* didn't want to be up there. This balcony had been built, Cook said, for dozens of VIPS and special guests to sit during concerts that were periodically held in the Bingo hall/showroom. I later learned that this balcony was built on one-inch by two-inch support beams (rather than 2x4s) holding sheets of plywood, with no additional support. The carpenter, who had built this substandard accident-waiting-to-happen, was overheard in a local bar laughing about that and other objects of his work, saying *"I stole so much money from those Indians and delivered them shit. I hope that doesn't change with the new guy there."* He was in for an unpleasant surprise.

At the far end of the Bingo hall was a stage, about 12 to 15 feet above the floor. The Bingo hall indeed was designed to double as an auditorium for concerts but rather than looking down at the stage (the traditional way), customers had to crane their necks to look up to see the performers. Those sitting closest to the stage could see nothing at all; and those in the flimsy balcony at the back of the room had the best view.

As we walked around the stage we discovered three doors, two in the front of the stage and one behind the stage. David had keys to the two front doors and behind each we found large rooms filled with folding metal chairs, most likely used to convert the room to a concert hall. But David did not have a key to the back door and neither did casino security or the Tribal police. With a sledge hammer, we broke the lock on that door and discovered a plush, carpeted, sound-proof room with couches, beds, refrigerator (filled with beer), televisions, paintings on the walls, and a telephone that did not go through the casino switchboard. The room looked like a giant hotel suite, but contained the stale smell of burned marijuana, warm beer, and assorted musk.

Subsequent investigation of the phone revealed that a "secret" phone line had been installed with a separate bill sent directly to the casino (rather than to Tribal headquarters where all other utility bills were sent). A review of the past year's bill showed more than $100,000 in long distance charges to locations all over the world. We later learned that the room itself had been furnished for some female members of the marketing staff to "entertain" performers, roadies,

234

and other "special guests" who might enjoy the carnal pleasures of the marketing girls. *This casino had it all!*

Behind the stage was another door…for which, like the secret room, no one could find a key. The solid-wood door had a deadbolt lock and the closest locksmith was two days from getting to us. I made the executive decision to have the door kicked in. Behind that door was the entrance to an entirely different world from the rustic casino. A hallway led to a private entrance hidden off the north side of the building; apparently a "secret" entrance for entertainers arriving on tour buses or by limo. (The casino's limo, incidentally, had disappeared and there was no record of it ever existing.)

Off of the hallway were two luxurious "dressing rooms"; one obviously for the "star" and one for the "band." Both were thickly carpeted and had large private bathrooms and showers. They were well-lit, had modern walls, and expensive ceramic tile leading to the carpeted rooms. Thinking about returning to the nicotine-poisoned General Manager's office, I turned to Cook and one of the maintenance men and said, *"welcome to the general manager's new office"*; I quickly gave instructions for cutting a doorway between the two rooms, putting a buzzer-controlled see-though glass security door where we had crashed through, dividing one room into a receptionist room and large boardroom, and turning the other room into an executive office. Ok, now at least I would not have to be detoxed from nicotine poisoning every time I walked into my office.

As I walked back through the Bingo hall/show room, I was almost overcome by a thick smoke cloud that had covered the room in the short time since I had walked through. The smoke was billowing through a large vent in the back side of the hall, spewing like an open fire and filling the room with a noxious greasy smell. Subsequent exploration revealed that the "hood" over the deep fryer and grill in the kitchen did not work and the smoke had been rerouted into this Bingo hall. A close look at the wall, where the vent was located, revealed a fire-hazard of caked grease dripping…or oozing…from the vent. Yuck.

Next stop on my tour was the "admin" building; the casino offices. There was no covered walkway between the casino and that building; I guessed that in rain or snow employees just covered their heads and ran from the offices to the casino. I had already seen many people smoking in the two-story wood-frame building (with no fire suppression nor smoke detectors); but it was not until I toured the building office-by-office that I realized how flimsy and "trailer-like" the construction was. The stairway to the second floor shook and creaked like the stairway to the balcony in the showroom; and the second story itself caved and dipped as I walked across it. I could see bows in the floor where file cabinets or desks weighted it.

Removed from the general manager and from the casino itself, it was obvious that the occupants of this building lived by their own rules and in their own little world. The marketing department lived and ruled from this building.

I immediately spotted a court-required ankle bracelet on one of the marketing employees. As Cook noticed that I was staring at it, he told me that the girl was a convicted felon (drugs and assault) who had served hard time and was now on house arrest. Though she could not "technically" be licensed to work in a casino, she was a relative of a high-ranking Tribal official. I glanced at a charmingly feminine tattoo across her right forearm that read, *"Fuck You Bitch"*, and continued my tour.

The rest of the administration building was a continuation of faulty construction, bad plumbing, coughing-heavy smoke, and more nepotism in key positions.

The final stop on my property-tour was another out-building; a long Quonset-hut looking storage building. At first glance it looked like a storage building for lawn mowers, ground equipment and various parts and supplies. However a more detailed examination revealed a universe of marketing supplies, two $20,000 go-carts, and a wealth of sorted "prizes" for players.

Most notably among the discarded displays and promotional items were banners and stands for several antique Harley Davidson motorcycles. According to Ellis, in a later investigation, the former GM had purchased the bikes at auction from the Venetian in Vegas following the closing of the Guggenheim's *"The Art of the Motorcycle"* collection. According to Ellis, the motorcycles had been purchased to be awarded in contest drawings for players but had been "won" by the carpenter (who did the questionable work) and the GM himself. Whether Ellis' allegations were true or false will probably never be known since there was no paper trail for the winners (which by the way is another MICS violation itself).

My property tour over, I set about reviewing contracts and relationships with slot machine vendors who were providing machines for the casino; a task I was already dreading because I had recognized the machines during my tour as being ones owned by those South Carolina transplants. Ellis had a hard-and-fast rule against ever purchasing slot machines; he wanted revenue share machines only. The treasure's thinking was that the speed of technology would make purchased machines obsolete by the time they paid for themselves. An "expensive" new machine sold for about $13,000 at that time; an Oklahoma revenue share (at that time) was about 35% of win-per-unit. Hence if a machine was averaging a win of $100 per day, then the vendor would get a rev share of $35 per day or $12,775 per year. Ellis felt that machine technology changed more frequently than that time frame. Unfortunately most rev-share contracts were for a minimum of 3 years so that $13,000 slot machine actually cost the Tribe $38,000. Further complicating the situation, the machines at Thunderbird were *not* $13,000 machines; they were (at most) $7,000 machines and would have paid for themselves in seven months. Nonetheless, Ellis was firm on his rule and the property was filled with lease-only machines. I, thus, set about the task of reviewing those revenue-share leases.

As I have discussed, in Indian Gaming a typical casino rev-share deal was what we called an 80/20 split; of that "win", the casino would keep 80% and the vendor would be paid 20%. Typically there were only two exceptions to that

236

standard: (1) a slightly higher vendor share was paid for "premium" game titles (such as themed-games for which manufacturers had to pay royalties for the theme license) and (2) an additional share for certain vendor-paid promotions or advertising. Unfortunately none of the "deals" in this casino's contracts were "typical".

The first contract I reviewed was for a 40/60 split. Note that is *not* a 60/40 split; this contract allowed the casino to keep only 40% of the revenue and the vendor was paid 60%. *What-the-hell was that all about?* I walked the floor seeking out the specific machines covered by that contract, hoping (at least) that they would be very popular machines that had *some* justification (albeit absurd) for a premium rev share. There was no excuse. Moreover, these were the machines in the "Nickel Corral" where who-the-hell-knows what is going on.

The next contract had a 60/40 rev share — still absurd but at least not upside down. However this one had what we call an "evergreen" clause; meaning that the contract never expired. To be legal in any state (and even in Indian Country), a contract needs to have three elements: a consideration (amount of money), an agreement, and a term (start and end dates). An end date can be flexible in that a contract can automatically renew if certain criteria are met. *This* bizarre contract renewed forever, providing that the vendor changed at least one game title ever three years. The contract went on to explain that changing a title literally meant that if the vendor had 50 machines with 25 of one title and 25 of a second title, that they could switch titles in any *one* of the physical boxes and that would qualify as meeting the contractual rollover. In effect, then, the contact with the Tribe was *forever*.

To make matters worse, this contract allowed that the vendor could cancel the contract at any time by giving the casino a 30-day written notice but the casino could *never* cancel the contract as long as the vendor met its obligations. The one exception to this non-cancellation rule was what the contract defined as "material breach". *Typically* material breach of a contract is a violation that is so substantial that it defeats the purpose of the parties in making the contract in the first place. In this case the contract language specifically said:

"in the event of material breach by either party, either party may notify the other party of said breach and either party may terminate this agreement immediately by notifying the other party either verbally or in writing of said breach by either party."

I am not certain who wrote this contract, though I am relatively confident it was not a competent attorney; but I was grateful for their overuse of the words "either party" and their inability to understand a noun clause. I immediately had my secretary call the vendor's representatives to meet with David Cook and me. At the meeting I informed the vendor, *"I want to report a material breach of the contract and we have to cancel the agreement immediately."*

"Oh my God, what breach? There is no way" the vendor responded assertively, as he followed-up with an arrogant smirk that had clearly been practiced.

237

"Well, I am not going to pay you anymore," I smirked, suspecting that since the contract was not written by an attorney the vendor would have no legal concept of the "constructive breach" that I was performing. *"You have 48 hours to get your fucking machines out of my casino; after that time I will have them removed from Indian trust land and placed on State Highway 9. Now get the fuck off of Tribal Land you Goddamn thieves. The days of stealing from this Tribe's members are over; there is a new sheriff in town and YOU are busted, motherfucker."*

At the same time, I had Wil Wimmer change the marquis sign at the entrance of the casino to read *"There Is A New Sheriff In Town,"* playing off of the Wild Wild West Casino theme. The machines were gone the next day and the contract was voided; the tribe saved tens of thousands if not hundreds of thousands of dollars. And I made a lifelong enemy of the owner of that South Carolina company.

The next contract I reviewed revealed a revenue share that was a three-way split rather than a two-way. While I did not know of anything illegal or in violation of MICS about such an arrangement, it still waved a red flag at me warning that something was unusual. The language bothered me so much that I invited the vendor in to meet with me and discuss the contract.

This vendor seemed sincere, honest, and very open about the contract. He explained, *"Mr. Green, I have never seen anything like this either; let me tell you what happened. We came to see the officials here at this casino to pitch our games and they seemed to love them. In fact the slot manager told me she wanted them on the floor immediately. I thought we had a deal and I told her that I would be back the next day with a contract. When I came back I was told that unfortunately there was no floor space available for my machines because this other vendor —the other name in your contract there— had signed an agreement for all of the remaining floor space. They went on to tell me that the other vendor had not used all of his allocated space and that perhaps he would give some of it up to me if I would call him directly. I called him and he agreed to sell me his floor space for 10% of the revenue of the machines. I had never heard of such a thing so I told the casino that if I was going to do such a thing I wanted it in the contract. That is why your rev share is with two companies; my percentage and the payoff to this other guy,"* he explained in obviously frustrated dismay. *"I later found out that of his 10% he only kept 5% and the other 5% was paid as marketing fees in personal checks to the casinos marketing director who I think was married to the general manager here,"* he added.

I am able to so vividly report this conversation, years later, because this vendor became a close friend and eventually a business partner with me in several ventures. He reminds me of the details constantly and has told the story over and over to industry operatives.

Russell Ellis later confirmed that part of the story, after he obtained copies of cancelled checks as well as a contract between that third-party vendor and the GM's wife. The "other guy" who orchestrated this scam, as of this writing is a multi-millionaire financier of Indian casinos with several currently-active "exclusive floor space" deals under his belt. In bidding for various development deals in recent years, my main competitor has been that company…which never misses the opportunity to give their version of how I sabotaged Tribal funding by thwarting that and other contracts.

The next contract I reviewed had a clause that excused that vendor from providing paper for their machines. These were all Class II machines; there was no TITO payout available and the machines did not pay in coin. When it was time to cash out, the machine would print a receipt ticket for the player to take to the cage and exchange for cash. Each vendor's machines used a different type of paper, often different sizes of paper. Typically paper, maintenance, parts, etc. are part of what the vendor provides for their portion of the rev share; but in *this* contract the paper was specifically excluded by agreement.

Again, I called for a sit-down with a vendor. This one explained to me that he had offered to provide the paper, of course, but was told "by the casino" that his paper would not be accepted and that he should exclude it from the contract. When I asked him where the casino got paper for his machines, he cited a printing company in Nashville Tennessee. A call to that company revealed that their contract was with a third-party company which they revealed to have the same name and address as the company partially owned by the GM's wife and that other vendor who had "sold" floor space at the casino.

Another vendor, when I questioned their contract, warned me that if I questioned their percentage, the way they heard that I had other vendors, they would close the casino by repossessing the building. It turned out that their company that had purchased the double-wide trailers that became the *Nickel Corral.* They were threatening to take away the trailers. Apparently, they had been promised that their machines and *only* their machines would fill those trailers forever at whatever contractual arrangement they dictated. Equally apparently, these geniuses had used the same legal scholars that had developed the "either party" language for that other contract; they overlooked the issue of Tribal sovereignty. I am guessing they never read *Bryan v. Itasca County* and had no clue that the original sovereignty issue that gave rise to Indian casinos in the first place was an issue over trying to remove a mobile home from Tribal land.

I called Russell Ellis and told him that I was about to go to war with a white-owned slot machine company trying to remove a building (actually four buildings) from Tribal trust land. He, in turn, notified Tribal Police, the Bureau of Indian Affairs, and the United States Marshall's office (I think he threw in the latter just for good measure; there was no jurisdiction that I could think of). David Cook's reaction was even stronger with a very direct, *"yeah, them and whose army is going to TRY to take our buildings?"* Sometimes it is very cool to have an "old boy" super-cop on the payroll. Eventually after a couple of nasty letter exchanges between the company and our attorneys, the vendor backed down and realized they didn't have a leg to stand on. A really funny footnote to that little adventure is that I ran into the owner of that company, some 5 years later, and he feigned never having heard of the incident.

Meanwhile, in the regular Bingo hall operation, I discovered mark-up pricing on Bingo paper and supplies contracts through another third-party vendor (rather than directly with one of the Bingo vendors) that would have been laughable if it had not been costing the casino so much money every week.

I found a contract with a bus company requiring the casino to pay the company $600 per trip to drive the 37-miles from Oklahoma City three times a week. Additionally, the casino paid the bus operators a bounty of $10 per person delivered to the casino. The casino also reimbursed the bus company for fuel (from presented diesel receipts) and provided each bus rider with $20 in free Bingo play. Finally, the casino was required to pay for advertising the bus trips in the Oklahoma City newspaper (though no one I talked with had ever seen one of the alleged ads).

I later learned that the "players" were picked up from homeless shelters in Oklahoma City and were required to split their winnings with the bus driver 50/50. Governor Blanchard told me that he witnessed a bus driver chase an elderly homeless woman through the parking lot and tackle her to the ground to collect his half of the $50 she had won one night.

Another vendor's contract had a revenue share of 37½% going to the vendor. The fine print explained that the actual was revenue share was *"only"* 32½% and the additional 5% was paid into a marketing fund which was spent at the vendor's discretion and not the casino's. A phone call turned into one of the most paternalistic (if not racist) explanations I had heard in a long time: *"you know, Mr. Green, a lot of these Tribes really aren't smart enough to know how to use marketing money, so we set this aside to make sure something gets done right."*

Beyond the paternalistic nonsense, I was outraged that a slot machine company THOUGHT they were going to tell ME how to market a casino. Maybe they had heard of Donald Trump; maybe they had heard of the only profitable casino in his chain; maybe $100-million-a-month coin-in had some meaning to them. Naw, probably not.

Not a single contract had the standard 80/20 revenue share. Moreover, not one of them had a rev share of less than 30% going to the vendor. (I later learned that no one in Oklahoma had "normal" rev shares.) None of the vendors were what I would have called "top-tier" slot machine companies (no IGT, Bally, Aristocrat, WMS, and so on); and though IGT had not yet entered the Class II market there were plenty of *legitimate* vendors in the space; though most of these were those very companies bred in the bowels of South Carolina and exposed by the scholars and journalists.

Unfortunately, this casino seemed to have a lot more "questionable" vendors than legitimate ones. Even the top names in Class II (VGT, Rocket, etc.) were missing from the floor of this casino; presumably not willing to pay the kickback/extortion fees to the third-party company. The floor was plagued with machines from companies that existed only for Oklahoma and in two cases only for this one casino. More dubious than the "third tier" companies that shark-infested the gaming landscapes of South Carolina, Alabama, Mexico and other "third world" jurisdictions, the companies that dominated this casino were on the surface at least quasi-criminal operations and at worst probably *Racketeer Influenced and Corrupt Organizations*.

I turned my orientation focus from the facility and the contracts to the staff; to human resources. Like the melodrama of corruption I had seen in the building and in the contracts, I found the staffing to be (at best) below the acceptable Minimum Internal Control Standards, despite the fact that David Cook had already fired more than 100 employees.

Nepotism was rampant; but that is often the case with Tribal casinos and there is little that can be done about that given the small size of most Tribes and the large families within them. However this casino was plagued with sibling supervising sibling, "untouchable" disciplinary problems protected by political connections, husbands supervising wives, and a really not-funny problem of the old cliché "they are all in bed together anyway" (in this case literally).

There were employees representing opposing Tribal political factions who held their positions to report to their outside political bosses. There were employees still loyal to former managers and were sending daily revenue reports to those fired managers. Even in the Human Resources department, personal files and background investigations (including my own) were forwarded to former employees. Vendor kick-backs to employees continued even after David Cook's initial house-cleaning of staff because the threads of corruption had been sewn so deeply into the fabric of the organization.

My staff and I were offered cash, sex, alcohol, drugs, and gifts to "protect" peoples' jobs, guarantee certain vendor contracts, and look the other way when family of fired employees came into the casino to play games under the control of close friends.

The head of my drop team was a convicted drug, prostitution, and extortion felon. The head of my cage and vault had pled *nolo contendere* to charges of embezzling from a national bank. One of my shift managers was a convicted armed robber. The manager of my valet parking had been convicted of man slaughter. The number of DUI, drug, and prostitution convicts on my staff was too numerous to keep count. The poker manager had been charged as an accessory to murdering an undercover police officer and stuffing the body in a plastic trash bag.

In addition to the activities I spotted in the OTB and the bar during my walk-through there on the first day, I came to observe a whole menu of unacceptable (if not criminal) behavior that, at very least, was ripping off the Tribe. The beer and wine distributor actually asked me who he should give the cash kickbacks to after we fired one of the bar managers. A player told me that she had come in on a particular day because she had been promised she would win a random drawing if she split payout with the employee conducting the drawing.

241

One of the Bingo managers was loan sharking to a large portion of casino employees; he held titles to their cars, got first dibs on their paychecks, and was running some serious vig on them. A local hardware store manager asked me if he still needed to increase his prices for goods sold to the casino to cover the cash he was required to kickback to casino employees. Several customers asked me if they would still be required to tip departmental managers in order to cash out from a slot machine. I observed two different employees on two different shifts actually removing money from cash register drawers and putting it in their own pockets; when questioned about it, one denied it and the other admitted that it was routine. Two different women (one married) vying for the position of one of my manager's secretary spontaneously (and unsolicited) undressed during his interviews with them. Hand-pays from slot machines (bypassing the printed ticket and the accounting system) always increased at night (a sure sign of fraud) …until I started requiring management verification of every hand pay.

One of the valet cart drivers (we had golf carts pick up patrons in the parking lot and deliver them to the front door) suped up the engines in the golf carts and was running (and betting on) drag races nightly between the carts. On one particular night security cameras recorded two girls removing their shirts and bras and riding topless on the back of one of the golf carts for over an hour. *(That sort of outlandish behavior was not so unusual in casino parking lots; one time at the Trump29 property we caught a clown (literally a guy we had hired for a party, dressed in a clown costume) having sex on the hood of a car with one of our cocktail waitresses (while he was in full clown costume.) I am not sure which of them was stranger.)* But clearly the incidents in this valet department were symptomatic of the property-wide problem of each little fiefdom running out of control without policies & procedures or strong management.

And just to top off the lovely image of the staff that I was getting, one of the first rules I had to enforce was that the female members of the staff should not spit their chewing tobacco juices onto the casino floor (most of the males apparently knew better). This, by the way, was a rampant problem at the casino I opened for a Montana Tribe as well (though there it was only the showgirls that chewed and spit on the floor).

As I said, David Cook had already fired (or listed to be fired) more than 100 people and he had hired a former district attorney's investigator to take over background checks on the remaining employees. Even without David's police work and preliminary firings, the normal turnover at the casino was abysmal. A typical employee lasted three months and had been employed by the casino at least three times. On the flip side there were some outstanding employees.

When I asked marketing employees "who are your best customers?" no one could give me a straight answer, but a housekeeper popped up *"well my best customer is Mr. Walker from Norman but he is only good on Tuesdays because his wife doesn't come with him. He usually plays $5 a spin for about six hours. Probably the next best is Verna Jackson, she…"* THAT was rattled off like a marketing person should do. (For years I have argued that the most important

242

customer service people at a casino are the valets, housekeepers, slot attendants, cashiers and security guards; because those are the only employees *most* customers ever see.)

There were *great* employees too. The blind girl that supervised the receptionists and telephone operators was one of the best customer-service reps I have ever seen in a casino. The gay cross-dresser that managed the "procurement" department was a former army quartermaster and was a brilliant supply organizer. The slot analyst (who David recommended for promotion to slot manager) was a paradigm of integrity. The young girl who managed the gift shop was meticulous in following instructions. The three housekeepers were phenomenal. The internal audit/accounting supervisor was amazing; both a bastion of integrity and a paragon of reliability. There was hope.

I quickly promoted all of those employees to management positions and put my Trump defectors in key spots. Wil Wimmer became my Director of Operations; Yuri, the Trump telephone operator, became my Customer Service Manager (she had outstanding customer service skills and training); Frank, of course, became the CFO; and Iram, the Trump valet guy, became my manager-on-duty when I was away and the go-to guy for covering any missing department. I brought in Tom Trimble to gain control of the computer systems for the Tribe and a brilliant network engineer from Boca Raton to administer the networks for Tom.

I assigned Frank to have absolute management of audit, accounting, cage, cashiers, vault, drop, count, IT, human resources, and administrative offices. In fact, I refused to ever enter the cage, vault, or drop areas; I wanted to make certain that security was the tightest. I asked David to have surveillance watch the drop and give 9instructions that even if I entered the area, security should stop me just like any other employee. I entered the audit and accounting departments at will, but I never discussed business with anyone from those departments. I had decided on this unusual removal of myself from anything fiscal because I knew that I was planning on making major personnel changes as well as equally major marketing expenditures; I did not want any possible cloud of impropriety over these major changes that were on the horizon.

With a good understanding of the situation, and not running back to Trump, I dug in for the job ahead: untangling this mess for the Tribe and trying to turn this dog into a money maker. Foremost in my mind was that the casino was still borrowing money to meet payroll.

Using my bag of Trump tricks, I had Tom Trimble create a *manual* player-tracking system, similar to what we had used at *Resorts International* in the 1980s but with a technology spin to the database. Since none of the South Carolina transplanted vendors allowed actual casino accounting and player tracking systems to be attached to their slot machines, Trimble had the daunting task of creating a manual process to create a customer database and a methodology for tracking player value.

243

I called Bunky Boger and within a few weeks Ginger and her sisters were playing chicken tic-tac-toe and the majority of casino players were joining Tom's new players club in order to challenge Ginger for the $10,000 top prize.

Under that first-ever compact with the State that Blanchard had signed, Thunderbird was the first casino in Oklahoma to offer legal blackjack (though a number of Tribes had been offering illegal blackjack for years). Under the provisions of the compact, Oklahoma-sanctioned blackjack was required to take a "rake" from the pot (just like poker) and establish a players' pool. The funds from that pool were legislatively required to be redistributed to the players rather than kept by the Tribe, though neither the compact nor the legislation defined how that was to be done. Thunderbird's blackjack games, again the only legal ones in the state, were so financially successful that in very short order that fund was several hundreds of thousands of dollars. To comply with the compact I decided to redistribute those funds through the creation of a blackjack tournament, somewhat akin to the World Series of Poker or the World Poker Tour. It turned, because of the sheer size of the players' pool, that I created what was at that time the world's largest-pot blackjack tournament with the top prize being $250,000 cash and an absurdly gaudy 25 karat gold winner's bracelet that I designed with a local jeweler. The tournament generated national news, including national cable television coverage of the event.

Continuing into the proven bag of tricks from the Trump property as well as from my commercial gaming experiences, I reached into a portfolio of celebrities with a propensity toward casinos and brought Johnny Carson's sidekick Ed McMahon to meet players...and draw in new players.

I began a direct mail program from Tom's database and launched a massive (for Oklahoma) branding campaign. Saturating, first Oklahoma City and eventually most of the state, with billboards, I again became the cartoonish image of casino. This image was reinforced in a series of television commercials with the

Above: Late night legend Ed McMahon with Gary Green at the launch of Ed McMahon-themed MGAM slot machines.

same theme: *"I am stealing Las Vegas and bringing it to Oklahoma."* Those television spots, produced by Jan Talamo and Frank Palmieri's *Media and Marketing Group* went on to win a national award for their creativity and originality. Those spots (to which I retained title, ownership, and copyright) are available on YouTube or at www.GaryGreenGaming.com. Since the Thunderbird experiences, I have used variations of those commercials at various casinos around the country, where it would be appropriate to have an over-the-top cartoonish branding.

These are the TV spots I talked about earlier that included filming an Elvis spot on his stage and in his jumpsuit. The 26 hours without sleep or break, filming those commercials in Las Vegas, was itself a series of adventures and exploits that ranged from: my pants catching fire during a sequence shot on the Vegas Strip; to one of our actors being arrested for impersonating a police office because we forgot to get the right permits; to having to wake up Mayor Oscar Goodman at 3:45am because did not know that the Freemont Street lights would be off at the time we were filming.

Above left: A page from the storyboard for the award-winning television sports. **Above right:** A cartoonish Gary Green bobble head distributed to players. **Below:** One of the series of themed billboards that peppered the State of Oklahoma.

245

Thunderbird had become the first casino in Oklahoma to have professional casino management, marketing, mainstream games, and by-the-book internal controls and regulation. David Cook was tapped by the State to help train the new compact-required regulators.

Without any debate, discussion, or misrepresentation, within one year the casino was profitable and able to pay every man, woman, and child member of the Tribe their first ever distribution of income from the casino. We transformed not only Oklahoma gaming, but we transformed Class II by bringing in the big vendors and reducing the role of the South Carolina boys.

As reported in *Indian Gaming Business Magazine*, the Tribe's revenue increased by $30-million. The majority of the exploitive South Carolina slot machine vendors were out and the first Class II games produced by giant IGT were shipping to Thunderbird; and for the first time in the Oklahoma casino industry, professionals from the industry were providing their expertise to Tribal government.

ABOVE: The cover story of *Indian Gaming Business Magazine* highlighting Gary Green's success at Thunderbird Casino and the transformation of the Class II universe.

Unfortunately for the Tribal membership, the supporters of all of those fired employees and kicked-out vendors spent the next two years marshaling their political forces to oust Blanchard, Ellis, and the other crusaders for a legal and profitable casino. The FBI approached me and forewarned that they had been monitoring Blanchard's chief opponent for years in drug and embezzlement investigations. *"You can't let this guy win the election,"* the agent warned me.

But it was too late; despite my best efforts to help Blanchard, including writing him a campaign plan, he was out. After a bitterly fought election and charges and counter-charges, the Blanchard team was defeated in the election.

The campaign against them revolved around the charge that Blanchard had turned the tribe's casino over to *"Las Vegas mafia greasers"* (that would be me and my team) who had pocketed millions of dollars that used to go to the tribal members (through personal deals, kickbacks, and "other methods"). The charges against Blanchard, Ellis, and other ousted Council members expanded to take my television spots literally and accused them of hiring a Las Vegas gangster to steal parts of Las Vegas and hide it on Indian land where, supposedly, Vegas law enforcement could never find the spoils I had hidden there.

Even I, personally, was targeted in the campaign against Blanchard with death threats, being followed to and from the casino, and posters claiming that there was no Bunky Boger and that I secretly owned a chicken farm that raised Ginger and the other chickens. One series of fliers proclaimed that I never worked for Trump and that he had obtained a court-order to have me stop from making that claim. Another flier claimed that I was an operative of an organized crime "family" that had decided to use Thunderbird as a stepping stone to sy-phon enough cash to *buy* Las Vegas. As evidence of that plot, they cited my employment contract and its very lucrative bonus structure which by now was in fact into seven-figures.

The ousted South Carolina vendors, one of which had hired the former General Manager (that Cook had fired), joined with Blanchard's opposition to provide their "expertise" in explaining how "the new slot machines" were de-signed to cheat the Tribe. Publically traded IGT, the largest slot machine com-pany in the world, was accused of paying $90,000 to buy my racing Jaguar and provide millions in kickbacks to me in exchange for ousting those "honest" companies from South Carolina.

The new Tribal government filed a bevy of criminal charges against Blanchard and the other former government officials and forced them all into Tribal court to answer to judges and an "Attorney General" appointed by the new government. After months of stomach-churning drama, all the charges were eventually dropped against Blanchard and his team. *(My team was never charged.)*

Meanwhile the new government reinstated the fired employees; reinstated the removed vendors; removed the IGT machines; fired me and my staff; turned casino management over to the new Tribal governor (whose first "official" act was to reinstitute the smoking policy); and in less than a year the casino was once again losing money and was in debt.

At one point the newly elected government's ferocious attacks on Blanchard spilled over to accusations against Cook, Haas, and my team. The newly-elected governor immediately announced that his "personal police force" was conducting a criminal investigation —a claim he quickly withdrew when a local newspaper reported that he had been charged with perjury and fraud two days earlier relating to his allegations against Blanchard. The nastiness continued for a couple of months, putting a cloud over Blanchard, my staff, and me.

As personally painful as all of that was to me, it was totally alleviated by one of the National Indian Gaming Commission's three commissioners telling me to *"ignore it; everybody knows that guy is crazy"* and FBI Special Agent who visited me to again tell me that the "Bureau" had a long-term investigation into the activities of the newly elected governor. That agent also told the leader of another Tribe that *"whatever you are hearing; you can't go wrong with Gary Green"*.

The vindication of the Blanchard government (and my team) continued with an investigation by the DEA into the new government's allegedly diverting of oxycodone from the Tribal clinic to the casino; the disbarring and commitment to a mental hospital of the new "Attorney General"; and *Casino Journal* magazine's assessment of the situation that *"it is hard to argue with a strategy that increased casino revenue by 59.1%"*

Still it was a rough few months through Tribal politics and if I had not been so steeped in Indian culture, I might have freaked out or taken it more seriously. Certainly most of my colleagues in the commercial gaming world would have freaked out over such things. And, sadly, Ten years later, Blanchard's reputation had still not recovered and for at least every two years during the next eight years he ran for re-election and was defeated time and time again...indicating that the false allegations really had done damage to Blanchard (and ultimately to the Tribe itself).

While the Thunderbird debacle and the Trump29 eccentricities are great anecdotal adventures into Indian Country, they are neither typical nor atypical. They are just *another day* in Indian casinos...in Indian Country.

After those two Tribal adventures I went on to work with dozens of other Tribes and almost none were as drama-filled as those two.

The Ottawa Tribe of Oklahoma and the creation of their *High Winds Casino* in Miami Oklahoma was not only drama-free but was a true joy of Tribal functionality and success-story. Working with my good friend the developer and financier Bill Caughey, Frank Haas and I were able to create *that* casino (which Frank still manages as of this writing). Caughey went on to develop dozens of other Tribal casinos working hand-in-hand with Tribal leadership across the country in some of the most successful and creative financing that I have ever seen.

My escapades with the Ho Chunk Nation in Wisconsin, the Akwesasne in New York, the Yakama in Washington State, and about 19 other Tribes all carried their own anecdotal adventures, though few carried the level of drama that compressed widespread long-term Tribal experiences into such compact little boxes as Thunderbird and Trump29 had done. The closest escapade to these adventures was my stint on behalf of the Blackfeet Tribe of Montana.

These once-feared mighty Algonquin warriors of the plains from the Great Lakes to the Northern Rockies, had been rounded up by U.S. imperialists and regulated to the slopes of what is now Glacier National Park —some of the harshest land in the continental United States. Clearly someone in the Department of War wanted to punish these legendary fighters even more than they had done with (true or false) smallpox-laced blankets deliberately distributed to the Tribe.

ABOVE: Casino Journal's Cover Story Proclaiming Gary Green a casino marketing *"Magic Man"* in conjunction with his development company (and his departure from Thunderbird Casino).

To understand the scale of the Montana project you need to understand the geography and natural surroundings of the new casino I developed there. It is located on the northern realm of Glacier National Park, northeast of the town of East Glacier — more than 50 miles from the closet four-lane highway; 60 miles from an Interstate Highway; two-and-a-half hours from the closest Airport or even a *Wal-Mart*. During much of the time that the casino was under construction it was accessible only by a 20-mile stretch of dirt and gravel road through open range; and the one highway south was closed for months due to snowfall (as it was every year).

The million-and-a-half acres of reservation land are populated by 8,600 people; but there are only 360 households and 254 families in the town. The annual per capita income was about $8,900 and 30% of the town was below the federal "poverty level". During the winter months the sun rises around 10 a.m. and sets as early as 2:30 p.m. On some evenings aurora borealis can be seen. The town of Browning, itself, is 30 miles northwest of the coldest spot ever recorded in the continental United States and during the one December (of the total 10 months) that I spent there, the *warmest* day I experienced was -11° (minus eleven degrees) below zero.

The nearby town of Cut Bank holds the world's record for the largest temperature drop in one day: from +44° down to -56°in a 24 hour period. "White outs" are common occurrences during much of the year *(a terrifying high-wind situation where no objects cast shadows, the horizon is not visible, only dark objects are discernible, and visibility is no more than a few inches)*. Most cars are equipped with electric block heaters as well as a glove-compartment stash of chocolate, matches, candles, and space blankets (for the *expected* (not "possible" but rather "probable") stranded times). Winds, trapped in the mountains, can reach hurricane-force with little or no warning. And with global warming, the area has recently been victim of uncontrolled wildfires and flash flooding.

Such a harsh climate was typical of many Indian reservations around the country; Tribes were forced to locate on callous, uninhabitable lands that white settlers did not want or could not tame. Such was clearly the case with the once warlords of the plains, the Blackfeet Nation. They must have really pissed off someone to be sent to such a place.

According to the *American Indian Studies Program* at the University of Arizona, this town, Browning Montana, of only 360 households sees at least 50-60 street drunks present every day and alcoholism there is twelve times the national average (from my personal observation, that is an *under-estimate*.) —in one way or another affecting 100% of the population. According to the regional Budweiser distributor, one convenience store / gas station in town sells more beer in a month than any five other sales outlets combined anywhere in the State of Montana. Following large holiday celebrations, I have personally witnessed the main street through town littered with beer cans more than a foot-deep along the curbs.

250

I will spare readers any more of my pent-up lectures on the tragedy of Native Americans and how white abuse, degradation, exploitation, piracy, and attempted genocide have forced the quality-of-life to this stage of unraveling and deconstruction. Less than a melodramatic calamity, the physical situation and the mental state of the people in the situation are byproducts of the last two centuries of white American expansionism. Sadly and painfully, this has manifest in hostility, anger, prejudices, and despair. Combined with the genetic predisposition for alcoholism, the behavior and living standards are disastrous.

Against that charming, if not tragic, backdrop, I was hired to supervise the completion of construction, hire & train staff, outfit the casino, and get it open.

Remember those vendor-provided "floor placement fees" (and kickbacks) that I discussed earlier? As you recall, those fees are actually paid (ultimately and over time) by the casino itself...many times over the actual cash value. Those rev share plans to pay kickbacks and fund casinos are, then, positioned as loans but paid back from revenue; hence avoiding taxes and are in the purest sense of the term a skim from the casino; especially if the money is paid to an individual. If a machine wins $100 per day for the casino and the vendor takes $35 a day of that, over a year that is $12,775 average; the game was paid off (if it was $8,000) in eight months and at the end of five years there would be a $56,000 profit or an investment return of 800% in five years. Good work if you can get it.

Aware of those inequities, I used a *legal* version of that very kickback scheme, myself, to benefit the Blackfeet's bad planning and duplicity with their original financing source. The original funding group did not provide enough money for basic casino supplies, payroll for staff during training, or even enough to do some of the finishing work on the structure. There was no money budgeted for signage. They did not even have money for staff uniforms or food and beverage supplies for the restaurant and bar.

To further complicate issues, the architect chosen by the business committee designed the casino with, frankly, some absolute absurdities (and financial nightmares) in the plans. Though lights and light poles had been designed for the muddy parking lot, there were no plans to run electricity to the lights. The roof was not designed to handle the weight of the HVAC (heating, ventilation, air conditioning) system necessary for the property and when that flaw was discovered, apparently the designers decided *"what-the-heck"* and added an unplanned second floor to the casino to have a place to put the unit. (And of course, each time it came on it shook the entire building, like a small earthquake on the second floor.)

A server room, housing multiple heat-generating computer servers for Class II Bingo, had neither ventilation nor air conditioning. *(Measured heat levels in the room eventually reached more than 115°.)* No study had been made of the water supply system nor the deep-ground well that fed it. When the water was turned on, large chunks of minerals (some over two-inches in diameter) rushed through pipes and instantly destroyed portions of internal plumbing of the build-

251

ing. A huge lobby center-piece fireplace faced the cashier cage so that if any long lines developed there, the customers would be rotisserized by the flames.

The cashier cage itself was strategically positioned as near as possible to the front door, making it easy for customers to cash-out and not have to be *"bothered"* by walking by slot machines to spend their winnings; as if it was designed to keep money from going back into slot machines. At the same time this location of the cashier cage also made it convenient for any would-be thieves to easily exit the casino without hindrance. And, with no "panic button" or alarms in the cage plans *(and being only a few miles from the Canadian border)*, the cage location was really an asset to any potential robber(s).

A floor-to-ceiling "two-way-mirror" in the General Manager's office looking onto the casino floor had the serious problem that if the lights were on in the office, then the occupants could not see the casino floor but all the customers on the floor could observe whatever might be going on in the office. In-floor wiring conduit was set in concrete rather than in a duct system, so once slot machines were placed on the floor the only way they could be moved was to cut through concrete and redirect wiring. Enough kitchen equipment had been ordered to outfit a large high school cafeteria (vast overkill); but no dishwashing equipment had been ordered; nor ice machines or pumping stations for the bar. Additionally there was no storage space for food and supplies (in this remote area where all deliveries halt during several road-impassible months, necessitating stockpiling).

A number of planning-related violations of the *Federal Minimum Internal Control Standards* included: No way to securely lock away Bingo paper (which has a cash-equivalent value); A cashiers' vault that could be entered through an unprotected drop-ceiling; A "vault" constructed with solid kitchen cabinets, allowing for no view of assets (by surveillance cameras) when the doors were closed; No controlled access to gaming servers; No controlled access to surveillance equipment (which itself was below minimum requirements for the projected income of the casino (and had been selected, provided and installed by the business committee-owned cable television company without competitive bid); *and a host of other Federal violations.*

The planning did not take into account the high winds common in the town and within a few weeks of opening, large metal sheets of roofing were flapping freely and flying around the parking lot like Frisbees thrown toward windshields. *(Yes there were insurance claims by several car owners.)* Within a month the winds had also destroyed the large freestanding outdoor sign.

On top of these construction-related nightmares, the project was equally plagued with organizational problems. There had been no planning for a players club, for a location for employees to take meals, for lockers for employees to store purses and coats, nor for almost any of the *back-of-the-house* operations (like slot techs, casino audit, alcohol storage, a surveillance room, etc.), as well as many more lack-of-experience omissions.

The original project manager, a Tribal member who had been identified to me as the COO, was fired in the two-week time frame between when I flew up to meet the business committee and then started to drive up from Florida. Apparently though, that did not resolve the problems. In fact, the casino secretary (and first employee of the new entity) told me that her observation was that the fired COO had tried to correct the problems and that is what had cost him his job; conflicts with the business committee's CEO and hired architect.

ABOVE: Gary Green (center in first picture; left in the second one) in hard hat surveys and discusses the Montana construction site in the packed-mud parking lot and discusses work-around solutions for the Tribe's planning shortfalls. **BELOW:** The casino sign shortly after installation and then several weeks later after a wind storm.

The whole project was under the auspices of a national-award-winning Tribal business committee, but was wrought with an amazing jumble of incompetence, lack of planning, and desperation to get funding. With an apparent long history of defaulting on project loans, the business committee was required to find a co-signer or underwriter for the loan to build the new casino.

This was not an unusual requirement for Tribes with little or (in this case) a *bad* credit history. In fact there is an entire cottage industry of white millionaires "underwriting" syndicated loan guarantees for tribes (in exchange for a variety of payback schemes). In reality these underwriters have credit at risk but no actual cash in the loan; they merely co-sign like a parent would for his son or

253

daughter's first car. If the Tribe were to default, the co-signer would have to make the payments. Since property on Indian lands cannot be seized to pay debts, the co-signer could potentially be left holding the bag with no collateral for his guarantee. Hence these cottage-industry loan-signers often charged usury-like fees or devised other quasi-legal kickback schemes to compensate them for their risk.

In a blatant violation of Federal regulations, one of the slot machine companies agreed to co-sign the loan in exchange for the *verbal* agreement that they would be the *only* company with slot machines at the new casino. Had such a violation been committed to paper, the *National Indian Gaming Commission* would have instantly nullified it; so it was shrewdly kept as a verbal "unwritten" agreement (and only revealed to me much later).

As if this shopping list of troubles were not enough, the HR (Human Resources) department, like finance, was kept separate from the casino and controlled exclusively by the business committee. HR positioned itself more as employee advocates than an entity to protect the casino. Consequently there were no job testing policies *(other than in-house conducted drug testing by a convicted drug felon who recently had been released from prison)*; and people were offered jobs literally based on judgments like, *"You look like a cashier."*

Among the gems that HR mandated the casino to hire were the cashiers and supervisors from the previous small Bingo-casino who, a week earlier, had accepted a $5 bill from a customer and given the guy change of two twenties and a ten. The excuse was that the five dollar bill had been mistaken for a fifty dollar bill.

I will let you be the judge; following is a photo of *the actual bill* accepted by the cashier. This is NOT a facsimile that I created later; this is the bill that was actually accepted.

ABOVE: This is the actual $5 bill *(not a later-copied facsimile)* with "50" written with a marking pen and was ACTUALLY accepted and cashed as a fifty-dollar bill by cashiers and supervisors. *Think something might have been up?*

In almost any other casino in America this would have set off all sorts of red-flag warnings in the mind of any stable casino boss. Most would have thought this was a criminal activity with the cashier and her supervisor being *"in on it"* with the perpetrator. In *some* casino jurisdictions, I might have had the employees taken to the back room and "interrogated". But at THIS casino it was just another of the regular daily HR issues. These employees *really and truly* were *that* oblivious to their jobs; they *really* did not notice.

Hmmm. Let's see; 600 slot machines projected to win $100 a day each, with an average hold of about 9%... that means about $1,111 would pass through each machine or a total of about $666-thousand dollars in and out of the casino that would have to be accurately counted every day. Oh yeah, this was going to be fun with the HR mandated hiring.

Though I had submitted an FTE (full time equivalent employee) projection of 110 employees, the Human Resources department insisted on hiring employees from the now-closing smaller casino as well as dozens of other unemployed tribal members. Based on their insistence, the employment list climbed to 308 before the casino even opened. I was not sure where the cash would come from to support that kind of payroll.

For a number of reasons, the Tribe's business committee did not make these failings known to their financial syndicator; in fact, they kept them hidden. Moreover, there was a border-line deceit *(in my opinion)* going on in a very conscious effort by the business committee to hide the specific spending and at the same time use the loan money to prop up other Tribal businesses, pay salaries and at least mislead (if not defraud) the funding syndicator when it came time for various construction-related draws.

These and other sordid absurdities *(such as the aforementioned relying on the Tribally-owned cable television company to provide surveillance cameras and a piece-mill video surveillance system)* left the business committee severely short of funds to finish the casino. It was against this backdrop that I began looking for sources to bail the Tribe out of their financial calamity.

So, on their behalf, I approached one of the slot machine vendors with, basically, this proposition: *"Hey, you know that kickback you give casino managers for placing your slot machines on the floor? Well I have never taken one but I will tell you what; I will let you put 300 slot machines on this casino floor if you will kickback $1,000 per slot machine. But I want you to pay it to the Tribe and not me. They need money to finish the casino."*

I was unaware of the deal with the original vendor to be the sole provider, so this slot company responded to my request and agreed that they *would* pay the kickback and increase the revenue-share percentage. However, since payments were going to a governmental body (the Tribe), rather than as bribing a General Manager, they wanted a loan guarantee document for the funds. I, in turn, suggested that if there were to be a loan-guarantee, then the increased revenue share would continue only until the "loan" was paid back, and not in perpetuity. Surprisingly, the slot vendor agreed and hence the loan was absolutely legal and enforceable.

Having no fiduciary authority whatsoever (not even the ability to sign a contract), I presented the proposition to the business committee which not only jumped at the prospect (and approved it) but also asked me to approach a second vendor with a similar proposition (without notifying the first vendor). Moreover, before a weekly conference call with the original lender and loan syndicators, I was instructed not to mention the $600,000 in loans from the slot machine manufacturers. Hence we finished the funding of the casino.

I positioned the grand opening as the biggest event to hit Montana since Little Big Horn. After talking with the business committee and its hired president, I began positioning this crapulent, remote, and icy perdition as the *Las Vegas of the Northwest*. It was my plan to bring the wealthy white tourist from Glacier National Park to the casino and avoid catering to the local population. I genuinely believed that building a glitter-place casino for no reason other than taking money from the already down-trodden local population would be both a viciously genocidal aggression and a financial disaster. *How could we possibly justify creating a casino to cater only to people whose annual income was less than $9,000?*

So I convinced the business committee that we would go after the tourists and not the locals; we would be a miniature Vegas. I would reuse my Thunderbird television spots and duplicate the formula that brought that casino from losing money to profitability.

This approach brought support from the business committee but met more than mere resistance from others. It was instantly denounced by the one slot vendor that had co-signed the loan with plans of an exclusive lock on the government relief checks of the reservation residents. *(The ferocious inhumanity of that slot machine company would ultimately further imprison the local population and lead to my own departure from the frozen hell.)*

Then there were the absurd assaults of *"we finally build something nice and its gets shared with white people allowed to come; only Indians should be allowed to play here."* These attacks were ultimately followed by the more sanguine *"we should operate more in line with the actual demand for business rather than high expectations."* Nonetheless, the business committee supported my change-in-direction for them and I moved forward with bringing *Vegas* to Montana.

For the grand opening, I hired the legendary Flying Elvi (also known as the *Flying Elvises)* a team of precision paratroopers dressed as Elvis impersonators, born from the film *Honeymoon in Vegas*. Since the movie, the Elvis paratroopers had become famous for hundreds of appearances nationwide, including television spots on *American Journal; Anthony Bourdain "No Reservations"; Best Damn Sports Show; British Broadcasting Corporation; CNN News; Current Affair; Dinner & A Movie; Donny & Marie; "E" Entertainment; ESPN; Fox Family Channel Promo; Fox FC Channel Promo; Good Morning America; Hard Copy; History Channel; Hoosier Lottery Commercial; Inside Edition; Jerry Lewis MDA Telethon; Nickelodeon; Real TV; Regis Live; The World (Japan's 31 Game Show); Travel Channel; Weddings Of A Lifetime*; and many others. Such a dazzling display of Vegas hokeyness was exactly the kind of start I needed to announce to the great Northwest that neon lights had arrived to compete with aurora borealis.

I also exploited some bastardized (and possibly-illegal) "class II" versions of blackjack, craps, and pai gow; games not available anywhere in the area (or, at time, anywhere in America in the versions we invented). I trumpeted "Vegas Style" games on television in nearby Alberta Canada and as far south as Great Falls Montana. In interview after interview and thousands of dollars in paid advertising, I touted the 600 slot machines, Vegas table games, and even Bingo along with free food, live music, and party-party-party.

Even by the accounts of those opposed to the strategy and some anti-Indian conservative press, the grand opening was huge. The one-street through town was lined with more-thousands of people than the casino could hold or the town of Browning had ever seen. As I discussed earlier, there was no doubt that the cash-flow situation was going to be a disaster; we would definitely run out of money. Five-thousand dollars that had been set aside by the lenders for the cage would not last the first hour; and if someone hit one of the progressive jackpots, I would be fucked. I discussed this situation in an earlier chapter, *but nothing could touch the crowning disaster looming.*

The flying Elvi thrilled the assembled mass by jumping from a plane and soaring over the heads of the crowd to land in the casino parking lot. Then, in the midst of the grandiose spectacle, the music was cut and the happy-go-lucky MC stopped his banter as one of the dozen parachuting Elvis impersonators, Paul Moran, came in too fast and hit the pavement at 50 mph.

LEFT: one of the Flying Elvi approaches safely over hundreds of cars lining the street.

ABOVE: Gary Green *(leaning back in white dinner jacket)* and others watch the sky divers jump above the parking lot landing area.

Moran was a Stockton California building contractor with a passion for water skiing, snowboarding, and unfortunately, sky-diving. News and amateur videos on the internet showed Moran crashing into the pavement on his right hip and immediately buckling with his head hitting the pavement as his Elvis wig/helmet bounced across the parking lot and his green glider-parachute fell over him like a too-foreboding shroud. The wig/helmet probably prevented a concussion, but the impact crushed his heel and broke his leg. More dangerously, a sharp broken bone fragment sliced his femoral artery and his body began filling with internal bleeding.

Other than an Indian health clinic, the practically inaccessible town of Browning had no medical facilities and no place to land a plane to fly Moran to a full service hospital. Transferred by ambulance to the originating airport two hours away, and then flown to *HarborView Medical Center* in Seattle, the flying Elvis died from the injuries.

Meanwhile, the national media made light of the tragic story announcing (in hundreds of newspapers and on television) *"Elvis broke his Pelvis"* and overlooking the heartbreakingly tragic death. Every editor in each medium thought that he or she was amazingly original and clever in penning the phrase…which was cliché-mimicked hundreds if not thousands of times by other "creative thinkers."

I, of course, in full-spin mode, did not announce his death and gave comments saying that he was taken to the Indian health clinic (which was *initially* true) and was expected to recover fully. My spin was supported by television interviews with the founder of the troupe announcing, *"He will be back; nothing can keep him out of the sky."*

Our spin-control announcements, unfortunately, only contributed to the media's comfort level of making light of the whole tragic affair. The *Associated Press* as well as several of the national television sensationalist magazine shows turned the entire affair into lighthearted Elvis story that

RIGHT: *The London Daily Mirror* webpage announcing the parachuting accident in Browning Montana.

also served as publicity for the casino. The story went international. The London Daily Mirror, among other papers worldwide, put the "funny" story on their front page.

In fact, as we watched the next day's national news coverage we were disappointed that some of the stories only said "a casino" rather than using the casino name and location. I put my Atlantic City based press agent to work correcting that oversight; by-god I used to work for Donald Trump and we believe that ALL media is GOOD media! I wanted our name in those stories.

Even after I successfully raised funds to pave the parking lot, buy advertising, and cover a number of the shortfalls, the business committee (unfortunately) elected to use none of the $600,000 to address that opening-cash shortfall that ultimately caused emergency drops and unbearably long lines at the casino cash cage for months to come. While I was not privy to exactly how the funds *were* used and never had the authority to either bind the business committee to funding nor to directly spend the funds, a few months later when I left the casino that committee *did* announce that *Gary Green had put them hundreds of thousands of dollars in debt.* Alas, they never explained how I performed this deed since only the business committee had that power.

In fairness to the business committee, a spokesman for the committee, discussing my departure, did give press statements saying *"Gary Green did what he could for us to date and he brought us to where we're at now,"* and *his departure "was not based on any monetary issue of theft or anything of that nature."*

As a final explanation, another business committee member reflected on the experience a year later, *"Our business plan had been predicated on a local market, but then we hired Gary Green and he brought Las Vegas to us."*

Gotta love Indian Country. I look at these anecdotes as testimony to the dysfunctional state that hundreds of years of "Indian Policy" from the United States have inflicted. Add to that dysfunctionality from the existence of sovereignty exempting Tribes from many State laws and allowing for Tribal Nation's own court systems, and there is clearly a recipe for confusion. Pour into the mix years of poverty, poor education, and a never-ending chorus line of white exploiters and profiteers and the stage is set for the trials of operating Indian casinos.

The greater issue here is the thread of commonality that non-Indian operators share in our own adventure stories operating in the world of Indian Gaming and on the reservation.

For every three dysfunctional anecdotes like these, I have days...or years...of perfectly functional and, in fact, stellar models for casino operations.

Chapter Fifteen
'Grey Area' ...illegal...Gambling

"We'd hear it from the people of the town
They'd call us Gypsys, tramps, and thieves
But every night all the men would come around
And lay their money down"
— Bob Stone's "Gypsies, Tramps And Thieves" as sung by Cher

My favorite question to ask my Las Vegas colleagues in 2009-2010 was *"Where is the largest non-Indian casino in the world?* None, not one, zero of my contemporaries ...nor the dozens of other "gaming" industry wags I sprung this on... ever answered correctly. Answer: *Alabama*[59]. No, seriously... Shorter Alabama with a population of 367 people. With more than six thousand slot machines, that was 16 slot machines for every man, woman, and child in town. Oh, and according to the Governor and the Attorney General of Alabama...casinos were then *and still are* illegal in their state.

"Grey area gaming" is a tidy little euphemism that at its best means "unregulated or under-regulated" gaming and at its worst means illegal gambling. They grey area exists in every state and most countries (and has forever). A close look at this kind of gambling is important because, as I have discussed here, in many cases that grey area has been the foundation of legal and regulated gaming. The founders of modern Las Vegas were all from the grey area. Gum-vending slot machines were created from the grey area. The foundation of games in Indian casinos began in grey area states.

The amount of money generated in unregulated, under-regulated, and criminal gambling is almost unimaginable —even in the face of the gigantic revenue numbers we have talked about in legal casinos. That much money draws all sorts of investments.

In 2010, after the Alabama State Police finally shut down that gigantic casino, slot machine giant IGT, a publically traded company, took a $53-million write off for their investment in Alabama and then paid a $375,000 fine in Missouri for failing to notify that state's gaming commission of a warning letter of illegal activity from Alabama authorities. (*How a large publically-traded company invests $53-million in an apparently illegal business is just the beginning of the "grey area" story.*)

As the Alabama example indicates, this is not backroom, hidden-away, bookie-like activity reserved for some B-movie stereotypical degenerate gambler. This is big business. That illegal Alabama casino with IGT's millions also boasted a 300-room gilded luxury hotel, a mass-appeal buffet, and a steady stream of daily buses.

The euphemistic genre is so vast and has so many permutations that it would take a full length book to just list and define the offerings in each state. That is certainly beyond the scope of *this* book.

What I will try to do is briefly describe the most pervasive of the grey area schemes and how they become *somewhat* legal in various jurisdictions. Indeed the complex yarn-ball is worth unwinding to see how the pattern of these unregulated markets morph into full-fledged legal, regulated gambling markets in multiple states.

The cash-flow is so massive that the genre attracts the sleaziest con men and criminals and at the same time large publically traded corporations (like the IGT example), and an entire universe of a middle world between the two. Even that middle world is filled with extremes from live-out-of-a-suitcase gypsy-like impresarios to entrepreneurially-driven businessmen and women to a group of take-the-cash-and-run schemers. I will also try to briefly describe some of these characters as well. Some are decent well-meaning people who operate on the fringes on the casino world because they lack the resources and wherewithal to buy or operate a regulated casino; others are just chasing fast cash; still others are wanna-be gangsters.

What the entire genre has in common is the legal status that allows it to gestate. Typically, gaming is outlawed in the targeted venue, whether out of fear of Las Vegas history being repeated, moral opposition to gambling, a desire to protect certain elements of society, or some other perception of noble principle. Where gambling is not overtly outlawed, gambling is usually under-regulated or poorly thought-through.

In most jurisdictions for a game to be considered "gambling", there are three requirements: (1) **Consideration**: players must pay cash or "something of value" to be eligible to participate; (2) **Value:** the prize must be money or ANYTHING of value; and (3) **Chance:** the outcome of the game must be determined by chance rather than any *application of skill*. In order for a game to be determined GAMBLING, it must meet ALL THREE of these criteria. Find an exemption from any one of these criteria and the game is *not* gambling...according to most laws.

Even in jurisdictions that have expanded those three requirements, in almost every case the "new" language outlawing gambling (or minimally regulating it) is at best anachronistic in the face of ev-

261

er-changing technology. The history of "Class II" gaming —*the bizarre evolution of invisible Bingo balls*— is the template for the business model; *loopholes and technology*. And the very vipers who created that template —*and a new generation of their successors*— have continued to flourish in these new frontiers.

"Alabama in 2007 was exactly like Oklahoma ten years earlier," assessed Joe Hight, the much-maligned and controversial founder of slot machine companies NexGaming, Penguin Gaming Systems, Kodiak Games, SlotMetrix, and a long-time supplier of slot machines to Indian casinos in Oklahoma, California and elsewhere.

The gypsy-like Hight, who often lives in the office of a temporary warehouse or in his car (taking baths in the swimming pools of easily-accessible hotels), is not terribly abnormal in the behind-the-curtains dwelling grey-area impresarios. One of the earliest of his genre to swoop into Alabama, his assessment was certainly accurate in terms of the types of slot machines and vendors —as well the level (or lack thereof) of casino management, marketing, floor design, tracking, and sophistication. I think I would take Hight's assessment a step further and say that Alabama in 2009 *mirrored South Carolina in 1993*…flip back to my chapter on the evolution of Class II Bingo games and the list of machine vendors there.

Initially, before IGT jumped into Alabama, the largest supplier of games in Alabama (in terms of number of machines) was *Gateway Gaming* (founded by Bob Mosley, former owner of South Carolina-based Nova Gaming). In fact, all the "usual suspects" from early Indian Country and/or South Carolina were sprinkled liberally through Alabama: Nova, SED, AGS, Multimedia, Rocket, Cadillac Jack, and whatever was the latest incarnation from my friend Hight's seem-

RIGHT: Logos from a few of the Class II companies active in Alabama at the time: Gateway, Nova, AGS, Rocket, SED, Cadillac Jack, Centurion, Capital Bingo, Synergy Gaming.

*logos used for Journalistic purposes to identify companies and not for commercial purposes

ingly shady world. Other Class II companies, notably led by VGT (the dominant Class II vendor in Oklahoma) took a more cautious and ultimately much wiser approach, waiting until the landscape was a little more clearly defined[60].

Joe D. Hight and his many gaming incarnations make for an interesting study of the prototypical live-out-of-the-car entrepreneurs in that one extreme niche on the fringe of the regulated and licensed gaming industry; he also makes for a case study of the dysfunctional vendors in that third tier of games and their history of leaving a string of enemies in their wake. *(And I saying that lovingly toward my friend Joe.)*

Almost a stereotypical nerd-geek, were it not for unfettered ambition, Hight was the only weight-lifting computer geek in his high school computer club in Georgia. Joe and his *Commode VIC-20* soon ran the computer club and he began planning entrepreneurial adventures while most of his contemporaries were debating the breast size of various female science fiction characters. His first venture was in 1989 as co-owner of an auto shop diagnosing car repairs by computer; by then Joe had become an ASC certified master car mechanic. He rose from being an Atlanta computer-driven greasemonkey to developing an intriguing knack for getting small non-gaming investors (the less-than a-million-dollars variety) to plunge into the grey area of gambling. Along the way, he created a long string of bitter enemies and vocal detractors gunning for him; but an equally long list of allies, supporters and partners. His decisively

RIGHT: Joe Hight at the grand opening of *Gary Green's Lil Vegas* in Florida, 2008.

non-business-like approach and style, his wild-and-free spending habits, his appetite for Crown Royal and various alternative intoxicants, as well as his general contempt for social convention have all served to make people either love or hate him. There is rarely a middle ground with Joe. And in that latter regard, he is absolutely 100% typical of that par-ticular ilk of grey area vendors.

He began his gaming career as a slot technician for Atlanta's World Touch Gaming — *one of those companies that migrated from South Carolina to Indian Gaming and later to the Sweepstakes grey market* — but after four years of being a combination technician, repairman, installer, salesman, customer service representative, route jobber, and slot machine builder he decided he could do better on his own. Pissing off World Touch in a series of accusations back and forth, he began a pattern of burning bridges rather than creating alliances. So intense was his knack, that in 2011 the owners of World Touch expressed hesitancy to do business with ME, because I was friendly with Hight.

In 2001, with $35,000 from one of those non-gaming investors, Joe started one of those dubious middleman companies distributing Mike Pace's stalwart *Pot-O-Gold* slot machines (the aforementioned *Leisure Time Technology)* to Indian casinos. In relatively short order he expanded his line to also distribute Cadillac Jack games.

Within a year of entering gaming, Joe Hight began developing his own slot machine games; games with outside-the-box creativity that could have only been created by a former nerd-boy geek. His *"Cookie Dough"* machine featured a *smell-a-vision* function that sprayed the scent of baking chocolate chip cookies when the player hit a bonus round. His *"Twister"* game, based on Oklahoma's history of tornados, featured a bonus round with electric fans blowing a hefty gust of wind and an electronically-vibrating chair to give the "twister" effect. His *"Big Ben"* game featured a three-dimensional hologram of a slot machine that resembled something out of *Star Trek's holodeck*; players could reach out to floating three-dimensional reels, view them from all angles, and literally stand in the middle of them as they spun all around. He took the Class II concept of video-representation of payouts based on virtual Bingo ball draws, and replaced the video representation of slot reels with a rotating roulette wheel and with oversized spinning dice...thus creating Class II Roulette and Class II Craps games.

Even his themed slot machines "boldly went where no man had gone before" when he had the guts to offer a *Pete Rose* themed slot machine. Endorsed by the baseball legend that was denied Hall of Fame admittance for gambling, Joe's machine celebrated the Baseball great's legacy though ...*of course*... a slot machine.

And I am personally partial to his creativity because he created and marketed a *"Gary Green"* themed slot machine.

On the "behind the scenes" side, unknown to players, Joe created some of the first downloadable games and structures by which a game could be changed in a physical box by a few software controls from casino staff, rather than radical hardware changes by company technicians. This, like many technology innovations, was created in the grey-area markets by the third-tier small operators long before the large publically traded companies decided downloadable games would be the next great thing.

The few hundreds of thousands dollars (as opposed to millions) that Joe raised for his slot machine ventures primarily came, as noted, from non-gaming investors; people who had made money in a variety of ways outside of the casino world. Of course that is the pattern for the majority of these vendors that could or would likely never be licensed in more legitimate venues like Nevada, New Jersey, or any of the Denny Gomes inspired venues.

Consequently, some of the eccentricities of the casino world that are examined in this book are lost on most non-gaming investors; especially the ones on the ladder rungs of Joe and his contemporaries. Generally speaking, less gaming-oriented investors expected to see business models, structures (and returns) similar to the industries they knew (real estate, retail, banking, etc.). The typical lack of diplomacy, tact, and investor management by the grey area companies (and taken to extremes by Joe) does nothing to comfort such investors; in many cases, his departure from various investors was *at best* hostile and adversarial, and in at least two cases was violent.

It is important to understand that this pattern is more-than-typical for those third-tier *wanna-be* companies, least some readers interpret my words as an attack on Joe rather than a critique of the processes. As a consequence of all that drama, Joe and his contemporaries have spent a half-decade bogged down in closing companies and starting new ones, crafting joint-venture agreements, filing and responding to lawsuits; and chasing more funding...all amidst the brilliant innovations Joe and these characters brought to gaming. Remember, these are the cats that invented "electronic Bingo" and virtual/invisible balls, and created that entire methodology that started "class II" universe; these are some VERY smart people. These are people who *IF* (notice the big "if" there) IF they could ever pass the licensing scrutiny of the real casino world, would probably choose not to do so because of all the restrictions that come with that licensing.

Hight is a typical of these off-the-books entrepreneurs; a man with a vision and energy. He has chosen an industry, though, dominated on one extreme by fly-by-night con men and schemers and on the other extreme by amazingly impersonal corporate America. Unfortunately in an industry as small and as incestuous as casino gaming, there is very little in-between the two extremes. Creatively-driven entrepreneurial firebrands inevitably have an uphill battle in the casino industry — especially in the shark-infested waters of slot machine vendors; hence they often deliberately choose the unregulated or grey area fringes of my industry.

Another vivid illustration of the characters that make up that grey-area world is the absolute opposite end of that particular spectrum from Joe Hight, my friend Luc Marcoux. When I began writing this book I knew of Luc only by reputation; but during the course of time for rewrites, proofs, and edits of this book I have had the time to come to know him well and to work closely with him as he explored the possibilities of breaking out of the grey area into regulated gaming; a prospect he later abandoned at least in part based on my input.

As noted, he is the polar opposite of my friend Joe Hight. Joe lives, from time to time, in his warehouse and bathes in a nearby Marriott swimming pool/hot tub when he is not living in hotels; Luc has penthouse condos in south Florida and in Montreal and commutes in his private jet or his $1.5-million rockstar touring bus. Yet both men are in the same business and have enjoyed the same financial successes and failures, likely to the same degrees.

With the tastes and style of a stereotypical "Frenchman", Luc is a French Canadian living in South Florida and heading a mini-empire of grey gaming that has been vastly successful in a series of ups and downs. From the hands-on struggles known by many of these entrepreneurs (driving trucks, assembling games, wiring the boards, painting, and trim) Marcoux has evolved his business into a world-class operation by sheer force of will. Unlike the scores of grey-area characters that make you feel like you need a fumigation after meeting with them, Marcoux leaves you with an understanding that you are dealing with success and reliability; *whether that was the reality or not.*

Since 1996 Luc has owned *Electromatic International* in Hollywood Florida and for the ten years before that he owned *Industries Electro-Jeux* in Quebec. Well known as a guru of the amusement, redemption, and sweepstakes gaming industry, by his mid-50s Luc had lived a highly successful (and profitable) career providing games and operating mini-casinos in the most notable grey-area locations: Georgia, Texas, Puerto Rico, Utah, Massachusetts, the Carolinas, Ohio and anywhere else where legal loopholes allowed placement of those kinds of games. The success of his game rooms, routes, and distribution network revolved around his keen eye for design, and an unrelenting drive for the next market; sometimes he was dead-on right and sometimes he lost his ass…just like Joe Hight and any number of other grey-area guys.

Marcoux entered the business as a young man in Canada continuing and expanding his father's jukebox and pinball route business there; the same pattern as many of the South Carolina vendors. From his base in a small asbestos-mining town outside of Montreal, Luc turned those routes into a highly successful network of unregulated mini-casinos ("game rooms") across Canada and provided games for a score of rooms he did not operate. When the Canadian government decided to nationalize (or province-ize) gaming and operate their own casinos, they shut down Luc's businesses; so he packed his family to headed south to the United States. In the USA, Luc's life was an intense series of hands-on gypsy-like adventures, as is the nature of the unregulated gaming markets. His gypsy existence, however, was punctuated by a high-flying style and shameless personal spending; even if his business was based on *"get in to a jurisdiction, make your money, bring out lots of cash, and get out before the law changes or the regulators catch up."*

Right: Luc Marcoux circa 2010

Below: (left to right) Gary Green, Alabama gaming attorney and former State Senator Bob Wilson, Luc Marcoux, Luc's son Pierre Marcoux, and casino regulator David Cook at Las Vegas' executive airport in front of Luc's private Citation II jet.

266

One of the primary tenets of that rung of the gaming ladder is that those markets are at best tenuous and at worst temporary. Typically, a grey area will "open up" — *meaning a particular court ruling or a newly-found loophole in a state law will become general knowledge* — and the swarms of grey-area vermin will infest the state like a biblical plague of locust putting slot-machine like devices in bars, convenience stores, and mini-casino/arcade/game rooms in 2,000 sq. ft. strip mall storefronts.

The vendors, route operators, and owners would flood the state with whatever device the loophole would allow, but always cloaked as a slot machine designed specifically to mislead consumers and players into thinking they were playing a Vegas-like device. Usually far more insidious than even the invisible ping-pong-balls of Class II devices, most of these "games" operate on Taiwanese-built computer boards with built in "cheats" *(as Luc calls them)* that allow the operator to reset the payout cycle at will and with holds as high as 35%. None of this-level of game could ever be approved or licensed in Nevada, New Jersey, Mississippi or any of the regulated gaming states.

Though the specific type of loophole exploited changes as quickly as legislators and Attorneys General can adapt, several game types re-skin and reemerge again and again like the 13-year cicadas surfaces from the muck, sheds its skin, and begins its cyclical plague. As of this writing the *flavor du jour* impersonating slot machines is the sweepstakes machine.

You go to McDonalds® and buy an order of fries; attached to the fries is a sweepstakes entry to participate in the Monopoly® sweepstakes with the potential of your winning thousands of dollars or a free order of fries. No purchase is necessary. You buy a bottle of Coca-Cola® and underneath the bottle cap is a *My Coke Rewards®* entry for a sweepstakes to win all sorts of cash and prizes. Again, no purchase is necessary. Clearly the reason for these sweepstakes is to sell more McDonalds food or Coke products. The sweepstakes is an age-old marketing scheme, proven successful for decades.

As noted early, in most jurisdictions in order to GAMBLE there must be some "consideration"; meaning that you had to put up some money to participate in the game. That is why all of these sweepstakes have a *"no purchase necessary"* disclaimer. McDonalds can run their Monopoly sweepstakes in the most conservative anti-gambling states where casinos are absolutely outlawed. Clearly, there is no connection between buying a Big Mac® and getting a sweepstakes piece and putting money into a slot machine. McDonalds uses the sweepstakes to get you to buy the Big Mac rather than run over to Burger King or Wendy's for your burger fix.

Simple enough; and certainly not gambling…right? Remember though, we are dealing with the mad genius entrepreneurs who gave us electronic Class II Bingo. This time around they outdid themselves; even surpassing their technology schemes around Bingo.

267

First they needed a product like French Fries or soft drinks. The easiest was "internet time". Renting a store-front in a strip mall, these entrepreneurs would open a "business center" that had rows of folding tables lined up like a family-style restaurant. Each eight-foot table had four touch-screen computers on each side of the table; eight computers on each table. Or, as the operations manual for one of these store-fronts instructs:

> Each location has been selected based on a specific target market that we have analyzed and researched. The demographic study that we have done on this location concludes that it is potentially a profitable location. The factors that go in to the selection of a location are the laws within the given state, traffic, demographic composure of the surrounding area, relation of certain living facilities and retail locations, and the size and shape of the building or space we have selected. We also look at price and parking to be able to accommodate our needs. The minimal size of any location is 2,000 square feet.

> It is necessary before we select a location, to research the legal parameters in each state to find out if our business is an acceptable practice within that state, county or city that we want to operate. Once we determine that our business is an acceptable practice within that state, we will move forward to secure a location.

A customer comes to the location and purchases "internet time" *(time at the computer terminals ostensibly to surf the Internet)* . Typically twenty-dollars purchased of 20 minutes. The business would have a high-speed internet connection so other than its monthly internet charge, there is no cost-of-goods for the time sold in the internet model. But for each minute of on-line time purchased (at $1 per minute) the customer is given 100 "free" sweepstakes entries.

Then came the brilliant loophole. To reveal whether each entry won or lost, the customer sits down at one of the internet-connected computers and touches an icon that says "reveal entries." The screen transforms to a slot-machine looking display with five reels (or three reels) and on-screen buttons that correspond to a slot machine's buttons. What resembles one slot machine spin is a typical 25-line game with each line requiring one credit (or sweepstakes entry) and each line taking up to nine credits; so with each spin of the reels, up to 225 sweepstakes entries are revealed ($2.25).

The symbols on the screen are electronic facsimiles of the actual reveal of wins. The sweepstakes software works exactly like the McDonalds paper sweepstakes in that there are a finite and limited number of entries per sweepstakes. For example, let's say there are one-million entries possible in *"Sweepstakes Number 101"*; in that sweepstakes we know that each entry is equal to one-cent in sales of "internet time" so one-million entries equals cash $10,000 in sales.

As I have repeatedly pointed out, typically these games hold about 35% so that means that there is a net profit of $3,500 from those one-million entries and $7,500 will be paid out. Depending on the game math, that might be paid as one "Grand Prize Winner" of $5,000 Cash and 2,500 winners of one-dollar...or any other variation of paying out the $7,500.

The flaw in this system, from a player standpoint, would *seem* to be that once a player —I mean internet customer— revealed the winning grand prize, the sweepstakes would fizzle out and no one would play (or buy additional Internet Time) beyond that. However, our mad scientists covered that as well. Remember we are using relatively high-powered computers for these sweepstakes. So rather than just one sweepstakes (that example "*Sweepstakes Number 101*") the software is simultaneously running hundreds (or thousands) of different sweepstakes games (numbers 101 through 999 for example). And

At Right: Screens of electronic "sweepstakes" games; very slot machine looking, no?

your "revealed" entries could be from any of those sweepstakes at any time during your play.

Now you get it! The customer keeps buying more and more internet time and, of course, never using it but revealing sweepstakes entries on the slot-machine-like screens.

The employees of these "internet cafes" are carefully trained to deflect law enforcement officials who might send undercover operatives in to determine if illegal gambling is taking place. Again, citing the training manual from one of these operations:

This is an Internet Café. What we sell is internet time. Our internet time will give each customer FREE Entries into our sweepstakes. This is the Game Promotion aspect of our business. We do not allow gambling, gaming, or any type

269

of wager, or betting in our facilities. We provide FREE Drinks, FREE Snacks, and FREE Meals for our customers and we also have promotions which give our customers FREE Internet Time.

It is very important for our employees to understand that when the internet time is purchased, the sweepstakes are given at NO COST to the customer. The customer can sit at a machine and reveal their entries one by one, up to 124 each time, or they may reveal all of their sweepstakes entries at once. *The sweepstakes winnings are determined at the time of purchase not during the process of revealing the sweepstakes.* Each day, our customers can receive 100 FREE sweepstakes entries. Each player is issued an Internet usage card when they become a new customer. Think of this card as having three separate readable components within the card.

- Internet Time: This is the service that customers can purchase.
- Sweepstakes Entries: This is the FREE entries that we give with the purchase of internet time.
- Prizes: This is the prizes that the customer has revealed.

Alternatives to the internet time scheme have been telephone cards (the customer purchases a card for long distance telephone time), discount coupons for an inflated-price on-line store, or any other "products" that can be purchased and are not expected to be used by the customer. One vendor told me candidly that only about 3% of their "sold" phone time is actually used by customers. Playing the game was just an exercise in purchasing the phone card, or internet time, or discount coupon. At first glance this might seem totally absurd; but when we remember that the original Vegas slot machines were just ways of purchasing flavored chewing gum, then the scheme becomes diabolically clear.

This sweepstakes scheme is actually an outgrowth of another very similar legal loophole to anti-casino laws: pull tabs. A number of states allow charities and other entities to sell pull tabs to raise money. In a traditional (non-electronic) pull-tab game, multi-layered paper tickets hide various combinations of symbols behind perforated "tabs". Certain symbols are designated as "winning" symbols. For example, three cherries may win the Jackpot; three bells may win Second Prize; three bars may win 3rd prize, and so on. If a "roll" of tickets contains, for example, 3,192 tabs, typically a casino will sell the tickets for a dollar each. In this example, that gives a gross income of $3,192. Typically, and for this example, there will be 15 "jackpots" in the role —winning $100 each (total $1,500 in payouts); four second prize tabs at $50 each (total payout of $200); four $15 payouts (total of $200); four $15 tabs (totaling $60 in payouts); twelve $5 tabs (for a total of $60); and 225 two-dollar tabs ($450) that double the player's one-dollar bet. This gives a total payout of $2,470 against the $3,192 gross or a net profit of $722 in this example. This translates to a casino hold of 28.88% or players odds of 1 in 12.28 of winning *something*. Not exactly what I would call good slot-machine odds for a player. From that $722 the operator of the pull tab had to buy the roll of tabs; which might cost $300, leaving a total net-net profit of only $422.

As I said, this methodology is not at all unlike the winning prize pieces attached to the side of the McDonalds' soft-drink cups or fry containers. In fact, it is basically the same deal: a pull tab is a form of a sweepstakes; add the element of allowing "no purchase necessary" for free play, and quite possibly the pull tab becomes a full-blow sweepstakes.

The purveyors of these sweepstakes games tried to revisit Indian Country with them, hoping to duplicate their successes with Class II before the big boys and regulations squeezed them out. Since pull-tabs are legal under NIGC definitions of Class II, the grey boys thought they could sneak the sweepstakes games in as well. The working of these sweepstakes games was best described by the National Indian Gaming Commission in an "opinion letter" dated October 17, 2003:

"The devices are stand-alone units that offer a patron the opportunity to play a video gambling game. Each device contains a bill acceptor, and for each dollar paid, the patron receives credits to play the "phone-card sweepstakes," a spinning reel game on a video screen. Typically, the player receives 20 credits for each dollar paid. The devices have the ability to accept several bills and will issue game credits based on the amount of money inserted. The player can win or lose credits while playing the game. The player wins by aligning similar figures on a pay line; in some versions there are eight such pay lines available depending on how many credits are applied. Some machines offer progressive prizes and special bonus features. All of the devices have common features including buttons to operate the game being shown or played on the video screen. Winners are paid in one of two ways. Some machines dispense a ticket that is equal to a specified number of credits. In the version reviewed, the player can receive a ticket worth one dollar for every 20 credits, the same value paid for the credits. When the ticket is dispensed, the credits available to the player on the device are reduced corresponding to the value of the ticket. Other machines provide receipts that are printed at the request of the player when the player decides to "cash out." Players redeem the tickets or the receipt for cash with the store operator.

"In addition to the game-play opportunity, the patron will also receive either a separate horoscope card or a phone-card when the player inserts money into the machine. The horoscope card contains a phone number to call for a recorded horoscope reading. The phone-card contains a number for a patron to call to obtain a two-minute long distance phone call.

"The argument that some players can play for free by requesting a voucher for a free play from the vendor may be useful to evaluating the individual transaction played with the free voucher but it does not serve to control the characterization of the device generally. Each transaction, or game, can be viewed independently. The free voucher method of play is seldom used, and may not be available for every device, depending on the vendor placing the device. When this free voucher is available, it is for a single game or for a limited number of credits, and must be obtained by sending a self-addressed stamped envelope to the gaming device vendor; the vendor will return only one voucher per request. Thus, it costs the patron two stamps ($.74) and two envelopes to obtain a $1.00 voucher, hardly a savings. This alternative method for obtaining play of a single or a limited number of game plays is intended to be

difficult for the patron so as to discourage its use. Common sense suggests that the alternative method is made available merely to allow the argument that consideration is not required rather than to actually facilitate game play using the alternative method. We understand that virtually all of the games are played in the traditional way: a player pays by inserting a bill into the bill acceptor on each machine; the player seeks to win a prize; and the player wins through the application of an element of chance."

As Far back as 2005, the Appellate Court in the State of North Carolina ruled: *"Prepaid phone cards that had an attached game piece were not an illegal method of gambling, a lottery, or a game of chance, because: (1) the purchase of the phone cards is made to obtain a valuable commodity, the sale of which is promoted by a process that is common in many promotional and sweepstakes type contests; (2) plaintiff's phone card provides the purchaser with a long-distance rate that is not merely competitive, but one of the best in the industry; (3) plaintiff's prepaid phone card is sufficiently compatible with the price being charged and has sufficient value and utility to support the conclusion that it, and not the associated game of chance, is the object being purchased; (4) consumers may receive free game pieces without purchasing the prepaid phone card via written request, which is some evidence that those who purchase the phone cards are doing so to receive the phone card and not the accompanying promotional game piece; and (5) states that permit lotteries do not give out free entries upon written request."*[61]

In early 2012, a Federal Judge in North Carolina gave further life to sweepstakes in that state following a 2011 U.S. Supreme Court ruling that the content of video games can't be regulated any more than books or films under the Constitution's Frist Amendment free-speech guarantee. In October of 2012, the state Supreme Court heard arguments in two cases in which vendors sought to overturn North Carolina's 2010 law banning video sweepstakes; the issue at hand was whether the state could label video sweepstakes parlors as gambling halls and outlaw the businesses, or whether the video screens give the owners those constitutional free-speech rights.

That silliness is indicative of the tangled grey area world. Pull-tabs, Sweepstakes, whatever one chooses to call them, they are just one more example of the brilliant madmen versus lawmakers who refuse to regulate and try to outlaw.

In 2008, the *Florida Department of Law Enforcement* recruited me to be an "expert witness" to help them determine if sweepstakes games as well as a number of "AWP redemption" games met the State exemptions from the ban on slot machines and the exemption defined in Florida's *Chuck E. Cheese* law. Working with them, I discovered firstly that each game has to be examined individually to determine what settings or grey-area nuances may have been applied to skirt certain regulations. Secondly, I discovered that law enforcement is (at best) ill-trained and ill-equipped to deal with the constant onslaught of technological challenges brought by the third-world grey vipers. Vendors work 24/7 to work around the loopholes; law enforcement generally has better things to do than spend every waking moment focusing on illegal gambling.

The other widely-distributed slot machine knock-offs are games called AWP: *"Amusement With Prizes."* Designed for the grey area markets like Florida and Texas, these games a dominant where lawmakers chose to "outlaw casinos" by making it illegal to pay cash winnings.

Like Class II Bingo games and electronic sweepstakes machines, AWP is another example of the devious brilliance of the grey area cockroaches.

Looking at the national amusement chains of *Chuck E. Cheese* and *Dave and Busters*, the same "usual suspects" of vendors/developers watched people play "amusement" games at those restaurants and "win" prizes ranging from free pizzas to blenders and portable televisions. Customers (children in the first example and twenty-somethings in the latter) would pay to play electronic games (video games), or physical games (like skeeball) and would win tickets or credits, which they could redeem for the prizes. Generally the model is/was totally legal because the games generally are skill-base.

From observing this business model, an entire industry of AWP mini-casinos was born. Not for nothing (as my Jersey friends would say) I, being part of the more legitimate (or at least *regulated*) casino world, was oblivious to these fringe casinos. In 2007 I first heard the operators of the racinos in Broward County (Ft. Lauderdale) Florida, near my home, whining that these mini-casinos were siphoning away their customers. At very least I wanted to know what sort of siphoning a mini *Chuck E. Cheese* could do from full-blown 2,000-game casinos; to me it sounded more like the excuse of bad management than the brilliance of *Pac Man* machine operators. So in 2007 I began to look at these little casinos.

I understood, they could not payout their customers in cash. Instead, I understood, "winners" would get tickets redeemable for near valueless prizes; I imagined the process to be like the old Bingo halls of the 1960s, where I could find the hot cards and win as many ashtrays, lamps, and stuffed animals as my heart desired.

Little did I know that operators of these arcade-casinos (and the State of Florida) have construed these "noncash" prizes to include non-cash redeemable gift certificates from merchants; and the courts have supported that interpretation. Okay, fair enough…that just meant that the operators didn't have to maintain a merchandise inventory, thus making the cost of entry to the business considerably less than I had expected.

A paper certificate with a store name on it was my (like many of my readers, I suspect) idea of what constituted a gift certificate. I had no idea that the gift certificate world has evolved into a billion-dollar business of gift cards with magnetic strips on the back, like ATM cards. Hence these redemption gift certificates offered as winning from these AWP machines were these plastic "gift cards" from scores of national merchants and gas stations.

Once operators, legislators, and the courts had made the leap from prizes to prepaid *gift cards*, it was a short hop to include prepaid "gift cards" from American Express, MasterCard and Visa. Those debit cards could, of course, be exchanged for cash, making these AWP games almost as good as slot machines (except for the "hold"/payout).

It was probably a tip to some of these entrepreneurs to see that Dave & Buster's advertises for new employees in such places as *CasinoCareers.com* under the heading of: *Category Casino Games & Slot Technology Operations*; giving at least the impression that the company considers itself to be in the casino business in one way or another.

While *Chuck E. Cheese* addresses the children market, and Dave and Busters addresses the young adult market, these mini-casinos usually go after the senior/retiree market that has proven so lucrative for the casino gaming industry in general.

To further complicate the AWP landscape, the Florida law

Above: A sampling of the gift cards offered as payout for Florida (and other States) redemption casinos. Note the top example is a VISA debit card. Also note the disclaimer sticker on the back of the VISA: in order to conform with the law the sticker says "THIS GIFT CARD CANNOT BE REDEEMED FOR CASH OR ALCOHOL; a disclaimer that carries no enforcement whatsoever.

(as well as those of several other states) enables: *"amusement games or machines which operate by means of the insertion of a coin and which by application of skill may entitle the person playing or operating the game or machine to receive points or coupons which may be exchanged for merchandise limited to noncash prizes, toys, novelties, and Florida Lottery products, excluding alcoholic beverages."*

The Florida legislation is written as an addendum to the *outlawing* of slot machines in the State (with the exception of counties that have legalized machines at pari-mutuel facilities). Once again, after outlawing slot machines and casinos, Florida (like MANY states) slammed the door on legitimate gaming businesses and (by refusing to regulate) invited in the sleazebags, hangers on, under-funded, and wanna-bees.

In an effort to keep these arcades from becoming full-blown gambling halls, the Florida legislation specifically excepts from the prohibition on slot machines:

- Nothing in the (slot machine) prohibition language applies to an arcade amusement center that meets the following criteria:
  1. Machines operate by inserting a coin;
  2. Application of skill allows player to receive points or coupons.
- Points or coupons can be exchanged for merchandise only, excluding cash, alcoholic beverages, or lottery tickets;
- The value of a prize awarded for points cannot exceed 75-cents *per game played* (this becomes very important in skirting the intent of the law);
- Any "arcade amusement center" must have a minimum of 50 games.

A number of bewildered law enforcers across the state (some genuinely unclear on the law and others under the direct political influence of either anti-gambling forces or the racinos feeling the competitive heat) repeatedly have tried to close some of the arcades. As of 2012, in the 16-year history of these arcades in Florida, there had never been a successful court-upheld closure. In every case that actually went to trial, seized games were returned and arcades were ordered reopened...except in cases where the operators got scared and pled guilty without a court battle.

Among the more absurd law enforcement arguments presented to the State Legislature was the assertion that the *75-cents-per-game-played* payout limit was being presented by arcade owners as 75-cents worth of plastic in a Visa card loaded with hundreds of dollars. If such were the case, then of course it would violate the law; but the fact is the machines themselves limit the number of credits that can be exchanged. Through the use of a game-counter built into the software of the game, even $100 "winnings" requires the player to spin 134 games before they can collect. This technical subtlety is lost on some operators, some law enforcers, some legislators, but almost no players... and certainly not on those mad-genius vendors like Joe, Luc, and others.

Additionally, the anti-arcade forces argued that the "application of skill" requirement of the games allowed players somehow to push a "stop" button to rapidly stop the spinning reels to a winning combination and that such a "skill" is humanly impossible. Of course *that* assumption is true; it would be humanly impossible to stop the reels to a winning combination. Firstly, as we have seen with Bingo machines or video slot machines, the video spinning reels do not determine the outcome of the game; they are merely a representation of the outcome. Stopping the reels based on observing the speed of the movie would have zero outcome on the game. However, no one in their right mind asserts that to be the skill. The skill, rather, is in recognizing patterns of game outcomes and symbols on the screen and then determining which symbols to "hold" for various respin options or in what order to stop reels. The skill is about patterns not hand-eye coordination (as is the required to be designated "skill" in North Carolina and some other states).

Nationwide this AWP redemption model has been around for years, especially in neighborhood bars and a number of small fortunes have been made by distributors, vendors, and route-jobbers who offer bar owners a revenue share in exchange for placing their machines in the bar. In States or jurisdictions that do not have the quagmire of Visa card and gift-card redemption options, route jobbers have created a number of creative payout schemes that generally last long enough for local law enforcement to crack down. As soon as that happens, the jobbers find another scheme to entice gamblers. One Georgia owner of a dozen or so convenience stores recently told me, in flagrant disregard for the law, *"I have three machine in each store. You are not supposed to pay cash just merchandise. But you know who your regular customers are and you can always pay them cash."*

Above: A Florida-legal AWP slot machine. **Below:** Florida players in one of the AWP "game room" mini casinos.

Not unlike "sweepstakes rooms", the typical arcade is located in a rented storefront in a strip shopping center in a community with a large retiree population. An average store is approximately 45 feet by 50 feet (2,250 square feet) and has the legislated minimum 50 sit-down (slant top) machines arranged in banks from two to 15 long, and back to back (2 and 30). A typical arcade space also includes room for a snack bar, a "desk" (which would be a cage in a normal casino), and restrooms. The "nicer" arcades also have a lounge area with a large-screen television surrounded by over-stuffed couches and chairs; some also have meeting rooms doubling as a dining room for buffet lunches, special parties, and community meetings. The properties are usually non-smoking and do not have alcohol licenses (though nothing prohibits that). As noted, generally these games have a hold of about 35% and if there is a revenue share with vendors that rev share is has high as 50/50. In most of the arcades, the walls, floors, and fixtures are bland to bleak and do not resemble a "casino" atmosphere at all. In the busier properties, the interior is designed to look like the clubhouse of a retirement neighborhood or a community center. The machines themselves are generally pressed-wood (MDF) slant tops (sit down units) with old style CGA monitors and that 1980s "board" technology that allows the games to "cheat".

One notable deviation from that norm has been the entrance into the American AWP market by Brazilian slot machine giant Ortiz Gaming. Ortiz operated

276

more than 40,000 Bingo-based slot machines (sort of Class II like) in Brazil until they were outlawed in 2005. The multi-billion-dollar company moved in Mexico and then into the AWP market here.

While AWP games *(often called "777 Games" in some states)* and Sweepstakes Games dominate the latest incarnation of the "grey area" some interesting exceptions have generated millions (if not billions) of dollars in gross revenue. Notable among those exceptions are non-Indian versions of electronic Bingo; what would be Class II games in Indian Country. This is where the Alabama behemoth was created.

So far in this "grey area" I have talked about what may sound like the fringes of the gambling business and what casually may seem to be of very little financial significance. That brings us to Alabama. One year of revenue from Alabama's illegal casinos was *equal to* the revenue of the entire automobile industry nationwide. Meyer Lansky had once famously boasted, *"We are bigger than US Steel."* Now he had been topped: one year of illegal gambling in Alabama, alone, was bigger than General Motors, Ford, Chrysler, and all auto sales in the entire United States. THAT is why I am spending so much time talking about Alabama. Can you even imagine what the state would have made had made if they had regulated *and taxed* gaming?

Alabama's bizarre story is a great amalgamation of all the different contingencies that contribute to a proliferation of grey area gaming. No other jurisdiction, in my knowledge or experience, has brought together all the key elements the way Alabama did; most jurisdictions will contain only one or two of their elements in their intrigue.

Okay...so the largest casino in the world was in Alabama AND casinos are totally illegal in Alabama. That absurd contradiction pretty well sums up Alabama in most realms, not just gaming. It is a state where the Governor of the state led a morality-based campaign against gambling expansion... funded by rival casinos that wanted their Alabama competition closed[62]. It is a state where a white man who grew up taking his childhood naps on the Governor's couch and calling George Wallace "Uncle George" was the close friend and partner in the casino business with the first African American Congressman elected from Alabama since reconstruction. It is a state where a "Master Trustee" for the Superior Court contracted with *me* to take control and *legally* operate one of the *illegal* casinos that the court had seized and kept open ...even though casinos had been outlawed; yes the Court was legally in the illegal casino business.

It is the state where, in furious anti-gambling ranting, a State Senator (and 2012 Republican candidate for U.S. Congress) denounced African American supporters of Alabama casinos as "aborigines, but they're not Indians." Historically along those sad lines, it is the state where Rosa Parks refused to go to the back of the bus, where Bull Connor was a police chief, and where I visited the *"White House of The Confederacy"* on the grounds of the Alabama State Capital

277

only to be given the tour and cake for Robert E. Lee's "birthday party" by an *African America* docent for the museum.

It is Alabama: a microcosm of the kind absurdities that allow the grey area of gambling. Rural, bible-belt, Southern, and arguably in a culturally different world than the gaming industry, Alabama was not only the home of one of the largest casinos in world, but it was home of at least 60 other casinos as well. Victoryland Greyhound Racing Complex in Shorter Alabama (24 miles east of Montgomery on I-85) with its 6,400 slot machines earned a reported net profit of about $1½-million *per day*. Approximately 125 miles north, in Walker County Alabama were another 10,000 slot machines in 30 or so casinos, earning a total net of about $2.5-million a day.

Those dollar-numbers were not *total revenue*; they represent total *net win* for the casino: a combined annual casino win of $1.4-billion in Alabama...where most people thought there were no casinos. And, there were another ten or fifteen casinos dotted around the state in other locations...as well as three Indian casinos. Total *gross revenue* (before payouts) for Alabama's illegal casinos was somewhere around $11.6-BILLION per year...EXACTLY what the entire Automobile industry made in gross sales nationwide for 2010[63]. THAT would explain why Joe Hight, Luc Marcoux, Bob Mosley, and publically-traded IGT all rushed to Alabama. *Big money.*

These Alabama casinos sprung from 17 State constitutional amendments (yes I said 17 different amendments) which expanded *"Charitable Bingo"* beyond its typical position in most states. Most importantly, the various constitutional amendments did not legalize gaming in a blanket across the state, but, rather allowed various local jurisdictions (select cities and counties independent of each other) to make their own legalization and rules. In fact, there was not one state-wide law legalizing charitable Bingo; rather there were a series of these constitutional amendments that were specific to each individual county jurisdiction but following the nationwide example of charitable Bingo laws.

At 357,157 words, the Alabama Constitution is 12 times longer than the average state constitution, 40 times longer than the U.S. Constitution, and is the second longest still-operative constitution anywhere in the world. *(Only India has it beat; but Alabama's is still growing.)* Amendments are plentiful and new ones are passed by the state legislature every year, similar to "private acts" are passed by most other state legislatures for individual towns or counties. Once the legislature passes an amendment it then must be ratified by the citizens of whichever specific jurisdiction it impacts (for example if the amendment is only for Birmingham, then the voters in Montgomery would not have a vote on it). This is how the Bingo constitutional amendments were passed.

Beginning in the late 1970s and continuing into the 21st century, various Volunteer Fire Departments, VFW halls, and other civic groups and charities across Alabama began to need funding that local governments or membership fees were not providing. Group leaders asked their state legislators to pass laws that would allow them to raise money the way their sister charities did in other states: through Saturday night Bingo games once a month; the age-old staple of the Catholic Church and volunteer fire departments nationwide.

Most states have some version of a "charitable Bingo" law, even if most are somewhat sleazy-feeling. Across the country, typically, a Bingo "operator" rents a large retail space in an inexpensive-rent shopping center and furnishes the shell bay with a bunch of eight-foot folding tables, a ball blower, lighted wall boards, Bingo paper and equipment, electronic daubers (like those 1980-ish very legitimate and legal T.E.D. machines we discussed), and a grill/restaurant operation. The operator then acts as a landlord "sub-leasing" the space and these "improvements" (by the hour) back to a licensed charity. Typically in these state laws a charity is allowed to raise funds by playing Bingo a limited number of hours per week. The hourly "lease" from the operator is usually at "banquet facility" rates; meaning hundreds or thousands of dollars per hour rather than the low-rent monthly rate the operator pays. Alternatively, the "rent" is based on a percentage of game revenue.

To fill a Bingo hall 12-15 hour day and seven days a week, the "operator" will "lease" to several different charities during a day. For the player it looks like one seamless Bingo hall operation; for accounting purposes each day of the week or time of day is leased to a different charity. Generally, state laws prohibit the "operator" from having employees run the game or profit from the game, so the employees all join the charity and become "volunteers" for their charity du jour...*or du heure*. They are "paid" only in "tips" from the players; tips which just happen to equal a salary when subsidized by the operator. The charity keeps all the proceeds from the Bingo games and pays their expenses (the rent) from those funds. Rent amounts generally increase based on the handle of the sessions (if the rent is not already based on revenue).

Typically this model will net the operator between $150,000 and $250,000 a year, depending on the amount of play and number of charities involved. It is not a big money-maker but it beats flipping

279

hamburgers at the local burger joint. And one "operator" rarely runs only *one* "charity Bingo" hall; they usually run three to ten such operations, making a decent income for their trouble. In addition to revenue for the operator, the Bingo equipment itself is usually leased and the paper, daubers, etc., have to be purchased; so often otherwise legitimate companies will list among their businesses "supplier for charitable Bingo." However, that is more often than not a code-phrase for being involved in a conspiracy to operate otherwise illegal gambling houses. Alas, again, such is the nature of that grey-area.

Besides making a livable income for the operator/local gambling impresario, the Bingo operation generates a nice revenue stream for the fire department, VFW hall, or other charity. Moreover, the charity gains this income without having to invest in a hall or equipment, and without needing the expertise to run the games and the required bank.

The problem with implementing such a statewide law in Alabama was an existing statewide ban on lotteries and many courts viewed Bingo as a form of lottery. Additionally, a State law to legalize charitable Bingo would not work in Alabama because of those eccentricities of their constitution. Hence, when over the three decades 17 different cities and counties wanted laws for their charities to raise funds with Bingo, 17 separate constitutional amendments fattened up Alabama's constitution.

Most states' charitable Bingo operations are limited to traditional paper Bingo; however, in Alabama, a December 2003 opinion letter from the state's Attorney General provided an official interpretation to further define the intent of those constitutional amendments. The Attorney General argued that the *electronic Bingo* –defined in his opinion letter as "media Bingo"— was legal under the Alabama Charitable Bingo amendments.

That letter sparked a wildfire of newly opening micro-casino and a firestorm of anti-gambling furor. Friendly *local* governments welcomed the tax dollars and jobs being created while conservative local prosecutors filed reams of legal pleadings demanding that the State Supreme Court define Bingo and prohibit the evil slot machine like Class II machines.

After avoiding the red-hot political issue for another five years, refusing to address the issue, eventually the high court took up the question...sort of. The politics of Alabama Bingo were clearly polarized by party lines and even as the court finally took up the general issue, the justices were too smart and too polarized themselves to risk the unpopularity of ruling for either side in such a publically divisive issue. The court ruled that Bingo is a lottery and while gambling is illegal, a lottery is not and equipment / devices used to play a lottery are not illegal if operated for and by a charity in one of the constitutional amendment venues.

2004 - 03 5

STATE OF ALABAMA
OFFICE OF THE ATTORNEY GENERAL

BILL PRYOR
ATTORNEY GENERAL

December 3, 2003

ALABAMA STATE HOUSE
11 SOUTH UNION STREET
MONTGOMERY, AL 36130
(334) 242-7300
WWW.AGO.STATE.AL.US

Honorable J. T. "Jabo" Waggoner
Member, Alabama State Senate
One HealthSouth Parkway
Birmingham, AL 35243

Bingo – Media Bingo – Gambling – Jefferson County

There is nothing preventing either the Town of White Hall or Jefferson County from conducting media bingo, provided that the game is kept solely on the premises of the nonprofit organization and is directly and solely operated by the organization. The game may not be broadcast to additional locations.

For the proposed media bingo plan to be legal, a statewide constitutional amendment would need to be passed repealing the requirements found in the county-specific amendments limiting the legality of bingo games to those located on the premises of and under the direct and sole control of the nonprofit organization operating the games in each location.

Dear Senator Waggoner:

This opinion of the Attorney General is issued in response to your request.

QUESTIONS

(1) Is media bingo legal in Jefferson County?

(2) Is media bingo legal in the Town of White Hall in Lowndes County?

ABOVE: First page of the Alabama Attorney General's opinion letter approving electronic Bingo (as "Media Bingo").

Then to further complicate the issue, in an appeal from a Circuit Court case, the State Supreme Court, without the benefit of gaming experience or expert witnesses, took it upon itself to define Bingo. Without actually addressing whether or not "electronic Bingo" was (in their opinion) actually Bingo, the court wimped by issuing six "guidelines" allegedly defining generic Bingo:

281

What Supreme Court Said:	Class II Application Of Guideline
Each player uses one or more cards with spaces arranged in five columns and five rows, with an alphanumeric or similar designation assigned to each space.	*A true "class II" machine displays this card ON THE GAME SCREEN (not on another screen, not invisible, not "hidden" or "virtual").*
Alphanumeric or similar designations are randomly drawn and announced one by one.	*The electronic balls appear on the screen one at a time...not all at once; as in the NIGC's most recent Class II regulations. Certified Class II machines have this functionality in their "true Bingo" setting.*
In order to play, each player must pay attention to the values announced; if one of the values matches a value on one or more of the player's cards, the player must physically act by marking his or her card accordingly.	*This is the "double daub" feature that has been so controversial in Indian Gaming. This requires the player to hit the DAUB button to match the Bingo card to the balls drawn. This function was a requirement of the 2005 third draft of the NIGC's current Class II regulations and all LEGAL Class II machines should have this functionality.*
A player can fail to pay proper attention or to properly mark his or her card, and thereby miss an opportunity to be declared a winner.	*This is also a function of that "double daub" feature. If the player fails to daub the marked card (i.e. fails to hit the daub button when there is a matching pattern, then that player does NOT win even though the matching pattern is a "winner". In order to win the player MUST daub ("properly mark") their card.*
A player must recognize that his or her card has a 'Bingo,' i.e., a predetermined pattern of matching values, and in turn announce to the other players and the announcer that this is the case before any other player does so.	*All LEGAL and properly installed Class II machines provide this functionality by ringing a bell and flashing the "candle" light on top of the winning player's machine — IF the player has properly daubed the winning pattern. This announces to other players that a Bingo has been one on that ball draw.*
The game of Bingo contemplates a group activity in which multiple players compete against each other to be the first to properly mark a card with the predetermined winning pattern and announce that fact.	*All LEGAL Class II machines REQUIRE two or more players in order for the game to be legitimate. Moreover, no two machines side-by-side should be operating from the same ball draw (thus preventing one person from playing two machines in order to operate the game).*

Apparently by design, the state's Supreme Court failed to say NO or say YES to electronic Bingo; to Class II games. Instead, they listed these six rules and left it up in the air to determine if they covered electronic and paper Bingo. As you can see from my chart above, the "Class II Application of Guideline" is my editorial explanation of how those items apply to electronic Bingo. My assessment was the prevailing thought of the pro-Bingo forces, while the anti-Bingo forces said that the six rules are so limited that ONLY paper Bingo can meet the requirements.

My interest in Alabama began in 2008 when, at Joe Hight's prodding, I visited the state to assess the situation at Victoryland and north in Walker County. I observed Joe's interpretation of the status being an early version of Oklahoma gaming and began my own inquiries into the legalities and potential. Once I realized that I was looking at a totally unregulated market, I "passed" on further interest in Alabama; apparently around the same time that Luc Marcoux, VGT, and several others decided to pass as well.

On that first trip I met with two of the state's best-known movers-and-shakers and supporters of legalized electronic Bingo: five time United States Congressman Earl Hilliard and former State Senator (and prominent attorney) Robert T. "Bob" Wilson, Jr.

Earl Hilliard was the first African American elected to the United-ed States Congress from Alabama since Reconstruction. Born in 1942 he matured and was shaped by the civil rights movement of the early 1960s in his native Birmingham ... the Bull Connor world. *Jet Magazine* quoted him as noting that *"if it hadn't been for Martin Luther King's march across the Edmund Pettus Bridge in Selma, I wouldn't have been a Congressman."* According to one biographer, before Congress, Earl first gained a reputation in the Alabama State Legislature *"as a sharp floor tactician, once marshaling the votes for a pension bill while the bill's opponents had gone out to eat dinner"*. At least 20-

Former Congressman Earl Hilliard with Gary Green in Birmingham in mid-2009.

years-ahead of his time, Hilliard ran his first congressional campaign on the primary issue of nationalizing health care. The winner of his last election without a clear majority, he was forced into a runoff election that resulted in a little more than a 3% loss and his retirement from Congress. Earl later joked to me, "that meant all I could do was become a *Statesman*."

By 2008, when I met him, Congressman Hilliard was a leading proponent of gaming in Alabama, seeing it primarily as an economic development tool to do for his state what it had done for Mississippi. For decades Mississippi ranked the lowly number 50 among the states in education, highways, infrastructure, pay, and social safety nets; after an influx of tax dollars from legalized gaming, Mississippi rose to the top ten in each of those categories.

When I met him, and Senator Wilson, Hilliard was deep into his search for economic development partners that could help him transform the crumbling Alabama infrastructure, the sinking economy (especially for his African American constituents), and the poor quality of life into a vibrant future with real prosperity for an otherwise backward state. Despite our immediate affinity, given my background and his, my pockets were not deep enough to become the development partner the Congressman needed.

Instead, he was approached by an entrepreneur who had made a small fortune from FEMA government contracts, clearing land and debris on a massive scale following hurricanes and other natural disasters. Wishing to personally own a large casino in Birmingham, the way the owner of the giant Victoryland had near Montgomery, this developer rented a 100,000 square foot building and began renovations for a 5,000-machine casino near Birmingham. He appointed the Congressman to his advisory board.

About the same time I was visiting Earl and Bob, my friend Luc Marcoux was looking at Walker County Alabama as a possible new market for his businesses, and despite taking the option on a property there, he opted (like myself) not to get involved in the highly-volatile market. At G2E (the Global Gaming Expo) in November of 2008, Luc's *Synergy Gaming* had taken their first booth in the regulated gaming world and was searching for business. Bob Wilson was wandering the floor of the giant gaming trade show looking for partners for his and the Congressman's economic development. One of his operatives stumbled across Synergy's booth and a week later Luc, his son Pierre, and some of their staff were in Alabama meeting with Bob and Earl.

Robert T. Wilson Junior is a great southern character that if he did not exist he would have been created by Faulkner, Tennessee Williams, or any one of the great Southern writers. His father was a stalwart of Alabama politics, a highly regarded populist Democrat, and the floor leader in the State Senate for Governor George Wallace. Bobby (Robert Junior / Bob) grew up calling Wallace *"Uncle George"*, taking his afternoon naps on the Governor's couch, and riding in the back seat of the Governor's limo. Bob Wilson, by that very pedigree is the last person on the planet that I would have predicted to become a Prius-driving liberal Democrat and friend of Congressman Earl Hilliard; let alone become his very best friend...which he was.

As an adult, Bob Wilson, by then an attorney like his father, became a major player in Democratic Party politics both on the state level and nationally. In addition to winning his father's old State Senate seat, he became a candidate for a U.S. Congressional seat and friend of Bill Clinton. Once out of the State Senate, he became a major lobbying force in the State. Though fiscally conservative and a darling of the business community, Bob was also a liberal Democrat and politically aligned with the seemingly-radical (especially by Alabama standards) Hilliard. With the mannerisms, poise, and charm of an almost fictional representation of a "Southern Gentleman", Bob Wilson became a real life model of integrity, play-by-the-rules, and old-style Southern genteel honor. His friendship with Hilliard was sincere, genuine, personal, political, built on respect and admiration, as well as genuinely caring.

Alabama Attorney Senator Bob Wilson

By the time Luc Marcoux and Wilson/Hilliard decided to follow-up on some economic development ideas for Alabama, I had teamed up with Synergy Gaming to help guide Luc toward the regulated gaming world. Apparently Bob was a little surprised when Pierre Marcoux told him that I had become involved in the Synergy project and wondered why I was needed in the mix, since my role would have been little more than another middle man in the process between the master vendor and the charities. Apparently Bob's initial understanding was that Synergy had contracted with me to open doors for them in Alabama; a role for which he and Earl were infinitely better suited. Once he understood that my relationship with Synergy Gaming was that of a paid consultant to help move Synergy from the cheat-board games to something that could compete with IGT, our relationship began to flourish and we became fast friends.

It was Wilson who first devised a legal working model for the charities to make money and at the same time have a developer create a true economic development model. Such a model was essential if gaming in Alabama was to be regulated, the public protected, and the casinos actually becoming a tool of economic development. Without such a model, the state had become twisted with operations scams.

One of my favorite of those scams was a sleaze-bag operator who opened a small casino —ten Class II Bingo machines— in the city of Birmingham. As soon as he opened what was being called an illegal operation, he anonymously called the police to report that his location was operating an illegal casino. A police raid followed and he was, of course closed down and forced into court. In court his attorney argued that since it had not been determined if these types of games were legal then it was not clear that his operation was illegal. Moreover, he argued that the location he rented had been operated by a particular charity as a paper-Bingo hall for a number of years before he installed his electronic machines. He petitioned the court for an injunction against the City Police to halt them from closing his business until the State Supreme Court could resolve whether their guidelines included electronic Bingo. The court gave him a 30-day pass, not an unlimited one. He immediately rented a 60,000 sq. ft. space and moved in 500 Class II machines. For 30 days he could operate the slot machines without police harassment...making hundreds of dollars per machine per day (at $300 per day 500 machines would net him $4.5-million in those 30 days; even at $150 a day he would net more than $2-million). By my personal observation, his machines appeared to be winning considerably more than $300 per day. At the end of the 30 days, he had to close...darn.

Another fraud that Bob Wilson was fighting against (and is typical of an unregulated jurisdiction) was demonstrated by one of those South Carolina companies operating in Alabama. The owner told me *"our machines are actually real slot machines; the Bingo card and balls are not server-based."* He confessed to me that since Alabama did not require independent laboratory certification and there was no state gaming regulatory agency, then his games were a complete sham. *"Who in Alabama is going to know the different,"* he laughed. Wilson was determined to assure regulation and consumer protections.

The Bingo battles dominated the evening news with new casinos opening daily and State Police raids occurring almost as frequently. As one gaming industry magazine summed it up *"E-Bingo, in essence, was illegal in Alabama ... except where it wasn't."*[64]

It is germane to understand some part of the then-Governor's motivation to fight the casinos. As far back as 1999 convicted wheeler-dealer Indian Casino lobbyist Jack Abramoff admitted to hiring Christian Coalition founder Ralph Reed on behalf of the Mississippi Choctaw Indian Tribe to defeat any legislation that would have legalized casinos in Alabama. According to Abramoff's testimony before the Senate Indian Affairs Committee (then headed by John McCain), the plan was to energize church-goers, pastors, and extremist religious groups to defeat Alabama gambling...on behalf of Mississippi gambling. The plan was that the religious right would be blind to the hypocrisy of being funded by gambling interests to halt gambling.

Lost in sanctimony, they would not even ask the motives of their benefactors. Mississippi gambling forces could protect their market by having the Christians halt competitors; sneaky huh?

For conspiracy theorists out there, add to the intrigue that the Alabama Governor's press secretary was Michael Scanlon, Abramoff's partner who turned state's evidence against Abramoff, Grover Norquist and Ralph Reed in various state and federal grand jury investigations related to the defrauding of Indian Tribes and corruption of public officials

Then in 2006, McCain's committee released a report citing a Tribal chief's testimony that Abramoff told him that the Mississippi Choctaw spent $13 million to get the governor of Alabama elected to keep down the expansion of gambling in Alabama so it wouldn't hurt their market in Mississippi.

When the Abramoff plan failed to stop the casinos *(because of the eccentricities of those constitutional amendments)*, Milton McGregor, the owner of the Victoryland dog track, began working on new legislation that would grant his county autonomy from the state laws. Not far from Victoryland, in Dothan Alabama, a country music promoter, Ronnie Gilley, partnered with McGregor and convinced a Baltimore-based hedge fund to put $86-million into the development of his *Country Crossings* casino project. The city government of Dothan wholeheartedly endorsed the project and the television airways were flooded with testimonials from Gilley's roster of country music stars, including George Jones, Randy Owens (of the group Alabama), Lori Morgan, and others.

Outraged Governor Robert Renfroe "Bob" Riley told the newspaper in Birmingham, *"Any community out there being enticed by organized gambling to bring in casinos and slot machines ought to take a close look at the law and these recent rulings. The law is clear. Only organized gambling and their allies will tell you otherwise."*

When the State's then Attorney General refused to back Governor Riley's interpretation of the Supreme Court's rules, the Governor hired a former prosecutor to head "a special task force against gambling" and conduct raids. A week later a McGregor-hired private detective photographed that task force leader playing at the slot machines in a Mississippi casino. The Governor embarrassingly removed his minion and appointed a more pliable dilatant as he set a deadline for all the Alabama casinos to close.

None complied and the Governor announced that he would raid them, seize and destroy the games, and arrest the gamblers. His first target was the Country Crossing complex where more than a hundred state troopers and several dozen tractor trailer trucks planned a 5 a.m. raid to seize the machines. Country Crossing owner Gilley told MSNBC, *"If that's what it takes to get this before a jury of my peers, by all means arrest me. Tell them to come put the cuffs on me."*

Meanwhile, as a registered lobbyist in Alabama on behalf of Luc Marcoux, I attended the 2009 and 2010 legislative sessions with Hilliard and Wilson, meeting regularly with the Lieutenant Governor (a Democrat who supported electronic Bingo) and other friendly legislators to try to pass statewide legislation that would have legalized *and regulated* Class II games in the state. As I noted earlier, the issue was clearly separated along party lines with the Republican majority under the Governor Riley's control. McGregor, Gilley, and the various operators all launched their lobbying efforts as well, though they were more focused on a statewide enabling law than on the regulatory and taxation economic development bills that Bob, Earl, and I were proposing.

The revenue numbers that brought giants like IGT and Bally into the state seemed to justify the risks of trying to pass legislation. The largest population center in Alabama is greater Birmingham (the City of Birmingham is an independent jurisdiction surrounded by Jefferson County Alabama). The 2007 census estimate gave greater Birmingham a population of 1.6-million; nearly one-fourth of the population of Alabama. Additionally, Birmingham is a two hour drive from Atlanta Georgia, which has a population of 5.2-million; Birmingham is three hours from Nashville Tennessee, which has a population of 1.5-million. Alabama is the closest gambling destination to either (compare the two-hour drive from Atlanta to Birmingham to six hours from Atlanta to Biloxi or eight hours to Tunica Mississippi). By further comparison, Southern gambling Mecca Biloxi/Gulfport Mississippi has a regional population base of less than 150,000. Demographically, Birmingham is an ideal match to a Class II Bingo machine market, based on comparable figures from other Class II jurisdictions (specifically Oklahoma).

IGT ranked number 717 in the Fortune 1000 that year and between them and the other publically traded companies lobbying in the state, the likelihood of fully regulated gaming looked promising; especially since the Democrats had controlled the Legislature for almost a century and a half. The real lobbying was about lining up enough votes to override a gubernatorial veto, which also looked very possible.

To try to head off that eventuality, the governor needed to get the big boys out of the picture. He responded to the lobbying effort by sending a letter to the CEO's of IGT, Bally, and Multimedia (as well as six smaller companies) warning them:

"While several local constitutional amendments have authorized "Bingo" in certain counties, no constitutional amendment has authorized slot machines...

"The Court held that the term "Bingo," as used in local constitutional amendment, means nothing other than "the ordinary game of Bingo"...

Given the force of these controlling judicial opinions, a company in this business would be taking an extraordinary risk of criminal liability were it to conclude that the Alabama Constitution's "narrow exception" for "the ordinary game of Bingo" somehow authorizes the use of machines that are slot machines or gambling devices...

Above: Governor's warning letter to manufacturers

As Governor, I am deeply concerned that many manufacturers, providers, and business operators may have a mistaken impression about the legality of certain activities... I fully intend to carry out my constitutional duty to faithfully execute the laws of Alabama."

Hence the line was drawn in the sand to chase the legitimate manufacturers out of the state and leave the door open for those who wish to defy the Governor's understanding of state law. The regulated companies were put on notice. The definition of Bingo was still being debated, notwithstanding the State Supreme Court's failure to define exactly what their six rules addressed. So the on-the-edge-of-legality grey boys launched a full scale invasion of Alabama with thousands of games of their own in the state with no persky regulation, taxation, or consumer protection.

In response to McGregor's hiring that private detective, political opponents targeted McGregor and devised plans to end the controversy once and for all. Governor Riley's campaign manager, who had overseen the Abramoff $13-million casino industry payola, was married to the Bush-appointed United States Attorney for Alabama. Prosecutors charged McGregor, Gilley, their lobbyists, and a handful of democratic legislators with various fraud and bribary felonies. Equivocating over the difference between a campaign contribution and a bribe, the prosecutor had sent wire-wearing Republican legislators to visit McGregor to ask for campaign contributions; no Democrats were wired for the sting.

A bribery, vote-buying, and corruption trial was scheduled. The governor called the charges "proof" of the "corrupting influence" of gambling. Riley was term limited from seeking re-election, but rejoiced that the scandal would tip the balance of power in the upcoming Alabama Legislature to the GOP for the first time in more than 135 years. Jess Brown, professor of Political Science at Athens State University told the *Montgomery Advertiser* the indictments were "an early Christmas present to Republicans." He and Riley were right; the Republicans seized the statehouse in the fall elections.

The anti-gambling forces were on a roll. Next, the governor's task force set a deadline for all of the state's casinos to be closed and the majority complied, including McGregor's and Gilley's.

Meanwhile, in Birmingham, the FEMA-funded casino, where Hilliard was on the board, closed its doors and the developers were photographed loading cash into plastic trash bags as they fled, hours before an expected State Police raid. Dozens of vendors were left unpaid and hundreds of employees were suddenly without jobs, as the assets had "disappeared" (in those plastic bags).

Hilliard immediately took the issue to a Superior Court Judge who issued a court order to seize the casino and locate its assets. The judge appointed a former judge as "Special Master." That Special Master of the Court hired a forensic accounting firm to follow the money and the Superior Court Judge ordered that the casino remain open during the investigation. From the revenue of the court-run casino, the Special Master ordered the accountants to rehire the employees and pay off the neglected vendors.

Despite Governor Riley's order to close all the casinos in the state, the *"Bamaco Bingo Casino"* remained open under the order *and protection* of the Judge and the Special Master. In March of 2010 the Special Master and the Judge appointed ME as their trustee and

General Manager to try to make some sense of the looted casino and operate it under regulated guidelines.

Above: "Bamaco" casino near Birmingham, operated by the Alabama Superior Court and Gary Green.

Meanwhile, as he promised the $13-million political donors, Riley launched his raids. At four o'clock one morning, more than 100 State Troopers arrived at McGregor's Victoryland with a convoy of tractor trailer trucks to seize the games. By six a.m. McGregor had obtained a temporary restraining order to keep the Troopers out. At Country Crossing, Gilley refused to allow the troopers access because they lacked a warrant. In Greene County Alabama the pro-Bingo Sheriff stationed snipers with high-powered rifles to repel any of the Governor's agents that might attempt to close the casino; they never showed up there.

After a two-day standoff, Gilley decided to close Country Crossing with the statement, *"With state troopers surrounding us, we've decided not to subject our customers to possible harassment by the police. We're not reopening until we get some (legal) protection."*

McGregor was able to extend his standoff for months, but after a series of openings and closings and reopenings, IGT finally sent trucks from Nevada to remove the majority of the 6,400 slot machines. As the decision was being made, I was sitting in the IGT corporate office in Las Vegas with the Vice President who was racking his brain on the sheer logistics of the number of trucks in the fleet necessary to move that many machines; it was a nightmare for the poor guy. I tenderly chided the guy for not having contracted with me as their advisor before pissing away that much money in illegal gambling. Now, for all practical purposes, the world's largest non-Indian casino was dead.

I was still operating the only regulated casino in the state (regulated by MICS that I had submitted to the Superior Court). I hoped that the example (and the power of the court) would rub off on the *other* casinos. The court's regulations were word-for-word the Minimum Internal Control Standards (MICS) that I had written years earlier for the Gaming Commission for the Ottawa Tribe of Oklahoma *(if you recall, they are contained in the endnotes of this book)*. Additionally, I asked the Special Master and the Judge implement Nevada Regulation 6.150 for minimal bankroll. (I have mentioned that regulation several times throughout this book; it is such an essential part of how I operate a casino that it is worth printing in its entirety in the endnotes.[65] *You remember what happens when there is not sufficient cash for the cage—emergency drops).*

Besides internal control standards, and in addition to a strong minimum cash rule, the third important control that I require (and actually is required by Federal law) is a strong adherence to Title 31 of the United States Code. Any casino that generates more than a million dollars in annual revenue (which is almost any casino) is required to report certain currency transactions to assist the *Financial Crimes Enforcement Network* of the Internal Revenue Service. Title 31 is the *Bank Secrecy Act* but because of the massive amounts of cash generated in casinos, the regulations also apply to our transactions. Consequently, at all of MY casinos, I institute a stringent Title 31 training and compliance program. The outline of my typical Title 31 program, specifically modified for Alabama Bingo, is in the endnotes of this book.[66]

I cannot stress enough the extreme importance of having regulatory controls in place; operating without them is an open invitation to corruption and a formula for loss of control. Our having the court endorse this first-in-the-state regulated casino was landmark, but unfortunately not precedent setting.

Nonetheless, since all of the cash had been carted out by the developer, there was no money for the cage or any expenses. Congressman Hilliard was working feverishly to find funding for the court-controlled casino; so intensely that his health was starting to fail. Bob Wilson was working equally zealously to alter state law and to find other jurisdictions that would be willing to adopt the Court's (and my) standards.

Despite the court protection and the regulatory controls, the governor's task force was eyeing us. The pressures increased on one of the last casinos standing and there was no source of investment funds. The few individuals who *had* provided investment funds were not happy with the stringency of my Internal Controls and insisted on the most absurd of nepotisms to grab cash. My bringing in super regulator David Cook to oversee the controls severed to create even more tension. Meanwhile, David's law enforcement contacts warned that a raid was imminent.

As Governor Riley's revenge trial of McGregor began, I approached the Court's Special Master and Congressman Hilliard about the future of the Court's casino. I recommended that until the laws could be clarified, the Governor had calmed down, and funding could be located, that we close the casino. Other than the Poarch Creek Indian casinos, that would leave open in Alabama only the one casino in Greene County —which remained under the armed patrol of the County Sheriff and his snipers. As of this writing, the Alabama Superior Court still owes me $160,971 for my last 10 weeks operating their casino and Greene County is *still* open.

The Governor's kangaroo court began with quibbling over recordings of McGregor indicating that he always supports lawmakers who are good for his business and would not support lawmakers that would be bad for business. Riley's campaign manager's wife had her prosecutors argued that McGregor's statements and attitude constituted bribery. Country Crossings co-owner Ronnie Gilley pled guilty to the charges and testified that he worked closely with McGregor in an illegal vote-buying scheme which McGregor bankrolled and coached him on what to say at meetings with politicians. In relatively short order, jurors returned multiple *not guilty* verdicts on *some* of the counts but said they were hopelessly deadlocked on others.

Nine months later, Riley's pocket prosecutor went back into court to retry the group on the deadlocked charges. This time the defense team attacked Gilley's motives and credibility and confronted the wire-wearing legislators, saying prosecutors had *"embraced in this case political manipulators, racists and crooks."*

The latter at least was empirically confirmed when one of the prosecution's key witnesses was heard on the undercover tape talking about economic development and the more than three-thousand jobs created by the casinos: *"That's y'all's Indians,"* one white legislator said; *"They're aborigines, but they're not Indians,"* the witness (also a legislator) replied. (The witness, Republican State Senator Scott Beason, a candidate for U.S. Congress, was on the racial hot seat again in 2012 when during a GOP meeting he suggested that the party should *"empty the clip"* and do what it takes to control illegal immigration."*

After seven days of deliberation, in March of 2012 the second jury returned 27 not-guilty verdicts against McGregor, two lobbyists, two former State Senators, and one sitting Senator. The jury agreed there was no direct quid pro quo, or explicit offering of a contribution for a vote. Gilley, who had pled guilty and testified against McGregor, was sentenced to six years and eight months in prison while two other lobbyists who had pled guilty received four and five year sentences. By this time, a new Governor and new Attorney General had been elected; but in the Bingo-fueled Republican seizure of the State Legislature, the new team was as fervently anti-gambling as their predecessors, though apparently not on the take.

Commenting on the political climate, IGT announced, *"The legality of electronic charitable Bingo in Alabama continues to be under challenge by the state's governor. The legal and political climate in Alabama has further deteriorated, and therefore we have determined that the recoverability of our assets in this market has been impaired."* Their $53-million write-off on its Victoryland investment sealed doom for regulated companies operating in the State (outside of Indian country).

Though the *new* governor abolished Riley's special "anti-gambling task force", during the next few months several small casinos opened and were immediately raided by the new Attorney General, who proclaimed that he needed no task force.

Several Alabama courts jumped onto the anti-slot machine bandwagon and ruled that "electronic" Bingo was not "real" Bingo and was therefore illegal. One judge righteously pontificated, *'I don't care about this new-fangled technology but if it walks like a duck and quacks like a duck, so whatever you want to call it, it is a slot machine and not Bingo."*

Even the armed encampment casino in Greene County modified their offering from Class II machines to a modification of table-top sweepstakes type machines with no bill acceptors or other accoutrements of Class II games or typically associated with slot machines. Attorneys in Alabama were unable to recreate the brilliance of the arguments given a decade earlier in Indian Country by Chickasaw lawyer Jess Green.

In Alabama, the gambling industry *(which two years earlier had generated more revenue in that one southern state than the entire automotive industry generated nationwide)* had all but disappeared. Victoryland remained closed. Alabama's non-Indian gambling offerings were limited to clones of those storefront sweepstakes style "game rooms" with flat screen monitors lined along folding tables. In place of that once ready-to-be-regulated industry, the State successfully drove out legitimate business and left the door open only for those companies who don't mind legal dodging.

Between the last rewrite of this book and the time it went to press for the first edition, I was approached by an intermediary for one of those less-scrupulous Alabama operators, offering to *sell me a charity*, a license and a lease for a Bingo casino in Birmingham. Unfucking-believable!

Meanwhile the South Carolina boys, the Joe Hight genre, the Luc Marcoux genre, and the Cher-esque *"Gypsys, Tramps, and Thieves"* moved on to the next grey area venues. Many of them zeroed in on Mexico which had some interesting loopholes that allowed a version of Class II slot machines if they were owned by Mexican nationals; but by 2010 the shootouts and violence over control between the operators/vendors and the drug cartels had many of them longing for the nice safe days of the Alabama governor's task force. Most of the grey area operators moved on to the sweepstakes racket and began unregulated infestations in new settings.

So what is the harm in "unregulated" gaming? Why the big deal? Is it really making THAT much money?

I have repeatedly pointed out the comparison of Alabama's gaming revenue to all car sales nationwide. Well, of course the big gaming vendors like IGT and Bally would come into the state. Of course the early-adopters like Joe Hight would think they found financial nirvana. But is that any reason to be concerned? Isn't that just business?

Consider that in 2011 the net income for the five-sisters of the U.S. oil industry was $132-billion. That is a pretty serious industry. Meanwhile, according to NBC news, in the same year (2011) the net revenue from illegal gambling (not including Las Vegas, Atlantic City, Indian casinos or any regulated jurisdictions)...ILLEGAL GAMBLING... was $380-billion; triple the oil companies combined.

But again, is keeping that money unregulated anything other than libertarian laissez faire capitalism? I have many friends who would debate on the global level that this money should be tax free, regulation free, and unaccounted; so what is the big deal in not wanting big government regulating everything?

By refusing to set state-regulations for gaming, Alabama (and the other jurisdictions) open two doors: Firstly, they tacitly invite the schemes and scams that circumvent prevention laws through a never-ending series of innovations, creations, and loop-holes; and secondly, without licensing individuals and setting standards for games, consumers are not protected from the unscrupulous, illegal, and out-and-out rip-offs.

It is, at very least, one of the great paradoxes of the gambling world that the laws and regulations that allowed all of these seeming-scams to exist...were all borne of anti-gambling forces trying to halt gambling rather than legalize and regulate it. Rather than halt gambling, they encouraged the most unregulated, (many times criminally un-licensable), unscrupulous elements of the gambling world to find ways to circumvent the restrictions.

Unaccounted for and non-taxed money (especially this much money) and the process of concealing the source of money *is clearly money laundering.* On that global level we can debate all day about the social consequences of not tracking that much money. Corrupt public officials need to be able to hide bribes, kick-backs, etc. Organized criminal groups need to be able to launder the proceeds of drug trafficking and commodity smuggling. Terrorist groups use money-laundering channels to get cash to buy arms.

There is a viable argument that, on a policy level, that the lack of regulation of this much cash can cause an actual deterioration of the national currency from money launderers easily moving their currency from one country to another, threatening the state's reserves of foreign exchange. The argument goes on that this threat will force the government to demand foreign loans to cover the external financing gap resulting from the smuggling of funds abroad. In any case, money laundering threatens the investment climate as investors lose confidence in the economic system and its regulatory legislation.

All of that aside, the lack of regulation *does* directly impact players. Without regulation, there is nothing that requires that winner are paid the proper amount; or paid at all, for that matter. There is nothing that requires that the machines pay out competitively or even fairly.

In Nevada, New Jersey, and other states there are strict regulations governing the minimum payback a consumer can expect from a slot machine. There are strict guarantees of what a player can expect to win (or lose) under those regulations. Without regulation, there is nothing in place to protect consumers.

Look at just the AWP market. Titles like *Queen Bee, Crazy Bugs, Fruit Bonus, Fruit Genie,* and even the venerable old *Cherry Master* and *Pot-O-Gold* are not slot machines as we know them, despite the look and feel. The majority of these games rip off players/consumers. Most of the games (regardless of the vendor or manufacturer) operate from one of those aforementioned dedicated software board produced by one of a handful of Taiwan-based companies (Astro, Dyna, ICS, etc.). Similar to the old barroom standby eight-liner games (Cherry Master, Pot-O-Gold, etc.) but with updated Asian technology; these games are indeed "cheat games" (as Luc calls them).

As I noted earlier, typically, the hold on these games is as high as 35% and can be reset at closing every night. Let's suppose for example the operator has a game set to pay out 65% (keeping in mind slot machines generally pay out in the 90%+ range). By now you understand that the payout level is over a long period of time — many plays of the game. These boards are designed so that the theoretical payout is 65%... over a *few* thousand plays; but they are also designed that during the first few hundred plays the payout is much less —perhaps as low as 25% payout in some cases. That means that to get up to the 65% figure, at some point after a few thousand plays the machine will have a large payout that will make up the difference. However, the "cheat" feature that Luc points out is that the operator of the game can reset that board every day so that the 65% figure (via a large payout) is never reached and in fact the game always pays only about 25% (and holds 75% or more). I have actually had operators of those games complain to me that some of their games were "only" holding 80% on some days; imagine how they would feel with a REAL slot machine that only holds 4% to 6%!

These are NOT casino gambling devices. These are sucker games and they masquerade as slot machines disguised under the pretext of "amusement games," "sweepstakes machines," and other legal loopholes through which they can slime.

The unscrupulousness and lack of regulatory control is certainly not limited to AWP and sweepstakes. I am no fan of Class II games; as is probably clear from my insistence on calling Class II *"invisible ping-pong balls"*). Even under the best Class II regulations (and I have written some and participated in the NIGC's rewrite of theirs), I still believe that these games are bullshit. But that is not to say they need to be outlawed. If the law is going to allow an *"electronic facsimile"* of Bingo, then clearly these games are legal.

My issue is much more global: I think *all* games should be regulated, protected, controlled, and fair. I think consumers should have expectations or fairness in gambling. If you go to the store to buy a product *...say a computer for example...* you expect it to be a computer. It has the HP logo on it; it is in an HP box; and it has what appears to be Microsoft Windows on it. As a consumer, you have every reason in the world to believe it is a computer like you would buy anywhere else. But what if, when you get the computer home, you find out it is a *"special Class II computer"* that doesn't really run Windows, won't run your e-mail program, doesn't do word processing, and doesn't compute anything? There was no sign on the box or the computer warning you of this and from looking at the product you had every reason in the world to believe it was the brand name computer you were seeking.

Hold that example and let's step back into this one aspect of Bingo-based slot machines and the *player experience*. You walk up to an IGT *Wheel Of Fortune®* brand slot machine. For all the world it looks to you like the same IGT machine you played in Las Vegas last year; but this one is at the Class II casino in your neighborhood (or in Alabama). It's cool though, because the advertisements for the casino tell you about *"Vegas style games"* and *"real slot machines."* The lights are there, the glitter is there, there are even showgirls. And the machine itself looks exactly like one you played in Vegas; the design of the machine, the logos, the sounds, everything. It even operates the same way...you push a button and spin the video reels. There is some little numbered card up in the corner of the screen that says something about Bingo, but you don't even have to look at that; you are focusing on the spinning reels of the machine.

Just like the example with the computer, you as the consumer, have every right to expect that machine to behave just like the machines you played in Vegas. But guess what? Just like the phony computer above, these slot machines are phony too. You, my friend, have just been ripped off, whether corporate American admits it or not.

Your expectation of *chances of winning* is totally wrong —*no matter what you expect.* This is because you are not playing against a slot machine with a random number generator churning the odds like you played in Vegas. Rather you are playing *against the other players in the casino.* You are playing against their pool of money, against virtual Bingo cards that they have on their machines, and you are not trying to get "three bars" at all but are trying to get a "Bingo" *before your neighbor does. That is a major difference and totally changes the outcome of the game.*

Read the National Indian Gaming Commission's technical standards for Class II machines and 25 C.F.R., part 547; the basis of the play of Class II machines is that the player is competing against other players (as opposed to against the casino). This is a fundamental difference in the nature of the game vs. slot machines; Hence in the payout structure.

In fact, mathematically speaking, Bingo is an entirely different universe than slot machine math. With a slot machine, the payout schedule can be anywhere the mathematician designs it to be. With Bingo, the payout schedule is necessarily a bell-curve (caused by the nature of the game). Since the minimum winning Bingo pattern requires four balls to be drawn (with the "free space" providing one of the five spots for winning), then it is impossible to win with the first three

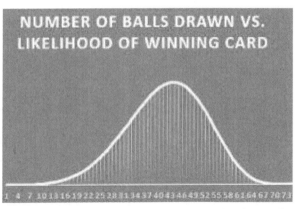

ball drawn. By the time the last ball is drawn there is a near-certain chance that some Bingo card will have already matched four spaces and a free space. At each end of that spectrum, the chances of winning are less than the chances after a substantial number of the balls have been drawn. This is in sharp contrast to the random number generator of a Class III machine where winning is determined at any point, rather than only within the bell's parameters.

Within the parameters of that bell curve it is possible to create different payout peaks and valleys thus artificially altering the nature of the play; frequency and volatility. Some game manufacturers have tried to compensate for this finite curve by having their games pay out in non-standard Bingo patterns. Besides serving to confuse players, this method only complicates the calcula-

298

tions. However, ultimately, it does not alter the fundamental mathematical difference between Bingo and slot machines.

If you examine the earlier bell curve illustration you will see that (for example) by the time the 27th random ball is drawn the winning cards begin to show up. However, that curve is based on the assumption of an even availability of the 75 number spread on various cards. What many manufacturers has do is

For example, the table at the right is taken from the actual payout table of one of the most popular Class II manufacturers. Within the parameters of that Bingo bell curve, this manufacturer (and many others) was able to change the frequency of winning combinations

Balls	Payout
26	10
27	800
28	40
37	5
40	2

withhold the availability of certain numbers showing up on cards until after a fixed number of balls have been drawn or certain combinations have occurred.

by limiting the correlation between the number of invisible balls drawn and numbers available on players' virtual Bingo cards.

This is really diabolically sneaky. If a virtual Bingo is won when the 26th ball is drawn, then the payout is 10 credits. Now comes the complication of a random numbers generator within the parameters of the bell curve. Let's consider just the range of "B" numbers available, 1 through 15. Every player's card has five of those numbers, seemingly at random. Just for this example, let's assume that four of those numbers are truly at random but one of those numbers is B-8. Now let's say that the likelihood of any of those numbers except B-8 coming up is equal after the 26th ball has been drawn. In this pay table, if a match is made, the player wins 10 credits. If, however, no one has won by the 26th ball then that could mean that the Bingo cards in play have number B-8 on them and in order to get that Bingo win, it requires that B-8 be drawn. However, for this example, the programmer has made the probability of B-8 being drawn before the 28th ball to be extremely unlikely. So if someone has a card on which the combination with B-8 is a "Bingo", then on the 27th draw the payout is much higher; 800 credits. By the time ball 28 has been drawn, the odds are more likely to obtain a Bingo in another column or pattern, so the payout for a "B" column Bingo is only 40 credits. By the 37th ball the pay is 5 credits; and by the 40th ball being drawn, the payout is only 2 credits.

With invisible Bingo cards and virtual balls, it is an easy technological step to repeat this deception for each of the five letters in "BINGO" and for all of the hundreds of permutations of winning patterns (which include shapes, letters, etc. rather than traditional straight lines or four corners).

With Vegas slot machines (and Class III machines in Indian Country) you are playing against the machine and such duplicity is simply not feasible. But with "virtual Bingo" you are playing from a "common ball drop" and against the other players competing for that drop. When the server computer picks the invisible ping-pong balls for a round of Bingo, the card on your machine goes up against the cards on every other machine where a player has put in money. That particular selection of invisible balls remains until either you or one of the other players gets a "Bingo" from that selection; the "session" does not end until then. A number of companies have further skewed the math by providing "interim" wins and "consolation" wins; in which prizes ranging from one-credit to thousands of credits are awarded via a random number generator (mimicking a slot machine) between Bingo wins but deducted from the payout percentage.

The odds of your winning then are, in part, based on the likelihood of your Bingo card having more matching numbers than your neighbor's Bingo card earlier in the game. To a mathematician this variable skews the odds so much that it makes the game vastly different from a slot machine.

Yet the game you are playing is designed to *look like* a slot machine and to hide this difference from you. You cannot even play on these machines unless at least one other player is playing at the same time (so that you can have the required Bingo ball drop *against other customers*).

In that regard, it reminds me a lot of the counterfeit drugs, baby formula, designer clothes, and even machinery pawned off on the third world. It is as if it these games were created to be substandard look-a-likes of the real thing; a cheap imitation without the substance of the real thing.

The percentage of payback that you might have come to expect in Vegas does not exist in the same manner with Class II. In Las Vegas, Mississippi, and Atlantic City, slot machine players are extremely aware of the payback of various machines in each casino. Casinos compete by offering higher paybacks than the casino down the street and players constantly switch properties to get the best payback. In Class II casinos, you won't see those big neon signs they put up in Vegas that announce "98% pay out".

In fact, the paybacks are nowhere near the Vegas odds. The odds for Class II casinos are set by the manufacturers of the machines and not by marketers in the slot department. While you can expect Vegas machines to pay back from a high of 98% to a low of about 85%, you can expect average Class II machines to payback 96% to down to a little as 75%, depending on the manufacturer. It is not totally unheard of for the machines to payback as little 65% (though as I noted earlier *some* of VGT's Class II machines do pay back almost 98%).

With Class II games, there is no legal minimum payout of any of the games. In Atlantic City no machine can pay back less than 83% and in Nevada it is 80% (though in either jurisdiction the payback rarely runs below 90% even on the very "worst" machines). Class II machines can be set to pay out 1/10th of what a Vegas machine might payout; you have no way of knowing the payout and there is no law compelling anyone to tell you. There is zero consumer protection on *that* front. In that "consumer" regard, the machines are indeed akin to the redemption and sweepstakes games.

The myth that one casino's Class II machines are "looser" or "tighter" than another's is just that: a myth. In Oklahoma, Southern California, and a few other jurisdictions where there are clusters of Indian casinos, the marketing myth is often that one casino has more winners than the one next door. As I just said, the payback percentage is determined and set by the manufacturer/owners of the games. It is the same everywhere; the Class II machines pay the same in every casino. Competition on that front does not exist.

My complaint is about the inherent deception, dishonesty, deceit, duplicity, and fraud of cloaking these slot machines in a loophole. My argument is this: in today's world, with technology ever changing, it is impossible to stop high-tech gambling. So whether it is electronic Bingo, sweepstakes, AWP, or Internet Poker; I want it regulated. As a consumer, as a player, I want to know the games are fair and have a standard. I want to know that, as a player, I actually CAN win.

The refusal of state governments (like Alabama) to *regulate* gambling leaves the door open for all sorts of schemes to circumvent laws that *ban* gambling. With technology constantly changing, there is just no way to anticipate the potential loopholes in even the best-crafted anti-gambling laws...given the level of pure genius, cunning, determination, and resilience of the grey area entrepreneurs (remember these guys invented virtual/invisible Bingo balls!).

As I said, the nature of that rung of the gaming ladder is short term. The loophole opens, the snakes move in, the loophole closes, and the snakes slither on to the next loophole state. In the meantime, they make a lot of money with minimal investment. And, if they are closed down or their games are seized and destroyed...well it is just the cost of doing business and there is another state waiting down the Interstate.

Chapter Sixteen
Marketing Donald Trump

"I'll tell you, it's Big Business. If there is one word to describe Atlantic City, it's Big Business. Or two words – Big Business."
— **Donald J. Trump**

God, I love Bunky's chickens. I think the Flying Elvis promotion is incredible. Fully decked out showgirls wandering the casino floor and mingling with players absolutely rocks (assuming the girls don't have a plug of chewing tobacco in their cheeks). No one can dispute the crowd-drawing power of shows from top rockers, country singers, and even the Chippendales. Car giveaways, postcards offering a premium of the week, in-casino interactive contests and promotions, all are incredible.

All of those creative marketing devices are tools for generating and responding to data. Remember: the real purpose of the tic-tac-toe chickens was to increase player's club card usage so I could gather more data about the customers. Once I had that data, then I could kick formulas into play and create "offers" that could motivate players to come more frequently, stay longer, and spend more money.

Most casinos use some combination of these and other creative devices to attract new customers, to retain existing customers who might defect to competing casinos, and to increase the amount of time that they play.

If you ask about in the casino business you are going to hear that I am a marketing pundit; that is what the magazines keep saying and that is what the numbers indicate. But if you stop there, then you miss the fact that my flavor of marketing involves every aspect of the casino operation —front of the house and back of the house. Yes, I am a marketer; but *all* casino operators *must* be marketers if they are to succeed. Running a casino is all about marketing. And marketing…is all about data that we gather about players and use for every management decision (as well as for customer service and branding).

In order to adequately use data, a number of casino factors must be totally symbiotic. Marketing and IT must be in sync; in fact, they need to be in love with each other. The casino marketers need to be well-trained in how to take the raw creativity of something like tic-tac-toe chickens and turn that into value. Casino operational management needs to be on board and understand the value of this kind of marketing. And the owner/operator needs to *"get it."*

It might seem that this synergy of internal casino forces would come easy when the track record of success is up to a 40% increase in revenue by applying a few simple marketing tracking, analytics, and targeting rules. Unfortunately, the combination of such hyperbole-sounding dramatic increases and the seemingly technical mumbo-jumbo of how those rules work are hard to swallow by hotel operators, general business accountants, and other top management that does not come from either the marketing world or the casino world.

Though advanced personalized marketing methodologies had been used by direct marketers and the catalog industry for decades, in the late 1990s when I began tossing around words like *"RFM targeting"*, they were completely alien to casino operators. Harrah's was winning marketing awards following the business direction of Harvard business professor Gary Loveman; but at that time Loveman was a consultant brought in by hotel boss Phil Satre. Today, Loveman is CEO of Caesars Entertainment Corporation, the successor to Harrah's; but even back then he and his protégé, Booz Allen Hamilton alumnae Richard Mirman, were apparently more interested in their own academic formulas than my proven catalog-industry methodologies.

After Bill Bennett's death, it was, at very least, challenging to find an operator willing to allow my hocus-pocus sounding methodology a live lab for development. I needed an operator who breathed, ate, and shit marketing and branding. I needed an operator who *lived* marketing, not from the Harrah's academia-to-live lab that Loveman was creating, but from a street-fighting "let's do it" attitude. I needed an operator who would *"get it."* Enter Donald J. Trump.

In 1987 or 1988 when Donald Trump's *Art of The Deal* came out, I absolutely hated it and hated him. I saw him as a real-life incarnation of Michael Douglas' *Gordon Gekko* pronouncing, "Greed is good." I read that book as a cliché of every absurd byproduct of the trickle-down-generation and a tome somewhere between Robert G. Allen's get-rich-by-buying-my-books, one of those "how to negotiate anything" books, and Michael Milken's 98 counts of racketeering and securities fraud. Not that Trump smelled of either Milkenesque crimes nor Allenese get-rich-quick schemes; but his book and his persona reeked of the zeitgeist of that epoch...at least to me it did...and *that* was not an appealing spirit. On my list of top 100 people I would like to meet, Donald Trump was probably number eight-billion down the list (keeping in mind there are only 6-billion people on the planet).

When his financial empire collapsed, for me it was not important enough to jump for joy; but it did cause me to note, in passing, that *what goes around comes around.* And ten years later when *Art of The Comeback* was released, I merely noted that some things (no matter how un-pleasant) just won't go away.

In 2000, when I kept an apartment in New York as a consultant to real estate mogul Bruce Ratner (who by the way developed the original concept for Vegas' Venetian), I actually met Trump for the first time at an upscale east side restaurant. He was sharing a private dining room with us; at his table was, among others, author Tom Wolfe (decked out in the white-suite and white fedora Tom Wolfe costume).

I was amused that Trump, while cordial, would not shake hands (I later learned he was a *Howie-Mandel-style* germaphobe). At that time Trump's casinos were going through one of their periodic financial crises. (I cannot *even* remember how many GM's the Taj Mahal has had; and I wonder if Donald can). It had not been *that* long since a Trump corporate helicopter crash had killed five people including three of his top casino executives: Steve Hyde, Mark Grossinger Etess and Jon Benanav; he definitely was suffering a brain-void in his casino empire. At that dinner, I thought it was a damned shame that he was not out of his seat begging for my advice; God knows I would have given him a free-of-charge earful. Nonetheless, he was THE *Donald Trump*, pre-Apprentice, but celebrity-like nonetheless.

I would have never, in a thousand lifetimes, predicted that I would either work for Trump or actually *like* the guy; hell most of the people that work for him don't even meet him. But experience and maturity do strange things to people *(and they certainly did for Donald Trump)*. The one thing at which Trump became brilliant —not just good, mind you, but brilliant— was (and is) branding. He turned the Trump name into a BRAND.

Even more difficult, he turned it into a brand of prestige, quality, and upscale value. Regardless of whether these perceptions were in reality 24-karat or merely plated gild, the brand awareness was identified with the BEST. *(And judging from my focus groups and due diligence at the Trump Plaza for a potential purchase of it in 2012, I can testify that it was mere perception; the property was a dump!)*

Never mind what those "tell-all" books written by any of his "insiders" purport to "know" to be "the truth," the Trump brand is iconic. Love him, hate him, or ignore him, there is no denying that the positioning of the Trump brand has been absolutely brilliant. It is that brilliance that I came to like about Trump...and learn from him.

Don't get me wrong. Outside of marketing, I disagree with almost everything Donald Trump says and does. That "birther" insanity of the 2012 presidential season was really over the line; and anyone who litigates as much as he does...well you get my point. Nonetheless, there is no denying that he is a marketing machine. In the 21st century, who would have thought that some huge percentage of Americans could name a famous real estate developer? Incredible.

When I was offered the job with Trump, I had already accepted a position with a casino in Washington State; in fact, I had already passed the background check, been issued a Washington State gaming license, and given a date to report to work. But who in their right mind would turn down an opportunity to be a marketing Vice President for Donald Trump?

Not only did I thrive in the job; not only did I increase monthly gross revenue by more than $60-million; not only did I create the only "successful" Trump-branded casino at that point in time; but I also got to learn branding from an undisputed grand master of the science: Donald J. Trump. And it gave me my much-needed laboratory to fully develop the methodologies that Bill Bennett had encouraged.

The culture of Trump Hotels and Casinos, either unfortunately or fortunately, was transient with that succession of General Managers and CEO's at the casino flagship Taj Mahal in Atlantic City. Every time a new CEO would take the helm, there would be a series of departures of top managers in various departments. It seemed that less than loyal to Trump, many executives were part of the team that traveled with the innumerable GM's.

I entered the Trump universe during the reign Mark Brown (rather than that of Nick Ribis, or Denny Gomes, or Jim Perry, or John O'Donnell (at the Plaza), Mark Juliano, Kevin DeSanctis, Rosalind Krause, Scott Butera, or...frankly I can't remember even a portion of them or what actual titles and positions they held). The Mark Brown epoch included Lou Creseenzo (slots), Vince Mascio (tables and casino management), Steve Gietka (entertainment), and in California Rich Williamson (finance), Rich Smith (F&B), and a handful of other key players.

Through a soap opera series of events *(from that tragic helicopter crash, to general incompetence, to corporate power plays)* the cast of characters constantly changed at every level in the organization. Complicated into that menagerie, out in California, we had the power struggle between the Tribe and the Trumpites and then internally within the Trump group another struggle between those loyal to the THCRM (Trump Hotels and Casino Resorts, Management Services, LLC) and those who thought independent management (dumping Trump) would be better for that Indian property. Absurd as it sounded and as much denial each of those then-"factions" might feign, the fact was the mere constant turnover of management staff indicated something was up. Most managers have chosen to say that the "something" was the quirks of Donald Trump's personality; but, frankly, that is such a ridiculous straw man copout that it makes me want to throw up. The truth is that Trump has consistently been *Trump*; good, bad, or indifferent, any of his various operatives and inner circles over the years should have been bright enough to recognize that fact. Even the stock-price-increasing departure of Nick Ribis and the strain on their longtime friendship was not a "quirk" but a Trump-analyzed business decision.

Through all of the turmoil, much of the glue and stability in the Trump gaming organization had been from an unassuming and deceptively brilliant attorney named Robert M. Pickus. At least since 1985 Trump had relied on Bob Pickus to guide him through the gaming universe. Apparently happy in the background of the larger-than-life Trump, Pickus brilliantly directed the ever-changing cast of characters in the Trump gaming drama. Even in the days of the Ribis' taking-the-company-public moves, Pickus was there as Trump's eyes and ears on the ground. At various times he filled roles of Chief Administrative Officer, General Counsel, Corporate Secretary, of Trump Resorts Funding, Trump Hotels and Casino Resorts, Trump Entertainment Resorts Holdings, Trump Casino Holdings, and whatever the Trump company of the day may have been. To my knowledge, he ran legal, H.R., risk management, government affairs, and development. He was successfully in charge of the two big restructurings of the Trump debt, 2005 and 2010 (reducing the 2010 debt by a billion-and-a-half dollars). He was in charge of compliance, training, the management contracts, trademarks, and licensing the Trump brand. He arranged the financing for Trump29 as well as the Trump riverboat casino in Gary Indiana. Bob Pickus is one of those things that took Donald Trump (at least in my mind) from that *Gordon Gekko* paperback bookseller to a serious business leader.

Though I did not work directly with him or really know him very well, I found him to be meticulous in detail *(one of his many employment contract addendums guaranteed him the right to have his laundry done in the Taj Mahal's laundry room)*. During the Mark Brown heyday, those of us in the field knew that talking to Pickus was the same as talking to the Trump organization itself, somehow bypassing Mark; hence most of us avoided Bob.

The cast of characters aside, the genius of Donald Trump's branding stands alone to move him from an "also ran" to a mogul with a brand-able hair style and then to a true icon. But even with that under his belt, there is a much more intense genius that is Donald Trump: the financial instruments guru that he became from his years of New York real estate finagling. From the in-your-face (he likes to call it "brash") disco-era asshole who fast-talked his way into the sweetheart Grand Hyatt tax abatement deal in New York, Donald J. Trump became a genuine guru of financially structuring deals that seemed impossible. That lower-key genius rivals even his branding genius.

His use of multiple companies' mortgage bond issues was at least dazzling...and a decade ahead of the hedge fund wags of the early 21st century who "invented" this technique. With debt sold in order to finance or expand casinos, Trump issued artificially low coupons (designed to sell considerably below par) for investors to profit from the difference between the purchase price and the value at maturity. His use of "leverage" permeated throughout the organization; even slot machines were revenue-share rather than purchased.

Beyond just usage of these instruments, Trump's management of them is viciously enlightening. Consider that much-publicized battle with entertainer Merv Griffin over ownership of the *Resorts International Casino and Hotel*. As I discussed earlier, Trump used these types of instruments to buy Resorts in 1987 but two years later sold it all ... including the bond *OBLIGATIONS* to Griffin.

Touted as a battle between two titans *(as I discussed, Griffin's holding included the Beverly (Hills) Hilton and a substantial interest in IGT's Wheel of Fortune slot machines)*, the publicity raged like a Saturday-night wresting card set for your local coliseum. One covenant of the final sale —in which Merv "won" Resorts and "kicked Trump's ass" (as he put it)— was that Trump would be "burdened" with ownership of the unfinished Taj Mahal project with its delays and cost overruns.

I discussed this battle in an earlier chapter, but to recap, Trump promptly financed the Taj with a new bond offering and other bondholders' monies. Merv, meanwhile, still had the Trump-created debt obligation at Resorts, but without the promise of the to-be-completed Taj on the horizon as a temptation for investors. Consequently, Griffin's Resorts had to file for bankruptcy-court protection, leaving the Resorts investors with a fraction of their original investment, the bonds virtually worthless, and Donald with the largest and newest casino resort in Atlantic City...with built-in equity. Take that kind of financial manipulative mastermind and meld it with the high-end branding machine that he has become... and you have a portrait of Donald J. Trump and his magic.

When I stepped into the Trump world, the casinos were on one of their periodic downward spirals, more a result of debt structure than the economy or operational issues. In Palm Springs California (actually Coachella), where the Trump name should have been the perfect tie-in, revenue was stagnate at about $40-million to $45-million a month; where it had been for months on end. Something was just...not working. And it was there that my marketing methodology was front and center.

The "magic" number that the Trump organization was looking for was a Saturday with gross revenue (coin-in) of $5-million. With that benchmark, the general feeling amongst the accountants was they could show growth with the property. That magical $5-million day had happened only once: during the grand opening. Since then, it had been elusive. A "really good" weekend would bring $4.2-million to $4.3-million. Once, in conjunction with a two-set concert by comedian George Lopez, a Saturday grossed $4.8-million, but the casino suffered during the following week and thus monthly revenue remained flat-lined. The magical $5-million number seemed just impossible to repeat.

Of course, from this build up, you obviously know that I turned that situation around. I consistently had *every* Saturday a $5-million day, along with many Fridays and Sundays as well. I moved the monthly gross revenue ("coin in" for the casino industry) from averaging $45-million to *consistently* at least $100-million. The "secret" for doing so was, again, formulaic, methodological, and executed from planning. And the success followed long after I left Donald Trump — as long as the formula was followed.

The marketing success was rooted in data; in the methodology that Bill Bennett and I had honed from my basics. The Trump property finally afforded me a replacement live lab; but there was no data. Hence the introduction of the tic-tac-toe chicken.

As you will recall from previous chapters, when I arrived at the property only 17% of the players were using their club cards. Consistently, the casino could not identify anything about 83% of their players. We had no data. By the end of the chicken promotion, 74% of my players were using their cards; finally a measurable base of my players.

Before I could begin using that player information, I needed to know exactly what it is that we had collected. I wanted to know really esoteric details like, how much money did white women age 45-50 from one zip code spend on the average; what was the average daily worth of customers, by demographic; what was the length of the relationship between those customers and the casino; what was the ratio between spending and mileage radius from the casino; and so on for (literally) several hundred pages. That would me a starting point from which to work.

Despite the fact that this data is available to every casino with a basic player tracking system, most good marketers (an all *wanna-be* marketers) often overlook a plethora of tangible and measurable revenue sources as well as the ability to attract new customers, to increase loyalty amongst existing customers, and increase

Above: Binders of the hundreds of pages of Trump data analysis reports

purchases from existing loyal customers…all hidden in that data.

Johnny Cash sang the powerful lyrics: "*It is dark as a dungeon way down in the mine.*" I always thought that imagery applied just as well to a *data* mine. All of that data the player tracking system collects about spending behavior was pretty worthless if it was idle in a dark bottomless pit somewhere in the process.

All good marketing preaches the use of data; and most CEOs and COOs are trained properly with the right buzzwords to feign grounding in data marketing. Almost all casinos have those frequent-player cards for recording and tracking customer behavior. Of course, there is *some kind* of mining of this behavioral data. In the 15 years since I began preaching my methodologies at trade shows and to a few selected clients (like Bill Bennett, Mandalay, and Wynn), every marketing consultant and agency has begun offering what they claim to be data analysis.

Most are using all the right buzz words of CRM (customer relationship management), Hybrid Marketing, Segmentation, Benchmarking, Customer Centric, Organic Campaigns, KPI (key performance indicators), Brand Loyalty, Integrated Marketing, Consumerization, and the ever-popular *Technology Fragmentation*. Few have a fucking clue as to what these terms mean when it comes to actual hands-on day-to-day casino operation.

At Trump, as I began the creatively over-the-top promotions (like the chickens) and then the mind-numbing process of sorting through the new data, Frank Haas (as comptroller) would immediately hammer me with "*how much incremental revenue did you generate with that.*" Frank wanted to know how much more money the casino made with the promotions than it would have made *without* the promotion.

Frank, and most of the people who review casino revenue, knew that, sadly, most marketers had no answer to that question. Sure all competent marketers look at their numbers following a promotion and compare to the same date last year or last month or whatever. But that sort of superficial accounting does not consider hundreds, if not thousands, of contingencies that could have impacted player behavior. In most cases there is no pro-forma in advance of a promotion; just accountant-driven post-forma reports.

My friend, Frank Haas, was in for a surprise from what he had been accustomed to receiving. Typically I would have not only pro and post forma (which then were rare enough) but I would also require a pre-event assessment for every promotion, mailing, or event. That way we surgically projected, evaluated, and analyzed the marketing function not just for a time period, but for each individual event, promotion, give-away, or mailing during any given time period. Suddenly he (and the analysts) had real data and real projections from which they could draw real-life conclusions.

For example, at the right you see the front cover of the eight-page monthly calendar I mailed to customers for January 2004. Below you see one of the inside pages actually listing the daily events for that month.

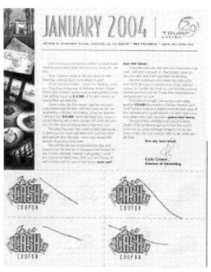

Many casino marketers would creatively visualize the events, giveaways, promotions, entertainment, and so on for the month and simply mail the calendar and see what happens.

That kind of haphazard shotgun approach just didn't work for me. I wanted to know in advance what I could expect from these month's calendar promotions.

More specifically, I wanted to measurable criteria for every promotion in the calendar. I wanted to project the start and end dates of each event; the measurable response that I WANTED (that could later be weighed against actual response); the number of test (or seed) mailings sent; the total number of pieces mailed; what method I would use to track the response to the calendar.

This would allow me to take the pre-event data and create a dollar-amount pro-forma of costs of the promotions versus expected revenue.

309

Moreover, I segmented even my calendar mailing the way catalog companies segment the catalogs they send out. Think about cataloguer L.L. Bean. They produce a nice paper catalog (at least as of this writing they still do) which they mail out all over America. The catalog is made of somewhere between 50 and 150 pages of their merchandise which is useful all over the country. The key to getting the customer to flip through those pages, however, is the front cover of the catalog. Now, let's think about what they can put on that front cover to get us to open the book and look at the merchandise. In their winter catalog, customers in Montana (for example) may be really excited about heavy coats, snow boots, and other cold-winter gear. But I live in South Florida where the temperature in February is 80-degrees rather than some-degrees-below-zero. The snowbound catalog isn't going to excite me to open the cover; though the pages inside have merchandise that may well appeal to me just as much as it appeals to the Montana well digger. *(As I type this page, I am wearing a nice cozy pair of L.L. Bean slippers which I put on right after I got out of my pool.)* To solve that problem, catalog companies send different front covers to different constituencies; in this example based on geographic location.

If they are going to go to all the trouble to create different versions of the catalog cover based on zip codes, then there are probably other common factors they can add in. For example, as a past customer who they want to encourage to reorder, I may be offered a 10% discount for returning customers and they may print that in huge red letters on the front of the catalog. My next door neighbor, right here in Florida, may have never ordered from them or have done so rarely enough that they are not considered regular customers; so to entice them the company may offer free shipping, printed in bright colors on the front of the catalog.

Using this method the catalog company is able to target customers on multi-dimensional levels. That also means that they have an entire selection of different covers for that winter catalog. Just in this example we know they have the northern and southern versions and within those versions they have regular customers and not-so-regular customers. Just in that simple example there are four different covers for that winter catalog. Every customer can be grouped into one of those categories.

Back in the casino world, we typically use players club membership to segment players by something called "ADT"; *Average Daily Theo*. ADT is the average theoretical WIN the casino makes from that customer's visit (remember from an earlier chapter the casino and players' juxtaposing the word "win"). Well-marketed casinos then add to the ADT a second segmentation: how recently a player was in the casino. I add a third dimension of how often the person comes in. That allows me to generate a three-dimension picture of an individual customer: how much I make when they visit; when they last played; and how often they come in. Below is the actual pre-event report for that January 2004 Trump calendar mailing.

Let's look at what we created, line by line:

Project Name	January 2004 Calendar
Goal	Retention
Start Date	January 1 2004
End Date	January 31 2004
Project Description	TRUMP 29 JANUARY 2004 CALENDAR HAS THE FOLLOWING PROMOTIONS: • Promotion 1: CHICKEN TIC-TAC-TOE, $10,000 CHALLENGE - every day from 12 noon to 8pm guests get a chance to challenge Ginger the chicken at tic-tac-toe. If they beat Ginger they win $10,000. • Promotion 2: SCRATCH CARD TUESDAYS - January 6, 13, 20, and 27, from 9am until Chairman's Club closing. Guests trade their coupon for a scratch card to win a share of $30,000 and are guaranteed to win a cash prize up to $1,000. • Promotion 3: APPRENTICE VIEWING PARTY - Premiering Thursday, January 8, at 8:30pm then showing the following Wednesdays in January: 14th, 21st and 28th at 8:00pm, in the Blue Bar. Weekly cash pool and series cash grand prize if guest picks who gets fired by Donald Trump, and who becomes the Apprentice. • Promotion 4: CHINESE NEW YEAR CELEBRATION - January 31, at 12 noon in the Spotlight Showroom. Festivities in-

	clude a D.J., Karaoke, Lion Dance and more.
	• Promotion 5: COUPONS - 30,012 members received coupons that are valid through the month of January for the following: 2 for 1 Buffet, Free $5 Cash, 2 for 1 Showtickets and $5 Matchplay.
	• Promotion 6: FOUR CASH COUPONS MEMBERS REDEEM WEEKLY
	o 3,850 members received $5 coupons
	o 1,891 members received $10 coupons
	o 1,603 members received $15 coupons
	o 1006 members received $25 coupons
	o 329 members received $50 coupons
	o 103 members received $100 coupons.
Desired Outcome	7%
Drop Date of Mail	December 23, 2003
In-house date	January 1
Mailing Type	Monthly Calendar
Number Mailed	38,794
Test (seed) mailings	15
Response desired	2,715 players
Geographic Target	CA, AZ, NV, & UT
Criteria for targeting	• Minimum $15 ADT • Minimum of one visit in last 12 months • Minimum of 2 visits during previous four months Additional criteria for Promotion #6 cash coupons: • ADT of $25-$49 receives $5 cash per week; • ADT of $50-$74 receives $10 cash per week; • ADT of $75-$124 receives $15 cash per week; • ADT of $125-$249 receives $25 cash per week; • ADT of $250-$499 receives $50 cash per week; • ADT of $500 or greater receives $100 cash per week;

Additionally, the report contains: a project ID number; a project reference number; any RSVP's required; any events that allow a player to bring a non-member guest; event codes; a succinct description of the offer; additional information identifying the tier segments; and the database operator/report generator's name and ID (in this example it was my aforementioned friend Steve Sohng).

The targeting criteria for this particular mailing also segmented players by ADA (Average Daily *Actual* casino win)weighted against the ADT. This measure came about from that debate between Steve and myself (that I talked about in Chapter Eight). My insistence on an Actual win number was based on an extreme example that had happened to me, as a player, and later was reported to me as having happened to a number of players.

A few years earlier I had walked through a casino on my way to a conference at the hotel. On my way across the floor, I stopped at a slot machine, put in my player's card, and played $20 before going on my way. My THEO for that brief play was a mere $1.70 because the casino hold was 8½%. The problem was that I lost the entire $20 without winning a damned thing. My ACTUAL was $20 despite what the system reported as my theoretical.

The next day I did the exact same thing. At the end of the conference, five days later, I had a few hours to kill and I gambled about $1,500 total. My theo was $127.50 for that day. But like my previous days, I was very unlucky and I actually lost $500 instead of $127.

The standard ADT measurement of my play for that multi-day casino visit showed $130.90. In reality, the casino had earned $540 from me; a little more than four-times my theo. Mathematically the odds were that I would eventually level-off and my theo would be near the 8½% of what I gambled.

Also, this simplistic explanation did not take into account my "reinvestment" …which the actual player tracking system does. For example, even though I lost my entire $20 on my first session, it probably was not on one spin (though it could have been). More likely, as we have seen in previous chapters, I won a little and lost a little and continued that pattern until eventually I lost the entire $20. But the theo data did not differentiate between whether I lost it all at once or through reinvestment play.

From a purely customer service standpoint, this sort of sucked for me as a player. The casino viewed my theo as $127. To be comped free meals at their restaurant during my stay I needed a theo of $150 and to get my hotel room free I needed a theo of $400. I was told by the players club that I was, basically, shit out of luck.

Had the casino measured my ADA in addition to my ADT, then there would have been no problem. Moreover, all of the player tracking systems track ADA; but marketers weren't using it. The casino world revolved around ADT. Hence, my introduction of ADA into the mix.

The calendar offer in the example here is more advanced than the average casino mailing at the time. Almost all casinos put out monthly calendars; but even today, very few track them like this. They simply do not know how.

Most casino offers segmented the database by ADT and by most recent trip to the casino. For this mailing, Steve used my methodology of adding a third dimension (of frequency) to the mixture as well as a balance between ADT and ADA.

I had wanted to use that January 2004 calendar as a transitional test mailing. Traditionally a casino calendar was not segmented; it was sent in a sort of "one size fits all" package. I wanted to segment. Also, traditionally, segmentation of letters or postcards involved two dimensions and not three (and certainly not ADT *and* ADA).

At the time, most casinos that had begun experimenting with customer segmentation were slicing their database into two to six segments; very similar to the way my January calendar was sliced for the cash coupons. Meanwhile Harrah's casinos were winning database awards for using, reportedly, 80 different segments in their direct mail letter offers *(though according to one of their IT managers they were not using anything like my RFM patent-pending formulas)*. I had devised a methodology with 250+ segments and that January calendar was the first transition. While on paper that reads as possible mind-boggling excessive, in reality it is merely a function of computing power. It was my methodology that had excited my friend and mentor Bill Bennett.

Long before my Trump foray, casino super-company Harrah's began applying that rudimentary (albeit effective) modeling from their data. They were able to increase response to their direct mail pieces from 3% to 8% (as early as May 2000, according to the *Wall Street Journal*). Much more importantly, annual earning and the P/E ratio had a direct correlation to this "new kind of marketing". Imagine what the last ten years could have added to that mix had they possessed the tools to take their modeling to the next steps.

Several times in this book I have talked about standard player targeting models usually measuring player behavior with demographics charted in two dimensions: usually recency of spending and amount of spending. Except in the aforementioned paper catalog industry, the model of R.F.M. measurements (**recency** of visit, **frequency** of visits, and **monetary** value of visits) were almost never matched as a trio against geographic data, basic census data, demographic data, and basic behavior data for those groups. Hence rather than target highly-specialized offers tailored —*almost personally*— for each individual potential player, casinos shotgun players with a barrage of offers that may or may not hit the mark.

I keep saying that the combined elements of **Recency, Frequency, and Monetary value** (RFM) of a player have driven the traditional paper-catalog direct marketing for years. Beyond the simple L.L. Bean example I cited, the RFM method has allowed the testing of new products, new pricing, and targeting specific offers to match specific types of players. It also has allowed highly accurate analyses and projections of profits.

On the other hand, RFM has moved into that collection of buzzwords mimicked by casino marketers, agencies, and consultants. But back in 1999 when we published my little booklet on the subject and started speaking at the casino trade shows, it was an unheard of concept. Since then it has crept into the assemblage of buzzwords and in some cases the methodology of casino marketers (though it is questionable as to how many have actually understood the application of RFM).

Recency. This is when a player last gambled in our casino. The knowledge of how recently a player gambled gives us the *beginning* ability to project the value that player has (to us or to other casinos, if we chose to sell that player's name). It does not reveal, however, if this is a repeat player; a less important factor in venues where tourism, foot traffic and convention traffic are in play, but still important.

Frequency. This is how often a player comes in. We should be able to measure the frequency of casino players as either one-time visitors or as repeat players. (It can also factor in hands-per -hour at tables or (more likely) handle-pulls (or button pushes) per quarter-hour of slot play). However, this measure does not identify the last time the player visited us. They may have played 5 times last year; or once a month for five months.

These different behavioral patterns are VERY important for creating a marketing offer that will attract additional betting from different types of players. These two measures, together, give us two of the axis we need to plot a player's value. If we consider the left axis to be Recency, then we should be able to begin a simple chart of repeat player activity that looks like the chart below:

Played Today					
Played Within A Week					
Played Within 30 days					
Played this Quarter					
Played within a year					

If we consider a top axis (I use top rather than bottom for reasons that will make sense shortly) to be Frequency, then we should be able to put together a full graphical analysis of two dimensions of our players. (For the purpose of this basic illustration, we will exclude the plays-per -hour portion of the Frequency plotting ... though in real application of this technique it is an essential element for accurate projections.

	Played 5 times or more	Played 4 times	Played 3 times	Played twice	Played once
Played Today					
Played Within A Week					
Played Within 30 days					
Played this Quarter					
Played within a year					

Having established two axes for player plotting, let's identify each of the positions where we should be able to enter data to plot player behavior. In each block we should be able to insert the number of (or the names of) players who match the criteria for that block.

To simplify this example, for illustration, I am using casino players but you could replace them with any type of customers in almost any business. Likewise, for the purpose of illustration I am only including 25 possible plotting positions for our players; in reality that number (for me) would be a minimum of 80 to 100, depending on the total size of the database.

To visualize the plotting for this example, we will identify each block with a letter of the alphabet.

315

	Played 5 times or more	Played 4 times	Played 3 times	Played twice	Played once
Played Today	A	B	C	D	E
Played Within A Week	F	G	H	I	J
Played Within 30 days	K	L	M	N	O
Played this Quarter	P	Q	R	S	T
Played within a year	U	V	W	X	Y

In this example above, players in block A played 5 times (or more) and played one of those times today. Likewise, players in Block F played 5 times and one of those times was this week. Continuing the plotting, players in Block Y played once last year. Players in block U played 5 times, but not in the past year...and so on.

This example-charting allows us to examine the behavior of our best players...either by number or by name (thanks to the miracle of database technology). This within itself is a powerful tool because it allows us immediately to tailor different offers to different players, based on this little bit of data.

In short, we can contact those players (for example) in Block U who spent with us five times but not recently. We can launch a marketing campaign to (a) determine why they have not been back, and (b) create an offer to entice them to come back. (That gets a little complicated, as we will see.)

Again, for the purpose of simplification in understanding the processes here, let's merge some of these blocks into quadrants so that we can easily see our best players, our worst players, and our borderline players. Even though we are using simple charts here, remember that in reality a computer is keeping track of all of this data for us and sorting the players into our categories. In reality, these seemingly time-consuming and expensive models are instant and virtually cost free.

Below, players in grid ABFGKL are our best players; while players in grid STXY are our worst players (in relative terms, of course). The other grids have varying values to us as good or bad players.

	Played 5 times or	Played 4 times	Played 3 times	Played twice	Played once
Played Today					
Played Within A Week	A, B, F, G, K, L		C H M R W	D, E, I, J, N, O	
Played Within 30 days					
Played this Quarter	P, Q, U, V			S, T, X, Y	
Played within a year					

Now if we also modify our axis to match our grids, we get a simplified chart that looks like this:

	Played 4 times or more	Played 3 times	Played once or twice
Played Today to 30 days ago	A, B, F, G, K, L	C H	D, E, I, J, N, O
Played this Quarter to one year ago	P, Q, U, V	M R W	S, T, X, Y

This over simplification very easily shows us how we, conceptually, should be able to rank players based on recency) and frequency data. We can also see how easy it is to start targeting specific offers to players based on their behavior (and therefore to what they are most like to respond).

This model holds true, unless we consider the possibility that each of the players in grid ABFGKL played 5¢ slots while the players in grid STXY each played $5 slots ...then suddenly our two dimensional graph is seriously skewed in any plan to use it to measure "good players". And it is herein that a lot of marketing fails in its striving for accuracy.

Fortunately, the Greek philosopher and mathematician Euclid taught us that the world is not two-dimensional. Equally fortunately, neither is the understanding of player history. The third dimension for us is Monetary Value.

Monetary Value. Pure and simple, this is how much money (a player gambles. Generally, for analytical purposes, this figure is the *average* spending for a repeat player.

Let's first consider the monetary value of players as a standalone chart. We will chart average bets placed in three per-gambling session categories: $1 to $100, $101 to $500, and $501 to ∞. This will be our left axis. The top axis, then, is a little more complex. If we rate the values as big spender, average spender, and worse spender, then the marketing task will be to determine what steps we must take in each category to increase a lower player to become a bigger spender. The top axis then is the category of spending:

	Big Spender	Average Spender	Worse Spender
$501-$1000	A		
$101-$500		B	
$1-$100			C

In the A block, all the players are already spending in our top (over simplified) segment, so no movement is necessary; however retention IS a major issue. In the B block, players must be retained AND move one level to become our best spending players. And in the C block the players must be retained and move two levels to become best...and move one level to even become average.

The Big Spender category, then, should receive the most attention in attempting to retain them, to get them to play more times and more often. The ones who spend almost nothing should have fewer resources dedicated to moving them toward spending more often and more times. This is one of many possible basic marketing strategies that most good marketers already deal with on a daily basis.

NOW...If we superimpose this model onto our "R" and "F" chart from above, we should be able to quickly see that a player who spends the most AND has recently played and plays often is our very best player. Likewise the player who spends the least, has only played once, and has not played in the past year...is the worst player. Everyone else falls somewhere between in a (vastly over simplified) three -dimensional graph of this RFM data.

Among the magical formulas that direct-marketing gurus talk about are rating formulas for players...using the RFM history that we keep for each player. Without taking the time here to teach an entire RFM rating systems (and thereby lose the focus of this look at Marketing Donald Trump), let us assume that we have developed a rating system that gives us 10 different categories of players, ranking from 0 to 9. For this simplified example: Category 9 players are those very best players who play often, gambled recently, and spend a lot of money; Category 0 casino visitors played twice, haven't played in more than a year, and their average spending was a mere $2; Categories 1-8 all fall mathematically between those two extreme poles.

With this method of sorting the player data, we now have a powerful personalization tool to add to our existing arsenal of explicit user ratings, observed behavior, and demographic/psychographic information. We can create an highly-targeted offer based on this RFM table. Of course, this table is vastly simplistic for the purpose of example; however it does illustrate the general technique.

For example, if I am a player who ranks in category 9, I might warrant personalized attention from a host, some outbound telemarketing, and a series of incentives that match other players like me. My offer would point me to specific games and even days of the week to visit (all based on my history as well as on my behavioral data). It would push up-sells and cross-sells to me based on casino. It would provide me with a personalized experience for my next visit based on my history and predicted behavior (measured against others in category 9). Creating an offer personalization with all the bells and whistles associated with suggestive selling is a monstrously complex process but, it is a process well worth the effort; and it can be further fine-tuned. Remember that this method has *proven* to increase revenue by 40% and more.

As I developed this methodology, I wanted to know how it stacked up against that award-winning Harrah's methodology that had Bill Bennett's attention. For my research to try to reverse engineer (or at least create a regression-analysis of) the Harrah's algorithms, I visited Harrah's in Tahoe twice, Harrah's in Las Vegas five times, Harrah's Las Vegas Rio Casino property twice, and Harrah's New Orleans' property once. In each case I deliberately played low-end 25¢ slot machines for a time-period of from one hour to up to three hours *(the proliferation of penny machines prevalent today had not begun in 1999, when I conducted the initial tests)*. My profile (which I filled out during my first Harrah's visit to get a "Total Rewards" player tracking card from them so they could rate me) clearly identified me as an executive with a high six-figure annual income who lives in a zip-code geo/demographic that is among the 5% most affluent in the United States.

After several hundreds of dollars of play at their properties across the country, my mail box was empty until the next quarter-year arrived. *Mental note number one: no instant letter generated to welcome me to their player's club.* Finally, Harrah's mailed me ONE offer (and only one): a FREE BUFFET in New Orleans valid only if I returned to play there. Where did their analysis came up with the supposition that I would (a) stand in line for a buffet anywhere, (b) visit New Orleans again (seeing as how 70% of my action was in Vegas), or (c) be enticed to fly from Florida to New Orleans for a free $7.95 meal?

The source of those mis-targeted was actually clear: They used typical limited dimensional analysis. They compared only certain elements of my behavior and not the full universe of information that SHOULD have been available to them to target me with a more suitable offer. Clearly they used geographic data and the subdivided that by theo; there was no other excuse. This one direct mail piece offering the buffet, instantly revealed the great failing and limitation of many so-called "state-of-the-art" systems.

Without analysis, the personalization of offers is little more than an attractive toy. Some readers will remember the 1970s and 1980s version of the PCH (Publishers Clearing House) "personalized" mailing that read something like:

> **GARY GREEN**   you have the opportunity to win millions for the   **GARY GREEN** household in   **PALM BEACH COUNTY FLORIDA** in this special offer created just for **GARY GREEN.**

That is pretty much "personalization" without analytical work. It is for the analysis, projections, budget management, marketing examination, advertising decisions, and a host of other operational considerations that we create *offers* rather than just random advertisements. Moreover, we need to be able to track the effectiveness of each offer targeted to each segment; this allows us to plan future offers.

At a bare minimum, an offer should analyze the cost per Promotion as well as the actual number of player visits driven by any given offer. We should be able to project spending from the offer, as well as project the number of plays. Far beyond merely providing reports, an offer should be incredibly configurable so that each personalized or suggested-action can be intensely analyzed for projections. Unfortunately, only a handful of marketers (even the ones using personalization and suggestive selling techniques) even now have learned how to target using these powerful formulas...or, alas, for that matter, even that such formulas exist beyond buzzwords.

Equally as important as calculating the formulas and creating offers, is the subsequent analysis of *effectiveness* and adding that follow-up analysis to the data mix (which also allows us to further segment and target players for future offers). There are a number of ways to do this, but for myself, I attach a "source code" to each offer.

I strongly recommend assigning a meaningful unique tracking and analysis number for each offer. A structured code for each offer will allow easier statistical analysis of an offer's variables; this is especially useful when dealing with dozens or scores of offers. If you look at a mailing that I send (or that most direct mailers send), you will notice a short code number above your name and address; that is the source code.

Typically I use a 16-digit alphanumeric code with the first eight digits identifying the offer itself, and the last eight identifying the use of that offer. The meaning of the distinction in these two terms (*offer code* and *use code*) will become apparent once we look at the structure of an offer itself.

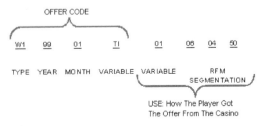

I begin the code by identifying the purpose of the offer (increase spending, increase visits, increase loyalty, acquire new players, retention, create a list, etc.). Next I need to know how the offer reached the player (direct mail; emails; advertisements; outbound telemarketing, junket affiliate networks; and so on). Using the example of that Trump29 calendar pre-event analysis, you saw that we listed the time frame

Above: A 16-digit source code strategy for offer and use allows analysis of return on advertising(for every dollar spent, how much comes back?).

that the offer would be available or repeated (including start date and stop dates of any particular offer).

Some offers may have required ADT or ADA levels (or "price points"); those need to be tracked. An offer should be able to specify which unit within the casino is responsible for the offer (players' club, slots department, table games, entertainment, F&B, etc.). We need to code a general description of the offer itself. In many cases my offers are tied to an analytical rebate (cash-back) table determined by either a percentage or a monetary amount.

A well-constructed offer should allow us to set up automatic promotional chains of subsequent events that help provide the ability to obtain an optimum conversion percentage. I say "optimum" because the *largest* conversion percentage may not be the most profitable for the casino to obtain. As we become able to define a virtually unlimited number of automatic promotional sequences, a good marketer should be able to test how many efforts (or the contents of efforts) yield the most profitable conversion percentage. Our source code should tie up-sells (and cross-sells) to offers at each player level.

In the source code, we need to track exactly what games or amenities of the casino are promoted for any specific offer. For pro forma analytical purposes, we should be able to specify expected revenue for each offer and then with post forma compare budget versus actual sales on an offer level. This too should be keyed to the first eight digits of that source code.

Moving to the next eight digits of *my* typical source code, I focus on the *use* of the offer. A use might be an RFM segment of the existing player base, or it might be the location and run of a particular advertisement, or the time slot for a TV spot. Think of a use as the distribution of the offer; what drove the player to that offer....how did the offer get into that player's hands. I include a code for when the offer begins and ends. My use code defines the date of the initial budget or when it is to be established and how often the offer ran. Beyond my RFM data, the use can allow additional segmentation clusters with criteria like average bet, game played most frequently, and, of course, demographics.

I also use this portion of the source code for more drilled-down analytical purposes, so I track cost of the offer here as well as well as the date the last forecast was produced (as it relates to this usage). Another operation of this use code can be to measure the "quantity" of that use, measured in player sessions or player visits per each one-thousand offers sent or viewed.

The rest of the use portion of the code may reflect advertising buys, junket affinity programs, bus programs, total impressions that reach the targeted market, etc. Finally, if the casino is supplementing their targeting with CRM type data, I attach that data to the "use" portion of my code. The combination of powerfully and flexibly configured offer and use codes together make a total source code that in turn can allow us to begin applying those magical formulas.

Keep in mind that the source code is an internal analytical tool and while I might include it on a mailing or a coupon for tracking (if for some reason I am not using bar codes), it does not need to be tied to the visual seen by the consumer/player.

Even at the time that I was doing that research, I was stunned at the number of major casino operators that were not (and still are not) using even this most simple player targeting methodology.

At the same time that I was testing the Harrah's award-winning techniques (that had sent me an offer to stand in line at a New Orleans buffet) I wanted to know how the rest of the industry was stacking up. I already had a good picture of Mirage Resorts (because of my encounter with Steve Wynn's issue between Mirage and Treasure Island), but I was curious how the other mega-operators were doing.

I decided my next target would be Park Place Entertainment's system. (Park Place, if you recall, was the spinoff of Hilton/Bally and has since been absorbed by Harrah's / Caesar's.) Over a three-month period I visited several of their Las Vegas casinos to play $1 slots for two to four hours per session with eight sessions during each visit. Painfully to me as a marketer, I discovered that any one of their casinos did not recognize me as having ever played at any of their other casinos because (as I was told) *"our computers do not talk to each other."* Even among their own brands I could not be identified as a rated player. It was the Steve Wynn problem all over again.

Most amusingly, I presented my Caesars' Las Vegas players' card to Caesars' in Tahoe and was informed that I needed a different card to play in Lake Tahoe (even though the cards themselves listed all of the Caesars' properties on them). Get this: the Tahoe plastic card actually had old-style computer punch-card holes in it so that it could be read without magnetic tape. I can't emphasize enough that this was in the 21st century...not decades ago.

ABOVE: The left photo is the Tahoe card *(check out the computer punch-holes)*; the right photo is the Vegas card *(look at the graphics on that card: the "Emperors Card" logo was haphazardly (and crooked) stuck on top of the background as if designed by a seventh grader)*.

To make matters worse, even though I had (by relative slot standards) a pretty high ADT, when I asked the *Las Vegas Hilton* (at that time the flagship of the chain) to comp a room for me based on my play over several weeks at their other properties, they quoted me a per-night rate that was *more than* the rack rate I could get booking the room on the Internet or through AAA. *This is the way to retain good players?*

Nonetheless, beginning the next quarter the Las Vegas Hilton did start (and continued to even though they have changed ownership twice) to mail to me almost every month a discounted room rate that is in fact a little less than rack.

No wonder Harrah's system was considered the industry's best; even with its absurdities it was heads and shoulders above the rest of the industry! Even the most rudimentary suggestive selling methodologies ...*the Harrah's package*... would indeed bring more visitors to a casino, convert more of those visitors to players, increase the number of returning players or additional play, and increase the average size of play. Even falling far short of a full targeting strategy, it was revolutionary for my industry.

It is indeed noteworthy, revolutionary, and a giant leap forward to have the best horse in the race at the county fair; but when everyone else is running Formula One race cars, that award-winning horse looks more and more like an old nag. The "state of the art" *CASINO* data-mining and marketing example is indeed THE best horse in the race. Unfortunately, this is a high-performance auto race in business and not a horse race.

Alone, the Harrah's personalization, cool as it was, allowed no means for analysis of the results...and especially no accurate method to *forecast* revenue. The technology just was not plugged into marketing.

A leading technologist for one of the major Nevada slot machine manufactures recently wrote to me: *"Every day I see how 'caveman' gaming is now. The simplest things — like using real TCP/IP STANDARD networking, NICs, CAT5 cable, routers and hubs you can buy at radio shack. NO they all have to invent their own bad systems of communication."*

In another sad example, a recent employment advertisement posted by giant MGM/Mirage (MGM Resorts International) warned potential *Marketing Manager* candidates:

"Must have ability to learn and master THREE DIFFERENT
Computer operating systems (hotel, slots, and casino)."

And this was for a *Marketing Manager* not for a computer technician! Yet no one stopped to ask, "WTF?" Bizarrely, in the casino industry this kind of nonsense is routine and doesn't raise a single eyebrow. In any other industry it would be laughable. *Personally*, I can't decide if I should laugh or cry.

A few years ago when Steve Wynn built *Wynn Las Vegas* (and later *Encore*), he spent millions of dollars to develop an in-house a system that solved many of these multi-system technology issues; but still did not address the marketing side of the issues.

With the exception of adherence to some basic business rules and decisions, the entire casino industry is saddled with these kinds of out-of-date methodologies...and not just in technology. When I initially addressed the management

323

prong of the equation I began by creating case studies of the management philosophies of the then-significant operators in the industry.

As I went through the early stages of formulating my methodology, Bill Bennett's former company, *The Mandalay Resort Group* gave me unprecedented access to their internal structure and organization. Now folded into the MGM giant, at the time they were the operators of Mandalay Bay, The Luxor, Excalibur, Circus-Circus, Slots of Fun, and several other properties.

Mandalay's corporate strategy at the time focused on what they called the *New Model vs. the Old Model.* Their "new model" revolved around earnings (EBITDA) being driven by a plan to link together the player data from all of their properties and then segment that mega-database into the largest groups. The plan was to focus those segments on "must see" destinations: Mandalay's various brands along what they called the "Masterplan Mile"—the stretch of the Las Vegas strip where their properties were all next door to each other (with the exception of Circus-Circus.

Specifically, Mandalay's stated corporate strategy was *"focusing on revenue management rather than unit group".* Their loyalty program was designed to identify the long-term value of those targeted players by *group* (rather than CRM-type focus on *individuals*). Consequently, their focus was on *rooms* rather than on *play* (this was congruent with Glenn Schaeffer's ferocious argument with me over concentrating on hotel average daily rate).

The Mandalay focus stood in sharp contrast to Harrah's focus on *relationship marketing.* Harrah's corporate focus was on nine specific corporate goals: (1) player card data collection; (2) data mining; (3) direct mail (4) telemarketing (5) yield management (6) internet functionality; (7) slot management; (8) e-commerce (separate from internet functionality); and (9) labor efficiency.

One remarkable thing about these contrasting philosophies was the year of these stated goals: 2001—a significantly forward-looking strategy take by Harrah's versus a very 1980-ish "new model" from Mandalay.

As dramatic illustration of these differences, consider the charts below. In each group, the first slide is from Mandalay Resort Group's internal management presentation and the following slide is from Harrah's investor presentation the same year and month:

Harrah's Investor Presentation:

324

Mandalay Management Presentation:

Value Creation

New Model	Old Model
Revenue Management	**Unit Growth**
• Raise spending-per-room-unit	• Add rooms and casino pieces in regular cycles
• Capture "leakage" of customer spending at competitor properties. Cluster resorts	• Count on new jurisdictional opportunities
• Loyalty programs, identify customer's "worth"	
• Cut loss leaders	

Mandalay Management Presentation:

Old Metric

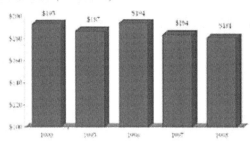

New Metric

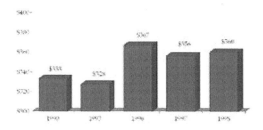

325

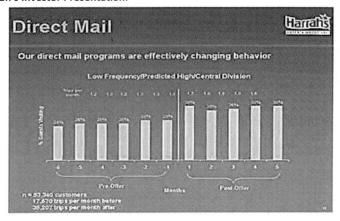

I realize that these decade-old internal documents are a little hard to read without straining, but they are important to understand the thinking at the time of the largest casino operators in the country.

The Mandalay model's understanding of data segmentation was driven by the genius-direction of Gregg Solomon, but in his role there he did not have the final authority to drive his insight into corporate policy as did Mandalay's CFO Glenn Schaeffer.

Neither approach was particularly right or wrong within the context of their corporate goals at the time. Disappointingly, neither even began to touch the real issues missing from such a player centric business; the personal level of marketing that I was developing.

The Mandalay model began on the right track but their own internal conflicts (including a power struggle to wrangle ownership away from my old mentor Bill Bennett) prohibited them from implementing the fundamentals that would allow the philosophy to translate to tangible operational procedures that would permeate through every level of the organization and have positive impact on the player base. Meanwhile, our friends at Harrah's, on the other hand, were focusing on the player experience and dictating company culture from the top down, but were doing so within the *retail* model of *CRM* rather than from the eccentricities of the world of gamblers.

That troublesome void became even more alarming when we realize that this was the "state-of-the-art" amongst large public corporations like Caesar's (Harrah's), MGM/Mirage, and the former Park Place Entertainment, Mandalay Resorts Group, Trump Casinos, etc. The smaller operators (second and third tier) were working in the 19th century compared to the rest of the business world and a good decade or two behind even the rest of the casino industry.

This would not be so bad if it were not for the size of the existing consumer market. During *that* time period, Harrah's reported 300+ million casino visits a year. A decade later the market had grown incredibly larger.

Even though the Las Vegas Convention and Visitors Authority reported that the prototypical Las Vegas visitor in 2011 was a 49-year-old, white, married, Southern California man who had a college degree and earned $100,000 a year or more, that is clearly not the demographic nationwide for visitors to hundreds of "local" casinos. In 2011 there were more than 956-million casino visits; Harrah's reported 40-million *members in their player's club*.

The scary thing is that the nuts-and-bolts of the marketing methodologies, the philosophy of top management and operators, and the relationships between technologists and marketers and operators have all changed very little in the past decade. Those intermediate steps from traditional segmentation to even rudimentary RFM targeting —*basically the same methodology I used for the January 2004 Trump29 calendar example*— represent "advanced" casino targeting almost a half-decade later.

What *has* changed is the technology itself. With the exception of large segments of the Class II universe, various casino management systems, accounting systems, and slot machine "backend" systems, all communicate universally. This has been primarily though the tireless work of a non-profit group called the *Gaming Standards Association* (GSA), its visionary president Peter DeRaedt and farsighted operators like Gregg Solomon. The simple technology "solution" that I had sketched on the back of a napkin for Steve Wynn was equaled, expanded, and far-surpassed by their brilliantly *forcing* the industry into technological common sense. Their work was so successful that the initial problem of systems communication disappeared.

My marketing issues, however, were beyond the scope of their mission. I had begun trying to address those marketing deficiencies with my appearance at that *World Gaming Congress* where I laid the ground work for my widely-distributed white paper *"Casino Executives Meet 21ˢᵗ Century Technology"*. That paper became one of the driving factors for many casino operators' move toward more advanced (and more profitable) player-tracking and decision-support systems. It also sparked my subsequent direct and indirect consulting for a half-dozen of the major Las Vegas strip operators and became the basis of that little booklet on the subject *(A Marketing-Driven Casino Operational Business Plan [ASIN: B000AOJA5M])*.

As I have mentioned several times, in the more than a dozen years since that first WGC seminar, gaming technology guru Tom Trimble and I even went so far as to create an automated system that would provide the marketing support and management decisions outlined in my RFM model.

Tom, who I have cited often in this book, is widely known in the industry as a highly skilled senior executive who has headed an extensive range of technology-based projects from casino management systems to slot operations. Combining that with a deep understanding of database structure and database marketing, in order to increase player loyalty and database productivity, Tom tackled my parameters from a technological standpoint. Tom is trained and certified Project Manager and experienced with casino operations from the smallest location to a major Las Vegas strip resort. He managed the software development and consulting team for Steve Wynn's aforementioned move to incorporate financial management, analytical reporting, and data warehouse, a player value analysis marketing system and an integrated web-based reservation system. He was also a VP-level distinguished member of the technical staff at Bell Laboratories.

Tom took my marketing management formulas to technology and created a management system called LogicComps; the system I discussed early in this book. Our goal was not only to automate my RFM methodology for hundreds of segments but also to automate the comping process based on surgical formulas. Since we began that project, several systems have created automated entire comping based on accumulation of points and assigning a point-based price tag to various casino amenities (meals, rooms, show tickets, gifts, playable credits, etc.). While those improvements in players' club technology have been more akin to an automated shopping list, Tom's innovations were light-years ahead by taking traditional casino-host functions to a highly personalized targeting, and thus arming hosts with tools which until now they could only dream.

Specifically, his methodology and business system involved the use of internet-type "Cloud" technologies, fed by real time communications between disparate point of sale software and hardware systems through a "third party" server. His data collection was based on Peter DeRaedt's GSA standards. He took an amalgamation of the combined data from multiple systems into one coherent, light weight and manageable database accessible through a web based interface (that required only minimal training to use).

Tom's system's automated creation of player offers, comps, and incentives (all based on my RFM data model) combined with behavioral, psychographic, and demographic targeting and matching in real-time player activity, point-of-sale, and other data. In short, the system automated the entire process so that any *clerical level* employee could implement what otherwise was expensive, time-consuming, manual, and management-heavy operations.

Keep in mind that when we *manually* implemented this methodology for Trump29, it rocketed revenue from $45-million monthly to a consistent $100-million monthly. In a nutshell, Tom Trimble automated a multi-million-dollar process so that *any* casino could afford it without specialized knowledge or expertise; Gary-In-A-Box

Remember earlier when I talked about casino the housekeeper in Oklahoma who was the only staff member able to identify the best players. I pointed out that the average visitor to the casino only sees valets, housekeepers, slot attendants, cashiers and security guards; No General Manager; no Marketing Director; and certainly, no Owner. The few people that the visitor does see are, regardless of their job title, are THE representatives of the casino; they are marketers. For those employees to be successful, top casino management must understand that marketing begins at that level. Beyond general management, the operators and owners need to "get it". You will see why, shortly.

I have talked a lot about marketing in this book; and spent an entire chapter talking about the importance of data and how to use it once we have it. Just as Tip O'Neil once said, *"all politics is local,"* so too is it true that all marketing is local: one-on-one contact (or the semblance thereof) is the most effective tool for generating player play. When I teach marketing seminars I almost always tell people that Marketing 101 is very simple: find out who your best players are and go get a lot more just like them.

Any marketer worth her or his salt — whether they are marketing slot machine play or Cheerios — lives and dies by data. Player information: who are the players; where are they; how often do they spend; how much will they spend; what is their behavior. Obviously you cannot target an audience, even with a brand as strong as Donald Trump, unless you know who is turned-on by that brand and what it represents (and conversely, who is turned off by it). You can't find more of the good players unless you know who the existing good players are, how they spend, and what excites them.

While casinos share many tenets of traditional marketing, there are many eccentricities to casino marketing. In casinos we have neither products with shelf-life nor a particular service. We don't have sales channels, price points (except game denominations), or many of the other standards of the marketing process.

As I noted in earlier chapters, casinos have the same slot machines with the same price points and payouts. Competing casinos all have similar buffets, high-end restaurants, interchangeable cocktail waitresses, entertainment, players clubs, staff, and even the same ugly carpet.

Casino marketing is, of course, part branding, part market-positioning and part player maintenance and expansion. Casino marketing is promotion-driven, event-driven, and incentive driven. I am a fan of effective bus programs, weekly premiums, and highly-targeted cash-back programs. I think high-end advertising programs (like the genius campaigns produced for me over a decade by companies like Frank Palmieri's *Media and Marketing*) are absolutely essential to branding and can (and should) be entwined with the direct mail programs.

Though I could certainly write a casino marketing manual (and someday may do so), that is not the intent here. What I can say though is that marketing is all about that player relationship. It is very personal player service. It is all about player service. As I have preached, lectured, begged, and demanded since before publication of that 1999 *World Gaming Congress* presentation, every single employee of the casino is a player service employee; every single employee is a marketing employee. Casino operational management must absolutely be marketing-driven, player-service-oriented management.

The branding, promotions, images, flash, and pomp are all essential features of casino marketing and absolutely necessary to the process of bringing in players and getting maximum play from them. Those are, very specifically, the *"front-of-the-house"* functions and that is where Bunky's chickens, and the Flying Elvi, and The Apprentice, my crazy television spots, all are indispensable. Make no mistake that a long-term successful casino cannot and should not operate without that flash. At the same time, make no mistake about it, such flash is just like a casino calendar; without the complex *"back-of-the-house"* elements it is a waste of time and resources.

Few casino marketers "get" that. Fewer casino operators get it. Odd as it may seem, Donald Trump did get it.

Chapter Seventeen
How To Manage, Finance, and Market Casinos

"Because a thing seems difficult for you, do not think it impossible for <u>anyone</u> to accomplish."
— **Marcus Aurelius**

How does a casino measure success? How profitable can (or should) a casino be? What *return on investment* should casino owners expect? How much debt can a casino realistically service? I have spent an entire book, here, tangentially ranting and raving about my proposition that the model for the *gambling racket* is fundamentally different from other business models. At the same time, whatever the model is, we need a way to project, measure, and analyze the *business*.

Without a basic understanding of seemingly intangible metrics, any promising casino enterprise cannot possibly expect to maintain long term revenue or support essential innovation and growth. Without answers to these basic questions, a casino cannot feasibly run smoothly, nor can investors confidently look ahead.

For those reasons (and others we will examine) I can instantly tell you that, statistically, a casino should expect a minimum 25% of its revenue to be left for earnings. We can call that a thumbnail measure and note that it cost about 75% of revenue to operate a casino. That number will vary wildly based on dozens of variables and can be reduced to 50% and less; however, it is a good concise representation and summary number.

This vast generalization is useful for owners, developers, operators, and analysts; but it is also interesting to serious players and patrons. If you are involved with a property not operating at least at that ratio, then it is time to make some major adjustments. If you are doing better: then more power to you (though some fine tuning formulas may be useful to you). And if you are thinking of becoming involved in a property, *now* you realistically know what to expect.

That is the axiomatic bottom line. The actual metrics that answer most of those questions are woven into ownership decisions about what to do with that 25% (or more). In every case, in order to drill down and identify those specific metrics, we need to begin with some fundamental data-gathering and analytical formulas. From those basics we can see where I came up with that 25% number and how we can translate that to a real number for any specific situation.

When I talk about valuation of casinos, I prefer to do so in terms of operating ratios rather than the old *"sum-of-the-parts"* analysis. Casino companies that have relied on that old analysis format have habitually been over valued; even in the great recession, consider the price of Vegas of land along the Vegas strip and properties on the market for obscene double-digit multiples of EBITDA (probably as much because of the high beta and preposterous cash flow within casino investments). Unfortunately, the more "street" traditional valuations have repeatedly gestated company finance and growth plans that have not come to fruition. Companies otherwise brilliant in Wall Street acumen (Harrah's, Colony Capital, and others) have track records that at least indicate they should focus on their core competencies.

Even as more and more casino operators focus their operating plans on loyalty cards (to track play time, spending, game preference, and frequency of visits) the investment-seekers continue to tout benchmarks like *"same store sales"* and *"business unit distinction"* when valuing casinos. This methodology is not helped by the Sheldon Adelson pronouncement that he is not in the *casino* business. In copycat fashion, many operators have focused investors on non-gaming amenities to drive spending-per-visitor; it is the old debate between Glenn Schaeffer and me in the transformation from gambling halls to destination resorts. While some of the Vegas properties can accurately report that gambling produces as little as 22% of their *revenue*, further analysis reveals that gambling also produces at least 48%-to-52% of their *profit* [67].

Outside of Vegas, the core Atlantic City demographic (for example) remains the 60-to-65-year-old female bus player who comes to play slot machines[68], the reality of which further drives a wedge between operational management and investment-fishing. Outside of Las Vegas, gaming continues to be responsible for upwards of 80% of casino property revenue. Thus my valuations are *casino* centric.

If we begin with that premise of gambling responsible for 80% of a property's revenue (with the remaining 20% spread between hotel, food & beverage, entertainment, retail, spas & salons, telephone & internet fees, etc.), then it is compulsory to drill down a bit into the gambling revenue itself. For properties that do not have that full range of amenities, this is even more essential.

Within the 80%+ revenue generated by gambling, the majority of *that* comes from slot machines. In fact, when we translate revenue to profit, only about 4% of a casino's profit comes from table games[69], primarily because of the high labor cost, credit expenses, and comp expenses tied to table operations. Only casinos that cater to high-end play (Venetian, Wynn, Bellagio, Caesar's, and so on) are likely to have a higher percentage of income from tables[70].

Consequently, a more accurate starting point to answer those pressing questions is to begin with some fundamental information about slot machine revenue. Once we have a good understanding of some of *those* basics, we can begin to measure the efficiency of a company's use of its assets in generating its revenue. From there, when we can determine how effectively those assets are deployed, *then* we can measure *risk tolerance* and discuss *debt to equity ratios* and other metrics that will actually be grounded in hard numbers rather than the ever-popular *forward-looking statements*.

332

Many important operating, investing, financing, and even player-choice decisions can be projected from some of the key indicators that will be generated from our starting point.

The ability of the casino to meet short-term obligations can be easily estimated from expected cash, cash-equivalents, receivables, inventory of owned games, and prepaid expenses all —weighed against payables and accrued expenses. If the value of current (or projected) assets is significantly greater than the current (or projected) liabilities, then we have a strong starting point for casino financing.

One important measure is the value of the slot machines (and other assets) weighed against the projected amount of play. This value also includes the *costs* of leased machines and helps us figure how many machines we can support at any given property.

Traditional debt management ratios are often misleading in gaming; and especially when financing Native American casinos. An unusually low debt ratio often means that a Tribe's funds (outside of gaming) may be supporting the property; this was certainly Treasurer Ellis' situation when I arrived at Thunderbird. Typically, in such cases, debt can be better understood if it is assessed against owner equity investment.

Ultimately, however, most of the answers to those pressing questions are going to be management-controlled judgments, measurable by looking at the decisions and plans for post-EBITDA net-net —compared to revenue *(as well as management's plans and ability to generate profits with its machine and marketing strategies)*. This provides a microscopic look at the return on actual equity after debt service.

So the first things I need to know about a casino are *where is it* and *who will be the players*. This information is best provided in an independent and *reputable* feasibility study or market analysis[71], but for initial analysis (and smaller properties) many times this can be self-generated. I need these statistics because they ultimately will tell me how many slot machines the property can support and what win-per-unit-per-day I can expect.

I need an economic/demographic analysis of the population, growth trends, income, employment, transportation, local attractions, potential traffic interception, and proposed targeted players.

I need a really good look at the competitive environment; to casinos within a 100-mile radius, including win-per-unit at those properties (in jurisdictions where it is available), number of games, types of games, and some measure of market saturation.

I need to know the propensity for gaming within the targeted population and the frequency of gaming at those competitive properties. As another sweeping generality rule-of-thumb, I generally posit gambling propensity of a population (excluding special circumstances) at around 40% for Class III slot machines and a little more than half that for a strictly Class II facility (again, barring special circumstances). This discrepancy in propensity between slot machines and Bin-

333

go-based machines is not so much based on my frenzied ranting about virtual Bingo as it is the *general* nature of Class II properties. Typically a non-compacted or Class II casino is geographically located rural, alone and away from other casinos and without the benefit of property clustering. More importantly the game selection is generally limited in Class II casinos, both in terms of variety and vendors.

With the amalgamation of this information we can determine the optimum number of slot machines, denominations, and projected win per unit per day.

Okay, let's start building an example here to see how all of this fits together. For the purpose of this example, let's assume the feasibility study (or a comparative analysis of the competition) tells us that we can support 500 slot machines that would win $100-per-machine-per-day. That translates to gross slot machine revenue of $50,000 per day or about $ 1.5-million per month ($18.25-million annually).

At this point we can look at our revenue one of two ways; we can stop at that $18.25-million figure and consider table games and the other amenities a "break even" wash that ultimately costs us nothing but sufficiently pays for itself. This model is useful for slot-only houses and for general "thirty-thousand-foot overviews" when looking at a full service casino with a full gaming complement. Alternatively, we can use the rule of thumb that slots account for about 80% of total revenue (outside of Vegas resort destinations). In that case, the total revenue number for this example would be $22,812,500 (with $18.25-million representing 80% of that).

Now let's see what it costs us to operate the casino. Goldman Sachs and some other investment banking analysts have suggested that the majority of casino expenses are fixed costs. In fact Goldman goes so far as to argue, *"The opportunity for meaningful margin expansion is somewhat difficult, as 60% -70% of operators' costs are fixed[72]."* Goldman cites labor as one of those fixed expenses due to unionization, regulatory issues, room cleaning issues, and intense player service required.

With all due respect to the investment banking giant, that is simply not true outside of Atlantic City, Las Vegas, and any jurisdiction where union contracts determine FTEs. It is prima-facie obvious, for example, if you have five table games you need less employees than a property with 200 tables and if you have 50 hotel rooms you need fewer housekeepers than if you have 500 rooms.

What *are* fixed, however, are cost *ratios* in which variances are only actual numbers, according to casino size, revenue, and competitive factors. Even Goldman acknowledges that methodology; they project maintenance costs at 10% to 15% of revenue and they recognize that marketing and promotional expenses can vary as well.

To formulate those ratios, there are a number of good sources for comparing revenue to operating expenses. Nevada Gaming Control publishes an annual *Nevada Gaming Abstract*, which makes a great companion to the Risk Management Association's *Hotel / Casinos, Credit Considerations* documents. Several gaming states publish similar casino reports that, when poured over, can help shape your expected fixed ratios of operating costs.

I generally add to that mix my own years of casino operational experience and the pundit advice of my various in-casino financial gurus like (the afore-often-mentioned Frank Haas, and others). I have saved the reader the trouble of having

ABOVE: An excerpt from the 240-page Nevada Gaming Abstract for 2011

to sort through abstracts and thirty-plus-years of operational experience by preparing an easy to follow table benchmarking what percentages of gross casino revenue should be spent on common line-categories. Again, these are generalizations (albeit accurate ones) and are subject to modification based on any number of specific factors for specific properties. Nonetheless, this thumbnail view is a good general overview of costs to be weighed against revenue.

Operational costs, excluding labor and rev-share deals for slot machines should come in at around 27%-28% of casino revenue and look like this (in order of largest costs):

Marketing & Promotions (including Advertising)	9.20%
Other G&A	6.70%
Comps & Cash Back	4.00%
Bank/credit card/check cashing/bad debt	1.98%
Supplies	1.06%
Utilities/telephone	0.98%
Repairs & Maintenance Expense	0.72%
Busing Expense	0.55%
Training, Travel, Meals & Entertainment	0.51%
Insurance	0.36%
Over/Short Expense	0.30%
Fees	0.25%
Printing, Postage, Dues & Subscriptions	0.21%
Donations and Sponsorships	0.10%
Equipment	0.10%
Laundry/Uniform Expense	0.10%

TOTAL 27.12%

If we throw into that mix the cost of labor, it significantly increases operating expenses to 54.43% of casino revenue.

Labor	23.35%
Employee Benefits	2.96%
Employee Incentives	0.51%
Contract Labor	0.49%
TOTAL LABOR COST	**27.31%**

Keep in mind that my management philosophy is heavily marketing oriented. In Nevada that marketing percentage averages only 1.4%, at Trump it was 7%, and the national figures float between 2.68% and 11.20% depending on local-specific factors. For a casino that I am not operating, let's cut the marketing line down to a closer-to-standard 4%. That reduces your operating costs, excluding labor, to 49.23%.

Additionally, I calculate expenses with a relatively high labor number (23.35%) and a generous incentive figure (.51% of revenue). I do that because I take into account the propensity toward considerable nepotism and its attendant over-compensation in many Native American casinos as well as (true to the Goldman commentary) regulatory staffing minimum in many jurisdictions. For a more "middle of the road" number, that 23.35% can be reduced to a more standard 14% of revenue and the incentives program cut to 0.30%.

With those changes (combined with the marketing changes), total casino operating costs can be posited at 39.67% of revenue.

Typically, when I discuss operational costs of a mature and well-run casino, I use the 39% to 42% range. I dramatically increase that number for start-ups that will be marketing intensive during the first couple of years; I also increase it for a variety of other special circumstances.

If we go back to my initial example of these valuations, we can take that $18.25-million annual revenue figure and project that it cost approximately $7,338,950 to operate that fictional casino leaving an EBITDA figure of $11,161,050.

What this number does *not* include is the issue of how the casino is going to pay for the slot machines. If the casino makes the decision exclusively to revenue share (lease) the games, then the cost comes off the top as a percentage of *casino win*. If the casino makes the decision to purchase games, then unless there is a huge cash reserve we are looking at servicing a sizable debt. In this one example 500 games at top-of-line-price $18,000 each would cost us $9-million.

As I have discussed elsewhere in this book, the standard revenue share lease fee is 20% of win per unit. Some premium games, as I have discussed, will cost more than the standard 20%; and progressives (the WAPS and LAPS that I have discussed) will require additional contribution from that win figure.

If the casino is going to lease slot machines, then for our purpose the initial revenue number must be reduced by 20.06% to cover the leases and contributions. In this method, actual operating costs are 59.73% to 74.49%. The latter number takes into account my higher marketing number, my higher labor number, and leasing games rather than purchasing them. In short, you go back to the beginning of this chapter where I began, *"I can instantly tell you that, statistically, a casino should expect a minimum 25% of its revenue to be left for earnings."*

The big variables, then, are: (1) how the casino pays for the slot machines; (2) what the casino spends on marketing and labor; and (3) how well operational management conforms to and meets my budgetary formulas. Therefore the answers to all of those questions, where we began, are all tied to management capabilities, competence, and ultimately management philosophy.

It comes down to following the formulas and sticking to them. If that can be done then this is a highly-predictable and formulaic business; if it is not done, then the business is not so predictable. A decade ago when I left Trump29, my parting words were *"don't change my formula; stick to it and you will continue to grow at this rate"*; and, for almost a year after I left for Oklahoma, they continued with my formulas and the indisputable successes those formulas generated. It wasn't until some wag came along who decided that "instinct" was somehow better than scientific formula that the numbers began to drop ... *dramatically.*

That critical determination of how to pay for the slot machines has such a dramatic impact on all of the key metrics that we need to make a detailed analysis of *that* management decision before we tackle those other two issues. In fact, all three of the determinant factors are functions of management.

In recent years more theme-licensed slot machines have been introduced and promoted; every casino industry trade show touts a bevy of new titles or themes. Most of the new games are the same platforms (the same math, the same winning patterns, same hold, same par sheets, etc.), but the pictures and sounds change to the new pop culture themes to make them high in consumer (player) demand. Recent years have brought us slot machines themed with *Batman, Michael Jackson, Dolly Parton,* the *CSI* television franchises, *Family Guy, Judge Judy, Sex and the City,* the *Hangover* movie, and the list goes on and on...and on...especially with downloadable games and the likes of the SbX platform (which is an entirely new platform and math).

More importantly for this discussion, revenue per machine has increased dramatically in recent years. In mid-2012, when doing due diligence for the purchase of the Trump Plaza in Atlantic City, I was pained to find the majority of the machines at the casino to be three-coin 25¢ stepper-reel old-style slot machines. Those games have a maximum bet of 75¢ and statistically a maximum of 7 spins per minute, 420 spins per hour, and 10,080 spins per day. The maximum daily possible win per unit with an 8½% hold was $642.60.

Let's compare that to the *modern* games that I would replace them with at Trump Plaza. Consider penny video slots; 25-lines with a maximum of nine credits per line and thus a maximum bet of $2.25 per spin. Video slots have more bonus rounds and video "things" going on the screen and hence they are a little slower in play that their stepper-reel predecessors. A video slot machine is good for only about 6 spins per minute, 360 spins an hour, or 8,640 plays per day; basically 14% fewer plays with a video slot. However, because of the increased maximum bet, the maximum win per unit at that same 8½% hold is $1,652.40 — two and a half times more earning potential than the older games. Moreover, the average bet on a 25¢ three-coin stepper is 57¢ where the average bet on the penny games is 83¢. *(This, by the way, opens a marketing opportunity to increase that number with holds, assigned points, etc. Silly as it sounds, most current player tracking systems assign a higher point-value to the quarter player with 75¢ per spin than the penny player at $4.95 a spin —because pennies are a smaller denomination than quarters. More absurdly, as recently as October 2012 one major manufacture told me that they adjust their penny machines to have a higher hold than quarter machines because pennies are such a small denomination; again, because even at $4.95 per spin for pennies and 75¢ per spin for quarters.)*

In addition, the technology itself has begun changing at a faster pace than in previous slot machine versions. For example, today server-based games are permeating the Class III market to allow downloadable games and the changing of themes on-the-fly. No matter how you stack it, it is absolutely necessary to have the latest-and-greatest in machine technologies; and the ability to swap-out machines quickly and easily.

You remember the constant debates I had with Shawnee Treasurer Russell Ellis over lease versus purchase of machines; in the long run Ellis was right about at least the constantly changing games. The life-cycles of slot machines have become shorter and shorter.

Remember, too, that some games are simply not for sale. As we have discussed in this book, many royalty-based themed games are for lease only because the manufacturer's deal with the theme copyright holder is for a percentage of win per machine. Other games are not for sale because they are part of WAP networks, while still others are not for direct sale because they are co-owned by various third parties. That means that if the decision is made to purchase games rather than lease games, still at least some portion of a fully-competitive floor *cannot* be purchased.

All of these factors, together, make the decision of *lease contrasted with purchase* even more critical for management. As noted earlier, purchasing a new slot machine cost (as of this writing) between $7,500 and $18,000 (varying so much because of vendor, theme and title, popularity, and other variables).

Let's contrast that price tag to the cost of a revenue-share lease agreement. We will assume the rev share to be the basic 20% of daily win per unit being paid as the lease fee. The first line of the chart below shows daily win per unit from $100 to $350. The second line of the chart below shows what the casino pays over five years of a lease agreement:

Amount paid for leased game over five year period:

win per unit per day	$100	$200	$250	$300	$350
20% rev share for 5 years	$36,500	$73,000	$91,250	$109,500	$127,750

If we take the purchase price of a machine and subtract that from the lease payments over the five year term, we can chart how much more, per machine, the lease costs the casino over purchasing the games:

Amount paid over and above retail price of machine:

win per unit per day	$100	$200	$250	$300	$350
at purchase price $7,500	$29,000	$65,500	$83,750	$102,000	$120,250
at purchase price $18,000	$18,500	$55,000	$73,250	$91,500	$109,750

Of course this simplistic comparison does not take into account the *costs of ownership* of the games. These costs include parts and servicing, depreciation, various conversion kits to update the games over the five-year lease term, machine down time, and so on. *Once again, what is better than owning a casino? Owning the games inside.*

At the same time, my revenue share chart only shows one type of revenue share: the 80/20 split. There are uncountable variations of leases ranging from daily fees to coin-in fees to combinations of fees. In any scenario, the daily operating cost per machine needs to be calculated into management's formula for the decision to lease or purchase.

Let's revisit the difference in revenue between purchase and lease, but this time let's look at that difference *per year* and *per day*:

win per unit per day	$100	$200	$250	$300	$350
lease cost per year	$7,300	$14,600	$18,250	$21,900	$25,550
Lease cost per day	$20	$40	$50	$60	$70

This is where experienced management becomes essential. In the third or fourth year of ownership, with a win-per-unit of only $100 per day... *$20 a day* might be worth it to the casino to be able to reduce some of those operating costs and have the latest-and-greatest titles and themes through no-cost lease change outs. At $70 per day, though, it might be a tougher pill to swallow. On the other hand, by the third or fourth year that $350 win-per-unit machine might not be competitive with the hottest theme and cutting-edge technology, so what may have been a $350 win-per-unit machine in the first year, by the fourth year it may be just a $100 win-per-unit machine. In this case a diminishing returns report kicks in and a complex calculation can determine the actual value of the machine.

A good slot manager should be able to produce a P&L for each individual game so that future management decisions can be based on the total cost of operating the machine, the revenue to per square foot of casino floor, hour performance, and a full accounting of the age of the game (as opposed to the age of the cabinet in which the game is housed). In many cases there may be a mixture of leased and purchased games on the floor; and in some cases the slot vendors will allow a rev-share that is actually a fixed-price lease-purchase agreement with a sales price and interest collected like a rev-share until the target return is reached.

In deciding between a lease and purchase, decisions have to be about such issues as whether the casino or the vendor will cover the costs of changing themes, converting denominations, refurbishing cabinets, changing location on the floor, marketing specific games, and dozens of other related decisions. Additionally, policy management and financial management executives need to determine the cost of money the casino will have to pay to borrow funds to buy the machines and then the depreciated value of the machines as an asset (as well as the tax value of that depreciation.)

I offer one more example of slot machine decision tables. Let's make some basic assumptions of buying the most expensive machine, having a WPUPD of $100 *(though most new machines perform considerably better, this is good for the math)*, and a 20% yearly decline in win because of new technologies and other aging factors.

PURCHASE IRR	1st year	2nd year	3rd year	4th year	5th year	Total
Price of machine	($18,500)	$0	$0	$0	$0	($18,500)
Annual win	$36,500	$29,200	$23,360	$18,688	$14,950	$122,698
Net Profit	$18,000	$29,200	$23,360	$18,688	$14,950	$104,198

Even with declining win per unit, the net profit on the machine is more than $100,000 or an IRR (internal rate of return) on the investment of 176.90% An IRR metric is standard for helping management decide if they should make an investment; it is a standard indicator of the efficiency or quality of an investment.

Where this becomes complex is when comparing purchased games' IRR to IRR for leased games —*assuming the lease terms and conditions are negotiated favorably by casino management and not just accepted as a form lease from the vendor.* With the right terms, the casino can require the vendor to replace the machine (without charge) whenever a new latest-and-greatest is released or when, over time, the machine's WPUPD falls below a pre-determined minimum.

Lease IRR	1st year	2nd year	3rd year	4th year	5th year	Total
Price of machine	$0	$0	$0	$0	$0	$0
Annual win	$36,500	$36,500	$36,500	$36,500	$36,500	$182,500
20% lease fee	$7,300	$7,300	$7,300	$7,300	$7,300	$36,500
Net Profit	$29,200	$29,200	$29,200	$29,200	$29,200	$146,000

From these two tables, leasing a machine actually gives the casino $41,802 net revenue *more than* buying the machines would provide. The lease model provides some incalculable IRR (something like 292,000% if we posit the casino's price of machine at an installation labor minimal $10).

The lease model, then, benefits both the vendor and the casino more than the purchase model benefits either —again, if and ONLY if management has the skills, ability, wherewithal, and experience to negotiate a contract *with those favorable terms.*

In short, while on the surface *lease versus purchase* may seem like a no-brainer, clearly the decision has such a major impact on the business model itself that the "no-brainer" becomes a complex key indicator of the soundness of the business. The decision involves performance, value, negotiations, availability of finance and cash flow options of the casino, and a headache-giving myriad of other management assessments and actions.

Those complexities of slot management decisions are indicative of the cosmos of issues relating to how well operational management conforms to and meets the budgetary formulas established by the policy management executives. Every area of casino management, finance, and marketing is equally (or more) complicated as the slot decisions, though not always as palpably so.

To answer those initial pressing questions for operators, then, we need to explore the rest of the equation: what the casino spends on marketing and labor; and how well operational management conforms to and meets my budgetary formulas. That brings us to a series of management necessities that unequivocally determine the outcome of those issues.

Paramount among these, I have discussed repeatedly throughout this book the dangers of *unregulated* or *under-regulated* gambling. The very integrity of a slot machine is a function of the regulatory process; a process designed to assure the machines are fair, secure, and able to be audited and operated correctly. We saw what happens in the unregulated *grey area.*

Remember the *"Tribal Internal Control Standards"* that I wrote for the Ottawa Tribe of Oklahoma? Such standards, usually mandated by law, provide not only slot machine standards but guidelines for surveillance, drop and count, security, employee and vendor background checks (approval, and licensing), and a dozen other areas.

Remember that nightmarish adventure of my first walk-though at Thunderbird Casino with David Cook? Without management enforcement of such regulations there are no guarantees that the calculation of WPUPD is accurate, that the person counting the cash is not a convicted thief, or that there are cameras actually trained on the cash (or even on slip-and-fall accidents).

With a strong regulatory compliance process, that five-dollar bill that was marked to look like a fifty at *Glacier Peaks Casino* could have never been passed. The only way to avoid such horror stories is to institute strict internal regulatory policies and procedures (P&P's), whether or not the jurisdiction requires them, regardless of who gets pissed off at the rules.

Compliance P&P's are absolutely necessary to ensure that casino assets are safeguarded; financial records are accurate and reliable; and that all casino transactions are performed only in accordance with management's authorization. Without such P&P's, there is no assurance that the casino can provide proper reporting of gaming revenue, fee, or taxes. Further, P&P's are necessary to assure that appropriate action is taken for any discrepancies in the accountability of assets (and to compare actual assets at specific intervals). Compliance also assures obedience of regulatory laws. It also defines employee functions, duties, and responsibilities.

In short, in order for any of the management policies or operational decisions to take effect, there *must* be a level of confidence and relative assurance that the basis of the business model is sound, protected, and verifiable. Hence, the very first step in the casino business is to create a strong compliance organization. That is exactly why the first phone calls I make for a new casino is to a cadre of regulatory consultants, agencies, trainers and advisors (the universe of David Cook, George Joseph, and others). I also make certain that written P&P's are in place and that every employee gets (and signs for) a copy of the policies and procedures that affect their jobs. P&P's are so essential that I have included a complete set of Tribal Casino P&P's in the Endnotes[73]. *(Again, I apologize for the ultra-fine print of such a long document.)*

Once compliance is in place, the next issue is staffing. After either reading or flipping through these pages, it should be obvious to the reader that one sure formula for disaster is the appointment of inexperienced operational managers without a mentoring or training program in place. Either experienced or mentored staff is unequivocally key to the success of a casino.

I walked into one casino (with almost 2,000 machines) whose marketing director's only experience was that he had sold real estate and worked in several political campaigns. I met a General Manager of another casino whose solitary experience was that he had been a general manager at a *Best Buy* store. One Tribe appointed a cage manager because "she looks like she could do that."

There are two good ways staff: either mentoring the uninitiated or hiring experienced experts; sometimes they are combined. Sometimes the decision is more political (at Tribal casinos or in ownership nepotism issues) and in other cases it is more financial. To hire a General Manager for a mid-sized casino-resort in Atlantic City I had to pay about a $500,0000 a year; the General Manager at a similar size (in terms of number of games) Indian casino near Tulsa Oklahoma was recently hired at $80,000. Such a dramatic disparity is not a simple function of marketing difference; it really is a matter of *"you get what you pay for"*.

I am a big fan of mentoring and providing training for employees who have potential to grow; this prevents me from having to require the manager "unlearn" mediocre or poor training. Remember that the majority of the casino woes I have talked about are related to what I have genteelly called *bad management*. Probably nine times out of ten (as the cliché goes) that *bad management* is more a function of poor (or no) training and mentoring than it is actual incompetence.

Not to sound like product placement (which it is not), but to succor that mentoring process, there are a plethora of really good consulting companies that train casino staff either on site or through a variety of seminars, conferences, and workshops. For the purest player service marketing, Dennis Conrad's *Raving Consulting* is almost unmatched; for table games it is hard to beat the expert training provided by Vic Taucer's *Casino Creations*; the aforementioned George Joseph's *Worldwide Casino Consulting* puts a lid on most casino crime (internal and external); and a list can go on and on.

Typically, I like to augment third-party training by personally mentoring managers for most departments. From a general HR standpoint, I tend to lean toward a more intense involvement than the ludicrously superficial approach of "team members" or "one big family." I recently saw an interview in which Steve Wynn proudly told Piers Morgan that he tries to cultivate a *"very familial kind of organization."* In a business generating a very visible $100-million-month or more cash flow, it is hard for a $9-an-hour employee to seriously feel like they are part of the "team" with a General Manager making a half-million-dollars-a-year[74] and the CEO making $4-million[75] annually.

Write it off to my years inside the American labor movement or to my 1960's acceptance of labor-value theory of capital, or accept it as a more productive methodology of human resources management, but I lean more toward the Google-esque democratic decision making styles with true profit sharing, bonusing, and day-to-day involvement in the success of not only the property but their own lives. Many companies are better at pushing employees to be *good* rather than *teaching them how* to be *great*. With a deeper and more thoughtful employee relationship, actually caring about the quality of life of the employees, the casino can be seen by employees not as locations where people *go to work*, but rather as an extension of their lives. The productivity gain from this is phenomenal.

Complex and *"touchy-feely"* as it sounds, that approach actually ultimately saves money and increases revenue. I was called into one casino where the average hourly-employee tenure was four weeks (through the first two paychecks). I cannot even begin to calculate what that cost was to the casino in terms of lost productivity, training, uniforms, and so on (though I suspect a good HR person could do so).

One of the tasks I assign my marketing department is to market to a different constituency; the *internal* constituency of employees. Few things irk me more than walking into a casino and asking a random employee about some casino promotion and getting the response *"I dunno"*; THAT, dear reader, is not a bad employee —it is bad management. *The best method of dealing with that is a "cheat sheet" card produced by marketing for each employee to carry with the uniform and license when they are on the casino floor (and drilled at departmental meetings attended by marketing).* Every employee is a marketing employee.

In situations in which budget, policy, expediency, and necessity decisions allow or require hiring skilled professional staff, I lean heavily toward top industry professionals. I compensate them well and I hire them under contract. In the Endnotes/Appendix of this book I proffer some samples of such contracts: Bob

343

Pickus' now-public-record employment agreement with Trump[76] and the same for Nick Ribis[77].

Once the major policy decisions have been made and compliance/HR protocols are in place, we can focus on the amenities that make up the remaining 20% of *revenue* outside of Vegas and 55% in Vegas. It is far beyond the scope this book, even as lengthy as this book is, to provide operating manuals for the casino, for restaurants, hotels, entertainment and the other amenities to the gambling racket. Nonetheless, each of these areas has its own career-length operational specifics for optimal performance. To get a flavor of that intensity, spend an hour watching my friend Anthony Melchiorri (another Trump alumnus) on his Travel Channel television series, *Hotel Impossible* or its Food Network cousin *Restaurant Impossible* with celebrity chef Robert Irvine, or my and Tom Trimble's development project creation *Casino Impossible*. For the purpose of this book, I will simply argue that each of these sectors has its own intense disciplines that, just like casino operational management, can *never* be haphazardly  operated. Each of the amenities...*but especially hotel and F&B because they are so customer-centric and essential to the operation*...require highly-focused management/business plans parallel and driven by the casino plan.

We can illustrate the revenue impact of each of these amenities by charting the typical or average contribution of each to that remaining 20% and to the total percentage of revenue of the property.

Amenity	percentage of remaining 20%	Percentage total revenue
Table & other Games	20%	4.0%
Hotel	40%	8.0%
F&B	22%	4.4%
Entertainment	8%	1.6%
Retail	5%	1.0%
Other	5%	1.0%

However, these revenue figures do *not* necessarily reflect a degree of *importance* of the amenity to the casino. For example, even though food and beverage typically only contributes to 4.4% of the property's bottom line, the property cannot possibly succeed without some sort of F&B operation. Just as we know that casinos which cater to high-roller players will have a greater percentage of revenue from table games, we know that all of these percentages are variable to the particulars of the venue.

Just as one example of location based eccentricities, we measure table game hold by the drop; the amount of money gamblers exchange for chips. However in international markets, Macau specifically, table game hold is measured as rolling chip hold. *(Rolling chips are non-cashable play-only chips that are sold at a discount rate or given to high-rollers; when they win from those chips they are paid in full value chips. It is part "playable credits" and part "rebate on losses. Rolling chip hold is a percentage of all bets made, including "reinvestment" from rolling chip wins. Hence the hold is lower.)* Gibberish as this reads, the distinction actually makes a huge difference in the table games are managed:

Table Game Hold Calculation	Normal Casino	Rolling Chip Casino
dollars spent on cheques	$10,000	$10,000
total amount wagered (with reinvestment)	$60,000	$60,000
base cash volume for hold calculation	$60,000	$10,000
Casino win from play	$1,700	$1,700
Hold	2.80%	17%

And that draws a perfect example of the specific types of variables that I am talking about which impact both the management and the calculations.

Managing the casino within these tightly defined formulas and parameters is really not simply a matter of saying *"okay I have this percentage of my revenue to spend on uniforms so order me that many dollars' worth of uniforms."* Far more complex are the countless of judgment calls, on-the-fly analyses, and formula modifications called for on a day-to-day basis. In my tirades on good and bad management, at the end of the day what I am preaching is that *good management* is based on a combination of knowledge, experience, accurate formulas, and especially a philosophical base of what the business model is.

Despite how formulaic the business is, there are countless examples of fiascos (I have quite a few of my own); but in almost every case of botches, the root is in one of those failings of philosophy. The typical issues *of failure to address the competition, theft, under capitalization, facility issues,* and the other typical explanations are all a result of policy management decisions.

The September 2012 federal investigation of Sheldon Adelson's Las Vegas Sands executives violating money-laundering laws; the April 2012 revocation of Foxwoods' casino license in Pennsylvania; the December 2007 revocation of the Tropicana gaming license in Atlantic City; the absolute collapse of Donald Trump's casino empire; The May 2011 shutdown of the Sahara in Vegas; the August 2012 bankruptcy of Jerry's Nugget in North Las Vegas; the 2009 financial calamities of Harrah's 2009 request to draw down the $740 million remaining on its credit line after doubling its debt load when it was taken private by Apollo Management and TPG Capital *(and their subsequent off-again-on-again going public again)*; Stations Casinos 2009 Chapter 11; the enormous failure of Colony's casino properties; —are all just recent manifestations of management decisions at the *policy management/ownership* level. What is remarkable about these decisions is that they are all from very large, some publically-traded, *successful* casino operators.

Either *"shit happens"* or the cycles of the national economy made (for example) Sands allegedly launder money or there is some widespread fundamental failing to act on what this business is all about. What do you think? I choose the latter.

All of my bitching about what business we are and are NOT in comes down to the twin issues of casino finance and operation. Even really good operators like Stations and Harrah's found themselves in 2008 and 2009 enmeshed in CMBS and RMBS (commercial mortgage-backed securities and residential mortgage-backed securities) as an integral of their financing; and we all know what happened to the mortgage backed securities world. Don't get me wrong, there are some brilliant people involved in the management of many of these organizations, especially Harrah's, Stations, and even the last incarnation of Trump. But, seriously, what the *fuck* are casino operators doing in the credit default swap and mortgage securities racket? Despite the pundit pronouncement that Wall Street is a giant casino, what-the-hell are casino operators doing gambling in any "game" where they do not own the odds? As I said back in an earlier chapter when I contrasted Doc Holliday and Meyer Lansky, "*THAT* is not gambling".

It is not my intent to write a primer tome on casino financing methodologies. Almost every conceivable approach has been tried, between Parry Thomas' and the "Mormon mafia's" Valley Bank, Michael Milken's junk bond *bromance* with Steve Wynn, and the Teamsters Central States Pension Fund. In early Vegas, some of them were even legal.

Funders have tried a library of alternative financing schemes from the NIGC rebuked MGAM floor-space deals to traditional real estate mortgage financing. I was even involved in one deal where the $55-million purchase price of a casino was paid by selling the land underneath the casino to an investor who in turn leased the land back to the casino operator for some usury-like rental rate.

One "barrier to entry" in funding casinos is the regulatory process. In most jurisdictions any equity owners of a casino are subject to heinously intrusive business and personal background investigations; in some jurisdictions that requires the licensee to produce record of every cancelled check written for the past two decades and a detailed explanation of source of funds and all expenditures for all those years. I know of at least one jurisdiction that sends agents to the investor's home town to interview neighbors, acquaintances, and even school teachers *(in my case, that is difficult, I started school 53 years ago).* Meanwhile in Indian Country, as I have discussed, the biggest barrier is the inability to secure funds with ownership of any real property on trust or reservation land (remember Minnesota's *Bryan v. Itasca County* from an earlier chapter). Consequently every few years new popular financing methods spring up.

Consider the management contract arrangement. The bar for management contract fees nationwide has been pretty established by the NIGC's rules for Indian Country. There, the NIGC allows a maximum of 30%-40%[78] of net revenue of the casino (after operating expenses). They go on very specifically to define net revenue as "*gross gaming revenues of an Indian gaming operation less (a) Amounts paid out as, or paid for, prizes; and (b) Total gaming-related operating expenses, including all those expenses of the gaming operation com-*

346

monly known as operating expenses and non-operating expenses consistent with professional accounting pronouncements, excluding management fees." In short management fees are 30% to 40% of EBITDA(M).

Now, let's think about that model. Remember our example earlier in this chapter of the casino that has 500 machines winning $100 per machine per day? After we apply the known operational formulas to that example, the casino has annual earnings of $11,161,050 (without slot lease). A management fee of 40% of that is $4.46-million a year or $22.3-million over a five-year contract period. Since that fee is after operating expenses, that means that the salaries, etc. are paid before that fee; so the $22.3-million is a simple fee for management expertise. If the casino needs to borrow say $9-million to buy 500 of the newest latest-and-greatest slot machines or needs $10-million for expansion, then I will be happy to loan them that money at a very low interest rate and unsecured (hence overcoming that barrier to entry in Indian Country). The security on my loan is that $22-million management contract. Think about it: I loan you $10-million which you pay me back at 3% simple interest for a total of $10,781,214 *plus* a $22-million management contract. I will finance deals like that all day.

There are, however, a few restrictions on such a seemingly simple deal. Under NIGC regs there is much debate over whether or not a slot machine rev-share lease agreement is included or not included in that "net revenue". Additionally, the NIGC puts restrictions on adding that additional 10% (above the 30% rate) if we are also going to position the $10-million financing as a loan. Outside of Indian Country, the regulations for management contracts vary by jurisdiction. In New Jersey, for example, the management company must buy a minimum of 5% equity in the casino to be managed, regardless of the fee charged. In Nevada, any entity that receives payment based on a percentage of casino revenue is subject to the same background and licensing requirements as the actual owner; not a less-intrusive key license like an employee manager, but an actual owners' license. Other regulations are determined jurisdiction-by-jurisdiction.

Even debt financing (rather than equity deals) generally require the loaning party showing source of funds and the receiving party showing proof of credit worthiness (for a billion-dollar casino?).

Another popular current funding method is a floor space deal. Let's look again at my example casino of 500 slot machines. Let's suppose that casino ownership decides to sell us 100 of those games and then lease them back from us at a standard 80/20 rev share for the maximum period of time allowed by NIGC (less than 7 years, so 6 years and 11 months). We ask for and receive a certified report of the floor average win-per-unit-per-day and that number is $215. The math seems to look really good: $215 per machine per day translates to $43 for our 20% fee; that is $1,308 per machine per month or $108,557 per machine for the six years and 11 months of the contract. Multiply that time 100 machines and the net revenue is $10,855,708.

Okay, these are used machines so we can buy them for the *"bargain price"* of only $10,000 each or a total of $5-million to the owners. Over the course of six years and 11 months we get back $10.8-million on our $5-million investment for a *profit* of $5.85-million. Seems like a no-brainer, doesn't it? *Whoops, not so fast.*

There are a few problems with this very common kind of deal. Firstly, consider the floor average win per unit. Remember my discussion of the new penny games versus the older 25¢ stepper reels at the Trump Atlantic City property? Let's assume the certified $215 win per unit floor average number is correct. That is the good news. The bad news is that 400 of the 500 games are new state-of-the-art penny games but the 100 we are buying are older games. The 400 new games are winning $250 per unit but our 100 games are only winning $75 per unit each. That still gives a floor average of $215 per unit. But over the term of the contract we only make a total of $3,786,875. For our $5-million investment we lost $1,213,215 rather than make a profit of $5.85-million. Whoops. My *"what is better than owning a casino; owning the slot machines inside the casino"* syllogism only holds if the games are competitive. If they are not competitive then it smacks of a scam.

Again, there are more casino finance techniques than I could possibly list here; but what all the *legitimate* ones require is a solid business model balanced against viable metrics. And those things, yet again, are a function of *management philosophy.*

Success or failure of casinos, machine deals, and financing is all formulaic; I cannot say that enough. Even the over-the-top marketing that had *Casino Journal* calling me a *"marketing magic man"* is purely formulaic. THE key is use of the formulas.

So, as I began, how *does* a casino measure success? How profitable *should* a casino be? What ROI should casino owners expect? How much debt *can* a casino realistically service?

The answers to all of these questions are in the formulas I have talked about since the beginning of this book and detailed in this chapter. When I look at taking over the operation of an existing casino I require a detailed analysis of an encyclopedia of formula-generating documents so that I can understand exactly where performance is before I take over. A partial list of these formula-generating documents includes:

Accounts receivables (trial balance and aging report)	Employment contracts/non-compete agreements
Actuarially-determined estimated liability and annual expense of post-retirement and post-employment benefits	Slot list, title manufacture, date, own/lease, denominations, hold, year, serial number, handle, win hold%,
Allowance for doubtful accounts	Administrative Expenses
Architectural and engineering reports	Appraisals of Property
Audited financial statements	Assets pledged as collateral
Balance sheets	Automobiles and other vehicles

Billboards lists	Bank Account Records
Budgets (by department)	Employee Bonus plans
Capital expenditures	Bus Tours / Wholesale sales reports
Casino Cash	Capital Leases
Convention information	Comp Rooms Report
Database count segmented by ADT, tier, last play day	Deferred charges and other current and non-current assets
Documents and agreements evidencing other financial arrangements of the company	Overview of restaurants bars meetings rooms, (cuisine, seating, square footage, leased, etc.)
Encumbrances	Accrued liabilities
Façade report	Environment assessment
Financial Statements	Federal and state tax returns
FTE list; Head count	Fixed Asset Detail
HR policies	Hotel, Food, Beverage statistics
Insurance information	Income Statements and Balance Sheet
Intellectual property report	Intangible assets
Land lease info	IT details
Legal claims	Licenses
Room statistics (cash revenue, comp, allowances; offers)	Letters from independent public accountants
Monthly Financial Statements	Litigation and suits
Organizational chart	Operating Budget
P&L documents	Player tracking system info
Prepaid expenses	Vendor list
Reserves for claims and assessments	Real estate tax billings
Corporate governance documents	Site plan
Table data (seats, game, drop, win, hold)	Surveys
Titles	Tax map
Union contracts	Total Revenue
Roof evaluation	

This list is presented here merely as a starting point for analysis before a final decision to manage (and especially to purchase) any existing casino. It is only from this starting point of data that we can draw a picture of the casino's existing condition and the prospects for improvement. That lengthy process only gives us the groundwork to plug in the right formulas. I examine every discretionary expenditure (from electricity usage, to physical plant maintenance to even travel and magazine subscriptions) to see if there was a better way to merge expenses into my formulas.

But beyond merely the right formulas, those answers require the right operational management and the right policy management.

To get management and ownership to the point that all of this makes sense requires a process-oriented focus on profitability, return on investment, and assuring a favorable ratio of assets to liabilities. For every $1-million in casino debt, I want to see on-hand a lot more money than that million. For every $1-million of equipment or building the casino owns, I want to see the casino owing only a tiny percentage of that. For every $1-million in slot machines and other assets the casino has, I want to see the casino generate a lot more every year than the value of that equipment. And these are all the functions of the management processes I have been discussing.

Things happen very fast in the casino world where so much money is transacted so quickly; where, as Elvis sang (and Mort Shuman and Doc Pomus wrote) there is *"a fortune won and lost on every deal"*. Sometimes management needs to react faster than many can normally react.

When I first went into Southern California I ran into an interesting culture shock. I would ask an employee to do a task "right now" and they would perform it superbly but not necessarily "right now" in *my* timeframe. This happened repeatedly with several employees and it bothered me more and more. One day, in the office of the players' club, I overheard two employees talking.

One was saying, *"I was talking to my cousin right now and she said..."*

I interrupted, *"excuse me, where is your cousin?"*

The employee responded, *"I don't know, I think at home."*

I did not see a cell phone. *"Then how can you talk to her right now if you are not on the phone,"* I asked.

"You don't understand anything, Mister Gary," the employee told me in a frustrated tone.

Perplexed, I sat down to ask for help from my friend (and employee), Yuri Dominguez (who later followed me from Trump to Oklahoma to work for me there).

"What does 'right now' mean to you?" I asked.

"Soon. Recently. Today sometime," she responded.

"Hmmmm. Ok. If I want something instantly, at this very moment, what do I need to say," I asked perplexed.

"Oh that is easy, just say *'en chinga',*" she said, laughing for apparently no reason.

I spoke some French, some German, some Russian, some Italian; but not a word of Spanish. I had no idea exactly what "en chinga" meant, but I did find out that when I added the term to a request, my bidding was carried out immediately. Yuri had been right on target with her recommendation.

Later when I moved to Oklahoma's Thunderbird, I wanted to change the uninspired lackluster work culture of the employees there. As part of the employee training program I instituted a sense of urgency for player service and for anything involving players interacting with staff. I called the program *En Chinga* and passed out embroidered Egyptian cotton polo shirts to staff members who excelled in my *En Chinga* program. The program and the shirts were a big hit and genuinely helped me literally brand the player service program that I was creating. Tribal council members requested shirts, employees competed with each other to provide higher-level player service to win one of the shirts, and my program was a huge success.

A few weeks into the program Yuri left California and she and her boyfriend came to work for me in Oklahoma. She took one look at the shirts and scolded me, *"I can't believe you put that on a shirt."*

"Why not? It means right now and that is what this is all about," I responded.

"Mister Gary, it means <u>*right fucking now,*</u>*"* she explained.

Hell, no wonder it worked in Southern California when I would tag it onto a request for action.

Despite the inadvertent expletive, the idea was superb and I think very appropriate for most casino

ABOVE: The "en chinga" embroidered shirt with a Tribal logo

issues. In fact, it describes my attitude, requirements, and disposition even today: I want it done right *fucking* now.

Back in Atlantic City at the end of the 1970s, that kid in the alley had asked, *"Who the hell are you?"* When I answered him, I was just a roving gambler not in a hurry to do anything.

Now, almost four decades later, I am a Gambling Man... *en chinga!*

ENDNOTES / APPENDIX

*I have elected to use the endnotes in this book a little unconventionally; placing foot-
notes at the end of the book rather than at the bottom of each page, but also using the
Endnotes in lieu of a never-ending number of appendixes. This approach makes the endnotes bulky and difficult to navigate but makes reading the book a lot more manageable.*

*I should also explain that the photographs, documents, emails, and letters contained
in this book are all my personal photos and documents or are in the public domain and
are presented here strictly for the journalistic purposes of telling the story.*

*Finally, please accept my advance apologies for the small print in this appendix; some
of these documents are absurdly long and while important enough to include here, you
may well need a magnifying glass.*

---

[1] MGM Resorts International 2011 Annual Report

[2] A Bob Stupak letter circa 1994:

From the Desk of
Bob Stupak *VEGAS WORLD*

Bob Stupak

*I have $1200 in Cash and Casino Action
for you*

Good Morning!

My name is Bob Stupak, and I'm the owner of one of the biggest
individually-owned hotel/casinos in the world.

Yes, I do have $1200 in cash and casino action for you.... If you
want it.

And oh, by the way, I'll throw in a great hotel room for you and
a companion, for 3 days and 2 nights here in Las Vegas — the most
exciting city in the world. And a lot more, too. I'm going to cram
this letter with benefits for you.

What's the reason for my being such a nice guy?

Your name didn't come to us by accident. I paid some high-
powered experts a lot of money for a list of people we'd like to have
visit us.

This is an elite list of people who are NOT the standard Las
Vegas "high rollers." We get plenty of those. What I'm after are
folks who might visit us occasionally, after having a pleasant
experience here as our guests.

Your name is on that very special list... and because I'm very
much aware I'm hitting you "cold" with this concept, I'm also aware
I'd better make this pot very, very sweet for you.

That's exactly what I propose to do.

I propose to hand you a combination of cash, chips, slot machine
action, shows, and bonuses totaling far more than $1200, in currency
and casino action. That's in addition to the fabulous room for two in
my hotel.

What do I get from you in return? Exactly $129 per person (which
you can charge to a credit card, if you like). Now, I guess it's
logical for me to assure you're willing to trade $129 each for you and

[3] The Trump Management Contract with the 29 Palms Band of Mission Indians follows. Sections or portions of sections that are not public record have been removed by the National Indian Gaming Commission:

GAMING FACILITY MANAGEMENT AGREEMENT

THIS AMENDED AND RESTATED GAMING FACILITY MANAGEMENT AGREEMENT (this "Agreement") is made as of the day of March 2002, by and between the **TWENTY-NINE PALMS BAND OF LUISENO MISSION INDIANS OF CALIFORNIA,** a sovereign Native American nation, with offices at 46-200 Harrison Place, Coachella, California 92236 (the "Tribe"), the **TWENTY-NINE PALMS ENTERPRISES CORPORATION,** a Federal corporation chartered by the Tribe pursuant to 25 U.S.C. Section 477, with offices at 46-200 Harrison Place, Coachella, California 92236 ("the Enterprise") and **THCR MANAGEMENT SERVICES, LLC,** a Delaware limited liability company with offices at 1000 Boardwalk, Atlantic City, New Jersey 08401.

RECITALS:

The Tribe is a federally-recognized Indian Tribe which possesses sovereign governmental powers pursuant to the Tribe's recognized powers of self-government. The Tribe occupies certain property located in Coachella, Riverside County, California, more specifically described on Exhibit A attached hereto, as "Indian lands" pursuant to 25 U.S.C. 2703(4) (the "Property"). The Tribe currently operates a Class II gaming facility on the Property.c

The Tribe desires to further develop the Property to promote increased tribal economic development, self-sufficiency and strong tribal government.

In order to obtain the benefit of Manager's management, marketing and technical experience and expertise, the Tribe and Manager entered into a Gaming Facility Management Agreement dated as of April 27, 2000.

The Tribe chartered the Enterprise to conduct Class II and Class III Gaming pursuant to the Indian Gaming Regulatory Act and the Compact at the Facility, and transferred all of its right, title and interest in and to the Facility to the Enterprise pursuant to an Assignment and Bill of Sale dated July 5, 2001.

With the assistance of Trump Hotels & Casino Resorts Development Company, LLC, the Enterprise intends to design, finance, construct, furnish and equip a permanent Class III gaming resort on the Property, which shall include a new casino facility, a hotel and other amenities and the renovation of the Tribe's

354

existing Class II gaming facility.

The Tribe, the Enterprise and Manager desire to amend and restate in its entirety the April 27, 2000 Gaming Facility Management Agreement in order to conform such agreement to comments received from the NIGC.

This Agreement is entered into pursuant to the Indian Gaming Regulatory Act of 1988, PL 100-497, 25 U.S.C. 2701 *et seq.* (the "IGRA") as that statute may be amended. All gaming conducted at the Facility will at all times comply with the IGRA, applicable Tribal law and the Compact.

SECTION 1 AMENDED AND RESTATED AGREEMENT;
DEFINITIONS

Amended and Restated Agreement. This Agreement amends and restates in its entirety the Gaming Facility Management Agreement entered into by the Tribe and Manager as of April 27, 2000.

Definitions. As they are used in this Agreement, the terms listed below shall have the meaning assigned to them in this Section:

"Affiliate" means as to Manager, the Enterprise or the Tribe, any corporation, partnership, limited liability company, joint venture, trust, department or agency or individual controlled by or controlling, directly or indirectly, Manager, the Enterprise or the Tribe.

"Articles of Association" shall mean the Articles of Association of The Twenty-Nine Palms Band of Luiseno Mission Indians of California as adopted by the Tribe on March 1, 1972 and approved by the Secretary of the Interior.

"BIA" shall mean the Bureau of Indian Affairs of the Department of the Interior of the United States of America.

"Capital Budget" shall mean the capital budget described in Section 3.10.

"Capital Replacement(s)" shall mean any alteration or rebuilding or renovation of the Facility, and any replacement of Furnishings and Equipment, the cost of which is capitalized and depreciated, rather than being expensed, applying generally accepted accounting principles, as described in Section 3.10.

"Capital Replacement Reserve" shall mean the reserve described in Section 3.12, into which periodic contributions are paid pursuant to Section 3.13.

"Charter" shall mean the Federal Charter of Incorporation of the Enterprise approved by the U.S. Department of the Interior on February 16, 2001 and ratified by the Tribe on March 28, 2001 pursuant to 25 U.S.C. Section 477.

"Class H Gaming" shall mean Class II Gaming as defined in the IGRA. "Class III Gaming" shall mean Class III Gaming as defined in the IGRA.

"Commencement Date" shall mean the first date that the approximately 50,000 square foot planned casino addition to the Facility is complete and open to the public for Gaming, which shall be the date upon which management services begin under this Agreement.

"Compact" shall mean the Tribal-State Compact between the Tribe and the State of California regarding Class III Gaming, executed by the Tribe on October 1, 1999 and signed by the Secretary of the Interior on May 5, 2000 and published in the Federal Register as provided in 25 U.S.C. 2710(d)(8)(D) on May 16, 2000; as the same may, from time to time, be amended, or such other Compact that may be substituted therefor.

"Compensation" shall mean the direct salaries and wages paid to, or accrued for the benefit of, any employee, including incentive compensation, together with all fringe benefits payable to or accrued for the benefit of such executive or other employee, including employer's contribution under FICA, unemployment compensation or other employment taxes, pension fund contributions, workers' compensation, group life, accident and health insurance premiums and costs, and profit sharing, severance, retirement, disability, relocation, housing and other similar benefits.

"Confidential Information" shall mean the information described in Section 8.22.

"Depository Account" shall mean the bank account described in Section 3.17.2.

"Disbursement Account" shall mean the bank account described in Section 3.17.3.

"Early Termination Fee" shall mean^r

"Effective Date" shall mean the date five (5) days following the date on which all of the following listed conditions are satisfied: written approval of this Agreement is granted by the Chairman of the NIGC; written approval of a Tribal Gaming Code is granted by the Chairman of the NIGC; written confirmation that the Tribe and the State (to the extent required by the Compact) have approved background investigations of Manager; Manager has received a certified copy of the Tribal Resolutions adopted by the Tribe in accordance with the Tribe's governing documents and the Corporate Resolutions adopted by the Enterprise in accordance with the Charter authorizing the execution of this Agreement;

execution of the Compact by the Secretary of the Interior and publication in the Federal Register as provided in 25 U.S.C. 2710(d)(8)(D); receipt by Manager of all applicable licenses for or related to management of the Facility; and Manager has satisfied itself that the Tribal Gaming Code and any other code adopted by the Tribe relative to any of the documents referenced in this Agreement do not have a material adverse effect on Manager's ability to operate the Facility under this Agreement.

"Emergency Condition" shall have the meaning set forth in Section 3.11.

"Enterprise" shall mean the "Twenty-Nine Palms Enterprises Corporation" chartered under 25 U.S.C. 477 by the Tribe to engage in Class II and Class III Gaming at the Facility and any other lawful commercial activity allowed in the Facility including, but not limited to the sale of alcohol, tobacco, gifts and souvenirs; or any ancillary non-Gaming activity within the Facility generally related to Class II or Class III Gaming.

"Enterprise Bank Accounts" shall mean those accounts described in Section

"Enterprise Employee" shall mean all Employees who are assigned to work at

"Enterprise Employee Policies" shall mean those employee policies described in Section 3.6.2.

"Excess Funds" shall have the meaning described in Section 5.4.1 so long as the Transfer and Deposit Agreement may be in effect, and thereafter "Excess Funds" shall have the meaning described in Section 5.4.2.

"Facility" shall mean all buildings, structures and improvements located on the Property used in connection with gaming or used for the operation of the Enterprise, and all fixtures, Furnishings and Equipment attached to, forming a part of, or necessary for the operation of such buildings, structures and improvements.

"Financing Agreements" shall mean all loan agreements, indentures, notes, security agreements and other documents to be entered into between the Tribe and/or the Enterprise and one or more Lenders pursuant to which the financing is issued including, without limitation, the Loan Agreement.

"Fiscal Year" shall mean the period commencing on January I of each year and ending on December 31 of such year, except that for purposes of calculating the Management Fee, the first Fiscal Year shall be deemed to commence upon the Commencement Date and end on December 31 of such year.

"Furnishings and Equipment" shall mean all furniture, furnishings and equipment required for the operation of the Facility, including, without limitation: cashier, money sorting and money counting equipment, surveillance and communication equipment and security equipment; electronic lottery terminals, video games of chance, table games, Bingo blowers and equipment, electronic displays, Class II pull-tab dispensers, table games, pari-mutuel betting equipment and other Class II and Class III gaming equipment permitted pursuant to the Compact and the IGRA; office furnishings and equipment; specialized equipment necessary for the operation of any portion of the Facility for accessory purposes, including equipment for entertainment facilities, hospitality facilities, kitchens, laundries, dry cleaning, cocktail lounges, restaurants, public rooms, commercial and parking spaces and recreational facilities; all decor, special effects and artwork; and all other furnishings and equipment hereafter located and installed in or about the Facility which are used in the operation of the Facility in accordance with the standards set forth in this Agreement.

"Gaming" shall mean any and all activities defined as Class II and Class III Gaming.

"General Manager" shall mean the person supplied by Manager and employed by the Enterprise to direct the operation of the Facility.

"Generally Accepted Accounting Principles or GAAP" shall mean those principles defined by the Financial Accounting Standards Board.

"Gross Gaming Revenue (Win)" shall mean the net win from gaming activities which is the difference between gaming wins and losses before deducting costs and expenses.

"Gross Revenues" shall mean all revenues of any nature derived directly or indirectly from the Facility including, without limitation, Gross Gaming Revenue (Win), food and beverage sales, and other rental or other receipts from lessees, sublessees, licensees and concessionaires (but not the gross receipts of such lessees, sublessees, licensees or concessionaires, provided that such lessees, sublessees, and licensees and concessionaires are not subsidiaries or affiliates of Manager), and revenue recorded for Promotional Allowances, but excluding any taxes the Tribe is allowed to assess pursuant to Section 7.

"House Bank" shall mean the amount of cash, chips, tokens and plaques that Manager from time to time determines necessary to have at the Facility daily to meet its cash needs.

"IGRA" shall mean the Indian Gaming Regulatory Act of 1988, PL 100-497, 25 U.S.C. 2701 *et seq.,* same may, from time to time, be amended.

"Internal Control Systems" shall mean the systems described in Section 3.16.

"Legal Requirements" shall mean any and all present and future judicial, administrative, and tribal rulings or decisions, and any and all present and future federal, state, local, and tribal laws, codes, rules, regulations, permits, licenses and certificates, in any way applicable to the Tribe, Manager, the Property, the Facility, and the Enterprise, including without limitation, the IGRA, the Compact, and the Tribal Gaming Code.

"Lender" shall mean First National Bank, as Administrative Agent, together with the "Lenders" identified in the Financing Agreement(s).

"Loan Agreement" shall mean the Loan Agreement dated October 17, 2001, by and among The Twenty-Nine Palms Enterprises Corporation, The Twenty-Nine Palms Band of Luiseno Mission Indians of California, the Lenders referred to therein, and First National Bank, together with all documents that constitute "Loan Documents" as defined therein.

"Management Agreement" shall mean this Agreement and may be referred **to herein** as the "Agreement."

"**Management Fee**" shall mean the management fee described in Section 5.1.

"**Manager**" shall mean TI-ICR Management Services, LLC, its successors and assigns.

"**Manager Advance**" shall mean any funds advanced by Manager or its Affiliates to the Enterprise, including on account of the Minimum Guaranteed Monthly Payment or the Manager Guaranty.

"**Manager Guaranty**" shall mean

"**Manager Proprietary Information**" shall mean the information described in Section 8.22.

"**Material Breach**" shall mean such material breach as described in Section 10.3.

"**Member of The Tribal Government**" shall have the meaning described in Section 9.5.

"**Minimum Balance**" shall mean the amount described in Section 3.17.1.

"**Minimum Guaranteed Monthly Payment**" shall mean that payment due the Tribe each month commencing in the month after the Commencement Date occurs in accordance with 25 U.S.C. 2711(b)(3) and Section 5.5 hereof.

"**National Indian Gaming Commission**" or "**NIGC**" shall mean the commission established pursuant to 25 U.S.C. 2704.

"**Net Revenues**" shall mean the sum of "Net Revenues (Gaming)" and "Net **Revenues (Other).**"

"**Net Revenues (Gaming)**" shall mean Gross Gaming Revenue (Win), of the Enterprise from Class II or Class III gaming less all gaming related Operating Expenses, excluding the Management Fee, and less the retail value of any Promotional Allowances, and less the following revenues actually received by the Enterprise and included in Gross Revenues: any gratuities or service charges added to a customer's bill; any credits or refunds made to customers, guests or patrons; any sums and credits received by the Enterprise for lost or damaged merchandise; any sales taxes, excise taxes, gross receipt taxes, admission taxes, entertainment taxes, tourist taxes or charges received from patrons and passed on to a governmental or quasi-governmental entity; any proceeds from the sale or other disposition of furnishings and equipment or other capital assets; any fire and extended coverage insurance proceeds other than for business interruption; any condemnation awards other than for temporary condemnation; any proceeds of financing or refinancing; and any interest on bank account(s). It is intended that this provision be consistent with 25 U.S.C. 2703(9).

"**Net Revenues (Other)**" shall mean all Gross Revenues of the Enterprise from all other sources in support of Class II or Class III gaming not included in "Net Revenues (Gaming)," such as food and beverage, entertainment, and retail, less all non-gaming related Operating Expenses, excluding the Management Fee and less the retail value of Promotional Allowances, if any, and less the following revenues actually received by the Enterprise and included in Gross Revenues: any gratuities or service charges added to a customer's bill; any credits or refunds made to customers, guests or patrons; any sums and credits received by the Enterprise for lost or damaged merchandise; any sales taxes, excise taxes, gross receipt taxes, admission taxes, entertainment taxes, tourist taxes or charges received from patrons and passed on to a governmental or quasi-governmental entity; any proceeds from the sale or other disposition of furnishings and equipment or other capital assets; any fire and extended coverage insurance proceeds other than for business interruption; any condemnation awards other than for temporary condemnation; any proceeds of financing or refinancing; and any interest on bank account(s). It is intended that this provision be consistent with 25 U.S.C. 2703(9).

"**Note**" shall mean the promissory note or notes to be executed by the Enterprise and/or the Tribe pursuant to the Financing Agreements.

"**Operating Budget and Annual Plan**" shall mean the operating budget and plan described in Section 3.9.

"**Operating Expenses**" shall mean all expenses of the operation of the Enterprise, pursuant to GAAP, including but not limited to the following: the payment of salaries, wages, and benefit programs for Enterprise Employees; Operating Supplies for the Enterprise; utilities; repairs and maintenance of the Facility (excluding Capital Replacements); interest on the Note; interest on installment contract purchases or other interest charges on debt approved by the Tribal Council; insurance and bonding; advertising and marketing, including busing and transportation of patrons to the Facility; accounting, legal and other professional fees; security costs; reasonable travel expenses for officers and employees of the Enterprise; lease payments for Furnishings and Equipment to the extent approved by the Tribe; costs of goods sold; other expenses designated as operating Expenses in accordance with the accounting standards as referred to in Section 3.19.3; expenses specifically designated as Operating Expenses in this Agreement; depreciation and amortization of the Facility based on an assumed thirty (30) year life, and depreciation and amortization of all other assets in accordance with GAAP; recruiting and training expenses; fees due to the NIGC under the IGRA; any required payments to the State or local governments made by or on behalf of the Enterprise or the Tribe pursuant to the Compact; license fees reflecting reasonable regulatory costs incurred by the Tribal Gaming Agency; and any budgeted charitable contributions by the Enterprise which are approved by the Tribe.

"**Operating Supplies**" shall mean food and beverages (alcoholic and nonalcoholic) and other consumable items used in the operation of the Facility, such as playing cards, tokens, chips, pull-tabs, Bingo paper, plaques, fuel, soap, cleaning materials, matches, paper goods, stationery and all other similar items.

"**Option Date**" **shall have** the meaning described in Section 10.10. "**Pre-Opening Budget**" shall have the meaning described in Section 3.8. "Pre-Opening Expenses" shall have the meaning described in Section 3.8.

"Promotional Allowances" shall mean the retail value of complimentary food, beverages, merchandise, and tokens for gaming, provided to patrons as promotional items.

"Property" shall mean the Tribe's "Indian lands" consisting of approximately of 240 acres of land located at 46-200 Harrison Place, Coachella, Riverside County CA 92236, pursuant to a declaration of trust by the United States of America dated May 18, 1978, recorded June 27, 1978 in the Official Records of Riverside County, California in Book 1978, Page 131619, more specifically described on Exhibit A attached hereto.

"Relative" shall have the meaning described in Section 9.5.

"Shortfall Amount" shall mean any amount necessary to pay Manager all or any portion of the Management Fee due but not paid to Manager as a result of a shortage of available funds.

"State" shall refer to the State of California.

"Term" shall mean the term of this Agreement as described in Section 2.2.

"Transfer and Deposit Agreement" shall mean that certain Transfer and Deposit Agreement dated as of October 17, 2001 between the Enterprise and First National Bank, as Depository.

"Tribal Council" shall mean the duly elected Tribal Council of the Tribe described in the Tribe's Articles of Association.

"Tribal Gaming Authority" shall mean the Tribal body created pursuant to the Tribal Gaming Code to regulate the Class II and Class III Gaming of the Tribe in accordance with the Compact, the IGRA and the Tribal Gaming Code.

"Tribal Gaming Code" shall mean the Gaming Ordinance adopted by the Tribe and approved by the Chairman of the NIGC regulating the conduct of gaming on tribal lands, as amended following the passage of Proposition 1A to permit Class III Gaming at the Facility in accordance with the Compact, together with the Tribal Gaming Commission Rules and Regulations.

"Tribal Priority Distribution" shall mean **"Tribal Resolution"** shall have the meaning described in Section 2.9.

SECTION 2
COVENANTS

In consideration of the mutual covenants contained in this Agreement, the parties agree and covenant as follows:

2.1 Engagement of Manager. The Enterprise hereby retains and engages Manager as the exclusive manager of the Enterprise pursuant to the terms and conditions of this Agreement, and Manager hereby accepts such retention and engagement, subject to receipt of all necessary regulatory approvals.

2.2 Term. The management services to be provided under this Agreement shall commence on the Commencement Date, and will terminate on the date which is the [1] anniversary of the Commencement Date. _
Manager shall be granted an additional two (2) year term of this Agreement; provided, however that the NIGC shall first have approved such extension of the term of this Agreement.

2.3 Status of Property. The Tribe represents and covenants that it will maintain the Property throughout the Term as Indian Lands, eligible as a location upon which Class II and Class III Gaming can occur. The Tribe covenants, during the term hereof, that Manager shall and may peaceably have complete access to and presence in the Facility in accordance with the terms of this Agreement, free from molestation, eviction and disturbance by the Tribe or by any other person or entity; provided, however, that such right of access to and presence in the Facility shall cease (i) in the event the Tribal Gaming Authority revokes any license issued by it to Manager which license is necessary for the lawful operation of the Facility by Manager, or (ii) upon the termination of this Agreement pursuant to its terms.

2.4 Manager Compliance with Law; Licenses. Manager covenants that it will at all times comply with all Legal Requirements, including the Tribal Gaming Code, the IGRA, the Compact, California statutes, to the extent applicable, and any licenses issued under any of the foregoing. The Tribe shall not unreasonably withhold, delay, withdraw, qualify or condition such licenses as the Tribe is authorized to grant.

2.5 Amendments to Tribal Gaming Code. The Tribe covenants that any amendments made to the Tribal Gaming Code will be a legitimate effort to ensure that gaming is conducted in a manner that adequately protects the environment, the public health and safety, and the integrity of the Enterprise. The adoption of any amendments to the Tribal Gaming Code or any other codes or resolutions that would materially and adversely affect Manager's rights under this Agreement shall be a Material Breach of this Agreement.

2.6 Compliance with Compact. The parties shall at all times comply with the provisions of the Compact.

2.7 Fire and Safety. Manager shall ensure that the Facility shall be constructed and maintained in compliance with all fire and safety statutes, codes, and regulations which would be applicable if the Facility were located outside of the jurisdiction of the Tribe although those requirements would not otherwise apply within that jurisdiction. Nothing in this Section shall grant any jurisdiction to the State of California or any political subdivision thereof over the Property or the Facility. The Tribe shall be responsible for arranging fire protection and police services for the Facility.

2.8 Compliance with the National Environmental Policy Act. With the assistance of Manager, the Tribe shall supply the NIGC with all information necessary for the NIGC to comply with any regulations of the NIGC issued pursuant to the National Environmental Policy Act (NEPA).

2.9 Satisfaction of Effective Date Requirements. Manager, the Enterprise and the Tribe each agree to cooperate and to use their best efforts to satisfy all of the conditions of the Effective Date at the earliest possible date. The Tribe shall adopt a resolution (the "Tribal Resolution") reciting that it is the governing law of the Tribe that the Management Agreement, the Financing Agreements and the exhibited documents attached thereto are the legal and binding obligations of the Tribe, valid and enforceable in accordance with their terms. Manager agrees to memorialize the satisfaction of each of the following requirements as well as the Effective Date in writings signed by Manager and delivered to the Tribe and to the Chairman of the NIGC: (i) Manager has satisfied itself as to the proper ownership and control of the Property, and that all of the Legal Requirements and other requirements for lawful conduct and operation of the Facility in accordance with this Agreement have been met and satisfied; and **(ii)** the satisfactory completion of all necessary and applicable feasibility studies required for the operation of the Facility.

2.10 Commencement Date. Manager shall memorialize the Commencement Date in a writing signed by Manager and delivered to the Tribe and to the Chairman of the NIGC.

2.11 Restrictions on Collateral Operations. During the term of this Agreement, Manager agrees that During the term of this Agreement, the Tribe agrees thatr

SECTION 3
BUSINESS AFFAIRS

3.1 Manager's Authority and Responsibility. Manager shall conduct and direct all business and affairs in connection with the day-to-day operation, management and maintenance of the Facility and the operation of the Enterprise, including the establishment of operating days and hours. It is the parties' intention that the Facility be open twenty-four (24) hours daily, seven (7) days a week. Upon the Commencement Date, Manager shall be deemed to have the necessary power and authority with respect to the Facility to fulfill all of its responsibilities under this Agreement. Nothing herein grants or is intended to grant Manager a titled interest to the Facility or to the Enterprise. Manager hereby accepts such retention and engagement.

The Tribe shall have the sole proprietary interest in and ultimate responsibility for the conduct of all Gaming conducted by the Enterprise, subject to the rights and responsibilities of Manager under this Agreement.

3.2 Duties of Manager. In managing, operating, maintaining and repairing the Facility, Manager's duties shall include, without limitation, the following:

3.2.1 Physical Duties. Manager shall use reasonable measures for the orderly physical administration, management, and operation of the Facility, including without limitation capital improvements, cleaning, painting, decorating, plumbing, carpeting, grounds care and such other maintenance and repair work as is reasonably necessary.

3.2.2 Compliance. Manager shall comply with all duly enacted statutes, regulations and codes of the State, the federal government, the Tribe and the Tribal Gaming Authority.

3.2.3 Required Filings. Manager shall comply with all applicable provisions of the Internal Revenue Code including, but not limited to, the prompt filing of any cash transaction reports and W-2G reports that may be required by the Internal Revenue Service of the United States or under the Compact. Manager shall also comply with all applicable reporting and filing provisions of all other federal, State, and Tribal regulatory agencies.

3.2.4 Contracts in the Name of the Enterprise and at Arm's Length. Contracts for the operations of the Facility shall be entered into in the name of the Enterprise, and signed by the General Manager.

Nothing contained in this section 3.2.4 shall be deemed to be or constitute a waiver of the Tribe's sovereign immunity.

3.2.5 Facility Operating Standards. Manager shall operate the Facility in a proper, efficient and competitive manner in compliance with all applicable provisions of the _ Compact and the standards promulgated by the NIGC at 25 C.F.R. 542.1 *et seq.,* as in effect at any time.

3.3 Security. Manager shall provide for appropriate security for the operation of the Facility. All aspects of the Facility security shall be the responsibility of Manager. All security officers shall be bonded and insured in an amount commensurate with his or her enforcement duties and obligations. The cost of any charge for security and increased public safety services will be an Operating Expense.

3.4 Damage, Condemnation or Impossibility of the Facility. If, during the term of this Agreement, the Facility is damaged or destroyed by fire, war, or other casualty, or by an Act of God, or is taken by condemnation or sold under the threat of condemnation, or if Gaming on the Property is prohibited as a result of a decision of a court of competent jurisdiction or by operation of any applicable legislation, Manager shall have the following options:

3.4.1 Recommencement of Operations. If Gaming on the Property is prohibited by Legal Requirements, Manager shall have the option to continue its interest in this Agreement and, with the approval of the Tribe, to commence or recommence the operation of Gaming at the Facility if, at some point during the Term of this Agreement, such commencement or recommencement shall be legally and commercially feasible.

3.4.2 Repair or Replacement. If the Facility is damaged, destroyed or condemned so that Gaming can no longer be conducted at the Facility, the Facility shall be reconstructed if the insurance or condemnation proceeds are sufficient to restore or replace the Facility to a condition at least comparable to that before the casualty occurred. If Manager elects to reconstruct the Facility and if the insurance proceeds or condemnation awards are insufficient to reconstruct the Facility to such condition, Manager may, in its sole discretion, supply such additional funds as are necessary to reconstruct the Facility to such condition and such funds shall, with the prior consent of the Tribe and the BIA or NIGC, as appropriate, constitute a loan to the Enterprise, secured by the revenues from the Facility and repayable upon such terms as may be agreed upon by the Enterprise and Manager. If the insurance proceeds are not sufficient and are not used to repair the Facility, the Enterprise and Manager shall jointly adjust and settle any and all claims for such insurance proceeds or condemnation awards, and such proceeds or award shall be applied first, to the amounts due under the Note (including principal and interest); second, any other loans; third, any undistributed Net Revenues pursuant to Section 5 of this Agreement; and fourth, any surplus shall be distributed to the Tribe.

3.4.3 Other Business Purposes. Manager shall have the option to use the Facility for other purposes reasonably incidental to Class II and Class III Gaming, provided the Enterprise has approved such purposes (which approval shall not be unreasonably withheld). For any purpose other than Gaming, Manager shall obtain all approvals necessary under applicable law.

3.4.4 Termination of Gaming. Manager shall have the option at any time within a sixty (60) day period following the cessation of Gaming on the Property to notify the Enterprise in writing that it is terminating operations under this Agreement, in which case Manager shall retain any rights Manager may have to undistributed Net Revenues pursuant to Section 5 of this Agreement and rights to repayments of amounts owed to it. If Manager does not elect to terminate this Agreement, it may take whatever action may be necessary to reduce expenses during such termination of Gaming.

3.4.5 Tolling of the Agreement. If, after a period of cessation of Gaming on the Property, the recommencement of Gaming is possible, and if Manager has not terminated this Agreement under the provisions of Section 3.4.4, the period of such cessation shall not be deemed to have been part of the term of this Agreement and the date of expiration of the term of this Agreement shall be extended by the number of days of such cessation period.

3.5 Alcoholic Beverages and Tobacco Sales. No Tribal legislation prohibiting the sale of tobacco and/or alcoholic beverages is now in force, and no such legislation will be enacted during the term of this Agreement. The Tribe agrees to enact any Tribal legislation necessary to allow sale of alcoholic beverages or tobacco products in the facility. The Enterprise and Manager mutually agree to include sale of tobacco and alcoholic beverages within the Facility to the fullest extent allowed by the Compact.

3.6 Employees.

3.6.1 Manager's Responsibility. Manager shall have, subject to the terms of this Agreement, the exclusive responsibility and authority to direct the selection, control and discharge of all employees performing regular services for the Enterprise in connection with the maintenance, operation, and management of the Facility and any activity upon the Property; and the sole responsibility for determining whether a prospective employee is qualified and the appropriate level of compensation to be paid; provided, however, the Tribal Gaming Authority shall have sole and exclusive control over the licensing of employees or prospective employees of the Enterprise, and the compliance by such employees with the conditions of their license.

3.6.2 Enterprise Employee Policies. Manager shall prepare a draft of personnel policies and procedures (the "Enterprise Employee Policies"), including a job classification system with salary levels and scales, which policies and procedures shall be subject to approval by the Enterprise. The Enterprise Employee Policies shall include a grievance procedure in order to establish fair and uniform standards for the employees of the Enterprise, which will include procedures for the resolution of disputes between Manager and Enterprise Employees. Any revisions to the Enterprise Employee Policies shall not be effective unless they are approved in the same manner as the original Enterprise Employee Policies. All such actions shall comply with applicable Tribal law.

3.6.3 Employees. The selection by the Manager of the General Manager, Chief Financial Officer, Director of Human Resources and Public Safety Director of the Enterprise shall be subject to the approval of the Enterprise, which approval shall not be unreasonably withheld. Manager shall provide the Tribal Council with sufficient information to adequately evaluate all recommendations for employment in the positions of General Manager, Chief Financial Officer, or Security Director. The terms of employment of the Enterprise Employees shall be structured as though all labor, employment, and unemployment insurance laws applicable in California employees would also apply to Enterprise Employees. The Enterprise agrees to take no action to impede, supersede or impair such treatment.

3.6.4 Off-Site Employees. Subject to approval of the Enterprise, Manager shall also have the right to use employees of Manager and Manager's Affiliates not located at the Facility to provide services to the

Enterprise ("Off-Site Employees"). All expenses, costs (including, but not limited to, salaries and benefits, but excluding pension, retirement, severance or similar benefits), which are related to such Off-Site Employees shall be paid by Manager.

3.6.5 No Manager Wages or Salaries. Neither Manager nor Manager's Affiliates nor any of their officers, directors, shareholders, or employees shall be compensated by wages from or contract payments by the Enterprise for their efforts or for any work which they perform under this Agreement, other than repayments of advances and the Management Fee to be paid to Manager under Section 5.1. Nothing in this subsection shall restrict the ability of an employee of the Enterprise to purchase or hold stock in Manager, or Manager's Affiliates where (i) such stock is publicly held, and (ii) such employee acquires, on a cumulative basis, less than five (5%) percent of the outstanding stock in the corporation.

3.6.6 Employee Background Checks. A background investigation shall be conducted by the Tribal Gaming Authority in compliance with all Legal Requirements, to the extent applicable, on each applicant for employment as soon as reasonably practicable, and in all events within the time necessary to enable the Tribal Gaming Authority to forward a report on such applicant for employment pursuant to 25 C.F.R. 556.5(b) within the 60 day time period provided in 25 C.F.R. 558.3(b). No individual whose prior activities, criminal record, if any, or reputation, habits and associations are known to pose a threat to the public interest, the effective regulation of Gaming, or to the gaming licenses of Manager or any of its Affiliates, or to create or enhance the dangers of unsuitable, unfair or illegal practices and methods and activities in the conduct of Gaming, shall knowingly be employed by Manager, the Enterprise, or the Tribe.

The background investigation procedures employed by the Tribal Gaming Authority shall be formulated in consultation with Manager and shall satisfy all regulatory requirements independently applicable to Manager and its Affiliates. Any cost associated with obtaining background investigations of the Manager, the Enterprise, or the Tribe for the Tribal Gaming Authority shall constitute an Operating Expense; costs associated with obtaining background investigations of Manager for the NIGC shall be paid by Manager.

3.6.7 Indian Preference, Recruiting and Training. Manager shall offer employment in the Enterprise to all employees in good standing of the Class II gaming facility operated by the Tribe prior to the Commencement Date. For additional employment needs, Manager shall, during the term of this Agreement, to the extent permitted by applicable law, including but not limited to the Indian Civil Rights Act, 25 U.S.C. 1301 *et seq.*, and the Compact, give preference in recruiting, training and employment to qualified members of a Native American Tribe recognized by the Federal government or the State of California, their spouses and children in all job categories of the Enterprise. Manager shall: conduct job fairs and skills assessment meetings for Native Americans; abide by any duly enacted Tribal preference laws; in consultation with and subject to the approval of the Tribe, develop a management training program for Native Americans. This program shall be structured to provide appropriate training for those participating to assume full managerial control at the conclusion of the Term of this Agreement; train and hire, to the maximum extent permitted by law, members of the local communities where the Facility is located. Whenever possible, Enterprise jobs shall be filled by Native Americans and persons living within Riverside County. Final determination of the qualifications of Native Americans and all other persons for employment shall be made by Manager, subject to any licensing requirements of the Tribe Gaming Authority.

3.6.8 Goals and Remedies. All hiring for the Enterprise shall be done by Manager, based on the hiring policies established by the Enterprise in consultation with Manager.

3.6.9 Removal of Employees. Manager will act in accordance with the Enterprise Employee Policies with respect to the discharge, demotion or discipline of any Enterprise Employee.

3.7 Marketing.

3.7.1 Nature of Marketing Services. The services described in this Section 3.7 ("Marketing Services") shall be provided by Manager.

3.7.2 Marketing Services. Manager shall provide the following Marketing Services:

3.8 Pre-Opening. Upon the later of (a) six (6) months prior to the scheduled Commencement Date and (b) fifteen (15) days following the Effective Date, Manager shall commence implementation of a pre-opening program which shall include all activities necessary to financially and operationally prepare the Facility for opening. To implement the pre-opening program, Manager shall prepare a comprehensive pre-opening budget which shall be submitted to the Enterprise for its approval upon the later of (x) seven (7) months prior to the scheduled Commencement Date and (y) fifteen (15) days following the Effective Date ("Pre-Opening Budget"). The Pre-Opening Budget sets forth expenses which Manager anticipates to be necessary or desirable in order to prepare the Facility for the Commencement Date, including without limitation,

The Enterprise agrees that the Pre-Opening Budget may be modified from time to time, subject to approval of the Enterprise in accordance with the procedure established by Article 3.9 of this Agreement for adjustments to the Operating Budget and Annual Plan.

3.9 Operating Budget and Annual Plan. Manager shall, prior to the scheduled Commencement Date, submit to the Enterprise, for its approval, a proposed Operating Budget and Annual Plan for the remainder of the current Fiscal Year. Thereafter, Manager shall, not less than sixty (60) days prior to the commencement of each full or partial Fiscal Year, submit to the Enterprise, for its approval, a proposed Operating Budget and Annual Plan for the ensuing full or partial Fiscal Year, as the case may be. The Operating Budget and Annual Plan shall include

The Operating Budget and Annual Plan for the Facility will be comprised of the following: The Enterprise's approval of the Operating Budget and Annual Plan shall not be unreasonably withheld or delayed. Manager shall meet with the Enterprise to discuss the proposed Operating Budget and Annual Plan and the Enterprise's approval shall be deemed given unless a specific written objection thereto is delivered by the Enterprise to Manager within thirty (30) days after Manager and the Enterprise have met to discuss the proposed Operating Budget and Annual Plan. If the Enterprise for any reason shall fail to meet with Manager to discuss a proposed Operating Budget and Annual Plan, the Enterprise shall be deemed to have consented unless a specific written objection is delivered to Manager within fifteen (15) days after the date the proposed Operating Budget and Annual Plan is submitted to the Enterprise. The Enterprise shall review the Operating Budget and Annual Plan on a line-by-line basis. To be effective, any notice which disapproves a proposed Operating Budget and Annual Plan must contain specific objections in reasonable detail to individual line items.

If the initial proposed Operating Budget and Annual Plan contains any disputed budget item(s), the Enterprise and Manager agree to cooperate with each other in good faith to resolve the disputed or objectionable proposed item(s). In the event the Enterprise and Manager are not able to reach mutual agreement concerning any disputed or objectionable item(s) prior to the commencement of the applicable fiscal year, the undisputed portions of the proposed Operating Budget and Annual Plan shall be deemed to be adopted and approved and the corresponding line item(s) contained in the Operating Budget and Annual Plan for the preceding fiscal year shall be adjusted as set forth herein and shall be substituted in lieu of the disputed item(s) in the proposed Operating Budget and Annual Plan. Those line items which are in dispute shall be determined by

The resulting Operating Budget and Annual Plan obtained in accordance with the preceding sentence shall be deemed to be the Operating Budget and Annual Plan in effect until such time as Manager and the Enterprise have resolved the items objected to by the Enterprise.

3.9.1 Adjustments to Operating Budget and Annual Plan. Manager may, after notice to and approval by the Enterprise, revise the Operating Budget and Annual Plan from time to time, as necessary, to reflect any unpredicted significant changes, variables or events or to include additional, unanticipated items of expense. Manager may, after notice to the Enterprise, reallocate part or all of the amount budgeted with respect to any line item to another line item and to make such other modifications to the Operating Budget and Annual Plan as

Manager deems necessary, provided that the total adjustments to the Operating Budget and Annual Plan shall not exceed one hundred ten percent (110%) of the aggregate approved Operating Budget and Annual Plan without approval of the Enterprise. Manager shall submit a revision of the Operating Budget and Annual Plan to the Tribe for review on a quarterly basis. In addition, in the event actual Gross Revenues for any period are greater than those provided for in the Operating Budget and Annual Plan, the amounts approved in the Operating Budget and Annual Plan for guest services, food and beverage, telephone, utilities, marketing and the repair and maintenance of the Facility for any month shall be automatically deemed to be increased to an amount that bears the same relationship (ratio) to the amounts budgeted for such items as actual Gross Revenue for such month bears to the projected Gross Revenue for such month. The Enterprise acknowledges that the Operating Budget and Annual Plan is intended only to be a reasonable estimate of the Facility's revenues and expenses for the ensuing Fiscal Year.

Manager shall not be deemed to have made any guarantee concerning projected results contained in the Operating Budget and Annual Plan.

3.10 Capital Budgets; Permitted Hotel Debt. Manager shall, prior to the Commencement Date and thereafter, not less than sixty (60) days prior to the commencement of each fiscal year, or partial fiscal year after the Commencement Date, submit to the Enterprise a recommended capital budget (the "Capital Budget") describing the present value, estimated useful life and estimated replacement costs for the ensuing full or partial year, as the case may be, for the physical plant, furnishings, equipment, and ordinary capital replacement items, all of which are defined to be any items, the cost of which is capitalized and depreciated, rather than expensed, using GAAP ("Capital Replacements") as shall be required to operate the Facility in accordance with sound business practices.

The Enterprise and Manager shall meet to discuss the proposed Capital Budget and the Enterprise shall be required to make specific written objections to a proposed Capital Budget in the same manner and within the same time periods specified in Section 3.9 with respect to an Operating Budget and Annual Plan. The Enterprise shall not unreasonably withhold or delay its consent. Unless the Enterprise and Manager otherwise agree, Manager shall be responsible for

3.11 Capital Replacements. The Enterprise shall effect and expend such amounts for any Capital Replacements as shall be required, in the course of the operation of the Facility, to maintain, at a minimum, the Facility in compliance with any Legal Requirements and to comply with Manager's recommended programs for renovation, modernization and improvement intended to keep the Facility competitive in its market, to maintain industry standards; or to correct any condition of an emergency nature, including without limitation, maintenance, replacements or repairs which are required to be effected by the Enterprise, which in Manager's sole discretion requires immediate action to preserve and protect the Facility, assure its continued operation, and/or protect the comfort, health, safety and/or welfare of the Facility's guests or employees (an "Emergency Condition"); provided, however, that the Enterprise shall be under no obligation to fund Capital Replacements in aggregate amount greater than its periodic required contributions to the Capital Replacement Reserve described in Section 3.12. Manager is authorized to take all steps and to make all expenditures from the Working Capital Account, described at Section 3.17.1 (in the case of non-capitalized repairs and maintenance), or Capital Replacement Reserve Account, described at Section 3.12, (in the case of expenditures for Capital Replacements) as it deems necessary to repair and correct any Emergency Condition, regardless whether such provisions have been made in the Capital Budget or the Operating Budget and Annual Plan for any such expenditures; or the cost thereof may be advanced by Manager and reimbursed from future revenues. Design and installation of Capital Replacements shall be effected in a time period and subject to such conditions as the Enterprise may establish to minimize interference with or disruption of ongoing operations.

3.12 Capital Replacement Reserve. Manager shall establish a Capital Replacement Reserve on the books of account of the Facility, and an account (the "Capital Replacement Reserve Account") in the Enterprise's name at a bank designated by the Enterprise in accordance with Section 3.17A of this Agreement.

3.13 Periodic Contributions to Capital Replacement Reserve. In accordance with Section 5.4 of this Agreement, Manager shall make monthly deposits into the Capital Replacement Reserve Account in amounts equivalent to if any adjustment of Net Revenues is made as a result of an audit or for other accounting reasons, a corresponding adjustment in the Capital Replacement Reserve Account deposit shall be made. In addition, all proceeds from the sale of capital items no longer needed for the operation of the Facility, and the proceeds of any insurance received in reimbursement for any items previously paid for from the Capital Replacement Reserve, shall be deposited into the Capital Replacement Reserve Account upon receipt.

3.14 Use and Allocation of Capital Replacement Reserve. Any expenditures for Capital Replacements which have been budgeted and previously approved may be paid from the Capital Replacement Reserve Account without further approval from the Enterprise. Any amounts remaining in the Capital Replacement Reserve Account at the close of any year shall be carried forward and retained in the Capital Replacement Reserve Account until fully used. If amounts in the Capital Replacement Reserve Account at the end of any year plus the anticipated contributions to the Capital Replacement Reserve Account for the next ensuing year are not sufficient to pay for Capital Replacements authorized by the Capital Budget for such ensuing year, then funds in the amount of the projected deficiency may be advanced by Manager to be repaid to Manager pursuant to Section 5.4 of this Agreement as a Manager Advance.

3.15 Contracting. In entering contracts for the supply of goods and services for the Facility, Manager shall give preference to qualified members of the Tribe, their spouses and children, and qualified business entities certified by the Tribe to be controlled by members of the Tribe.

"Qualified" shall mean a member of the Tribe, a member's spouse or children, or a business entity certified by the Tribe to be controlled by members of the Tribe, who or which is able to provide services at competitive prices, has demonstrated skills and abilities to perform the tasks to be undertaken in an acceptable manner, in Manager's opinion, and can meet the reasonable bonding and/or financial requirements of Manager.

3.16 Internal Control Systems. Manager shall install systems for monitoring of all funds (the "Internal Control Systems"), which systems shall comply with all Legal Requirements, and shall be submitted to the Enterprise and the Tribal Gaming Authority for approval in advance of implementation, which approval shall not be unreasonably withheld. The Enterprise shall have the right to retain an auditor to review the adequacy of the Internal Control Systems prior to the Commencement Date. If the Enterprise elects to exercise this right, the cost of such review shall be a Pre-Opening Expense. Any significant changes in such systems after the Commencement Date also shall be subject to review and approval by the Tribal Gaming Authority in advance of implementation. The Tribal Gaming Authority and Manager shall have the right and duty to maintain and police the Internal Control Systems in order to prevent any loss of proceeds from the Facility. The Tribal Gaming Authority shall have the right to inspect and oversee the Internal Control System at all times. Manager shall install a closed circuit television system to be used for monitoring all cash handling activities of the Facility sufficient to meet all Legal Requirements.

3.17 Banking and Bank Accounts.

3.17.1 Enterprise Bank Accounts. The Enterprise shall select a bank or banks for the deposit and maintenance of funds and shall establish in such bank or banks accounts as Manager deems appropriate and necessary in the course of business and as consistent with this Agreement, including, but not limited to, a Depository Account, Disbursement Account, a Working Capital Account and a Capital Replacement Reserve Account ("Enterprise Bank Accounts"). Establishment of any Enterprise Bank Account shall be subject to the approval of the Enterprise. The sum of money agreed upon by the Manager and the Enterprise to be maintained in the Working Capital Account to serve as working capital for Facility operations, shall include

Attached hereto as Exhibit E is the form of Irrevocable Banking Instructions to be executed by the Enterprise with regard to each Enterprise Bank Account and to be in effect during the Term of this Agreement, other than with respect to the accounts maintained by the Enterprise with the "Collection Bank" and the "Depository Bank" pursuant to the Transfer and Deposit Agreement.

The parties agree that so long as the

Transfer and Deposit Agreement shall be in effect, the "Accounts" specified therein shall constitute the Disbursement Account of the Enterprise.

3.17.2 Daily Deposits to Depository Account. Manager shall

3.17.3 Disbursement Account. Manager shall, consistent with and pursuant to the approved annual Operating Budget and Annual Plan, have responsibility and authority for making or otherwise authorizing all payments for Operating Expenses, debt service, Management Fees, and disbursements to the Tribe from the Disbursement Account in accordance with the provisions of Section 5.

3.17.4 Transfers Between Accounts. Manager has the authority to

3.18 Insurance. Manager, on behalf of the Tribe and the Enterprise, shall arrange for, obtain and maintain, or cause its agents to maintain, with responsible insurance carriers licensed to do business in the State of California, insurance satisfactory to Manager and the Enterprise covering the Facility and the operations of the Enterprise, naming the Tribe, the

Enterprise, Manager, and Manager's Affiliates as insured parties, in at least the amounts which are set forth in Exhibit F.

3.19 Accounting and Books of Account.

3.19.1 Statements. Manager shall prepare and provide operating statements to the Enterprise on a monthly, quarterly, and annual basis. The operating statements shall comply with all Legal Requirements and shall include an income statement, statement of cash flows, and balance sheet for the Enterprise. Such statements shall include the Operating Budget and Annual Plan and Capital Budget projections as comparative statements, and which, after the first full year of operation, will include comparative statements from the comparable period for the prior year of all revenues, and all other amounts collected and received, and all deductions and disbursements made therefrom in connection with the Facility.

3.19.2 Books of Account. Manager shall maintain full and accurate books of account at an office in the Facility. The Enterprise and the Tribe shall have the right to immediate access to the daily operations of the Facility and shall have the unlimited right to inspect, examine, and copy all such books and supporting business records. Any such copies are to be considered confidential and proprietary and shall not be divulged to any third parties without the express written permission of the Enterprise. Such rights may be exercised through the Tribal Gaming Agency or through an agent, employee, attorney, or independent accountant acting on behalf of the Tribe or the Enterprise.

3.19.3 Accounting Standards. Manager shall maintain the books and records reflecting the operations of the Facility in accordance with the accounting practices of Manager in conformity with Generally Accepted Accounting Principles consistently applied and shall adopt and follow the fiscal accounting periods utilized by Manager in its normal course of business (i.e., a month, quarter and year prepared in accordance with the Enterprise Fiscal Year). The accounting systems and procedures shall comply with Legal Requirements and, at a minimum: include an adequate system of internal accounting controls; permit the preparation of financial statements in accordance with generally accepted accounting principles; be susceptible to audit; permit the calculation and payment of the Management Fee described in Section 5; provide for the allocation of operating expenses or overhead expenses among the Tribe, the Enterprise, and any other user of shared facilities and services; and (vi) allow the Enterprise, the Tribe and the NIGC to calculate the annual fees required under 25 C.F.R. 514.1.

3.19.4 Annual Audit. An independent certified public accounting firm of national recognition engaged by the Enterprise or the Tribe shall perform an annual audit of the books and records of the Enterprise and of all contracts for supplies, services or concessions reflecting Operating Expenses. The BIA and the NIGC shall also have the right to perform special audits of the Enterprise on any aspect of the Enterprise at any time without restriction. The costs incurred for such audits shall constitute an Operating Expense. Such audits shall be provided by the Tribe or the Enterprise, as the case may be, to all applicable federal and state agencies, as required by law, and may be used by Manager for reporting purposes under federal and state securities laws, if required.

3.20 Retail Shops and Concessions. With respect to the operation of the shops and concessions lo-cated within the Facility, the Enterprise shall approve in advance in writing the specific type or types of shops or concessions proposed by Manager to be authorized for inclusion in the Facility.

SECTION 4
LIENS

4.1 Liens. Subject to the exceptions hereinafter stated in Section 5.1, the Tribe and the Enterprise specifically warrant and represent to Manager that during the term of this Agreement neither the Tribe nor the Enterprise shall act in any way whatsoever, either directly or indirectly, to cause any person or entity to become an encumbrancer or lienholder of the Property or the Facility, other than the Lender, or to allow any person or entity to obtain any interest in this Agreement without the prior written consent of Manager, and, where applicable, consent from the United States. Manager specifically warrants and represents to the Tribe and the Enterprise that during the term of this Agreement Manager shall not act in any way, directly or indirectly, to cause any person or entity to become an encumbrancer or lienholder of the Property or the Facility, or to obtain any interest in this Agreement without the prior written consent of the Tribe or the Enterprise, and, where applicable, the United States. The Tribe, the Enterprise and Manager shall keep the Facility and Property free and clear of all enforceable mechanics' and other enforceable liens resulting from the construction of the Facility and all other enforceable liens which may attach to the Facility or the Property, which shall at all times remain the property of the United States in trust for the Tribe. If any such lien is claimed or filed, it shall be the duty of Manager, utilizing funds of the Enterprise, to discharge the lien within thirty (30) days after having been given written notice of such claim, either by payment to the claimant, by the posting of a bond and the payment into the court of the amount necessary to relieve and discharge the Property from such claim, or in any other manner which will result in the discharge or stay of such claim.

4.2 Exceptions. The Enterprise shall have the right to grant security interests in Facility revenues, as well as first priority security interests in any Facility assets other than personal property purchased with the proceeds of the Loan, but only if such security interests are granted to secure loans made to and for the benefit of the Enterprise.

SECTION 5
MANAGEMENT FEE, REIMBURSEMENTS AND DISBURSEMENTS BY MANAGER

5.1 Management Fee. In consideration of the services rendered by Manager pursuant to this Agreement, Man-ager shall be entitled to an annual Management Fee equal to The Management Fee shall be payable monthly in an amount equal to the accrued Management Fee for the preceding month plus any Shortfall Amount. Notwith-standing anything contained in this Agreement to the contrary, Manager shall not be entitled to any compensation for providing management services pursuant to this Agreement other than the annual Management Fee.

5.2 Disbursements for Operating Expenses. Each month, Manager shall, for and on behalf of the Enterprise, cause funds to be disbursed from the Disbursement Account, to the extent available, to pay Operating Expenses due and payable. So long as the Transfer and Deposit Agreement shall be in effect, such disbursements shall be from the "Operating Account" specified therein.

5.3 Disbursements for Debt Service. After the disbursements pursuant to Section 5.2, Manager shall, for and on behalf of the Enterprise, disburse funds from the Disbursement Account, to the extent available, to pay debt service due and payable in accordance with the Loan Agree-ment. Thereafter, Manager shall, for and on behalf of the Enterprise, cause funds to be disbursed from the Disbursement Account, to the extent available, to pay debt service due and payable in accordance with Financing Agreements other than the Loan Agreement in accordance with the payment priorities specified in the Loan Agreement and the Financing Agreements. So long as the Transfer and Deposit Agreement shall be in effect, such disbursements shall be from the "Debt Service Account," "Permitted Equipment Debt Account," and "Permitted Other Debt Account" specified therein, respectively.

5.4 Payment of Fees and Tribal Disbursement. Within twenty-one (21) days after the end of each calendar month of operations, Manager shall calculate Gross Revenues, Operating Expenses, and Net Revenues of the Facility for the previous month's operations and the year's operations to date.

5.4.1 Disbursements Pursuant to Transfer and Deposit Agreement. After the disbursements pursuant to Sec-tions 5.2 and 5.3, so long as the Transfer and Deposit Agreement shall be in effect, Manager shall cause funds to be disbursed from the Enterprise Bank Account(s) in accordance with the provisions of Section 3.6, 3.7 and 3.8 there-of.

(iv) the balance of Excess Funds shall be disbursed to the Enterprise.

5.4.2 Disbursements Other Than Pursuant to Transfer and Deposit Agreement. In the event the Transfer and Deposit Agreement shall no longer be in effect, after the disbursements pursuant to Sections 5.2 and 5.3, Manager shall cause the funds remaining in the Enterprise Bank Account(s) ("Excess Funds") to be applied in the following order:

5.4.3 Shortfall Amounts and Manager Advances. Shortfall Amounts due Manager and Manager Advances shall be paid at such time as sufficient Excess Funds exist to pay such Shortfall Amounts or Manager Advances in accordance with Section 5.4,

5.5 Minimum Guaranteed Monthly Payment. Manager shall pay the Tribe
from Net Revenues per month (the "Minimum Guaranteed *lq*
Monthly Payment"), beginning on the Commencement Date and continuing for the remainder of the Term in
accordance with Section 5.4. The Minimum Guaranteed Monthly Payment shall have preference over the retirement of development and construction costs of the Facility. The Minimum Guaranteed Monthly Payment shall be
payable to the Tribe in arrears on the twenty-first (21') day of each calendar month following the month in which
the Commencement Date occurs, which payment shall have priority over the Management Fee. If the Commencement Date is a date other than the first day of a calendar month, the first payment will be prorated from the Commencement Date to the end of the month. Minimum Guaranteed Monthly Payments shall be charged against the
Tribe's distribution of Net Revenues for each month provided, however,
In the event Class II and/or Class III gaming is suspended for any portion of a month, the Guaranteed Monthly
Payment shall be prorated and payable for the portion of the month during which gaming was conducted at the
Facility. No Minimum Guaranteed Monthly Payment shall be owed for a month in the event Class II and/or Class
III gaming is suspended or terminated at the Facility pursuant to Section 3.4 for the entire month. The obligation of
Manager to make Minimum Guaranteed Monthly Payments shall cease upon termination of this Agreement. Ex-
cept as provided in the preceding sentence of this Section 5.5, Manager's obligation to pay the Tribe the Minimum
Guaranteed Monthly Payment is unconditional, and shall not be affected by the actual level of funds generated by
the Facility.

5.6 Distribution of Excess Funds. The distributions of Excess Funds to the
Enterprise pursuant to this Section 5 shall be deposited in the Enterprise's bank account specified by the Enterprise
in a notice to Manager pursuant to Section 8.2.

5.7 Manager Guaranty. Manager shall

5.8 Development and Construction Costs. Manager and the Tribe agree that

SECTION 6

TRADE NAMES, TRADE MARKS AND SERVICE MARKS

6.1 Facility Name. The Facility shall be operated under the name "Trump Spotlight 29 Casino Hotel" or such other
name as the parties may agree upon (the "Facility Name") during the Term of this Agreement, subject to and in
accordance with the terms and conditions of the Trademark License Agreement dated May 31, 2000, between
Trump Hotels & Casino Resorts Holdings, L.P. and the Tribe, as amended by the First Amendment to Trademark
License Agreement dated as of March, 2002.

6.2 Signs. Prior to the Commencement Date and from time to time during the
Term hereof, Manager agrees to erect and install, in accordance with local codes and regulations, all signs Manager
deems necessary in, on or about the Facility, including, but not limited to, signs bearing the Facility Name.

SECTION 7

TAXES

7.1 State and Local Taxes. If the State of California or any local government attempts to impose any tax including
any possessory interest tax upon any party to this Agreement or upon the Enterprise, the Facility or the Property, the
Tribal Council, in the name of the appropriate party or parties in interest, may resist such attempt through legal
action. The costs of such action and the compensation of legal counsel shall be an Operating Expense of the Facility.
Any such tax shall constitute an Operating Expense of the Facility. This Section shall in no manner be construed to
imply that any party to this Agreement or the Enterprise is liable for any such tax.

7.2 Tribal Taxes. The Tribe agrees that neither it nor any agent, agency,
affiliate or representative of the Tribe will impose any taxes, fees, assessments, or other charges of any
nature whatsoever on payments of any debt service to Manager or any of its Affiliates or to any lender
furnishing financing for the Facility or for the Enterprise, or on the Enterprise, the Facility, the revenues therefrom or on the Management Fee as described in Section 5.1 of this Agreement; provided,
however, the Tribe may assess license fees reflecting reasonable regulatory costs incurred by the Tribal
Gaming Agency to the extent not paid as Operating Expenses; the Tribe further agrees that neither it nor
any agent, agency, affiliate or representative will impose any taxes, fees, assessments or other charges
of any nature whatsoever on the salaries or benefits, or dividends paid to, any of Manager's stockholders, officers, directors, or employees, any of the employees of the Enterprise; or any provider of goods,
materials, or services to the Facility, other than with respect to any such provider of goods, materials, or
services to the Facility, license fees reflecting reasonable regulatory costs incurred by the Tribal Gaming Authority.

Nothing in this Section 7.2 shall be construed to prohibit the Tribe from taxing the sale of goods at the Facility in
amounts equivalent to any state taxes that would otherwise be applicable but for the Tribe's status as an Indian
tribe; provided that no such tax shall be applied to any goods supplied as Promotional Allowances.

7.3 Compliance with Internal Revenue Code. Manager shall comply with all applicable provisions of the
Internal Revenue Code.

SECTION 8

GENERAL PROVISIONS

8.1 Situs of the Contracts. This Agreement, as well as all contracts entered into between the Tribe, the Enterprise and any person or any entity providing services to the Facility, shall be deemed entered into in California, and shall be subject to all Legal Requirements of the Tribe and federal law as well as approval by the Secretary of the Interior where required by 25 U.S.C. 81 or by the Chairman of the NIGC where required by the IGRA.

8.2 Notice. Any notice required to be given pursuant to this Agreement shall be delivered to the appropriate party by Federal Express or by Certified Mail Return Receipt Requested, addressed as follows:

If to the Tribe or the Enterprise, to:

Dean Mike, Chairman

Twenty-Nine Palms Band of Luiseno Mission Indians of California

46-200 Harrison Place

Coachella CA 92236

with a copy to: Gene R. Gambale, Esq.

Vice President-General Counsel

Spotlight 29 Enterprises

46-200 Harrison Place Coachella CA 92236

If to Manager, to: Robert M. Pickus

Executive Vice President and General Counsel Trump Hotels & Casino Resorts, Inc.

Huron Avenue & Brigantine Boulevard

Atlantic City NJ 08401

with copies to: John M. Peebles, Esq.

Monteau, Peebles & Marks, L.L.P. 12100 West Center Road, Suite 202 Bel Air Plaza

Omaha NE 68144-3960

and: Peter Michael Laughlin, Esq.

Graham, Curtin & Sheridan, PA

4 Headquarters Plaza

Morristown NJ 07962-1991

or to such other different address(s) as Manager, the Enterprise or the Tribe may specify in writing using the notice procedure called for in this Section 8.2. Any such notice shall be deemed given two (2) days following deposit in the United States mail or upon actual delivery, whichever first occurs.

8.3 Authority to Execute and Perform Agreement. The Tribe, the Enterprise and Manager represent and warrant to each other that they each have full power and authority to execute this Agreement and to be bound by and perform the terms hereof. On request, each party shall furnish the other evidence of such authority.

8.4 Relationship. Manager, the Enterprise and the Tribe shall not be construed as joint venturers or partners of each other by reason of this Agreement and neither shall have the power to bind or obligate the other except as set forth in this Agreement.

8.5 Manager's Contractual Authority. Manager is authorized to make, enter into and perform in the name of and for the account of the Enterprise, such contracts deemed necessary by Manager to perform its obligations under this Agreement, provided such contracts comply with the terms and conditions of this Agreement, including, but not limited to, Section 3.2.4, and provided such contracts do not obligate the Enterprise to pay sums not approved in the Operating Budget and Annual Plan or the Capital Budget.

8.6 Further Actions. The Tribe, the Enterprise and 'Manager agree to execute all contracts, agreements and documents and to take all actions necessary to comply with the provisions of this Agreement and the intent hereof.

8.7 Defense. Except for disputes between the Tribe, the Enterprise and Manager, and claims relating to the Tribe's status as a Tribe or the trust status of the Property, Manager shall bring and/or defend and/or settle any claim or legal action brought against Manager, the Enterprise or the Tribe, individually, jointly or severally, or any Enterprise Employee, in connection with the operation of the Facility. Subject to the Tribe's approval of legal counsel, Manager shall retain and supervise legal counsel, accountants and such other professionals, consultants and specialists as Manager deems appropriate to defend any such claim or cause of action. All liabilities, costs and expenses, including reasonable attorneys' fees and disbursements incurred in defending and/or settling any such claim or legal action which are not covered by insurance, shall be an Operating Expense. Nothing contained herein is a grant to Manager of the right to waive the Tribe's or the Enterprise's sovereign immunity. That right is strictly reserved to the Tribe and the Enterprise. Any settlement of a third party claim or cause of action shall require approval of the Enterprise.

8.8 Waivers. No failure or delay by Manager, the Enterprise or the Tribe to insist upon the strict performance of any covenant, agreement, term or condition of this Agreement, or to exercise any right or remedy consequent upon the breach thereof, shall constitute a waiver of any such breach or any subsequent breach of such covenant, agreement, term or condition. No covenant, agreement, term, or condition of this Agreement and no breach thereof shall be waived, altered or modified except by written instrument. No waiver of any breach shall affect or alter this Agreement, but each and every covenant, agreement, term and condition of this Agreement shall continue in full force and effect with respect to any other then existing or subsequent breach thereof.

8.9 Captions. The captions for each Section and Subsection are intended for convenience only.

8.10 Severability. If any of the terms and provisions hereof shall be held invalid or unenforceable, such invalidity or unenforceability shall not affect any of the other terms or provisions hereof. If, however, any material part of a party's rights under this Agreement shall be declared invalid or unenforceable, (specifically including Manager's right to receive its Management Fees) the party whose rights have been declared invalid or unenforceable shall have the option to terminate this Agreement upon thirty (30) days written notice to the other party, without liability on the part of the terminating party.

8.11 Interest. Any amounts advanced by Manager related to the operation of the Facility shall accrue interest at the rate specified in the Note; provided, however, no interest shall accrue or be payable in respect of the Minimum Guaranteed Monthly Payment funded by Manager.

8.12 Travel and Out-of-Pocket Expenses. Subject to the Operating Budget and Annual Plan, all travel and out-of-pocket expenses of Enterprise Employees reasonably incurred in the performance of their duties shall be an Operating Expense.

8.13 Third Party Beneficiary. This Agreement is exclusively for the benefit of the parties hereto and it may not be enforced by any party other than the parties to this Agreement and shall not give rise to liability to any third party other than the authorized successors and assigns of the parties hereto as such are authorized by this Agreement.

8.14 Brokerage. Manager, the Enterprise and the Tribe represent and warrant to each other that none of them has sought the services of a broker, finder or agent in this transaction, and none of them has employed, nor authorized, any other person to act in such capacity. Manager, the Enterprise and the Tribe each hereby agrees to indemnify and hold the other harmless from and against any and all claims, loss, liability, damage or expenses (including reasonable attorneys' fees) suffered or incurred by the other party as a result of a claim brought by a person or entity engaged or claiming to be engaged as a finder, broker or agent by the **indemnifying party.**

8.15 Survival of Covenants. Any covenant, term or provision of this Agreement which, in order to be effective, must survive the termination of this Agreement, shall survive any such termination.

8.16 Estoppel Certificate. Manager, the Enterprise and the Tribe agree to furnish to any other party, from time to time upon request, an estoppel certificate in such reasonable form as the requesting party may request stating whether there have been any defaults under this Agreement known to the party furnishing the estoppel certificate and such other information relating to the Facility as may be reasonably requested.

8.17 Periods of Time. Whenever any determination is to be made or action is to be taken on a date specified in this Agreement, if such date shall fall on a Saturday, Sunday or legal holiday under the laws of the Tribe, federal government, or the State of California, then in such event said date shall be extended to the next day which is not a Saturday, Sunday or legal holiday.

8.18 Exhibits. All exhibits attached hereto are incorporated herein by reference and made a part hereof as if fully rewritten or reproduced herein.

8.19 Successors, Assigns, and Subcontracting. The benefits and obligations of this Agreement shall inure to and be binding upon the parties hereto and their respective successors and assigns. Manager shall have the right to assign its rights under this Agreement to one or more directly or indirectly wholly-owned subsidiaries of Trump Hotels & Casino Resorts, Inc., or its successor. The Enterprise's consent shall be required for the assignment or subcontracting by Manager of its rights, interests or obligations as Manager hereunder to any person or entity other than an Affiliate of Manager, or any successor corporation to Manager, provided that any such assignee or subcontractor agrees to be bound by the terms and conditions of this Agreement, and the Enterprise shall consent to any such assignee or subcontractor provided that such assignee or subcontractor has, in the discretion of the Enterprise, the competency and financial capability to perform as required by this Agreement. The acquisition of Manager or its parent company by a party other than an Affiliate of Manager, or its successor corporation, shall not constitute an assignment of this Agreement by Manager and this Agreement shall remain in full force and effect between the Tribe, the Enterprise and Manager, subject only to Legal Requirements. In all respects, any assignment or subcontracting permitted pursuant to this Section 8.19 shall be subject to the notification requirements provided in Section 13.4 of this Agreement and any required approval by the NIGC.

8.20 Permitted Assignment. Any assignment of this Agreement permitted under the Agreement, to the extent mandated by the IGRA, shall be subject to approval by the Chairman of the NIGC or his authorized representative after a complete background investigation of the proposed assignee. The Tribe or

Enterprise shall, without the consent of Manager but subject to approval by the Secretary of the Interior or the Chairman of the NIGC or his authorized representative, have the right to assign this Agreement and the assets of the Facility to an instrumentality of the Tribe or to a corporation wholly-owned by the Tribe organized to conduct the business of the Enterprise for the Tribe that assumes all obligations herein. Any assignment by the Tribe shall not prejudice the rights of Manager under this Agreement. No assignment authorized hereunder shall be effective until all necessary government approvals have been obtained.

8.21 Time is of the Essence. Time is of the essence in the performance of this Agreement.

8.22 Confidential Information. The parties agree that any information received concerning any other party during the performance of this Agreement, regarding the parties' organization, financial matters, marketing plans, or other information of a proprietary nature (the "Confidential Information"), will be treated by both parties in full confidence and except as required to allow Manager, the Enterprise and the Tribe to perform their respective covenants and obligations hereunder, or in response to legal process or appropriate and necessary inquiry, and will not be revealed to any other persons, firms or organizations. This provision shall survive the termination of this Agreement for a period of two (2) years.

The obligations not to use or disclose the Confidential Information shall not apply to Confidential Information which (i) has been made previously available to the public by the Tribe, the Enterprise or Manager or becomes generally available to the public, unless the Confidential Information being made available to the public results in a breach of this Agreement; **(ii)** prior to disclosure to the Tribe, the Enterprise or Manager, was already rightfully in any such person's possession; or **(iii)** is obtained by the Tribe, the Enterprise or Manager from a third party who is lawfully in possession of such Confidential Information, and not in violation of any contractual, legal or fiduciary obligation to the Tribe, the Enterprise or Manager, with respect to such Confidential Information and who does not require the Tribe, the Enterprise or Manager to refrain from disclosing such Confidential Information to others.

8.23 Patron Dispute Resolution. Manager shall submit all patron disputes concerning play to the Tribal Gaming Authority pursuant to the Tribal Gaming Code, and the regulations promulgated thereunder.

8.24 Modification. Any change to or modification of this Agreement must be in writing signed by all parties hereto and shall be effective only upon approval by the Chairman of the NIGC, the date of signature of the parties notwithstanding.

SECTION 9
WARRANTIES

9.1 Noninterference in Tribal Affairs. Manager agrees not to interfere in or attempt to wrongfully influence the internal affairs or government decisions of the Tribal Council or the Enterprise by offering cash incentives, by making written or oral threats to the personal or financial status of any person, or by any other action, except for actions in the normal course of business of Manager that relate to the Facility. As of the date of this Agreement, the Tribe and the Enterprise acknowledge that Manager has not interfered or wrongfully interfered in the internal affairs of the Tribe and the Enterprise. For the purposes of this Section 9.1, if any such undue interference in Tribal affairs is alleged by the federally recognized Tribal government in writing and the NIGC finds that Manager has unduly interfered with the internal affairs of the Tribe government and has not taken sufficient action to cure and prevent such interference, that finding of interference shall be grounds for termination of the Agreement. Manager shall be entitled to immediate written notice and a complete copy of any such complaint to the NIGC.

9.2 Prohibition of Payments to Members of Tribal Government. Manager represents and warrants that no payments have been or will be made by Manager or Manager's Affiliates, to any Member of the Tribal Government, any Tribal official, any relative of a Member of Tribal Government or Tribal official, or any Tribal government employee for the purpose of obtaining any special privilege, gain, advantage or consideration.

9.3 Prohibition of Hiring Members of Tribal Government. No Member of the Tribal Government, Tribal official, or employee of the Tribal government may be employed at the Facility or Manager or its Affiliates without a written waiver of this Section 9.3 by the Tribe. For this purpose, the Tribe will identify all such persons to Manager in a writing and take reasonable steps to keep the list current; Manager shall not be held responsible if any person not on such written list is employed.

9.4 Prohibition of Financial Interest in Enterprise. No Member of the Tribal Government or relative of a Member of the Tribal Government shall have a direct or indirect financial interest in the Enterprise greater than the interest of any other member of the Tribe. No Member of the Tribal Government or relative of a Member of the Tribal Government shall have a direct or indirect financial interest in Manager or Manager's Affiliates.

9.5 Definitions. As used in this Section 9, "Member of the Tribal Government" means any member of the Tribal Council, the Tribal Gaming Authority or any independent board or body created to oversee any aspect of Gaming and any Tribal court official; "Relative" means an individual residing in the same household who is related as a spouse, father, mother, son or daughter.

SECTION 10

TERMINATION

10.1 <u>Voluntary Termination and Termination for Cause.</u> This Agreement may be terminated pursuant to the provisions of Sections 3.4.4, 10.2, 10.3, 10.4, 10.5 and 10.6 and 10.10.

10.2 <u>Voluntary Termination.</u> This Agreement may be terminated upon the mutual written consent and approval of the parties.

10.3 <u>Termination for Cause.</u> Either the Tribe or the Enterprise may terminate this Agreement if Manager commits or allows to be committed any Material Breach of this Agreement, and Manager may terminate this Agreement if either the Tribe or the Enterprise commits or allows to be committed any Material Breach of this Agreement,. A Material Breach of this Agreement means a failure of any party to perform any material duty or obligation on its part for any thirty (30) consecutive days after notice, and shall include, but not be limited to, those events identified as a Material Breach in Section 13.5 of this Agreement. Any action taken or the adoption of any statute or code that taxes, materially prejudices or materially adversely affects or imposes additional costs or burdens on Manager's rights or duties under this Agreement shall be a Material Breach of this Agreement by the Tribe. No party may terminate this Agreement on grounds of Material Breach unless it has provided written notice to the other parties of its intention to declare a default and to terminate this Agreement and the defaulting party thereafter fails to cure or take steps to substantially cure the default within sixty (60) days following receipt of such notice. During the period specified in the notice to terminate, any party may submit the matter to arbitration under the dispute resolution provisions of this Agreement at Section 16. The discontinuance or correction of a Material Breach shall constitute a cure thereof.

An election to pursue damages or to pursue specific performance of this Agreement or other equitable remedies while this Agreement remains in effect pursuant to the provisions of Sections 10.7 or 10.8 shall not preclude the injured party from providing notice of termination pursuant to this Section 10.3. Neither shall termination preclude a suit for damages.

10.4 <u>Involuntary Termination Due to Changes in Legal Requirements.</u> It is the understanding and intention of the parties that the establishment and operation of the Facility shall conform to and comply with all Legal Requirements. If during the term of this Agreement, the Facility or any material aspect of Gaming is determined by the Congress of the United States, the Department of the Interior of the United States of America, the NIGC, or the final judgment of a court of competent jurisdiction to be unlawful under federal law, the obligations of the parties hereto shall cease, and this Agreement shall be of no further force and effect; provided that:

Manager shall have the rights described in Section 3.4 of this Agreement;

Manager, the Tribe and the Enterprise shall retain all money previously paid to them pursuant to Section 5 of this Agreement; funds of the Enterprise in any Enterprise account shall be paid and distributed as provided in Section 5 of this Agreement;

The Enterprise shall retain its interest in the title (and any lease) to all Facility assets, including all fixtures, supplies and equipment, subject to any requirements of financing arrangements.

10.5 <u>Manager's Right to Terminate Agreement.</u> Manager may terminate this Agreement by written notice effective upon receipt if:

Any Tribal, State or Federal authority where approval is required fails to approve this Agreement or otherwise objects to the performance by Manager of any obligation imposed on it under this Agreement. Manager has been notified by any Federal regulatory agency that the performance by it of any obligation imposed by this Agreement will jeopardize the retention of any license, or approvals granted thereunder, held by Manager or any of its Affiliates in other jurisdiction, and the Tribe or the Enterprise refuses to allow Manager to immediately rectify any such complaint. Manager has reason to believe that the performance by it, by the Enterprise or by the Tribe of any obligation imposed under this Agreement may reasonably be expected to result in the breach of any Legal Requirement and the parties have been unable to agree upon waiver of such performance within ten (10) days written notice by Manager.

Through its own actions, the Tribe or the Enterprise fails to make any payment to Manager when due within the time specified in this Agreement and a grace period of thirty (30) days.

10.6 <u>Tribe's and Enterprise's Right to Terminate Agreement.</u> In addition to the suspension of Manager pursuant to Section 10.9 herein, the Tribe or the Enterprise may terminate this Agreement by written notice effective upon receipt if:Any Federal or State authority, where approval is required, fails to approve this Agreement or otherwise objects to the performance by Manager of any obligation imposed on it under this Agreement and Manager has not cured the circumstance giving rise to the failure to approve or the objection to performance within thirty (30) days.

The Tribe has reason to believe that the performance by it, the Enterprise or Manager of any obligation imposed under this Agreement may reasonably be expected to result in the breach of any Legal Requirement (other than a Legal Requirement imposed or created by the Tribe or any agency thereof) and the parties have been unable to agree upon waiver of such performance within ten (10) days of written notice given by the Tribe. Manager fails to make any payment to the Tribe or the Enterprise when due, including but not limited to any Minimum Guaranteed Monthly Payment to the Tribe within the time specified in this Agreement and a grace period of thirty (30) days. Manager has had its license withdrawn because Manager, or a director or officer of Manager, has been convicted of a criminal felony or misdemeanor offense in the performance of Manager duties hereunder, or where Manager has failed to disclose any such conviction to the Tribal Gaming Authority promptly upon Manager receiving notice thereof; provided, however, the Tribe or the Enterprise may not terminate this Agreement based on a director or officer's conviction where Manager terminates such individual within ten (10) days after receiving notice of the conviction.

10.7 <u>Consequences of Manager's Breach.</u> In the event of the termination of this Agreement by the Tribe or the Enterprise for cause under Section 10.3, Manager shall not, prospectively from the date of termination, except as provided in Section 10.3, have the right to its Management Fee from the Facility, but such termination shall not affect Manager's rights relating to recoupment and reimbursement of monies owed to Manager and/or guaranteed by Manager and/or Manager's Affiliates (to the extent Manager or Manager's Affiliate has paid under such guarantee) under this Agreement, the Financing Agreements, the Note, the Manager Guaranty or any other agreements entered pursuant hereto, including a Shortfall Amount, and such right of recoupment and reimbursement shall survive any termination of this Agreement. Any Net Revenues accruing through the date of termination shall be distributed in accordance with Section 5 of this Agreement. Manager, the Tribe and the Enterprise acknowledge and agree that termination of this Agreement may not be a sufficient or appropriate remedy for breach by Manager, and further agree that pursuant to the other provisions of this Agreement, including, but not limited to, Section 16, the Tribe or the Enterprise shall, upon breach of this Agreement by Manager, have the right to pursue such remedies (in addition to termination) at law or equity as it determines are best able to compensate it for such breach. Manager specifically acknowledges and agrees that there may be irreparable harm to the Tribe or the Enterprise and that damages will be difficult to determine if Manager commits a Material Breach, and Manager therefore further acknowledges that an injunction and/or other equitable relief may be an appropriate remedy for any such breach. In any event, the Tribe shall have the right to all payments due to the Tribe accruing until the date of termination.

10.8 <u>Consequences of Tribe's Breach.</u> In the event of termination of this Agreement by Manager for cause under Section 10.3, Manager shall not be required to perform any further services under this Agreement and the Enterprise shall indemnify and hold Manager harmless against all liabilities of any nature whatsoever relating to the Facility, but only insofar as these liabilities result from acts within the control of the Tribe or the Enterprise or their respective agents or created by the termination of this Agreement. Manager, the Tribe and the Enterprise acknowledge and agree that termination of this Agreement may not be a sufficient or appropriate remedy for breach by the Tribe or the Enterprise, and further agree that pursuant to the other provisions of this Agreement, including but not necessarily limited to, Section 16, Manager shall, upon breach of this Agreement by the Tribe or the Enterprise, have the right to pursue such remedies (in addition to termination) at law or equity as it determines are best able to compensate it for such breach, including, without limitation, specifically actions to require payment of the Management Fee pursuant to Section 5 for a term equal to the then remaining term of this Agreement at the percentage of Net Revenues specified in Section 5. The Tribe and the Enterprise specifically acknowledge and agree that there may be irreparable harm to Manager and that damages will be difficult to determine if the Tribe or the Enterprise commits a material breach, and the Tribe and the Enterprise therefore further acknowledge that an injunction and/or other equitable relief may be an appropriate remedy for any such breach.

10.9 <u>Suspension of Manager for Cause; Notice and Opportunity to Cure.</u> In the event of any breach of this Agreement by Manager involving a violation by Manager of any Legal Requirements, the Enterprise may immediately suspend the right and authority of Manager to manage the Facility unless and until such breach is remedied or cured by Manager. The Enterprise will give Manager notice of any alleged violation of the Tribal Gaming Code by Manager and twenty (20) days opportunity to cure before the Tribal Gaming Authority may take any action other than suspension of the Manager based on such alleged violation.

10.10 <u>Enterprise's Buy-Out Option.</u> The Enterprise shall have the right to
If the Enterprise fails to satisfy any of the above conditions on or before the dates specified above, then this option and any attempted exercise thereof shall be null and void and of no further force or effect, and this Agreement shall continue in full force and effect according to its terms.

SECTION 11
CONCLUSION OF THE MANAGEMENT TERM
11.1 <u>Conclusion of the Management Term.</u> Upon the conclusion or the termination of this Agreement, Manager shall have the following rights and obligations:
11.2 <u>Transition.</u> Manager shall take reasonable steps for the orderly transition of management of the Facility to the Tribe, the Enterprise or its designee pursuant to a transition plan as described in Section 17 of this Agreement.

11.3 <u>Undistributed Net Revenues.</u> If the Facility has accrued Net Revenues which have not been distributed under Section 5 of this Agreement, Manager shall receive that Management Fee equal to that Management Fee it would have received had the distribution occurred during the term of the Management Agreement (including any Shortfall Amount, but upon termination at the conclusion of the Term, only to the extent of Excess Funds).

SECTION 12
CONSENTS AND APPROVALS

12.1 <u>Tribal.</u> Where approval or consent or other action of the Tribe is required, such approval shall mean the written approval of the Tribal Council evidenced by a resolution thereof, certified by a Tribal official as having been duly adopted, or such other person or entity designated by resolution of the Tribal Council. Any such approval, consent or action shall not be unreasonably withheld or delayed; provided that the foregoing does not apply where a specific provision of this Agreement allows the Tribe an absolute right to deny approval or consent or withhold action.

12.2 <u>Manager.</u> Where approval or consent or other action of Manager is required, such approval shall mean the written approval of an officer of Manager. Any such approval, consent or other action shall not be unreasonably withheld or delayed.

SECTION 13
DISCLOSURES

13.1 <u>Shareholders and Directors.</u> Manager warrants that on the date of this Agreement its Affiliates, shareholders, directors and officers are those listed on Exhibit G.

13.2 <u>Warranties.</u> Manager further warrants and represents as follows: no person or entity has any beneficial ownership interest in Manager other than as set forth herein; no officer, director or owner of ten (10%) percent or more of the stock of Manager has been arrested, indicted for, convicted of, or pleaded *nolo contendere* to any felony or any gaming offense, or had any association with individuals or entities known to be connected with organized crime; and no person or entity listed on Exhibit G to this Agreement, including any officers and directors of Manager, has been arrested, indicted for, convicted of, or pleaded nolo contendere to any felony or any gaming offense, or had any association with individuals or entities known to be connected with organized crime.

13.3 <u>Criminal and Credit Investigation.</u> Manager agrees that all of its shareholders, directors and officers (whether or not involved in the Facility), shall:

consent to background investigations to be conducted by the Tribe, the State of California, the Federal Bureau of Investigation (the "FBI") or any other law enforcement authority to the extent required by the IGRA and the Compact; be subject to licensing requirements in accordance with Tribal law and this Agreement; consent to a background, criminal and credit investigation to be conducted by or for the NIGC, if required; consent to a financial and credit investigation to be conducted by a credit reporting or investigation agency at the request of the Tribe; cooperate fully with such investigations; and disclose any information requested by the Tribe which would facilitate the background and financial investigation.

Any materially false or deceptive disclosures or failure to cooperate fully with such investigations by an employee of Manager or an employee of the Tribe shall result in the immediate dismissal of such employee. The results of any such investigation may be disclosed by the Tribe to federal officials and to such other regulatory authorities as required by law.

13.4 <u>Disclosure Amendments.</u> The Tribe and Enterprise acknowledge that Manager is wholly-owned by a publicly traded company, and that Manager's Affiliates, shareholders, directors and officers may change from time to time without the prior approval of the Tribe or the Enterprise. Manager agrees that whenever there is any material change in the information disclosed pursuant to this Section 13 it shall notify the Tribe of such change not later than ten (10) days following the change or within ten (10) days after it becomes aware of such change, whichever is later. In the event the change relates to information provided or required to be provided to the NIGC pursuant to 25 C.F.R 537.1, Manager shall notify the NIGC in sufficient time to permit the NIGC to complete its background investigation by the time the individual is to assume management responsibility for the gaming operation, and within ten (10) days of any proposed change in financial interest. All of the warranties and agreements contained in this Section 13 shall apply to any person or entity who would be listed in this Section 13 as a result of such changes.

13.5 <u>Breach of Manager's Warranties and Agreements.</u> The material breach of any warranty or agreement of Manager contained in this Section 13 shall be grounds for immediate termination of this Agreement; provided that (i) if a breach of the warranty contained in clause (ii) of Section 13.2 is discovered, and such breach was not disclosed by any background check conducted by the FBI as part of the BIA or other federal approval of this Agreement, or was discovered by the FBI investigation but all officers and directors of Manager sign sworn affidavits that they had no knowledge of such breach, then Manager shall have thirty (30) days after notice from the Tribe to terminate the interest of the offending person or entity and, if such termination takes place, this Agreement shall remain in full force and effect; and (ii) if a breach relates to a failure to update changes in financial position or additional gaming related activities, then Manager shall have ten

(10) days after notice from the Tribe to cure such default prior to termination.

SECTION 14
RECORDATION

At the option of the Lender, Manager, the Enterprise or the Tribe, any security agreement related to the Financing Agreements may be recorded in any public records. Where such recordation is desired in any relevant recording office maintained by the Tribe, and/or in the public records of the BIA, the Tribe or the Enterprise will accomplish such recordation upon the request of the Lender or Manager, as the case may be. No such recordation shall be deemed to waive the Tribe's or the Enterprise's sovereign immunity.

SECTION 15
NO LIEN, LEASE OR JOINT VENTURE

The parties agree and expressly warrant that neither the Management Agreement nor any exhibit thereto is a mortgage or lease and, consequently, does not convey any present interest whatsoever in the Facility or the Property, nor any proprietary interest in the Facility itself. The parties further agree and acknowledge that it is not their intent, and that this Agreement shall not be construed, to create a joint venture between the Tribe or the Enterprise and Manager; rather, Manager shall be deemed to be an independent contractor for all purposes hereunder.

SECTION 16
DISPUTE RESOLUTION

16.1 General. The parties agree that binding arbitration shall be the remedy for all disputes, controversies and claims arising out of this Agreement, any documents referenced by any of this Agreement, any agreements collateral thereto, or any notice of termination thereof, including without limitation, any dispute, controversy or claim arising out of any of these agreements; provided, however, that actions or decisions by the Tribe that constitute the exercise of its sovereign governmental powers shall not be subject to arbitration, including decisions or actions by the Tribal Gaming Authority regarding the issuance or denial of licenses, and actions by the Tribal Council regarding the approval of budgets or the enactment of ordinances relating to Gaming. The Tribe acknowledges, however, that while the exercise of its governmental powers in a manner contrary to a provision of this Agreement may not be avoided through arbitration, Manager may compel arbitration pursuant to this Section 16 to redress any injury suffered by Manager as a result of such exercise. The parties intend that such arbitration shall provide final and binding resolution of any dispute, controversy or claim, and that action in any other forum shall be brought only if necessary to compel arbitration, or to enforce an arbitration award or order. All initial arbitration or judicial proceedings shall be instituted within twelve (12) months after the claim accrues or shall be forever barred.

Each party agrees that it will use its best efforts to negotiate an amicable resolution of any dispute between Manager and the Enterprise or the Tribe arising from this Agreement. If the Tribe or the Enterprise and Manager are unable to negotiate an amicable resolution of a dispute within fourteen (14) days from the date of notice of the dispute pursuant to the notice section of this Agreement, or such other period as the parties mutually agree in writing, either party may refer the matter to arbitration as provided herein.

16.2 Initiation of Arbitration and Selection of Arbitrators. Arbitration shall be initiated by written notice by one party to the other pursuant to the notice section of this Agreement, and the Commercial Arbitration Rules of the American Arbitration Association shall thereafter apply. The arbitrators shall have the power to grant equitable and injunctive relief and specific performance as provided in this Agreement. If necessary, orders to compel arbitration or enforce an arbitration award may be sought before the United States District Court for the Central District of California and any federal court having appellate jurisdiction over said court. If the United States District Court for the Central District of California finds that it lacks jurisdiction, the Tribe and the Enterprise consent to be sued in the California State Court system. This consent to California State Court jurisdiction shall only apply if Manager exercises reasonable efforts to argue for the jurisdiction of the federal court over said matter. The arbitrator shall be a licensed attorney, knowledgeable in federal Indian law and selected pursuant to the Commercial Arbitration Rules of the American Arbitration Association.

Unless the parties agree upon the appointment of a single arbitrator, a panel of arbitrators consisting of three (3) members shall be appointed. One (1) member shall be appointed by the Tribe and one (1) member shall be appointed by Manager within ten (10) working days' time following the giving of notice submitting a dispute to arbitration. The third member shall be selected by agreement of the other two (2) members. In the event the two (2) members cannot agree upon the third arbitrator within fifteen (15) working days' time, then the third arbitrator shall be chosen by the American Arbitration Association. Alternatively, the parties may, prior to any dispute, agree in advance upon a panel of arbitrators or a single arbitrator to which any dispute that may arise shall be submitted for resolution pursuant to this Section 16.2. Choice of Law. In determining any matter the arbitrators shall apply the terms of this Agreement, without adding to, modifying or changing the terms in any respect, and shall apply federal and applicable State law. Place of Hearing. All arbitration hearings shall be held at a place designated by the arbitrators in Los Angeles or Los Angeles County, California. Confidentiality. The parties and the arbitrators shall maintain strict confidentiality with respect to arbitration.

16.3 Limited Waiver of Sovereign Immunity. The Tribe and the Enterprise expressly and irrevocably waives its respective immunity from suit as provided for and limited by this Section. This waiver is limited to the Tribe's and the Enterprise's consent to all arbitration proceedings, and actions to compel arbitration and to enforce any awards or orders issuing from such arbitration proceedings which are sought solely in United States District Court for the Central District of California and any federal court having appellate jurisdiction over said court, provided that if the United States District Court for the Central District of California finds that it lacks jurisdiction, the Tribe and the Enterprise consent to such actions in the California State Court system. This consent to California State Court jurisdiction shall only apply if Manager exercises reasonable efforts to argue for the jurisdiction of the federal court over said matter. The arbitrators shall not have the power to award punitive damages. Time Period. The waiver granted herein shall commence as of the Date of this Agreement and shall continue for following expiration, termination or cancellation of this Agreement, but shall remain effective for the duration of any arbitration, litigation or dispute resolution proceedings then pending, all appeals therefrom, and except as limited by this Section, to the full satisfaction of any awards or judgments which may issue from such proceedings, provided that an action to collect such judgments has been filed within one year of the date of the final judgment. Recipient of Waiver. This limited waiver is granted only to Manager and not to any other individual or entity. Limitations of Actions. This limited waiver is specifically limited to the following actions and judicial remedies: The enforcement of an arbitrator's award of money damages provided that the waiver does not extend beyond the assets specified in Subsection (iii) below. No arbitrator or court shall have any authority or jurisdiction to order execution against any assets or revenues of the Tribe or the Enterprise except as provided in this Section or to award any punitive damages against the Tribe or the Enterprise. An action to compel or enforce arbitration or arbitration awards or orders. Damages awarded against the Tribe or the Enterprise shall be satisfied solely from the distributable share of Net Revenues of the Tribe from the Facility, the tangible assets of the Facility and the business of the Enterprise, provided, however, that this limited waiver of sovereign immunity shall terminate with respect to the collection of any Net Revenues transferred from the accounts of the Enterprise to the Tribe or the Tribe's separate bank account in the normal course of business in accordance with this Agreement. In no instance shall any enforcement of any kind whatsoever be allowed against any assets of the Tribe other than those specified in this subsection.

SECTION 17
NEGOTIATE NEW AGREEMENT
17.1 Intent to Negotiate New Agreement. On or before thirty (30) days after the Enterprise shall give Manager notice of its intent regarding its willingness to enter into negotiations for a new Management Agreement to be effective upon the conclusion of this Agreement.
17.2 Transition Plan. If the Enterprise and Manager are unable to agree to the terms of a new agreement or if the Enterprise decides not to enter into negotiations for a new agreement, then the Enterprise and Manager shall agree upon a transition plan within thirty (30) days' notice from the Enterprise of its intention not to negotiate a new Management Agreement, which plan shall be sufficient to allow the Tribe and/or the Enterprise to operate the Facility and provide for the orderly transition of the management of the Facility.

SECTION 18
ENTIRE AGREEMENT
This Agreement, including the Schedules and Exhibits referred to herein, constitutes the entire understanding and agreement of the parties hereto and supersedes all other prior agreements and understandings, written or oral, between the parties. The parties acknowledge that the Tribe is entering into a Gaming Facility Construction and Development Agreement and a Trademark License Agreement with affiliates of Manager contemporaneously with this Agreement.

SECTION 19
REQUIRED AMENDMENT
Each of the parties agrees to execute, deliver and, if necessary, record any and all additional instruments, certifications, amendments, modifications and other documents as may be required by the United States Department of the Interior, BIA, the NIGC, the office of the Field Solicitor, or any applicable statute, rule or regulation in order to effectuate, complete, perfect, continue or preserve the respective rights, obligations, liens and interests of the parties hereto to the fullest extent permitted by law; provided, that any such additional instrument, certification, amendment, modification or other document shall not materially change the respective rights, remedies or obligations of the Tribe, the Enterprise or Manager under this Agreement or any other agreement or document related hereto.

SECTION 20
PREPARATION OF AGREEMENT
This Agreement was drafted and entered into after careful review and upon the advice of competent counsel; it

shall not be construed more strongly for or against any party.

SECTION 21
STANDARD OF REASONABLENESS

Unless specifically provided otherwise, all provisions of this Agreement and all collateral agreements shall be governed by a standard of reasonableness.

SECTION 22
EXECUTION

This Agreement may be executed in four counterparts, one to be retained by each of the Tribe and the Enterprise, and two to be retained by Manager. Each of the four originals is equally valid. This Agreement shall be deemed "executed" and shall be binding upon both parties when properly executed and approved by the Chairman of the NIGC.

IN WITNESS WHEREOF, the parties hereto have executed this Agreement on the day and year first above written.

THCR MANAGEMENT SERVICES, LLC

By: _____
Donald J. Trump, President

TWENTY-NINE PALMS BAND OF LUISENO
MISSION INDIANS OF CALIFORNIA

By: _____
Dean Mike, Chairperson

TWENTY-NINE PALMS
ENTERPRISES CORPORATION

Approved by:

_____
Montie R. Deer, Chairman
National Indian Gaming Commission

April 15-2002
Date

By: _____
Dean Mike, President

By: _____
Gene Gambale, Secretary

[4] Harper Paperbacks, June 2009, ISBN 978-0061712746

[5] The Ten-Cent Plague: The Great Comic-Book Scare and How It Changed America by David Hajdu; Macmillan Picador, New York, February 2009, ISBN 978-0312428235

[6] http://www.economist.com/node/16507768?story_id=16507768&fsrc=rss, July 8th 2010

[7] www.cnnmoney.com Jun 13, 2005

[8] The **"Hubbart Room Rate Formula"**, recommended by the *American Hotel and Lodging Association*, sets an ADR (average daily room rate) to pay all the expenses and leave something for the investor. In their formula, estimated expenses are listed on an annual basis.

1. So step one is to list the following ANNUAL costs:
   Operating Expenses: Room expenses; Telephone & Internet; G&A (general and administrative); Payroll taxes and employee benefits; Utilities; Marketing; Maintenance
   Taxes and Insurance: Real Estate & Personal Property Taxes; Franchise taxes & fees; Insurance on building and contents; Leased equipment
   Depreciation (Standard rates based on present fair value): Building; FF&E (Furniture, Fixtures, Equipment)
   R.O.I. for investors: Land ($___ at __%); Building ($___ at __%); FF&E ($___ at __%); Take the total of all of those items and deduct the following credits from non-room income: Rental from contracted out stores; Profit (or loss) from F&B (food and beverage); Net income from any other operating departments or miscellaneous income
2. THAT total (all of #2 subtracted from all of #1) gives the total annual amount of money needed annually from guest-room sales to cover costs and a reasonable return for investors.
3. List the total number of guest rooms available in the hotel.
4. List total number of rooms available annually (#4 multiplied by 365 nights).

375

5. Deduct an allowance for vacancies. Take the percentage of expected nightly occupancy (*the national average is 70% the Las Vegas number is higher, depending on specific location*) and subtract that number from #5 above. This gives you the number of rooms to be occupied at the estimated average occupancy.

6. Divide #3 by #6 to get the ADR (average daily rate) per-occupied-room needed to cover costs and a reasonable return on investment.

[9] Forbes.com 6/12/2012:"Exclusive: Adelson's Pro-Romney Donations Will Be 'Limitless,' Could Top $100M"

[10] One of the few publically available Par Sheets:

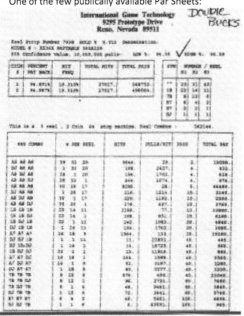

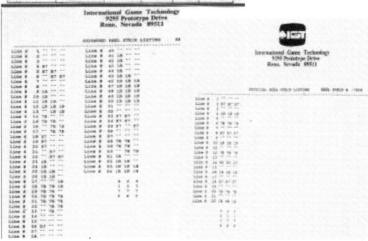

PAY COMBO	$ PER REEL	HITS	PULLS/HIT	PAYS	TOTAL PAY
[illegible]	1 11 1	12.	21845.	160.	1920.
[illegible]	8 1 1	8.	32768.	160.	1280.
[illegible]	6 4 1	24.	10923.	200.	4800.
[illegible]	6 1 2	12.	21845.	200.	2400.
[illegible]	1 4 2	8.	32768.	200.	1600.
[illegible]	2 2 1	4.	65536.	200.	800.
[illegible]	1 1 2	2.	131072.	400.	800.
[illegible]	1 4 1	4.	65536.	400.	1600.
[illegible]	6 1 1	6.	43691.	400.	2400.
[illegible]	1 2 1	2.	131072.	400.	800.
[illegible]	2 1 1	2.	131072.	400.	800.
[illegible]	2 2 1	4.	65536.	400.	1600.
[illegible]	1 1 1	1.	262144.	800.	800.
			Coin # 2	1600P	
[illegible]	1 2 1	2.	131072.	800.	1600.
			Coin # 2	1600P	
[illegible]	2 1 1	2.	131072.	800.	1600.
			Coin # 2	1600P	
[illegible]	1 1 1	1.	262144	1800.	1800.
			Coin # 2	3600P	

[illegible] 11832 Total Coins Paid [illegible] 248732

90% CONFIDENCE VALUES VOLATILITY INDEX = 12.670

HANDLE PULLS	LOWER PERCENTAGE	UPPER PERCENTAGE
1000.	54.92	135.05
10000.	82.32	107.66
100000.	90.98	98.99
1000000.	93.72	96.25
10000000.	94.59	95.39

PAY TABLE FILE NAME : PTDAT:S57938.PAY
REEL STRIP FILE NAME : RSDAT:S57938.LAY
OPERATOR'S INITIALS: DL

[11] The Thunderbird was built by Marion Hicks (a partner in the El Cortez downtown) and Nevada's then Lieutenant Governor, 34-year-old Cliff Jones. (Jones went on to become a highly regarded attorney in Vegas and founder of the law firm (that I have used many times) currently known as Jones and Vargas.) Though Hicks was listed as the President and General Manager, Meyer Lansky's brother, Jake, managed the place...reporting to Meyer back in Miami Beach.

On opening night, two local casino operators —the owner of the Pioneer Club downtown and his friend, the owner of the El Rancho (across the street from Thunderbird)— spent an all-night session at a craps table at the Thunderbird. With no limit on the bets, by morning the pair had won more than the casino had available to pay them. *(Remember that "running out of cash" problem that I talked about in Chapter Four?)*

Asked to come back the next day, while Jake called his brother and figured out what to do, they demanded security for what was owed to them. The only security available was the casino itself. So by the end of the grand opening night, the owners of the new casino had lost the casino...gambling. Only in Vegas; gotta love it! Eventually the Hicks, Jones (and Lansky) were able to pay the $145,000 debt and take their casino back.

The Thunderbird itself had a pretty colorful history over its lifespan; a history that included Hicks and Jones losing their license. By 1955, seven years into the casino's history, the Las Vegas Sun published reports that Jake Lansky was actually the General Manager of the casino. The state Tax Commission, which at that time was the only regulatory body for casinos, investigated and discovered that Hicks in fact had built the property with a loan from Lansky. In typical western-state independence, fearing that the press attention might bring the Kefauver Committee and Federal scrutiny to the State, the Governor created a new Gaming Control Board to investigate applicants for casino licenses. The new board revoked the Thunderbird licenses and the owners sold to a Los Angles investment company. After a year-long court battle, Hicks finally won back both his license and control of the Thunderbird.

Finally legitimately sold in 1976, Thunderbird's name was changed to Silverbird; 1982 brought another name change, borrowing the name of the Strip's first casino: El Rancho. In 2000 the new El Rancho, which had been closed for eight years, was sold and imploded. The new owner was Turnberry Associates (a South Florida condo developer that had built a palace on the site of the old Landmark Casino). By 2007 Glen Schaeffer and Mark Lefever's Fontainebleau, broke ground for a $3-billion resort, which by 2009 had bankrupted, and was sold to Carl Icon in 2012 for $150-million.

[12] Paul Mann Publishing Co., 1973

[13] The Insiders' Guide to Myrtle Beach and the Grand Strand--4th Edition Paperback: 333 pages; Publisher: Insiders Guides; 4th edition (April 1997); ISBN-10: 1573800171; ISBN-13: 978-1573800174

[14] Source: Nevada Gaming Control Board, Quarterly Revenue Report, by location

[15] ibid

[16] We are required file *Suspicious Activity Reports* (SARs) when we know or even have reason to *suspect* that a transaction (or a group of transactions) involving at least $5,000: came from illegal activity; or *"has no apparent business or other lawful purpose"*; or is more than a regular customer normally plays.

[17] Max played "Jethro Bodine" in the original TV series in the 1960s, had a highly successful career as a director and producer, and today he is in the slot machine and casino business.

LEFT: Max Baer Jr. and Gary Green at the introduction of the *Beverly Hillbillies* progressive slot machines from IGT. **RIGHT:** Max Baer Jr. in his best-known roll as Jethro Bodine in the *Beverly Hillbillies* television series *(274 episodes, 1962-1971).* Max and Gary remained in contact over the years as Max pursued his dream of creating and owning a *Beverly Hillbillies* casino/resort. In 2008 Gary attempted (and failed) to put together financing to purchase the small working-class *Beverly Hillbillies Gamblers Casino* in North Las Vegas and free Max and a partner from that grandfather-able license.

[18] http://www.igt.com/company-information/news-room/news-releases.aspx?NewsID=650311

[19] National Indian Gaming Association Library (www.indiangaming.org/library/indian-gaming-facts/index.shtml)

[20] Time Magazine, December 16, 2002, "Wheels of Misfortune" by Donald L. Barlett and James B. Steele

[21] Tribal Ordinances of The Absentee Shawnee Tribe of Oklahoma

[22] Time Magazine, December 16, 2002, "Wheels of Misfortune" by Donald L. Barlett and James B. Steele

[23] Open Letter to Time Magazine from Ernest L. Stevens, Jr., Chairman National Indian Gaming Association (NIGA), issued as an NIGA Press Release December 10, 2002.
[24] History of the Santa Ynez Band of Chumash Indians, History of Native American Gaming, http://www.santaynezchumash.org/gaming_history.html
[25] US Constitution, Article I Section 2 cl. 3 and Amendment XIV Section 2
[26] US Constitution, Article I Section 8 cl. 3
[27] http://www.doi.gov/bureau-indian-affairs.html
[28] William Shakespeare (1564–1616), Henry VI, Part 2, act 4, sc. 2, l. 76-7.
[29] Cherokee Nation v. Georgia, 30 US 1 (1831)
[30] Bryan v. Itasca County, 426 US 373, 96 S.Ct. 2102, 48 L.Ed.2d 710
[31] Seminole *Tribe of Florida v. Butterworth,* 658 F.2d 310 5th Cir. 1981
[32] California Cabazon Band of Mission Indians, 480 US 202 (1987)
[33] 25 CFR, Part 501 and 502
[34] Ibid, Part 502.2
[35] Ibid, Part 502.3
[36] Ibid , Part 502.4
[37] Mission and Responsibilities of the NIGC, http://www.nigc.gov/nigc/nigcControl?option=ABOUT_MISSION
[38] National Indian Gaming Association Factsheet, 2005, Suzette Brewer, Washington DC
[39] US Code: Title 15, Sections 1171-1178
[40] 15 U.S.C. 1175
[41] Op cit
[42] "Busted Flush: SC's Video Poker Operators Run A Political Machine," by David Plotz, Harpers Magazine, August 1999, volume 299, issue 1791, p63
[43] Video Game Machines Act; S.C. Code Ann. § 12-21-2770
[44] Op cit
[45] Op cit
[46] Atlanta Business Chronicle, March 20, 2001
[47] Harpers Op cit.
[48] Indianz.com, Senators' letter questioned NIGC's agenda, Wed. January 26, 2005
[49] The Daily Oklahoman, newspaper, November 18, 2004
[50] Indianz.com, April 23, 2004, *Multimedia Games determined to have Management Contract*
[51] Indianz.com, March 9, 2004, *"Did your Tribe waive its Sovereignty to Multimedia Games or How to Manage a Casino without a Management Contract"*; http://indianz.com/InTheHoop/archive/002104.asp

[52] Lectric Law Library's stacks; http://www.lectlaw.com/files/ban02.htm
[53] CBS Marketwatch, Herb Greenberg, April 23, 2004
[54] This information is from firsthand accounts with Cadillac Jack staff claiming ownership of a casino building managed by the author.
[55] Not to be deterred by a little thing like an order from the Federal regulatory agency overseeing Indian gaming, MGAM continued to pursue these manager agreements...or "development" agreements, if you prefer. And where would MGAM look next? Where else? MGAM headed to South Carolina, of course, with a proposed development deal for the Catawba Tribe in that state.
Five years after South Carolina outlawed video poker, The Columbia State (the largest newspaper in South Carolina) interviewed Robert Stewart, the chief of the State Law Enforcement Division. Stewart warned, "Everybody is trying to find some loophole so they can find a machine that's legal. There is a lot of money being put into that effort. "
Among South Carolina law enforcement's targets were the Catawba Tribe . In 2003 the Tribe was found guilty in state court of failure to pay taxes on their Bingo operation. Since that time the

state's ultra-conservative newspapers and religious lobby have been pushing State lawmakers to prohibit casino gaming in the Tribe's Bingo hall. Despite the talks and pending deal with MGAM, the Tribal chief was quoted in another South Carolina newspaper as saying his tribe had no interest in slot machines. It was these kinds of mixed signals that made investigators take a closer look. And it was probably these kinds of signals that had the Tribe withdraw plans for a second facility to be built and MGAM's decision to withdraw plans to build in that state.

In fact, despite all the righteousness about assisting poor tribes (for a mere 85%+ interest rate), by mid-2005 MGAM began withdrawing from management-looking development contracts completely.

[56]The entirety of MGAM's official press release said:

NIGC's Acting General Counsel Interprets Development Agreement as Management Contract; Multimedia Games Differs With Interpretation

AUSTIN, Texas --(Business Wire)-- April 23, 2004 -- Multimedia Games, Inc. (NASDAQ: MGAM) today reported that the acting General Counsel of the National Indian Gaming Commission (NIGC) has issued a letter to Multimedia Games and one of its Native American tribal customers opining that their development agreement regarding the WinStar Casino in Thackerville, Oklahoma constitutes a "management contract."

Clifton Lind, President and Chief Executive Officer of Multimedia Games, stated: "We were surprised by the letter and differ with the opinions expressed therein. The development agreement was furnished to the NIGC in June 2003 prior to the WinStar Casino's opening in July 2003. Prior to receiving the letter, neither Multimedia Games nor the tribe was ever contacted by the acting General Counsel to indicate that she was reviewing the agreements for this purpose or consulted in this matter."

The agreement provides that Multimedia Games would fund the construction and development of an expanded Class II gaming facility for the tribe in return for committed floor space for MGAM games for a specified term. The agreement was drafted and reviewed by legal counsel who specialize in Native American gaming regulation.

The authority of the NIGC to review and approve gaming related contracts is limited to management contract and related collateral agreements. According to the acting General Counsel, the performance of any planning, organizing, directing, coordinating or controlling with respect to any part of a gaming operation constitutes management for purposes of determining whether an agreement for any of these activities is a management contract.

Mr. Lind continued: "We respectfully disagree with the acting General Counsel's recent interpretation that the development agreement and collateral agreements constitute a management contract. We invest significant resources to ensure that our activities are compliant with applicable laws and regulations. We believe that the acting General Counsel's view of management is broader than was intended and that counsel's interpretation in this case was based in part on collateral agreements not in effect, without the benefit of discussions with MGAM or tribal representatives."

Mr. Lind concluded by saying, "We have requested a meeting with NIGC representatives to discuss and hopefully resolve these matters. As we have done in the past, we intend to support our tribal customer and work closely with our customer and the NIGC to clear up these uncertainties."

Under the Indian Gaming Regulatory Act (IGRA), a management contract is an agreement with a tribe that provides for the third-party management of all or part of a gaming operation. NIGC approval of management contracts is required by IGRA. The acting General Counsel has requested that Multimedia Games and the tribe submit within twenty (20) days the development agreement and any related agreements for approval by the NIGC Chairman.

About the Company

Multimedia Games, Inc. is the leading supplier of interactive electronic games and player stations to the rapidly growing Native American gaming market. The Company's games are delivered through a telecommunications network that links its player stations with one another both within and among gaming facilities. Multimedia Games designs and develops networks, software and content that provide its customers with comprehensive gaming systems. The Company also offers systems and products for the growing racino, charity and commercial Bingo markets. The Company's ongoing development and marketing efforts focus on new Class II gaming systems and products, Class III video lottery systems for use by Native American tribes throughout the United States, and products for charity Bingo opportunities. Additional information may be found at www.multimediagames.com.

Cautionary Statements

[57] The American Indian Movement was founded in 1968 in the midwest by urban Native Americans activists Dennis Banks, Clyde Bellecourt, Russell Means, George Mitchell,and others. Gary Green

380

founded TAIMSG (Tennessee American Indian Movement Support Group) and later AIMSG (the national American Indian Movement Support Group).

58 OTTAWA TRIBAL GAMING COMMISSION TRIBAL INTERNAL CONTROL STANDARDS
1. GENERAL PROVISIONS

The following are Minimum Internal Controls Standards (TICS) adopted by the Tribal Gaming Commission of the Ottawa Tribe for all Tribal gaming facilities.

These TICS are designed to provide a basic framework for any and all Ottawa Tribal gaming facilities in establishing and maintaining their Internal Control System (ICS). The casino's internal control systems are reflected and codified in the casino's written policies and procedures. These policies and procedures must be submitted to, and approved by, the Ottawa Tribal Gaming Commission before live gaming may proceed at any location.

The Casino's responsibility is to ensure that Casino internal control systems comply with *at least* these minimum standards adopted by the Tribal Gaming Commission. If a minimum standard is not consistent with a Casino system, The Gaming Commission mandates that Ottawa Casino management's responsibility is to see that compensating internal controls are developed and submitted to the Ottawa Tribal Gaming Commission for approval. *Immediate (within the same regular scheduled shift of a gaming day) notification of discovery of the inconsistency is to be reported to the Tribal Gaming Commission.*

Ottawa Tribal Gaming Commissioners, Ottawa Tribal Internal Audit Personnel, Commission Compliance Officers/Inspectors, Agents of the State Gaming Agency, Officers and Agents of the National Indian Gaming Commission, and other persons authorized by the Tribal Gaming Commission are to be afforded instant access to any and all areas requested in the gaming facilities. These individuals requesting to view documents and records will be afforded *immediate* access and consideration. Copies of records requested shall be provided immediately (within the same regular scheduled shift of a gaming day), except in those instances where an illegal act may have occurred, in which case the copies will be provided instantly (without any delay).

Internal auditors, financial statement auditors, and employees of the Tribal gaming facility operations are required to report violations of the Casino TICS to Casino management and to the Tribal Gaming Commission simultaneously (within the same regular scheduled shift of the gaming day). Deviations that violate the TICS may result in disciplinary actions.

A license number issued by the Ottawa Tribal Gaming Commission is the only valid identification number to be used in gaming operations and activities.

CHANGES TO OTTAWA TRIBAL GAMING COMMISSION TICS (per 25 CFR 542.3)

Before any Ottawa Tribal gaming facility receives Tribal Gaming Commission approval for initial TICS and changes to the approved TICS, the Casino shall comply with the following procedures for requesting approval of changes to the TICS. The Casino shall not alter the approved TICS unless and until the Tribal Gaming Commission approves such changes and evidences such approval in writing.

DEFINITIONS OF TYPES OF CHANGES TO TICS

Changes required by the Tribal Gaming Commission shall be enacted immediately (within the same regular scheduled shift of a gaming day).

1. Each proposed change to the TICS shall be classified per category and each category shall be submitted separately. The categories are:

• Emergency; An Emergency is a change to the TICS that if not approved and implemented by a given date would negatively impact the internal controls or cause serious interruption to gaming activities. Changes designated as Emergency may be submitted for approval at any time (The Emergency classification of changes to the TICS is expected to be rare).

• Substantive; Substantive is a change to the TICS that affects the method of complying with the TICS.

• Administrative; Administrative is a change to the TICS that is editorial, clarifies procedures or changes position descriptions or titles, but has no effect on the existing TICS. and New Games; internal control changes needed for the casino to run a Tribal/Gaming Commission-approved Game that was not previously included in the TICS

TIMING OF SUBMISSION OF CHANGES TO TICS

The Tribal gaming facility shall be permitted to submit requested Substantive, Administrative or New Games changes to the TICS at any regularly scheduled meeting of the Tribal Gaming Commission. These requests for change shall be submitted to the Tribal Gaming Commission.

METHOD FOR TRIBAL GAMING FACILITIY TO SUBMIT PROPOSED CHANGES TO TICS

The Tribal gaming facility shall comply with the following provisions to propose changes to the TICS. No changes shall be implemented by the Casino until Tribal Gaming Commission written approval is granted.

1. Each request for changes shall contain redlined copies of the pages of the TICS containing the proposed changes. A letter requesting approval for the changes and the reason for the change shall accompany the changes. One redlined and one clean copy of the pages shall be delivered to the Tribal Gaming Commission.

2. If the addition of information on a page causes text to be moved to the next page, these pages must also be submitted.

3. Any proposed modifications and changes should ensure that all Tables of Contents, References, and Indexes are also updated, if applicable.

4. A log must be kept for all TICS changes. At a minimum this log should include:

(i) The page number.

(ii) The revised date and the effective date.

(iii) The change number.

5. Each changed page should include the revision and Tribal Gaming Commission approval dates.

6. Any changes which are required to be made as a result of an independent certified public accounting firm's audits and related reportable conditions must be submitted at the next submission date following the issuance of the auditor's report.

TRIBAL GAMING COMMISSION APPROVAL PROCEDURES

1. After receipt of the proposed changes, Tribal Gaming Commission staff shall read each proposed change to determine that it is complete, carefully prepared, and that extensive comments are not necessary.

2. The Tribal Gaming Commission staff shall proceed with a detailed review to determine compliance with the Commission, the Compact, and that the specific internal control is consistent with the overall TICS.

(i) When revised pages of a change are resubmitted, the proposed changes shall not include further new changes to the TICS. If new changes are requested, these pages shall be submitted as a new change at the next submission date within the specified time periods.

(ii) When changed pages are resubmitted after revisions only those pages that require additional revisions shall be resubmitted and the revision date on all pages of the change shall be updated to coincide with the revised submission date.

(iii) When the Tribal Gaming Commission approves a change, a letter of approval from the Tribal Gaming Commission shall be delivered to the Tribal gaming facility.

(iv) The effective date shall be stated in the aforementioned letter. No changes shall be implemented until Tribal Gaming Commission written approval is granted.

(v) The Tribal Gaming Commission may reject or disallow any proposed modifications or changes at its discretion.

3. The General Manager and/or one individual of the operation designated by the General Manager shall be assigned the responsibility for submitting TICS changes to the Tribal Gaming Commission. A letter should be on file with the Tribal Gaming Commission stating who this individual will be. If said responsibility is designated to a different individual, an updated letter shall be mailed to the Tribal Gaming Commission. If a submission is received from any other individual, the submission in its entirety will be returned.

POLICIES AND PROCEDURES

1. All manual procedures and forms, as well as computerized procedures and forms, if applicable, shall be described throughout the Casino's internal control system (casino Policies and Procedures).

2. When the term "non-gaming employee" is used throughout these Policies and Procedures, that "non-gaming employee" must be employed in maintenance, housekeeping, food service or another area as determined by the Ottawa Tribal Gaming Commission.

3. The lowest level of employee with the authority for any specific employee's respective duty should be listed in the procedures. Employees with higher authority within the same department may perform these duties, except where specifically noted in the TICS. When a higher-level employee performs the duties of a lower-level employee, he/she may not then perform verification of his/her own work.

4. Sensitive areas are those areas that the Ottawa Tribal Gaming Commission considers susceptible to potential weaknesses in the internal control system of the Casino's operation and, therefore, require strict control over access (i.e., pits, count rooms, cages, surveillance rooms, vaults, etc.).

5. The casino's Policies and Procedures (internal control system) shall include organizational charts for the Casino including the General Manager and all Casino gaming related departments including live games, electronic gaming devices, drop and count team participants, casino cashiering, internal audit, casino accounting, surveillance, security, purchasing and contract administration, and management information systems.

6. The casino's Policies and Procedures shall include detailed job description of each of the Casino employee positions shown on the organizational chart that includes:

(i) Duties and responsibilities.

(ii) Immediate supervisor.

(iii) Signatory ability including alternate procedures in cases in which the required signatory is unable to perform his/her duty.

(iv) Access to sensitive assets and areas.

7. Officers, executives, external auditors, and other employees shall not have unaccompanied access to sensitive areas of the Casino. If a reason exists for such person or persons to access a sensitive area, the Tribal Gaming Commission must be notified prior to each access. A Tribal Gaming Commissioner or Inspector must accompany such person or persons while in any sensitive area. A Tribal Gaming Commissioner or Tribal Compliance Officer/Inspector must also accompany such person or persons into the surveillance room. Procedures to allow for these accesses are to be included in the casino's Policies and Procedures.

8. All occupational licensees, other than the General Manager and certain key executives authorized by the Tribal Gaming Commission, shall wear Tribal Gaming Commission issued identification badges at all times unless otherwise authorized by the Tribal Gaming Commission. All licensees are to use only the license number issued by the Tribal Gaming Commission for identification purposes in gaming operations.

MANAGEMENT INFORMATION SYSTEMS (MIS)

1. The Casino's Policies and Procedures shall include a description of all Casino *gaming* computer systems used, and all systems (on or off site) that *interface with gaming computer* systems and that track, control, monitor, or account for gaming

382

facility activities including microcomputer data input templates developed from applications *such as* Microsoft Word and Excel (See each specific gaming section for additional Computer Activities).

2. The gaming operation shall comply with the following items to ensure that procedures are established to:

(i) Notify and obtain prior approval of the Ottawa Tribal Gaming Commission for proposed changes to the computer monitoring system using the procedures outlined for changes in the TICS.

(ii) Update or change information (passwords, etc.).

(iii) Establish back-up files.

(iv) Protect files (off-site storage of back-up files).

(v) Limit access to computer software and equipment (restricted access, locked doors).

(vi) Provide the Ottawa Tribal Gaming Commission timely lists of authorized access personnel.

(vii) Test program changes or implementation of new or upgraded hardware and software.

(viii) Control the ability to access computer programs and equipment at each level (key access, time-out restrictions, and passwords).

(ix) Compare computer-generated information affecting gaming revenues through physical count, management analysis, and other methods.

(x) Ensure that a department independent of the slot department performs maintenance of the computerized slot monitoring system data files. Alternatively, maintenance may be performed by slot supervisory employees if sufficient documentation is generated and it is randomly verified by employees independent of the slot department on a monthly basis.

(xi) Ensure updates to the computerized slot monitoring system to reflect additions, deletions or movements of slot machines are made at least weekly prior to in-meter readings and the weigh process.

(xii) Provide documentation regarding each change to the MIS system in the same manner as changes to the TICS are requested.

(xiii) Provide records for review immediately (within the same regular scheduled shift of a gaming day) upon request from the Tribal Gaming Commission.

3. Instant access to computer-contained information shall be furnished to Ottawa Tribal Gaming Commission Compliance Officers, Tribal Internal Auditors, State Gaming Agency Agents, and other Tribal Gaming Commission authorized individuals.

TIPS AND GRATUITIES

1. No gaming employee shall accept currency as a tip or gratuity from any patron unless the Casino Management allows such a practice and has provided procedures for accepting such tip or gratuity in its internal controls, which have been approved by the Tribal Gaming Commission.

2. NO EMPLOYEE SHALL SOLICIT ANY TIP OR GRATUITY.

3. No gaming key person or any other employee who serves in a supervisory position shall accept tips or gratuities from a patron.

4. Additionally, a log listing the employee, the date, and that employee's social security number will be maintained in the main casino cage. The names of those employees exchanging chips and/or tokens received as tips or gratuities shall be filled out by the cashier upon the exchange, and initialed by the employee. The log will be submitted to and maintained by the accounting department. A December 31 year-end total-per-employee of these transactions will be maintained and are included as part of the reporting requirements of the Ottawa Tribal Gaming Commission.

CASINO ACCOUNTING STANDARDS

A. RESPONSIBILITIES:

The Accounting Department (Accounting) is responsible for the complete analysis and reporting of all gaming revenue. Accounting is responsible for reviewing, analyzing, comparing, reconciling, filing, and maintaining all source documents. Additional responsibilities include preparing statistical reports, and analyzing and documenting variances noted as a result of reviewing these statistical reports. The results of all reviews and investigations must be documented in writing as evidence that required procedures (adequate explanation criteria) have been performed. Adequate explanation criteria must include the procedures used to investigate the variance and the results of the investigation.

Additionally, Accounting must implement a process to identify continued variances on the same gaming device from drop to drop in order to initiate a different level of review (e.g., a review by a more experienced gaming employee, performance of different tests, contact slot manufacturer, etc.). The point at which a different level of review will be initiated is specific to each gaming operation (depending upon the frequency of statistical report generation) and must be incorporated into the gaming operation's written accounting plan, which is discussed below. It is the gaming operations' responsibility through the segregation of duties, redundancy of task and tracking of statistical performance to ensure the effective detection and deterrence of irregularities.

Accounting personnel cannot participate in any gaming transactions or activities (i.e., drops, counts, fills, cashiering, shift manager functions, etc.) other than reading and recording slot machine and poker progressive meters. The objective of this restriction is to ensure accounting personnel maintain independence of the creation of original source documents and do not have a vested interest in transactions pertaining to gaming or gaming related activities.

B. SYSTEM OVERRIDES:

Gaming operations must have procedures in place that address how to handle any necessary overrides to system-generated information. All system overrides must be independently authorized. Additionally, accounting must review all overrides for reasonableness and proper authority. Accounting's review must be evidenced on the supporting documentation with the date of the review and the initials of the reviewer.

C. WRITTEN ACCOUNTING PLAN:
The gaming operation must develop a detailed written accounting plan which outlines their methodology, process, and procedures regarding the preparation, review, analysis, and maintenance of the statistical reports. The objective of the plan is to provide sufficient detail for each member of the Casino's gaming accounting staff to adequately perform their job. This plan includes at a minimum:
1. Job positions responsible for preparing the reports, reviewing the reports, investigating variances, correcting erroneous information, and ensuring corrective action has been taken.
2. List of source documents used to obtain meter information and actual drop information.
3. Procedures for:
(i) Preparing reports;
(ii) Reviewing the reports for accuracy;
(iii) Investigating variances that exceed the allowable threshold (includes thresholds used to initiate the investigation, method of documenting variance review and investigation, events that signal and initiate a different level of review or investigation, etc.);
(iv) Correcting erroneous information; and
(v) Identifying and communicating noncompliance issues to employees.
4. Time frames for each step of the processes (e.g., reports are prepared and reviewed, variances are investigated, etc.).
To ensure an adequate control environment and proper segregation of duties, the person who prepares the reports must be someone other than the person who performs the final review of the reports. The final review of the reports includes reviewing corrections made to the reports and reviewing variance investigation results. Any corrections by the accounting department to gaming documents, forms, reports, etc., must be made in accordance with the gaming operation's written accounting plan. In the case where reports are reprinted to reflect any corrections and/or adjustments made by accounting personnel (e.g., "final run" reports), corrected and/or adjusted information reflected on these "final run" reports must be reviewed by someone other than the individual who made the correction/adjustment. This review must be evidenced by the reviewer's initials and date of review. The first run and the final run of reports are considered gaming documents and must be maintained.

D. ACCOUNTING STANDARDS:
1. Each gaming operation shall prepare accurate, complete, legible, and permanent records of all transactions pertaining to revenue and gaming activities.
2. Each gaming operation shall prepare general accounting records according to *Generally Accepted Accounting Principles* (GAAP) on a double entry system of accounting, maintaining detailed, supporting, subsidiary records, including, but not limited to:
(i) Detailed records identifying revenues, expenses, assets, liabilities, and equity for each gaming operation;
(ii) Detailed records of all markers, IOU's, returned checks, hold checks, or other similar credit instruments;
(iii) Individual and statistical game records to reflect statistical drop, statistical win, and the percentage of statistical win to statistical drop by each table game, and to reflect statistical drop, statistical win, and the percentage of statistical win to statistical drop for each type of table game, by shift, by day, cumulative month-to-date, and cumulative year-to-date, and individual and statistical game records reflecting similar information for all other games;
(iv) Gaming machine analysis reports which, by each machine, compare actual hold percentages to theoretical hold percentages.
(v) The records required by §542 and by the tribal internal control standards.
(vi) Journal entries prepared by the gaming operation and by its independent accountants, and
(vii) Any other records specifically required to be maintained.
3. Each gaming operation shall establish administrative and accounting procedures for the purpose of determining effective control over a gaming operation's fiscal affairs. The procedures shall be designed to reasonably ensure that:
(i) Assets are safeguarded;
(ii) Financial records are accurate and reliable;
(iii) Transactions are performed only in accordance with management's general and specific authorization;
(iv) Transactions are recorded adequately to permit proper reporting of gaming revenue and of fees and taxes, and to maintain accountability of assets;
(v) Recorded accountability of assets is compared with actual assets at reasonable intervals and appropriate action is taken with respect to any discrepancies; and
(vi) Functions, Duties, and responsibilities are appropriately segregated in accordance with sound practices by competent, qualified personnel.
4. Gross revenue computations
(i) For table games gross revenue equals the closing table bankroll plus credit slips for cash, chips, or tokens returned to the cage, plus drop, less opening table bankroll and fills to the table.
(ii) For gaming machines gross revenue equals drop less fills, jackpot payouts and personal property awarded to patrons as gambling winnings.
(iii) For each counter game, gross revenue equals:

384

(A) The money accepted by the gaming operation on events or games that occur during the month or will occur in subsequent months, less money paid out during the month to patrons on winning wagers; or

(B) The money accepted by the gaming operation on events or games that occur during the month plus money, not previously included in gross revenue, that was accepted by the gaming operation in previous months on events or games occurring in the month, less money paid out during the month to patrons as winning wagers.

(iv) For each card game and any other game in which the gaming operation is not a party to a wager, gross revenue equals all money received by the operation as compensation for conducting the game. A gaming operation shall not include either shill win or loss in gross revenue computations.

5. Each gaming operation shall establish internal control systems sufficient to ensure currency (other than tips or gratuities) received from a patron in the gaming area is promptly placed in a locked box in the table, in the case of cashier, in the appropriate place in the cashier's cage, or on those games which do not have a locked drop box or on card game tales, in an appropriate place on the table, in the cash register or other approved repository.

6. Periodic payment of winnings awarded to a patron may be made if the method of funding the periodic payments assures such payments to the winning patron by establishing an irrevocable method of funding.

7. Maintenance and preservation of books, records and documents.

(i) All original books, records and documents pertaining to the conduct of wagering activities shall be retained by a gaming operation in accordance with the following schedule. A record that summarizes gaming transactions is sufficient provided that all documents containing an original signature(s) attesting to the accuracy of a gaming related transaction is independently preserved. Original books, records or documents shall not include copies of originals, except for copies that contain original comments or notations or parts of multi-part forms. The following original books, records and documents shall be retained by a gaming operation for a minimum five (5) years:

(A) Casino cage documents;

(B) Documentation supporting the calculation of table game win;

(C) Documentation supporting the calculation of gaming machine win;

(D) Documentation supporting the calculation of revenue received from the games of keno, pari-mutuel, Bingo, pull-tabs, card games, and all other gaming activities offered by the gaming operation;

(E) Table games statistical analysis reports;

(F) Gaming machine statistical analysis reports;

(G) Bingo, pull-tab and keno statistical reports;

(H) Internal audit reports;

(I) Documentation supporting the write-off of gaming credit instruments and named credit instruments;

(J) All other books, records and documents pertaining to the conduct of wagering activities that contain original signature(s) attesting to the accuracy of the gaming related transaction.

(ii) Unless otherwise specified in §542, all other books, records, and documents shall be retained until such time as the accounting records have been audited by the gaming operation's independent Certified Public Accountants.

(iii)   The above definition shall apply without regards to the medium through which the book, record or document is generated or maintained (paper, computer generated, magnetic media, etc.).

ACCOUNTING RECORDS

1. The Casino will maintain complete, accurate, and legible records of all transactions relating to the revenues, costs, assets and liabilities and equity of the gaming operation. All original records and documents of The Casino shall be maintained on trust land.

2. General accounting records will be maintained on a double entry system of accounting with transactions recorded on the accrual basis using generally accepted accounting principles, and detailed, supporting subsidiary records, sufficient to meet the requirements of paragraph three (3) below.

3. The detailed accounting and subsidiary records will include, but not be limited to:

(i) Records of all patrons' checks initially accepted, deposited, and returned as "uncollected", and ultimately written off as "uncollectible".

(ii) Statistical game records to reflect drop and win amounts for each table and for each game type.

(iii) Records of investments in property and services, including equipment used directly in connection with the operation of Class II and Class III gaming.

(iv) Records of amounts payable.

(v) Records which identify the purchase, receipt, and destruction of gaming chips used in wagering.

(vi) Revenues, expenses, assets, liabilities, and equity for each facility at which any component of each gaming activity or operation is conducted.

(vii) Daily cash transactions for each game at each facility at which any gaming activity or operation is conducted, including but not limited to transactions relating to each gaming table bank, game drop box and gaming room bank.

(viii) Individual and statistical game records to reflect statistical drop, statistical win, statistical drop by table for each game, and individual and statistical game records reflecting similar information for all other games.

(ix) For electronic games of chance, analytic reports that, by each machine, compare actual hold percentages to theoretical hold percentages.

(x)   All audit reports prepared by or for the Tribe.

(xi)   Records required from other sections of the TICS are to be incorporated into the system.

(xiii) All pertinent accounting records shall be kept for a period of time not less than five (5) years from their respective date pursuant to applicable law and Tribal Ordinance.

FORMS, RECORDS, DOCUMENTS, AND RETENTION

1. All information required by the system of internal controls is to be placed on a form, record, or document in, or stored data shall be recorded in ink, or on a computer disk, or other permanent form.

2. Sensitive forms shall be sequentially pre-numbered using numeric or alpha-numeric coding schemes. Only one iteration of a series of numbering should be used in a fiscal year.

3. Whenever duplicate or duplicate copies are required of a form, record, or document:

(i) The original, duplicate, and duplicate copies shall be color-coded.

(ii) Forms, records, or documents that are required to be inserted in a locked dispenser must be maintained with the last copy being retained in a continuous unbroken form in the dispenser.

(iii) When exceptions are noted regarding forms or serial numbers of forms required to be accounted for or copies of forms required to be compared for agreement, the Tribal Gaming Commission must receive immediate (within the same regularly scheduled shift of a gaming day), written notification of said exceptions. Once the investigation is completed the Tribal Gaming Commission must receive immediate (within the same regularly scheduled shift of a gaming day), timely (within the same gaming day) notification.

4. Unless otherwise specified or exempted by the Tribal Gaming Commission, all forms, records, and documents, and stored data required to be prepared, maintained, and controlled shall:

(i) Have the title of the form, record, document, or stored data imprinted or pre-printed thereon or therein.

(ii) Be located on Ottawa Tribe lands or such other location as approved by the Tribal Gaming Commission.

(iii) Be retained for a period of at least five (5) years in a manner that assures accessibility to Inspectors of the Tribal Gaming Commission, personnel of the State Gaming Agency (Agency) (if applicable), and other Tribal Gaming Commission authorized individuals.

SIGNATURES

1. All signatures required on forms, records, and documents outlined in the Policies and Procedures shall:

(i) Include at a minimum, the signer's first initial and last name in the same manner as recorded on a signature control record maintained in the Tribal Gaming Commission office and Revenue Audit department.

(ii) Be immediately adjacent to the signer's Ottawa Tribal Gaming Commission license number.

2. Signify that the signer has prepared forms, records, and documents, and/or authorized to a sufficient extent to attest to the accuracy of the information recorded thereon, in conformity with the system of internal controls.

3. Signature records shall be prepared for each person required by these standards to sign or initial forms, records, and documents. The records shall:

(i) Include specimens of signatures and initials of signers.

(ii) Be maintained on a dated signature card file, alphabetically by name.

(iii) Be adjusted on an immediate basis to reflect changes in personnel with simultaneous (within 8 hours) notification to the Tribal Gaming Commission.

4. Signature records will be securely stored concurrently in the Tribal Gaming Commission Office and Revenue Audit Department.

5. Records maintained by the Tribal Gaming Commission are the control documents.

CASHING-IN/PRIZE PAYOUTS

1. Ottawa Casino(s) will comply with all applicable provisions of the Internal Revenue Code including, but not limited, to, the prompt filing of any cash transaction reports, W-2G reports and any 1099 reports that may be required by the Internal Revenue Service of the United States. (Title 31)

2. The patron will be required to produce an identification card confirming information required by the forms prior to completion of the transaction, e.g., acceptance of cash or disbursement of winnings. A Social Security card need not be presented to verify a patron's Social Security Number. (Title 31)

SENSITIVE KEYS (SEE ALSO SECURITY)

Sensitive keys are those keys that the Tribal Gaming Commission considers sensitive to the Casino's operation and, therefore, require strict control over custody and issuance.

1. The Casino Security Department shall maintain:

(i) Location of all sensitive key boxes and whether any of the boxes are portable or controlled by dual locks.

(A) Personnel positions which have authorized access to the sensitive key box, how the keys are issued and controlled.

(B) Sensitive key name, location, custodian, and job titles authorized to sign out each sensitive key.

(C) Location and custodian of duplicate sensitive keys.

2. Each sensitive key box custodian shall be issued a sensitive key access list noting authorized job titles that may access each sensitive key.

3. Whenever two (2) sensitive keys are required to access a controlled area, the keys shall be issued to different employees and each key shall be independently signed out.

4. Sensitive keys that require issuance under security, management, or Tribal Gaming Commission escort, shall be identified as such in the sensitive key access list.

5. Casino Management shall detail which management employee or designee has the authority to make changes, deletions, and/or additions to the sensitive key access list.
6. A sensitive key access list shall be maintained at each sensitive key box and a current copy given Immediately (within the same regular scheduled shift of a gaming day) at the time any changes are made to the Tribal Gaming Commission, and shall include:
(i) Name of sensitive key.
(ii) Location of sensitive key.
(iii) Custodian of sensitive key.
(iv) Quantity of sensitive key(s).
(v) Job titles authorized to sign out sensitive key and, if applicable, escort requirements and specific limitations.
(vi) Custodian/location of duplicate keys.
7 All sensitive keys and duplicate keys shall be issued after proper completion of a sensitive key log, which shall include:
(i) Key number
(ii) Key name
(iii) Signature of individual giving out key
(iv) Signature of individual receiving key
(v) Date
(vi) Time key signed out
(vii) Time key signed in
(viii) Signature of individual receiving returned key
(ix) Signature of individual returning key
8. Sensitive keys shall be returned to custody and signed in by the same employee to whom they were issued. If keys must be passed on at shift change, identify these keys and indicate the procedural controls over their transfer.
9. Completed sensitive key logs shall be forwarded at specified intervals to the accounting department with simultaneous (within the hour) copies to the Tribal Gaming Commission where they shall be reviewed and retained.
DEFINITIONS As Stated In 25 CFR 542.2
Accountability: All inventory items of currency, chips, coins, tokens, receivables, and customer deposits constituting the total amount for which the bankroll custodian is responsible at a given time.
Accounting Department: The department established in the operations system of organization complying with these standards.
Accumulated Credit Payout: A credit earned in a gaming machine that is paid to a customer manually in lieu of a machine payout.
Actual Hold: Coins-in less coins-out, less manual payouts, less hopper fills.
Actual Hold Percentage: The percentage calculated by dividing the win by the drop or coin-in. Can be calculated for individual tables or slot machines, type of table games or slot machines, on a per-day or cumulative basis.
Adjustment Form: A document used to describe and identify any change to player's cage account balance not generated directly by player gaming activity.
AICPA: The American Institute of Certified Public Accountants.
Analysis Report: A report prepared that compares theoretical to actual hold by a gaming machine on a monthly or other periodic basis.
Applicable Law: Ottawa Tribal Gaming Ordinance approved by Ottawa Tribal Executive Committee, any applicable Federal law, any applicable State law, and the Tribal/Oklahoma State Gaming Compact (when applicable).
Authorized: Used in conjunction with other terms to attest someone has approval from the Tribal Gaming Commission for specified duties listed on a master authority sheet maintained by the Tribal Gaming Commission, or that some action has such approval.
Award Schedule Card: A statement printed on cards, paper, Plexiglas, etc., of the payoffs or awards applicable to a particular game or device. Also known as "Award Schedule" or "Payout Schedule."
Bank (Bankroll): The inventory of currency, coins, chips, checks, tokens, receivables, and customer deposits in the cage, pit area, gaming booths, and on the playing tables and cash in bank which is used to make change or pay winnings, bets, and pay gaming machine jackpots.
Bank Number: A unique number assigned to identify a network of player terminals.
Base Jackpot: The fixed, minimum amount of a progressive gaming or electronic gaming device payout for a specific combination.
Bill Validator Box *(See also Currency Acceptor):* A locked container securely
attached to the electronic gaming device for the purpose of collecting bills or a device that accepts and reads currency by denomination in order to accurately register customer credits at a gaming machine. The machine number is clearly visible on the box.
Bingo: The game of chance commonly known as Bingo (whether or not electronic, computer, or other technologic aids are used in connection therewith) which is played for prizes, including monetary prizes, with cards bearing numbers or other designations, in which the holder of each card covers such numbers or designations when objects, similarly numbered or designated,

are drawn or electronically determined, and in which the game is won by the first person covering a previously designated arrangement of numbers or designations on such cards.

Blackjack: The card game played by a maximum of seven players and one dealer wherein each player plays his hand against the dealer's hand with the object of obtaining a higher total card count than the dealer by reaching 21 or as near 21 as possible without exceeding 21.

Buy In: The amount of money a player must present for coin and chips in a poker game. Usually put in a separate drop box by the dealer. May also refer to chips bought from the "house" or operator by the player upon entering any other card game.

Cage: A secure work area within the gaming facility for cashiers, and a storage area for the gaming facility or operation bankroll.

Cage Accountability Form: An itemized list of the components that make up the cage accountability.

Cage Cashier: The person in charge of the central banking function or the cashiers performing any of the functions of the Cashier's Cage.

Calibration Module: The section of a weight scale used to set the scale to a specific amount or number of coins to be counted.

Card Games: A game in which the gaming facility is *not* party to wagers, and from which the gaming facility receives compensations in the form of a rake, a time buy-in, or other fee or payment from a player for the privilege of playing.

Card Room Bank: The operating fund assigned to the card room or main card room bank.

Cash: Legal tender issued by the United States Treasury in various denominations made of paper and metal.

Cash Equivalent: A treasury check, personal check, travelers check, wire transfer of funds, money order, certified check, cashiers check, a check drawn on the tribal gaming operation payable to the patron or to the tribal gaming operation, or a voucher recording cash drawn against a credit card or charge card. Items are included with cash to aggregate the Bank Total.

Cash count sheet: The form used to record the contents of the bankroll as they are counted.

Cash loads: The initial currency, coins, chips, and tokens issued from a bankroll to a gaming table or put into an electronic gaming device.

Cash Transaction Report Form: The form used for reporting under Title 31 requirements.

Cashier's Count Sheet *(check out sheet)*: An itemized list of the components that make up the cage accountability.

Cashier's count sheet reconciliation: A detailed reconciliation of the beginning to the ending cage accountability.

Casino: The facility in which several gaming activities or enterprises are operated.

Change Bin: A booth or small cage in the gaming area that is used to provide change to customers, store change banks, make electronic gaming device fills, account for jackpot payouts, and make gaming receipt payouts, store change aprons, extra coin, and account for jackpot and other payouts.

Change Person: A person who has an imprest fund of coins, tokens, and currency for making change for customers.

Cheating: A person operating or playing in any game in a manner in violation of the written or commonly understood rules of the game, with the intent to create for himself, or someone in collusion with him, an advantage over and above the chance of the game.

Chief Operating Officer or Chief Executive Officer: The senior executive exercising the overall management or authority over all the operations of the operation and the carrying out by employees of the tribal gaming operation of their duties.

Chip or Gaming Chip or Check or Cheque: A non-metal or partly metal disc or plaque representative of value or money substitutes in various denominations issued by the casino for value at table games or the cashier's cages (See Value of Chips and Tokens).

Chip Tray: A container located on gaming tables where chips are stored that are used in the game.

Chip and Token Float: The monetary value of chips and tokens held by customers.

Class III Gaming: Defined in Indian Gaming Regulatory Act (IGRA) as any gaming that is not Class I or Class II gaming.

Closer: The original of the table inventory slip upon which each table inventory is recorded at the end of each shift.

Counter Game: Games whose gross revenue is computed as total write or amount wagered less payouts (such as Bingo).

Count Sheet: A form used to record the count of currency, coins, chips, etc. from the drop box for a game. Also, a form used to count the currency, coin, and chips in the game trays. Occasionally referred to as the Master Game Report.

Count team: Personnel that perform count of the gaming machine drop.

Credit (Credit Slip): Is the document reflecting the authorization for preparation of a credit with respect to removal of gaming chips and coins from a gaming table. A casino form initiated to record the amount of money or chips removed from a gaming table or the transfer of a negotiable check from a gaming table to a casino cage, bankroll, or pit bank.

Cross Fill: The transfer of cash or chips from one gaming table to another or an even-money transfer.

Currency Acceptor *(also known as a bill validator or bill changer)*: The device that accepts and reads currency by denomination in order to accurately register customer credits at a gaming machine.

Currency Acceptor Drop: Cash contained in currency acceptor drop boxes.

Currency Acceptor Drop Box *(also known as a cash storage box)*: Box attached to currency acceptors used to contain currency received by currency acceptors.

Currency Acceptor Drop Box Release Key: The key used to release currency acceptor drop box from currency acceptor device.

Currency Acceptor Box Rack: A locked cabinet or rack where bill validator boxes are securely stored when not attached to an electronic gaming device.

Currency Acceptor Drop Storage Rack Key: The key used to release currency acceptor drop boxes from the storage rack.

Customer Deposits: The amounts placed with a cage cashier by customers for the customers' use at a future time.

Dealer/Boxman: An employee who operates a game, individually, or as a part of a crew, administering house rules and making payoffs.

Deal-In Pull-Tabs Games: The numerical sequence of all pull-tabs in a specific pull-tab game that are sold or available for sale to patrons.

Discard Tray: A tray, box, or specific area where cards used in a game are held awaiting the next shuffle. Used primarily in baccarat and twenty-one.

Drop-In Table Games: The total amount of cash and chips contained in the drop box and the total amount of credit slips reflecting transfers. In electronic gaming devices, the "drop" is the total amount of money removed from the drop buckets and bill validator boxes.

Drop Box: A locked container affixed to the gaming table into which the drop/rake is placed and for deposit of cash, coin, and gaming chips and certain documents received at a gaming table. The game type, table number, and shift are indicated on the box.

Drop Box Contents Key: The key used to open drop boxes.

Drop Box Release Key: The key used to release drop boxes from tables.

Drop Box Storage Rack Key: The key used to release drop boxes from the storage rack.

Drop Bucket: A container located in the drop cabinet (or in a secured portion of the gaming machine in coin less/cashless configurations) for the purpose of collecting coins, tokens, cash-out tickets and coupons from the gaming machine or a container located beneath an EGD tokens from the device.

Drop Cabinet: The wooden or metal base of the gaming machine that contains the gaming machine drop bucket.

Drop Count Card: A document prepared by the count team to record the amount of cash, chips, or tokens by denomination, in a drop box or electronic gaming device.

Drop Period: The period of time that occurs between sequential drops.

Electronic Gaming Device (EGD), (Slot, Slot Machine. Gaming Machine): An electronic or electromechanical machine that allows a player to play games of chance, some of which may be affected by skill, which contains a microprocessor with random number generator capability for outcome selection or computer terminal that accesses an outcome that is subsequently and randomly selected in drawings that are electronically conducted by central computer or other such methods of chance selection, whether mechanical or electronic. The machine is activated by the insertion of cash or cash equivalents and which awards cash, cash equivalents, merchandise, or a written statement of the player's accumulated credits, which written statements may be redeemable for cash. All EGDs must be connected at all times online/real-time to a central computing devices for purposes of accounting, auditing, security, and monitoring.

Electronic Gaming Device Drop/Win Report: A record of the computation of win/loss by denomination of each device.

Electronic Gaming Device Supervisor: An individual with responsibility for electronic gaming devices area and jackpots, but does not include a person within the security department.

Employee: Any executive, employee, independent contractor, or agent of the Tribe or management contractor that works for or at a gaming facility.

EPROM: An erasable programmable read only memory chip.

Enterprise: Any tribally owned gaming operation.

Even Money Transfers: The act of exchanging currency and chips for coin or other chips of equivalent value.

Eye, "Eye in the sky', "The Peek", Surveillance Cameras: Placement of cameras in a casino located in the overhead structure of a building from which the casino area can be viewed without detection from the casino.

False Drop: The amount of cash or cash equivalents used to purchase chips at a gaming table at which the customer does not play the chips.

Fill: A transaction whereby a supply of chips, coins, and tokens is transferred from a bankroll to a table, an electronic gaming device, or Bingo.

Fill Slip: A document evidencing a transfer of chips, tokens, or cash from the casino cage to the gaming table, Bingo or an EGD. Fill Slip is the document reflecting the request for the distribution of gaming chips and coins to a gaming table, or a document prepared by a pit supervisor or runner to authorize the preparation of a fill slip.

Final Fill/Credit: Transfer of chips, tokens, or cash to or from a gaming table at a shift-end to restore the table to its impress amount.

Fiscal Year: The annual period used by a tribal gaming operation for internal accounting of its gaming operations.

Fixed Camera (Stationary Camera): A camera fixed into a set view position. Such camera view can only be moved manually from its set position. The camera lens can zoom in or out from this set view position but the camera itself cannot otherwise move.

Flare: The information sheet provided by the manufacturer that sets forth the rules at a particular game of pull-tabs and that is associated with a specific deal of pull-tab tickets. The flare shall contain the following information: Name of the Game; Manufacturer's name or manufacturer's logo; Ticket count; and Prize structure.

Floor Par: The sum of the theoretical hold percentages of all machines within a gaming machine denomination weighted by the coin-in contribution.

Foreign Chips and Tokens: Chips and tokens of another casino that are found or redeemed for cash or Tribal chips or tokens from other casinos following the Tribe's prescribed procedures (Such Items are included in the Bank).

Foreign Currency and Coins: Currency and coins other than those issued by the United States Treasury which are found or redeemed for cash or house chips or tokens (Such items are included in the Bank).

Game, Gaming Activity: Any activity or operation in which any valuable consideration may be wagered upon the outcome determined by chance, skill, and in which any valuable prize is awarded to the player so wagering, and any activity in further-ance thereof, including owning, financing, managing, participating in, conducting or assisting in any way in any such activity which it is being conducted, directly or indirectly, whether at the site in person or off tribal land.

Gaming Day: The 24-hour period adopted by casino management and approved by the Ottawa Tribal Gaming Commission for daily accounting of gross gaming revenues.

Gaming Enterprise: Any gaming activity or operation subject to the provisions of this TICS and Compact.

Gaming Equipment: Any device, machine, paraphernalia, or equipment that is used or usable in the playing phases of any gaming activity, whether or not specifically designed for the purpose, but excluding tables and chairs normally used in the occupancy of any gaming facility.

Gaming Facility: Means any building, room or rooms in which Class II and Class III gaming is conducted as authorized by the NIGC and/or the Tribal/State Compact.

Gaming Facility Supervisor (Manager on Duty or MOD): A person in a supervisory capacity required to perform certain functions or under the TICS.

Gaming Facility Manager: The executive who has the authority and responsibility for all gaming operations.

Gaming Machine Booths, Change Banks, or Change Bins: A booth or small cage in the gaming machine area used to provide change to players, store change aprons, extra coin, and account for jackpot and other payouts.

Gaming Machine Monitoring System: A system used by a gaming operation to monitor gaming machine meter reading activity on an online basis.

Gaming Operation: Any enterprise owned by the Tribe on its Reservation located within the boundaries of Oklahoma for the conduct of Class II gaming in a gaming facility.

Gaming Services: Any goods or services to the Tribe directly in connection with each Class II gaming activity or operation in a gaming facility, including but not limited to equipment, maintenance, or security services for such gaming facility and conces-sions.

General Manager: See Chief Operating Officer.

Gross Gaming Revenue: The net win from gaming activities, which is the difference between gaming wins and losses plus table and card fees before deducting costs and expenses.

Gross Receipts: Any money collected or received from gaming activity or operation.

Hard Count: The total amount of coins and tokens removed from a slot machine drop bucket or bag. The amount counted is entered on the Slot Count Sheet and is considered the drop. Also, the procedure of counting the coins and tokens, or the process of verifying slot coin and token inventory.

Ottawa Tribe Casinos *(Tribal gaming facility)*: The gaming operations owned by the Ottawa Tribe of Oklahoma in accordance with the requirements approved under IGRA.

Hold: In the case of table games, the comparison of win to drop. In the case of slots, the total coins counted compared to the drop. In the case of Bingo, total amount wagered (write, card sales) compared to win. Hold may also be used to refer to the gross revenue or amount won or held by the house from a particular game or device. Also called PC (per cent) or Hold Per-centage. See Theoretical Hold and Gross Revenue.

Hold Percentage: The relationship of hold to drop.

Hopper: A piece of equipment in a electronic gaming device used to retain coins or tokens used to make electronic payouts.

House Bank Game: Each player opposes the gaming facility and the gaming facility opposes each player.

IGRA: The Indian Gaming Regulatory Act, Public Law 100-497, 102 Stat.
2426, 25 U.S.C. 2701, et seq. (1988), as amended.

Immediate Notification: Communication to specified parties within the same regularly scheduled shift of a gaming day. Said information is required under the TICS.

Imprest Bank: An advance or loan of money to be used to transact business outside the primary area where money is centrally stored which is usually the cashier's cage. A change bin contains an imprest bank to make change for customers, pay off Jackpots, etc.

Imprest Basis: The basis on which funds are replenished from time to time by exactly the amount of the net expenditures made from the funds and amounts received and in which a review of the expenditure is made by a higher authority before replenishment.

Income Control (Revenue Audit): That group of individuals in the accounting department who are responsible for the daily audits of records generated on the casino floor, both gaming and non-gaming. There are no incompatible functions in this department as the staff reports directly to the Revenue Audit Supervisor who in turn reports to the Financial Controller.

Incompatible Function: A function, for accounting and internal control purposes, that places any person or department in a position to either perpetrate and/or conceal errors or fraud in the normal course of his/her duties. Anyone both recording trans-actions and having access to the relevant assets is in a position to perpetrate or conceal errors or fraud.

Independent Accountant: An independent certified public accountant licensed by the State of Oklahoma with a current permit to practice, suitably qualified and sufficiently independent to act as auditor of the tribal gaming operation.

Indian Gaming Commission (NIGC): The National Indian Gaming Commission established pursuant to the IGRA.

Inspector: An employee and agent of the Tribal Gaming Commission duly appointed by the Tribal Gaming Commission as an inspector also known as a Compliance Officer.

Instant Notification: Communication to specified parties without any delay being purposely introduced. Said information is required under the TICS.

Internal Audit: Individuals or organizations that perform an audit function of a gaming operation that are independent of the operation subject to audit. Independence is obtained through the organizational reporting relationship as the internal auditor shall not report to management of the gaming operation. Internal audit activities should be conducted in a manner that permits objective evaluation of areas examined. Results of audits are generally communicated to management. Audit exceptions generally require follow-up. Internal audit personnel may provide audit coverage to more than one operation within a tribe's gaming operation holdings.

Internal Controls: See Internal Controls Procedures.

Internal Control Procedures (See also Procedure): The detailed description of steps or processed taken or to be followed to meet the intent of the TICS as approved by the Tribal Gaming Commission.

Internal Controls System: Plan of organization and all of the coordinated methods and measures adopted within a business to safeguard its assets, check the accuracy and reliability of its accounting data, provide adequate separation of incompatible procedures and functions, promote operational efficiency, and encourage adherence to prescribed managerial policies.

IRS: The United States Internal Revenue Service.

Jackpot Payout: The portion of a jackpot paid by gaming facility personnel. The amount is usually determined as the difference between the total posted jackpot amount and the machine payout. May also be the total amount of the jackpot.

Jackpot Payout Slip: A form on which the portion of a jackpot paid by gaming facility personnel is recorded.

Key Control Ledger: A ledger which authorized personnel sign to receive keys to sensitive areas, such as drop boxes, count room and cashier's cage.

Kobetron: A machine that reads the identification signature from EPROM chips located in the slot machines.

Layout: In games like roulette or craps, a diagram - usually on felt - with spaces for bets, odds, and payoffs. Part of table inventory ledger card.

Limit: The minimum and maximum amount that customers may wager.

Load: The amount of coins or tokens in the hopper.

Loose Coin: Coin held in a cage, change bin, vault, or count room or on gaming tables, that has not been put in wrappers. Usually in denominations other than dollars. May also include bent or damaged coins.

Log: Document used for recording and tracking information and activity.

Main Card Room Bank: A fund of currency, coin, and chips used primarily for card room use. Used to make even money transfers between various games as needed. May be used similarly in other areas of the gaming operation.

Manager on Duty (MOD, Shift Supervisor, Shift Boss): The person with overall responsibility for gaming facility operations during a shift.

Manufacturer/Distributor: Any individual, sole proprietorship, partnership or corporation which assembles, produces, makes, prints, or supplies Class II gaming equipment or supplies for sale, lease, use, or distribution to the Tribe or a licensed gaming operator for a Class II gaming activity.

Master Game Program Number: The game program number listed on a gaming machine EPROM.

Master Gaming Report/Game Report (Game Count Sheet): A form used to record, by shift and day, each table games winnings and losses. This form reflects the opening and closing table inventories, the fills and credits, and the drop and win.

Meter: An electronic or a mechanical apparatus in an electronic gaming device. May record the number of coins wagered, the number of coins dropped, the number of times the handle was pulled, and/or the number of coins paid out to winning players.

Meter Reading Summary: A report reflecting the meter readings on electronic gaming devices. The number is recorded when the drop bucket and/or bill validator is removed from the cabinet.

TICS: Tribal Internal Control Standards of the Tribal Gaming Commission or the National Indian Gaming Commission.

Tribal Internal Control Standards: The Tribal Gaming Commission's adopted and published minimum standards through its authority to promulgate rules that are comprehensive and establish minimums for internal control procedures required of gaming operations that in the Tribal Gaming Commission's opinion satisfy the Tribal Gaming Commission and the NIGC. Such standards may be changed periodically by the Tribal Gaming Commission (See Section on changes to TICS).

National Indian Gaming Commission: The commission by that name established by the IGRA.

Net Revenues: Gross gaming revenues, less amounts paid out as, or paid for, prizes, and total gaming-related operating expenses, excluding management fees.

Non-House Banking Card Game: A card game where the house does not participate in or have any interest in the outcome of the wager.

Opener: The duplicate copy of the table inventory slip upon which each table inventory is recorded at the end of each shift and serves as the record of each table inventory at the beginning of the next or succeeding shift.

Operator: A person contracted, appointed, or hired by the Tribe to perform, promote, conduct, or operate any lawful, tribally licensed gaming activity or operation on tribal lands at a gaming facility. In the case of a gaming activity owned and operated solely by the Tribe, this person shall be the senior gaming management official employed to operate the game or games. In the case of game or games operated pursuant to a management contract, that person shall be the senior management official designated by the management contract on its management contractor's license application.

Par Percentage: The percentage of each dollar wagered that the house wins (i.e., gaming operation advantage).

Participate: Manage, operate, direct, own, finance, furnish, supply or in any way assist in the establishment of, or operation of, any class II gaming activity or operation, directly or indirectly, whether at the site in person or off of the reservation.

Payout: The total amount of money paid to customers as winnings on various games.

Pit: The area enclosed or encircled by an arrangement of gaming stations in which gaming facility personnel administer and supervise the games played at the tables by the patrons located on the outside perimeter of the area. There may be more than one pit in a casino.

Pit Boss: The person who supervises all games in a particular pit area.

Pit Floorman/Table Supervisor: The person who supervises specific gaming tables in a pit and is responsible to a pit boss.

Pit Podium: A stand located in the middle of the tables used as a work space and record storage area for gaming operation supervisory personnel.

Pit Supervisor: The employee who supervises all games in a pit.

Player: One person to whom a hand has been dealt or means any person participating in any gaming with the chance of winning money or other benefit, but does not include an operator, or any assistant of an operator.

Player Tracking System: A system typically used in gaming machine departments that can record the gaming machine play of individual patrons.

Poker: A card game using a single 52-card deck. Players, preferably five or more, wager against each other based on the value of their hands, the bets forming a pool or pot to be taken by the winner.

Policy: A plan or course of action designed to influence and determine decisions and actions.

Procedure *(See also Internal Control Procedure)*: A way of performing, or a method used, in dealing with the affairs of a business.

Progressive Gaming Machine: A gaming machine, with a payoff indicator, in which the payoff increases as it is played (i.e., deferred payout). The payoff amount is accumulated, displayed on a machine and will remain until a player lines up the jackpot symbols that result in the progressive amount being paid.

Progressive Jackpot: Deferred payout from a progressive gaming machine.

Progressive Table Game: Table games that offer progressive jackpots.

Promotional Payouts: Personal property or awards given to players by the gaming operation as an inducement to play. Promotions vary but a promotion example might be a program developed where a player receives a form of personal property based on the number of games or sessions played.

Promotional Progressive Pots/pools: Funds contributed to a table game or card game by and for the benefit of players. Funds are distributed to players based on a predetermined event.

Pull-Tabs: Any gaming utilizing preprinted cards bearing symbols or numbers in random order, which are uncovered by random choice in expectation of cash prizes whenever prescribed combinations of symbols and numbers are revealed.

Rake: The fee the gaming facility charges a customer for using a position at a gaming table.

Rake Circle: The area of a table where rake is placed.

Rake-Off: The amount of coin or chips taken from certain card game pots by the dealer to be put in the drop box. The rake-off is the casino's fee for running the game.

Randomness: The observed unpredictability and absence of pattern in a set of events that have definite probabilities of occurrence.

Random Number Generator: A device that generates numbers in the absence of a pattern. May be used to determine numbers selected in various games such as keno and Bingo. Also commonly used in gaming machines to generate game outcome.

Reasonable Notification: Communication to specified parties within seven (7) gaming days. Said information is required under the TICS.

Reel Strip Settings: Setting positions on electronic gaming machine reels so that they correspond to the calibrations regulating winning combinations and payoffs.

Reel Symbols: Symbols listed on reel strips of gaming machines.

Ottawa Tribe Trust Land: All lands in Oklahoma, Ohio, or any other state of the United States owned by the Ottawa Tribe of Indians of Oklahoma.

Revoke: To permanently void and recall all rights and privileges to obtain or hold a license.

Runner: An employee in the pit who reports to the cage cashier and who prepares documentation such as requests for fills and credits, markers, etc.

Security Department: A department within, or utilized by, a gaming operation whose employees primary responsibility is for the protection of company and guest assets, while also insuring the safety of casino guests and employees. This department also assists in maintaining compliance with all internal controls but do not participate in operating table games or electronic gaming devices, and do not participate in cashier cage operations.

Security Department Representative/Member: Any person who is a member of the Security Department as provided in the organization of the operation.

Series Number: The unique identifying number printed on each sheet of Bingo paper that identifies the Bingo paper as a series or packet. The series number is not the free space or center space number located on the Bingo paper.

Shift: Any time period designated by management up to 24 hours.

Shift Boss (Manager on Duty, MOD): The person with overall responsibility for gaming facility operations during a shift.

Shoe: A device used to hold cards before dealing.

Short Pay: A payoff from an electronic gaming device that is less than the listed amount.

Signature: At a minimum, the first initial and full last name accompanied by the Tribal Gaming Commission license number.

Simultaneous Notification: Communication to specified parties within the hour. Said information is required under the Tribal Internal Control Standards.

Slip Dispenser (Whiz Machine): A locked device used primarily in a cage to dispense fill and credit slips in numerical sequence.

Slot Machine: An electronic gaming device.

Slot Fills: Coin required to fill tubes or hoppers of a slot machine when it is first put into operation. Subsequently, additional coins placed in a machine so that it can continue to make automatic payouts.

Slug: A non-gaming counterfeit coin used to cheat a slot machine.

Soft Count: The amount counted that is entered on the Game Count Sheet, as part of the drop. The total amount of currency and chips removed from the drop box and bill validators. The entire procedure of counting drop box and bill validator contents of card and table games and EGDs is referred to as the soft count.

Standard Operating Procedure: Refers to an established procedure to be followed in a given situation. As part of its standard operating procedure, a gaming operation is required to provide step-by-step instructions so that anyone coming into the operation would be able to follow the instructions and actually perform the task.

State Gaming Agency (Agency): Such agency of the State of Oklahoma as the State of Oklahoma may designate as the Agency responsible for oversight of Class III gaming conducted pursuant to the Tribal/State Compact.

Surveillance/Observation Room: Designated area that contains the surveillance equipment that monitors the gaming facility.

Table Bank: Coins and house chips assigned to a gaming table as an imprest fund or inventory.

Table Chip Tray: A device to hold coin and chips on a gaming table. Facilitates inventory counts. Usually designed with clear locking covers to secure the table bank when the game is "closed" or not open for play. Also called Table Rack or Table Tray.

Table Game: Games such as Craps, Roulette, Blackjack, Poker, etc.

Table Game Drop: The sum of the total amounts of currency, coin, tokens, gaming chips, customer checks, and other cash equivalent(s) removed from a drop box.

Table Game Win or Loss: Determined by adding the amount of cash or coin, closer, funds removed from a drop box (drop), plus credits, and subtracting the opener and fills removed from a drop box.

Theoretical Hold: The intended hold percentage or win of an individual electronic gaming device as computed by reference to its payout schedule and reel strip settings.

Theoretical Hold Sheet: A form that lists the characteristics of an individual electronic gaming device, such as reel settings, award schedule, number of coins that may be played, number of reels, theoretical hold, and other data applicable to an electronic gaming device.

Timely Notification: Communication to specified parties within the same gaming day. Said information is required under the TICS.

Token/Slot Token: A metal disk representative of value issued by the Tribe for use in electronic gaming devices or at table games at a Tribal gaming facility or a coin-like money substitute, in various denominations, used for gambling transactions (See Value of Chips and Tokens).

Tokes: A euphemism for tokens, i.e., gratuities, given to the casino employees by players.

Tribal Gaming Commission: The Ottawa Tribal Gaming Commission established by the Tribe as the agency primarily responsible for regulatory oversight of Class II/III gaming conducted pursuant to the IGRA and the NIGC.

Tribal Gaming Regulations: Those regulations adopted by the Tribe to regulate Class II/III gaming conducted pursuant to the IGRA and other applicable law.

Tribe: The Ottawa Tribe of Oklahoma, recognized by the federal government and operating pursuant to the Tribal Constitution and By-laws, and "tribal" means belonging or pertaining to the Tribe.

Twenty-One or Blackjack: The card game played by a maximum of seven players and one dealer wherein each player plays his hand against the dealer's hand with the object of obtaining a higher total card count than the dealer by reaching 21 or as near 21 as possible without exceeding 21.

Value of Chips and Tokens: Chips and tokens are solely representative as evidence of a debt owed to their custodian by the Tribal gaming facilitiy and are not the property of anyone other than the Tribal gaming facilitiy. Use of the Tribal gaming facilitiy's chips or tokens for any monetary purpose whatsoever is prohibited. The Tribal gaming facilitiy will redeem the chips and tokens from its patrons by cash or check drawn on an account of the gaming facility. Promotional chips and tokens shall bear an inscription "No Cash Value".

Vice President and General Manager: See Chief Operating Officer

Wager: A sum of money or thing of value risked on an uncertain occurrence.

Weigh/Count and Wrap: The comparison of the weighed gaming machine drop to counted and wrapped coin.

Weigh Scale: A scale that calculates (by weight) the amount of money in a given bucket/bags from an electronic gaming device/slot.

Win: Synonymous with Gross Gaming Revenue.

Work Papers: Documents containing the evidence to support the auditors findings, options, conclusions, and judgments.

Wrap: The procedure of wrapping coins. May also refer to the total amount or value of the wrapped coins.

393

Write: Total dollar amount collected for all tickets written in Bingo operations for a specified shift or period.

COMPLIANCE WITH NIGC MANDATES (25 CFR 542.3)

1. Tier A gaming operations (More than $1 million but less than $5 million annual gross revenue) must comply with Secs. 542.1 through 542.18, and Secs. 542.20 through 542.23.

2. Tier B gaming operations (Between $5 - $15 million in annual gross revenue) must comply with Secs. 542.1 through 542.18, and Secs. 542.30 through 542.33.

3. Tier C gaming operations (More than $15 million in annual gross revenue) must comply with Secs. 542.1 through 542.18, and Secs. 542.40 through 542.43. The Tribal gaming facilitiy is a Tier C gaming operation.

1. The determination of tier level shall be made based upon the annual gross gaming revenues indicated within the gaming operation's audited financial statements. Gaming operations moving from one tier to another shall have nine (9) months from the date of the independent certified public accountant's audit report to achieve compliance with the requirements of the new tier.

2. The Tribal Gaming Commission may extend the deadline by an additional six (6) months if written notice is provided to the Commission no later than two weeks before the expiration of the nine (9) month period.

Tribal Gaming Commission shall, in accordance with the Tribal gaming ordinance, establish and implement tribal internal control standards that shall:

1) Provide a level of control that equals or exceeds those set forth in this part;
2) Contain standards for currency transaction reporting that comply with 5 CFR part 103;
3) Establish standards for games that are not addressed in this part; and
4) Establish a deadline, which shall not exceed nine (9) months from June 27, 2002, by which a gaming operation must come into compliance with the tribal internal control standards. However, the Tribal Gaming Commission may extend the deadline by an additional six (6) months if written notice is provided to the Commission no later than two weeks before the expiration of the nine (9) month period.

D. GAMING OPERATIONS.

Each gaming operation shall develop and implement an internal control system that, at a minimum, complies with the tribal internal control standards.

1. Existing gaming operations.

All gaming operations that are operating on or before June 27, 2002, shall comply with this part within the time requirements established in paragraph (c) of this section. In the interim, such operations shall continue to comply with existing tribal internal control standards.

2. New gaming operations.

All gaming operations that commence operations after August 26, 2002, shall comply with this part before commencement of operations.

E. SUBMISSION TO COMMISSION.

Tribal regulations promulgated pursuant to this part shall not be required to be submitted to the Commission pursuant to 25 CFR 522.3(b).

F. CPA TESTING.

1. An independent certified public accountant (CPA) shall be engaged to perform procedures to verify, on a test basis, that the gaming operation is in material compliance with the tribal internal control standards or a tribally approved variance that has received NIGC concurrence. The procedures may be performed in conjunction with the annual audit. The CPA shall report its findings to the Tribe, Tribal Gaming Commission, and management. The Tribe shall submit a copy of the report to the NIGC within 120 days of the gaming operation's fiscal year end.

2. CPA Guidelines. : In connection with the CPA testing pursuant to paragraph (f)(1) of this section, the NIGC shall develop recommended CPA Guidelines available upon request.

TRIBAL – OKLAHOMA STATE GAMING COMPACT (25 CFR 542.4)

1. If there is a direct conflict between an internal control standard established in a Tribal-State compact and a standard or requirement set forth in this part, then the internal control standard established in a Tribal-State compact shall prevail.

2. If an internal control standard in a Tribal-State compact provides a level of control that equals or exceeds the level of control under an internal control standard or requirement set forth in this part, then the Tribal-State compact standard shall prevail.

3. If an internal control standard or a requirement set forth in this part provides a level of control that exceeds the level of control under an internal control standard established in a Tribal-State compact, then the internal control standard or requirement set forth in this part shall prevail.

OKLAHOMA STATE JURISDICTION (25 CFR 542.5)

Nothing in this part shall be construed to grant to the State of Oklahoma jurisdiction in Class II gaming or extend the State of Oklahoma's jurisdiction in Class III gaming.

SMALL AND CHARITABLE GAMING OPERATIONS (25 CFR 542.6)

The Ottawa Tribe has no plans, intentions, nor provisions to operate charitable gaming pursuant to this section of 25 CFR.

BINGO BASED GAMES (25 CFR 542.7)

The Ottawa Tribal Gaming Commission does not at this time authorize the playing of traditional or paper Bingo games. Bingo-based Class II machines, as long as authorized by the NIGC are acceptable under these provisions. For any of these computer applications utilized, alternate documentation and/or procedures that provide at least the level of control described by the standards in this section, as approved by the Tribal Gaming Commission, will be acceptable.

The gaming operation is authorized to utilize electronic Bingo equipment in connection with the play of Bingo, provided the following sections of 25 CFR are hereby adopted and shall apply:

(i) If the electronic equipment contains a bill acceptor, then Sec. 542.21(e) and (f), Sec. 542.31 (e) and (f), or Sec. 542.41 (e) and (f) (as applicable) shall apply.

(ii) If the electronic equipment uses a bar code or microchip reader, the reader shall be tested periodically by a person or persons independent of the Bingo department to determine that it is correctly reading the bar code or the microchip.

(iii) If the electronic equipment returns a voucher or a payment slip to the player, then Sec. 542.13(n) (as applicable) shall apply.

Management shall ensure that all agreements/contracts entered into a to provide linked electronic games shall contain language requiring the vendor to comply with the standards in this section applicable to the goods or services the vendor is providing.

HOST REQUIREMENTS/GAME INFORMATION (FOR LINKED ELECTRONIC GAMES).

1. Providers of any linked electronic game(s) shall maintain complete records of game data for a period of one (1) year from the date the games are played (or any other time frame established by the Tribal Gaming Commission). This data may be kept in an archived manner, provided the information can be produced within twenty-four (24) hours upon request. In any event, game data for the preceding seventy-two (72) hours shall be immediately accessible.

2. Data required to be maintained for each game played includes:
(i) Date and time game start and game end;
(ii) Sales information by location;
(iii) Cash distribution by location;
(iv) Refund totals by location;
(v) Cards-in-play count by location;
(vi) Identification number of winning card(s);
(vii) Ordered list of Bingo balls drawn; and
(viii) Prize amounts at start and end of game.

3. Linked electronic game providers shall maintain on-line records at the remote host site for any game played. These records shall remain on-line until the conclusion of the session of which the game is a part. Following the conclusion of the session, records may be archived, but in any event, must be retrievable in a timely manner for at least seventy-two (72) hours following the close of the session. Records shall be accessible through some archived media for at least ninety (90) days from the date of the game.

STANDARDS FOR PLAYER ACCOUNTS (FOR PROXY PLAY AND LINKED ELECTRONIC GAMES).

1. Prior to participating in any game, players shall be issued a unique player account number. The player account number can be issued through the following means:
(i) Through the use of a point-of-sale (cash register device);
(ii) By assignment through an individual play station; or
(iii) Through the incorporation of a "player tracking" media.

2. Printed receipts issued in conjunction with any player account should include a time/date stamp.

3. All player transactions shall be maintained, chronologically by account number, through electronic means on a data storage device. These transaction records shall be maintained on-line throughout the active game and for at least twenty-four (24) hours before they can be stored on an "off-line" data storage media.

4. The game software shall provide the ability to, upon request, produce a printed account history, including all transactions, and a printed game summary (total purchases, deposits, wins, debits, for any account that has been active in the game during the preceding twenty-four (24) hours).

5. The game software shall provide a "player account summary" at the end of every game. This summary shall list all accounts for which there were any transactions during that game day and include total purchases, total deposits, total credits (wins), total debits (cash-outs) and an ending balance.

PULL-TABS (25 CFR 542.8), PARA MUTIAL AND OTHER GAMES

The Ottawa Tribal Gaming Commission does not at this time authorize the playing of pull-tab games or para-mutual betting. The Ottawa Tribal Gaming Commission reserves the right to amend these TICS in the future to add Pull-Tabs or Bingo or any other games that may become legal.

CARD GAMES (25 CFR 542.9)

A. COMPUTER APPLICATIONS.

For any computer applications utilized, alternate documentation and/or procedures that provide at least the level of control described by the standards in this section, as approved by the Tribal Gaming Commission, will be acceptable.

B. STANDARDS FOR DROP AND COUNT.

The procedures for the collection of the card game drop and the count thereof shall comply with Sec. 542.41.

C. STANDARDS FOR SUPERVISION.

1. Supervision shall be provided at all times the card room is in operation by personnel with authority equal to or greater than those being supervised.

2. Exchanges between table banks and the main card room bank (or cage, if a main card room bank is not used) in excess of $100.00 shall be authorized by a supervisor. All exchanges shall be evidenced by the use of a lammer unless the exchange of chips, tokens, and/or cash takes place at the table.

3. Exchanges from the main card room bank (or cage, if a main card room bank is not used) to the table banks shall be verified by the card room dealer and the runner.

4. If applicable, transfers between the main card room bank and the cage shall be properly authorized and documented.

5. A rake collected or ante placed shall be done in accordance with the posted rules.

D. STANDARDS FOR PLAYING CARDS.

1. Playing cards shall be maintained in a secure location to prevent unauthorized access and to reduce the possibility of tampering.

2. Used cards shall be maintained in a secure location until marked, scored, or destroyed, in a manner approved by the Tribal Gaming Commission, to prevent unauthorized access and reduce the possibility of tampering.
3. The Tribal Gaming Commission, or the gaming operation as approved by the Tribal Gaming Commission, shall establish and the gaming operation shall comply with a reasonable time period, which shall not exceed seven (7) days, within which to mark, cancel, or destroy cards from play.

(i) This standard shall not apply where playing cards are retained for an investigation.
(ii) [Reserved]

4. A card control log shall be maintained that documents when cards and dice are received on site, distributed to and returned from tables and removed from play by the gaming operation.

E. PLASTIC CARDS.

Notwithstanding paragraph (d) of this section, if a gaming operation uses plastic cards (not plastic-coated cards), the cards may be used for up to three (3) months if the plastic cards are routinely inspected, and washed or cleaned in a manner and time frame approved by the Tribal Gaming Commission.

F. STANDARDS FOR SHILLS.

1. Issuance of shill funds shall have the written approval of the supervisor.
2. Shill returns shall be recorded and verified on the shill sign-out form.

3. The replenishment of shill funds shall be documented.

G. STANDARDS FOR RECONCILIATION OF CARD ROOM BANK.

1. The amount of the main card room bank shall be counted, recorded, and reconciled on at least a per shift basis.
2. At least once per shift, the table banks that were opened during that shift shall be counted, recorded, and reconciled by a dealer or other person, and a supervisor, and shall be attested to by their signatures on the check-out form.

H. STANDARDS FOR PROMOTIONAL PROGRESSIVE POTS AND POOLS.

1. All funds contributed by players into the pools shall be returned when won in accordance with the posted rules with no commission or administrative fee withheld.
2. Rules governing promotional pools shall be conspicuously posted and designate:
(i) The amount of funds to be contributed from each pot;
(ii) What type of hand it takes to win the pool (e.g., what constitutes a "bad beat");
(iii) How the promotional funds will be paid out;
(iv) How/when the contributed funds are added to the jackpots; and
(v) Amount/percentage of funds allocated to primary and secondary jackpots, if applicable.
3. Promotional pool contributions shall not be placed in or near the rake circle, in the drop box, or commingled with gaming revenue from card games or any other gambling game.
4. The amount of the jackpot shall be conspicuously displayed in the card room.
5. At least once a day, the posted pool amount shall be updated to reflect the current pool amount.
6. At least once a day, increases to the posted pool amount shall be reconciled to the cash previously counted or received by the cage by personnel independent of the card room.
7. All decreases to the pool must be properly documented, including a reason for the decrease.

I. PROMOTIONAL PROGRESSIVE POTS AND POOLS WHERE FUNDS ARE DISPLAYED IN THE CARD ROOM.
1. Promotional funds displayed in the card room shall be placed in a locked container in plain view of the public.
2. Persons authorized to transport the locked container shall be precluded from having access to the contents keys.
3. The contents key shall be maintained by personnel independent of the card room.
4. At least once a day, the locked container shall be removed by two persons, one of whom is independent of the card games department, and transported directly to the cage or other secure room to be counted, recorded, and verified.
5. The locked container shall then be returned to the card room where the posted pool amount shall be updated to reflect the current pool amount.

J. PROMOTIONAL PROGRESSIVE POTS AND POOLS WHERE FUNDS ARE MAINTAINED IN THE CAGE.
1. Promotional funds removed from the card game shall be placed in a locked container.
2. Persons authorized to transport the locked container shall be precluded from having access to the contents keys.
3. The contents key shall be maintained by personnel independent of the card room.
4. At least once a day, the locked container shall be removed by two persons, one of whom is independent of the card games department, and transported directly to the cage or other secure room to be counted, recorded, and verified, prior to accepting the funds into cage accountability.
5. The posted pool amount shall then be updated to reflect the current pool amount.

ADDITIONAL TABLE GAME REGULATIONS AS PROVIDED BY (25 CFR 542.12)
A. COMPUTER APPLICATIONS.
For any computer applications utilized, alternate documentation and/or procedures that provide at least the level of control described by the standards in this section, as approved by the Tribal Gaming Commission, will be acceptable.
B. STANDARDS FOR DROP AND COUNT.
The procedures for the collection of the table game drop and the count thereof shall comply with Sec. 542.41.
C. FILL AND CREDIT STANDARDS.
1. Fill slips and credit slips shall be in at least triplicate form, and in a continuous, prenumbered series. Such slips shall be concurrently numbered in a form utilizing the alphabet and only in one series at a time. The alphabet need not be used if the numerical series is not repeated during the business year.
2. Unissued and issued fill/credit slips shall be safeguarded and adequate procedures shall be employed in their distribution, use, and control. Personnel from the cashier or pit departments shall have no access to the secured (control) copies of the fill/credit slips.
3. When a fill/credit slip is voided, the cashier shall clearly mark "void" across the face of the original and first copy, the cashier and one other person independent of the transactions shall sign both the original and first copy, and shall submit them to the accounting department for retention and accountability.
4. Fill transactions shall be authorized by pit supervisory personnel before the issuance of fill slips and transfer of chips, tokens, or cash equivalents. The fill request shall be communicated to the cage where the fill slip is prepared.
5. At least three parts of each fill slip shall be utilized as follows:
(i) One part shall be transported to the pit with the fill and, after the appropriate signatures are obtained, deposited in the table game drop box;
(ii) One part shall be retained in the cage for reconciliation of the cashier bank; and
(iii) For computer systems, one part shall be retained in a secure manner to insure that only authorized persons may gain access to it. For manual systems, one part shall be retained in a secure manner in a continuous unbroken form.
6. For Tier C gaming operations, the part of the fill slip that is placed in the table game drop box shall be of a different color for fills than for credits, unless the type of transaction is clearly distinguishable in another manner (the checking of a box on the form shall not be a clearly distinguishable indicator).
7. The table number, shift, and amount of fill by denomination and in total shall be noted on all copies of the fill slip. The correct date and time shall be indicated on at least two copies.
8. All fills shall be carried from the cashier's cage by a person who is independent of the cage or pit.
9. The fill slip shall be signed by at least the following persons (as an indication that each has counted the amount of the fill and the amount agrees with the fill slip):
(i) Cashier who prepared the fill slip and issued the chips, tokens, or cash equivalent;
(ii) Runner who carried the chips, tokens, or cash equivalents from the cage to the pit;
(iii) Dealer or boxperson who received the chips, tokens, or cash equivalents at the gaming table; and
(iv) Pit supervisory personnel who supervised the fill transaction.
10. Fills shall be broken down and verified by the dealer or boxperson in public view before the dealer or boxperson places the fill in the table tray.
11. A copy of the fill slip shall then be deposited into the drop box on the table by the dealer, where it shall appear in the soft count room with the cash receipts for the shift.
12. Table credit transactions shall be authorized by a pit supervisor before the issuance of credit slips and transfer of chips, tokens, or other cash equivalent. The credit request shall be communicated to the cage where the credit slip is prepared.
13. At least three parts of each credit slip shall be utilized as follows:

397

(i) Two parts of the credit slip shall be transported by the runner to the pit. After signatures of the runner, dealer, and pit supervisor are obtained, one copy shall be deposited in the table game drop box and the original shall accompany transport of the chips, tokens, markers, or cash equivalents from the pit to the cage for verification and signature of the cashier.

(ii) For computer systems, one part shall be retained in a secure manner to insure that only authorized persons may gain access to it. For manual systems, one part shall be retained in a secure manner in a continuous unbroken form.

14. The table number, shift, and the amount of credit by denomination and in total shall be noted on all copies of the credit slip. The correct date and time shall be indicated on at least two copies.

15. Chips, tokens, and/or cash equivalents shall be removed from the table tray by the dealer or boxperson and shall be broken down and verified by the dealer or boxperson in public view prior to placing them in racks for transfer to the cage.

16. All chips, tokens, and cash equivalents removed from the tables and markers removed from the pit shall be carried to the cashier's cage by a person who is independent of the cage or pit.

17. The credit slip shall be signed by at least the following persons (as an indication that each has counted or, in the case of markers, reviewed the items transferred):

(i) Cashier who received the items transferred from the pit and prepared the credit slip;

(ii) Runner who carried the items transferred from the pit to the cage;

(iii) Dealer who had custody of the items prior to transfer to the cage; and

(iv) Pit supervisory personnel who supervised the credit transaction.

18. The credit slip shall be inserted in the drop box by the dealer.

19. Chips, tokens, or other cash equivalents shall be deposited on or removed from gaming tables only when accompanied by the appropriate fill/credit or marker transfer forms.

20. Cross fills (the transfer of chips between table games) and even cash exchanges are prohibited in the pit.

D. TABLE INVENTORY FORMS.

1. At the close of each shift, for those table banks that were opened during that shift:

(i) The table's chip, token, coin, and marker inventory shall be counted and recorded on a table inventory form; or

(ii) If the table banks are maintained on an imprest basis, a final fill or credit shall be made to bring the bank back to par.

2. If final fills are not made, beginning and ending inventories shall be recorded on the master game sheet for shift win calculation purposes.

The accuracy of inventory forms prepared at shift end shall be verified by the outgoing pit supervisor and the dealer. Alternatively, if the dealer is not available, such verification may be provided by another pit supervisor or another supervisor from another gaming department. Verifications shall be evidenced by signature on the inventory form.

4. If inventory forms are placed in the drop box, such action shall be performed by a person other than a pit supervisor.

E. TABLE GAMES COMPUTER GENERATED DOCUMENTATION STANDARDS.

1. The computer system shall be capable of generating adequate documentation of all information recorded on the source documents and transaction detail (e.g., fill/credit slips, markers, etc.).

2. This documentation shall be restricted to authorized personnel.

3. The documentation shall include, at a minimum:

(i) System exception information (e.g., appropriate system parameter information, corrections, voids, etc.); and

(ii) Personnel access listing, which includes, at a minimum:

(A) Employee name or employee identification number (if applicable); and

(B) Listing of functions employees can perform or equivalent means of identifying the same.

F. STANDARDS FOR PLAYING CARDS AND DICE.

1. Playing cards and dice shall be maintained in a secure location to prevent unauthorized access and to reduce the possibility of tampering.

2. Used cards and dice shall be maintained in a secure location until marked, scored, or destroyed, in a manner as approved by the Tribal Gaming Commission, to prevent unauthorized access and reduce the possibility of tampering.

3. The Tribal Gaming Commission, or the gaming operation as approved by the Tribal Gaming Commission, shall establish and the gaming operation shall comply with a reasonable time period, which shall not exceed seven (7) days, within which to mark, cancel, or destroy cards and dice from play.

(i) This standard shall not apply where playing cards or dice are retained for an investigation.

(ii) [Reserved]

4. A card control log shall be maintained that documents when cards and dice are received on site, distributed to and returned from tables and removed from play by the gaming operation.

G. PLASTIC CARDS.

Notwithstanding paragraph (F) of this section, if a gaming operation uses plastic cards (not plastic-coated cards), the cards may be used for up to three (3) months if the plastic cards are routinely inspected, and washed or cleaned in a manner and time frame approved by the Tribal Gaming Commission.

H. STANDARDS FOR SUPERVISION.

Pit supervisory personnel (with authority equal to or greater than those being supervised) shall provide supervision of all table games.

I. ANALYSIS OF TABLE GAME PERFORMANCE STANDARDS.

1. Records shall be maintained by day and shift indicating any single-deck blackjack games that were dealt for an entire shift.

2. Records reflecting hold percentage by table and type of game shall be maintained by shift, by day, cumulative month-to-date, and cumulative year-to-date.

3. This information shall be presented to and reviewed by management independent of the pit department on at least a monthly basis.

4.   The management in paragraph (I)(3) of this section shall investigate any unusual fluctuations in hold percentage with pit supervisory personnel.

5. The results of such investigations shall be documented, maintained for inspection, and provided to the Tribal Gaming Commission upon request.

J. ACCOUNTING/AUDITING STANDARDS.

1. The accounting and auditing procedures shall be performed by personnel who are independent of the transactions being audited/accounted for.

2. If a table game has the capability to determine drop (e.g., bill-in/coin-drop meters, bill acceptor, computerized record, etc.) the dollar amount of the drop shall be reconciled to the actual drop by shift.

3. Accounting/auditing employees shall review exception reports for all computerized table games systems at least monthly for propriety of transactions and unusual occurrences.

4. All noted improper transactions or unusual occurrences shall be investigated with the results documented.

5. Evidence of table games auditing procedures and any follow-up performed shall be documented, maintained for inspection, and provided to the Tribal Gaming Commission upon request.

6. A daily recap shall be prepared for the day and month-to-date, which shall include the following information:

(i) Drop;

(ii) Win; and

(iii) Gross revenue.

K. MARKER CREDIT PLAY.

The Ottawa Tribe does not currently authorize the issuance of credit in their gaming facilities. Should that change due to recommendations from managment, the following Tribal Internal Control Standards will be followed:

If a gaming operation allows marker credit play (exclusive of rim credit and call bets), the following standards shall apply:

(i) A marker system shall allow for credit to be both issued and repaid in the pit.

(ii) Prior to the issuance of gaming credit to a player, the employee extending the credit shall contact the cashier or other independent source to determine if the player's credit limit has been properly established and there is sufficient remaining credit available for the advance.

(iii) Proper authorization of credit extension in excess of the previously established limit shall be documented.

(iv) The amount of credit extended shall be communicated to the cage or another independent source and the amount documented within a reasonable time subsequent to each issuance.

(v) The marker form shall be prepared in at least triplicate form (triplicate form being defined as three parts performing the functions delineated in the standard in paragraph (k)(1)(vi) of this section), with a preprinted or concurrently printed marker number, and utilized in numerical sequence. (This requirement shall not preclude the distribution of batches of markers to various pits.)

(vi) At least three parts of each separately numbered marker form shall be utilized as follows:

(A) Original shall be maintained in the pit until settled or transferred to the cage;

(B) Payment slip shall be maintained in the pit until the marker is settled or transferred to the cage. If paid in the pit, the slip shall be inserted in the table game drop box. If not paid in the pit, the slip shall be transferred to the cage with the original;

(C) Issue slip shall be inserted into the appropriate table game drop box when credit is extended or when the player has signed the original.

(vii) When marker documentation (e.g., issue slip and payment slip) is inserted in the drop box, such action shall be performed by the dealer or box person at the table.

(viii) A record shall be maintained that details the following (e.g., master credit record retained at the pit podium):

(A) The signature or initials of the person(s) approving the extension of credit (unless such information is contained elsewhere for each issuance);

(B) The legible name of the person receiving the credit;

(C) The date and shift of granting the credit;

(D) The table on which the credit was extended;

(E) The amount of credit issued;

(F) The marker number;

(G) The amount of credit remaining after each issuance or the total credit available for all issuances;

(H) The amount of payment received and nature of settlement (e.g., credit slip number, cash, chips, etc.); and

(I) The signature or initials of the person receiving payment/settlement.

(ix) The forms required in paragraphs (K)(1)(v),(vi), and (viii) of this section shall be safeguarded, and adequate procedures shall be employed to control the distribution, use, and access to these forms.

(x) All credit extensions shall be initially evidenced by lammer buttons, which shall be displayed on the table in public view and placed there by supervisory personnel.

(xi) Marker preparation shall be initiated and other records updated within approximately one hand of play following the initial issuance of credit to the player.

(xii) Lammer buttons shall be removed only by the dealer or boxperson employed at the table upon completion of a marker transaction. (xiii) The original marker shall contain at least the following information:

(A) Marker number;

(B) Player's name and signature;

(C) Date; and

(D) Amount of credit issued.

(xiv) The issue slip or stub shall include the same marker number as the original, the table number, date and time of issuance, and amount of credit issued. The issue slip or stub shall also include the signature of the person extending the credit, and the signature or initials of the dealer or boxperson at the applicable table, unless this information is included on another document verifying the issued marker.

(xv) The payment slip shall include the same marker number as the original. When the marker is paid in full in the pit, it shall also include the table number where paid, date and time of payment, nature of settlement (cash, chips, etc.), and amount of payment. The payment slip shall also include the signature of pit supervisory personnel acknowledging payment, and the signature or initials of the dealer or boxperson receiving payment, unless this information is included on another document verifying the payment of the marker.

(xvi) When partial payments are made in the pit, a new marker shall be completed reflecting the remaining balance and the marker number of the marker originally issued.

(xvii) When partial payments are made in the pit, the payment slip of the marker that was originally issued shall be properly cross-referenced to the new marker number, completed with all information required by paragraph (K)(1)(xv) of this section, and inserted into the drop box.

(xviii) The cashier's cage or another independent source shall be notified when payments (full or partial) are made in the pit so that cage records can be updated for such transactions. Notification shall be made no later than when the customer's play is completed or at shift end, whichever is earlier.

(xix) All portions of markers, both issued and unissued, shall be safeguarded and procedures shall be employed to control the distribution, use and access to the forms.

(xx) An investigation shall be performed to determine the cause and responsibility for loss whenever marker forms, or any part thereof, are missing. These investigations shall be documented, maintained for inspection, and provided to the Tribal Gaming Commission upon request.

(xxi) When markers are transferred to the cage, marker transfer forms or marker credit slips (or similar documentation) shall be utilized and such documents shall include, at a minimum, the date, time, shift, marker number(s), table number(s), amount of each marker, the total amount transferred, signature of pit supervisory personnel releasing instruments from the pit, and the signature of cashier verifying receipt of instruments at the cage.

(xxii) All markers shall be transferred to the cage within twenty-four (24) hours of issuance.

(xxiii) Markers shall be transported to the cashier's cage by a person who is independent of the marker issuance and payment functions (pit clerks may perform this function).

NAME CREDIT INSTRUMENTS ACCEPTED IN THE PIT.

1. For the purposes of this paragraph, name credit instruments means personal checks, payroll checks, counter checks, hold checks, traveler's checks, or other similar instruments that are accepted in the pit as a form of credit issuance to a player with an approved credit limit.

2. The Ottawa Tribe does not currently authorize Name Credit Instruments to be accepted in the pit. Should that change, the following Tribal Internal Control Standards will be observed:

(i) A name credit system shall allow for the issuance of credit without using markers;

(ii) Prior to accepting a name credit instrument, the employee extending the credit shall contact the cashier or another independent source to determine if the player's credit limit has been properly established and the remaining credit available is sufficient for the advance;

(iii) All name credit instruments shall be transferred to the cashier's cage (utilizing a two-part order for credit) immediately following the acceptance of the instrument and issuance of chips (if name credit instruments are transported accompanied by a credit slip, an order for credit is not required);

(iv) The order for credit (if applicable) and the credit slip shall include the customer's name, amount of the credit instrument, the date, time, shift, table number, signature of pit supervisory personnel releasing instrument from pit, and the signature of the cashier verifying receipt of instrument at the cage;

(v) The procedures for transacting table credits at standards in paragraphs (C)(12) through (19) of this section shall be strictly adhered to; and

(vi) The acceptance of payments in the pit for name credit instruments shall be prohibited.

CALL BETS.

The Ottawa Tribe does not currently authorize the acceptance of call bets in the pit.

RIM CREDIT.

The Ottawa Tribe does not currently authorize the extension of rim credit in the pit.

FOREIGN CURRENCY.

The Ottawa Tribe does not currently accept any foreign currency in its gaming facilities:

GAMING MACHINES (25 CFR 542.13)

A. STANDARDS FOR GAMING MACHINES.

1. For this section only, credit or customer credit means a unit of value equivalent to cash or cash equivalents deposited, wagered, won, lost, or redeemed by a customer.

2. Coins shall include tokens.

3. For all computerized gaming machine systems, a personnel access listing shall be maintained, which includes at a minimum:

(i) Employee name or employee identification number (or equivalent); and

(ii) Listing of functions employee can perform or equivalent means of identifying same.

B. COMPUTER APPLICATIONS.

For any computer applications utilized, alternate documentation and/or procedures that provide at least the level of control described by the standards in this section, as approved by the Tribal Gaming Commission, will be acceptable.

C. STANDARDS FOR DROP AND COUNT.

The procedures for the collection of the gaming machine drop and the count thereof shall comply with Sec. 542.41.

D. JACKPOT PAYOUTS, GAMING MACHINES FILLS, SHORT PAYS AND ACCUMULATED CREDIT PAYOUTS STANDARDS.

1. For jackpot payouts and gaming machine fills, documentation shall include the following information:

(i) Date and time;

(ii) Machine number;

(iii) Dollar amount of cash payout or gaming machine fill (both alpha and numeric) or description of personal property awarded, including fair market value. Alpha is optional if another unalterable method is used for evidencing the amount of the payout;

(iv) Game outcome (including reel symbols, card values, suits, etc.) for jackpot payouts. Game outcome is not required if a computerized jackpot/fill system is used;

(v) Preprinted or concurrently printed sequential number; and

(vi) Signatures of at least two employees verifying and witnessing the payout or gaming machine fill (except as otherwise provided in paragraphs (D)(1)(vi)(A), (B), and (C) of this section).

(A) Jackpot payouts over a predetermined amount shall require the signature and verification of a supervisory or management employee independent of the gaming machine department (in addition to the two signatures required in paragraph (d)(1)(vi) of this section). Alternatively, if an on-line accounting system is utilized, only two signatures are required: one employee and one supervisory or management employee independent of the gaming machine department. This predetermined amount shall be authorized by management (as approved by the Tribal Gaming Commission), documented, and maintained.

(B) With regard to jackpot payouts and hopper fills, the signature of one employee is sufficient if an on-line accounting system is utilized and the jackpot or fill is less than $1,200.

(C) On graveyard shifts (eight-hour maximum) payouts/fills less than $100 can be made without the payout/fill being witnessed by a second person.

2. For short pays of $10.00 or more, and payouts required for accumulated credits, the payout form shall include the following information:

(i) Date and time;

(ii) Machine number;

(iii) Dollar amount of payout (both alpha and numeric); and

(iv) The signature of at least one (1) employee verifying and witnessing the payout.

(A) Where the payout amount is $50 or more, signatures of at least two (2) employees verifying and witnessing the payout. Alternatively, the signature of one (1) employee is sufficient if an on-line accounting system is utilized and the payout amount is less than $3,000.

(B) [Reserved]

3. Computerized jackpot/fill systems shall be restricted so as to prevent unauthorized access and fraudulent payouts by one person as required by Sec. 542.16(a).

4. Payout forms shall be controlled and routed in a manner that precludes any one person from producing a fraudulent payout by forging signatures or by altering the amount paid out subsequent to the payout and misappropriating the funds.

PROMOTIONAL PAYOUTS OR AWARDS.

If a gaming operation offers promotional payouts or awards that are not reflected on the gaming machine pay table, then the payout form/documentation shall include:

(i) Date and time;

(ii) Machine number and denomination;

(iii) Dollar amount of payout or description of personal property (e.g., jacket, toaster, car, etc.), including fair market value;

(iv) Type of promotion (e.g., double jackpots, four-of-a-kind bonus, etc.); and

(v) Signature of at least one employee authorizing and completing the transaction.

GAMING MACHINE DEPARTMENT FUNDS STANDARDS.

1. The gaming machine booths and change banks that are active during the shift, shall be counted down and reconciled each shift utilizing appropriate accountability documentation.

2. The wrapping of loose gaming machine booth and cage cashier coin shall be performed at a time or location that does not interfere with the hard count/wrap process or the accountability of that process.

3. A record shall be maintained evidencing the transfers of wrapped and unwrapped coins and retained for seven (7) days.

EPROM CONTROL STANDARDS.

1. At least annually, procedures shall be performed to insure the integrity of a sample of gaming machine game program EPROMs, or other equivalent game software media, by personnel independent of the gaming machine department or the machines being tested.

2. The Tribal Gaming Commission, or the gaming operation subject to the approval of the Tribal Gaming Commission, shall develop and implement procedures for the following:

(i) Removal of EPROMs, or other equivalent game software media, from devices, the verification of the existence of errors as applicable, and the correction via duplication from the master game program EPROM, or other equivalent game software media;

(ii) Copying one gaming device program to another approved program;

(iii) Verification of duplicated EPROMs before being offered for play;

(iv) Receipt and destruction of EPROMs, or other equivalent game software media; and

(v) Securing the EPROM, or other equivalent game software media, duplicator, and master game EPROMs, or other equivalent game software media, from unrestricted access.

3. The master game program number, par percentage, and the pay table shall be verified to the par sheet when initially received from the manufacturer.

4. Gaming machines with potential jackpots in excess of $100,000 shall have the game software circuit boards locked or physically sealed. The lock or seal shall necessitate the presence of a person independent of the gaming machine department to access the device game program EPROM, or other equivalent game software media. If a seal is used to secure the board to the frame of the gaming device, it shall be pre-numbered.

5. Records that document the procedures in paragraph (G)(2)(i) of this section shall include the following information:

(i) Date;

(ii) Machine number (source and destination);

(iii) Manufacturer;

(iv) Program number;

(v) Personnel involved;

(vi) Reason for duplication;

(vii) Disposition of any permanently removed EPROM, or other equivalent game software media;

(viii) Seal numbers, if applicable; and

(ix) Approved testing lab approval numbers, if available.

6. EPROMS, or other equivalent game software media, returned to gaming devices shall be labeled with the program number. Supporting documentation shall include the date, program number, information identical to that shown on the manufacturer's label, and initials of the person replacing the EPROM, or other equivalent game software media.

STANDARDS FOR EVALUATING THEORETICAL AND ACTUAL HOLD PERCENTAGES.

1. Accurate and current theoretical hold worksheets shall be maintained for each gaming machine.

2. For multi-game/multi-denominational machines, an employee or department of the gaming machine department shall:

(i) On a weekly basis, record the meters that contain the number of plays by wager (i.e., one coin, two coins, etc.);

(ii) On a quarterly basis, record the coin-in meters for each paytable contained in the machine; and

(iii) On an annual basis, adjust the theoretical hold percentage in the gaming machine statistical report to a weighted average based upon the ratio of coin-in for each paytable and

(iv) The adjusted theoretical hold percentage shall be within the spread between the minimum and maximum theoretical payback percentages.

3. For those gaming operations that are unable to perform the weighted average calculation as required by paragraph (H)(2) of this section, the following procedures shall apply:

(i) On at least an annual basis, calculate the actual hold percentage for each gaming machine;

(ii) On at least an annual basis, adjust the theoretical hold percentage in the gaming machine statistical report for each gaming machine to the previously calculated actual hold percentage; and

(iii) The adjusted theoretical hold percentage shall be within the spread between the minimum and maximum theoretical payback percentages.

4. The adjusted theoretical hold percentage for multi-game machines may be combined for machines with exactly the same game mix throughout the year.

5. The theoretical hold percentages used in the gaming machine analysis reports should be within the performance standards set by the manufacturer.

6. Records shall be maintained for each machine indicating the dates and type of changes made and the recalculation of theoretical hold as a result of the changes.

7. Records shall be maintained for each machine that indicate the date the machine was placed into service, the date the machine was removed from operation, the date the machine was placed back into operation, and any changes in machine numbers and designations.

8. All of the gaming machines shall contain functioning meters that shall record coin-in or credit-in, or on-line gaming machine monitoring system that captures similar data.

9. All gaming machines with bill acceptors shall contain functioning bill-in meters that record the dollar amounts or number of bills accepted by denomination.

10. Gaming machine in-meter readings shall be recorded at least weekly (monthly for Tier A and Tier B gaming operations) immediately prior to or subsequent to a gaming machine drop. On-line gaming machine monitoring systems can satisfy this requirement. However, the time between readings may extend beyond one week in order for a reading to coincide with the end of an accounting period only if such extension is for no longer than six (6) days.

11. The employee who records the in-meter reading shall either be independent of the hard count team or shall be assigned on a rotating basis, unless the in-meter readings are randomly verified quarterly for all gaming machines and bill acceptors by a person other than the regular in-meter reader.

12. Upon receipt of the meter reading summary, the accounting department shall review all meter readings for reasonableness using pre-established parameters.

13. Prior to final preparation of statistical reports, meter readings that do not appear reasonable shall be reviewed with gaming machine department employees or other appropriate designees, and exceptions documented, so that meters can be repaired or clerical errors in the recording of meter readings can be corrected.

14. A report shall be produced at least monthly showing month-to-date, year- to-date (previous twelve (12) months data preferred), and if practicable, life-to-date actual hold percentage computations for individual machines and a comparison to each machine's theoretical hold percentage previously discussed.

15. Each change to a gaming machine's theoretical hold percentage, including progressive percentage contributions, shall result in that machine being treated as a new machine in the statistical reports (i.e., not commingling various hold percentages), except for adjustments made in accordance with paragraph (H)(2) of this section.

16. If promotional payouts or awards are included on the gaming machine statistical reports, it shall be in a manner that prevents distorting the actual hold percentages of the affected machines.

17. The statistical reports shall be reviewed by both gaming machine department management and management employees, independent of the gaming machine department on at least a monthly basis.

18. For those machines in play for more than six (6) months, large variances (three percent (3%) recommended) between theoretical hold and actual hold shall be investigated and resolved by a department independent of the gaming machine department with the findings documented and provided to the Tribal Gaming Commission upon request in a timely manner.

19. Maintenance of the on-line gaming machine monitoring system data files shall be performed by a department independent of the gaming machine department. Alternatively, maintenance may be performed by gaming machine supervisory employees if sufficient documentation is generated and it is randomly verified on a monthly basis by employees independent of the gaming machine department.

20. Updates to the on-line gaming machine monitoring system to reflect additions, deletions, or movements of gaming machines shall be made at least weekly prior to in-meter readings and the weigh process.

GAMING MACHINE HOPPER CONTENTS STANDARDS.

1. When machines are temporarily removed from the floor, gaming machine drop and hopper contents shall be protected to preclude the misappropriation of stored funds.

2. When machines are permanently removed from the floor, the gaming machine drop and hopper contents shall be counted and recorded by at least two employees with appropriate documentation being routed to the accounting department for proper recording and accounting for initial hopper loads.

PLAYER TRACKING SYSTEM.

The following standards apply if a player tracking system is utilized:

(i) The player tracking system shall be secured so as to prevent unauthorized access (e.g., changing passwords at least quarterly and physical access to computer hardware, etc.).

(ii) The addition of points to members' accounts other than through actual gaming machine play shall be sufficiently documented (including substantiation of reasons for increases) and shall be authorized by a department independent of the player tracking and gaming machines. Alternatively, addition of points to members' accounts may be authorized by gaming machine supervisory employees if sufficient documentation is generated and it is randomly verified by employees independent of the gaming machine department on a quarterly basis.

(iii) Booth employees who redeem points for members shall be allowed to receive lost players club cards, provided that they are immediately deposited into a secured container for retrieval by independent personnel.

(iv) Changes to the player tracking system parameters, such as point structures and employee access, shall be performed by supervisory employees independent of the gaming machine department. Alternatively, changes to player tracking system parameters may be performed by gaming machine supervisory employees if sufficient documentation is generated and it is randomly verified by supervisory employees independent of the gaming machine department on a monthly basis.

(v) All other changes to the player tracking system shall be appropriately documented.

IN-HOUSE PROGRESSIVE GAMING MACHINE STANDARDS.

1. A meter that shows the amount of the progressive jackpot shall be conspicuously displayed at or near the machines to which the jackpot applies.

403

2. At least once each day, each gaming operation shall record the amount shown on each progressive jackpot meter at the gaming operation except for those jackpots that can be paid directly from the machine's hopper;

3. Explanations for meter reading decreases shall be maintained with the progressive meter reading sheets, and where the payment of a jackpot is the explanation for a decrease, the gaming operation shall record the jackpot payout number on the sheet or have the number reasonably available; and

4. Each gaming operation shall record the base amount of each progressive jackpot the gaming operation offers.

5. The Tribal Gaming Commission shall approve procedures specific to the transfer of progressive amounts in excess of the base amount to other gaming machines. Such procedures may also include other methods of distribution that accrue to the benefit of the gaming public via an award or prize.

WIDE AREA PROGRESSIVE GAMING MACHINE STANDARDS.

1. A meter that shows the amount of the progressive jackpot shall be conspicuously displayed at or near the machines to which the jackpot applies.

2. As applicable to participating gaming operations, the wide area progressive gaming machine system shall be adequately restricted to prevent unauthorized access (e.g., changing passwords at least quarterly, restrict access to EPROMs or other equivalent game software media, and restrict physical access to computer hardware, etc.).

3. The Tribal Gaming Commission shall approve procedures for the wide area progressive system that:

(i) Reconcile meters and jackpot payouts;

(ii) Collect/drop gaming machine funds;

(iii) Verify jackpot, payment, and billing to gaming operations on pro-rata basis;

(iv) System maintenance;

(v) System accuracy; and

(vi) System security.

4. Reports, where applicable, adequately documenting the procedures required in paragraph (1)(3) of this section shall be generated and retained.

ACCOUNTING/AUDITING STANDARDS.

1. Gaming machine accounting/auditing procedures shall be performed by employees who are independent of the transactions being reviewed.

2. For on-line gaming machine monitoring systems, procedures shall be performed at least monthly to verify that the system is transmitting and receiving data from the gaming machines properly and to verify the continuing accuracy of the coin-in meter readings as recorded in the gaming machine statistical report.

3. For weigh scale and currency interface systems, for at least one drop period per month accounting/auditing employees shall make such comparisons as necessary to the system generated count as recorded in the gaming machine statistical report. Discrepancies shall be resolved prior to generation/distribution of gaming machine reports.

4. For each drop period, accounting/auditing personnel shall compare the coin-to-drop meter reading to the actual drop amount. Discrepancies should be resolved prior to generation/distribution of on-line gaming machine monitoring system statistical reports.

5. Follow-up shall be performed for any one machine having an unresolved variance between actual coin drop and coin-to-drop meter reading in excess of three percent (3%) and over $25.00. The follow-up performed and results of the investigation shall be documented, maintained for inspection, and provided to the Tribal Gaming Commission upon request.

6. For each drop period, accounting/auditing employees shall compare the bill-in meter reading to the total bill acceptor drop amount for the period. Discrepancies shall be resolved before the generation/distribution of gaming machine statistical reports.

7. Follow-up shall be performed for any one machine having an unresolved variance between actual currency drop and bill-in meter reading in excess of an amount that is both more than $25 and at least three percent (3%) of the actual currency drop. The follow-up performed and results of the investigation shall be documented, maintained for inspection, and provided to the Tribal Gaming Commission upon request.

8. At least annually, accounting/auditing personnel shall randomly verify that EPROM or other equivalent game software media changes are properly reflected in the gaming machine analysis reports.

9. Accounting/auditing employees shall review exception reports for all computerized gaming machine systems on a daily basis for propriety of transactions and unusual occurrences.

10. All gaming machine auditing procedures and any follow-up performed shall be documented, maintained for inspection, and provided to the Tribal Gaming Commission upon request.

CASH-OUT TICKETS.

For gaming machines that utilize cash-out tickets, the following standards apply. This standard is not applicable to Tiers A and B. Tier A and B gaming operations shall develop adequate standards governing the security over the issuance of the cash-out paper to the gaming machines and the redemption of cash-out slips.

1. In addition to the applicable auditing and accounting standards in paragraph (M) of this section, on a quarterly basis, the gaming operation shall foot all jackpot cash-out tickets equal to or greater than $1,200 and trace totals to those produced by the host validation computer system.

2. The customer may request a cash-out ticket from the gaming machine that reflects all remaining credits. The cash-out ticket shall be printed at the gaming machine by an internal document printer. The cash-out ticket shall be valid for a time period

specified by the Tribal Gaming Commission, or the gaming operation as approved by the Tribal Gaming Commission. Cash-out tickets may be redeemed for payment or inserted in another gaming machine and wagered, if applicable, during the specified time period.

3. The customer shall redeem the cash-out ticket at a change booth or cashiers cage. Alternatively, if a gaming operation utilizes a remote computer validation system, the Tribal Gaming Commission, or the gaming operation as approved by the Tribal Gaming Commission, shall develop alternate standards for the maximum amount that can be redeemed, which shall not exceed $2,999.99 per cash-out transaction.

4. Upon presentation of the cash-out ticket(s) for redemption, the following shall occur:

(i) Scan the bar code via an optical reader or its equivalent; or
(ii) Input the cash-out ticket validation number into the computer.

5. The information contained in paragraph (N)(4) of this section shall be communicated to the host computer. The host computer shall verify the authenticity of the cash-out ticket and communicate directly to the redeemer of the cash-out ticket.

6. If valid, the cashier (redeemer of the cash-out ticket) pays the customer the appropriate amount and the cash-out ticket is electronically noted "paid" in the system. The "paid" cash-out ticket shall remain in the cashiers bank for reconciliation purposes. The host validation computer system shall electronically reconcile the cashier's banks for the paid cashed-out tickets.

7. If invalid, the host computer shall notify the cashier (redeemer of the cash-out ticket). The cashier (redeemer of the cash-out ticket) shall refuse payment to the customer and notify a supervisor of the invalid condition. The supervisor shall resolve the dispute.

8. If the host validation computer system temporarily goes down, cashiers may redeem cash-out tickets at a change booth or cashier's cage after recording the following:

(i) Serial number of the cash-out ticket;
(ii) Date and time;
(iii) Dollar amount;
(iv) Issuing gaming machine number;
(v) Marking ticket "paid"; and
(vi) Ticket shall remain in cashier's bank for reconciliation purposes.

9. Cash-out tickets shall be validated as expeditiously as possible when the host validation computer system is restored.

10. The Tribal Gaming Commission, or the gaming operation as approved by the Tribal Gaming Commission, shall establish and the gaming operation shall comply with procedures to control cash-out ticket paper, which shall include procedures that:

(i) Mitigate the risk of counterfeiting of cash-out ticket paper;
(ii) Adequately control the inventory of the cash-out ticket paper; and
(iii) Provide for the destruction of all unused cash-out ticket paper.
(iv) Alternatively, if the gaming operation utilizes a computer validation system, this standard shall not apply.

11. If the host validation computer system is down for more than four (4) hours, the gaming operation shall promptly notify the Tribal Gaming Commission or its designated representative.

12. These gaming machine systems shall comply with all other standards (as applicable) in this part including:

(i) Standards for bill acceptor drop and count;
(ii) Standards for coin drop and count; and
(iii) Standards concerning EPROMS or other equivalent game software media.

ACCOUNT ACCESS CARDS.
For gaming machines that utilize account access cards to activate play of the machine, the following standards shall apply:

1. Equipment.
(i) A central computer, with supporting hardware and software, to coordinate network activities, provide system interface, and store and manage a player/account database;
(ii) A network of contiguous player terminals with touch-screen or button-controlled video monitors connected to an electronic selection device and the central computer via a communications network;
(iii) One or more electronic selection devices, utilizing random number generators, each of which selects any combination or combinations of numbers, colors, and/or symbols for a network of player terminals.

2. Player terminals standards.
(i) The player terminals are connected to a game server;
(ii) The game server shall generate and transmit to the bank of player terminals a set of random numbers, colors, and/or symbols at regular intervals. The subsequent game results are determined at the player terminal and the resulting information is transmitted to the account server;
(iii) The game server shall be housed in a game server room or a secure locked cabinet.

3. Customer account maintenance standards.
(i) A central computer acting as an account server shall provide customer account maintenance and the deposit/withdrawal function of those account balances;
(ii) Customers may access their accounts on the computer system by means of an account access card at the player terminal. Each player terminal may be equipped with a card reader and personal identification number (PIN) pad or touch screen array for this purpose;

(iii) All communications between the player terminal, or bank of player terminals, and the account server shall be encrypted for security reasons.

4. Customer account generation standards.

(i) A computer file for each customer shall be prepared by a clerk, with no incompatible functions, prior to the customer being issued an account access card to be utilized for machine play. The customer may select his/her PIN to be used in conjunction with the account access card.

(ii) The clerk shall sign-on with a unique password to a terminal equipped with peripherals required to establish a customer account. Passwords are issued and can only be changed by information technology personnel at the discretion of the department director.

(iii) After entering a specified number of incorrect PIN entries at the cage or player terminal, the customer shall be directed to proceed to the Gaming Machine Information Center to obtain a new PIN. If a customer forgets, misplaces or requests a change to their PIN, the customer shall proceed to the Gaming Machine Information Center.

5. Deposit of credits standards.

(i) The cashier shall sign-on with a unique password to a cashier terminal equipped with peripherals required to complete the credit transactions. Passwords are issued and can only be changed by information technology personnel at the discretion of the department director.

(ii) The customer shall present cash, chips, coin or coupons along with their account access card to a cashier to deposit credits.

(iii) The cashier shall complete the transaction by utilizing a card scanner that the cashier shall slide the customer's account access card through.

(iv) The cashier shall accept the funds from the customer and enter the appropriate amount on the cashier terminal.

(v) A multi-part deposit slip shall be generated by the point of sale receipt printer. The cashier shall direct the customer to sign the deposit slip receipt. One copy of the deposit slip shall be given to the customer. The other copy of the deposit slip shall be secured in the cashier's cash drawer.

(vi) The cashier shall verify the customer's balance before completing the transaction. The cashier shall secure the funds in their cash drawer and return the account access card to the customer.

(vii) Alternatively, if a kiosk is utilized to accept a deposit of credits, the Tribal gaming commission, or the gaming operation as approved by the Tribal gaming commission, shall establish and the gaming operation shall comply with procedures that safeguard the integrity of the kiosk system.

6. Prize standards.

(i) Winners at the gaming machines may receive cash, prizes redeemable for cash or merchandise.

(ii) If merchandise prizes are to be awarded, the specific type of prize or prizes that may be won shall be disclosed to the player before the game begins.

(iii) The redemption period of account access cards, as approved by the Tribal Gaming Commission, shall be conspicuously posted in the gaming operation.

7. Credit withdrawal.

The customer shall present their account access card to a cashier to withdraw their credits. The cashier shall perform the following:

(i) Scan the account access card;

(ii) Request the customer to enter their PIN, if the PIN was selected by the customer;

(iii) The cashier shall ascertain the amount the customer wishes to withdraw and enter the amount into the computer;

(iv) A multi-part withdrawal slip shall be generated by the point of sale receipt printer. The cashier shall direct the customer to sign the withdrawal slip;

(v) The cashier shall verify that the account access card and the customer match by:

(A) Comparing the customer to image on the computer screen;

(B) Comparing the customer to image on customer's picture ID; or

(C) Comparing the customer signature on the withdrawal slip to signature on the computer screen.

(vi) The cashier shall verify the customer's balance before completing the transaction. The cashier shall pay the customer the appropriate amount, issue the customer the original withdrawal slip and return the account access card to the customer;

(vii) The copy of the withdrawal slip shall be placed in the cash drawer. All account transactions shall be accurately tracked by the account server computer system. The copy of the withdrawal slip shall be forwarded to the accounting department at the end of the gaming day; and

(viii) In the event the imaging function is temporarily disabled, customers shall be required to provide positive ID for cash withdrawal transactions at the cashier stations.

CAGE (25 CFR 542.14)

A. COMPUTER APPLICATIONS.

For any computer applications utilized, alternate documentation and/or procedures that provide at least the level of control described by the standards in this section, as approved by the Tribal Gaming Commission, will be acceptable.

B. PERSONAL CHECKS, CASHIER'S CHECKS, PAYROLL CHECKS, AND COUNTER CHECKS.

1. If personal checks, cashier's checks, payroll checks, or counter checks are cashed at the cage, the Tribal Gaming Commission, or the gaming operation as approved by the Tribal Gaming Commission, shall establish and the gaming operation shall comply with appropriate controls for purposes of security and integrity.

2. The Tribal Gaming Commission, or the gaming operation as approved by the Tribal Gaming Commission, shall establish and the gaming operation shall comply with procedures for the acceptance of personal checks, collecting and recording checks returned to the gaming operation after deposit, re-deposit, and write-off authorization.

3. When counter checks are issued, the following shall be included on the check:

(i) The customer's name and signature;

(ii) The dollar amount of the counter check (both alpha and numeric);

(iii) Customer's bank name and bank account number;

(iv) Date of issuance; and

(v) Signature or initials of the person approving the counter check transaction.

4. When traveler's checks or other guaranteed drafts such as cashier's checks are presented, the cashier shall comply with the examination and documentation procedures as required by the issuer.

C. CUSTOMER DEPOSITED FUNDS.

The Ottawa Tribe does not currently authorize any customer to deposit funds on account with the Casino Cage.

D. CAGE AND VAULT ACCOUNTABILITY STANDARDS.

1. All transactions that flow through the cage shall be summarized on a cage accountability form on a per shift basis and shall be supported by documentation.

2. The cage and vault (including coin room) inventories shall be counted by the oncoming and outgoing cashiers. These employees shall make individual counts for comparison of accuracy and maintenance of individual accountability. Such counts shall be recorded at the end of each shift during which activity took place. All discrepancies shall be noted and investigated.

3. The gaming operation cash-on-hand shall include, but is not limited to, the following components:

(i) Currency and coins;

(ii) House chips, including reserve chips;

(iii) Personal checks, cashier's checks, counter checks, and traveler's checks for deposit;

(iv) Customer deposits;

(v) Chips on tables;

(vi) Hopper loads (coins put into machines when they are placed in service); and

(vii) Fills and credits (these documents shall be treated as assets and liabilities, respectively, of the cage during a business day. When win or loss is recorded at the end of the business day, they are removed from the accountability).

4. The Tribal Gaming Commission, or the gaming operation as approved by the Tribal Gaming Commission, shall establish and the gaming operation shall comply with a minimum bankroll formula to ensure the gaming operation maintains cash or cash equivalents (on hand and in the bank, if readily accessible) in an amount sufficient to satisfy obligations to the gaming operation's customers as they are incurred. A suggested bankroll formula will be provided by the Commission upon request.

E. CHIP AND TOKEN STANDARDS.

The Tribal Gaming Commission, or the gaming operation as approved by the Tribal Gaming Commission, shall establish and the gaming operation shall comply with procedures for the receipt, inventory, storage, and destruction of gaming chips and tokens.

F. COUPON STANDARDS.

Any program for the exchange of coupons for chips, tokens, and/or another coupon program shall be approved by the Tribal Gaming Commission prior to implementation. If approved, the gaming operation shall establish and comply with procedures that account for and control such programs.

G. ACCOUNTING/AUDITING STANDARDS

1. The cage accountability shall be reconciled to the general ledger at least monthly.

2. A trial balance of gaming operation accounts receivable, including the name of the customer and current balance, shall be prepared at least monthly for active, inactive, settled or written-off accounts.

3. The trial balance of gaming operation accounts receivable shall be reconciled to the general ledger each month. The reconciliation and any follow-up performed shall be documented, maintained for inspection, and provided to the Tribal Gaming Commission upon request.

4. On a monthly basis an evaluation of the collection percentage of credit issued to identify unusual trends shall be performed.

5. All cage and credit accounting procedures and any follow-up performed shall be documented, maintained for inspection, and provided to the Tribal Gaming Commission upon request.

H. EXTRANEOUS ITEMS.

The Tribal Gaming Commission, or the gaming operation as approved by the Tribal Gaming Commission, shall establish and the gaming operation shall comply with procedures to address the transporting of extraneous items, such as coats, purses, and/or boxes, into and out of the cage, coin room, count room, and/or vault.

CREDIT (25 CFR 542.15)

The Ottawa Tribe does not currently allow its gaming operations to extend credit to patrons.

INFORMATION TECHNOLOGY (25 CFR 542.16)

A. GENERAL CONTROLS FOR GAMING HARDWARE AND SOFTWARE.

1. Management shall take an active role in making sure that physical and logical security measures are implemented, maintained, and adhered to by personnel to prevent unauthorized access that could cause errors or compromise data or processing integrity.

(i) Management shall ensure that all new gaming vendor hardware and software agreements/contracts contain language requiring the vendor to adhere to tribal internal control standards applicable to the goods and services the vendor is providing.

(ii) Physical security measures shall exist over computer, computer terminals, and storage media to prevent unauthorized access and loss of integrity of data and processing.

(iii) Access to systems software and application programs shall be limited to authorized personnel.

(iv) Access to computer data shall be limited to authorized personnel.

(v) Access to computer communications facilities, or the computer system, and information transmissions shall be limited to authorized personnel.

(vi) Standards in paragraph (A)(1) of this section shall apply to each applicable department within the gaming operation.

2. The main computers (i.e., hardware, software, and data files) for each gaming application (e.g., keno, race and sports, gaming machines, etc.) shall be in a secured area with access restricted to authorized persons, including vendors.

3. Access to computer operations shall be restricted to authorized personnel to reduce the risk of loss of integrity of data or processing.

4. Incompatible duties shall be adequately segregated and monitored to prevent error in general information technology procedures to go undetected or fraud to be concealed.

5. Non-information technology personnel shall be precluded from having unrestricted access to the secured computer areas.

6. The computer systems, including application software, shall be secured through the use of passwords or other approved means where applicable. Management personnel or persons independent of the department being controlled shall assign and control access to system functions.

7. Passwords shall be controlled as follows unless otherwise addressed in the standards in this section.

(i) Each user shall have their own individual password;

(ii) Passwords shall be changed at least quarterly with changes documented; and

(iii) For computer systems that automatically force a password change on a quarterly basis, documentation shall be maintained listing the systems and the date the user was given access.

8. Adequate backup and recovery procedures shall be in place that include:

(i) Frequent backup of data files;

(ii) Backup of all programs;

(iii) Secured off-site storage of all backup data files and programs, or other adequate protection; and

(iv) Recovery procedures, which are tested on a sample basis at least annually with documentation of results.

9. Adequate information technology system documentation shall be maintained, including descriptions of hardware and software, operator manuals, etc.

B. INDEPENDENCE OF INFORMATION TECHNOLOGY PERSONNEL.

1. The information technology personnel shall be independent of the gaming areas (e.g., cage, pit, count rooms, etc.). Information technology personnel procedures and controls should be documented and responsibilities communicated.

2. Information technology personnel shall be precluded from unauthorized access to:

(i) Computers and terminals located in gaming areas;

(ii) Source documents; and

(iii) Live data files (not test data).

3. Information technology personnel shall be restricted from:

(i) Having unauthorized access to cash or other liquid assets; and

(ii) Initiating general or subsidiary ledger entries.

C. GAMING PROGRAM CHANGES.

Program changes for in-house developed systems should be documented as follows:

(i) Requests for new programs or program changes shall be reviewed by the information technology supervisor. Approvals to begin work on the program shall be documented;

(ii) A written plan of implementation for new and modified programs shall be maintained, and shall include, at a minimum, the date the program is to be placed into service, the nature of the change, a description of procedures required in order to bring the new or modified program into service (conversion or input of data, installation procedures, etc.), and an indication of who is to perform all such procedures;

(iii) Testing of new and modified programs shall be performed and documented prior to implementation; and

(iv) A record of the final program or program changes, including evidence of user acceptance, date in service, programmer, and reason for changes, shall be documented and maintained.

D. SECURITY LOGS.

1. If computer security logs are generated by the system, they shall be reviewed by information technology supervisory personnel for evidence of:

(i) Multiple attempts to log-on, or alternatively, the system shall deny user access after three attempts to log-on;

(ii) Unauthorized changes to live data files; and

408

(iii) Any other unusual transactions.

2. This paragraph shall not apply to personal computers.

E. REMOTE DIAL-UP.

If remote dial-up to any associated equipment is allowed for software support, the gaming operation shall maintain an access log that includes:

(i) Name of employee authorizing modem access;

(ii) Name of authorized programmer or manufacturer representative;

(iii) Reason for modem access;

(iv) Description of work performed; and

(v) Date, time, and duration of access.

F. DOCUMENT STORAGE.

Documents may be scanned or directly stored to an unalterable storage medium under the following conditions.

(i) The storage medium shall contain the exact duplicate of the original document.

(ii) All documents stored on the storage medium shall be maintained with a detailed index containing the gaming operation department and date. This index shall be available upon request by the Commission.

(iii) Upon request and adequate notice by the Commission, hardware (terminal, printer, etc.) shall be made available in order to perform auditing procedures.

(iv) Controls shall exist to ensure the accurate reproduction of records up to and including the printing of stored documents used for auditing purposes.

(v) The storage medium shall be retained for a minimum of five years.

(vi) Original documents must be retained until the books and records have been audited by an independent certified public accountant.

COMPLIMENTARY SERVICES OR ITEMS (25 CFR 542.17)

A. COMPLIMENTARY PROCEDURES

Each Tribal Gaming Commission or gaming operation shall establish and the gaming operation shall comply with procedures for the authorization, issuance, and tracking of complimentary services and items, including cash and non-cash gifts. Such procedures must be approved by the Tribal Gaming Commission and shall include, but shall not be limited to, the procedures by which the gaming operation delegates to its employees the authority to approve the issuance of complimentary services and items, and the procedures by which conditions or limits, if any, which may apply to such authority are established and modified (including limits based on relationships between the authorizer and recipient), and shall further include effective provisions for audit purposes.

B. REPORTS

At least monthly, accounting, information technology, or audit personnel that cannot grant or receive complimentary privileges shall prepare reports that include the following information:

1. Name of customer who received the complimentary service or item;

2. Name(s) of authorized issuer of the complimentary service or item;

3. The actual cash value of the complimentary service or item;

4. The type of complimentary service or item (i.e., food, beverage, etc.); and

5. Date the complimentary service or item was issued.

C. LIMITATIONS

The report required by paragraph (B) of this section shall not be required to include complimentary services or items below a reasonable amount to be established by the Tribal Gaming Commission, or the gaming operation as approved by the Tribal Gaming Commission.

D. REPORT REVIEW

The internal audit or accounting departments shall review the reports required in paragraph (B) of this section at least monthly. These reports shall be made available to the Tribe, Tribal Gaming Commission, audit committee, other entity designated by the Tribe, and the Commission upon request.

VARIANCE FROM STANDARDS (25 CFR 542.18)

A. TRIBAL GAMING COMMISSION APPROVAL.

1. A Tribal Gaming Commission may approve a variance for a gaming operation if it has determined that the variance will achieve a level of control sufficient to accomplish the purpose of the standard it is to replace.

2. For each enumerated standard for which the Tribal Gaming Commission approves a variance, it shall submit to the chairman of the NIGC, within thirty (30) days, a detailed report, which shall include the following:

(i) A detailed description of the variance;

(ii) An explanation of how the variance achieves a level of control sufficient to accomplish the purpose of the standard it is to replace; and

(iii) Evidence that the Tribal Gaming Commission has approved the variance.

3. In the event that the Tribal Gaming Commission or the Tribe chooses to submit a variance request directly to the NIGC, it may do so without the approval requirement set forth in paragraph (A)(2)(iii) of this section. And such request shall be deemed as having been approved by the Tribal Gaming Commission

B. NIGC CONCURRENCE.

1. Following receipt of the variance approval, the Chairman or his or her designee shall have sixty (60) days to concur with or object to the approval of the variance.

2. Any objection raised by the Chairman shall be in the form of a written explanation based upon the following criteria:

(i) There is no valid explanation of why the gaming operation should have received a variance approval from the Tribal Gaming Commission on the enumerated standard; or

(ii) The variance as approved by the Tribal Gaming Commission does not provide a level of control sufficient to accomplish the purpose of the standard it is to replace.

3. If the Chairman fails to object in writing within sixty (60) days after the date of receipt of a complete submission, the variance shall be considered concurred with by the Chairman.

The 60-day deadline may be extended, provided such extension is mutually agreed upon by the Tribal Gaming Commission and the Chairman.

C. CURING CHAIRMAN'S OBJECTIONS.

1. Following an objection by the Chairman to the issuance of a variance, the Tribal Gaming Commission shall have the opportunity to cure any objections noted by the Chairman.

2. A Tribal Gaming Commission may cure the objections raised by the NIGC by:

(i) Rescinding its initial approval of the variance; or

(ii) Rescinding it's initial approval, revising the variance, approving it, and re-submitting it to the Chairman.

3. Upon any re-submission of a variance approval, the Chairman shall have thirty (30) days to concur with or object to the re-submitted variance.

If the Chairman fails to object in writing within thirty (30) days after the date of receipt of the re-submitted variance, the re-submitted variance shall be considered concurred with by the Chairman.

5. The thirty (30) day deadline may be extended, provided such extension is mutually agreed upon by the Tribal Gaming Commission and the Chairman.

D. APPEALS.

1. Upon receipt of objections to a re-submission of a variance, the Tribal Gaming Commission shall be entitled to an appeal to the full National Indian Gaming Commission in accordance with the following process:

(i) Within thirty (30) days of receiving an objection to a re-submission, the Tribal Gaming Commission shall file its notice of appeal.

(ii) Failure to file an appeal within the time provided by this section shall result in a waiver of the opportunity for an appeal.

(iii) An appeal under this section shall specify the reasons why the Tribal Gaming Commission believes the Chairman's objections should be reviewed, and shall include supporting documentation, if any.

(iv) The Tribal Gaming Commission shall be provided with any comments offered by the Chairman to the Commission on the substance of the appeal by the Tribal Gaming Commission and shall be offered the opportunity to respond to any such comments.

(v) Within thirty (30) days after receipt of the appeal, the NIGC shall render a decision based upon the criteria contained within paragraph (B)(2) of this section unless the appellant elects to provide the NIGC additional time, not to exceed an additional thirty (30) days, to render a decision.

(vi) In the absence of a decision within the time provided, the Tribal Gaming Commission's re-submission shall be considered concurred with by the NIGC and become effective.

2. The Tribal Gaming Commission may appeal the Chairman's objection to the approval of a variance to the full Commission without resubmitting the variance by filling a notice of appeal with the full Commission within thirty (30) days of the Chairman's objection and complying with the procedures described in paragraph (D)(1) of this section.

E. EFFECTIVE DATE OF VARIANCE.

The gaming operation shall comply with standards that achieve a level of control sufficient to accomplish the purpose of the standard it is to replace until such time as the NIGC objects to the Tribal Gaming Commission's approval of a variance as provided in paragraph (b) of this section. Concurrence in a variance by the Chairman of the NIGC is discretionary and variances will not be granted routinely. The gaming operation shall comply with standards at least as stringent as those set forth in this part until such time as the NIGC concurs with the Tribal Gaming Commission's Approval of the variance.

GAMING OPERATION TIERS (25 CFR 542.20; 25 CFR 542.30; 25 CFR 542.40)

A Tier A gaming operation is one with annual gross gaming revenues of more than $1 million but not more than $5 million. If the Ottawa Tribe of Oklahoma operates a tier A gaming facility, regulatory standards will be those set forth in the Federal Register, 25 CFR part 542.20.

A Tier B gaming operation is one with gross gaming revenues of more than $5 million but not more than $15 million. If the Ottawa Tribe of Oklahoma operates a tier B gaming facility, regulatory standards will be those set forth in the Federal Register, 25 CFR part 542.30.

A Tier C gaming operation is one with annual gross gaming revenues of more than $15 million.

TIER C DROP AND COUNT (25 CFR 542.41)

A. COMPUTER APPLICATIONS.

For any computer applications utilized, alternate documentation and/or procedures that provide at least the level of control described by the standards in this section, as approved by the Tribal Gaming Commission, will be acceptable.

410

B. TABLE GAME DROP STANDARDS.

1. The setting out of empty table game drop boxes and the drop shall be a continuous process.
2. At the end of each shift:
(i) All locked table game drop boxes shall be removed from the tables by a person independent of the pit shift being dropped;
(ii) A separate drop box shall be placed on each table opened at any time during each shift or a gaming operation may utilize a single drop box with separate openings and compartments for each shift; and
(iii) Upon removal from the tables, table game drop boxes shall be transported directly to the count room or other equivalently secure area with comparable controls and locked in a secure manner until the count takes place.
3. If drop boxes are not placed on all tables, then the pit department shall document which tables were open during the shift.
4. The transporting of table game drop boxes shall be performed by a minimum of two persons, at least one of whom is independent of the pit shift being dropped.
5. All table game drop boxes shall be posted with a number corresponding to a permanent number on the gaming table and marked to indicate game, table number, and shift.
6. Surveillance shall be notified when the drop is to begin so that surveillance may monitor the activities.

C. SOFT COUNT ROOM PERSONNEL.

1. The table game soft count and the gaming machine bill acceptor count shall be performed by a minimum of three employees.
2. Count room personnel shall not be allowed to exit or enter the count room during the count except for emergencies or scheduled breaks. At no time during the count, shall there be fewer than three employees in the count room until the drop proceeds have been accepted into cage/vault accountability. Surveillance shall be notified whenever count room personnel exit or enter the count room during the count.
3. Count team members shall be rotated on a routine basis such that the count team is not consistently the same three persons more than four (4) days per week. This standard shall not apply to gaming operations that utilize a count team of more than three persons.
4. The count team shall be independent of transactions being reviewed and counted. The count team shall be independent of the cage/vault departments, however, an accounting representative may be used if there is an independent audit of all soft count documentation.
5. Count Team members shall wear a pocketless jumpsuit at all times while in the count room. The jumpsuit will be removed each time the employee leaves the count room and shall not under any circumstances be worn to the restroom, the employee locker room, the break room, nor any other location outside of the count room.

D. TABLE GAME SOFT COUNT STANDARDS.

1. The table game soft count shall be performed in a soft count room or other equivalently secure area with comparable controls.
2. Access to the count room during the count shall be restricted to members of the drop and count teams, with the exception of authorized observers, supervisors for resolution of problems, and authorized maintenance personnel.
3. If counts from various revenue centers occur simultaneously in the count room, procedures shall be in effect that prevent the commingling of funds from different revenue centers.
4. The table game drop boxes shall be individually emptied and counted in such a manner to prevent the commingling of funds between boxes until the count of the box has been recorded.
(i) The count of each box shall be recorded in ink or other permanent form of recordation.
(ii) A second count shall be performed by an employee on the count team who did not perform the initial count.
(iii) Corrections to information originally recorded by the count team on soft count documentation shall be made by drawing a single line through the error, writing the correct figure above the original figure, and then obtaining the initials of at least two count team members who verified the change.
5. If currency counters are utilized and the count room table is used only to empty boxes and sort/stack contents, a count team member shall be able to observe the loading and unloading of all currency at the currency counter, including rejected currency.
6. Table game drop boxes, when empty, shall be shown to another member of the count team, or to another person who is observing the count, or to surveillance, provided the count is monitored in its entirety by a person independent of the count.
7. Orders for fill/credit (if applicable) shall be matched to the fill/credit slips. Fills and credits shall be traced to or recorded on the count sheet.
8. Pit marker issue and payment slips (if applicable) removed from the table game drop boxes shall either be:
(i) Traced to or recorded on the count sheet by the count team; or
(ii) Totaled by shift and traced to the totals documented by the computerized system. Accounting personnel shall verify the issue/payment slip for each table is accurate.
9. Foreign currency exchange forms (if applicable) removed from the table game drop boxes shall be reviewed for the proper daily exchange rate and the conversion amount shall be recomputed by the count team. Alternatively, this may be performed by accounting/auditing employees.
10. The opening/closing table and marker inventory forms (if applicable) shall either be:
(i) Examined and traced to or recorded on the count sheet; or
(ii) If a computerized system is used, accounting personnel can trace the opening/closing table and marker inventory forms to the count sheet. Discrepancies shall be investigated with the findings documented and maintained for inspection.
11. The count sheet shall be reconciled to the total drop by a count team member who shall not function as the sole recorder.

12. All members of the count team shall sign the count document or a summary report to attest to their participation in the count.

13. All drop proceeds and cash equivalents that were counted shall be turned over to the cage or vault cashier (who shall be independent of the count team) or to an authorized person/employee independent of the revenue generation and the count process for verification. Such person shall certify by signature as to the accuracy of the drop proceeds delivered and received.

14. The count sheet, with all supporting documents, shall be delivered to the accounting department by a count team member or a person independent of the cashiers' department. Alternatively, it may be adequately secured (e.g., locked container to which only accounting personnel can gain access) until retrieved by the accounting department.

15. Access to stored, full table game drop boxes shall be restricted to authorized members of the drop and count teams.

E. GAMING MACHINE BILL ACCEPTOR DROP STANDARDS.

1. A minimum of three employees shall be involved in the removal of the gaming machine drop, at least one of who is independent of the gaming machine department.

2. All bill acceptor canisters shall be removed only at the time previously designated by the gaming operation and reported to the Tribal Gaming Commission, except for emergency drops.

3. Surveillance shall be notified when the drop is to begin so that surveillance may monitor the activities.

4. The bill acceptor canisters shall be removed by a person independent of the gaming machine department then transported directly to the count room or other equivalently secure area with comparable controls and locked in a secure manner until the count takes place.

(i) Security shall be provided over the bill acceptor canisters removed from the gaming machines and awaiting transport to the count room.

(ii) The transporting of bill acceptor canisters shall be performed by a minimum of two persons, at least one of who is independent of the gaming machine department.

5. All bill acceptor canisters shall be posted with a number corresponding to a permanent number on the gaming machine.

F. GAMING MACHINE BILL ACCEPTOR COUNT STANDARDS.

1. The gaming machine bill acceptor count shall be performed in a soft count room or other equivalently secure area with comparable controls.

2. Access to the count room during the count shall be restricted to members of the drop and count teams, with the exception of authorized observers, supervisors for resolution of problems, and authorized maintenance personnel.

3. If counts from various revenue centers occur simultaneously in the count room, procedures shall be in effect that prevent the commingling of funds from different revenue centers.

4. The bill acceptor canisters shall be individually emptied and counted in such a manner to prevent the commingling of funds between canisters until the count of the canister has been recorded.

(i) The count of each canister shall be recorded in ink or other permanent form of recordation.

(ii) A second count shall be performed by an employee on the count team who did not perform the initial count.

(iii) Corrections to information originally recorded by the count team on soft count documentation shall be made by drawing a single line through the error, writing the correct figure above the original figure, and then obtaining the initials of at least two count team members who verified the change.

5. If currency counters are utilized and the count room table is used only to empty canisters and sort/stack contents, a count team member shall be able to observe the loading and unloading of all currency at the currency counter, including rejected currency.

6. Canisters, when empty, shall be shown to another member of the count team, or to another person who is observing the count, or to surveillance, provided that the count is monitored in its entirety by a person independent of the count.

7. The count sheet shall be reconciled to the total drop by a count team member who shall not function as the sole recorder.

8. All members of the count team shall sign the count document or a summary report to attest to their participation in the count.

9. All drop proceeds and cash equivalents that were counted shall be turned over to the cage or vault cashier (who shall be independent of the count team) or to an authorized person/employee independent of the revenue generation and the count process for verification. Such person shall certify by signature as to the accuracy of the drop proceeds delivered and received.

10. The count sheet, with all supporting documents, shall be delivered to the accounting department by a count team member or a person independent of the cashiers' department. Alternatively, it may be adequately secured (e.g., locked container to which only accounting personnel can gain access) until retrieved by the accounting department.

11. Access to stored bill acceptor canisters, full or empty, shall be restricted to:

(i) Authorized members of the drop and count teams; and

(ii) Authorized personnel in an emergency for the resolution of a problem.

12. All bill acceptor canisters shall be posted with a number corresponding to a permanent number on the gaming machine.

G. GAMING MACHINE COIN DROP STANDARDS.

The Tribal gaming facility does not currently maintain any coin-operated video gaming machines. Should that change with the advent of Class III gaming, the following Tribal Internal Control Standards will apply:

1. A minimum of three employees shall be involved in the removal of the gaming machine drop, at least one of whom is independent of the gaming machine department.

2. All drop buckets shall be removed only at the time previously designated by the gaming operation and reported to the Tribal Gaming Commission, except for emergency drops.

3. Surveillance shall be notified when the drop is to begin in order that surveillance may monitor the activities. Security shall be provided over the buckets removed from the gaming machine drop cabinets and awaiting transport to the count room.

4.　　　　As each machine is opened, the contents shall be tagged with its respective machine number if the bucket is not permanently marked with the machine number. The contents shall be transported directly to the area designated for the counting of such drop proceeds. If more than one trip is required to remove the contents of the machines, the filled carts of coins shall be securely locked in the room designed for counting or in another equivalently secure area with comparable controls. There shall be a locked covering on any carts in which the drop route includes passage out of doors. Alternatively, a smart bucket system that electronically identifies and tracks the gaming machine number, and facilitates the proper recognition of gaming revenue, shall satisfy the requirements of this paragraph.

6. Each drop bucket in use shall be:

(i) Housed in a locked compartment separate from any other compartment of the gaming machine and keyed differently than other gaming machine compartments; and

(ii) Identifiable to the gaming machine from which it is removed. If the gaming machine is identified with a removable tag that is placed in the bucket, the tag shall be placed on top of the bucket when it is collected.

7. Each gaming machine shall have drop buckets into which coins or tokens that are retained by the gaming machine are collected. Drop bucket contents shall not be used to make change or pay hand-paid payouts.

8. The collection procedures may include procedures for dropping gaming machines that have trays instead of drop buckets.

H. HARD COUNT ROOM PERSONNEL.

The following Tribal Internal Control Standards apply specifically to any Class III gaming machines if Casino Management elects to use and the Ottawa Tribal Gaming Commission approves such machines:

1. The weigh/count shall be performed by a minimum of three employees.

2. At no time during the weigh/count shall there be fewer than three employees in the count room until the drop proceeds have been accepted into cage/vault accountability. Surveillance shall be notified whenever count room personnel exit or enter the count room during the count. If the gaming machine count is conducted with a continuous mechanical count meter that is not reset during the count and is verified in writing by at least three employees at the start and end of each denomination count, then one employee may perform the wrap.

3. Count team members shall be rotated on a routine basis such that the count team is not consistently the same three persons more than four (4) days per week. This standard shall not apply to gaming operations that utilize a count team of more than three persons.

4. The count team shall be independent of transactions being reviewed and counted. The count team shall be independent of the cage/vault departments, unless they are non-supervisory gaming machine employees and perform the laborer function only (A non-supervisory gaming machine employee is defined as a person below the level of gaming machine shift supervisor). A cage cashier may be used if this person is not allowed to perform the recording function. An accounting representative may be used if there is an independent audit of all count documentation.

I. GAMING MACHINE COIN COUNT AND WRAP STANDARDS.

The Tribal gaming facility does not currently maintain any coin-operated video gaming machines. Should that change with the advent of Class III gaming, the following Tribal Internal Control Standards will apply:

1. Coins shall include tokens.

2. The gaming machine coin count and wrap shall be performed in a count room or other equivalently secure area with comparable controls. Alternatively, an on-the-floor drop system utilizing a mobile scale shall satisfy the requirements of this paragraph, subject to the following conditions:

(A) The gaming operation shall utilize and maintain an effective on-line gaming machine monitoring system, as described in Sec. 542.13(m)(3);

(B) Components of the on-the-floor drop system shall include, but not be limited to, a weigh scale, a laptop computer through which weigh/count applications are operated, a security camera available for the mobile scale system, and a VCR to be housed within the video compartment of the mobile scale. The system may include a mule cart used for mobile weigh scale system locomotion.

(C) The gaming operation must obtain the security camera available with the system, and this camera must be added in such a way as to eliminate tampering.

(D) Prior to the drop, the drop/count team shall ensure the scale batteries are charged;

(E) Prior to the drop, a videotape shall be inserted into the VCR used to record the drop in conjunction with the security camera system and the VCR shall be activated;

(F) The weigh scale test shall be performed prior to removing the unit from the hard count room for the start of the weigh/drop/count;

(G) Surveillance shall be notified when the weigh/drop/count begins and shall be capable of monitoring the entire process;

(H) An observer independent of the weigh/drop/count teams (independent observer) shall remain by the weigh scale at all times and shall observe the entire weigh/drop/count process;

(I) Physical custody of the key(s) needed to access the laptop and video compartment shall require the involvement of two persons, one of whom is independent of the drop and count team;

413

(J) The mule key (if applicable), the laptop and video compartment keys, and the remote control for the VCR shall be maintained by a department independent of the gaming machine department. The appropriate personnel shall sign out these keys;

(K) A person independent of the weigh/drop/count teams shall be required to accompany these keys while they are checked out, and observe each time the laptop compartment is opened;

(L) The laptop access panel shall not be opened outside the hard count room, except in instances when the laptop must be rebooted as a result of a crash, lock up, or other situation requiring immediate corrective action;

(M) User access to the system shall be limited to those employees required to have full or limited access to complete the weigh/drop/count; and

(N) When the weigh/drop/count is completed, the independent observer shall access the laptop compartment, end the recording session, eject the videotape, and deliver the videotape to surveillance.

3. Access to the count room during the count shall be restricted to members of the drop and count teams, with the exception of authorized observers, supervisors for resolution of problems, and authorized maintenance personnel.

4. If counts from various revenue centers occur simultaneously in the count room, procedures shall be in effect that prevent the commingling of funds from different revenue centers.

5. The following functions shall be performed in the counting of the gaming machine drop:

(i) Recorder function, which involves the recording of the gaming machine count; and

(ii) Count team supervisor function, which involves the control of the gaming machine weigh and wrap process. The supervisor shall not perform the initial recording of the weigh/count unless a weigh scale with a printer is used.

6. The gaming machine drop shall be counted, wrapped, and reconciled in such a manner to prevent the commingling of gaming machine drop coin with coin (for each denomination) from the next gaming machine drop until the count of the gaming machine drop has been recorded. If the coins are not wrapped immediately after being weighed or counted, they shall be secured and not commingled with other coin.

(i) The amount of the gaming machine drop from each machine shall be recorded in ink or other permanent form of recordation on a gaming machine count document by the recorder or mechanically printed by the weigh scale.

(ii) Corrections to information originally recorded by the count team on gaming machine count documentation shall be made by drawing a single line through the error, writing the correct figure above the original figure, and then obtaining the initials of at least two count team members who verified the change.

If a weigh scale interface is used, corrections to gaming machine count data shall be made using either of the following:

(1) Drawing a single line through the error on the gaming machine document, writing the correct figure above the original figure, and then obtaining the initials of at least two count team employees. If this procedure is used, an employee independent of the gaming machine department and count team shall enter the correct figure into the computer system prior to the generation of related gaming machine reports; or

(2) During the count process, correct the error in the computer system and enter the passwords of at least two count team employees. If this procedure is used, an exception report shall be generated by the computer system identifying the gaming machine number, the error, the correction, and the count team employees attesting to the correction.

7. If applicable, the weigh shall be converted to dollar amounts before the reconciliation of the weigh to the wrap.

8. If a coin meter is used, a count team member shall convert the coin count for each denomination into dollars and shall enter the results on a summary sheet.

9. The recorder and at least one other count team member shall sign the weigh tape and the gaming machine count document attesting to the accuracy of the weigh/count.

10. All members of the count team shall sign the count document or a summary report to attest to their participation in the count.

11. All drop proceeds and cash equivalents that were counted shall be turned over to the cage or vault cashier (who shall be independent of the count team) or to an authorized person/employee independent of the revenue generation and the count process for verification. Such person shall certify by signature as to the accuracy of the drop proceeds delivered and received.

12. All gaming machine count and wrap documentation, including any applicable computer storage media, shall be delivered to the accounting department by a count team member or a person independent of the cashier's department. Alternatively, it may be adequately secured (e.g., locked container to which only accounting personnel can gain access) until retrieved by the accounting department.

13. If the coins are transported off the property, a second (alternative) count procedure shall be performed before the coins leave the property. Any variances shall be documented.

14. Variances. Large (by denomination, either $1,000 or 2% of the drop, whichever is less) or unusual (e.g., zero for weigh/count or patterned for all counts) variances between the weigh/count and wrap shall be investigated by management personnel independent of the gaming machine department, count team, and the cage/vault functions on a timely basis. The results of such investigation shall be documented, maintained for inspection, and provided to the Tribal Gaming Commission upon request.

J. SECURITY OF THE COUNT ROOM INVENTORY DURING THE GAMING MACHINE COIN COUNT AND WRAP.

The Tribal gaming facility does not currently plan to maintain any coin-operated video gaming machines.

TABLE GAME DROP BOX KEY CONTROL STANDARDS.

1. Procedures shall be developed and implemented to insure that unauthorized access to empty table game drop boxes shall not occur from the time the boxes leave the storage racks until they are placed on the tables.

414

2. The involvement of at least two persons independent of the cage department shall be required to access stored empty table game drop boxes.

3. The release keys shall be separately keyed from the contents keys.

4. At least three (two for table game drop box keys in operations with three tables or fewer) count team members are required to be present at the time count room and other count keys are issued for the count.

5. All duplicate keys shall be maintained in a manner that provides the same degree of control as is required for the original keys. Records shall be maintained for each key duplicated that indicate the number of keys made and destroyed.

6. Logs shall be maintained by the custodian of sensitive keys to document authorization of personnel accessing keys.

TABLE GAME DROP BOX RELEASE KEYS.

1. The table game drop box release keys shall be maintained by a department independent of the pit department.

2. Only the person(s) authorized to remove table game drop boxes from the tables shall be allowed access to the table game drop box release keys; however, the count team members may have access to the release keys during the soft count in order to reset the table game drop boxes.

3. Persons authorized to remove the table game drop boxes shall be precluded from having simultaneous access to the table game drop box contents keys and release keys.

4. For situations requiring access to a table game drop box at a time other than the scheduled drop, the date, time, and signature of employee signing out/in the release key must be documented.

BILL ACCEPTOR CANISTER RELEASE KEYS.

1. The bill acceptor canister release keys shall be maintained by a department independent of the gaming machine department.

2. Only the person(s) authorized to remove bill acceptor canisters from the gaming machines shall be allowed access to the release keys.

3. Persons authorized to remove the bill acceptor canisters shall be precluded from having simultaneous access to the bill acceptor canister contents keys and release keys.

4. For situations requiring access to a bill acceptor canister at a time other than the scheduled drop, the date, time, and signature of employee signing out/in the release key must be documented.

TABLE GAME DROP BOX STORAGE RACK KEYS.

1. A person independent of the pit department shall be required to accompany the table game drop box storage rack keys and observe each time table game drop boxes are removed from or placed in storage racks.

2. Persons authorized to obtain table game drop box storage rack keys shall be precluded from having simultaneous access to table game drop box contents keys with the exception of the count team.

BILL ACCEPTOR CANISTER STORAGE RACK KEYS.

1. A person independent of the gaming machine department shall be required to accompany the bill acceptor canister storage rack keys and observe each time canisters are removed from or placed in storage racks.

2. Persons authorized to obtain bill acceptor canister storage rack keys shall be precluded from having simultaneous access to bill acceptor canister contents keys with the exception of the count team.

TABLE GAME DROP BOX CONTENTS KEYS.

1. The physical custody of the keys needed for accessing stored, full table game drop box contents shall require the involvement of persons from at least two separate departments, with the exception of the count team.

2. Access to the table game drop box contents key at other than scheduled count times shall require the involvement of at least three persons from separate departments, including management. The reason for access shall be documented with the signatures of all participants and observers.

3. Only count team members shall be allowed access to table game drop box content keys during the count process.

BILL ACCEPTOR CANISTER CONTENTS KEYS.

1. The physical custody of the keys needed for accessing stored, full bill acceptor canister contents shall require involvement of persons from two separate departments, with the exception of the count team.

2. Access to the bill acceptor canister contents key at other than scheduled count times shall require the involvement of at least three persons from separate departments, one of who must be a supervisor. The reason for access shall be documented with the signatures of all participants and observers.

3.   Only the count team members shall be allowed access to bill acceptor canister contents keys during the count process.

GAMING MACHINE COMPUTERIZED KEY SECURITY SYSTEMS.

1. Computerized key security systems which restrict access to the gaming machine drop and count keys through the use of passwords, keys or other

means, other than a key custodian, must provide the same degree of control as indicated in the aforementioned key control standards; refer to to paragraphs (L), (O), (Q), and (S) of this section. Note this standard does not apply to the system administrator. The system administrator is defined in paragraph (T)(2)(i) of this section.

2. For computerized key security systems, the following additional gaming machine key control procedures apply:

(i)   Management personnel independent of the gaming machine department assign and control user access to keys in the computerized key security system (i.e., system administrator) to ensure that gaming machine drop and count keys are restricted to authorized employees.

(ii)   In the event of an emergency or the key box is inoperable, access to the emergency manual key(s) (a.k.a. override key), used to access the box containing the gaming machine drop and count keys, requires the physical involvement of at least three persons from separate departments, including management. The date, time and reason for access, must be documented with the signatures of all participating employees signing out/in the emergency manual key(s).

(iii)   The custody of the keys issued pursuant to paragraph (T)(2)(ii) of this section requires the presence of two persons from separate departments from the time of their issuance until the time of their return.

(iv)   Routine physical maintenance that requires accessing the emergency manual key(s) (override key) and does not involve the accessing of the gaming machine drop and count keys, only requires the presence of two persons from separate departments. The date, time and reason for access must be documented with the signatures of all participating employees signing out/in the emergency manual key(s).

3. For computerized key security systems controlling access to gaming machine drop and count keys, accounting/audit personnel, independent of the system administrator, will perform the following procedures:

(i)   Daily, review the report generated by the computerized key security system indicating the transactions performed by the individual(s) that adds, deletes and changes user's access within the system (i.e., system administrator). Determine whether the transactions completed by the system administrator provide an adequate control over the access to the gaming machine drop and count keys. Also, determine whether any gaming machine drop and count key(s) removed or returned to the key cabinet by the system administrator was properly authorized.

(ii)   For at least one day each month, review the report generated by the computerized key security system indicating all transactions performed to determine whether any unusual gaming machine drop and count key removals or key returns occurred.

(iii)   At least quarterly, review a sample of users that are assigned access to the gaming machine drop and count keys to determine that their access to the assigned keys is adequate relative to their job position.

(iv)   All noted improper transactions or unusual occurrences are investigated with the results documented.

4.   Quarterly, an inventory of all count room, drop box release, storage rack and contents keys is performed, and reconciled to records of keys made, issued and destroyed. Investigations are performed for all keys unaccounted for, with the investigation being documented.

TABLE GAMES COMPUTERIZED KEY SECURITY SYSTEMS.

1.   Computerized key security systems which restrict access to the table game drop and count keys through the use of passwords, keys or other means, other than a key custodian, must provide the same degree of control as indicated in the aforementioned key control standard; refer to paragraphs (m), (n), (p) and (r) of this section. Note: This section does not apply to the system administrator. The system administrator is defined in paragraph (u)(2)(ii) of this section.

2.   For computerized key security systems, the following additional table Game key control procedures apply:

(i)   Management personnel independent of the table game department assign and control user access to keys in the computerized key security system (i.e., system administrator) to ensure that table game drop and count keys are restricted to authorized employees.

(ii)   In the event of an emergency or the key box is inoperable, access to the emergency manual key(s) (a.k.a override key), used to access the box containing the table games drop and count keys, requires the physical involvement of at least three persons from separate departments, including management. The date, time and reason of access, must be documented with the signatures of all participating employees signing out/in the emergency manual key(s).

(iii)   The custody of the keys issued pursuant to paragraph (U)(2)(ii) of this section requires the presence of two persons from separate departments from the time of their issuance until the time of their return.

(iv)   Routine physical maintenance that requires accessing the emergency manual key(s) (override key) and does not involve the accessing of the table games drop and count keys, only requires the presence of two persons from separate departments. The date, time and reason for access must be documented with the signatures of all participating employees signing out/in the emergency manual key(s).

3.   For computerized key security systems controlling access to table games drop and count keys, accounting/audit personnel, independent of the system administrator, will perform the following procedures:

(i)   Daily, review the report generated by the computerized key security system indicating the transactions performed by the individual(s) that adds, deletes and changes user's access within the system (i.e., system administrator). Determine whether the transactions completed by the system administrator provide an adequate control over the access to the table games drop and count keys. Also, determine whether any table games drop and count key(s) removed or returned to the key cabinet by the system administrator was properly authorized.

(ii)   For at least one day each month, review the report generated by the computerized key security system indicating all transactions performed to determine whether any unusual table games drop and count key removals or key returns occurred

(iii)   At least quarterly, review a sample of users that are assigned access to the table games drop and count keys to determine that their access to the assigned keys is adequate relative to their job position.

416

(iv)   All noted improper transactions or unusual occurrences are investigated with the results documented.
4.   Quarterly, an inventory of all count room, table game drop box release, storage rack and contents keys is performed, and reconciled to records of keys made, issued, and destroyed. Investigations are performed for all keys unaccounted for, with the investigations being documented.

EMERGENCY DROP PROCEDURES.

Casino Management shall develop emergency drop procedures to be approved by the Tribal Gaming Commission.

INTERNAL AUDIT (25 CFR 542.42)

A. INTERNAL AUDIT PERSONNEL.

1. For Tier C gaming operations, a separate internal audit department shall be maintained whose primary function is performing internal audit work and that is independent with respect to the departments subject to audit.
2. The internal audit personnel shall report directly to the Tribe, Tribal Gaming Commission, audit committee, or other entity designated by the Tribe in accordance with the definition of internal audit in Sec. 542.2.

B. AUDITS.

1. Internal audit personnel shall perform audits of all major gaming areas of the gaming operation. The following shall be reviewed at least annually:
(i) Bingo, including but not limited to, Bingo card control, payout procedures, and cash reconciliation process;
(ii) Pull-tabs, including but not limited to, statistical records, winner verification, perpetual inventory, and accountability of sales versus inventory;
(iii) Card games, including but not limited to, card games operation, cash exchange procedures, shill transactions, and count procedures;
(iv) Keno, including but not limited to, game write and payout procedures, sensitive key location and control, and a review of keno auditing procedures;
(v) Pari-mutuel wagering, including write and payout procedures, and pari-mutuel auditing procedures;
(vi) Table games, including but not limited to, fill and credit procedures, pit credit play procedures, rim credit procedures, soft drop/count procedures and the subsequent transfer of funds, unannounced testing of count room currency counters and/or currency interface, location and control over sensitive keys, the tracing of source documents to summarized documentation and accounting records, and reconciliation to restricted copies;
(vii) Gaming machines, including but not limited to, jackpot payout and gaming machine fill procedures, gaming machine drop/count and bill acceptor drop/count and subsequent transfer of funds, unannounced testing of weigh scale and weigh scale interface, unannounced testing of count room currency counters and/or currency interface, gaming machine drop cabinet access, tracing of source documents to summarized documentation and accounting records, reconciliation to restricted copies, location and control over sensitive keys, compliance with EPROM duplication procedures, and compliance with TICS procedures for gaming machines that accept currency or coin(s) and issue cash-out tickets or gaming machines that do not accept currency or coin(s) and do not return currency or coin(s);
(viii) Cage and credit procedures including all cage, credit, and collection procedures, and the reconciliation of trial balances to physical instruments on a sample basis. Cage accountability shall be reconciled to the general ledger;
(ix) Information technology functions, including review for compliance with information technology standards;
(x) Complimentary service or item, including but not limited to, procedures whereby complimentary service items are issued, authorized, and redeemed; and
(xi) Any other internal audits as required by the Tribe, Tribal Gaming Commission, audit committee, or other entity designated by the Tribe.
2. In addition to the observation and examinations performed under paragraph (B)(1) of this section, follow-up observations and examinations shall be performed to verify that corrective action has been taken regarding all instances of noncompliance cited by internal audit, the independent accountant, and/or the Commission. The verification shall be performed within six (6) months following the date of notification.
3. Whenever possible, internal audit observations shall be performed on an unannounced basis (i.e., without the employees being forewarned that their activities will be observed). Additionally, if the independent accountant also performs the internal audit function, the accountant shall perform separate observations of the table games/gaming machine drops and counts to satisfy the internal audit observation requirements and independent accountant tests of controls as required by the American Institute of Certified Public Accountants guide.

C. DOCUMENTATION.

1. Documentation (e.g., checklists, programs, reports, etc.) shall be prepared to evidence all internal audit work performed as it relates to the requirements in this section, including all instances of noncompliance.
2. The internal audit department shall operate with audit programs, which, at a minimum, address the TICS. Additionally, the department shall properly document the work performed, the conclusions reached, and the resolution of all exceptions. Institute of Internal Auditors standards are recommended but not required.

D. REPORTS.

1. Reports documenting audits performed shall be maintained and made available to the Commission upon request.
2. Such audit reports shall include the following information:
(i) Audit objectives;
(ii) Audit procedures and scope;

417

(iii) Findings and conclusions;
(iv) Recommendations, if applicable; and
(v) Management's response.

E. MATERIAL EXCEPTIONS.
All material exceptions resulting from internal audit work shall be investigated and resolved with the results of such being documented and retained for five years.

F. ROLE OF MANAGEMENT.
1. Internal audit findings shall be reported to management.
2. Management shall be required to respond to internal audit findings stating corrective measures to be taken to avoid recurrence of the audit exception.
3. Such management responses shall be included in the internal audit report that will be delivered to management, the Tribe, Tribal Gaming Commission, audit committee, or other entity designated by the Tribe.

SURVEILLANCE (25 CFR 542.43)

A. SURVEILLANCE ROOM
The surveillance system shall be maintained and operated from a staffed surveillance room and shall provide surveillance over gaming areas.

B. ENTRANCE
The entrance to the surveillance room shall be located so that it is not readily accessible by either gaming operation employees who work primarily on the casino floor, or the general public.

C. ACCESS
Access to the surveillance room shall be limited to surveillance personnel, designated employees, and other persons authorized in accordance with the surveillance department policy. Such policy shall be approved by the Tribal Gaming Commission. The surveillance department shall maintain a sign-in log of other authorized persons entering the surveillance room.

D. OVERRIDE CAPABILITY
Surveillance room equipment shall have total override capability over all other satellite surveillance equipment located outside the surveillance room.

E. AUXILLIARY POWER
In the event of power loss to the surveillance system, an auxiliary or backup power source shall be available and capable of providing immediate restoration of power to all elements of the surveillance system that enable surveillance personnel to observe the table games remaining open for play and all areas covered by dedicated cameras. Auxiliary or backup power sources such as a UPS System, backup generator, or an alternate utility supplier, satisfy this requirement.

F. DATE AND TIME GENERATORS
The surveillance system shall include date and time generators that possess the capability to display the date and time of recorded events on video and/or digital recordings. The displayed date and time shall not significantly obstruct the recorded view.

G. TRAINING
The surveillance department shall strive to ensure staff is trained in the use of the equipment, knowledge of the games, and house rules.

H. CAMERA INSTALLATION
Each camera required by the standards in this section shall be installed in a manner that will prevent it from being readily obstructed, tampered with, or disabled by customers or employees.

I. MONITORING AND RECORDING
Each camera required by the standards in this section shall possess the capability of having its picture displayed on a monitor and recorded. The surveillance system shall include sufficient numbers of monitors and recorders to simultaneously display and record multiple gaming and count room activities, and record the views of all dedicated cameras and motion activated dedicated cameras.

J. TIMELY REPAIRS
Reasonable effort shall be made to repair each malfunction of surveillance system equipment required by the standards in this section within seventy-two (72) hours after the malfunction is discovered. The Tribal Gaming Commission shall be notified of any camera(s) that has malfunctioned for more than twenty-four (24) hours.
In the event of a dedicated camera malfunction, the gaming operation and/or the surveillance department shall immediately provide alternative camera coverage or other security measures, such as additional supervisory or security personnel, to protect the subject activity.

K. CARD GAMES.
The surveillance system shall monitor and record general activities in each card room with sufficient clarity to identify the employees performing the different functions.

L. PROGRESSIVE CARD GAMES.
Progressive card games with a progressive jackpot of $25,000 or more shall be monitored and recorded by dedicated cameras that provide coverage of:
(i) The table surface, sufficient that the card values and card suits can be clearly identified;
(ii) An overall view of the entire table with sufficient clarity to identify customers and dealer; and

(iii) A view of the posted jackpot amount.

M. GAMING MACHINES.

1. Except as otherwise provided gaming machines offering a payout of more than $250,000 shall be monitored and recorded by a dedicated camera(s) to provide coverage of:

(i) All customers and employees at the gaming machine, and

(ii) The face of the gaming machine, with sufficient clarity to identify the payout line(s) of the gaming machine.

2. In-house progressive machine.

In-house progressive gaming machines offering a base payout amount (jackpot reset amount) of more than $100,000 shall be monitored and recorded by a dedicated camera(s) to provide coverage of:

(i) All customers and employees at the gaming machine; and

(ii) The face of the gaming machine, with sufficient clarity to identify the payout line(s) of the gaming machine.

3. Wide-area progressive machine.

Wide-area progressive gaming machines offering a base payout amount of more than $1.5 million and monitored by an independent vendor utilizing an on-line progressive computer system shall be monitored and recorded by a dedicated camera(s) to provide coverage of:

(i) All customers and employees at the gaming machine; and

(ii) The face of the gaming machine, with sufficient clarity to identify the payout line(s) of the gaming machine.

4. If the gaming machine is a multi-game machine, the Tribal Gaming Commission, or the gaming operation subject to the approval of the Tribal Gaming Commission, may develop and implement alternative procedures to verify payouts.

N. CAGE AND VAULT.

1. The surveillance system shall monitor and record a general overview of activities occurring in each cage and vault area with sufficient clarity to identify employees within the cage and customers and employees at the counter areas.

2. Each cashier station shall be equipped with one (1) dedicated overhead camera covering the transaction area.

3. The surveillance system shall provide an overview of cash transactions. This overview should include the customer, the employee, and the surrounding area.

O. FILLS AND CREDITS.

1. The cage or vault area in which fills and credits are transacted shall be monitored and recorded by a dedicated camera or motion activated dedicated camera that provides coverage with sufficient clarity to identify the chip values and the amounts on the fill and credit slips.

2. Controls provided by a computerized fill and credit system maybe deemed an adequate alternative to viewing the fill and credit slips.

P. CURRENCY AND COIN.

1. The surveillance system shall monitor and record with sufficient clarity all areas where currency or coin may be stored or counted.

2. Audio capability of the soft count room shall also be maintained.

3. The surveillance system shall provide for:

(i) Coverage of scales shall be sufficiently clear to view any attempted manipulation of the recorded data.

(ii) Monitoring and recording of the table game drop box storage rack or area by either a dedicated camera or a motion-detector activated camera.

(iii) Monitoring and recording of all areas where coin may be stored or counted, including the hard count room, all doors to the hard count room, all scales and wrapping machines, and all areas where uncounted coin may be stored during the drop and count process.

(iv) Monitoring and recording of soft count room, including all doors to the room, all table game drop boxes, safes, and counting surfaces, and all count team personnel. The counting surface area must be continuously monitored and recorded by a dedicated camera during the soft count.

(v) Monitoring and recording of all areas where currency is sorted, stacked, counted, verified, or stored during the soft count process.

Q. CHANGE BOOTHS.

The surveillance system shall monitor and record a general overview of the activities occurring in each gaming machine change booth.

R. VIDEO RECORDING AND/OR DIGITAL RECORD RETENTION.

1. All video recordings and/or digital records of coverage provided by the dedicated cameras or motion-activated dedicated cameras required by the standards in this section shall be retained for a minimum of seven (7) days or the length of time proscribed by any compact with The State of Oklahoma.

2. Recordings involving suspected or confirmed gaming crimes, unlawful activity, or detentions by security personnel, must be retained for a minimum of thirty (30) day or the length of time proscribed by any compact with The State of Oklahoma.

3. Duly authenticated copies of video recordings and/or digital records shall be provided to the NIGC upon request.

S. VIDEO LIBRARY LOG.

A video library log, or comparable alternative procedure approved by the Tribal Gaming Commission, shall be maintained to demonstrate compliance with the storage, identification, and retention standards recorded required in this section.

T. MALFUNCTION AND REPAIR LOG.

1. Surveillance personnel shall maintain a log or alternative procedure approved by the Tribal Gaming Commission that documents each malfunction and repair of the surveillance system as defined in this section.

2. The log shall state the time, date, and nature of each malfunction, the efforts expended to repair the malfunction, and the date of each effort, the reasons for any delays in repairing the malfunction, the date the malfunction is repaired, and where applicable, any alternative security measures that were taken

3. Such log shall be maintained by surveillance room personnel and shall be stored securely within the surveillance department.

4. At a minimum, the following information shall be in a surveillance log:

(i) Date;
(ii) Time commenced and terminated;
(iii) Activity observed or performed; and
(iv) The name or license credential number of each person who initiates, performs, or supervises the surveillance.

4. Surveillance personnel shall also record a summary of the results of the surveillance of any suspicious activity. This summary may be maintained in a separate log.

[59] Though as of this writing that number has repeatedly changed month-to-month, in 2010 for the entire year when I was playing "stump the experts" the largest casinos in the world (strictly in terms of number of slot machines) were: Foxwoods Resort Casino in Ledyard, Connecticut with more than 7,400 slot machines; Mohegan Sun in Uncasville, Connecticut with 6,780; and Victoryland Race Track and Casino in Shorter Alabama with a little more than 6,400 machines. The two largest are Indian Casinos; the third was privately owned. (By the way, the Venetian in Macau had 3,400 machines, the Horseshoe in Hammond Indiana had 3,200, MGM Grand in Vegas had 2,300; Morongo in California had 2,200.)

[60] In a universe dominated by the sleaziest elements of gaming, surprisingly for one those South Carolina born companies, VGT (Video Gaming Technologies) has stood out as a paragon model of integrity and game excellence. Founded in 1991 by an entrepreneur Jon Yarbrough, VGT has viewed unregulated gaming more as "restricted" gaming and has taken extraordinary steps to maintain their distance from the sleaze.

[61] NO. COA04-1065; Judges Timmons-Goodson and Geer concur.

[62] Capitol Punishment: The Hard Truth About Washington Corruption From America's Most Notorious Lobbyist; Jack Abramoff; WND Books November 7, 2011

[63] Booz & Company 2012 Automotive Industry Perspective, December 7, 2011 By Scott Corwin, Jan Miecznikowski, Mike Beck, Evan Hirsh, Brian Collie

[64] Casino Enterprise Management, November 2010

[65] On February 23, 2006, the Nevada Gaming Commission adopted a new bankroll formula for licensees. The new formula modified the decades-old Regulation 6.150. Below is both the amendment and the current regulation:

AMENDMENTS TO REGULATION 6.150

PURPOSE: To establish that the chairman of the Board may adopt or revise a bankroll formula that specifies the minimum bankroll requirements applicable to restricted gaming licensees, nonrestricted gaming licensees and persons licensed as an operator of an inter-casino linked system or as an operator of a slot machine route, along with instructions for computing available bankroll; to establish that at least 30 days before adopting or revising the bankroll formula, the chairman shall (a) publish notice of the proposed adoption or revisions, together with the effective date thereof, once a day for seven (7) consecutive days in a newspaper of daily general circulation, one of which is published in Reno, Nevada, and the other published in Las Vegas, Nevada, (b) mail a copy of the proposed bankroll formula or revisions, together with the effective date thereof, to each restricted gaming licensee, nonrestricted gaming licensee, operator of an inter-casino linked system, operator of a slot machine route, and every other person who has filed a request therefore with the board or commission; and (c) provide a copy of the proposed bankroll formula or revisions and their effective date to the commission; to establish that any affected licensee may object to the proposed bankroll formula or revisions, by filing a request for a review of the chairman's administrative decision, pursuant to Regulation 4.190 and that if no requests for review are filed with the board, then the bankroll formula or revisions shall become effective on the date set by the chairman; to establish that each restricted gaming licensee, nonrestricted gaming licensee and each person licensed as an operator of an inter-casino linked system or as an operator of a slot machine route shall maintain in accordance with the bankroll formula adopted by the chairman, cash or cash equivalents in an amount sufficient to reasonably protect the licensee's or operator's patrons against defaults in gaming debts owed by the licensee or operator; to establish that except in the case restricted locations, if at any time the licensee's or operator's available cash or cash equivalents should be less than the amount required, the licensee or operator shall immediately notify the board of this deficiency and shall also detail the means by which the licensee shall comply with the minimum bankroll requirements; to establish that the failure to maintain the minimum bankroll, or a higher bankroll as required by the chairman, or failure to notify the board as required, is an unsuitable method of operation; to establish that records reflecting accurate, monthly computations of bankroll requirements and actual bankroll available shall be maintained in accordance with Regulation 6.060; to establish that nothing within the new regulation or a bankroll formula adopted pursuant to it alters, amends, supersedes or removes any condition of any licensee or approval imposed on any licensee by the commission; to establish that the chairman, for good cause shown by the licensee, may waive one or more of the requirements or provisions of the minimum bankroll requirements and that the chairman is granted the authority to revoke any waiver that may have been granted for any cause deemed reasonable; to repeal Regulation 5.130 in its entirety and incorporate bankroll requirements for restricted gaming licensees into Regulation 6.150; and to take such additional action as may be necessary and proper to effectuate these stated purposes.

REGULATION 6
ACCOUNTING REGULATIONS

1. The chairman may adopt or revise a bankroll formula that specifies the minimum bankroll requirements applicable to restricted gaming licensees, nonrestricted gaming licensees and persons licensed as an operator of an inter-casino linked system or as an operator of a slot machine route, along with instructions for computing available bankroll.

2. At least 30 days before adopting or revising the bankroll formula, the chairman shall:

   a. Publish notice of the proposed adoption or revisions, together with the effective date thereof, once a day for seven (7) consecutive days in a newspaper of daily general circulation, one of which is published in Reno, Nevada, and the other published in Las Vegas, Nevada;

   b. Mail a copy of the proposed bankroll formula or revisions, together with the effective date thereof, to each restricted gaming licensee, nonrestricted gaming licensee, operator of an inter-casino linked system, operator of a slot machine route, and every other person who has filed a request therefore with the board or commission; and

   c. Provide a copy of the proposed bankroll formula or revisions and their effective date to the commission.

3. Any affected licensee may object to the proposed bankroll formula or revisions, by filing a request for a review of the chairman's administrative decision, pursuant to Regulation 4.190. If any licensee files a request for review, then the effective date of the proposed bankroll formula or revisions will be stayed pending action by the board, and if the board's decision is appealed pursuant to Regulation 4.195, pending action by the commission. If no requests for review are filed with the board, then the bankroll formula or revisions shall become effective on the date set by the chairman.

4. Any licensee may propose the repeal or revision of any existing bankroll formula by submitting a request to the chairman, who shall consider the request at his discretion. If such a request is approved by the chairman, then the proposed repeal or revision must be processed in accordance with subsections 2 and 3. If such a request is denied by the chairman, then the licensee may file the request for a review as an administrative approval decision with the board pursuant to Regulation 4.190, and the commission, pursuant to Regulation 4.195.

5. Each restricted gaming licensee, nonrestricted gaming licensee and each person licensed as an operator of an inter-casino linked system or as an operator of a slot machine route shall maintain in accordance with the bankroll formula adopted by the chairman pursuant to the requirements of this section, cash or cash equivalents in an amount sufficient to reasonably protect the licensee's or operator's patrons against defaults in gaming debts owed by the licensee or operator. If at any time the licensee's or operator's available cash or cash equivalents should be less than the amount required by this section, the licensee or operator shall immediately notify the board of this deficiency and shall also detail the means by which the licensee shall comply with the minimum bankroll requirements. Failure to maintain the minimum bankroll required by this section, or a higher bankroll as required by the chairman pursuant to this section, or failure to notify the board as required by this section, is an unsuitable method of operation.

6. Records reflecting accurate, monthly computations of bankroll requirements and actual bankroll available shall be maintained by nonrestricted gaming licensees, operators of inter-casino linked systems and operators of slot routes in accordance with Regulation 6.060. The chairman, in his sole discretion, may require more frequent computations, require additional recordkeeping not specified in the formula, or require the licensee to maintain a bankroll higher than is or would otherwise be required by the bankroll formula, or require recordkeeping by restricted gaming licensees.

7. Neither this section nor a bankroll formula adopted pursuant to it alters, amends, supersedes or removes any condition of any licensee or approval imposed on any licensee by the commission.

8. The chairman, for good cause shown by the licensee, may waive one or more of the requirements or provisions of the minimum bankroll requirements.

9. The chairman is hereby granted the authority to revoke any waiver granted pursuant to this section for any cause deemed reasonable. Notice of the revocation of a waiver shall be deemed delivered and effective when personally served upon the licensee, or if personal service is impossible or impractical, when deposited, postage prepaid, in the United States mail, to the licensee at the address of the establishment as shown in the records of the commission. If a notice revoking or suspending the waiver of a bankroll requirement is issued, the affected licensee may request that the decision of the chairman be reviewed by the board and commission pursuant to NGC Regulation 4.185 through 4.195, inclusive.

66 Title 31 Requirements:

Section I—Title 31 Compliance Oversight

Section II—Title 31 Compliance Program
Section III—Title 31 Compliance Program Risk Assessments
Section I—Title 31 Compliance Oversight

1. **Title 31 Compliance Officer.** Person(s) independent of electronic gaming machines and cage departments shall provide on-going oversight of the enterprise's compliance with anti-money laundering and suspicious activity regulations as they pertain to the gaming industry.

2. **Non-Compliance Resolution.** Title 31 Compliance Officer(s) shall ensure corrective actions are undertaken in a timely manner.

Section II—Title 31 Compliance Program

1. **Deviation.** Any deviation to this program by any team member Fairfield Bingo may be subjected to:

a. Progressive disciplinary action up to and including termination;

b. Civil penalty of up to $100,000 fine, per violation, assessed on them personally by the Federal Crimes Enforcement Network (31 CFR 103.57 (2008)); and

c. Criminal penalty of up to $500,000 fine assessed on them personally and imprisoned up to five (5) years. (31 CFR 103.59 (2008))

2. **Gaming Day.** The normal business day for the Bingo halls shall be referred to as the "gaming day," which is a twenty-four (24) hour period. The Bingo hall shall establish the specific time by hour and minute in which their gaming day commences and ends (e.g., 2:00 a.m. to 01:59 a.m.). The Bingo hall shall keep its books and records for business, accounting, and tax purposes based on their gaming day. The Bingo hall shall disseminate their gaming day time period to their team members. The gaming day may not be disclosed to the general public. (31 CFR 103.64(b)(4) (2008))

3. **Business Year.** The annual accounting period, calendar or fiscal year, shall be established by the Bingo hall for which the Bingo hall maintains its books and records for purposes of subtitle A of Title 26 of the United States Code. The Bingo hall shall disseminate their business year to their team members. (31 CFR 103.64(b)(1) (2008))

4. **Provisions.** The following five (5) requirements shall be expounded on in this program:

a. A system of internal controls to assure ongoing compliance;

b. Internal and/or external independent test for compliance. The scope and frequency of the testing shall be commensurate with the money laundering and terrorist financing risks posed by the products and services provided by the Bingo hall;

c. Training of personnel, including training in the identification of unusual or suspicious transactions, to the extent that the reporting of such transactions is required by Title 31, by other applicable law or regulation, or by the enterprise's own administrative policies;

d. An individual or individuals to assure day-to-day compliance;

e. Procedures for using all available information to determine:

i. When required by Title 31, the name, address, social security number, and other information, and verification of the same person;

ii. The occurrence of any transactions or patterns of transactions required to be reported pursuant to 31 CFR 103.21;

iii. Whether any record as described in Title 31, pertaining to gaming, must be made and retained; and

5. **Agent.** For Title 31 purposes, any individual who conducts a currency transaction on behalf of another individual or organization shall be denoted as an "agent." (FinCEN Form 103 pg.3 *Definitions* (2008))

6. **Recording and Reporting.**

a. Multiple Transaction Log (MTL). Player's Club and Cage departments shall maintain a one-part log to record any, single or aggregate, transaction(s) of three-thousand dollars ($3,000) and greater.

i. A MTL shall be maintained in each monitoring location per gaming day.

ii. Cash-in (e.g., Bingo hall is receiving the currency) and cash-out (e.g., Bingo hall is issuing the currency) transactions shall **not** be combined for a net total. All cash-in transactions shall be aggregated per guest. All cash-out transactions shall be aggregated per guest.

iii. Each MTL shall have "page # of #" annotated with the appropriate number of pages used for that particular gaming day to ensure all pages of the MTL for that particular monitoring location is properly maintained and forwarded to the Title 31 Compliance Officer.

iv. Each MTL shall contain the following information for each logged transaction:

1. Description of the guest, and agent if applicable, which shall include at a minimum, age, sex, race, eye color, hair, weight, and height;

2. Guest's name, and agent's name if applicable, if known;

3. Guest's type of identification and the identification's number, if known;

4. Specific location where the transaction occurred (e.g., Main Cage , Window 3);

5. Military time and date of transaction (e.g., 4:00 p.m. is 16:00 and full date is 12/11/2008);

6. Type of transaction (e.g., chips purchased, cash deposit, check cashed, promotion payout);

7. U.S. dollar amount of transaction;

8. Any Bingo hall account number, available to that monitoring location, by which the Bingo hall identifies the guest with (e.g., player's card number);

9. Aggregate total of all like transactions (e.g., cash-in or cash-out) of the guest for the respective monitoring location; and

10. Signature of the team member and license number recording each transaction.

v. A MTL shall be completed for each monitoring location each gaming day. In the event no recordable transactions occurred for a monitoring location within a gaming day, "no activity" shall be written across the entire MTL, signed, and dated by the management designee for that monitoring location. The MTL shall be forwarded to the Title 31 Compliance Officer each gaming day.

vi. Single and aggregate transaction(s) less than three-thousand dollars ($3,000) may be recorded on the MTL.

vii. Corrections on a MTL shall be made by drawing a single line through the error. The team member making the correction shall sign their initials and employee license number next to the line. The team member then shall write the correct information in the appropriate area of the MTL.

viii. Management in each monitoring area shall ensure, per shift:

1. MTLs have been initiated for their respective areas;

2. Recordable transactions were documented immediately;

3. Guests with recorded, or potentially recordable, transactions on the MTL are made known to team members in their monitoring location as well as monitoring locations with similar currency transactions (e.g., cash-in or cash-out).

ix. Management in each monitoring location shall, at the end of the gaming day:
1. Ensure MTLs have been accurately completed for their respective monitoring location;
2. Review all available source documents (e.g., player rating, negotiable instrument log) for their respective monitoring location to ensure all recordable transactions have been recorded on the MTL;
3. Ensure any required *Currency Transaction Report by Casinos* (CTRC) have been accurately completed based on each guest's aggregate total transactions for that particular gaming day's MTLs;
4. Sign the MTL to attest and document who conducted the aforementioned three (3) steps; and
5. Forward all MTLs and CTRCs to the Title 31 Compliance Officer.
b. Negotiable Instrument Log (NIL). The Cage department and Player's Club, if applicable, shall maintain a chronological log of transactions between the Bingo hall and its guests involving negotiable instruments with face value of three-thousand dollars ($3,000) and greater. (31 CFR 103.36(b)(9)(i) (2008)
c. *Note: This program does not authorize the issuance or acceptance of any type of negotiable instrument. This program merely states how negotiable instruments shall be recorded and reported for Title 31 purposes. Refer to other internal controls, policies, procedures, and management directives to determine whether negotiable instruments stated within this program are authorized for issuance or acceptance.*
   i. Negotiable instruments to be logged shall be:
1. Personal checks
2. Business checks
3. Official bank checks;
4. Cashier's checks;
5. Third-party checks;
6. Promissory notes;
7. Traveler's checks; and
8. Money orders. (31 CFR 103.36(b)(9)(i)(A-H) (2008))
   ii. NIL shall contain the following for each logged negotiable instrument:
1. Military time (e.g., 4:00 p.m. is 16:00), date (e.g., 12/11/08), and U.S. dollar amount of the transaction;
2. Name and permanent address (*not* a P.O. Box) of the guest;
3. Type of negotiable instrument;
4. Name of the drawee or issuer of the instrument;
5. All reference numbers (e.g., player's club card number, personal check number, et cetera); and
6. Name and number of the team member who conducted the transaction. (31 CFR 103.36(b)(9)(ii) (2008)
   iii. Transactions shall be recorded in chronological order in which they occurred. (31 CFR 103.36(b)(9)(ii) (2008))
   iv. Whenever a record of a negotiable instrument is retained on microfilm or other copy or reproduction, both the front and back of the instrument shall be retained except in that there is no need to retain the back of any negotiable instrument when it is completely blank.
   v. A NIL shall be completed for each monitoring department each gaming day. In the event no recordable transactions occur for a monitoring department within a gaming day, "no activity" shall be written across the entire NIL, signed, and dated by the management designee for that monitoring location. The NIL shall be forwarded to the Title 31 Compliance Officer for each gaming day.
   vi. Cage and Player's Club, if applicable, management shall, at the end of the gaming day:
1. Ensure NILs have been accurately completed
2. Ensure all cash transactions resulting from the logged negotiable instruments have been accurately documented on the MTL;
3. Ensure any required *Currency Transaction Report by Casinos* (CTRC) have been accurately completed based on the logged negotiable instruments;
4. Sign the NIL to attest and document who conducted the aforementioned three (3) steps; and
5. Forward all NILs, MTLs, and CTRCs to the Title 31 Compliance Officer.
d. Safekeeping/Cage Deposit Receipt (inclusive of Front Money). A receipt shall be created for each deposit of funds, account opened or line of credit extended. (31 CFR 103.36 (a) (2008)
e. *Note: This program does not authorize the acceptance of guests' currency for deposit with the Bingo hall. This program merely states how guests' currency deposits shall be recorded and reported for Title 31 purposes. Refer to other internal controls, policies, procedures, and management directives to determine whether guests' currency deposits stated within this program are authorized.*
   i. At the time the funds are deposited or withdrawn, the account is opened or credit is extended, the following is secured and documented on the receipt:
1. Guest's name;
2. Permanent address (*not* P.O. Box);
3. Guest's social security number;
4. Guest's type of identification and identification number (if applicable);
5. Guest's signature;
6. Type of the transaction; and
7. U.S. dollar amount of the transaction by individual denominations and in total. (31 CFR 103.36(a) (2008)
   ii. Preprinted serial numbers shall be on safekeeping receipts and issued in sequential order.
   iii. In the event the deposit, account or credit is in the names of two (2) or more guests, the Bingo hall shall secure the name, permanent address, social security number of each guest having a financial interest in the deposit, account or line of credit. (31 CFR 103.36(a) (2008); ONGR § 404(a)(4) (2007))
   iv. The name and address of the guest shall be verified by the Bingo hall at the time the deposit is made and withdrawn, account opened, or credit extended. The verification shall be made by examination of valid government issued picture identification. (31 CFR 103.36(a), 103.28 (2008))

1. A guest who is a nonresident alien shall also have their passport number or a description of some other government document used to verify their identity. (31 CFR 103.36(a) (2008)
2. [reserved]
   v. In the event that the Bingo hall was unable to secure the social security number for a safekeeping receipt, it shall **not** be deemed to be in violation of Title 31 if:
1. The Bingo hall made a reasonable effort to obtain the social security number; and
2. The Bingo hall maintains a list containing the names and permanent addresses of those guests from who it has been unable to obtain social security numbers and makes the names and addresses of those guests available to FinCEN/IRS upon request. (31 CFR 103.36(a) (2008)
   vi. A copy of each safekeeping receipt, for that respective gaming day, documenting when funds are deposited or withdrawn, the account is opened or credit is extended shall be forwarded to the Title 31 Compliance Officer at the end of each gaming day.
f. <u>Currency Transaction Report by Casinos (CTRC; FinCEN Form 103).</u> A CTRC shall be reported for any single or aggregate currency transaction(s) exceeding ten-thousand dollars ($10,000) in a single gaming day by a guest(s), and their agent(s) if applicable. (31 CFR 103.22 (2008)
   i. Player's Club, if applicable and Cage departments shall maintain on file within their departments an unused FinCEN Form 103, inclusive of instructions, in both hard-copy and electronic format.
   ii. FinCEN Form 103 shall be available to all departments by contacting the Title 31 Compliance Officer.
   iii. Management in each monitoring area shall ensure, per shift:
1. Guests with recorded, or potentially recordable, transactions on the MTL are made known to team members in their monitoring location as well as monitoring locations with similar currency transactions (e.g., cash-in or cash-out); and
2. Guests who have reportable, or potentially reportable, transactions on a CTRC are made known to team members in their monitoring location to ensure guests do not exceed $10,000 in a gaming day without providing required information and to ensure all cash-in and cash-out transactions are accurately reported on a CTRC.
   iv. Team members shall obtain and verify all required guest information **prior** to a guest, or an agent on their behalf, completing a transaction that in itself exceeds $10,000 or makes their aggregate currency transaction total to exceed $10,000 for the gaming day. (31 CFR 103.28 (2008)
1. In the event a transaction occurs on behalf of more than one guest, required information shall be obtained and verified for each guest. (e.g., a check made jointly out to two (2) guests, two (2) guests sharing the same buy-ins and bankroll on table games) (31 CFR 103.28 (2008); FinCEN Form 103 pg.3 *Specific Instructions* Section A (2008))
2. In the event a transaction occurs on behalf of an organization, required information shall be obtained and verified for the organization. (e.g., a check made out to a business) (31 CFR 103.28 (2008); FinCEN Form 103 pg.3 *Specific Instructions* Section A (2008))
   v. In the event required information cannot be obtained, team members shall **not** conduct a currency transaction with the guest, or agent, when the currency transaction in itself exceeds $10,000 or makes their aggregate currency transaction total exceed $10,000 for the gaming day.
   vi. Team members who know the guest, and agent if applicable, who is conducting the transaction may, in lieu of requesting the required information, use information previously obtained from the guest, and agent if applicable, which is maintained on file.
1. Prior to relying on information on file, the team member shall review the information on file to ensure it has not expired and it is inclusive of all required information.
2. Information on file shall be periodically reviewed to ensure the identification on file has not expired and noted when the verification occurred. (FinCEN Form 103 pg.2 *General Instructions* Identification Requirements (2008))
3. Information on file shall be periodically reviewed to ensure it is still accurate (e.g., permanent address) and noted when the verification occurred. (FinCEN Form 103 pg.2 *General Instructions* Identification Requirements (2008))
4. Information shall be updated by examination of an original valid government issued picture identification. (FinCEN Form 103 pg2. *General Instructions* Identification Requirements (2008))
5. Information shall be reported on the CTRC. Documenting "known customer" in lieu of reporting the specifics of the guest's identifying information is strictly prohibited. (31 CFR 103.28 (2008); FinCEN Form 103 pg.3 *Specific Instructions* Section A Item 14 (2008))
   vii. The guest's and agent's, if applicable, required information is:
1. Guest's name;
2. Guest's address;
3. Guest's Player's Club account number, if applicable;
4. Guest's social security number or taxpayer identification number;
5. Type of guest's identification;
6. Government who issued the guest's identification; and
7. Guest's identification number. (31 CFR 103.28 (2008); FinCEN Form 103 pg.3 *Specific Instructions* Section A (2008))
   viii. The guest's and agent's, if applicable, information shall be verified with a valid government issued picture identification. (31 CFR 103.28 (2008))
   ix. Team members shall obtain and retain a copy of the guest's and agent's, if applicable, valid government issued picture identification.
   x. In the event a reportable transaction occurred without obtaining the required information:
1. The guest and agent, if applicable, shall be prohibited from further currency transactions until such time required information is provided and properly verified;
2. An immediate e-mail notification shall be sent to the Director of Compliance;
3. An immediate e-mail notification shall be sent to the Title 31 Compliance Officer
4. An incomplete CTRC shall be prepared and reported; and
5. An amended CTRC shall be prepared and reported once the required information is obtained and properly verified.
   xi. The Bingo hall is **not** obligated to report the following currency transactions:

1. Transactions between the Bingo hall and a currency exchange dealer or exchanger, or between a Bingo hall and a check cashing service so long as such transactions are conducted pursuant to a contractual or other arrangement with the Bingo hall covering the financial services;

2. Bills inserted into electronic gaming devices in multiple transactions unless the Bingo hall has knowledge of such transactions by any sole proprietor, partner, officer, director, or team member of the Bingo hall, while acting within the scope of their employment, has knowledge that such transactions have occurred, including knowledge from examining the books, records, logs, information retained on magnetic disk, tape or other machine-readable media, or in any manual system, and similar documents and information, which the Bingo hall maintains pursuant to any law or regulations or within the ordinary course of its business, and which contain information that such transactions have occurred; and

3. Jackpots from slot machines or video lottery terminals. (31 CFR 103.22(b)(iii) (2008)

xii. Disclosure.

1. Team members may, but are not required to, disclose to the persons, whom a CTRC was reported on based on their currency transactions, that a CTRC was reported regarding their currency transactions.

2. Upon the request of the persons, whom a CTRC was reported on based on their currency transactions, a copy of the CTRC reported regarding their currency transactions shall be provided to the persons making the request.

xiii. Management shall, at the end of the gaming day:

1. Review all available source documents (e.g., MTL, player rating, NIL, Safekeeping Receipt) for their respective monitoring location to ensure all reportable transactions have been reported on a CTRC;

2. Inquire with management from the other monitoring locations to ensure all reportable transactions are included on a CTRC;

3. Ensure one (1) CTRC was accurately completed for each guest and their agent, if applicable, who had currency transactions exceeding ten-thousand dollars ($10,000) for that particular gaming day;

4. Ensure that "NOT APPLICABLE" was documented in *item 16* of the CTRC in the event the guest does not have a Players Club account number

5. Ensure that *item 30* is marked when the guest had multiple transactions without any of them in themselves exceeding $10,000;

6. Ensure that *item 15* is thoroughly completed even if *item 14's b* "Known Customer" was marked;

7. Sign the CTRC to attest and document who conducted the aforementioned six (6) steps; and

8. Forward all CTRCs and copies of identifications to the Title 31 Compliance Officer.

xiv. Title 31 Compliance Officer shall file all CTRCs with the IRS by the fifteenth (15th) calendar day after the transaction(s) occurred. (31 CFR 103.27(a)(1) (2008); FinCEN Form 103 pg.2 *General Instructions* (2008)

xv. Title 31 Compliance Officer shall file an amended CTRC in the event CTRC previously filed with the IRS had incomplete or inaccurate information.

1. Title 31 Compliance Officer shall mark *item 1* on the CTRC to designate the CTRC is amending a prior CTRC. (FinCEN Form 103 pg.3 *Specific Instructions* Item 1 (2008))

2. Title 31 Compliance Officer shall complete *Part 3* on the CTRC in its entirety. (FinCEN Form 103 pg.3 *Specific Instructions* Item 1 (2008))

3. Title 31 Compliance Officer shall only complete the other parts of the CTRC that need amending. (FinCEN Form 103 pg.3 *Specific Instructions* Item 1 (2008))

4. Title 31 Compliance Officer shall file the amended CTRC with a copy of the original CTRC being amended. In the event of electronic filling, Title 31 Compliance Officer shall follow the current instructions provided by the IRS regarding the copy of the original CTRC. (FinCEN Form 103 pg.3 *Specific Instructions* Item 1 (2008))

xvi. Statistical Log. Title 31 Compliance Officer shall maintain a statistical log stating, at the minimum, the following:

1. Quantity of CTRCs amended per month for each property;

2. Quantity of CTRCs filed per month for each property; and

3. Quantity of CTRCs filed per calendar year for each property.

g. Suspicious Activity Report by Casinos and Card Clubs (SARC; FinCEN Form 102 and FinCEN Form 102a). A SARC shall be reported for a transaction or pattern of transactions that are conducted or attempted by, at, or through the Bingo hall, and involves or aggregates at least five-thousand dollars ($5,000) in funds or other assets, and the Bingo hall knows, suspects, or has reason to suspect that the transaction:

Involves funds derived from illegal activity or is intended or conducted in order to hide or disguise funds or assets derived from illegal activity (including, without limitation, the ownership, nature, source, location, or control of such funds or assets as part of a plan to violate or evade any federal law or regulation or to avoid any transaction reporting requirement under federal law or regulation;

Is designed, whether through structuring or other means, to evade any requirements of Title 31;

Has no business or apparent lawful purpose or is not the sort in which the particular customer would normally be expected to engage, and the Bingo hall knows of no reasonable explanation for the transaction after examining the available facts, including the background and possible purpose of the transaction; or

Involves use of the Bingo hall to facilitate criminal activity. (31 CFR 103.21(a)(2), 103.64(a)(2)(v)(B), 103.120(d) (2008)

SARC may be voluntarily reported whenever a team member believes activity is relevant to the possible violation of any law or regulation but whose reporting is not required by Title 31. (31 CFR 103.21(b)(1) (2008))

i. The Bingo hall is not required to file a SARC for a robbery or burglary committed or attempted that is reported to appropriate law enforcement authorities. (31 CFR 103.21(c) (2008)

ii. Security, Food and Beverage, Player's Club, Player Development, Gaming Machine and Cage departments shall maintain on file within their departments an unused FinCEN Form 102, inclusive of instructions (FinCEN Form 102a), in both hard-copy and electronic format.

iii. FinCEN Form 102 shall be available to all departments by contacting the Title 31 Compliance Officer.

iv. Team members shall inform their immediate management representative whenever they believe possible suspicious activity has or is occurring.

v. Management shall have the team member who witnessed the possible suspicious activity complete, in clear chronological detail, the *narrative, Part VI*, of a SARC. There are twenty (20) critical checklist items provided as guidance within *Part VI* when completing the narrative. (FinCEN Form 102 (2008))

vi. Upon completion of their narrative, the team member shall sign the SARC.

vii. Management shall notify surveillance immediately of any possible suspicious activity.

viii. Management shall be due diligent in investigating the possible suspicious activity to determine all available information pertaining to the guest(s) that has or is conducting possible suspicious activity. During the investigation, management shall review FinCEN Form 102 to determine what information to attempt to obtain and document.

ix. After the end of the gaming day, SARCs shall be forwarded to the Title 31 Compliance Officer for review.

x. The Title 31 Compliance Officer shall review, and investigate as needed, all completed SARCs within one (1) calendar week of when the possible suspicious activity occurred.

xi. The Title 31 Compliance Officer shall make the final determination of whether activity is reportable under Title 31 Code of Federal Regulations Part 103. The Title 31 Compliance Officer shall either:

1. Complete and file a SARC with FinCEN in the event the Title 31 Compliance Officer determines reportable suspicious activity has occurred; or

2. Complete a summary of their investigation and reasoning why the activity was not reportable and noting a SARC was not filed with FinCEN.

xii. A required SARC shall be filed with FinCEN within thirty (30) days of the date of the initial detection by the Bingo hall of the facts that may constitute the required basis for filing a SARC. (31 CFR 103.21(b)(2)-(3) (2008)

xiii. In the event the guest cannot be identified for a required SARC, a required SARC shall be filed with FinCEN within sixty (60) days of the date of the initial detection by the Bingo hall of the facts that may constitute the required basis for filing a SARC. During the additional thirty (30) day period, the Bingo hall shall be due diligent in attempting to identify the guest for the SARC. (31 CFR 103.21(b)(2)-(3) (2008)

xiv. Urgent Filing/Notification. The Title 31 Compliance Officer shall contact the appropriate law enforcement authorities via telephone, in addition to filing a SARC, in the event the suspicious activity requires immediate attention (e.g., ongoing money laundering scheme). (31 CFR 103.21(b)(3) (2008))

xv. Terrorist Related Transactions. Bingo hallss may voluntarily report suspicious transactions that may relate to terrorist activity by calling FinCEN's Financial Institutions Hotline at 1-866-556-3974 in addition to filing a SARC. (31 CFR 103.21(b)(3) (2008)) ·

xvi. Notification Prohibited. Team members may **not** notify any person involved in the suspicious activity that has been reported. Thus, any person subpoenaed or otherwise requested to disclose a SARC or the information contained in a SARC, except where such disclosure is requested by FinCEN or another appropriate law enforcement or regulatory agency, shall decline to produce the SARC or to provide any information what would disclose that a SARC has been prepared or filed and shall notify FinCEN of any such request. (31 U.S.C. 5318(g)(3) (2008); 31 CFR 103.21(e) (2008)

xvii. Safe Harbor. The enterprise and team members are protected from liability for any disclosure contained in, or for failure to disclose the fact of, such report, or both, to the extent provided by 31 U.S.C 5318(g)(3). (31 CFR 103.21(e) (2008))

xviii. Statistical Log. Title 31 Compliance Officer shall maintain a statistical log stating, at the minimum, the following:

1. Quantity of SARCs investigated per month for each property;

2. Quantity of SARCs filed per month for each property; and

3. Quantity of SARCs filed per calendar year for each property.

7. **Auditing and Monitoring.** The enterprise shall implement and maintain on ongoing system of auditing and monitoring of the Title 31 requirements.

a. Day-to-Day Compliance. The Title 31 Compliance Officer shall be the primary person to assure the ongoing day-to-day compliance with Title 31 requirements. (31 CFR 103.64(a)(2)(iv) (2008)

i. On a daily or weekly basis, the Title 31 Compliance Officer shall perform a compliance audit to ensure enterprise-wide:

1. Supporting Title 31 documentation is accounted for;

2. Qualified cash transactions have been properly documented in the Bingo halls Title 31 records;

3. Qualified cash transactions have been properly aggregated for the purpose of determining if they meet the reporting requirements of Title 31;

4. Reportable transactions have been filed on a CTRC and/or a SARC to IRS/FinCEN in the required timeframe; and

5. The CTRC and/or SARC filed are completed in an accurate manner and reflect the enterprise's internal records.

ii. It is the affirmative duty of the Title 31 Compliance Officer to augment the Title 31 compliance audit process when necessary to ensure ongoing compliance with Title 31 requirements.

iii. The Title 31 Compliance Officer shall design processes that utilize the enterprise's automated data processing systems, when the enterprise or Bingo has an automated data processing system, to aid in assuring compliance with Title 31 reporting requirements. (31 CFR 103.64(a)(2)(vi) (2008)

b. Audited Documents. In order to perform a thorough and efficient audit, the following documents shall be obtained by the Title 31 Compliance Officer from the areas in the Bingo hall charged with Title 31 record keeping responsibilities. The receipt of these documents shall be recorded on a Title 31 Document Control Log.

i. The Title 31 Document Control Log shall document the receipt of the following documents:

1. All cash-in MTLs;

2. All cash-out MTLs;

3. All NILs;

4. All Safekeeping/Cage Deposit receipts, if applicable;

5. All CTRCs; and

6. All SARCs.

ii. Other documents deemed helpful or necessary by the Title 31 Compliance Officer to conduct an adequate compliance audit shall be obtained, such documents may include, but not limited to:

1. Checks cashed report;
2. Table game pit rating summary report; or
3. Table game pit rating slips.
c. Audit. The Title 31 Compliance Officer shall agree all source documents to the Title 31 documents (e.g., all checks of $3,000 were documented on the NIL accurately, all rated cash buy-ins of $3,000 were documented on the MTL, and et cetera).
d. Exception Reports. The Title 31 Compliance Officer shall issue exception reports to the appropriate department head in the event Title 31 documentation or source documents were not completed and processed according to the enterprise's established Title 31 procedures.
   i. The exception report shall be issued within one (1) calendar day of detecting the exception.
   ii. The Title 31 Compliance Officer shall retain a copy of the exception report.
   iii. Within three (3) calendar days of receiving an exception report, the department head shall respond to the Title 31 Compliance Officer with any information as necessary to complete the Title 31 audit or adequate corrective action to ensure ongoing compliance.
   iv. In the event a response has not been issued within the required timeframe, the Title 31 Compliance Officer shall e-mail the department head, director of compliance, and general manager stating the response is past due.
e. Filing Reports. The following are the team members who shall file reports with the IRS/FinCEN and be those agencies' point of contact in regards to reports filed with those agencies.
   i. The Title 31 Compliance Officer shall file all necessary CTRCs and SARCs on the enterprise's behalf with approval from the Director of Compliance, who acts as the enterprise's "approving official."
   ii. The Title 31 Compliance Officer shall be the "person to contact" for filed CTRCs and SARCs.
f. Independent Review. The Compliance department, which is independent of the Title 31 Compliance Officer and all Title 31 processes, shall, at a minimum, conduct one (1) compliance risk assessment annually to ensure ongoing compliance with Title 31 requirements. (31 CFR 103.64(a)(2)(ii) (2008)
   i. The compliance review shall be inclusive of:
1. Sufficient sampling of documents that were generated to comply with this program;
2. Procedural observations and team member inquiries concerning the effective implementation of this program;
3. Determination of the adequacy and documentation of the training program implemented to comply with this program;
4. Determination if previously noted remedies to deviations of this program have been effectively implemented; and
5. Any perceived enhancements to policies, processes, and documentation as they relate to Title 31 requirements.
   ii. Compliance shall issue a report inclusive of:
1. Period of time reviewed;
2. Any noted deviations from this program;
3. Any needed remedies to noted deviations;
4. Department's and enterprise's location accountable for deviations and remedies;
5. Time period in which remedies are to be implemented;
6. Management responses to any noted deviations from this program; and
7. All enterprise team members the report was disseminated to.
B. **Training.** A comprehensive training program shall be implemented to provide Bingo hall personnel the requirements of this program including the identification of unusual or suspicious transaction. (31 CFR 103.64 (a)(2)(iii) (2008)
a. Orientation. Team members shall successfully participate in Title 31 training before they are permitted to function in any capacity that may include Title 31 reporting, record keeping, and compliance.
b. Required Participants. The following team members shall successfully participate in the Title 31 training program, at a minimum, annually:
   i. Player's Club: all team members;
   ii. Player Development: all team members;
   iii. Finance: Controller, Revenue Audit Manager/Supervisor, any auditors conducting or assisting in the Title 31/BSA audit;
   iv. Cage: all team members;
   v. Food and Beverage: Beverage Servers, Bartenders, and F & B Managers/Supervisors;
   vi. Security: all team members;
   vii. Gaming Machine Department: all team members
c. Permitted Participants.
   i. Any team member, who is not required to participate in training, may participate in the training program at the Title 31 Compliance Officer's discretion.
d. Increased Frequency. More frequent participation may be required if updated regulations, procedures, or other related information must be incorporated into the training.
e. Approval. The training program shall be approved by the Title 31 Compliance Officer.
. Content. Training shall be inclusive of:
   i. Presenting materials such as a copy of CTRC, SARC, MTL, NIL, Safekeeping/Cage Deposit Receipt, if applicable, this program, and/or any other appropriate training exhibits;
   ii. Reviewing and explaining the purpose, use, and completion requirements of each Title 31 form and how they are used;
   iii. Explaining prohibited transactions, loggable transactions, reportable transactions, and suspicious transactions;
   iv. Reviewing duties, responsibilities, and procedures associated with each team member's position; and
   v. Explaining the consequences of noncompliance with Title 31.
g. Additional Content. More exhaustive training shall be incorporated within the training program on the identification of suspicious and unusual activity, which shall include, at a minimum, the following activity:
   i. Attempt to evade or avoid CTRC filing;
   ii. Pressure not to file CTRC or other form;

427

iii. Minimal Play;
iv. Identification Issues;
v. Currency Exchanges;
vi. Using Bingo hall for Financial Transactions; and
vii. Illegal or Unusual Activity. (*Suspicious Activity Reporting Guidance for Casinos* (12/03); *Examples of Suspicious Bingo hall Transactions and Activities* (7/98))

9. **Forms**. Only approved forms disseminated by the Title 31 Compliance Officer shall be utilized in logging and reporting transactions governed by this program. Such forms shall include, but not limited to, the following:
a. Title 31 Document Control Log;
b. Multiple Transaction Log;
c. Negotiable Instrument Log;
d. Safekeeping/Cage Deposit Receipt, if applicable;
e. Currency Transaction Report by Casinos; and
f. Suspicious Activity Report by Card Clubs and Casinos.

10. **Document Retention**. Documentation generated to comply with this program shall be retained, at a minimum, for five (5) years. (31 CFR 103.38(d) (2008)

11. **Note:** This program does <u>not</u> authorize the issuance of credit or acceptance of guests' currency for deposit with the Bingo hall. This program merely states how guests' extension of credit and currency deposits shall be recorded and reported for Title 31 purposes. Refer to other internal controls, policies, procedures, and management directives to determine whether issuance of credit or currency deposits stated within this program are authorized.

a. Required Documents. Either the original or a microfilm or other copy or reproduction of each of the following documents shall be retained:
i. Safekeeping/Cage Deposit receipt for each deposit and withdrawal;
ii. Record of each bookkeeping entry comprising a debit or credit to a guest's deposit account or credit account with the Bingo hall;
iii. Each statement or other record of each deposit or credit account with the Bingo hall, showing each transaction in or with respect to, a guest's deposit account or credit account with the Bingo hall;
iv. A record of each advice, request or instruction received or given by the Bingo hall or itself or another person with respect to a transaction involving a guest, account or place outside the United States;
v. Records prepared or received by the Bingo hall in the ordinary course of business which would be needed to reconstruct a guest's deposit account or credit account with the Bingo hall or to trace a check deposited with the Bingo hall through the Bingo hall's records to the bank of deposit;
vi. All records, documents or manuals required to be maintained by a Bingo hall under local laws or regulations;
vii. All records which are prepared or used by a Bingo hall to monitor a guest's gaming activity;
viii. NILs and negotiable instruments logged on the NILs;
ix. Copy of this compliance program;
x. MTLs;
xi. Filed CTRCs;
xii. Filed SARCs; and
xiii. Non-filed SARCs and supporting investigation summary. (31 CFR 103.21(d), 103.27(a)(3), 103.36(b) (2008))

b. Electronic Records.
i. If the Bingo hall inputs, stores, or retains, in whole or in part, for any period of time, any record required to be maintained for Title 31 purposes on computer disk, tape, or machine-readable media shall retain the same on computer disk, tape, or machine-readable media. (31 CFR 103.36(c)(1) (2008))
ii. All indexes, books, programs, record layouts, manuals, formats, instructions, file descriptions, and similar materials which would enable a person readily to access and review the records for Title 31 purposes that are input, stored, or retained on computer disk, tape, or other machine-readable media shall be retained. (31 CFR 103.36(c)(2) (2008))

c. Training Records. Documents and manuals demonstrating the training program and the training that was provided to individual team members shall be kept for a minimum of one (1) year after the date it is superseded.

Section III—Title 31 Compliance Program Risk Assessments

1. **Risk Assessment**. Risk based assessment shall be conducted for each gaming facility to determine sufficiency of the current Title 31 Compliance Program.

a. **Risk Factors**. Risk assessment shall take into consideration the following factors, at the minimum:
i. Size of gaming facility;
1. Quantity of electronic gaming machines;
2. Quantity of cage windows;
ii. Location of the gaming facility;
iii. Volume of annual revenues;
iv. Type of games at the gaming facility;
v. Type of services at the gaming facility; and
vi. Nature of patrons. (31 CFR 103.64(a)(1)(ii) (2008))
vii. **Assessor**. Risk assessment shall be conducted by the Title 31 Compliance Officer(s). (ONGR § 405(a) (2007))
b. **Frequency**. Risk assessment shall be conducted annually for each gaming facility. (31 CFR   103.64(a)(1)(ii) (2008); ONGR § 405(c)(2) (2007))

c. **Results.**
i. Title 31 Compliance Officer(s) shall report results to:
1. General Manager; and
2. Director of Compliance.

428

ii.   Report shall contain:
1.   Whether the Title 31 Compliance Program is sufficient for the gaming facility;
2.   Any discovered deficiencies in the Title 31 Compliance Program; and
3.   Any recommendations to remediate deficiencies in the Title 31 Compliance Program.
2.   **Risk Assessment Documentation.** Title 31 Compliance Officer(s) shall retain risk assessment documentation for five (5) years. (31 CFR 103.38(d) (2008);

[67] Goldman Sachs Global Investment Research, Americas: Gaming, Steven Kant, CFA

[68] ibid

[69] ibid

[70] ibid

[71] I have seen some really shyster documents purporting to be feasibility studies. For a legitimate study I usually turn to one of the well-established independent companies like The Innovation Group, Klas Robinson, or one of the other well-established and reputable providers.

[72] Op. cit.

[73] Following is an example of Tribal Policies and Procedures:

DEFINITIONS
The Tribal Gaming Ordinance contains definitions that explain different phrases contained in the Ordinance. These definitions relate to standard gaming industry terminology.

PUBLIC POLICY
The Tribe's public policy is:

Section 102   A.   The Public Gaming Commission shall be charged with the sole responsibility of administering and enforcing the provisions of this Code.

B.   It shall be the responsibility of the Public Gaming Commission to promulgate regulations necessary to administer the provisions of this Code. These duties shall include but are not limited to the following:

1.   Printing and making available application forms for initial and renewal licenses, as well as any other necessary licenses.
2.   Supervising the collection of all licensing fees prescribed in this Code and other ordinances in regard to gaming and gaming related activities.

3.   Processing all license applications.
4.   Issuing licenses.
5.   Determining applicable license fees.

6.   Auditing all casino revenues.
7.   Review all gaming operation contracts, records, documents, and anything else necessary and pertinent to the financial accountabilities of licensees or enforcement of any provision of gaming operation contracts, and agreements of this and related ordinances.
8.   The Public Gaming Commission shall have the power and authority to deny any application, to limit, condition, suspend, or restrict any license, make a finding of suitability or approval of the license, or a finding of suitability or approval of or the imposition of a fine upon any person licensed for any cause deemed reasonable by the Public Gaming Commission, or to make assessment for money owed the Tribe of State by contract or taxation and to levy collection of the same with or without notice.
9.   The performance of any other duties required in the Code or any amendments thereto or other duties that may hereafter be specified by the Public Gaming Commission.
10.   Defend their actions in any court of competent jurisdiction or initiate any actions with consent of the Executive Committee.

Section 103   The Public Gaming Commission may exercise any proper power and authority necessary to perform the duties assigned by this Code, and is not limited by any enumeration of powers in this chapter.

Section 104   The Public Gaming Commission may refuse to reveal, at any court proceedings, the identity of any informant, if such revelation would subject the informant to bodily harm.

Section 105   Regular and special meetings of the Public Gaming Commission may be held, at the discretion of the Public Gaming Commission, at such time and places as may be convenient and open to tribal members, with notice posted in a public place at le twenty-four (24) hours prior to the meeting.

Section 106   The Public Gaming Commission may organize and form divisions as may be necessary and from time to time alter such plan of organization as may be expedient. The Public Gaming Commission shall recommend the budget for operations to the Executive Committee, and take any other steps necessary to fulfill duties and responsibilities under the Code.

Section 107   In adopting, amending, or repealing any regulations under this Code, the Public Gaming Commission shall give prior notice of the proposed action to all licensees and other persons whom the Public Gaming Commission has reason to believe have a legitimate and bona fide interest in such proposed action.

Section 108   The Public Gaming Commission shall afford an applicant for a license or permit an opportunity for a hearing prior to final action denying such applications and shall afford a licensee or any other person(s) subject to the Code the opportunity for a hearing prior to taking final action resulting in terminating, revoking, suspending, or limiting a license or any other adverse action the Public Gaming Commission deems appropriate; provided, that the Public Gaming Commission may summarily temporarily suspend or extend suspension of license for sixty (60) days in those cases where such action is deemed appropriate by the Public Gaming Commission. In cases where a license is suspended prior to a hearing, an opportunity for a hearing shall be provided.

Section 109   Whenever upon a specific factual finding the Public Gaming Commission determines that any person has failed to comply with the provisions of this Code or any regulation promulgated hereunder, the Public Gaming Commission shall make a certification of findings with a copy

429

thereof to the subject or subjects of that determination. After five (5) days notice, and within ninety (90) days thereof, the Public Gaming Commission shall hold a hearing at which time the subject shall have opportunity to be heard and present evidence.

Section 110   At such hearing it shall be the obligation of the subject to show cause why the determination is incorrect, why the application in question shall not be denied, why the license, licenses, or permit in question shall not be revoked or suspended, why the period of suspension should not be extended, or to show cause why special conditions or limitations upon a license or permit should not be imposed, or to show cause why any other action regarding any other person or persons subject to any action should not be taken.

Section 111   Following such hearing the Public Gaming Commission shall within seven (7) days, reach a determination concerning the accuracy of the preliminary certification of facts and whether the license in question should be granted, continued or suspended, revoked, conditioned or limited, and whether or not any other action recommended to or by the Commission (including but not limited to forfeitures or fines) should be taken.

Section 112   Wherever else in the Tribal Gaming Code the term "Commissioner" is used it shall mean the Public Gaming Commission.

ESTABLISHMENT
The Tribal Gaming Commission has been previously established and shall consist of three (3) members (Section 101).

AUTHORITY AND INSPECTION ACCESS
The Commission shall exercise all powers to enforce the Ordinance. The Commission shall have the power and authority to limit, revoke, restrict or suspend any license. The Commission can impose fines and sanctions for any cause deemed reasonable by the Commission (section 102). Gaming Commissioners and Gaming Commission employees and representatives (including but not limited to the Executive Director, the Internal Auditor, the Compliance Officer, the Background Investigator, or any other approved gaming commission representative) have the right to inspect any area of the gaming facility, as well as any record, report, or document, etc., at any time. Inspections shall be unrestricted, immediate, and unhindered. Gaming Commissioners and employees have the authority:

1.   To inspect and examine all premises wherein gaming is conducted or gaming devices or equipment are used, manufactured, sold or distributed.

2.   To inspect all equipment and supplies in, upon, or about a gaming establishment, or inspect any equipment or supplies wherever located, which may, or have been, used in the gaming establishment.

3.   To summarily seize and remove from the gaming establishment (or wherever located) and impound such equipment or supplies for the purpose of examination, inspection, evidence, or forfeiture.

4.   To seize and impound any patron's winnings which the Gaming Commission has reason to believe may have been won or obtained in violation of the Tribal Gaming Ordinance pending a civil forfeiture hearing on such seizure.

EXECUTIVE DIRECTOR
The Executive Director is responsible for the protection of the integrity of all gaming and gaming related activities at the Gaming Center. He/she is also accountable for ensuring all policies and procedures are in compliance with the Indian Gaming Regulatory Act (IGRA), the National Indian Gaming Commission (NIGC) Rules and Regulations, the Tribal Gaming Ordinance, the Minimum Internal Control Standards as adopted by the tribe, and the Tribal-State Compact (when applicable). The Executive Director oversees the Licensing Division, Compliance, and Gaming Commission Auditing Departments.

LICENSE PROCEDURES
The following are required to be licensed:
1.   Management Entity or Shareholder
2.   Primary Management Official
3.   Key Employees
4.   Suppliers of Gaming goods and services
5.   Any other employee deemed necessary to be licensed.
6.   Gaming Establishment.

Violations of any provision of the Ordinance or the rules shall be deemed contrary to public health, safety of the Tribe and shall be grounds for license revocation or suspension (Section 102.B.08).

The Gaming Commission shall license every key employee of the gaming operation. The Gaming Commission shall formulate decisions regarding the suitability or eligibility of each applicant to be issued or denied a gaming license, or to have a license suspended or revoked.

Gaming licenses shall serve as the only acceptable identification badge to be worn by all employees. Every employee shall at all times, while on duty, wear the license plainly visible and at approximately chest height.

BACKGROUND INVESTIGATION
Background Investigations shall be conducted by the Commission on all Management Officials, Key Employees, Gaming Suppliers and Vendors, and any other employee of the Gaming Center as directed by the gaming ordinance (section 102).

Licensees shall be legally responsible for any violation of this Ordinance, rules, Tribal-State Compact (when applicable), or IGRA. Any license can be limited, revoked, suspended by the Commission after a hearing as provided in the Tribal Gaming Ordinance (section 102).

HEARING PROCEDURES
Section 108 of the Tribal Gaming Ordinance shall govern all license hearings, enforcement hearings, and exclusion hearings conducted by the Gaming Commission. The Commission shall afford an Applicant an opportunity for a hearing prior to any final action by the Commission on an application.

The Commission shall afford a Licensee the opportunity for a hearing prior to taking final action resulting in the revocation of the License or the imposition of any penalties, which the Commission is authorized to impose pursuant to this Ordinance.

The Commission shall provide written notice to the Applicant or Licensee of the hearing at le ten (10) business days excluding weekends and holidays prior to the date set for the hearing.

Any member of the Commission who receives an ex parte communication shall immediately report such communication to the Commission's legal counsel.

All evidence, including records and documents in the possession of the Commission or which the Commission desires to avail itself, shall be duly offered and made a part of the record in the case.

APPEALS
A person directly affected by any finding of the Commission pursuant to this Ordinance, or any licensing decision of the Commission under this Ordinance, shall have the right to appeal such finding by filing for a rehearing before the Commission (Section 109).

AUDITING
The Commission shall promulgate rules governing the control of internal fiscal affairs of all Gaming Operations (Section 102).

Any delay or action of any kind, which, in the opinion of the Commission, is effectuated by any Licensee to unlawfully or improperly divert Gaming or other proceeds properly belonging to the Tribe, shall constitute grounds for taking disciplinary action against that Licensee.

If the Commission finds an unlawful diversion was attempted, it may sanction the Licensee, report the matter to appropriate law enforcement and gaming regulatory agencies for further action, and take such action as it deems necessary or appropriate. Sanctions may include the imposition of fines and/or the revocation, suspension, or limitation of or refusal to renew and license (Section 102).

Failure to comply with any of the requirements of this Chapter or the rules promulgated hereunder may be found to constitute a violation of this Ordinance (Section 102).

EXCLUSION PROCEDURES

It shall be a violation of this Ordinance for any Licensee to knowingly fail to exclude or eject from the gaming area of a Gaming Establishment any individual who:

1. Is visibly under the influence of liquor, a drug or other intoxicating substance.
2. Is under the age of 21.
3. Is displaying disorderly conduct.
4. Is a person known to have committed a gaming related felony.
5. Is known to have a reputation for cheating or manipulation of games.
6. Has been personally excluded or is a member of any group or type of persons which has been excluded for cause from the Gaming Establishment by a resolution of the Commission (Section 111).

If the Commission deems it in the best interest of the Tribe, the Commission may exclude or remove any persons from the venues of any Gaming Operation.

The General Manager of any Gaming Operation shall also have the authority to exclude or remove any persons.

PROHIBITED ACTS

Pursuant to the Tribal Gaming Ordinance it is unlawful for any person to:

1. Alter or misrepresent the outcome of a game or other event on which wagers have been made after the outcome of such game or event has been determined but before such outcome is revealed to the players.
2. Place, increase or decrease a bet after acquiring knowledge of the outcome of the game (i.e. p posting or pressing a bet).
3. Aid anyone in acquiring such knowledge for the purposes of increasing or decreasing any bet or wager, or for the purpose of determining the course of play.
4. Defraud by claiming, taking, collecting, or attempting to claim money or anything of value from a game. Collecting or taking an amount greater that the amount actually won in such game.
5. Reducing the amount of the wager (i.e. pinching a bet).
6. Manipulating with the intent to cheat or defraud any component or part of a game in a manner contrary to the designed and normal operational purpose for such component or part.
7. Defrauding the tribe, employee or patron in any gaming operation;
8. Participating in any gaming not authorized under this Ordinance;
9. Knowingly provide false information or making any false statement with respect to an application for employment;
10. Knowingly provide false information or making any false statement to the Tribe, the Commission, or the Executive Director in connection with any contract for services or property related to gaming;
11. Knowingly provide false information or making any false statement in response to any official inquiry by the Commissions or its agents;
12. Offering or attempting to offer anything of value to an employee in an attempt to induce the employee to act or refrain from acting in a manner contrary to the official duties;
13. Acceptance by a employee of anything of value with the expectation that receipt of such thing of value is intended or may be perceived as intended to induce the employee to act or refrain from acting in a manner contrary to the official duties of the employee under this Ordinance;
14. Falsifying, destroying, erasing or altering any books, computer data, records or other information relating to a Gaming Operation in ways other than is provided in the approved MICS;
15. Taking any action that interferes with or prevents the Gaming Commission from fulfilling its duties and responsibilities under the Ordinance;
16. Entering into any contract or making payment on any contract for the delivery for goods or services to the Gaming Operation, when such contract fails to provide for or result in the delivery of goods or services of fair value for the payment made.

Additionally, no person shall possess with the intent to use, or actually use, at any table game, either by himself or in concert with others any calculator, computer or other electronic, electrical, or electromechanical device to assist in projecting an outcome of the game, to keep track of or analyze the cards having been dealt, or to change the probabilities of any game.

THE NATIONAL INDIAN GAMING COMMISSION AND THE TRIBAL/STATE COMPACT

Notwithstanding any provision in this Ordinance or the rules, the Tribal Gaming Commission is hereby fully empowered to comply with all regulations promulgated by the NIGC.

Each Class II Gaming operation is under statutory requirement of the National Indian Gaming Commission to pay a fee to the NIGC. These fees are based on the assessable gross revenues of the prior calendar year. The assessable gross revenues for each Class II Gaming operation are the annual total amount of money wagered in Class II gaming, admission fees (including table or card fees), less any amounts paid out as prizes or paid for prizes awarded, and less an allowance for amortization of capital expenditures for structures. The allowance for amortization of capital expenditures for structures shall not exceed 5% of the cost of the structures in use throughout the year, and 2.5% of the cost of structures in use only a part of the year. All fee payments must be remitted to the National Indian Gaming Commission by the set due date.

Notwithstanding any provision in this Ordinance or the rules, the Tribal Gaming Commission is hereby fully empowered to comply with all provision of the Tribal-State State Compact (when applicable).

GENERAL REQUIREMENTS

Each Gaming Establishment must provide for full security and surveillance within the Gaming Establishment at all times (Section 103).

Any winnings, whether property or cash, which are due and payable to a participant in any Gaming activity and which remain unclaimed at the end of a Gaming session, shall be held in safekeeping for the benefit of such participant if his or her identity is known.

Any person who has any dispute, disagreement or other grievance with the Gaming Operation that involves currency, tokens, coins or any other thing of value may seek resolution of such dispute from the following persons an in the following order: a member of the staff relevant to the Gaming Operation, the supervisor of the department where the dispute arose, the manager of the Gaming Operation, and the Gaming Commission.

All disputes submitted to the Gaming Commission shall be decided by the Commission based on information provided by the complainant, including any witnesses for or documents provided by or for the complainant.

The Gaming Commission has the authority to initiate civil and criminal actions in court to enforce provisions of this Ordinance, Tribal Gaming Regulations, or the IGRA (Section 102.10).

The Commission has the authority to demand access to and inspect, examine, copy and audit all papers, books, and records concerning activities and revenues of any gaming activity conducted on the tribal land (Section 102.7).

The Commission has the authority when information is received through audits or other investigation that indicates a violation of Tribal, Federal or applicable State ordinances, laws, or regulations to treat as confidential and provide such information to the appropriate law enforcement officials (Section 102.10).

Beginning January 1, 2003, the Gaming Center will be assessed a fee commensurate with the cost of Compliance activities. These fees will be established in December of 2002, and will be based on percentages and operating costs of Compliance in 2002.

GCP&P.002   TRIBAL GAMING COMMISSION

OVERVIEW

The Tribal Gaming Commission has the authority and responsibility to conduct investigations and file reports related to the following activity:

1.   Patron disputes with the Gaming Operation.
2.   Minimum Internal Controls Standard violations.
3.   Tribal-State compact violations
4.   Tribal Gaming Ordinance violations
5.   Casino policy and procedure violations
6.   Any real or suspected State and Federal law violations.
7.   Any civil law violations.

STRUCTURE

The Tribal Gaming Commission currently consists of the following personnel:

TITLE	NUMBER OF EMPLOYEES
Gaming Commissioners	3
Executive Director	1
Compliance Officer	2
Internal Auditor	1
Background Investigator	0
Administrative Assistant	1
TOTAL STAFFING:	8

AUTHORITY

Tribal governments are recognized as having the right to engage in gaming. This authority is confirmed through the IGRA. Under the IGRA and the regulations of the NIGC, tribal governments are responsible for the regulation of gaming conducted on Indian lands. Comprehensive regulation is a necessary component in the system of checks and balances needed to ensure the integrity of the games and to protect the interest of the tribe. Effective regulatory oversight requires that there be a separation between the regulations and operation of tribal gaming activities. Also, the regulatory entity should have no involvement in the operational or managerial decisions of gaming activities, except to the extent that such issues may involve tribal law or regulations. The tribal gaming commission is an arm of the tribal government, established for the exclusive purpose of regulating and monitoring gaming on behalf of the tribe.

INTERNET AND E-MAIL ACCESS

All computer systems, on-line accounts, email, and email facilities are the property of the Tribe, and the Tribe reserves the right to monitor and audit all internal and external email sent by employees, as well as all use of tribally provided Internet resources.

The Internet is for business use only. The Executive Director must approve any personal use. Access to sexually oriented material is prohibited. No software will be downloaded without the permission of the Information Technology Manager.

Violation of this policy may result in disciplinary action up to and including termination.

GAMING COMMISSION STAFF ETHICS AND INTEGRITY

The Gaming Commission staff, and their immediate families, shall receive no personal compensation, gift, reimbursement, or payment of any kind from any person doing or wishing to do business with the Tribe relating to gaming, nor with any person wishing to obtain an unfair advantage in any authorized wager or gaming. Any property received in violation of this provision, including cash payments, shall be immediately forfeited to the Tribe, and the offending person or persons shall be prosecuted to the fullest extent possible.

WORK SCHEDULES

The Gaming Commission staff currently works a variety of shifts and schedules. Compliance Officers may work a 4 day 10 hour schedule that rotates every four months, while the Executive Director, Internal Auditor, Background/Licensing Investigators, and administrative personnel work 5 day 8 hour schedules. These schedules are subject to change in response to critical incidents, employee leaves, employee illnesses, or other events at the casino. All leave (vacation/time-off) requests must be approved by the Executive Director in advance. Absences due to illness or emergency must be called in to the Executive Director or immediate supervisor within 30 minutes of the beginning of the employee's shift.

At le one (1) Compliance Officer must remain on duty at all times. Peak days and hours will call for additional Compliance Officers to be assigned as needed.

GAMING COMMISSIONER

SUMMARY:

Commissioners are appointed by and serve at the direction of the Tribal Executive Committee and shall be compensated on a per diem and stipend basis contingent upon attendance at required Tribal Gaming Commission meetings and hearings.

ORDINANCE:

1.   The tribal gaming commission's responsibilities, powers, and enforcement authority are specifically set forth in the tribal ordinance.
2.   The Tribal Gaming Ordinance includes provisions regarding the number of commissioners, the method of selecting commissioners, including the qualifications needed and the background requirements, their terms of office, and the methods and grounds for removal of commission members. The ordinance requires staggering the terms of the commissioners so as to provide continuity in the tribal gaming commission's activities during transition of commission members.
3.   This ordinance defines the basic procedures for conducting official commission business. Included are provisions regarding appeal procedures of tribal gaming commission actions.
4.   Commissioners shall be compensated at a rate to be established annually by the Tribal Executive Committee. Commissioners shall be reimbursed for actual expenses incurred on Commission business, including necessary travel expenses.
5.   The Commission shall meet at le once a month at the Commission's main office or at any other designated meeting place. Special meetings shall be convened by the Commission Chair as necessary to carry out the official duties of the Commission. Proper notice of each special

meeting shall be given by the Gaming Commission Chairperson by telephone, by email, or by mail to each Commissioner. Notice shall be received at le 24 hours in advance of such meeting and shall include the date, time and place of the proposed meeting.

ESSENTIAL DUTIES & RESPONSIBILITIES:

1. Promulgate tribal gaming regulations pursuant to tribal law.
2. Take testimony and conduct hearings on regulatory matters, including matters related to the revocation of primary management official and key employee licenses.
3. Approve minimum internal control standards or procedures for the gaming operation, including the operation's credit policies and procedures for acquiring supplies and equipment.
4. Establish any supplemental criteria for the licensing of primary management officials, key employees, and other employees that the tribe deems necessary.
5. Establish standards for issuance of licenses or permits to persons and entities who deal with the gaming operations such as manufacturers and suppliers of machines, equipment, and supplies.
6. Resolve patron disputes, employee grievances, and other problems, pursuant to the tribal gaming ordinance.

SUPERVISORY RESPONSIBILITIES

This position does not require supervisory responsibilities.

QUALIFICATIONS

To perform this job successfully, an individual must be able to perform each essential duty satisfactorily. The requirements listed below are representative of the knowledge, skill, and/or ability required. Reasonable accommodations may be made to enable individuals with disabilities to perform the essential functions.

EDUCATION AND EXPERIENCE

A Bachelor's degree from a four-year college or university is preferred; or a minimum of four years regulatory, auditing, or investigative-related experience and/or training; or equivalent combination of education and experience on a one-for-one basis.

EXECUTIVE DIRECTOR

The Executive Director is responsible for the protection of the integrity of all gaming and gaming related activities at the Gaming Center. He/she is also accountable for ensuring all policies and procedures are in compliance with IGRA, NIGC Rules and Regulations, Tribal Gaming Ordinance, Internal Control Standards as adopted by the tribe, and Tribal-State Compact (when applicable). The Executive Director oversees the Licensing Division, the Compliance Division, and the Gaming Commission Auditing Department.

The Executive Director supervises and directs all administrative actions of the Gaming Commission. He/she employs the services of Compliance Officers, Licensing Inspectors, Background Investigators, Internal Auditors, and other such persons considered necessary for the purposes of consultation or investigation. The Executive Director also performs any other such duties deemed necessary by the Gaming Commission.

ESSENTIAL DUTIES & RESPONSIBILITIES:

1. The Executive Director is responsible for administering gaming control regulations.
2. Reviews Internal Audit reports of all gaming department and investigates deviations.
3. Reviews for recommendation, all changes requested by the Gaming Center to the Tribal Internal Controls System, Table Games Regulations, and Gaming Equipment rules and requirements. Determines if changes requested would affect game integrity.
4. Ensures confidentiality of all information, including but not limited to, gaming license applications, background investigations, license suspensions or revocations, and information from Tribal, Federal and State agencies.
5. Oversees investigations and resolution of customer disputes concerning gaming, gaming equipment, and prizes. Will include initial investigation, witness interviews, analysis of machine information, securing of surveillance videotapes, if appropriate, and request for appropriate tests by technicians. Provides recommendations to the Gaming Commission for reaching a fair and equitable disposition of the dispute.
6. Responsible for the timely filing of all reports and documentation required by IGRA, NIGC, Tribal Gaming Ordinance, Internal Control Standards, and Tribal-State Compact (when applicable).
7. Provides weekly reports to the Tribal Executive Committee on activities, violations, licensing, deficiencies, and discrepancies. Responsible for the preparation and submission of an annual budget for review and approval, as well as for the preparation and submission of quarterly budget reports to the Tribal Executive Committee.
8. Exercise professional and technical leadership in enforcing IGRA, NIGC, Tribal Gaming Ordinance, Internal Control Standards, and Tribal-State Compact (when applicable).
9. Analyzes violations cited against the Gaming Operations to ensure the Gaming Operations conform with approved procedures. Assists the Gaming Operations in achieving the result when necessary.
10. Responsible for the inventory of all gaming equipment and the maintenance of all gaming equipment. Ensures all gaming equipment in use complies with all applicable requirements of the IGRA, NIGC, Tribal Gaming Ordinance, Internal Control Standards, and Tribal-State Compact, if any.
11. The final decision on the types of games offered and gaming equipment utilized in the Gaming Center is reserved to the Tribal Executive Committee; however, the Executive Director may make recommendations to the Executive Committee.

SUPERVISORY RESPONSIBILITIES

Carries out supervisory responsibilities for all Gaming Commission employees in accordance with the organization's policies and applicable laws. Responsibilities include interviewing, hiring, and training employees, planning, assigning, and directing work, appraising performance, rewarding and disciplining employees, addressing complaints, and resolving problems.

QUALIFICATIONS

To perform this job successfully, an individual must be able to perform each essential duty satisfactorily. The requirements listed below are representative of the knowledge, skill, and/or ability required. Reasonable accommodations may be made to enable individuals with disabilities to perform the essential functions.

1. Develop licensing procedures for all employees of the gaming operations pursuant to 25CFR §558.1(b).
2. Issue, suspend, revoke, and review licenses of primary management officials and key employees upon completion of background investigations and after following the procedures contained in 25 CFR §556 and 558.
3. Conduct background investigations on primary management officials and key employees according to requirements that are at le as stringent as those in 25 CFR §556 and §558 pursuant to 25 CFR §522.4(b)(5).
4. Forward completed employment applications for primary management officials and key employees to the NIGC pursuant to 25 CFR §558.3. These applications should include the Privacy Act notice and the notice regarding false statements contained in 25 CFR §556.2 and §556.3.
5. Forward completed investigative reports on each background investigation for each primary management official or key employee to the NIGC prior to issuing a license pursuant to 25 CFR §556.5.

433

6. Review a person's prior activities, criminal record, if any, and reputations, habits, and associations to make a finding concerning the eligibility of a key employee or primary management official for employment in a gaming operation pursuant to 25 CFR §558.2.

7. Notify the NIGC if, after conducting a background investigation on a primary management official or a key employee, the tribe does not license the individual pursuant to 25 CFR § 556.6(d)(1).

8. Retain applications and reports of background investigations of primary management officials and key employees for no less than three years from termination of employment pursuant to 25 CFR §558.1(c).

9. Issue separate licenses to each place, facility or location on Indian lands where a tribe elects to allow gaming pursuant to 25 CFR §552.4(b)(6).

10. Ensure that gaming facilities are constructed, maintained and operated in a manner that adequately protect the environment and the public health and safety pursuant to 25 CFR §552.4(b)(7).

11. Obtain annual independent outside audits and submit these audits to the NIGC pursuant to 25 CFR §522.4(b)(3). Ensure that Internal Audits are performed in accordance with 25 CFR 542.14. The scope of these audits should include all gaming-related contracts that result in purchases of supplies, services, or concessions for more than $25,000 in any year pursuant to 25 CFR §522.4(b)(4).

12. Promulgate tribal gaming regulations pursuant to tribal law.

13. Monitor gaming activities to ensure compliance with tribal law/regulations through the Internal Audit and Compliance departments.

14. Interact with other regulatory and law enforcement agencies regarding the regulation of gaming.

15. Conduct investigations (through Internal Audit and/or Compliance) of possible violations and take appropriate enforcement action with respect to the tribal gaming ordinances and regulations.

16. Provide independent information to the tribe on the status of the tribe's gaming activities.

17. Establish or approve minimum internal control standards of procedures for the gaming operation, including the operation's credit policies and procedures for acquiring supplies and equipment.

18. Establish any supplemental criteria for the licensing of primary management officials, key employees, and other employees that the tribe deems necessary.

19. Establish standards for issuing licenses or permits to persons and entities that deal with the gaming operation such as manufacturers and suppliers of machines, equipment, and supplies.

20. Maintain records on licensees and on persons denied licenses including persons otherwise prohibited from engaging in gaming activities within the tribe's jurisdiction.

21. Perform audits (through the Internal Audit department) of business transactions to ensure compliance with regulations and/or policies.

22. Establish or approve rules of various games, and inspect games, tables, equipment, machines, cards, dice, and chips or tokens used in the gaming operations. Establish or approve video surveillance standards. Establish standards/criteria for gaming machines and facilitate the testing of machines.

EDUCATION AND EXPERIENCE
A Bachelor's degree from a four-year college or university; or a minimum of four years law enforcement, regulatory, auditing, or investigative-related experience and/or training; or equivalent combination of education and experience on a one-for-one basis.

COMPLIANCE OFFICER
SUMMARY:
This is a critical gaming commission position responsible for monitoring casino activities, observing customers, employees, transactions and requirements reporting to ensure compliance with Federal, State, and Tribal gaming laws and regulations as well as compliance with required internal controls. The Compliance Officer, along with the Internal Auditor, investigates and reports deficiencies or violations and conducts follow-up to ensure implementation of appropriate corrective action.

ESSENTIAL DUTIES & RESPONSIBILITIES
1. Report directly to the Executive Director of the Gaming Commission.

2. Maintains control over access to sensitive areas of gaming devices.

3. Conducts testing of gaming device computer control chips for verification of validity and authorized programming.

4. Monitors shipping, receiving, installation, relocation, removal, storage of gaming devices for security and compliance.

5. Inspects all gaming equipment and supplies for integrity and compliance with applicable laws and regulations. Ensures accurate records are maintained.

6. Randomly audits (through the Internal Audit department) any gaming-related transaction documents for compliance with regulation and internal controls.

7. Monitors table games and money drops for compliance in conjunction with Internal Audit.

8. Monitors count room activities for compliance in conjunction with Internal Audit.

9. Monitors other non-gaming departments and personnel activities and transactions for compliance in conjunction with Internal Audit.

10. Conducts investigations on criminal and internal theft violations in conjunction with Internal Audit.

11. Makes arrests as necessary and in conjunction with Security and Tribal Police.

12. Writes reports and conducts necessary follow-up investigations on reported or observed violations or deficiencies.

13. Conducts follow-up monitoring (along with Internal Audit) for implementation of appropriate corrective action.

14. Maintains Gaming Commission records, files, and statistics on compliance monitoring activities.

15. Works closely with Gaming Commission Internal Auditors and Background Investigators as well as appropriate casino personnel to fulfill responsibilities.

16. Works with outside regulatory or Law Enforcement officials as necessary.

17. Ensures that the casino fulfills all of its reporting requirements including, but not limited to, Title 31, IRS, NIGC, State and Gaming Commission reports, and assessments.

18. Other duties as assigned by the Gaming Commission.

COMPUTER NETWORK
1. In support of day-to-day operations, Compliance Officers should have access to desktop computers with software applications installed that facilitate investigations and the submission of Incident Reports to the Gaming Commission.

2. Regardless of which Compliance Officer generates a report, all Incident Reports should be maintained in a common file named "Gaming Reports", and should be given filenames which correspond to the Incident Report number assigned to the written report. A report template should be developed to standardize the report writing process, which will enable each Compliance Officer to efficiently create the narrative supplement to every Incident Report.

3.   Compliance Officers should have access to the Employee Database, which provides basic personnel information on all Gaming Center employees. The database should also include an employee photograph and any p disciplinary action that has taken place. This database, which is normally maintained by the Casino's Human Resource department, should have a search feature that permits the user to pull up an employee's file when only a limited amount of information on the employee is available. It is especially helpful when trying to obtain the employee's full name for an Incident Report, when the only available information is the employee number. On the Compliance Officer's computer, this database should have a "read only" feature that will prevent unauthorized editing of the employee file.

4.   Another very useful database in the Compliance Officer computer is the Exclusion Database, which is a file of all patrons who have been excluded from the Casino. For any one patron, it provides a picture, the grounds for the exclusion, and the effective dates. This is helpful information when seeing an excluded patron in the Casino and trying to determine if exclusion is still in effect. It also should have a "read only" feature and cannot be edited.

REPORT WRITING

As oversight agents for the Tribal Gaming Commission, Compliance Officers may enter the casino at any time without notice. Compliance Officers may enter any area of a gaming facility without notice, except Soft Count, Hard Count, and the General Manager's Office, unless so directed by a Higher Authority. The Tribal Executive Committee is a Higher Authority. Compliance Officials are required to identify themselves upon entering the casino, but they are not required to have their License (ID Badge) visible while on the Gaming Floor.

Class II (and Class III when applicable) Gaming Facility compliance is accomplished through oversight activities. Compliance Officials will report a violation of the Tribe's Ordinances, the Internal Controls, Policies & Procedures, or the Indian Gaming Regulatory Act, through an Incident Report. Three copies of the violation(s) will be made. One copy will be retained by the writer, one copy will be forwarded to the facility Management, and one copy will be sent to the Gaming Commission Compliance Office.

A dub of the relevant surveillance video will be made when appropriate. Approval to retain the dub will be obtained from the Surveillance Manager. Once the facility Management receives the Incident (Violation) Report regarding the compliance violation(s), the Casino or Bingo Management is responsible for the corrective action(s), the disposition of the report(s), and should forward the corrective action information to the Gaming Commission Compliance Office. Again, the role of Compliance is that of oversight. However, in cases of non-action by the facility Management, or in cases of repeated compliance violations, this information will be forwarded to the Tribal Gaming Commission. The Tribal Gaming Commission may then call for enforcement activities to be taken, up to and including revocation of individual gaming licenses, or the suspension or revocation of the facility's Gaming License to operate.

All Incident Reports will require various pieces of documentation depending on the complexity of the incident. However, all reports require a face sheet, a narrative, and any relevant attachments.

The face sheet is a standard incident report with places for required information such as Date, Time, Location of incident, names and addresses of participants and witnesses, names and employee numbers, the manner in which the incident was reported (Surveillance observation, Security, employee report, etc.), etc. It is imperative that this document be completed in full. Segments of the document that do not apply to a particular incident should contain the letters "N/A" for not applicable.

The narrative segment of the report, which is completed using word processing equipment, is the factual description of what took place regarding a specific incident. Written in third person style, the narrative should answer the following basic investigative questions:

1.   Who: who was involved?
2.   What: what took place?
3.   When: when did it take place?
4.   Where: where did it take place?
5.   Why: why did it occur? i.e. causative factors
6.   How: how did it occur?
7.   The narrative must conform to the following general format: an origin or introduction, victims' statements, witnesses' statements, the Compliance Officer's investigation to include any suspect's statements, a tape review narrative, a list of applicable violations, a detailed tape review and a list of attachments to the report. If an Incident Report is lengthy, it is appropriate to include a synopsis or executive summary section at the beginning of the report.
8.   The nature and number of attachments to the report will depend on the complexity of the incident. Items that are typically included as attachments are copies of driver's licenses, voluntary written statements, receipts or vouchers, evidence, photos, logs, Counterfeit Note Reports and exclusion letters. The assigned Incident report number should be included on all attachments as appropriate.
9.   The Incident Report should be page numbered, copied, and submitted to the Supervisor correctly. Copies of the narrative and attachments should always result in three complete copies of the report. Although Counterfeit Note Reports are multi-copy forms, three parts of the form are required for the Secret Service; thus, two copies of the form must be made for the Incident Report. When copying Exclusion Letters, three copies of the top page, which have the individual's driver's license and photo attached, are required. If a surveillance tape review was conducted in conjunction with the Incident Report, one copy of the face sheet should be copied, folded and included with the tapes when the report is submitted to the Supervisor.
10.   Once reviewed and approved by the Department Director, the original copy of the Incident Report is filed in the Surveillance Office, one copy is forwarded to the Gaming Commission Compliance Officer and the third is returned to the originating Compliance Officer. Note: a copy of the face sheet, without narrative or attachments, should be forwarded to the Security Department for inclusion in their database.
11.   Often times, after a report has been reviewed and filed, an Incident Report Addendum will be required to document additional elements of an investigation. In those cases, the Addendum is submitted in the form of a narrative with attachments as required. To assist in the Department Manager's review, the original Incident Report should be temporarily removed from its file and attached to the Addendum report.
12.   Incident Reports should be submitted in a timely fashion. Under normal circumstances, reports should submitted prior to the Compliance Officer completing his or her shift. In the event the report cannot be completed due to the requirement to obtain additional information, an Incident Report pending sheet should be submitted to the Supervisor. Reports on patron disputes should be submitted within twenty-four hours of the incident and must include voluntary written statements from all personnel involved. If an Exclusion Letter was initiated, the Compliance Officer, prior to leaving the Casino for the day, must complete the Incident Report.

JACKPOT VERIFICATION

Jackpot verification by a Gaming Commission Compliance Officer is required for all jackpots of $25,000.00 and over won on a slot machine or Wide Area Progressive (WAP). The following is the procedure for verification.

1.   Receive notification from Slot Shift Manager.
2.   Respond to the location of the slot machine.
3.   Verify that the slot machine is in a valid jackpot mode.
4.   Exam the outside of the slot machine cabinet for any signs of tampering.
5.   Open the machine's main door.

6.   Inspect the bill/coin comparitor for validity.
7.   Inspect the hopper for slugs (if applicable).
8.   If the diverter is active, the coin drop bucket must be inspected for slugs.
9.   Power down the machine.
10.   Verify the logic board door is secured and sealed with Gaming Commission tamper-proof tape.
11.   Document the seal number on the tamper-proof tape.
12.   If the tamper-proof tape has been compromised, remove the logic board and verify the EPROMs with the Kobetron Unit.
13.   If the EPROMs match the GLI standards, reinstall the EPROM into the proper socket.
14.   Reseal the logic board door with tamper-proof tape.
15.   If the EPROMs signature does not match the GLI standard, advise Casino Management that the jackpot winnings are going to be held pending further investigation by the Gaming Commission.
16.   Power up the machine.
17.   Verify the machine has returned to the jackpot mode.
18.   Reset the jackpot on the machine.
19.   Conduct a l game recall to determine that the jackpot has registered into the machine's history.
20.   Verify the jackpot via the slot reporting system (if applicable).
21.   Ensures that Casino Management completes all necessary tax paperwork.
22.   Request Surveillance hold the videotape and a still photograph of the patron.
23.   Complete Slot Machine Jackpot Verification report.
With WAP jackpots, assist the WAP representative with their verification process.

BACKGROUND INVESTIGATOR
SUMMARY:
The Background Investigator conducts investigations to determine the suitability of individual and corporate applicants to obtain an Tribal Gaming License. The investigator will access various criminal databases, and interface with Law Enforcement and credit agencies in an attempt to properly evaluate an applicant's suitability for employment at the Gaming Center, or their fitness to provide gaming-related goods and services to the casino.

ESSENTIAL DUTIES & RESPONSIBILITIES:
1.   Development of his/her working knowledge of the Tribal Gaming Ordinances, Federal, State and local laws that pertain to the Gaming Center, Gaming Commission/casino Minimum Internal Control Standards, Gaming Commission policies and procedures, and the Tribal-State Compact (when applicable).
2.   Ensure applications are complete. Confirm/clarify gaps in employment and residence, confirm phone numbers, completion of 2nd half of applications for key employees, assist prospective employees with the completion of application. Make sure applications are notarized.
3.   Maintain applicant files, remove terminated employees from active investigation file, recover and properly destroy employee's license.
4.   Maintain statistical applicant information. Sustain database with date application received, date preliminary background investigation completed, date fingerprints mailed, date fingerprints received.
5.   Issue Tribal Gaming License utilizing proper software system. Photograph applicants and print out respective licenses. Deliver license to the Gaming Center Human Resource department or mail to commercial applicants. Maintain licensing system hardware items.
6.   Perform all related and compatible duties as assigned.

SUPERVISORY RESPONSIBILITIES
This position has no supervisory responsibilities.

QUALIFICATIONS
To perform this job successfully, an individual must be able to perform each essential duty satisfactorily. The requirements listed below are representative of the knowledge, skill, and/or ability required. Reasonable accommodations may be made to enable individuals with disabilities to perform the essential functions.

EDUCATION AND/OR EXPERIENCE
Two years college or equivalent. At le one-year investigative experience with a Law Enforcement or regulatory agency is preferred. Additional years of experience may substitute for college.

INTERNAL AUDITOR
SUMMARY:
The Internal Auditor is responsible for ensuring that the Gaming Operation meets the Minimum Internal Control Standards (MICS) of the National Indian Gaming Commission (NIGC), and that the policies and procedures as approved by the Executive Committee, as well as policies and procedures established by the other Tribal Departments are being followed on a routine basis. The Internal Auditor is also responsible for communicating any instances of non-compliance, or any material weaknesses in the casino's Internal Control System, to casino management and to the Gaming Commission. The Internal Auditor will work closely with Compliance Officers in investigating criminal activities, and will have the lead in directing investigations of casino-related financial improprieties, such as shortages, cage or vault theft, accounting fraud, and etc.

ESSENTIAL DUTIES AND RESPONSIBILITIES:
1.   Report results of Internal Audits to casino management and to the Gaming Commission.
2.   Investigate and resolve material exceptions or deviations.
3.   Test count room currency counters quarterly.
4.   Audit Table Games fill and credit procedures, soft drop and count procedures, transfers of funds, sensitive key controls, and trace source documentation and reconciliation at le twice per year.
5.   Audit Slot Machine jackpot payouts, drop and count procedures, transfers of funds, sensitive key controls, and trace source documentation and reconciliation at le twice per year.
6.   Examine Bingo procedures, Complimentary services, cage and vault procedures, electronic data processing, etc., at le once per year.
7.   Follow-up on previously reported violations and deviations to ensure that management corrective action has been taken.
8.   Assist external auditors and Compliance Officers as necessary.
9.   Any other duties assigned by the Executive Director, the Gaming Commission, or the Tribal Executive Committee.

SUPERVISORY RESPONSIBILITIES
This position does not currently require supervisory responsibilities.

QUALIFICATIONS

To perform this job successfully, an individual must be able to perform each essential duty satisfactorily. The requirements listed below are representative of the knowledge, skill, and/or ability required. Reasonable accommodations may be made to enable individuals with disabilities to perform the essential functions.

1.   Assist with the preparation and implementation of an internal control policy and procedures to be performed at the Gaming Center.

2.   Prepare and document audit reports for all major gaming areas that include objectives, audit procedures and scope, findings and conclusions, and recommendations in accordance with 25 CFR 542.14(f).

3.   Understand and implement coin/bill drop procedures and internal control standards pursuant to 25 CFR 542.12(d).

4.   Understand and implement gaming equipment procedures and internal control standards pursuant to 25 CFR 542.12(e).

5.   Understand and implement gaming machine count and wrap procedures and internal control standards in accordance with 25 CFR 542.12(f)

6.   Evaluate cage, credit, and collections functions compliance with minimum internal control standards pursuant to 25 CFR 542.13(l).

7.   Perform any other duties and responsibilities as directed by the Executive Director, the Gaming Commission, or the Tribal Executive Committee.

EDUCATION AND EXPERIENCE

A Bachelor's degree in Accounting or Business Finance from a four-year college or university. A Certified Public Accountant with auditing experience is preferred.

ADMINISTRATIVE ASSISTANT

SUMMARY:

The Gaming Commission Administrative Assistant helps the Executive Director meet the various reporting deadlines for the Tribe, State, and Federal requirements. Schedules Gaming Commission meetings, responds to requests for information, and provides a professional office environment.

ESSENTIAL DUTIES & RESPONSIBILITIES:

1.   Performs special assignments directly related to the management policies or general business operations. Customarily and regularly exercises discretion and independent judgment.

2.   Provides analytical and specialized administrative support of non-routine, non-repetitive nature.

3.   Independently investigates assigned problems.

4.   Determines method of research, data and information requirements as well as analysis techniques.

5.   Prepares reports/recommendations for action by superior.

6.   Contacts casino and tribal personnel at all organizational levels to gather information and prepare reports.

7.   Performs clerical duties as requested.

8.   Promotes positive public/employee relations at all times.

9.   Acts with discretion and confidentiality in handling sensitive material; required to sign and adhere to a confidentiality agreement.

10.   Maintains a clean, safe, hazard-free work environment within area of responsibility.

11.   Ensures employee applications are complete. Confirm/clarify gaps in employment and residence, confirm phone numbers, completion of 2nd half of applications for key employees, assist prospective employees with the completion of application. Make sure applications are notarized, and if not, notarize.

12.   Maintain employee applicant files, remove terminated employees from active investigation files, recover and properly destroy employee's license.

13.   Maintain statistical applicant information. Sustain database with date application received, date preliminary background investigation completed, date fingerprints mailed, date fingerprints received.

14.   Assist in issuing Gaming Licenses utilizing proper software system. Photograph applicants and print out respective licenses. Deliver license to Gaming Center's Human Resource department personnel.

15.   Maintains all building inspection files and acts as liaison with building inspector.

SUPERVISORY RESPONSIBILITIES

There are no supervisory responsibilities.

QUALIFICATIONS

To perform this job successfully, an individual must be able to perform each essential duty satisfactorily.

EDUCATION AND EXPERIENCE

High school graduate; some college preferred.

LICENSING POLICIES AND PROCEDURES

OVERVIEW

The Gaming Center shall not employ or retain any employee who has not met the licensing standards of the Tribe. No casino employee shall be on any gaming floor without a valid license on their person. In order to meet licensing criteria, the casino employees must meet or exceed the standards set by the Tribe's Tribal Gaming Ordinance, the Tribe's approved Internal Controls and Policies & Procedures, the Indian Gaming Regulatory Act, and the National Indian Gaming Commission's rules and regulations.

Licenses are also issued to the gaming facility on a yearly basis by the Tribal Gaming Commission. In order to meet licensing criteria, the gaming facility must meet or exceed the standards set by the Tribe's Tribal Gaming Ordinances, the Tribe's approved Internal Controls and Policies & Procedures, the Indian Gaming Regulatory Act, and the National Indian Gaming Commission's rules and regulations.

LICENSING OF PRIMARY MANAGEMENT OFFICIALS, KEY EMPLOYEES, AND NON-KEY EMPLOYEES

OVERVIEW

The Tribe of State established these licensing regulations to ensure the integrity of the Operation. Employees are licensed on a yearly basis, which begins on their start date. Requirements and conditions for licensing are established and employees must meet the standards of licensing and be issued a license before they can begin work in any Gaming Operation. Gaming Center employees are classified and licensed in three categories:

LICENSED EMPLOYEES

1.   Primary Management Official: As defined by NIGC, a Primary Management Official is any person with the authority to:

a.   Establish working policies and procedures.

b.   Hire and terminate employees.

c.   Direct financial management activities.

d.   The definition also includes employees in the Casino Shift Manager position and above (GM, CFO, Controller, Table Games Manager, OTB Manager, Slot Manager, etc.).

2.   Key Employee: As defined by NIGC, a Key Employee is any person who performs one or more of the following functions:

437

a.	Bingo caller.	
b.	Counting room supervisor.	
c.	Chief of Security.	
d.	Custodian of gaming supplies or cash.	
e.	Floor manager.	
f.	Pit boss.	
g.	Dealer.	
h.	Croupier.	
i.	Approver of credit.	
j.	Custodian of gambling devices including persons with access to cash and accounting records within such devices.	
k.	If not otherwise included, any other person whose total cash compensation is in excess of $50,000 per year.	
l.	If not otherwise included, the four most highly compensated persons in the gaming operation.	
3.	In addition to the NIGC definition, the Tribal Gaming Operation has included the following as Key Employees:	

	a.	Security Officer
b.	Food/Beverage Supervisor	
c.	Blackjack Dealer	
d.	Compliance Official	
e.	Blackjack Floor Person	
f.	Slot Attendant	
g.	Auditing	
h.	Accounting	
i.	Benefits Manager	
j.	Pull Tab Clerk	
k.	Shipping / Receiving Clerk	
l.	T.L.C. (Players Club)	
m.	Gaming Manager	
n.	Change Attendants (All positions)	
o.	Vault / Count (All positions)	
p.	Concessions	
q.	Systems Specialist	
r.	Dining Cashier	
s.	Group Sales Manager	
t.	Promotions Manager	
u.	Cage (All positions)	
v.	Hotel Desk	
w.	M.I.S. (All staff positions)	
x.	Kitchen Manager / Assistant Mgr.	
y.	Bartender	
z.	Executive Administrative Assistant	
aa.	Bingo (All positions)	
bb.	Gift Shop Cashier	
cc.	Payroll	
dd.	Creative Services	
ee.	Slot Technician	
	ff.	Blackjack Pit Supervisor

3.   A Non-Key Employee is any employee in the gaming facility that does not meet the guidelines of Key Employee or Primary Management Official.

LICENSING APPLICATION POLICY

All applicants for positions in the Gaming Center must complete and submit a Privacy Act Statement, Release of Information, and a Personal History Statement so that a Background Investigation can be conducted. The Background Investigation will include all of the information given on the Personal History Statement, Fingerprinting and Criminal checks on the State and Federal level. A Financial check will also be conducted for Key and Primary Management Official Employees. The applicant must receive a "Suitable for Licensing" status upon completion of the investigation by a Compliance Investigator, and/or approval from the Tribal Gaming Commission for licensing.

All employees are required to meet the standards of the Tribal Ordinances, Internal Controls, and Policies & Procedures, and the standards and regulations of the Indian Gaming Regulatory Act. Failure to meet any of these requirements may result in the suspension or revocation of their license.

Once an individual has received a License, they are responsible for their conduct and must follow the Tribe's Ordinances, Internal Controls, Policy & Procedures, and the Indian Gaming Regulatory Act. They are also responsible for maintaining their integrity, a good reputation, and positive associations.

Again, the role of Compliance is that of oversight. However, a licensed individual's negative conduct will result in Compliance reporting such conduct to the Gaming Commission. Enforcement action(s) up to and including suspension or revocation of the individual's license may occur.

LICENSING FEE POLICY

No person may be employed or retained in a casino position unless they have been issued a valid gaming license for that facility. There are three types of Gaming licenses that are issued according to a person's position and responsibilities. The types and fees for such licenses are listed below. License fees must be paid by the Employee. Employees must sign a voucher for their license fees, which if paid by the employee, may be paid in installments per pay period:

1.   Gaming Facility Employee Licenses

a.   Primary Management Officials will pay a license fee of $200.00 in up to four (4) installments.

b.   Key Employees will pay a license fee of $100.00 in up to four (4) installments.

c.   Non-Key Employees will pay a license fee of $40.00 in up to two (2) installments.

2.   It is mandatory for all employees to have their license with them when they report for work. Gaming Management has the option of utilizing a Temporary One Day License which Compliance will have available should an employee report to work without their license. A special form must be filled out and signed by the employee to obtain this license. The fee is $10.00, and the license must be returned upon completion of the employee's shift. The employee will be charged an additional $10.00 for each day the license is not returned. Continued or repetitive requests for a Temporary One Day License may result in suspension or revocation of the employee's gaming license.

3.   Any employee who misplaces their license will be issued a replacement license at a cost of $20.00. Repetitive requests for Re-placement may result in suspension or revocation of the employee's gaming license.

4.   If any license is defective in any way, it will be replaced free of charge.

5.   All questions or problems concerning the licensing process or the license (ID Badge) itself, should be brought directly to the Executive Director of the Tribal Gaming Commission, the Licensing/Investigations Staff, or to the Compliance staff.

LICENSING APPLICATION PROCEDURE

1.   Applicant is directed to Human Resources by Employment Coordinator to obtain licensing application paperwork.

2.   Applicant is directed to the Gaming Commission Licensing Office with their completed application paperwork to be interviewed by Licensing or Investigative Staff. A preliminary background check will be conducted and Application documents will be reviewed with the Applicant to determine licensing suitability.

3.   If Applicant does not meet the licensing standards according to information presented on the application or obtained through the initial interview and background check, the Applicant is informed that they do not qualify for licensing and their denied application paperwork is returned to Human Resources.

4.   Upon satisfactory interview and preliminary background check and acceptance of license application, the Applicant will be finger-printed, photographed, and issued a Temporary Gaming License. Applicant will sign a Voucher for the license.

5.   Upon issuance of a Temporary License, Applicant may be scheduled for work. No person may begin working until they have been issued a Temporary License.

6.   Background and licensing investigative staff shall further review a person's prior activities, employment, education, criminal record, (if any) and reputation, habits and associations to make a finding concerning the eligibility for permanent employment.

7.   If, upon completion of a background investigation, the Applicant does not meet the licensing standards set by NIGC, or the Tribe, or if the Tribe determines that employment of the person poses a threat to the public interest or to the effective regulation of gaming, or creates or enhances dangers of unsuitable, unfair, or illegal practices, methods, and activities in the conduct of gaming, the Tribe may deny issuance of a permanent license and the person's employment shall be terminated.

8.   Under no circumstances shall any individual be employed in the Gaming Operation who has been convicted of, or entered a plea of guilty or no contest to, any of the following, unless the person has been pardoned:

a.   Any gambling-related offense.

b.   Fraud or misrepresentation in any connection.

c.   A violation of any provision of the Tribal Gaming Ordinance regulating or prohibiting gaming.

d.   A felony, other than a felony conviction for an offense in a, b, or c, listed above, during the immediately preceding 10 years.

e.   Any theft or drug-related misdemeanor.

f.   Who has been determined by the Tribe to be a person whose prior activities, criminal record if any, or reputation, habits, and associations pose a threat to the public interest or to the effective regulation and control of gaming, or create or enhance the dangers of unsuitable, unfair, or illegal practices, methods, or activities in the operation of gaming or the carrying on of the business and financial arrangements incidental thereto.

9.   The prohibitions contained in the preceding paragraphs may be waived by the Tribal Executive Committee, by Resolution, if the applicant or employee demonstrates to the satisfaction of the Tribe, evidence of sufficient rehabilitation and present fitness.

LICENSING APPEAL POLICY AND PROCEDURE

1.   Gaming Employees who are denied licensing may be eligible to file a grievance, and may do so through the Gaming Commission Office.

2.   The Grievance process is confidential.

3.   The Grievance:

a.   Must be filed in writing.

b.   The issues must relate to licensing policy issues only.

c.   The Grievance Letter must be turned in to the Gaming Commission Office within five (5) days after receiving licensing denial notification.

4.   The Executive Director of the Tribal Gaming Commission or an Official designee will take the Grievance Letter along with the employee/applicant file to the Tribal Attorney and the Tribal Gaming Commission.

5.   Any person who presents false information on the License Application or Personal History Statement, or presents false documents to support the Application, or falsifies information on any documents, will not be eligible for the Appeal Process.

LICENSING GLOSSARY

1.   Revocation of License: The license is voided or annulled by recall.

2.   Suspension of License: The license is rendered temporarily ineffective due to violations of licensing criteria and the facility must not operate until it has met the criteria. In the case of an employee license, the employee may not work until the license is rendered effective.

3.   National Indian Gaming Regulatory Act: Law enacted by Congress of the United States which provides in part, that a tribal/state compact may be negotiated between a tribe and a state to set forth the rules, regulations and conditions under which a tribe may conduct Class III gaming, as defined in the Act, on Indian lands within a state permitting Class III gaming.

4.   Internal Controls: Strict rules and/or procedures for operations of gaming facilities established or approved by the tribal gaming commission designed to protect our guests, our employees and the assets of the Tribe.

5.   Policy & Procedure Manuals: Standards and procedures for departmental operations within the Tribe's gaming facilities.

6.   Primary Management Official: Gaming employee who has authority to hire and fire personnel, or set up working policies and procedures, or has responsibility for financial management, or any person performing as a Casino Shift Manager or above.

7.   Key Employee: Any gaming employee who performs functions involving gaming revenue, gaming devices or equipment, gaming supplies or cash, or who has access to any gaming accounting records or supplies and equipment.

8.   Non-Key Employee: Any gaming employee who does not meet the criteria for a Primary Management Official or Key Employee.

9.   Class II Gaming: Bingo Facilities, Electronic Bingo, and Pull-Tabs, etc.

10.   Class III Gaming: Casinos with true slot machines and house-banked Blackjack.

11.   Tribal Ordinances: Laws enacted by the Tribe of State.

12.   Higher Authority: As it relates to tribal gaming, the Tribal Executive Committee of the Tribe constitutes Higher Authority.

GCP&P.003   TRIBAL GAMING COMMISSION MINIMUM INTERNAL CONTROL STANDARDS

OVERVIEW

Internal controls are essential to assure the integrity and fairness of Indian Gaming and to assure that gaming is conducted fairly, honestly and safely by both the operator and the players. The Minimum Internal Control Standards (MICS) provide for the protection of Tribal assets and permits accountability of gaming enterprises to the Tribal Government, management, and Tribal regulatory entities. Internal control systems and procedures vary from casino to casino, and they are typically developed based on the unique operating environment of a particular tribal casino. MICS establish an internal control system that permits the timely preparation of accurate financial statements in accordance with generally accepted accounting principles. In addition, they provide management with reasonable assurance that Tribal assets are safeguarded against loss from unauthorized use or disposition, and that transactions are executed in accordance with management's authorization and recorded properly to permit the preparation of financial statements.

MICS are intended to cover Class II and Class III gaming currently conducted in the United States. Games covered by the MICS include Bingo and other games such as pull-tabs, electronic Bingo, and other electronic gaming machines. Card games, specifically house-banked Blackjack, and pari-mutuel horse racing are also covered by the Gaming Center's MICS.

1.   The Tribe derives its authority for establishing MICS from the National Indian Gaming Commission. The Gaming Commission and the Gaming Center have expanded upon or used alternate procedures to assure that its MICS comply with all regulatory standards. The MICS are designed to reasonably ensure that:

a.   Assets are safeguarded and accountability of such assets is maintained.

b.   Liabilities are properly recorded and contingent liabilities are properly disclosed.

c.   Financial records, which should include revenues, expenses, assets and liabilities, are accurate and reliable.

d.   Transactions are conducted in accordance with generally accepted accounting principles, the Tribe's rules and regulations, and/or management's specific authorization.

e.   Access to assets is limited to management's specific authorization.

f.   Accountability of assets is compared to records at reasonable intervals, with appropriate action being taken for noted discrepancies.

g.   Functions, duties and responsibilities are appropriately segregated and that they are properly performed by competent, qualified personnel.

Additional detail concerning specific gaming-related topics can be found in the Tribal Minimum Internal Control Standards.

SLOT MACHINE OPERATIONS

OVERVIEW

During the course of casino history, the slot machine department has grown from one of little importance (a gaming device that wives or girlfriends could play while their male counterparts played the "real games" such as Craps, Blackjack, and Roulette) to one that now contributes in excess of 80-85% of casino revenues. As such, it's very important that proper controls and procedures be put in place to ensure that revenues and expenses are properly accounted for.

SLOT MACHINE GUIDELINES

1.   Prior to new machines being put into play the Gaming Machine Revenue Analyst will perform the following steps:

a.   Assign a unique number to each gaming machine, and print labels to be affixed to the front of each machine.

b.   Record the serial number of each machine and if applicable the serial number of each logic board.

c.   Record both the hard and soft meter reading for each machine (if applicable).

d.   Prepare a Machine Log form.

e.   Enter the new machines into the machine accounting system.

f.   Prepare a Video Machine Door Log.

g.   Notify the Shift Manager on duty, and the Casino Cage that the machine is now ready to be turned on for customer play.

2.   A Video Machine Door Log will be kept inside each gaming machine at all times. The Gaming Machine Revenue Analyst will prepare a Video Machine Door Log for each new gaming machine prior to the game being put into play. Any time a machine is opened for any reason an entry will be made on the Video Machine Door Log indicating the reason for opening the machine, and the date and time that the machine was opened.

3.   During the drop, or anytime there are uncounted funds in the room, there shall be no less than three (3) authorized persons in the room.

4.   When a gaming machine door needs to be opened for any reason the following steps must be strictly adhered to:

a.   A Security Officer must be present

b.   The Surveillance department must be given the following information prior to the machine being opened:

1.   The machine number.

2.   The zone number.

3.   The technician employee number.

4.   The reason for opening the machine.

c.   The person relaying the information to the Surveillance Department must wait for acknowledgement indicating that all the above information has been noted by the Surveillance Operator.

5.   The gaming machine drop supervisor shall notify Surveillance when the drop is ready to begin so that monitoring can be performed.

6.   Surveillance shall record any exceptions or variations to established procedures observed during the drop. Such records shall be available to Compliance, Internal Audit, Gaming Commission, and casino management personnel only.

7.   Currency acceptor boxes shall be individually emptied and counted, and their totals recorded in ink, and the empty boxes shall be shown to Surveillance.

8.   Each Jackpot payout form shall have the signatures of at le two employees verifying and witnessing the payout.

9.   Jackpot payouts in excess of $1200 require the signature of a management employee independent of the gaming machine depart-ment.

10.   Accurate and current theoretical and actual hold percentages shall be maintained for each gaming machine to ensure that payouts are within acceptable and authorized limits.

11.   Large variations between theoretical and actual hold percentages must be investigated by management employees independent of the gaming department. The findings must be documented.

12.   Accounting/auditing personnel shall review exception reports for all gaming machine systems on a daily basis and review the transactions for propriety and unusual occurrences.

TABLE GAMES OPERATIONS (BLACKJACK)

OVERVIEW

Because the State of State has not yet negotiated a Gaming Compact with State tribes, only Class II gaming is authorized. Class II status prohibits the tribe from offering "house-banked" table games, and limits the Gaming Center to offering "player-banked" Blackjack. In "player-banked" table games, Blackjack players pay an annual membership fee, and a "commission" on each Blackjack hand played based on the amount of the bet. For example, for a bet of between $5-$10, a $0.25 commission is paid by the player to the casino. For bets in excess of $11 but less than $25, a $0.50 commission is paid. For bets placed between $26-$50, a commissin of $0.75 is paid. Finally, for all bets in excess of $50, and commission of $1.00 is paid. These commissions are the only actual revenues received by the casino. The table games profits and losses are paid to and deducted from the player's pool, and excess player's pool funds are paid out in the form of tournament prizes, etc.

TABLE GAMES GUIDELINES

1.   No person under 21 years of age may play any game. If any person below the age of 2l plays and otherwise qualifies for a prize or winnings, the prize or winnings shall not be paid.

2.   No person who is obviously intoxicated shall be permitted to play any game.

3.   All dealers and players must speak English only during play at the table.

4.   The Casino shall conspicuously post general game rules and play procedures.

5.   The Casino shall conspicuously post a notice that all gaming conducted is regulated by the Tribal Gaming Commission and the procedures that customers can follow to resolve player disputes.

STANDARDS FOR SUPERVISION

1.   Personnel with authority equal to or greater than those being supervised shall provide supervision at all times when the card room is in operation.

2.   Chips and monetary equivalents transferred to or from the Cashier's cage to the table banks or Player Pool fund shall be properly authorized and documented. An individual who is independent of the cage or Table Games personnel shall carry all transfers.

PLAYING CARDS CONTROL

1.   Playing cards are stored in Inventory Control until issued.

2.   Inventory Control maintains a log that documents when cards are received on site, distributed to, returned from tables, destroyed, and removed from the gaming operation.

3.   Playing cards are to be issued to the floor supervisor.

4.   New cards must remain in the original sealed box and are to be locked in the dealer's shoe, podium, or secured area until put in use.

5.   When the cards are put in use, the floor supervisor must break the seal on the table surface in full view of the Surveillance cameras.

6.   The dealer spreads, sorts, and checks both sides of the cards at the table.

7.   Cards should be used a maximum of 24 hours or three shifts. When replacing decks, the used cards are sorted and put back in their original boxes. The boxes are tagged with the game number and returned to Surveillance to be replaced with the new decks.

PLAYERS POOL ACCOUNTING & ADMINISTRATIVE PROCEDURES

The Player's Pool Account is a fund from which money can be withdrawn, in chip form to facilitate the play of Table Games. The account balance will fluctuate depending on whether the fund increases or decreases. A positive balance on the Player's Pool record board represents a liability to the Casino. Separate general ledger liability accounts are maintained for each type of Player's Pool (e.g.: 21, Pai Gow, etc.) when applicable.

1.   Gaming Center Player's Pool accounts are payable to the players through jackpots, prizes and awards. Records of transactions for each of these accounts are kept separate from other Gaming Center operational records.

2.   The initial fund (seed) account was a one-time contribution authorized by the Tribal Gaming Commission, and which was an expense to the Casino.

3.   All other contributions to the Player Pool account are paid in as designated by the Tribal Gaming Commission from the revenues generated from the play of the game. Gaming Center's function regarding the Players Pool account is that of the Trustee.

4.   In compliance with the Tribal MICS, the current balance of the Player's Pool Fund will be conspicuously posted in the Casino. These balances are updated on a daily basis by the Table Games staff when informed of the new balances by the Accounting Department.

CARD GAME GIVEAWAY PROMOTIONS

Excess Player Pool Funds are to be made available for distribution to the players.

1.   To eliminate any potential misconceptions, Casino employees are not allowed to participate in card game giveaway of excess Player Pool Funds.

2.   The Director of Gaming Operations develops a plan identifying which giveaways should be held. The plan is to be in the form of a written proposal prepared for the review and approval signature of both the Gaming Commission and the casino General Manager. The Chief Financial Officer must also sign the plan to confirm the amounts requested are within the limit ranges. An approved, signed off copy of this plan must be distributed to Accounting by the Director of Gaming Operations. This will be their authorization to transfer funds between applicable general ledger accounts.

PLAYER RATING & REDEMPTION SYSTEM

The Player Rating and Redemption System (when applicable) is designed to identify and reward players who deserve redemption privileges, while at the same time exerting sufficient control to prevent abuses and protect Tribal Assets.

1.   Players receive redemption points (good toward food, non-alcoholic beverages, etc.) base on their playing time and average bet. At the Blackjack tables, players receive redemption points on a per-hour basis for hours played.

2.   For example, each redemption point may have a value of $0.333 (3 points equals $1.00).

3.   Redemption points can only be used to purchase food and/or nonalcoholic beverages from any Casino restaurant. They cannot be use to purchase alcoholic beverages, to cover gratuities, or to purchase any other product or service offered by the Casino.

4.   Players present their Player's Club Card at the Blackjack table at the start and end of each playing session.

5.   Hostesses and/or supervisors may also perform regular checks to log points every hour for the players, as well as to insure that players that are no longer playing have been clocked out.

TABLE GAMES CHIP AND CASH HANDLING

1.   The clearing of hands must be performed anytime the dealer reaches below the table surface, touches his/her own person or another person, passes any object to another person, or disposes of any object. This consists of simply extending both palms upward and then turning the palms down in one motion.

2.   The dealer will count all cash facedown in vertical columns on the table surface so that the denomination of each bill is visible. Cash is counted in columns of five (5), or large amounts may be counted in columns of ten (10), so that the count can be easily verified by Surveillance.

3.   All $100 and $50 bills must be checked with the Counterfeit Bill Pen before being exchanged for chips.

4.   Four or more $20.00 bills handed in by the same guest must be checked with the Counterfeit Bill Pen before being exchanged for chips.

5.   When counting out chips, do so in stacks and spread the I stack in a way that all chips can be counted by Surveillance. $1, $5, and $100 chips are counted in stacks of five (5). $25 chips are counted in stacks of four (4). $500 chips (if applicable) are counted in stacks of two (2). $1000 chips (if applicable) are counted one-by-one.

6.   The dealer calls out "Change $, table #__" on all cash transactions. The dealer must receive approval from a Floor Supervisor before completing a cash transaction of $100 or more.

7.   When changing smaller denomination chips to larger denomination chips, it is called "coloring up", and should be performed when the player finishes his playing session and prepares to leave the table.

TABLE GAMES PROTECTION
OVERVIEW
Protection of tribal assets from fraud and theft through illegal gaming play and/or employee misconduct requires not only the careful placement of security cameras and electronic equipment, but also the direct involvement of highly skilled surveillance staff members, well-trained Table Games Supervisors, Pit Bosses, Dealers, and Floor Runners, as well as competent and involved Gaming Commission Compliance and Investigative officers.

PROTECTION PROCEDURES
1.   CAMERA PLACEMENT: In order to observe both dealer and player actions during a card game, surveillance cameras should be placed directly over each gaming table. These cameras are constantly being recorded to a VCR in the event there is a patron dispute, a jackpot, or a requirement to investigate suspected cheating by either an employee or a patron. Occasionally, in support of routine housekeeping requirements or table maintenance, Blackjack tables may occasionally be moved out of position; therefore, it is imperative that the Surveillance Office monitors the tables locations and adjusts their camera positions as required.

2.   CARD CHEATING METHODS: There are some basic assumptions that can be made when considering the topic of cheating. The first, and probably most important, is that where there is money, someone will find a way to steal it. There is always someone that will try and take advantage of any given situation. Sloppy dealers and inattentive supervisors contribute to ideal situations for a cheater to take advantage of the casino. However, good dealer "procedures" will always beat a cheater's "move". Cheating may be divided into a number of general categories, which are discussed below.

a.   Dealer Dumping: Whenever a dealer cheats either a player or the house, a procedure must be broken. Dumping the game may happen in a variety of ways. False shuffling, dealing seconds, peeking, and rolling the deck are single-deck methods used to dump a game. In almost all cases, the dealer's "move" is disguised by diverting attention to the other end of the table, perhaps by moving an ashtray. Dealers using a combination of a "peek" and a "second" deal are a common method of cheating when a dealer and a player are in collusion.

b.   With a "peek", the dealer learns the value of the top card. If it is high, and the dealer wishes to keep it, the second card is dealt. Dealers who deal "seconds" or "peek" must use a "mechanic's grip". The deck not being squared when offered for the cut indicates a false shuffle. It is a technique used by the dealer to apparently shuffle the cards in the normal manner, but the original order of cards is not disturbed by the shuffling activity. A "hop" cut is used to false-cut the deck. Tipping or flashing the hole card can be done by the dealer turning the deck over while it is held in the deck hand and pushing the top card off slightly to expose the value of the next card to the accomplice. Other ways of dumping a game are by overpaying bets and making incorrect change. Finally, "coolers", i.e. prearranged replacement decks or shoes can be put into a game as part of a scam.

c.   Cutting: Stutter cutting, Drop cutting, Knuckle cutting and cutting to either a crimp or a nick are single-deck techniques used by the cheater only when the house rules permit lift cutting. A skilled cutter using these techniques is able to manipulate, or steer, favorable cards into play for themselves, or manipulate unfavorable cards out of play. It is also possible to identify a card and then force it into the dealer's hand as the hole card. Crimping Aces and then cutting to them is an easy method for the cheater to guarantee getting one. A slight hesitation as the cards are lifted is a good indicator of a bad cut. Use of a pl ic cut card is an extremely effective way for the house to control the cut.

d.   Hole Card Play: There are a variety of ways for a player to spot the dealer's hole card. Common methods include using shiners and prisms, spooking, TV cameras, first or third basing, or sloppy dealing techniques. A glim, or shiner, is a small-concealed mirror used to get a reflection of the face of the hole card as it is buried. Shiners may be concealed in a variety of items such as in a cigarette pack or in an ice cube in a drink. Any flat reflective surface can also serve as a shiner, even something as simple as the surface of a cup of coffee.

e.   Gaffing: Cards can be marked, or "gaffed", in a variety of ways to include daubs, crimps, nicks, sanding, shaving and dimpling. This so called "paperwork" is a fairly common form of cheating at casinos.

f.   Cheating techniques that use a fingernail or device to mark the edges of a key card are called "edgework". Cards can be nicked, sanded, shaved or dimpled on the side to help the cheater locate the valuable card. An equally effective method of marking cards is to bend them in some fashion that allows them to stand out from the rest of the deck. Another way of gaffing a deck of cards is by daubing, crimping or dimpling the top of the cards. Numerous substances that are easily obtainable can be used to daub a deck. Examples are cigarette ash, dirt from a shoe, or "shade", an alcohol based substance that is very difficult to detect. The most sophisticated sort of daubed deck is called the "juice" deck, and only the person who put them there can usually detect the markings. One way to tell if the backs of cards are marked is to use the "riffle" test, also called "going to the movies". If the cards are marked, a quick riffle through the deck will often times reveal a moving picture with spots and lines jumping in different directions compared to the pattern of the back design.

g.   Mucking: Another method of cheating that requires a sleight-of-hand skill like a magician is "mucking". Hand muckers will work as a team or individually. The individual will muck cards in and out of the game from a cache of cards hidden under their leg or from inside their coat. Card switching is another mucking technique. A single player, who plays multiple hands may do it, or it may be done by a team who will switch cards from one person's hand to another. No cards are brought in from the outside, rather, dealt cards are switched from one hand to another.

h.   Pinching and Pressing: Although a crude method of cheating, pinching and pressing/capping bets are probably the most common and easiest to detect. When a player pinches a bet, he decreases the bet after acquiring knowledge of the game's outcome. When a player caps or presses a bet, he increases the bet.

442

i.   Electronics: The newest and most sophisticated method of cheating involves the use of computers and other electronic devices. The most common use of the device is to keep track of the card values, so that an increase or decrease of the bet can be made. These devices can be concealed on a person's body under his clothes, or in a vehicle in the parking lot using concealed transmitters and receivers.

j.   Magnets and Loaded Dice: In those table games that use dice as part of the play, such as Pai Gow and Pan 9, cheaters may try to introduce dice that have been weighted with metal in order to influence the outcome of the dice roll. Sometimes a magnet is placed under the table, and used in conjunction with loaded dice, in an attempt to control the game where the action begins.

CASH OPERATIONS
OVERVIEW
The casino's Cash Operation system deals with accounting for the operations of a casino's business. The Cash Operations are tied to the internal control system that should be in place to comply with the NIGC Minimum Internal Control Standards. At the same time, Cash Operations should focus specifically on accounting operations and procedures to ensure that the system provides proper control over tribal assets.

CASH OPERATIONS GUIDELINES
Management is responsible for establishing, implementing, and maintaining casino's accounting and finance system. One of the primary goals of the system should be to provide management with reliable financial information for carrying out its operations. The policies and procedures are designed to provide reasonable assurance that five (5) basic objectives are being met:

1.   Validation: The examination of documentation by someone with an understanding of the accounting system, for evidence that a recorded transaction actually took place, and that it occurred in accordance with prescribed procedures.

2.   Accuracy: Concerned with amounts and account classification as achieved by establishing control tasks to check calculations, extensions, additions, and account classifications.

3.   Completeness: Ensures that all transactions are recorded on a control document and accepted for processing once and once only.

4.   Maintenance: Monitor accounting records after the entry of transactions to ensure that they continue to reflect accurately the operations of the business.

5.   Physical: Requires that access to assets be limited to authorized personnel only.

STANDARDS FOR SUPERVISION
1.   Personnel with authority equal to or greater than those being supervised shall provide supervision at all times in the Cage, in the Vault, and in Accounting and Finance when the casino is in operation, and when monies are being counted, transferred, and recorded.

2.   Chips and monetary equivalents transferred to or from the Cashier's cage to the gaming operations or to the bank shall be properly authorized and documented. An individual who is independent of the cage or the gaming operations shall carry all transfers.

DROP AND COUNT PROCEDURES
The collection of monies will be on a regular and consistent basis, and the monies will be immediately counted and recorded in accordance with NIGC MICS requirements.

1.   Access to the count room during the count will be limited to only count team members and others authorized by the General Manager. Gaming Commission staff members will also have unlimited access to the count room. It is preferred, although not mandatory, that a Compliance Officer be present during each count.

2.   Count team members will where a smock or a jumpsuit (without pockets) at all times while in the count room, and will take the smock or jumpsuit off immediately outside the count room before exiting for breaks or shift changes.

3.   The casino Shift Manager will notify Surveillance when the count is about to begin and at le one Surveillance Officer will monitor the drop in its entirety.

4.   The recorder and at le one other member of the count team shall each verify the summary document and attest by signature to the accuracy of the count.

CAGE AND VAULT PROCEDURES
1.   The door to the Cage/Vault area is to be secured at all times.

2.   Security must accompany non-cage personnel such as external auditors who need access to the cage/vault. Gaming Commission staff (Compliance Officers, Internal Auditors) does not require an escort.

3.   All cage banks and cash drawers are to be verified before personnel leave the cage area.

4.   Personal items such as purses, bags, coats, lunch bags, etc., are not to be in the cage, vault, or count room areas at any time.

5.   Each cashier must count down their chips and cash at shift end, and complete a Cashier's Shift Report that tracks all transactions that occurred during the shift.

ACCOUNTING AND FINANCE PROCEDURES
1.   Mail is to be picked up from the box by an Accounting department staff member and delivered to the Receptionist where it will be opened, dated, and time-stamped. Checks will immediately be endorsed with a restrictive "For Deposit Only" stamp and recorded on a deposit slip. Once the day's receipts are recorded, the checks and deposit slip are to be delivered to the Vault for inclusion in the day's deposit.

2.   Account classification titles will be descriptive enough to indicate specific General Ledger accounts.

3.   Accounts will be arranged in the same sequence as they appear in the financial statements (i.e. Asset Accounts, Liability Accounts, Capital Accounts, Revenue Accounts, Direct Expense Accounts, and Operating Expense Accounts).

4.   The Accounts Payable Clerk will ensure that proper documentation is completed before payments are made to vendors. The documentation will include the original Purchase Requisition, the packing slip, the Vendor Invoice, and any other supporting documentation.

5.   All vendor payments in excess of $550 must be paid by check. Invoices of less than $550 may be paid from petty cash funds.

6.   The Controller shall prepare all bank reconciliation statements within 3 days of receiving the monthly bank statements. Financial statements may not be issued until the bank reconciliation process is complete.

7.   Authorized check signers must be approved in writing and require a majority vote of the Tribal Executive Committee. All checks require two authorized signatures.

8.   The Revenue Audit Department is responsible for the distribution of daily, weekly, and monthly gaming operation revenue reports to the Accounting Department for recording in the General Ledger.

9.   The Chief Financial Officer and the Controller are responsible for the timely and efficient preparation and distribution of monthly financial statements to the General Manager and the Executive Committee.

10.   A comprehension annual budget shall be prepared by the General Manager and the Controller, and approved by the Executive Committee of the Tribe each year.

GCP&P.010   SURVEILLANCE OPERATIONS
OVERVIEW

The Surveillance Department's goal is to provide adequate video camera coverage to reasonably assure the protection of Tribal assets and assist in the safety and security of patrons, employees, and their personal property. In support of that goal, several hundred cameras, which are being recorded by VCRs 24 hours a day, are located throughout the Casino and are positioned to provide coverage of key gaming and cash operations locations. Additionally, other operational and storage areas in the Casino, such as offices, kitchens, storerooms, and hallways are covered to monitor general employee activity.

1.   SURVEILLANCE REQUIREMENTS: In order to comply with the Internal Controls of the Tribal Gaming Commission, the Casino's surveillance system must meet the following requirements:

a.   One pan-tilt-zoom camera shall be provided for every two gaming tables with sufficient clarity to identify the patrons and the dealers and with sufficient coverage to simultaneously view the red rack and determine the configuration of wagers, card values and game outcome.

b.   Each progressive table game with a potential progressive jackpot of $25,000 or more (if any) must have sufficient camera coverage of the table to determine the card values and an overall view of the entire table to identify the patrons and the dealer.

c.   The capability to monitor the Bingo random generator, the game board and the activities of the Bingo caller.

d.   Gaming machines offering payouts must be monitored by a dedicated camera and provide coverage of all patrons and employees at the gaming machine and the face of the gaming machine with sufficient clarity to identify the payout line on the machine.

e.   The surveillance system must be able to monitor and record a general overview of activities occurring in each cash cage and the main bank area with sufficient clarity to identify employees within the cage and patrons and employees at the counter areas.

f.   The cages in which fills and credits are transacted shall be monitored and recorded with sufficient clarity to identify the chip values and the amounts on the fill and credit slips.

g.   The system shall monitor and record the soft and hard count rooms (as applicable), all surfaces where money is counted, and all money counters and sorters.

h.   All video recordings must be retained for a minimum of seven days. Recordings involving suspected gaming crimes, unlawful activity, or detentions by Security personnel must be retained for at le thirty days.

i.   The surveillance department must maintain adequate logs and records of system malfunction/repair, video libraries and surveillance activities.

STRUCTURE
The Surveillance Department is directed by the Surveillance Manager, who is assisted by a Surveillance Supervisor. In addition, on every shift there is a Surveillance Lead and at le one additional Surveillance Officer.

DUTIES AND RESPONSIBILITIES
The Surveillance Department observation room is manned 24 hours a day, and is located so that it is not readily accessible by either employees or the general public. Shift personnel maintain continuous surveillance of the Casino by monitoring various cameras, and as required, they adhere to standard procedures for the following routine activities:

1.   Daily VCR tape change.

2.   Table game jackpot reviews.

3.   Slot jackpot review.
4.   Card issue.

5.   Casino management tape review requests.

6.   Tape pull and review for investigations.
7.   Casino alarm response.

GCP&P.004   GAMING CENTER'S MANAGEMENT TEAM
OVERVIEW
Gaming Commission personnel must all be familiar with the topics that are covered by the Gaming Center's Policies and Procedures. Violations of Policies and Procedures must be addressed in reports generated by Commission Staff; therefore, a good working knowledge of them is essential.
DEPARTMENTS
1.   The casino's Human Resources department is responsible to research, develop, write and coordinate implementation of Policies and Procedures (P&Ps) that are required in the conduct of Casino business and are in compliance with applicable government regulatory requirements. New or revised P&Ps are sent to all affected Departments and the Gaming Commission for review, input and approval. After the Gaming Commission's final approval, the Gaming Center's General Manager must approve and sign the new Policy and Procedure. The following is a brief description of the major sections of the P&P manual:
a.   Under the direction of the General Manager, the Gaming Center is organized into various functional departments, each with their own manager.
1.   Support Services (Housekeeping, Maintenance, etc.)
2.   Gaming
3.   Finance and Accounting
4. Marketing
                              5. Security
6.   Cage Operations
7.   Human Resources
8.   Facilities
9.   Video Gaming Department
10.   Bingo
11.   Blackjack
12.   Off Track Betting
13.   Administration
14.   Snack Bar (Food and Beverage)
2.   The Gaming Center is open for gaming operations 24 hours a day. In support of that schedule, Casino employees are organized into three shifts: day, swing and graveyard. Each shift has the following key personnel on duty:

a.	OTB Supervisor
b.	Casino Manager on Duty (MOD)
c.	Food and Beverage Shift Manager
d.	Cage Operations Shift Manager
e.	Slot Shift Supervisor
f.	Maintenance Shift Supervisor
g.	Security Shift Watch Commander
h.	Black Jack Shift Supervisor
i.	Bingo Supervisor
j.	Compliance Officer
k.	Vault Personnel

DISCIPLINARY ACTIONS

Any employee activity that is detrimental to the public health, safety, morals, good order and general welfare of the Tribe, or would reflect or tend to reflect discredit upon the Tribe or the Gaming Operation shall be considered an unsuitable method of operation and shall be grounds for disciplinary action by the Gaming Commission.

Casino management may first be given an opportunity to take corrective action. The following acts are examples of unsuitable methods of operations:

a.	Permitting persons who are obviously intoxicated to participate in gaming activity.
b.	Failure to comply with Tribal laws and regulations.
c.	Denying Gaming agents access to any information.
d.	Abuse of comp privileges.
e.	Theft or misappropriation of Tribal assets.

GAMING COMMISSION LICENSES

Gaming Center employees must display their current Gaming License at all times while on the gaming floor. The license should be worn or displayed at about chest height, similar to the manner in which a name tag is normally worn. No employee may work a shift at the Gaming Center without a valid license in their possession. If necessary, the employee must return home to obtain their license, and will not be paid for the time away from their job.

UNIFORMS

Gaming Employees working in gaming operations, snack bar (Food and Beverage), Off-Track Betting, Security and the Cage or main Bank will wear the approved Gaming center uniforms at all times.

ACCESS CONTROL

The Casino's Cash Cage area may only be entered by authorized casino employees, gaming commissioners, gaming commission staff, security, and authorized representatives such as external auditors.

GCP&P.005   CASINO EMERGENCIES

OVERVIEW

An emergency is any sudden and unpredictable occurrence, which causes partial or total disruption to Casino operations. Examples of emergency situations include, but are not limited to, earthquakes, power outages, fires, explosions, flooding, water pipe breaks, bomb threats, computer network difficulties, and criminal conduct, etc. The Gaming Center General Manager has overall responsibility for handling emergency situations so that any adverse impact on tribal assets, casino operations, customers, and employees is minimized. In support of that responsibility, the General Manager is required to establish and maintain a documented, standardized Action Plan to be implemented automatically in the event of an emergency. To facilitate implementation of the Action Plan, the General Manager uses a "recall roster" containing current information on key personnel (usually selected department heads), to form the Action Team for the current emergency. The actual makeup of the team depends on the nature of the emergency. For each Action Plan, applicable departments are responsible for establishing, maintaining, and using written procedures, which provide detailed descriptions of the tasks to be performed during the emergency.

1.   **EMERGENCY VEHICLES:** In the event the nature of the emergency requires the use of an emergency vehicle, designated parking is available at the Main Entrance and at the Employees' Entrance.

2.   **EMERGENCY CODES AND PROCEDURES:** In support of certain emergencies, the Security Department has developed specific standard operating procedures (SOP) and uses the standard Public Safety Ten Code code words.

3.   **CASINO ALARMS:** The Gaming Center has an alarm system. The alarm panels for the system are in the Surveillance Office, which is the only location where the alarm sounds if activated. If an alarm sounds, controlling actions for the Surveillance Officer on shift are as follows:

a.	Contact Security and identify the type of alarm (Smoke, fire, intrusion, weather).
b.	Identify the location.
c.	Align a surveillance camera on the location.
d.	Notify the Shift Manager and follow instructions for contacting 911 emergency services.
e.	In the event of an evacuation, Surveillance will do a check of surveillance cameras and ensure no patrons or employees remain in the facility.

AUTHORITY

The Tribe of State is a federally recognized tribe exercising all inherent sovereign rights, and operates under a constitution approved by the Department of Interior. The Tribal Executive Committee is empowered by the Constitution to conduct business on behalf of the Tribe, and has granted authority to the Gaming Center General Manager to prepare for and respond to casino emergencies.

GCP&P.006   INVESTIGATIONS

OVERVIEW

In accordance with the Tribal Gaming Ordinance, any and all unusual occurrences and all violations or suspected violations with the gaming operation are to be recorded, investigated, and filed. There are two recognized investigative authorities at the Gaming Center: the Tribal Gaming Commission and the Security Department. Each entity shall have distinctively different reporting and investigative responsibilities.

1.   Tribal Gaming Commission Compliance Officers shall have sole authority and responsibility to conduct investigations and file reports related to the following activity:

445

a.   Patron disputes with the Gaming Operation.

b.   Internal control violations.

c.   Any real or suspected criminal activity including but not limited to theft, fraud, counterfeit slot tickets and/or currency, assault, cheating, property damage, etc., whether by patron or employee.

d.   Any civil violations of any applicable Federal, State, or Tribal gaming regulations or laws.

2.   The Security Department is responsible for filing reports in the following incidents and Compliance Officers will assist by request only:

a.   Disorderly conduct and/or exclusions of patrons for conduct not in the best interests of Gaming Center.

b.   Accident or injury reports involving patrons or employees.

c.   Accidental property damage reports.

d.   Safety, health or security hazards.

e.   Lost and Found items.

3.   Investigating a counterfeit bill is a common occurrence for Gaming Commission Compliance Officers. A requirement for this type of investigation is to complete a Counterfeit Note Report, which is a four-copy (white, blue, yellow, pink) carbon-backed document. This form is used to record information regarding the subject who had possession of or "passed" the counterfeit bill and the counterfeit bill itself. It is imperative that all necessary information be recorded on this document. When the Surveillance Department is contacted regarding counterfeit currency, the situation should be referred to by a code name, such as a "Mr. Smith", to avoid tipping off the patron who passed the counterfeit note. When investigating counterfeit currency, it is necessary for the Compliance Officer to perform several counterfeit tests on the suspect bill. Compliance Officers will encounter counterfeit bills of varying quality with the higher quality counterfeit bills being capable of thwarting some of the basic examination points. Read the material "Know your Money" and "New Designs for Your Money" provided by the US Treasury Department for reference. The following tests should be conducted at a minimum until a conclusion can be drawn regarding the bill as genuine or counterfeit:

a.   Visual: Inspect the bill for crispness and clarity of important features (Portrait of President, Concentric lines, Denomination of bill over the Treasury Seal, etc.). If the bill appears to not look right, it probably isn't. Hold the bill up to adequate lighting and check for the inscribed security thread. The security thread is located to the left of the Federal Reserve Seal and runs vertical. It will have the letters USA, the written denomination of the bill (Twenty, Five, Ten) on lower denominations, or "USA 50" and "USA 100" on larger denominations. Use a magnifying glass to visually inspect suspected bills, if you are unable to draw a conclusion, consult with a fellow Compliance Officer, Surveillance Supervisor, or the Director of Surveillance for guidance and/or assistance.

b.   Metallic Ink Test: The Money Tester ST-008 is one of the more reliable testing devices for detecting counterfeit bills as it is difficult to replicate the metallic ink that is in genuine bills. The ST-008 checks the metallic content of the ink in the bill. If the ST-008 "Beeps" and the red indicator light comes on, the bill may be genuine. Place the suspect bill on top of the felt cover, depress the button on the top of the ST-008 and slide it back and fourth across the bill. Listen for the "Beep" and look for the red indicator light.

c.   Counterfeit Detection Pen: The counterfeit detection pen is not a foolproof detection device and should not be used as the primary testing device for counterfeit bills. Take the counterfeit pen and make a mark on the suspect bill. If the mark stays clear, the bill is less suspect, and if the mark turns to a dark brown or black color, the bill is highly suspect. Counterfeit artists will often dip their counterfeit bills in a waxy or oily substance to defeat the counterfeit detection pen.

4.   Anytime suspected counterfeit notes are seized from a patron, a Cash Receipts Voucher should be used to record the amount of money. A copy of the receipt should be given to the customer as proof that the Gaming Center has seized the suspected counterfeit notes. In the event that the money is genuine, the dollar amount recorded on the receipt will be returned to the patron. The Incident Report number should also be recorded on the receipt for later reference.

5.   During the course of an investigation voluntary statements from witnesses, suspects, or victims should be recorded. The witness, suspect, or victim should verbally describe what took place during the incident. The investigative officer should then ask the individuals involved to read and sign the voluntary statement, which acknowledges that their voluntary cooperation. At that point, the individuals would write out their voluntary statement. Investigating officers should then question the individuals regarding omitted information, added information, or other inconsistencies between their verbal description and their written statement.

6.   Be On the Lookout (BOL) Procedures: In the course of conducting an investigation, there are many instances when the suspect(s) of the investigation are not immediately identified or found in the Casino at the time of the incident. In those cases, it is appropriate for the Investigating Officer to initiate and post a BOL for the suspect in order that other Surveillance Department personnel on subsequent shifts can identify the suspect in the event they to return to the Casino. A BOL is generated by obtaining the best possible surveillance camera picture of the suspect, and attaching the picture to the designated BOL form. Once completed, the BOL must be approved and initialed by a Supervisor before it can be posted on the designated clipboard and included as an attachment to an associated Incident Report. When reproducing a BOL for an Incident Report, three copies should be made and submitted, so that the original can be posted.

7.   Gaming Commission Letter Service Procedures: Often times, as a result of an investigation, Compliance Officers are asked to serve various types of letters to Casino employees from the Gaming Commission outside the normal working hours of Commission personnel. Examples include requests to contact Background Investigators, notification of planned hearings, letters of warning, and occasionally, summary suspension of employee gaming licenses. Under normal circumstances, service of these letters is very routine, and there is no requirement for witnesses or video recording of the service. In these cases, it is appropriate to serve the letter off the Casino floor in some type of privacy, so as not to cause any embarrassment to the employee. However, when serving a summary suspension of a gaming license, prior coordination with Casino management, Human Resources employee relations personnel, and the Security Department is required.

AUTHORITY

Tribal Gaming Commission investigative authority is derived from Section 102 of the Tribal Gaming Ordinance, and from the regulatory responsibilities granted to Tribal Regulatory bodies in the Indian Gaming Regulatory Act.

CRIMINAL ACTIVITY

Suspected criminal activity may be investigated by authorized Tribal Gaming Commission staff members (Compliance Officers and Internal Auditor), but early coordination with Tribal Police, city and county law enforcement agencies, and State and Federal agencies (when necessary), regarding the suspected criminal activity, is mandatory. The Gaming Commission Executive Director has the responsibility to establish effective communication and coordination with his law enforcement counterparts.

MICS VIOLATIONS

Violations of Tribal Minimum Internal Control Standards may be identified by Surveillance, discovered in the course of routine or special auditing work by the Internal Auditor, or observed by Compliance Officers in the course of their normal duties. These observed violations will be investigated, and a report written for the Gaming Commission, for the Department Manager, and for the casino General Manager. Corrective action is to be taken by the casino management team, and a written response detailing that action is due to the Gaming Commission within 14 days. The incident will be followed up by Gaming Commission staff members within six (6) months to determine whether the violations have been corrected.

TRIBAL GAMING ORDINANCE VIOLATIONS

Violations of the Tribal Gaming Ordinance will be investigated by Compliance and Internal Audit, and if confirmed, the subject will served with a copy of the findings and notified of a Gaming Commission Hearing in which the subject will have the opportunity to be heard and present evidence to the contrary in accordance with Sections 109-111 of the Tribal Gaming Ordinance.

CASINO POLICY & PROCEDURE VIOLATIONS

Violations of Gaming Center Policies and Procedures observed by Gaming Commission staff members will be reported to casino management for corrective action. Management responses should be returned to the Gaming Commission within fourteen (14) days. If violations persist, the Gaming Commission may be required to suspend or revoke the subject's gaming license pursuant to Section 108 of the Tribal Gaming Ordinance.

GCP&P.007   INTERVIEW PROCEDURES AND TECHNIQUES

OVERVIEW

Interviews are a necessary part of any criminal investigation, and can be very effective if conducted properly.

INTERVIEW PROCEDURES

Interviews should be conducted in a secure room with both camera and audio coverage, and the sessions must be recorded by VCR with the tapes maintained for at le thirty (30) days. In the event that the tape becomes part of a criminal or civil legal matter, it must be maintained until the conclusion of those proceedings.

Prior to and after conducting any interview, the immediate area around the interview desk must be checked for proof of any evidence that the person being interviewed might have tried to discard during the interview. The interview is recorded by ensuring that the VCR associated with the dedicated camera is placed in the record mode, and that the associated audio recorder on top of the VCR is turned on and adjusted per the posted instructions. A dedicated log sheet is located with the interview VCR tape, which must be completed after each interview.

When conducting an interview, a Surveillance Supervisor, if available, should also sit in on the interview as a witness for the Compliance Officer, as well as to assist the Compliance Officer if required. If a Supervisor is not available, then another Compliance Officer or a Surveillance Officer on duty should be used. In those cases when others are not available, it is permissible to have a security officer act as a witness. Depending on the nature of the interview, or if it is likely that an exclusion from the Casino may result at the end of the interview, the presence of a security officer is always appropriate.

In all cases when a male Compliance Officer is interviewing a female subject, the witness must also be a female to protect against any accusations of sexual harassment. With the exception of the security officer, all witnesses should be seated behind the Compliance Officer, and all witnesses must remain clear of the camera recording the interview. To ensure that privacy is maintained during the interview, Compliance Officers should post the designated sign on the door so as to prevent unauthorized access to the interview room.

INTERVIEW TECHNIQUES

While questioning an individual, it is important to read the person's body language. People for the most part will answer a question without a verbal response. Studies have shown that when a person looks off to their left in the thought process, they are referring to the creative side of their brain for answers. When a person looks off to their right side, they are referring to the factual side of their brain. In other words, a person who looks off to their right when thinking of an answer to a question generally will tell the truth.

Additionally, if the person being interviewed is threatened by the line of questioning or the subject brought to their attention, that individual will generally want to move away from the interviewer. They will re-position themselves in their seat or push away from the desktop to get space between themselves and the person conducting the interview.

GCP&P.008   INCIDENT REPORTS

OVERVIEW

Incident reports are prepared by Compliance Officers, Security Officers, and Surveillance Officers, and include pertinent information involving patron disputes, criminal activity, or violations of tribal minimum internal control standards and/or Gaming Center policies and procedures. Incident reports are used to keep the Gaming Commissioners and casino management informed of all casino activities related to their regulatory responsibilities.

REPORT FORMAT

Below is a list of procedures to follow regarding the Gaming Commission's Incident Reports.

1.   Select Microsoft ACCESS thru the Program menu on the computer.
2.   Select C: Incident Report.
3.   Select "OK"
4.   Input password into dialog box.
5.   Press enter.
6.   When the Incident report format appears, select the enlarge button in the upper right hand corner of the report format.
7.   The first incident report will appear. Select the scroll arrow in the lower left corner of the report format.
8.   Scroll through the reports until you reach the next blank report.
9.   Begin the report writing process.
10. IR Number: automatic and cannot be changed.
12. Date and Time: automatic.
13. Type of Incident: Use only one item from the drop-down box.
i)   Description of Incident: Use a short description of the incident.
ii) (i.e. Petty Theft, Failure to clear jackpot, Overpayment, etc.)
iii) Location of Incident: Stand number (07/07/01), West Parking Lot, Main Cage, Soft Count, etc.
14. Officers Name: Use only one item from the drop-down box.
15. Department: Department affected, i.e. Slot, F & B, Security, etc.
16. Department Supervisor: Example: Doe, Jane.
17. Machine Number: 4-digit casino number.
18. Subject 1 Name: L Name, First Name.
19. Subject 1 Address: Address and City.
20. Subject 1 Phone: Contact number.
21. Exclusion: Select Yes or No.
22. Date Start: Current Date.
23. Date End 1: Next Day or 30 Days.
24. If the Subject is an employee, use the following format:
Subject 1 Name: "Doe, John".
Subject 1 Address: "Slot Technician".
Subject 1 Phone: "246" (GC License number).

447

26.   Witness 1 Name: use steps 19-21 or 25.

27.   Witness 1 Address: use steps 19-21 or 25.

28.   Witness 1 Phone: use steps 19-21 or 25.

29.   Follow-up Action: If the incident is resolved (i.e. employee's supervisor was advised of the P & P violation) select "no". If the investigation is pending and needs additional information select "yes".

30.   Evidence Seized: Select Yes or No.

31. Video Camera: Obtain information from surveillance if needed.

32. Associated Security: Security or Surveillance case number.

33. Location of Evidence: GC, Surveillance, Security or Other.

34. Detailed Explanation of Incident:

a. Use Third person format on reports.

b. Use paragraph form with indentations.

c. Skip a line between paragraphs.

d. List employees by their title and first and l name.

e. After listing the employee's name at the beginning of the report, refer to them by their l name for the remainder of the report.

f. After completing the narrative section, use the following section:

1ATTACHMENTS: List all attachments to the report (i.e. copy of security report, count room report, etc.).

2FOLLOW-UP: List any follow-up information needed.

3CONCLUSION: Use a short narrative regarding the conclusion of the report and the specific violation that occurred. (i.e. Jones violated Slot Host P& P Page 21, section 3; Failure to carry Gaming License, etc.).

35. Place "N/A in every blank area.

36. Proofread your report.

37. Select PRINT from top dropdown box.

38. Select SELECTED RECORD from Print Range box.

39. Select "OK".

40. Place completed report with any attachments in the INCOMING basket in the mailbox in the compliance office.

GCP&P.009   PATRON DISPUTES

OVERVIEW

Gaming Center management shall make every effort to resolve patron disputes over payment of alleged winnings or other disputes involving money to the satisfaction of all parties. Whether or not a Gaming Commission employee (Compliance Officer) gets involved in the dispute depends on the amount of money involved and whether management is able to satisfactorily resolve the issue.

POLICY

For disputes involving $100 OR Less, the Casino Shift Manager On Duty (MOD) is allowed to exercise discretionary authority to pay patrons disputed amounts up to a limit of $100. The decision to pay can be made even if technical evidence indicates that the patron is not entitled to it. However, this judgment is to be based on an analysis regarding:

1.   Whether it is in the best interest of the Tribe for public relations purposes.

2.   Whether the cost of conducting the investigation exceeds the benefit (cost-benefit analysis).

3.   Whether this is a known, valued patron, or one whose complaints are frequent and without merit.

4.   Whether the dispute appears to be a simple scam attempt.

For disputes involving between $100 - $500, the casino's General Manager shall attempt to resolve the dispute. However, if after negotiation the patron is still dissatisfied with the decision, management is required to inform the patron that he or she has the right to have a Gaming Commission Compliance Officer conduct an investigation. Should the patron remain unhappy with the results of Compliance Officer's investigation, they must be informed of their right to appeal the decision at a regularly scheduled Gaming Commission meeting.

For disputes involving funds in excess of $500, casino management must immediately notify a Gaming Commission Compliance Officer, who will initiate an Incident Report for the record. After discussing the situation with the Compliance Officer and reviewing relevant surveillance tapes, management will make a decision on how to resolve the dispute. If the decision does not satisfy the patron, or if the Compliance Officer disagrees with the decision, the Compliance Officer must notify the patron of appeal rights and procedures. The Compliance Officer will then conduct an investigation and submit an Incident Report to the Gaming Commission. Should the patron remain unhappy with the results of that investigation, they may appeal the decision at a regularly scheduled Gaming Commission meeting. The Executive Director will review the incident and make recommendations to the Gaming Commission. Following the patron's appeal, the Gaming Commission will render a binding decision.

GCP&P.010   ARREST AND DETENTION

OVERVIEW

An arrest is defined as the act of taking an individual or group of individuals into custody in a case, and in the manner defined by law.

POLICY

An arrest may be made by a peace officer or by a private person (OK Penal Code).

Tribal Compliance Officers do not have peace officer arrest powers and are considered a private person, and may effect an arrest under the following conditions:

1.   A private person may arrest another for a public offense committed or attempted in his presence.

2.   A felony is a crime, which is punishable with death or by imprisonment in the state prison. Every other crime or public offense is a misdemeanor except those offenses that are classified as infractions (OK Penal Code).

3.   A private person who has arrested another for the commission of a public offense must, without unnecessary delay, take the person arrested before a magistrate or deliver him to a peace officer (OK Penal Code).

Tribal Compliance Officers have authority to detain persons involved in criminal acts only until Tribal Police or other local or county law enforcement officials arrive at the scene. Tribal Compliance Officers may interview suspects and witnesses, on a voluntary basis, without the presence of duly appointed law enforcement officers, but may not detain them unless law enforcement representatives are called.

GCP&P.011   EXCLUSION PROCEDURES

OVERVIEW

The Tribal Gaming Commission may establish a list of persons who are to be excluded from the Casino. This list may include any person whose presence is determined to pose a threat to the interests of the Tribe, the gaming public, or to licensed gaming. Such conduct shall include, but is not limited to, violations of Federal or State law, violations of any Tribal-State compact, violations of the Tribal Gaming Ordinance, or any conduct which adversely affects the health, security and welfare of the Casino, such as cheating, assault, theft, panhandling, misrepresentation, fraud, threatening

448

or intimidating behavior, intoxication, or disorderly conduct. Any person on the exclusion list who enters the Casino or engages in any game shall be considered trespassing.

AUTHORITY
Only casino Security personnel or employees of the Gaming Commission in coordination with Casino management can exclude a person from the casino. The initial notice of exclusion is valid for a period of up to 30 days. Any desire to exclude a person for more than 30 days must be submitted in writing to the Gaming Commission along with justification.

PATRON EXCLUSION
Exclusion of a patron requires the service of an Exclusion Letter. Before issuing the letter, the Director of the Surveillance Department must be notified, and if he is not available, then the approval from a Surveillance Supervisor must be obtained. In such cases, a phone message must be left on the Director's answering machine or voice mail.
The form letter must be completely filled out and signed by the patron and the issuing Compliance Officer. A photocopy of the patron's driver's license or identification card must be made. There should be one normal size copy for the Exclusion Letter and three 150% zoom size copies for attachment to the Incident Report. In addition, two photos of the patron must be taken. One should be a Polaroid picture for the Exclusion Letter and the other should be a digital photo for inclusion in the Exclusion database. To complete the form, the normal size copy of the patron's identification card and the Polaroid photo are attached to the Exclusion Letter. The Exclusion Letter should be copied and attached to all copies of the associated Incident Report generated by the Compliance Officer. The patron should be given one copy and must be escorted out of the building and off casino property by a Security Officer.

EMPLOYEE EXCLUSION
In the event that the person to be excluded is an employee, a special Gaming Commission memo is used, versus the standard Exclusion Letter. That letter is maintained on the Compliance Officer computer under a special file and is completed and printed out as needed. Similar to a patron's exclusion, an excluded employee must be escorted off of casino property by a Security Officer. Caution should be observed so that the employee is not embarrassed during the removal.

SELF-EXCLUSION
Patrons may request a Self-Exclusion from the Tribal Gaming Commission. The application will be considered in a regular gaming commission meeting, and if granted, notification will be sent to casino management, Security, and Surveillance.

74 My aforementioned hire for Atlantic City

75 Steve Wynn gets annual salary boost of $1 million, Las Vegas Sun Feb. 28, 2011

76 Sample executive employment contract:

April 17, 2000
Dear Mr. Pickus:
This letter will serve to confirm our understanding and agreement pursuant to which Trump Hotels & Casino Resorts, Inc. ("THCR"), Trump Hotels & Casino Resorts Holdings, L.P. ("Holdings"), and Trump Atlantic City Associates ("TACA"), (THCR, Holdings and TACA collectively referred to as "Trump") have agreed to employ you, and you have agreed to be employed by Trump commencing as of April 17, 2000, and expiring April 16, 2003 ("Expiration Date"), unless terminated earlier pursuant to Paragraph 12 or 13 hereof:

1. You shall be employed by Trump in the capacity of Executive Vice President and General Counsel, as well as President of Trump Casino Services, LLC, to perform such duties as are commonly attendant upon such offices and shall report directly to THCR's Chief Executive Officer.
2. During the term of this Agreement, you shall be paid an annual base salary at a rate not less than your current salary, payable periodically in accordance with Trump's regular payroll practices.
3. During each year of your employment with Trump, you shall be eligible to receive a bonus in an amount determined in the sole and absolute discretion of Trump's Chairman based upon the performance and profitability of Trump.
4. You shall be afforded coverage under Trump's employee insurance programs in such form and at such levels as Trump, in its sole and absolute discretion, may hereafter elect to provide for similarly situated executives.
   a. You shall be entitled to participate in Trump's executive benefit programs in such form and at such levels as Trump, in its sole and absolute discretion, may hereafter elect to provide similarly situated executives.
   b. You shall also have free use of hotel valet and laundry services and executive comping privileges at such levels, if any, as Trump in its sole and absolute discretion, shall establish from time to time for similarly situated executives.
5. You agree that until the Expiration Date and so long as Trump continues to pay your salary as provided herein, you shall not accept employment, either as an employee, consultant or independent contractor, with any other casino hotel located in Atlantic City, New Jersey. You
   acknowledge and agree that this restrictive covenant is reasonable as to duration, terms and geographical area and that the same is necessary to protect the legitimate interests of Trump, imposes no undue hardship on you and is not injurious to the public.
6. You hereby agree that throughout the term of this Agreement you shall devote your full time, attention and efforts to Trump's business and shall not, directly or indirectly, work for, consult with or otherwise engage in any other activities of a business nature for any other person or entity, without Trump's prior written consent. You will promptly communicate to Trump, in writing when requested, and marketing strategies, technical designs and concepts, and other ideas pertaining to Trump's business which are conceived or developed by you, alone or with others, at any time (during or after business hours) while you are employed by Trump. You acknowledge that all of those ideas will be Trump's exclusive property. You agree to sign any
   documents which Trump deems necessary to confirm its ownership of those ideas, and you agree to otherwise cooperate with Trump in order to allow Trump to take full advantage of those ideas.
7. You acknowledge that you have access to information which is proprietary and confidential to Trump. This information includes, but is not limited to, (1) the identity of customers and prospects, (2) names, addresses and phone numbers of individual contacts, (3) pricing policies, marketing strategies, product strategies and methods of operation, and (4) expansion plans, management policies and other business strategies and policies. You acknowledge and understand that this infor-

449

mation must be maintained in strict confidence in order for Trump to protect its business and its competitive position in the marketplace. Accordingly, both during and after termination of your employment, you agree that you will not disclose any of this information for any purpose or remove materials containing this information from Trump's premises. Upon termination of your employment, you will immediately return to Trump all correspondence files, business card files, customer and prospect lists, price books, technical data, notes and other materials which contain any of this information, and you will not retain copies of those materials.

8. You represent to Trump that there are no restrictions or agreements to which you are a party which would be violated by our execution of this Agreement and your employment hereunder.

9. You hereby agree to comply with all of the rules, regulations, policies and/or procedures adopted by Trump during the term of this Agreement, as well as all applicable state, federal and local laws, regulations and ordinances.

10. You hereby represent that you presently hold the New Jersey Casino Control Commission ("Commission") license required in connection with your employment hereunder and will take appropriate steps to renew said license in a timely manner.

11. Prior to the Expiration Date, Trump may terminate your employment hereunder only under the following circumstances (herein referred to as "Cause"):
    (i) Upon revocation by the Commission of your casino key employee license and the exhaustion of all appeals therefrom, or in the absence of an appeal, the exhaustion of any appeal period from such action;
    (ii) Your conviction of a crime under the law of any jurisdiction which constitutes a disqualifying crime described in N.J.S.A. 5:12-86;
    (iii) You shall become permanently disabled and unable to perform the essential functions of your position;
    (iv) You die; or
    (v) Any breach by you of your duty of trust to Trump, such as theft by you from Trump or fraud committed by you upon Trump.
    In the event of a termination pursuant to this paragraph, Trump shall pay to you your compensation under Section 2 hereof earned to the date of termination and shall have no further liability or obligation to you under this Agreement.

12. You may terminate this Agreement upon written notice to Trump at any time following a Change of Control, which termination shall be effective on the thirtieth day after such notice. For purposes of this Paragraph, a Change in Control means (i) the acquisition of Trump or over thirty-five (35%) percent of THCR's common stock or equivalent limited partnership interests by an unrelated entity, or (ii) the sale or long-term lease of all or substantially all of the assets of Trump. In the event of a termination pursuant to this Paragraph, you will receive in a lump sum payment the full amount of the unpaid compensation payable pursuant to Paragraph 2 hereof through the Expiration Date and the restrictions contained in Paragraph 6 hereof

    shall be null and void.

13. Trump shall indemnify, defend and hold you harmless, including the payment of reasonable attorney fees, if Trump does not directly provide your defense, from and against any and all claims made by anyone, including, but not limited to, a corporate entity, company, other employee, agent, patron or member of the general public with respect to any claim which asserts as a basis, any acts, omissions or other circumstances involving the performance of your employment duties hereunder unless such claim is based upon your gross negligence or any

    willful and/or wanton act.

14. You represent that you are a citizen of the United States or that you possess the proper visa and/or work permits necessary to perform your functions hereunder.

15. You acknowledge that it would be extremely difficult to measure the damages that might result from any breach by you of your promises in Sections 6, 7, and 8 of the Employment Contract and that a breach may cause irreparable injury to Trump which could not be compensated by money damages. Accordingly, Trump will be entitled to enforce this Employment Contract by obtaining a court order prohibiting you (and any others involved) from breaching this Agreement. If a court decides that any part of this Agreement is too broad, the court may limit that part and enforce it as limited.

16. This Agreement shall be governed by and construed in accordance with the laws of the State of New Jersey and in any lawsuit involving this Agreement, I consent to the jurisdiction and venue of any state or federal court located in New Jersey. This Agreement represents the entire agreement between the parties, superseding all previous agreements, including the January 15, 1998 letter agreement, and may not be modified, amended, extended or renewed without the written agreement of both parties.

If the foregoing correctly sets forth our understanding, kindly sign and return to me the duplicate copy of this letter enclosed herewith.

Very truly yours,

TRUMP HOTELS & CASINO RESORTS, INC. TRUMP HOTELS & CASINO RESORTS HOLDINGS, L.P. By: Trump Hotels & Casino Resorts, Inc.

General Partner

And

TRUMP ATLANTIC CITY ASSOCIATES By: Trump Atlantic City Holding, Inc.

General Partner

Agreed and Consented to:

BY: /s/ Donald J. Trump /s/ Robert M. Pickus

January 9, 2003

Re: Employment Agreement dated April 17, 2000 between Robert M. Pickus and Trump Hotels & Casino Resorts, Inc., Trump Hotels & Casino Resorts Holdings, L.P. and Trump Atlantic City Associates (collectively "Trump") (the "Agreement")

Dear Mr. Pickus:

This letter will confirm that the Agreement is hereby amended as set forth below:

1. the Expiration Date is extended to December 31, 2006;

2. paragraph 2 is amended to reflect the annual base salary of $400,000; and

3. paragraph 3 is amended to state that commencing January 1, 2004 the annual salary shall be increased at a rate not less than 5% per annum.

Except to the extent modified herein, you and Trump hereby ratify the Agreement and agree that all other terms, conditions and obligations contained therein remain in full force and effect as stated in the Agreement.
Very truly yours,
/s/ MARK A. BROWN, Chief Operating Officer
Agreed and Consented to:
/s/ ROBERT M. PICKUS

SEVERANCE AGREEMENT
This Agreement is entered into this 10th day of January, 1994 by and between Trump Plaza Associates (hereinafter "TPA") with offices located at Boardwalk and Mississippi Avenue, Atlantic City, New Jersey and Robert M. Pickus residing at 663 Weilers Lane, Absecon, New Jersey (hereinafter "Employee").
WITNESSETH
Whereas, on and before December 3, 1993 Employee was for many years employed by the Trump's Castle Casino Resort; and
Whereas, TPA desires to employ Employee as Vice President/General counsel and is willing to enter into this severance agreement;
Now therefore, based upon the execution of this Agreement, Employee's employment, and other good and valuable consideration, TPA and Employee agree as follows:
    1. In the event TPA terminates the employment of Employee for a reason set forth below, TPA shall pay Employee on the date of termination the full amount of compensation and any reimbursements due him through the date of termination whereupon TPA shall have no further liability or obligation to Employee.
        a. Upon revocation or termination of the Employee's casino key employee license;
        b. Upon an act committed by the Employee constituting "cause" which is defined to mean: an act by the Employee constituting a breach of any of the material terms of his employment; the indictment and/or conviction of any criminal offense constituting a felony; the deliberate refusal by the Employee to perform his duties as Vice President/General Counsel; or if the Employee:
            i. Files a petition in bankruptcy or is adjudicated as bankrupt;
           ii. Institutes or suffers to be instituted any procedure in bankruptcy court for reorganization or arrangement of his financial affairs;
          iii. Has a receiver of his assets or property appointed because of insolvency; or
          iv. Makes a general assignment for the benefit of creditors;
        c. Upon the death or permanent disability of the Employee;
        d. Upon the voluntary resignation by Employee.
    2. If Employee's employment should be terminated by TPA for any reason, other than those specified in Section (1) above (it being understood that a purported termination for Cause which is contested by Employee and finally determined not to have been proper shall be treated as a termination under this Section (2)), then TPA shall on the date of termination pay Employee his salary and any reimbursements due to the date of termination and as severance payment the full amount of his salary at its then current rate for a period of one year whereupon TPA shall have no further liability or obligation to Employee under this Agreement or otherwise.
In Witness Whereof, TPA and Employee have set their hands and seals the date and year first above written.
TRUMP PLAZA ASSOCIATES
Kevin DeSanctis, President and Chief Operating Officer
Robert M. Pickus

77 AGREEMENT, dated as of September ___, 1993, between TRUMP PLAZA ASSOCIATES (the "Company"), and NICHOLAS L. RIBIS (the "Executive").
    1. Employment. The Company agrees to employ the Executive and the Executive agrees to be employed by the Company under the terms and conditions hereinafter set forth.
    2. Term. The term of this Agreement (the "Term")shall be for three years, commencing on the date hereof.
    3. Salary. During the first year of the Term, the Company shall pay the Executive an annual salary of $550,000,payable in accordance with the Company's normal payroll practices. The salary shall be increased by ten percent for each of the second and third years of the Term.
    4. Duties. The Executive shall serve as Chief Executive Officer of the Company and hereby promises to perform and discharge well and faithfully the duties which may be assigned to him from time to time by the Board of Directors of the Company, provided such duties are consistent with Executive's position as Chief Executive Officer.
    5. Signing Bonus. Upon execution of this Agreement, the Company shall pay the Executive a one-time signing bonus of $250,000.
    6. Benefits/Expenses. During the Term, Executive shall participate in all employee benefit plans of the Company, subject to the eligibility, enrollment and other requirements of such plans, and, in addition, shall continue to receive his current automobile allowance and such other benefits as he is presently receiving. The Executive shall be entitled to reimbursement by the Company for reasonable expenses incurred in connection with the performance of his duties hereunder, on the same basis and under the same terms applicable to other Executive officers of the Company.
    7. Roll-Up; Public Offering. In the event that the Company, or any entity which acquires substantially all of the stock or assets of the Company, proposes to engage in an offering of common shares to the public (a "Public Offering"), the parties hereto shall negotiate in good faith to adopt new employment compensation arrangements for Executive which shall include equity participation for Executive.
    8. Termination for Cause. The Company may at any time terminate the Executive's employment for "Cause" and shall thereafter have no obligations to the Executive for continued payment of salary, benefits or other amounts payable to Executive hereun-

der accruing after the date of termination. For purposes of this Agreement, Cause shall mean either (i) Executive's conviction of a felony, or (ii) the revocation or termination of Executive's casino key employee license issued by the New Jersey Casino Control Commission.

9. Covenant Not to Compete. In the event that, during the Term, either (i) the Company terminates the Executive's employment for Cause, or (ii) the Executive voluntarily terminates his employment (other than following any material breach of this Agreement by the Company), the Executive shall not, for a period of the lesser of (A) one year from such termination, or (B) the period then remaining in the Term as of the date of such termination, engage directly or indirectly, as an employee, consultant or otherwise, in the management or operation of any gambling casino located in the Atlantic City, New Jersey market; provided, however, that this covenant shall not be applicable in the event that a Public Offering occurs and Executive voluntarily terminates his employment as a result of the parties' failure to negotiate mutually satisfactory compensation arrangements as contemplated by Section 7 hereof.

10. Board Approval. This Agreement is subject to the approval of the governing board of the Company.

11. Law to Govern. This Agreement shall be governed by and construed and enforced in accordance with the laws of the State of New Jersey, without giving effect to the principles of conflicts of laws thereof.

12. Entire Agreement. This instrument contains the entire agreement of the parties with respect to the subject matter hereof. The execution of this Agreement by the parties shall make null and void any prior agreement or understanding between the parties with respect to terms and conditions of employment. It may not be changed orally but only by an agreement in writing signed by the party against whom enforcement of any waiver, change, modification, extension or discharge is sought.

IN WITNESS WHEREOF, the parties have executed this Agreement as of the day first hereinabove written.

[78] 25 USC § 2711 specifically sets management contract fees at no more than 30% of net revenue but then allows that fee to be extended to "40% of the net revenues if the Chairman of NIGC is satisfied that the capital investment required, and income projections, for such tribal gaming activity require the additional fee requested by the Tribe."

452

INDEX

454

456